Mental Health and
Productivity in the Workplace

Mental Health and Productivity in the Workplace

A Handbook for Organizations and Clinicians

Jeffrey P. Kahn, M.D.
Alan M. Langlieb, M.D., M.B.A.
Editors

Foreword by Marcia Kraft Goin, M.D., Ph.D.

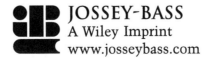

JOSSEY-BASS
A Wiley Imprint
www.josseybass.com

Published by Jossey-Bass
A Wiley Imprint
989 Market Street, San Francisco, CA 94103-1741   www.josseybass.com

An earlier edition of this book edited by Jeffrey Kahn was published
in 1993 by Van Nostrand Reinhold with the title *Mental Health in the
Workplace: A Practical Psychiatric Guide,* from which this edition
has been substantially revised and expanded.

The five-point bulleted list on page 331 is from Colledge, A. L.,
Johns, R. E., & Thomas, M. H. (1999). Functional ability assessment:
Guidelines for the workplace. *Journal of Occupational and Environmental
Medicine, 41,* 172–180 by permission of Lippincott Williams & Wilkins.

Jossey-Bass books and products are available through most bookstores. To
contact Jossey-Bass directly, call our Customer Care Department within the U.S.
at (800) 956-7739, outside the U.S. at (317) 572-3993, or fax (317) 572-4002.

Jossey-Bass also publishes its books in a variety of electronic formats. Some
content that appears in print may not be available in electronic books.

Library of Congress Cataloging-in-Publication Data

Mental health and productivity in the workplace: a handbook for
organizations and clinicians/Jeffrey P. Kahn, Alan M. Langlieb,
editors; foreword by Marcia Kraft Goin.—1st ed.
p. cm.
Includes bibliographical references and index.
ISBN 0-7879-6215-5 (alk. paper)
1. Industrial psychiatry—Handbooks, manuals, etc.   I. Kahn, Jeffrey
P.   II. Langlieb, Alan M., date.
RC967.5 .M455 2002
616.89—dc21   2002014344

Printed in the United States of America
FIRST EDITION
HB Printing   10 9 8 7 6 5 4 3 2 1

CONTENTS

Figures and Tables   xiii

Foreword   xvii
Marcia Kraft Goin

Preface   xix

PART ONE: THE WORKPLACE AND MENTAL HEALTH   1

1   Workplace Mental Health Quality: Effective Recognition, Management, Evaluation, Treatment, and Benefits   3
Jeffrey P. Kahn
Recognition, Management, and Referral • Evaluation: Define the Problem to Define the Treatment • Treatment: Techniques of Psychotherapy and Consultation • Assessing Treatment and Consultation Response • Building a Better Benefit: Quality Mental Health Care Guidelines

2   Mental Health Care Providers and Delivery Systems   28
Alan M. Langlieb, Anne M. Stoline, Steven S. Sharfstein
Providers • Delivery Systems

3   Cost-Effectiveness, Cost Containment, and Worker Productivity   48
Alan M. Langlieb, Benjamin G. Druss, Robert Rosenheck
Cost-Benefit and Cost-Effectiveness • Cost-Offset • Cost Containment • Productivity

4 Mental Health Ethics and Confidentiality in the Organization   60
Robert C. Larsen
Medical Ethics • Role of the Physician • Mental Health Referral Situations with Potential for Moral Conflict • Appendix

5 Psychiatry, Productivity, and Health: A Brief History of Psychiatry in the Workplace   71
Len Sperry, Alan A. McLean
Early History • 1920s: Psychiatrists in the Workplace • 1930s and 1940s: War Stress and Initial Academic Efforts • 1950s and 1960s: Increasing Clinical Involvement • 1970s, 1980s, and 1990s: Expanding Psychiatric Horizons • The Third Millennium: New Directions

PART TWO: COMMON OCCUPATIONAL CONCERNS   89

6 Executive Development: Assessment, Coaching, and Treatment   91
Jeffrey P. Kahn, Len Sperry
Executive Assessment • Leadership Development • Executive Coaching • Personal Treatment • Organizational Intervention • Appendix

7 Executive Distress and Organizational Consequences   113
Jeffrey P. Kahn, Mark P. Unterberg
Narcissism: Patching over the Uncaring World • Competition Gone Awry: Intergenerational Oedipal Conflict • When It Looks Like Character Is Destiny: Rigid Personalities Under Stress • Hiding Away Those Pesky Emotions: Repression of Emotional Distress

8 Job Loss and Employment Uncertainty   135
Nick Kates, Barrie Sanford Greiff, Duane Q. Hagen
The Impact of Impending Job Loss • How the Effect of Job Loss Is Transmitted • An Integrated Model • Assessing the Impact of Impending Job Loss • Impact on Those Who Remain at Work • Intervention • Preventive Interventions

9 Sending Employees and Families Overseas: Mental Health in the Workplace Abroad   155
Thomas H. Valk
Mental Health and Psychosocial Issues in Expatriate Populations • Costs of Overseas Moves and Early Curtailment Rates • Mental Health Services and Legal Issues Overseas • Policy and Procedures to Minimize Disruption from Mental Health Issues

10 Office Politics: The Good the Bad, and the Ugly 171
Roy H. Lubit, Robert P. Gordon
*Knowing and Understanding Personality Styles • Knowing and Understanding
Leadership Styles • Issues in Managing Your Boss • Understanding What
Motivates Leaders' Behavior • Attitudes Toward Authority • Organizational
Culture • Hidden Agendas • Boundary Issues and Regression • Male-Female
Relationships • Competition*

PART THREE: COMMON ORGANIZATIONAL ISSUES 203

11 How Leadership and Organizational Structure Can Create a
Winning Corporate Culture 205
Howard E. Book
*What Is Corporate Culture? • Organizational Cultures: The Two Extremes
• How the CEO's Style Shapes Culture • How Organizational Structures Affect
Culture • Other Factors That Influence Culture*

12 A Comprehensive Overview of Organizational Change 233
Gerald A. Kraines
*Leveraging a Company's Potential • Moving to Action • Forging Psychological
Contracts • Managing for Changing Realities • Adapting to Change • The
Casualties of Change • Successfully Leading Change • Changing Times: What Is
Coming Next?*

13 Organizational Consequences of Family Problems 254
David E. Morrison, David A. Deacon
Literature and Research • Family Problems: Cases and Discussion • Interventions

14 Psychiatric Causes of Workplace Problems 276
Steven E. Pflanz, Stephen H. Heidel
*Common Work Problems • Causes • Effects on the Employee and the Organiza-
tion • Assessment • Interventions • Prevention*

15 Emotional Crises in the Workplace 297
Stephen H. Heidel
*Disaster and Emotional Trauma • Traumatic Events at the Work Site • Substance
Abuse Emergencies • Suicide • Psychotic Behavior*

16 Violence in the Workplace 314
Ronald Schouten
*Defining Workplace Violence and Threat Assessment • Potential Roles for Mental
Health Professionals in Threat Assessment • Knowledge Base for Threat Assessment
and Violence in the Workplace • Responding to Workplace Threats and Violence*

17 Psychiatric Fitness-for-Duty Examinations 329

Robert C. Larsen

*Fitness-for-Duty Guidelines • The Sensitive Nature of Psychiatric
Information • Appropriate Situations for Psychiatric Examinations • Work
Function Assessment • Information Exchange • Administrative
Minefields • Appendix A • Appendix B*

18 Disability and Workers' Compensation 347

Brian L. Grant, David B. Robbins

*Workplace Disability Problems and Definitions • The Treating Physician's
Role • The Psychiatric Disability Consultative Examination • Determination of
Causality • Administrative Medical Review • Adopting the Disability Role: A
Psychological Process • Prevention of Disability • Work-Related Impairments and
Workers' Compensation*

19 Workplace Forensic Psychiatry: The Americans with Disabilities
Act and the Family and Medical Leave Act 369

Sara Eddy, Ronald Schouten

Understanding the ADA • Family and Medical Leave Act • Appendix

20 Organizational Ethics in the Company: Beyond Personal, Professional,
and Business Ethics 387

Len Sperry

*Ethics: Definitions, Classification System, and Ethical Perspectives • Commonly
Encountered Ethical Issues in Corporations • Organizational Ethics in
Action • Two Ethical Perspectives Germane to Organizational Ethics • Systemic
Factors with an Impact on Organizational Ethics*

PART FOUR: COMMON EMPLOYEE PROBLEMS 405

21 Anxiety and Stress 407

Dan J. Stein, Eric Hollander

*Adjustment Disorder with Anxiety, Generalized Anxiety Disorder, and Other Ten-
sion States • Panic Disorder: Intense Anxiety and Phobias • Social Anxiety Disorder: Stage Fright and Shyness • Obsessive-Compulsive Disorder • Posttraumatic
Stress Disorder*

22 Depression and Burnout 433

Philip M. Liu, David A. Van Liew

*Adjustment Disorder with Depressed Mood • Major Depression • Dysthymia and
Atypical Depression • Bipolar Disorder*

23 Personality: Personalities, Personal Style, and Trouble
    Getting Along   458
    Mark P. Unterberg
    Obsessive Compulsive: Overinvolved, Underachieving Employees • Histrionic:
    Overemotional, Overreactive Employees • Antisocial: Criminal or Aggressive
    Employees • Paranoid: Isolated or Litigious Employees • Borderline: Impulsive or
    Divisive Employees • Narcissistic: Grandiose or Demanding Employees • Passive-
    Aggressive: Compliant or Underachieving Employees

24 **Drugs: Abuse and Dependence**   481
    Avram H. Mack, Jeffrey S. Rosecan, Richard J. Frances
    Possible Causes of Workplace Drug Abuse • Workplace Management and Referral
    • Drug Use, Drug Abuse, and Addiction • Individual Drug-Dependence
    Syndromes • Testing for Drug Use • Public Policy and Law • Psychiatric
    Management • Appendix

25 **Alcohol: Abuse and Dependence**   502
    Carlotta Lief Schuster
    Workplace Recognition and Referral • Causes and Effects of Alcoholism in the
    Workplace • Psychiatric Management • Return to Work

26 **Psychosis: Peculiar Behaviors and Inflexible Bizarre Beliefs**   517
    Corinne Cather, Kim T. Mueser, Donald C. Goff
    Delusional Disorders • Affective Disorders with Psychotic Features • Substance-
    Induced Psychotic Disorder • Schizophrenia Spectrum Disorders

27 **Emotion and Illness: The Psychosomatic Interface**   540
    Brian L. Grant
    Somatoform Disorders: Physical Symptoms of Emotional Origin • Factitious
    Disorders and Malingering: Falsely Reported Symptoms • Psychiatric Disorders
    with Frequent Physical Symptoms • Controversial Medical Illnesses: Functional
    Somatic Syndromes • Emotional Aspects of Physical Disease • Organic
    Behavioral Syndromes

    About the Editors   569

    About the Contributors   571

    Name Index   579

    Subject Index   587

FIGURES AND TABLES

FIGURES

8.1   An Integrated Model of the Impact of Job Loss   143

12.1   *We Che*   245

12.2   Attachment and Change: Roots of Identification   246

12.3   Critical Change Sequence   247

24.1   Factors Involved in the Development of an Addiction   487

TABLES

10.1   Myers-Briggs Personality Dimensions   173

10.2   Coping with Narcissistic Managers   179

10.3   Managing Aggressive Managers   180

10.4   Working with Different Leadership Styles   185

11.1   Emotional Intelligence and Cognitive Intelligence: A Comparison   217

11.2   Components of Emotional Intelligence   217

13.1   Subtle Organizational Consequences of Family Problems   255

13.2   Family Impacts on Work   260

20.1   Definitions of Terms   389

22.1   Comparison of Depression and Bereavement   436

24.1   Pros and Cons of Mandatory Urine Testing for Illicit Drugs   496

MEDICAL AND LEGAL DISCLAIMER

This volume contains information about mental health and medical diagnosis, treatment, and prognosis intended only for business and clinical professionals. Every effort has been made to ensure accuracy; however, the field is evolving, and new information may later emerge. Neither the authors, editors, nor publisher are responsible for any errors. This book is not intended as a layperson's manual of mental health or medical care. The accurate diagnosis and effective treatment of any distressed individual requires attention by a professional in the field, with comprehensive and appropriate training and full knowledge of the specific case. Similarly, proper training and experience are also required when addressing the issues of organizational concern described in Parts Three and Four. In addition, information in this book about legal considerations for certain mental health and management issues is not a substitute for professional legal services about any specific circumstance. Except where specifically noted, all case material in this book is either fictitious or a fictionalized composite. Similarity of characters presented in the text to any person living or dead is coincidental.

FOREWORD

The worlds of mental health and work have elaborated two cultural traditions, speak different languages, are philosophically distinct, and believe in two separate truths: the relative and the absolute. But psychiatry conveys invaluable perspectives on mental health in the workplace: informing relationships, uncovering interactions, and analyzing organizational behavior. Psychiatrists respond to the specific distress of individuals and corporations. The tragic events of a Tuesday in September 2001 have sharply heightened the already growing awareness of the prevalence, importance, and economic costs of mental health problems among employees and their bosses. Many executives and employees know how effective modern psychiatric treatment can be, but organizational use requires effective problem recognition and the best possible diagnostic and treatment resources.

This book offers a comprehensive and invaluable tool for businesspeople who want to use their workforce in the best way possible and ameliorate everyday concerns in the workplace. It provides thoughtful and practical guidance on a wide range of skills essential for any business operation or organizational task. The book starts with a review of significant issues in mental health care, from diagnosis and treatment, to providers, to cost-effectiveness, and to ethics and the history of organizational and occupational psychiatry. It provides informed readers with a perspective on occupational concerns that include the nature of business culture and the inevitable and never-ending changes made imperative by market forces and world events. Workplace violence and crises, the complexities of the Americans with Disabilities Act, work-life balance, disability and fitness-for-duty evaluations, and corporate ethics are central issues that require ongoing attention. Commonly observed employee problems are thoroughly discussed from the perspective of both workplace and clinical considerations. This unique book offers clear guidance for resourceful management of human resources. This is an outstanding reference that presents invaluable insights in nontechnical language for readers who are not formally trained in mental health. For the clinically sophisticated audience, the book will optimize its understanding of the human experience in the workplace. Importantly, it explores family conflicts and the personal problems of workers embarked on a competitive career path. These issues are even more important with the growth of single-parent families and of families where both parents spend long hours at work.

This thorough compendium illuminates a field that has not been well understood or addressed in the past.

September 2002   Marcia Kraft Goin, M.D., Ph.D.
Clinical Professor of Psychiatry,
Keck School of Medicine,
University of Southern California, and
President Elect, American Psychiatric Association

PREFACE

Emotional problems can have profound effects on employees, families, and employers. Those effects can range from hidden internal distress, to outwardly obvious emotional, drug abuse, and behavioral problems and can have workplace consequences for morale, productivity, retention, absenteeism, executive effectiveness, and organizational functioning. The complex interplay of individual emotions and organizational function has long been a focus of attention. Recent years, though, have seen an enormous growth in that attention.

There has been greater awareness of the considerable emotional, financial, and organizational costs of these problems, a growing research literature, and an ongoing need for thorough understanding of causes and solutions. Good managers have always known the importance of maintaining individual and group morale. Such long-standing concerns have been highlighted recently by the ongoing restructuring of many American industries, implementation of the Americans with Disabilities Act, federal consideration of mental health parity legislation, and the profound workplace awareness of mental health issues after the attacks of September 11, 2001. Organizational effectiveness requires careful attention to both individuals and organizational functioning. In addition, the impact of managed care and a renewed interest in quality mental health care are becoming increasingly important variables that are also essential considerations.

This book reviews common individual and organizational mental health concerns at a relatively sophisticated level of discussion but in nontechnical language. Discussions include a particular focus on workplace considerations and solutions. Workplace emotional problems can usually be understood and resolved, with benefits for employee, family, and the workplace itself. There is no substitute for comprehensive understanding of problems and careful implementation of practical and effective solutions.

The audience for this book is broad. Psychiatrists and other mental health professionals can learn about specific occupational and organizational problems (Parts Two and Three) as well as about workplace considerations for syndromes that they may already know well (Part Four). Managers, occupational health professionals, human resource and benefits professionals, business students, and others who are concerned with workplace mental health and organizational development will find valuable information throughout this book. It serves as an introduction to a comprehensive psychiatric perspective on the emotional problems and issues that are so important for effective management and organizational success. As noted in the Disclaimer, this book should not be used as a substitute for the efforts of fully informed mental health, medical or legal professionals.

There is a nearly endless list of teachers, colleagues, students, clients, patients, and friends whose teachings, guidance, or other support made this book possible. Stephen Heidel, Thomas Valk, Donald Williams, Ronald Schouten, Sandy Cohen, Drew Clemens, Seth Aidinoff, Edward Anselm, Marcia Scott, Harvey Barten, Jeffrey Speller, Leonard Moss, James Oher, Norman Wyloge, Michael Kaminsky, Paul McHugh, J. Raymond DePaulo Jr., Stephen Teret, Erica Frank, Gary Nyman, Jonathan Reader, Louis Hugo Francescutti, Donald Steinwachs, Alfred Sommer, Raymond Ralph, Thomas Peace, Louis Lasagna, Robert Carr, George Lundberg, Darrel Regier, Larry Lesh, David Clews, and all of the indefatigable chapter authors have offered a wealth of knowledge and skill in organizational and occupational psychiatry. In particular, Alan McLean, now deceased, was a mentor and a source of inspiration since the inception of this project so long ago. We will miss him. The Departments of Psychiatry at Cornell and Johns Hopkins have been steady sources of inspiration and support. Stephen Zollo, Robert Esposito, and Bernice Pettinato at Van Nostrand Reinhold, along with Thomas Phillips, offered wise and tolerant editorial guidance on the first edition and have been more than ably followed by Alan Rinzler and Amy Scott at Jossey-Bass and Beverly H. Miller for this revised and expanded second edition.

Most of the contributors are members of the Academy of Organizational and Occupational Psychiatry (AOOP; www.aoop.org). Founded in 1990 to address the contributions of psychiatry to workplace mental health solutions, the rapid growth and strength of AOOP is testimony to the ongoing importance of those issues. AOOP offers information and collegial support to interested psychiatrists, and provides a referral service to corporations concerned about the broad range of employee or larger organizational problems.

Most important, we are forever indebted for the warm affection and wise counsel of Stephen, Eva, Nancy, Jessica, and Tara (J.P.K.) and of Muriel, Martin, Nannette, Irvin, Tammara, Marin, Emlyn, and Jonah (A.M.L.).

September 2002   Jeffrey P. Kahn, M.D.
                                                 New York, New York

                                                 Alan M. Langlieb, M.D., M.B.A.
                                                 Baltimore, Maryland

PART ONE

THE WORKPLACE AND MENTAL HEALTH

Past, Present, and Future

These first five chapters lay the foundation for the study and science behind mental health and productivity in the workplace. Beginning with a provocative overview of the nature of mental health and the mechanisms of quality mental health care, the chapters also offer a framework by which mental health care is delivered and judged effective in the United States today. They proceed to demystify the subjects of cost-effectiveness and cost containment, of vital importance for employers today. Mental health ethics and confidentiality issues are addressed here because they are of paramount importance to the effectiveness of psychiatry in general, and to the role of psychiatry in the workplace in particular. Part One concludes with a review of the historical underpinnings, origin, and recent history of workplace psychiatry. Elmer Southard (in the early twentieth century) and Alan McLean (in the later twentieth century) were founding fathers of this field. Dr. McLean, deceased since the first edition of this book, would surely be pleased to know his vision for the future of this exciting field is thriving in the new millennium.

CHAPTER ONE

Workplace Mental Health Quality

Effective Recognition, Management, Evaluation, Treatment, and Benefits

Jeffrey P. Kahn

Workplace mental health problems pose special challenges for management, human resource and benefits officers, and occupational and mental health professionals. Recognition and management of emotional problems require careful attention. Referral and proper initial evaluation of personal and organizational problems involve awareness of the complex and often hidden causes of surface symptoms. Once causal factors are identified, defined treatment can effect helpful solutions. Educational, supportive, behavioral, cognitive, insight-oriented, organizational, and medication approaches are among the many different types of therapy. Basic principles of psychoanalytic thought are useful for understanding many of these approaches. Without considered attention, it can be hard to distinguish treatment response from treatment failure. As with other organizational tasks, a thorough initial approach will reduce future costs and complications. These issues are especially important for understanding and implementing quality mental health care benefits programs.

The scientific principles that define psychiatric thought are not always obvious to the casual observer. Common belief often suggests that psychiatric illness is largely willful or hopeless. Psychiatric (and other mental health) treatment is sometimes dismissed as nonspecific hand holding, as based on outdated and rigid psychoanalytic theory, or as inappropriate or abusive use of dangerous medications. Such views are reinforced by media representations of psychiatrists and other mental health professionals as treating only the most disturbed and untreatable patients, as themselves disturbed, or as unnecessarily confusing patients no more eccentric than themselves. And last but not least, much of mental health care is indeed much less than it could be.

Actually, psychiatric knowledge and skills have changed enormously since the work of Sigmund Freud and his predecessors. While Freud was perhaps the first to offer a systematic approach to understanding mental processes and underlying hidden emotions, there are few today who would directly emulate his specific techniques. Freud himself predicted that psychiatric knowledge would require an understanding of biological underpinnings, and even the most orthodox of psychoanalysts today would offer far more refined and flexible psychotherapeutic principles than Freud did. Today's complex blend of scientific skills in diagnosis, psychotherapy, medicine, and medication use makes it possible for patient and psychiatrist to resolve distressing problems. Syndromes once considered untreatable are now readily brought under the patient's control, often with short-term methods.

Psychiatry has focused much of its attention on interpersonal interactions and specific illnesses as the centerpiece of treatment. Less attention has been given to the personal meanings of work and the role of emotional issues in the workplace. Although home life usually has a greater emotional significance to people, working people often spend more waking hours at the job than at home. And workplace problems are to some extent determined by the emotions, personalities, and problems of the people who work there.

As companies adapt to changing markets, new economic conditions, and increasing workforce diversity, mental health issues are easily overlooked until they cause overriding interpersonal, performance, or organizational problems. This is not surprising, because emotional issues typically are more complex than they seem, involve hidden and deeply personal emotions, and can be uncomfortable to address. At first glance, they do not seem as if they can be understood, much less effectively resolved. And there are good reasons to avoid dealing directly with personal problems in the workplace. It is usually more empathic for managers to address issues of work performance and to suggest effective outside attention for contributory personal problems. Nevertheless, informed, specific, and empathic interventions benefit worker and company alike and require scientific understanding of both people and their distress and of organizational contexts and problems. Superficial attempts at remedy yield disappointingly superficial results. This principle applies to both consideration of individual employees and, as we will see, evaluation of employer benefits.

RECOGNITION, MANAGEMENT, AND REFERRAL

Problems need to be recognized before they can be helped, and even that can be a difficult task. Less enmeshed in the personal emotional turmoil, workplace colleagues and management often recognize problems before the family does. Problems at work often show up only in such subtle ways as decreased productivity, ambition, quality, or interpersonal effectiveness. And larger-scale problems of the organization itself can creep up gradually, invisible to management until the organizational effects are pressing or severe. The first step is to realize that a problem exists. It also requires technical skill to know when and how to manage the problem and when to look for outside help.

Management and Mental Health

Management plays many roles in fostering emotional health of worker and workplace. Perhaps most of all, management structure and style define interactions at all levels and the sort of an emotional environment that will exist in the organization (see Chapter Eleven). Increasing attention is being directed to the role of organizational structure on employee morale and productivity. Major emotional problems of managers themselves are sometimes obvious, but more subtle distress can alter the emotional culture of a division or an entire company (see Chapter Seven). Management also plays the largest role in determining mental health insurance benefits, and thus the availability and quality of mental health care for employees (a topic addressed later in this chapter, as well as in Chapter Two on mental health providers and delivery systems). With the limitations that come with managed mental health care, there has been greater awareness of the value of quality mental health care for all employees.

Managers are in a position to notice and point out employee and organizational problems that can be helped by treatment. They can create a climate where appropriate psychiatric care is encouraged and its benefits recognized. And they are in a position to counsel employees about performance problems in a way that points out any need for outside help. Many companies have a psychiatric consultant on call for emergencies, available for specific employee problems, and offering consultation on more general organizational concerns.

Human Resources and Mental Health

In most large companies, much of management's attention to employee mental health problems is through the human resource (HR) department. HR officers help determine insurance coverage. They often play a major role in sorting out workplace problems and in the development of improved organizational models and are thus often the first to be presented with a distressed employee, a dysfunctional supervisor, or a problematic work area. Recognition and correction of problems is a difficult task, always complicated by complex office politics (see Chapter Ten). HR in many companies is well situated to help manage mental health issues and often has established relationships with outside consultants.

Workplace Employee Counseling

Many companies offer limited counseling at the workplace, often through an employee assistance program (EAP; see Chapter Two). Counseling can cover issues of elder care, substance abuse, financial planning, and emotional problems. Such programs can identify employees in particular distress and at risk and are valuable benefits for employees who use them. Many in-house programs have ongoing consultation arrangements with outside mental health providers. A few have part-time psychiatrists who supervise or work directly with the program.

In-house programs must be very careful in what services they offer and with what degree of training. There is a natural tendency to operate such programs at minimum cost and with attention largely to immediate and obvious crises. Insufficient attention or professional skill often results in failures of evaluation and treatment, and consequent increases in long-term costs. Prompt attention to less obvious problems can also be cost-efficient in the long run. There can be real or perceived problems of conflict of interest and confidentiality when in-house treatment is provided by someone who works for the same employer (see Chapter Four).

Psychiatry in the Medical Department

Medical departments are another common site for presentation of emotional problems. Many large companies have medical departments that offer such services as employee examinations, disability reviews, urgent medical care, health promotion programs, and referral for quality medical treatment. Employees on disability or medical leave commonly have concurrent depressive or anxiety disorders that often remain unrecognized and untreated (see Chapters Twenty-One and Twenty-Two). The emotional component can prolong absence from work long after an actual physical impairment has improved (see Chapters Eighteen and Twenty-Seven). A psychiatric consultant to the medical department can offer direct consultation and make treatment referrals. On-site consultation is often more acceptable to employees who are reporting physical symptoms or workplace causes. Even when an EAP is present, many employees often make discreet requests for psychiatric referral through the medical department.

Outside Consultation

There are advantages and disadvantages to outside referral for consultation. The advantages lie largely in the availability of greater expertise and improved outcome, and in diminished concern about confidentiality and potential conflicts of interest. As with outside management consultants and advertising agencies, an outside psychiatric consultant may have a higher fee but offer advantages in quality, independence of company politics, and reduced long-term costs. Effective consultation to any part of a company requires identification of skilled clinicians and a comfortable working relationship. The consultant must be able to conduct rapid and thorough evaluations of functioning individuals in an organizational setting, communicate that understanding to employee or manager, and be committed to preserving function in the workplace. And it is imperative to know the difference between a consultation for the company and a confidential treatment relationship (see Chapter Four).

Barriers to Effective Treatment and Referral

Even with the best of intentions, it is often difficult to bring about effective referrals for treatment. The reasons are varied but mostly not surprising.

Fears of Stigma, Employment Effects, and Punishment. Employees and managers are often afraid that seeking any sort of mental health care will stigmatize them and adversely affect their careers. People in the midst of emotional distress may have difficulty realizing that much of their concern may come from their inner fears of rejection or of failure. And concerned managers and coworkers, who are naturally reluctant to seem insensitive, readily sense those inner fears. Employees with severe depressions can even convince others of the hopelessness of their situation, and therefore of the pointlessness of treatment. Employees who are especially sensitive may see a supervisor's suggestion as punitive rather than helpful. In reality, effective treatment most often improves workplace performance and contentment, and psychotherapy is a commonplace in the culture.

Low Treatment Expectations and Previous Ineffective Treatment. Even aside from low expectations that derive from the distress itself, employees, families, and managers may not think that treatment will help much. Low expectation can be caused by an absence of obviously treatable causes of distress. It can also be caused by a conscious conviction or wish that the distress has a single and emotionally acceptable cause, such as workplace unfairness or physical illness. In fact, emotional distress is usually multiply determined, and the major contributors are often not apparent. A careful diagnostic evaluation sorts out the various contributors and allows for treatment that specifically addresses actual causes.

Low expectations can also stem from previously ineffective treatment and awareness of the great variations in the quality of mental health care. Many clinicians are not as effective as they could be. Some have limited skills or training (or sometimes little training at all). Others' training or temperament leads them to stereotype illness and treatment. They fail to focus on individualized evaluation, diagnosis, and treatment (see Chapter Two). Employees are also sometimes more comfortable with treatments that reinforce beliefs in irremediable external causes for distress but offer only limited symptomatic improvement.

Self-Reliance, Time, and Money. While effective treatment does require some commitment of emotional, financial, and time resources, magnified concerns about those costs can also reflect inner emotional concerns. For instance, many people think of themselves as self-reliant, and they find distasteful the idea of making an emotional investment in seeking help from someone else. While self-reliant abilities are generally adaptive, they can be used in self-defeating ways to deny emotional or adaptational problems. Exaggerated self-reliance reflects a heightened natural reluctance to address painful hidden fears and emotions. For instance, self-reliance can be a protection against a hidden fear that other people are unreliable. Those fears can make people feel that any attempt at resolving problems will only make their worst fears come true. In a similar way, people who would benefit from treatment can have disproportionate concerns about investing time and money in their emotional well-being. Any investment can seem unwise when there is a hidden expectation of certain disappointment.

Effective Management and Referral of Mental Health Problems

The art of effective management always involves understanding and responding to people's personal characteristics. In the case of mental health problems, the management issue is the personal characteristics themselves. Emotional problems at work can pose a dilemma for managers: a natural tendency to leave intense emotions untouched and an equally natural urge to help the employee. In addition, there are corresponding managerial responsibilities to stay out of personal matters and to maximize employee performance. Emotional problems evident in the workplace are best addressed with discretion, respect for privacy, and genuine concern. Every employee and circumstance is different, so the usefulness of the following suggestions differs for each case.

Timing is important, and it is never easy to tell the difference between early recognition of a real problem and exaggerated concern about a minor issue. Some basic considerations include evidence of significant emotional distress, maladaptation at work, or references to major personal problems or concerns. Often it is helpful to ask an employee whether she would like to talk to someone about the problem. At other times, effective treatment referral requires skillful management.

Most important, people respond to empathic advice. Empathy reflects awareness of inner feelings and is not the same as sympathy for expressed concerns. The best approach is nonintrusive, nonthreatening, and nonconfrontational. Look for an opening in what the employee says. When the employee refers to a problem, point out his concern about it. Even when other problems or causes are obvious, referrals are most readily accepted for conscious concerns rather than for hidden causes or for management's purposes. At the same time, though, mention any specific workplace problems. Point out that all emotional distress is complex and that careful psychiatric consultation can help sort out the details. Know that catchphrases like *stress* and *burnout* are useful shorthand that often reflect problems requiring a skillful initial evaluation. Major depression, panic disorder, and other common problems have medical causes and should not be a cause for shame. Acceptance of a consultation does not require any commitment to treatment.

Be reassuring. Proper treatment makes problems better, and while genuine life problems may exist, emotional distress makes everything look worse than the reality. Point out that therapy is confidential and commonplace. Note explicitly that referral is not evidence of rejection, a hopeless situation, or punishment. Be sensitive to the possibility of your own conscious or unwitting emotional reactions to employee distress. Depressed employees often leave other people sharing their hopelessness (see Chapter Twenty-Two), while other employees may generate hostility toward themselves. Most of all, do not be frustrated if the employee cannot easily recognize a need for help.

Review available referral resources and the kinds of credentials to look for, and be aware of the advantages and disadvantages of the different kinds of treatments and clinicians. Where possible, offer flexible work schedules to accommodate treatment. Within legal and ethical limits, it is sometimes appropriate to use authority to encourage treatment. For instance, grossly disruptive or dysfunctional workplace behavior may require treatment to allow continued employment. Lesser problems may limit an employee's potential for future promotion. Such referrals can at first be colored by resentment that impedes treatment response. Ultimately, though, employees usually feel grateful after effective treatment. Some problems are so serious or acute that intervention is mandatory. Employees with significant suicidal, violent, or psychotic features often need immediate attention, and perhaps police assistance (see Chapter Fifteen).

EVALUATION: DEFINE THE PROBLEM TO DEFINE THE TREATMENT

Effective solutions for medical, business, and emotional problems all require skillful evaluation, detailed understanding, and focused implementation. All are multiply determined, but emotional problems nearly always involve unpleasant feelings that hide important causes from view.

Stress and Burnout

There is a natural reluctance to address directly intense feelings such as fear, sadness, and anger, which typically underlie emotional distress and organizational dysfunction. Instead, less threatening words are more useful to describe certain kinds of problems in ordinary language. *Stress* is certainly the most familiar such word and has a variety of meanings. Perhaps most often, it is used as a catchall for forms and degrees of anxiety (see Chapter Twenty-One). But the useful vagueness of its meaning fails to convey useful understanding of the real problem, and it also fails to differentiate unpleasant stress (distress) from less disagreeable pressures of work and circumstance (eustress).

Burnout, another familiar term, most commonly refers to various forms and degrees of depression (see Chapter Twenty-Two). Here, too, ordinary language has found a less threatening word for a set of distressing problems. Although these common phrases make initial recognition of emotional problems easier, effective resolution ultimately requires more careful evaluation.

Problems in Adaptation Are Not Always Obvious

The causes of emotional and adaptational problems are always more complex than they appear. Feeling unhappy at home, for instance, individual employees may be more readily aware of long work hours or interpersonal conflicts at the office. The more pressing family concerns are too overwhelming to really think about (see Chapter Thirteen). In fact, people sometimes get so wrapped up in what otherwise might be a minor concern that they become almost unaware of things that really distress or frighten them. This shifting of attention is common, especially when past emotional experiences leave the belief that family problems are essentially unresolvable. The reverse shift is equally common, as in the common metaphor of "kicking the dog" in response to unacceptable angry feelings toward the boss.

Finding the true causes of distress is a complex and demanding process that is essential for gaining control of feelings and solving problems. People may be aware of some causes for their distress, but ferreting out others requires careful evaluation of personal history, experience, and style. Distressed employees usually have experienced a recent event of emotional significance. Both positive and negative life events—family births, deaths, marriages, and retirements, for example—can be significant. The most emotionally important events are often overlooked ("You mean I never told you that my best friend died last month?"), hidden ("Our relationship hasn't changed in three years. Well, okay, so now he's pressing me to marry him."), or their significance denied ("How could a new baby bring anything but happiness?"). Similarly, people are largely unaware of personality traits that can contribute to their distress. Because the traits were a way of adapting to early emotional environments, people are not aware when they sometimes cause problems in adulthood (see Chapter Twenty-Three).

An employee may deliberately overemphasize specific issues in an honest attempt to make sure that they are not disregarded. For example, fears of stigma or honest belief that work factors caused disability can lead an employee to focus only on workplace issues (see Chapter Eighteen). Unscrupulous employees may deliberately hide details so as to mask substance abuse (see Chapters Twenty-Four and Twenty-Five), hide dishonest behavior, or abuse disability entitlements.

Deliberate and skilled effort is needed to make accurate psychiatric diagnoses in medical and psychosocial contexts. Patients with common syndromes such as major depression or panic disorder will not usually present themselves specifically for treatment of those conditions. Instead, their conscious concerns will be about distressing events in their lives. Faced with any depression or anxiety disorder, psychiatrists routinely take a brief medical history and arrange for further medical evaluation if necessary. Medical problems themselves can present with emotional symptoms or exacerbation of existing emotional problems (see Chapter Twenty-Seven).

Psychiatrists also need to evaluate the organizational context of an individual's distress. Organizations are collections of people with complicated goals, motivations, and methods. While an employee who feels stymied in her career may have disadvantageous personality traits or mixed feelings about advancement, consultants must acknowledge the organizational context as well as hidden organizational impediments (see Chapter Six).

Organizations can be highly political and do not always operate on meritocratic, rational, or even obvious principles (see Chapters Ten and Eleven). Problems of the organization itself are also demanding to assess. Although the emotions and goals of key individuals are always important, much of the problem can lie in corporate culture, idiosyncratic group process, or changing economic circumstances.

Value of Defined Treatment

Specific evaluation is important because it allows for carefully defined treatment. The most effective approaches for individual and organizational problems are those that resolve underlying causes. Although not all such problems require resolution of underlying causes, it is always useful to know what those causes are and essential to know the difference between treatment of causes and treatment of symptoms. Nonspecific treatments for individuals (such as relaxation therapy and some kinds of support groups) can offer some temporary relief of symptoms but leave unaddressed the underlying family problems, work conflicts, or significant medical psychiatric problems such as anxiety disorders. Specific treatments include psychotherapy aimed at uncovering sources of distress and overreaction, problem solving to facilitate adaptation, and medication for some syndromes that are not treated well by psychotherapy alone. Organizational programs that encourage effective communication and appropriate workplace interactions can stimulate individual problem solving and recognition of personal dysfunction. Sometimes the process of careful evaluation makes underlying causes more apparent and thus effects a partial resolution of the immediate problem.

The DSM-IV Diagnostic System

Personality and adaptability are a result of thoughts and feelings derived from experience. Illness is the dysfunction that occurs when adaptation fails in the face of internal or external change. Diagnosis simply defines the nature of dysfunctions that can include adjustment, anxiety, depressive, or personality disorders. Historically, psychiatric diagnosis has sometimes been viewed as vague, nonspecific, and of limited practical value. Since the early 1980s, though, the *Diagnostic and Statistical Manual of Mental Disorders,* Fourth Edition (DSM-IV), developed by the American Psychiatric Association, has become the standard for psychiatric diagnosis. DSM-IV criteria allow emotional diagnoses to have specific meanings and clearer implications for treatment and prognosis (see the chapters in Part Four). By design, DSM-IV describes discreetly recognizable syndromes and avoids reliance on psychodynamic, biological, and sociological theories. The continuing efforts at diagnostic specificity have led to greater knowledge about the psychotherapeutic and medication responsiveness of diagnoses and have spurred interest in still further improvements. (DSM-V is in preparation.)

DSM-IV has become an invaluable tool for recognition and treatment of both mild and severe emotional problems. It is not, however, a replacement for clinical skills in general or knowledge of individual, family, and organizational interactions in particular. And diagnosis itself is not as important in predicting future functioning as an individual's ability to recognize and tolerate distress, and then to seek and accept emotional support and the most effective treatment.

TREATMENT: TECHNIQUES OF PSYCHOTHERAPY AND CONSULTATION

Psychotherapy can be many different things, but it is always based on a therapeutic relationship that is intended to address emotional distress or maladaptive traits. There are many varieties of psychotherapeutic ideology, and no matter how hard they tried, no two therapists could use exactly the same technique. Within limits, variety in technique allows therapists to find effective approaches that mesh with their own personalities and those of their patients. Selecting a therapist or consultant requires attention to diagnostic and psychotherapeutic training, ability, and integrity (see Chapter Two). Depending on the nature of the problem, treatment goals, economic constraints, and individual preference, many different psychotherapeutic approaches are commonly used.

Education: Awareness Programs and Stress Management

All psychotherapy is education of a sort, and some problems call for a straightforward teaching approach. For instance, there are often educational programs in the workplace that increase awareness of problems such as depression and substance abuse. The goal of the program is to increase knowledge and recognition of the problem, with the intent of encouraging early treatment. Many stress management programs also use an educational approach. Increased awareness of the stresses of work, family, and holidays allows some relief. Other common techniques include relaxation therapy and biofeedback. Such approaches can be beneficial for mild situational anxiety that is largely related to a specific stressor, but they should not be a replacement for focused evaluation.

Support: Counseling and Self-Help Groups

Supportive counseling and self-help groups may include problem recognition, advice about specific problems, and direction to available community resources. They can be useful for guidance through a stressful period. In contrast to purely educational approaches, the process of discussing a practical problem and its solutions offers indirect emotional support from a therapist or other group members. Supportive approaches are most useful for helping people adapt in crisis situations (such as initial treatment after a major trauma), for long-term support (such as people with chronic illness that make stable adaptation difficult, or who prefer supportive therapy), and for group interventions (such as large numbers of employees who need to address shared concerns about organizational change). Some self-help groups offer this kind of support, while others have a more limited focus on members' mutual troubles.

Supportive therapies are not designed to address or recognize underlying emotional, medical, or organizational problems. They are not a replacement for more reflective therapy, but their more limited goals can improve individual adaptation where distress is overwhelming or a more limited approach is initially preferred. Effectiveness depends on the skill of the therapist and the receptiveness of the patient. The most distressed patients are often least able to feel emotionally supported, and less distressed patients may feel frustrated by the circumscribed approach. It is not always easy to give useful advice. Most people are intelligent and knowledgeable enough to look for solutions to their interpersonal problems. When they are unaware of practical solutions, it may be that their emotions have unwittingly hidden those solutions from view. Helping people to overcome their emotions and use suggested solutions is a challenging task in supportive therapy.

Surface Behavior and Thought: Behavior and Cognitive Therapy

Behavior therapy focuses on problematic external behaviors and attempts to modify them through the instruction and practice of new behavioral techniques. For example, a behavioral approach to an elevator phobia in a patient with panic disorder might attempt progressively longer periods of time in an open elevator, leading ultimately to an elevator ride. Strictly applied, behavioral approaches do not directly address underlying emotions or to associated psychiatric syndromes. The hope is that tolerating unpleasant feelings in small doses will allow the maladaptive behavior to cease.

Cognitive therapy focuses on reworking unrealistic thoughts (cognitive distortions) that are associated with emotional distress and maladaptive behaviors. For instance, a cognitive approach to depression would involve identification of recurring thoughts of worthlessness and hopelessness, and attempt to replace them with more rationally accurate thoughts of self-worth and future possibility. In its pure form, cognitive therapy does not attempt to address underlying emotions or associated psychiatric syndromes directly. Rather, the focus is on developing adaptive new cognitions. Behavior therapy and cognitive therapy are often used together. Recent research has suggested that such approaches may have benefit for some depressive and anxiety disorders.

Relationship Patterns and Inner Emotions: Insight-Oriented Therapy

Insight-oriented psychotherapy is a more thorough form of psychotherapy, often used for patients who already have generally high levels of social functioning. Low-functioning patients and those in severe acute distress are less likely to benefit from the goal of understanding the hidden long-term emotional determinants of their relationship patterns. In some cases, looking for such feelings can increase distress and dysfunction. The names for the many different forms of insight-oriented therapy are derived largely from psychoanalytic theories, but they can be very similar in clinical practice. As a group, they are also called *psychoanalytic, psychodynamic,* and *uncovering psychotherapies.*

In contemporary psychiatric practice, insight-oriented psychotherapy is often combined with other forms of therapy for specific purposes. Supportive therapy may be used just after an emotional crisis or behavior therapy used for phobic avoidance. Medication may be used for problems when psychotherapy alone is not fully effective (such as panic disorder and social phobia), or its benefits are not reliable, prompt, or complete (such as major depression). Insight-oriented therapy relies on a set of basic concepts and techniques. The further significance of these concepts for organizational interactions is discussed in Chapters Eleven, Twelve, and Thirteen.

Session Frequency and Goals of Insight-Oriented Psychotherapy. The extent to which psychoanalytic techniques are employed depends on the nature of the insight-oriented therapy employed. Generally, more intensive forms are suitable for patients who are already psychologically minded and functioning at least reasonably well. Formal psychoanalysis is an intensive treatment for certain deep-seated personality problems. Typically conducted four times per week on a couch, treatment may last for several years. Only a few patients opt for this major commitment of time, money, and emotional effort. Psychoanalytic psychotherapy is conducted once or twice a week. Its basic principles are similar to those of psychoanalysis, but the goal is limited to uncovering maladaptive emotions and perceptions hidden from conscious awareness. Similar principles are essential to understanding even the most supportive psychotherapy.

Treatment should not continue indefinitely. Rather, certain goals are sought, and a continuing process of reevaluation is part of the treatment itself. At a certain point, continuing benefits for the patient are outweighed by the costs, and a specific termination phase of therapy is started. That does not mean that therapy should stop any time the question comes up. In fact, the question often arises at exactly those times when anxiety increases while important issues start to emerge. Care must be taken not to see these signs of impending therapeutic progress as evidence for termination of therapy.

Emotional Development, Unconscious Expectation, and Conflict. People grow up in a particular emotional environment, usually their biological family. From their early relationships, they unwittingly (unconsciously) acquire direct and indirect expectations about what relationships are like and about how best to interact with other people. These expectations derive from experience and observation of family behavior and from inner experience of their personal emotional reactions. The expectations remain unwittingly present into adulthood; they color perceptions of other people and influence behavior and emotion. Without realizing it, all people thus have certain expectations about what the world is like and are limited in their ability to see people and situations for what they really are. Depending on the strength and kind of these unconscious expectations, they can have detrimental effects on social adaptation and emotional well-being. An example might be a manager who has trouble completing a prestigious project because he unwittingly fears the envy of his peers. The fear may derive from his experience of envious siblings in childhood. It may also derive from attribution onto his peers (referred to as projection) of his own defiant anger about anticipated lack of recognition for his success. Similarly, avoidance of success may be an unwitting attempt at avoiding punishment from a powerful authority figure. Such concerns about intergenerational competition (referred to as oedipal conflict) are particularly well known in psychotherapeutic and popular culture (see Chapter Seven).

Transference and Countertransference. People experience varying degrees of unwitting expectation and feeling with all other people, and relationship problems can be a result. In the particular setting of psychotherapy, persistent expectations and feelings can become focused on the therapist (a process known as transference), without any real basis in the therapeutic relationship itself. In the psychotherapeutic setting, transference can be more readily recognized and understood than in social relationships. The psychotherapeutic relationship is designed to allow transferential expectations and feelings to become evident and therapeutically useful. Transference thus becomes a major tool in understanding the hidden factors that adversely influence relationships.

Therapists too have hidden expectations and feelings in the therapeutic setting (countertransference). For this reason, psychotherapy training programs always include direct individual supervision. Programs should also include a primary focus on keeping trainees constantly aware of their own inappropriate expectations and feelings, which would otherwise impose limitations on psychotherapeutic progress. Many psychiatric resident and other training programs encourage trainees to complete a formal personal psychoanalysis. Such treatment is a requirement for psychoanalytic certification.

Defense, Resistance, Interpretation, and Insight. Because hidden emotional dilemmas (referred to as unconscious conflicts) can be distressing, people develop a variety of unwitting mechanisms known as psychological defenses to protect themselves from emotional pain. For example, repression is a process of removing a painful thought from awareness, such as failure to remember childhood sadness or angry impulses. Counterphobia involves attempts at conquering a feared situation in order to hide the fear itself from awareness (such as hidden competitive fears of success leading to an ever more intense drive for accomplishment). These two mechanisms are among the mature defenses that are ordinary parts of adult personality development. Recent decades have also seen increasing attention to other defenses that protect against more primitive fears of an overwhelmingly inattentive world. Splitting, for instance, involves seeing all people as either all good or all bad, as a way of avoiding a perception of rejection by everyone.

These emotional defenses also operate within the psychotherapeutic setting (resistance). Resistance is the largely unwitting process of keeping transferential feelings toward the therapist out of awareness. From one perspective, psychoanalytic process involves an empathic and progressive interpretation of resistance. The process thus allows awareness of transferential expectations and feelings, corresponding hidden emotional dilemmas, and painful childhood experiences. At the same time, other relationships are examined for evidence of similar emotional and behavioral patterns. The same patterns are reviewed many times and from different perspectives ("working through") in the process of working through. As a result, there is insight: increased awareness of relationship patterns and their emotional determinants ("insights"). Newly alerted to unwitting expectations and feelings, patients feel less distressed and better able to change their circumstances and relationships. Introspective self-awareness ("I always foul up when the deal is about to close"), in contrast to insight, rarely brings either the same kind of emotional relief or the capacity for personal change.

Therapeutic Alliance, Neutrality, Advice, Free Association, and Dreams. As therapy begins, one of the first tasks is development of a therapeutic alliance. Therapy is not a social relationship, and the therapeutic alliance calls for recognition of the therapist's role in offering insight into self-defeating unconscious expectations and feelings. In that capacity, the therapist maintains therapeutic neutrality. This does not mean neutrality toward the well-being of the patient. Rather, the therapist is neutral toward patients' conflicting hidden motivations. The assumption is made that the inability to make choices is usually a function of unwitting emotional conflict. Understanding those conflicts is the most important goal, and specific practical advice is sometimes counterproductive. Instead, attempts are made to uncover the emotional dilemma and allow comfortable conscious decisions to emerge. When advice is given or other deliberate breaks in therapeutic neutrality occur ("parameters"), there are specific emotional meanings for patients that should be understood. For instance, some patients might feel that they are not permitted to solve their own problems.

Once therapy is underway, patients are encouraged to say whatever comes to mind, no matter how irrelevant, disconnected, painful, or silly it might seem ("free association"). The idea is that a common emotional thread ties the thoughts together, and this free association allows recognition and interpretation of that thread. Since this is so different from normal social conversation, it takes some effort and practice. Difficulty in free association also reflects expectations and feelings about the therapist, and thus also becomes useful information for the therapy. The therapist allows free association and transference to emerge by saying comparatively little and maintaining an attentive nonjudgmental attitude. Dreams are another source of useful information in this type of therapy. Because dreams are put together by the mind, they symbolically reflect the kinds of relationship patterns that people unwittingly perceive in the world around them. There are no textbook or mystical explanations for dreams. The patterns of the dream become clear in the overall context of relationships, but particularly those in childhood, family, and the therapy itself.

Career Enhancement: Executive Development

While the process of psychotherapy can offer many kinds of personal advantages, one particular area of interest is career success and satisfaction. Transference, emotional conflict, and personality style have major effects in the workplace. There are many different psychotherapeutic methods of enhancing career development (see Chapter Six). They range from educational models that are like business courses, to supportive advice and mentoring models, to executive coaching. This last approach often relies on both standardized skill evaluation and a modified form of psychotherapy. Although many of the techniques are similar to insight-oriented psychotherapy, there are important differences. Less attention is paid to inner emotional life and more to the effects of expectations, feelings, and behaviors on business skills and relationships. People who are primarily interested in improving their management or sales skills sometimes prefer executive coaching. At the same time, though, resulting career benefits may be accompanied by heightened tension. That tension is often responsive to appropriate interpretation and may thus lead to further benefits beyond career advancement alone.

Organizational Development: Organizational Consulting

There are also emotional and interpersonal factors that affect the organization as a whole and that managers may recognize as needing outside consultation. On the largest scale, there are often concerns about issues of organizational structure (see Chapter Eleven), especially in times of change. For example, changing external circumstances can include increased competition, shifting customer preferences, or a major lawsuit. Changing internal circumstances include mergers and acquisitions, growth, and downsizing (see Chapter Eight). Stagnation in the face of change is a problem that needs attention. There are also many smaller-scale issues, including team building, conflict resolution, fostering intrapreneurship and creativity, succession planning, and general aspects of employee motivation and management.

Addressing these problems requires a wide variety of psychiatric skills. Behavioral approaches are useful for understanding surface effects of performance evaluation and promotional systems. Psychometric approaches use interviews and questionnaires to develop a detailed perspective on management and interactional problems. Group process and family systems theories are useful in understanding interactions within the organization. More psychoanalytic approaches help explore and improve management and employee morale and motivations. True employee empowerment comes about through the creation of a healthy organizational culture. But any change in emotional environment can be threatening to entrenched interests and hidden emotions. Changing organizational culture is a true challenge for managers and consultants. Perhaps most important, a psychiatric perspective is essential for understanding the organizational and individual behavior of key personnel. Consultation to an organization often results in identification and referral of a distressed executive. Sometimes the distress is most obvious through its organizational effects (see Chapter Seven).

Medication and Therapy

Optimal treatment of emotional problems often requires more than psychotherapy alone, and the importance of adding medication is not always obvious. For instance, there are several common syndromes that psychotherapy alone does not treat well and that respond much better when appropriate medication is added. Notable among these are chronic low-grade problems such as dysthymia, panic disorder, social phobia, and obsessive-compulsive disorder (see Chapters

Twenty-One and Twenty-Two). These problems can be easily missed unless a skilled clinician seeks specific history. Ineffective psychotherapies commonly result from failure to diagnose and treat such conditions. Major depression is a more acute syndrome, which may show a delayed, partial, or unreliable response to psychotherapy alone. Recent studies have shown that the fastest and most complete response is to combined medication and psychotherapy. The need for medication is most obvious in patients with overt mania or psychosis (see Chapter Twenty-Six).

The process of prescribing medication for emotional problems is complex. Beyond the issues of careful diagnosis, specific and adequate treatment, and medication side effects are issues of the emotional meaning of the medication itself. The medication is seen both consciously and unconsciously in many different ways—as a gift or a penalty, an opportunity or an impediment. Some patients jump at the chance to use medication instead of psychotherapy; others fear that medication will be a crutch that prevents self-reliance or psychotherapeutic benefit. Most patients react to effective medication with relief, although some experience that relief with anxiety and even treatment noncompliance.

Appropriate medication is rarely an alternative to some equally effective psychotherapy. Specific medications should be used for specific syndromes. They should not be used just because psychotherapy does not seem to be working, because a patient is considered hopeless, or because of some feelings toward the patient of which the therapist is unaware. And neither should medication be withheld because of some need to make psychotherapy work where it cannot, failure or inability to recognize medication responsive syndromes, or some unwitting feelings toward the patient. Psychotherapy and medication work together, each primarily addressing symptoms unresponsive to the other. Once medication-responsive syndromes are treated, patients often find it easier to understand the emotional issues that confront them and find solutions for their practical and interpersonal problems.

ASSESSING TREATMENT AND CONSULTATION RESPONSE

Just as optimal psychiatric evaluation and treatment require focused approaches, assessing treatment response requires equally careful attention. Changes are often gradual or subtle. And people do not usually tell coworkers when symptoms or conflicts are newly improved, nor should they. Only occasionally is it appropriate for colleagues or supervisors to receive direct feedback from a treating psychiatrist (see Chapter Four). So although subtle improvements are easy to overlook, it is important for everyone to recognize workplace changes when they occur.

Employee Changes: Symptoms, Demeanor, Style, and Family

Some changes are relatively easy to see. For instance, return to work after a major depression or the absence of intoxication on the job is evidence of symptomatic improvement. But even for these more overt problems, improvement may become evident only as subtle changes in demeanor. The always reserved but now depressed worker who stays on the job may seem only more reserved than usual. When the depression resolves (typically after three weeks of medication), the employee will seem more alert and well rested. Less obvious to coworkers will be the resolution of unremitting sadness, insomnia, and suicidal thoughts. Similarly, the alcoholic worker who had always been sober on the job may show a subtle decrease in irritability once he stops drinking.

More subtle still are changes in interpersonal style. These kinds of changes can occur gradually after treatment of chronic mild depressive and anxiety disorders and after effective insight-oriented psychotherapy. Subtle style changes are followed by gradual self-awareness and gradual recognition by others. For instance, an employee with social phobia might have been tense and withdrawn in meetings and even at lunch. Initial treatment effects might include relief of the tension. Only later is there greater social interaction and increasingly comfortable efforts at meeting participation. And when those changes do occur, it may take a while before anyone recognizes them.

Personality changes through psychotherapy are often the most subtle of all. Insight-oriented psychotherapy has the potential for gradually effecting substantial change in rigid and self-defeating styles (see Chapter Twenty-Three). Even once change has occurred, it may take close attention to see that personality style has become more flexible and that workplace interactions have become more productive. Effective treatment benefits family life as well. Those changes are typically unapparent at work, although often with secondary benefits for workplace functioning.

Workplace Changes: Productivity, Decisions, Interactions, and Leadership

Beyond benefits for the individual worker, personal treatment and organizational consultation can bring about changes for the organization as a whole. Some changes are readily apparent—for instance, if treatment or consultation causes clear changes in productivity, clear reductions in infighting, or clearly beneficial organizational streamlining. But less tangible changes can have just as important effects on the workplace. Careful observation is needed to recognize such benefits as wise planning, recognition of both short- and long-term effects of decisions, effective management style, and visionary leadership. The better someone feels inside about herself and her work, the better the job she will do for herself, coworkers, and the organization as a whole. At the same time, there are limits to the benefits that can accrue. Productivity, decisions, interactions, and leadership are functions of individuals, organizational structure and style, and external economic and social factors.

Treatment Resistance and Entrenched Reputation

When people do not seem to get better, there are many possible explanations. Perhaps most common is real improvement that is not very apparent. Sometimes people have trouble seeing improvement in themselves. For instance, shortly after resolution of a depression, some hopeless thoughts may persist despite a more cheerful mood. Or a pessimistic outlook makes outward acknowledgment of improvement uncomfortable. Within an organization, people often develop entrenched reputations. Even when there is definite change in both acute problems and long-term style, the old reputation can linger. The same is true for changing the organization. Even if effective changes are brought about, plainly the old images may linger for a while within the organization and longer still to customers on the outside.

It is important to allow enough time for treatment to work. Medications might take effect in days or weeks (and sometimes months), but psychotherapy is often more gradual. Still, treatment quality varies considerably, and questions about ineffectiveness are sometimes appropriate. When contact with the clinician is appropriate, the clinician's opinion and the employee's can be sought. Alternatively, there are some situations where a consultation with a nontreating psychiatrist can provide useful reevaluation of diagnosis, treatment, and prognosis. When treatment does not seem to be going well, there are certain kinds of questions to keep in mind.

Incorrect Diagnosis, Therapy, or Goals. The first question is whether there was a complete and accurate evaluation before treatment began. Frequently, important problems are overlooked. For example, treatment might have focused on reducing stress in the office, when problems at home were a more pressing issue. Depressive or anxiety disorders may have gone undiagnosed and untreated. It is also possible that the treatment used was unsuited for the goals at hand or that the therapist is insufficiently skilled. For instance, supportive therapy may not be sufficient for helping to uncover and change maladaptive personality styles. And insight-oriented therapy by itself may not be sufficient for acute family crises, sudden job loss, or panic disorder. And even appropriate medication, without psychotherapy, is usually insufficient for most problems. Less frequently, treatment may be impaired by noncompliance or deliberate misrepresentation.

Family, Organizational, Medication, or Medical Problems. Even if the evaluation and treatment seem appropriate, other factors may keep progress at a minimum. For instance, families often develop habitual patterns of interaction that can impede progress. As the employee starts to feel better, relatives may unwittingly protect the family structure by discouraging further change. The same thing can happen within an organization, where people get used to certain patterns of behavior. When a colleague starts to feel or act differently, that threatens the organizational equilibrium. Similarly, when efforts are made to change the organization itself, individuals may feel threatened and resist the change.

Both mild and serious medication-responsive symptoms are often overlooked, and their treatment can require specific expertise. Different kinds or combinations of medication are often tried, and proper integration with psychotherapy is important. Medical illness is commonly mistaken for emotional problems. Even demoralization at work can sometimes be a surface presentation of undetected illnesses such as thyroid disease, anemia, vitamin deficiency, or cancer.

BUILDING A BETTER BENEFIT: QUALITY MENTAL HEALTH CARE GUIDELINES

Quality mental health care for individuals is possible, better than ever, and always improving. The question, though, is whether employers and employees are getting the full benefit of these advances on the larger scale. Alas, mental health delivery systems and benefits are not all what they could be.

Quality Care Components: Access, Evaluation, and Treatment

There are some basic components to keep in mind and to review from the employer's perspective. And while defining quality mental health care may seem almost easy, implementation is far more complex.

Ready Employee Access. Once employees have set out to find good care, easy access is important. Barriers to care sometimes put off people in emotional distress. And as the old saying goes, it is best to help people strike while the iron is hot and their motivation is strong.

There are a number of programs that employers can use to enhance access. For example, many companies have programs to increase management and employee awareness of problems like depression and drug abuse, or to educate management about recognizing the role of emotional distress in workplace problems (see Chapter Fourteen). Paper-and-pencil or Internet-based self-rating tools can help employees recognize and label their distress. Perhaps most helpful are managers who recognize that value of good care and encourage appropriate treatment.

Start with Skilled Evaluators. It is very important that the initial clinical contact is with a well-trained clinician. Too often, important problems are not recognized at the outset, and the diagnostic omission is never corrected. Unrecognized personal and career problems are extremely common, especially when an employee calls an 800 number or has an initial session for evaluation only. People are understandably cautious about what they reveal, and more so when they perceive issues about confidentiality. More than that, most people cannot put their finger on the issue that may actually be bothering them the most. Equally common are subtle but important anxiety, depressive, or substance use problems. Much less common, but obviously important, are undiagnosed medical problems masquerading as emotional distress.

A broadly trained clinician can help to recognize the contributing problems at the outset and arrange for appropriate treatment. The most complete training includes a thorough understanding of personal, family, and workplace issues; psychiatric diagnosis; psychotherapy; medication; and medical problems (see Chapter Two).

Beyond the training itself, finding skilled evaluators involves considering their clinical experience, academic credentials, attention to confidentiality and ethics, interpersonal skills, emotional self-awareness, and knowledge of their own clinical limitations.

Thorough and Precise Initial Diagnosis. Having the right evaluators in place dramatically improves the odds of doing it right the first time for both the evaluation and subsequent treatment. In any emotional crisis, issues are usually more complex than they appear, and evaluators are never aware of what they miss. Common omissions (with ballpark prevalence speculations for ordinary psychotherapy cases) are specific depression and anxiety disorders (50 percent); the most central personal, family, or workplace issue (30 percent); alcohol and drugs (20 percent); medical problems as symptom triggers (5 percent); and undiagnosed major medical problems as hidden cause of symptoms (1 percent). Making the right diagnoses is essential for making effective referrals for optimal treatment.

People Really Can Get Better. Most emotional problems of employed individuals can be readily and swiftly treated as long as the diagnoses are correct and the best treatment is chosen. Here, too, it is important to have well-trained and highly experienced clinicians. Most mental health treatment is some form of psychotherapy, often with use of medication.

The psychotherapy used should be specifically appropriate for each individual patient. It should have focused goals, but without an oversimplified view of problems and their emotional contributors. Supportive psychotherapies that offer little more than sympathy and reassurance have limited benefit. And psychotherapy alone is not usually sufficient for the commonplace anxiety and depressive disorders.

Medication and psychotherapy do not replace each other. Rather, they complement and enhance each other. Unmedicated anxiety and depressive disorders can continue to be problematic and interfere with progress in psychotherapy. At the same time, appropriate medication is rarely sufficient by itself. Even biological imbalances come attached to important personal and life issues that medication alone will leave unresolved. A small but important percentage of patients also need medical care for undiagnosed illnesses and other changes in their health.

A few cautions about treatment are important in thinking from the employer's perspective. Confidentiality and perceived confidentiality are always essential for full clinical effectiveness. Problems arise when treating clinicians act as patient advocates (for example, for disability claims; see Chapter Eighteen). Length of psychotherapy treatment varies depending on the patient, diagnosis, goals, insurance, and clinician, and it should not be an endless process. Even with privately paid psychoanalyses, there comes a time where limited continuing benefit no longer justifies the ongoing investment of time, money, and emotional energy. Finally, all clinicians need to be aware that they do have limitations in their abilities and that patients' diagnoses and circumstances frequently change over time.

Assessment and Quality Control. Quality control is popular for mental health care, and important research is underway. Nevertheless, the science is still a long way from accurate data that can be usefully applied. Some managed care companies conduct self-assessments, though most of these rely on patient satisfaction measures that are largely unrelated to evaluation and treatment quality. Employers can gather some additional data through exploration of employee surveys, diagnostic patterns, treatment patterns, and workplace feedback (with due caution about confidentiality). Some studies have also started to look at the workplace cost-effectiveness and cost benefit of mental health care (see Chapter Three).

It stands to reason that better help for employees will also help the bottom line. Employees get better faster, stay on the job, stay at the company, have fewer future problems, have greater initiative and creativity, and often are more productive than they were before. In particular, studies have suggested that the largest cost of anxiety disorders (88 percent) is in lost productivity (Greenberg et al., 1999). A study found that employees were already less productive six months before they started an antidepressant, suggesting a long time lag between onset of depression and treatment (Claxton, Chawla, & Kennedy, 1999). Yet another study reported that depression with anxiety is the best predictor of absenteeism and that absenteeism then improved with treatment (Tollefson, Souetre, Thomander, & Potvin, 1993).

Most internists say that most outpatient visits have significant emotional determinants. So mental health care can have some degree of medical care cost offset, though probably not 100 percent. Quality care should also offset some of the costs of mental health care coverage. For example, some psychotherapy (without medication) for panic disorder can be lengthy but yet of limited benefit. A workplace-focused executive coach may overlook a central family problem and have limited effectiveness (though the coaching cost is not generally covered by health insurance; see Chapter Six). Finally, early and effective treatment may reduce disability claims for both mental illness and medical illness.

Less tangible workplace benefits include reduced conflict and improved communication at work. This is especially important for executives, whose emotions and perspective affect management quality, judgment, and employee morale (see Chapter Seven).

Recognizing Quality Care: Why Isn't It Obvious?

These basic principles may seem straightforward at first glance, yet assessment of mental health systems for quality turns out to be a complicated process. Not surprisingly, employers generally have low expectations of mental health care. While most organized systems of care stress that they offer a quality product, much of the self-assessment that they provide is based largely on patient satisfaction measures. This is obviously important, but it is not necessarily a measure of accurate diagnosis, effective treatment, positive outcomes, or even cost-effectiveness.

Although diagnosis and treatment are better studied and more reliably effective in psychiatry than most other fields of medicine, it is also far easier to imitate quality care in mental health than in, say, surgery or cardiology. In fact, patients can be quite pleased with a friendly clinician in a pleasant office, even while both may be unaware that more positive or rapid outcomes are possible.

Some outside agencies have started to develop some useful, though limited, assessment methodologies. For example, the Health Plan Employer Data and Information Set looks at such rudimentary measures as length of hospitalization, follow-up after hospitalization, employee utilization rates, and basic issues of depression medication management. Further efforts are underway, but standardized measures of diagnostic accuracy and treatment use may prove to be quite complex.

Proactive Approaches to Improve Employee Benefits

There are good ways to improve the quality of care that employers make available to their employees. Careful attention must be provided to both benefits and delivery systems (see Chapter Two).

Carefully Assess Current Mental Health System. The benefits package is a good place to start studying quality of care. It is important that benefits costs are viewed as an investment with potential advantages for both employees and employer. An investment poorly planned, funded, or monitored will not pay off. Are employees offered more than one kind of insurance (for example managed care, indemnity, preferred provider)? Is managed care "carved out" from the health insurance package? While carve-outs ostensibly offer mental health care from more specialized companies, they may actually be an opportunity to reduce short-term costs at the expense of quality of care. What kinds of limits are there on access, length of treatment, fees or providers?

If the benefits use a predetermined set of providers, then it is important to know how evaluations are done, who provides clinical care, what the mix is of providers in the system, and how well experienced and credentialed they are. Further information can be found by examining claims data for diagnostic and treatment data, again with attention to issues of confidentiality. Are common diagnoses commonly made? Are rare or controversial diagnoses too common? Are treatments appropriate for diagnoses and goals? Do employees feel that they are getting effective care, and do managers feel that employees return to their previous levels of functioning?

Develop Guidelines to Improve Quality of Care for Your Company's Needs. Based on the initial assessment, employers should formulate guidelines that reflect their needs and expectations of mental health care. Guidelines should be drawn up with the help of independent outside consultants rather than relying solely on internal expertise, existing brokers, or vendors themselves. The guidelines should address the issues in this chapter and also draw on the several evolving sets of treatment guidelines (many are cited by the chapters in Part Four). A few employers have even started proprietary clinical networks to maximize benefit. This allows direct application of guidelines, built-in follow-up and improvement mechanisms, better analysis of cost and cost benefit, and outside clinical oversight.

Understanding and resolving mental health problems in the workplace require careful attention by management, HR officers, and occupational and mental health professionals. Individual and organizational problems have multiple causes, some of which may be hidden from casual observation. Referral for proper initial evaluation calls for special knowledge and skills. Once underlying causal factors are identified, defined treatment can effect helpful solutions. The many different types of therapy include educational, supportive, behavioral, cognitive, insight oriented, organizational, and medication approaches. These approaches are often combined, and basic principles of psychoanalytic thought are useful for understanding many of them. Once treatment is underway, special attention is needed to assess changes in workplace performance. The best results and lowest long-term costs are obtained through careful initial evaluation, followed by optimal treatment.

References and Additional Sources

American Psychiatric Association. (2000). *American Psychiatric Association practice guidelines for the treatment of psychiatric disorders: Compendium 2000.* Washington, DC: Author.

American Psychiatric Association. (2000). *Diagnostic and statistical manual of mental disorders (text rev.).* Washington, DC: Author.

Beitman, B. D., & Klerman, G. L. (1991). *Integrating pharmacotherapy and psychotherapy.* Washington, DC: American Psychiatric Press.

Bernstein, A. E., & Warner, G. M. (1995). *An introduction to contemporary psychoanalysis.* Northvale, NJ: Aronson.

Claxton, A. J., Chawla, A. J., & Kennedy, S. (1999). *Journal of Occupational and Environmental Medicine, 41,* 605–611.

Greenberg, P. E., Sisitsky, T., Kessler, R. C., Finkelstein, S. N., Berndt, E. R., Davidson, J. R., Ballenger, J. C., & Fyer, A. J. (1999). The economic burden of anxiety disorders in the 1990s. *Journal of Clinical Psychiatry, 60,* 427–435.

Herman, R. C., & Palmer, R. H. (2002). Common ground: A framework for selecting core quality measures for mental health and substance abuse care. *Psychiatric Services, 53,* 281–287.

McLean, A. A. (1979). *Work stress.* Reading, MA: Addison-Wesley.

Schatzberg, A. F., & Nemeroff, C. B. (Eds.). (1998). *American psychiatric textbook of psychopharmacology* (2nd ed.). Washington, DC: American Psychiatric Press.

Sperry, L. (1993). *Psychiatric consultation in the workplace.* Washington, DC: American Psychiatric Press.

Tollefson, G. D., Souetre, E., Thomander, L., & Potvin, J. H. (1993). Comorbid anxious signs and symptoms in major depression: Impact on functional work capacity and comparative treatment outcomes. *International Clinical Psychopharmacology, 8,* 281–293.

CHAPTER TWO

Mental Health Care Providers
and Delivery Systems

Alan M. Langlieb
Anne M. Stoline
Steven S. Sharfstein

A variety of professionals are available within the mental health care system for employees who seek or need mental health evaluation. The choice of health care provider will depend on the employee's problem, as well as the goals for the evaluation or treatment. Selecting a provider will be constrained by financial considerations, including whether the employee has mental health insurance benefits. Some health insurance programs constrain provider selection. Employees without mental health insurance benefits can receive evaluation or treatment in the public sector mental health care system. Rising health care expenditures motivated third-party payers, including government, corporations, and insurance companies, to implement cost-containment approaches, including programs to oversee resource use. Many managed care systems and employee assistance programs employ gatekeepers (with variable training) to regulate the use of mental health care resources. These oversight methods have uncertain effects on quality of care.

The U.S. mental health care system is funded through myriad sources, including government programs, private insurance companies, and out-of-pocket payment from individuals. Many people receive insurance coverage through their place of employment; in that case, the employer becomes the payer either directly (with self-insurance) or indirectly (through an insurance company).

The private sector has various reimbursement mechanisms, including the traditional method of fee for service (FFS), discounted FFS such as preferred provider organizations (PPOs), and prospective arrangements such as health maintenance organizations (HMOs). Employees without insurance coverage pay for mental health care services out of pocket.

Thanks to R. Benoit, D. Edwin, J. Hedblom, and S. Proctor for their help in preparing this chapter.

Those who are unable to afford these costs have a number of alternatives. The public mental health care sector includes a network of state hospitals for inpatient care. State and local clinics provide income-adjusted outpatient care to the population. In large urban areas, city-funded hospital clinics provide low-fee care to the poor. Private agencies, often run by religious groups, are another low-fee alternative found in most urban areas. Additional sources of reduced-fee care include teaching clinics staffed by physicians in training, research clinics treating persons with designated conditions, and psychoanalytic training institutes. These services are sought by the uninsured, including those whose traditional policy does not include mental health care or those who have exhausted their mental health coverage.

The provision of mental health care in the United States has been heavily influenced in the past two decades by a crisis in health care costs caused by a number of factors, including general price inflation, an aging and expanding population, and the inflationary incentives of FFS reimbursement. Specific to the mental health care sector, inpatient units and treatment of substance abuse were the main additional causes of rising expenditures before managed care became widespread. Greater use of these services reflected increases in societal stress, as well as a weakening of church and work relationships that formerly provided channels for handling personal problems. They also reflected a growth of for-profit hospitals, many of which specialize in these services.

The health care cost crisis motivated payers to implement a number of cost-containment strategies. These include restrictions on health insurance benefits, in many cases resulting in severe constraints on mental health care coverage. Cost sharing by employees has been increased, usually with greater copayments and deductibles for mental health care than for other conditions.

Several methods of resource management at the level of the patient-provider encounter have been implemented by managed care. These include case management, gatekeeper programs, and utilization review. The effects of these programs on mental health care are explored.

PROVIDERS

A wide variety of health care professionals are available within the mental health care system in diverse settings. The type of professional who is selected depends on the employee's particular problem, as well as on the goals of evaluation or treatment. In managed care, gatekeepers often refer employees to mental health care providers. Many gatekeepers tend to have minimal (if any) clinical training, a problem because anyone who refers a troubled employee with a low mood should be able to distinguish among major depression, demoralization, and other possible underlying emotional and medical conditions. Distinguishing these causes of low mood will affect the selection of an appropriate professional to evaluate the employee. The selection of a professional should be based on quality and depth of training, as well as an impressionistic opinion of the person's skills.

Whether the various provider types can be substituted (for example, a psychologist or social worker instead of a psychiatrist) is a hotly debated issue because little basic research to compare treatment outcomes among various providers has been done. A gatekeeper may be charged with finding the most economical provider, leaving quality of care a secondary concern (if that). Similarly, little information is available about the benefits of the different types of treatment (such as those endorsed by the various schools of psychotherapy). Lack of data should not be interpreted to mean that certain therapies are ineffective; rather, it reflects the difficulty in studying treatment. In fact, studies of psychotherapy reveal its economic benefits (reflected in improved productivity and lower costs of other types of medical care), in addition to its clinical benefits.

Clergy, social welfare agencies, teachers, and medical care providers without specialized training in mental health may interact with a troubled employee. However, this chapter focuses on the professionals who typically provide initial clinical evaluation. Other professionals may be called on as specialized services are needed, including marital and family counselors, expressive art therapists, occupational therapists, group therapists, vocational rehabilitation counselors, and nurses.

Each type of education in mental health has a particular emphasis, which then partly characterizes the professionals it prepares to provide mental health care. There are also areas common to every mental health professional. To varying extents, the knowledge of all mental health professionals broadens and deepens with time, clinical experience, and contact with other health care professionals.

The issue of market value influences the decision process. Although psychiatric care is sometimes more expensive than care by other mental health professionals, higher price generally reflects higher perceived quality. The concept of "doing it right the first time" also applies. Without realizing it, those with lesser training may be ill prepared to treat a particular case and not recognize their clinical limitations. At risk is the lack of recognition by a lesser trained professional of the need for more sophisticated psychotherapeutic approaches, the need for medication, or the presence of a medical or psychiatric diagnosis. False starts delay or prevent effective treatment and increase the eventual total cost. All health care professionals must know their limitations and refer to or consult with another clinician when appropriate.

Psychiatrists

A psychiatrist is a physician and has thus obtained an undergraduate degree with a number of basic science course requirements, followed by medical school where the M.D. (or D.O.) degree is obtained. Extensive patient care and medical skills are developed in this training, under the supervision of both experienced physicians and those in residency training. The physician then spends four years in postgraduate specialty training in an approved psychiatry residency program. The overall length of training before independent practice is at least eight years after the undergraduate degree is obtained.

Psychiatrists are the only mental health specialists with medical school training. As a result, they have a number of unique skills, including the education required to prescribe medications. They are trained to recognize and treat unsuspected organic or physical causes of mental disorders. Of all the mental health professionals, they receive the most training in diagnosing mental disorders through a systematic examination of the patient's thoughts, emotions, mental life, and relationships. This process of systematic conversation, known as the mental status examination, is in many ways analogous to physical examination of the body. Psychiatrists are extensively trained to perform individual, group, and family psychotherapy. Psychotherapy training includes academic course work, supervised clinical experience, seminars, and often personal psychotherapy.

Many elect to seek further training within specific areas of psychiatry in a fellowship, a period of advanced training. Potential areas of specialization include psychopharmacology (the use of medications), geriatrics, forensics (concerning psychiatry and the law), research, psychotherapy, addictions, consultation-liaison (evaluating inpatients on medical and surgical units with suspected psychiatric conditions), and child and adolescent psychiatry. Some fellows focus on the treatment of a particular disease, such as depression or eating disorders; such clinical work is often combined with basic scientific research on the condition. Psychiatrists may undergo extended training to practice psychoanalysis, a form of intensive psychotherapy. Many psychiatrists undergo personal psychoanalysis to develop their own psychotherapeutic skills.

Psychiatrists are credentialed at a number of steps in the educational process. During medical school and residency, they must pass either the U.S. Medical Licensing Exam or the Federal Licensing Exam, both of which test for basic science knowledge and general clinical knowledge. Physicians who pass one of these tests can qualify for state licensure to practice medicine. State requirements for licensure vary. In order to remain licensed, physicians must complete a predetermined number of hours of continuing medical education with credits toward recertification.

One year after completing residency, psychiatrists may take an optional two-stage board certification exam, with written and oral components. The oral component requires interviewing a patient, followed by an examination of the results of the interview with two board-certified psychiatrists. Psychiatrists who pass both phases are board certified. Until recently, there was no requirement for recertification. However, this regulation has been changed, and psychiatrists tested after 1993 will be required to take a written test every ten years.

Nearly all patients treated by psychiatrists receive some type of psychotherapy, depending on their diagnosis and the goals of treatment. In addition, surveys by the American Psychiatric Association (APA) indicate that about two-thirds of the people treated by psychiatrists receive care that depends in some way on the clinician's medical skills. Such treatment includes medication management and evaluation or consultation (often for patients being treated on hospital medical or surgical units). The other one-third of the psychiatric patient population receives psychotherapy or psychoanalysis without medication.

Ideally, a well-trained psychiatrist provides the best initial evaluation for any troubled employee. Several directories are available that list physicians in active practice, facilitating selection of a provider. One guide, the *American Psychiatric Association Biographical Directory,* lists psychiatrists by state and city, as well as alphabetically. The citation includes the psychiatrist's name, address, type of practice, birthdate, professional titles, education, and special interests. Such guides often note whether the psychiatrist is board certified. The local chapter of the APA or the state psychiatric association can also assist with private referrals. The Academy of Organizational and Occupational Psychiatry (AOOP) was established in 1990 by psychiatrists with a special interest and expertise in organizational mental health issues. (Many of this book's contributors are AOOP members.)

Psychiatrists are available in nearly every area of the country. A local practitioner can be found in the *Who's Who Directory of Medical Specialists,* which lists information similar to that in the *American Psychiatric Association Biographical Directory.* APA surveys reveal that about half of the mental health services in the United States are provided by nonpsychiatric physicians, including general practitioners, family physicians, emergency room physicians, neurologists, internists, and pediatricians. Of note, where there is a shortage of psychiatrists, there is an equal shortage of other mental health professionals.

Selection of a psychiatrist is based on several other factors. First is availability. Of approximately 200,000 mental health professionals in the United States, only about 30,000 are psychiatrists. This is one of the few undersupplied specialties in the United States, and waiting lists for treatment in many areas (particularly rural areas) can be long. A second consideration is whether the psychiatrist has specialized in a particular type of treatment or group of patients. Certain considerations become important when obtaining treatment for employees with some conditions, as will become clear in Part Four of this book. For example, an employee with a known medical condition or suspected illness should be evaluated by a psychiatrist. Furthermore, because only a psychiatrist is trained to recognize these conditions, a decision to refer the employee to another type of specialist for evaluation or treatment may preclude accurate diagnosis and appropriate treatment. Similarly, an employee already taking prescribed medication or will likely require medication as part of treatment should be evaluated by a psychiatrist, the only medical specialist trained in mental disorders and the only mental health professional trained to prescribe medications.

Psychologists

A clinical psychologist is a mental health professional who obtained an undergraduate degree and then completed requirements for a Ph.D. in clinical or counseling psychology (exceptions include psychology associates, licensed in some states with a master's degree), or for an Ed.D. Graduate programs in psychology are diverse, but most include course work and practica or clerkships in the various areas of psychology, followed by a one- to two-year internship. A thesis is required by most programs, an exception being the Psy.D. degree in applied psychology, which has no requirement for original research. Psychologists receive a significant amount of systematic training in psychotherapy. They are also trained to perform tests on patients, including tests of intelligence, memory, and personality. Psychology is a broad field that includes training in education and industrial organization. Supervision is generally provided by experienced psychologists, as well as by psychiatrists. Following completion of a basic program, psychologists may specialize in cognitive-behavioral therapy, psychoanalysis, neuropsychology (focusing on the impact of brain disease on human behavior and mental life), and other areas. The overall length of training after the undergraduate degree before qualifying for independent practice is four years.

Just as a major part of a psychiatric evaluation focuses on inner conflicts and relationship problems, psychological evaluation of a patient focuses primarily on inner conflicts or problems within an individual. This professional is also trained to be attuned to the quality of an individual's relationships at work, as well as with family and friends. It could be said that nonphysician mental health professionals study "dis-ease," not disease per se in the sense of physical illness. Psychologists do not prescribe medication and are not trained to diagnose physical conditions that can influence a patient's mental state.

As Sharfstein and Koran (1990) note,

> Psychologists have . . . been pressing for hospital admitting privileges, and they debate with psychiatrists the qualifications necessary for practicing psychotherapy. On the one hand, a medical education is not needed to be a skilled psychotherapist or to counsel or treat physically well individuals whose mental disorders do not require medications. On the other hand, only psychiatric physicians can prescribe indicated psychotherapeutic drugs, knowledgeably treat the large proportion of mentally disordered patients who suffer from both physical disease and mental disorder, and be relied on to recognize organic diseases masquerading behind mental symptoms [p. 221].

Psychologists are licensed by forty-eight states, with unregulated practice in the remaining two states. Licensure requires that the psychologist complete the educational requirements, then pass a national written examination, followed by a separate state examination. The content and form of this exam vary by state and may be written or oral. State licenses generally permit psychologists to perform psychological services, including psychotherapy and testing. Licenses are renewable every two years and include continuing-education requirements. Whether psychologists can bill third-party payers independently varies by state. Medicare accepts claims for financial reimbursement from psychologists.

Several directories list psychologists in active practice, facilitating selection of a psychologist. These guides include the American Psychological Association membership directory and the *National Register of Health Services Providers in Psychotherapy.* Both list psychologists separately by geographical area and alphabetically. Citations include the education, experience, and professional membership of the clinician, as well as any areas of specialization or particular expertise. The local chapter of the American Psychological Association or the state psychological association (almost every state has one) can also assist with private referrals.

Selection of a psychologist is based on several factors. Availability is one. Of approximately 200,000 mental health practitioners in the United States, about 73,000 are psychologists; of those, about one-third are clinical psychologists. Other considerations include the type of treatment anticipated for the employee and the specialization or expertise of the psychologist. Again, it is important to note that employees likely to need medication, those with complicated medical histories, or those suspected of having a medical condition contributing to their problem should be referred for evaluation first by a psychiatrist. Furthermore, it is not usually initially obvious which patients have an illness or need medication.

Social Workers

Social workers in the mental health system have completed an undergraduate degree, usually in a social sciences major, followed by master's (M.S.W.) or doctoral (D.S.W.) degree in social work. Their education focuses on interventions in the social system, from the individual in the family to a group in the community or greater society. This discipline draws on sociology and most of the behavioral sciences, such as psychology. After completing this broadly based degree, social workers obtain specialty training, pursuing either a clinical or a policy- and community-level track. Education of clinical social workers in mental health includes an internship. Some obtain advanced training in a particular school of psychotherapy or family treatment. The overall length of training before a social worker qualifies for independent practice, averages three years.

Supervision is provided by experienced social workers, as well as by psychologists and psychiatrists.

While sharing skills with other mental health professionals, such as the ability to perform psychotherapy, clinical social workers strongly emphasize the interaction of the person within the environment: job, family, community, or some other social system (factors also considered in evaluation by psychiatrists and psychologists). Social workers focus heavily on the family and the community system's impact on the individual. Thus, they are uniquely skilled to serve as an interface with community resources such as health and welfare agencies, often assisting their clients in obtaining social services such as medical assistance, housing, and food stamps.

The process for credentialing social workers is only twenty-five years old. In most states, social workers obtain licensure by passing a test. Many states have different levels of licensure, depending on the clinician's degree and amount of experience. Most states have continuing social work education requirements. In most states, social workers can be licensed for independent practice, and they can submit claims for financial reimbursement to Medicare.

Referral to a social worker can be facilitated by use of a directory such as the *2000 Diplomate Directory,* published by the American Board of Examiners in Clinical Social Work, which lists practicing clinicians by geographical area, licensure, type of practice, and other information. About half of the approximately 200,000 mental health professionals in the United States are social workers.

Considerations in the selection of a social worker include the focus of treatment. A social worker is particularly appropriate for work with the family or conflicts on the job. As with any other professional, licensure is an important sign of quality because it indicates that the individual has met the standards set by the profession. Cost may be a consideration as well: social workers' fees are generally in a lower range than those of psychologists or psychiatrists, which is a consideration particularly for employees who will be paying for treatment out of pocket. Psychologists, and to a lesser extent psychiatrists, find themselves in competition with social workers (and family and marital counselors), who believe that they provide the same psychotherapy and counseling services at less cost.

Other Clinicians

Employees can be referred to a number of other mental health professionals for initial evaluation. These professionals may be employed by hospitals, clinics, or clinicians such as psychiatrists (who can provide the supervision required by law, medical backup, and prescriptions for medication). These clinicians are generally supervised by other mental health professionals, primarily psychologists and psychiatrists (as well as other physicians), although some are licensed for independent practice. The length of training following the undergraduate degree varies by specialty.

Psychiatric nurses and psychiatric nurse practitioners have completed requirements for a nursing degree, the latter obtaining additional specialized training and certification in mental health. They may provide counseling or therapy. With their nursing training, they can also administer medications orally and by injection, when that medication has been prescribed by a physician.

Mental health counselors represent a small, diverse group of professionals who received training as a result of programs established in the 1960s in response to the shortage of psychiatrists and other therapists in the United States. Their training varies from one- to three-year programs, usually following undergraduate work. Most obtain a master's degree or the doctorate, although some clinicians have an associate degree. Their education focuses strongly on psychotherapy and includes a clinical internship. Other clinicians include certified alcoholism counselors and marriage and family counselors, whose training and orientation are reflected in their titles.

Although none of these clinician types can bill for services provided to Medicare enrollees, licensure to practice independently or to receive reimbursement from insurance companies is available to some of these clinician types in some states. These practice privileges have been brought about mainly as a result of lobbying efforts of professional organizations representing these clinicians. For example, nurses have recently begun following the lead of social workers in lobbying for increased autonomous practice privileges such as the right to bill independently for services. To date, however, their scope of practice remains quite limited.

Selection of one of these professionals is made on the availability of the most appropriately trained provider, licensure of available professionals, and costs. Most of these providers have state or local associations, which can be contacted for referrals.

DELIVERY SYSTEMS

Just as there is a spectrum of mental health professionals, there are a number of organizational settings in which individuals receiving treatment for mental disorders are seen. Similarly, payment for treatment can be arranged in various ways. The choice of setting is determined by a number of factors, including insurance coverage, type of professional assessed to be most likely needed, prior arrangements between health care organizations and corporate representatives, and employee choice.

Many insurance and other financing arrangements may restrict selection of a provider. Some policies exclude mental health care, in which case the employee must be able to afford to pay for treatment out of pocket in the private sector or otherwise be willing to seek treatment in the public sector.

Payment issues are often central to the treatment of mental disorders. Mental health professionals, in contrast to most other health professionals, often prefer that their patients deal directly with their insurance companies. Under this arrangement, the patient receives reimbursement for covered services from the insurance company, and the patient pays the clinician. This arrangement is more common in mental health for several reasons, including the greater degree of confidentiality possible for the patient, and also because in psychotherapy, payment of the fee is often a central emotional issue in the therapy itself. It is thus important that the payment relationship between patient and therapist be pure, not "contaminated" by third-party payers.

Fee for Service

Since health insurance began in the United States in the late 1930s, FFS has been the traditional reimbursement method, and today, with managed care, it is the method most commonly used. Under this system, the mental health professional bills for services after they are provided. For example, a fee is charged for each separate service provided, such as a therapy session.

Employees may have coverage for mental health services under a number of arrangements that use FFS reimbursement. In what is likely the most common arrangement in large corporations, the business insures its employees through the purchase of private indemnity coverage. Most private insurance companies use FFS reimbursement. Employees in corporations that do not provide health insurance can purchase such coverage independently (at a much higher premium price).

In addition, FFS is also used by many organizations that self-insure medical care for their employees. Self-insuring corporations commonly pay an insurance company to provide administrative services for the business, the insurance company then processing claims and serving as a conduit for payment. The corporation pays for these administrative services but does not pay policy premiums to the insurance company. Instead, it takes on the financial risk for its employees and pays medical bills as they are incurred.

Under FFS reimbursement for covered benefits, the bill (or more commonly some portion of it) is paid by the insurance company. Under some arrangements, the patient is responsible for the portion of the bill the insurance company does not pay. Under other arrangements, the care provider accepts insurance company reimbursement as payment in full.

Costs under a FFS system are not wholly predictable: they are dependent on the incidence of problems and the services received in treating them. The insurance industry profits by charging higher premiums than estimated payouts. Such prediction, based on the methods of actuarial science, is sophisticated, complicated, and not easily replicated. Insurance premiums under this type of reimbursement tend to be more expensive than for other payment methods, because the clinician's incentive is to provide all the care that the patient could logically need. This can have optimal treatment potential, but also the potential for cost escalation.

The setting in which care is delivered is not restricted under this arrangement. Similarly, any clinician who is licensed to bill independently or is working under the supervision of a billing professional can provide services to an employee under FFS reimbursement. In general, there is unlimited flexibility under this system for choice of provider.

There are pros and cons to FFS reimbursement, as is true with any form of reimbursement. One potential disadvantage is the possibility of higher expenditures under this system. Another disadvantage for the risk-taking entity, whether it be the self-insuring business or the insurance company, is the inability to predict costs. Yet another disadvantage is that employees may be billed for costs not reimbursed by the insurance company; leeway for fee negotiation is variable.

Optimal initial psychiatric care may reduce both psychiatric and medical costs, as well as having productivity benefits. In a true free market, higher fees reflect a higher perceived value. There are other advantages in FFS payment as well: corporate management can be assured that the mental health professional has no financial incentive to skimp on the care provided to employees. In addition, FFS offers the most flexibility in choice of provider.

Self-insurance under FFS has other nuances: with a population of healthy employees, a self-insured company will not pay out much for medical care, in contrast with other methods examined here. If the corporation pays in advance for care, expenditures for the same hypothetical group of healthy employees could be greater than necessary. Conversely, if the employee population of a self-insured corporation has a high incidence of illness and treatment, medical expenditures will be high, with insurance reducing the out-of-pocket costs to the employee who receives services. In a company with choice of coverage types, healthy individuals will seek coverage under PPOs, HMOs, and similar systems. Those who expect to need treatment are more likely to stay with conventional insurance coverage (termed adverse selection). This can create an artificial appearance of cost reduction in non-FFS systems.

The effects of adverse selection on health care costs created the need for mandated benefits for insurance coverage, which specify legal limits for minimum coverage of psychiatric conditions and substance abuse. Requirements vary widely among the states, ranging from parity with coverage for medical and surgical conditions to very limited coverage. Drug abuse treatment is covered by nearly all states and alcohol treatment by all but one. Of note, self-insured corporations are exempt from state mandates: as more and more Americans come under self-insurance or become uninsured, the mandates have less of an impact on access to care than was originally hoped.

Preferred Provider Organizations

Another reimbursement method is discounted FFS payment. This has become possible in the era of cost control as a result of a confluence of factors, including the recent oversupply of mental health care providers and payers' desire to minimize expenditures. As a result, third-party payers and self-insuring corporations have been able to negotiate discounted FFS reimbursement with providers.

One type of discounted FFS arrangement is the PPO, in which a group of providers agrees to accept a discounted fee (typically 10 to 30 percent below customary charges) as reimbursement for a group of employees. They also agree to accept this fee as payment in full and not bill patients for the balance. PPO managers seek providers who give resource-efficient care, and the providers they enroll agree to utilization management oversight by PPO administrators.

The discounted FFS method does not usually restrict the setting in which care is provided. However, it does restrict the employee to receiving care from the "preferred" providers: enrollees agree not to see providers outside the PPO, on penalty of paying a large portion or the full fee. Physicians are the mental health professionals most commonly involved in PPO arrangements.

The mental health care provider's advantage in this arrangement is the guarantee of a potential patient population. The disadvantage to the provider is a reduced fee for caring for these patients.

The patient's disadvantage is limited choice of providers. The advantage is financial, in that the arrangement creates reduced fees and eliminates the need for copayments. However, the personal cost of this arrangement may be steep if the employee leaves an established relationship with a provider outside the PPO. The financial cost can be substantial if the employee elects to seek treatment outside the PPO roster of providers. It should be remembered that "preferred" providers often are those clinicians who meet minimal qualifications and agree to accept reduced fees.

Health Maintenance Organizations

Capitation is another reimbursement method: the self-insured corporation or the insurer pays a provider organization in advance on a per head, or capitated, basis for the care of a group of employees. In return for this payment, the provider organization agrees to provide all necessary care to the group for a predetermined period of time; thus, total payment is independent of the amount of services eventually given.

Such an arrangement usually occurs only within nontraditional delivery settings such as HMOs. From the provider's perspective, capitation is often viewed more as an organizational arrangement than an insurance program. From the business or employee perspective, however, capitation is an insurance mechanism that protects enrollees against financial loss from illness, with the prepayment analogous to purchasing an insurance premium.

Capitation plans rarely require cost sharing except for small copayments for some services. Services are usually comprehensive in scope, although with limited depth. HMOs usually offer a broader benefit package than conventional private insurance policies, including preventive care, immunizations, and annual check-ups. The enrollee has no financial disincentive to use the HMO because there is no significant additional cost once the capitation payment is made. Therefore, financial survival of the organization requires that services be limited. Nonfinancial barriers may include time delays between appointment and visit, telephone triage using gatekeepers, and visit limits. Because all psychotherapy depends on development of a therapeutic alliance, many mental health patients are put off by bureaucratic procedures, in many cases opting to forgo treatment.

Federal standards have been developed for HMOs. Minimal mental health care benefits include short-term (up to twenty visits) outpatient evaluation and crisis intervention mental health services, medical treatment, and referral services for alcohol and drug abuse or addiction. It is thus possible to meet federal standards without offering inpatient psychiatric coverage. Furthermore, the federally legislated benefits do not entitle the enrollee to care; although gatekeepers and other bureaucratic procedures concurrently used to minimize resource use do not technically prohibit the use of services, in reality that is often the result.

The financial incentives facing the HMO organization may be different from the incentives facing the providers it employs. However, these incentives may be tightly linked through contractual arrangements that pass along financial risk to the provider. Alternatively, the link may be quite loose, with the organization absorbing the financial risk. It is therefore difficult to generalize about the effects of financing on care received within an HMO. However, it is clear that because the HMO receives lump payment in advance for the care of all patients, the incentive is to provide as few services as possible so as to maximize revenue. The provider organization and its practitioners (depending on the contractual financial arrangement), instead of the third-party payer or enrollee, bear the financial risk. Because the capitation payment depends only on the number of people cared for rather than on the quantity of services, there is no incentive to maximize the volume of services provided. In fact, there is some incentive to enroll more members and provide fewer services for each.

As a result of this potential for compromise, much has been written about HMOs concerning their financial incentives and the resulting quality of care that patients receive compared to other health care delivery systems. Opinions about quality of care differ, although anecdotal evidence suggests that at least some enrollees receive suboptimal care. However, the main conclusion is that HMOs save money over FFS systems because of the low rate of patient hospitalization (for medical and surgical conditions), which is about 40 percent lower than within FFS systems. The lower rate of hospitalization within HMOs does not represent a higher quality of medical care. Apart from the financial incentive not to hospitalize, healthier enrollees self-select into HMOs. Given that HMOs are not mandated to provide inpatient psychiatric care, their rate of hospitalization for these conditions is likely even less than 40 percent of the rate within FFS systems.

Treatment sites depend on the arrangement between the provider and the HMO. Care may be rendered in a private office or a central site. Choice of clinician is limited to those employed by or on the HMO staff. To save money, many HMOs use lowest-cost nonphysician providers, particularly to provide psychotherapy. This may be adequate for some patients, but it often results in suboptimal care. Because of the nonfinancial barriers, employees may have difficulty getting an appointment with a staff psychiatrist (assuming there is one). Alternatively, primary mental health care may be provided by a family or general practitioner. These arrangements keep costs (and probably quality) down. Enrollees may receive fewer visits than they think they need.

For a healthy employee population with good overall mental health, an HMO may be a good option. And because the corporation knows in advance how much it will be paying for employee care, there are yearly budgeting advantages to using an HMO.

The major disadvantages are a consequence of the HMOs' financial incentives to minimize care and the existence of nonfinancial barriers to care. It is generally agreed that most HMOs have problems providing care for psychiatric conditions and substance abuse. In the hypothetical situation of the employee with a crisis, a long wait for an appointment with a caregiver could mean the difference between outpatient resolution of the problem and the need for hospitalization or for employee termination.

Employee Assistance Programs

Employee assistance (or alcoholism) programs (EAPs) provide various mental health services from a program that has traditionally been organized within the corporation itself. EAPs were originally focused on the treatment of alcoholism and its related problems as reflected in the workplace. The identified alcoholic might be the employee or a family member.

EAPs proliferated in the 1970s. Later, some EAPs broadened their scope to include other drug problems, wellness programs, and mental health programs.

The Department of Health and Human Services (DHHS, 1986) describes the goals of an EAP "to restore valuable employees to full productivity" (p. 36). Specifics were delineated by DHHS (p. 20):

1. Identify employees with alcohol, drug abuse, emotional or behavior problems resulting in a pattern of deficient work performance.
2. Motivate such individuals to seek help.
3. Provide short-term professional counseling assistance and referral.
4. Direct employees towards the best assistance available.
5. Provide continuing support and guidance throughout the problem solving period.

To carry out these goals, EAPs should provide clinical services and referrals. An EAP should offer consultation to corporate supervisors, as well as employee orientation to the program. EAPs should also offer preventive health education programs.

EAP staffs vary, determined to some extent by the goals of a particular program. Some EAPs employ treatment staff, which may include psychiatrists, nonpsychiatric physicians, psychologists, social workers, nurses, family therapists, and marital therapists. Some use clinicians or administrators to triage employees into appropriate services.

Historically, EAPs have been organized within the corporation. Now, many programs are contracted out to providers or to external EAPs in the community. In a further variation, some businesses are developing joint EAP programs. Some employees receive mental health or substance abuse treatment on a contract basis within the community after referral from the EAP. In some corporations, the EAP staff act as gatekeepers, liaisons between employees, and community-based providers.

An employee can self-refer to the EAP or be referred by management. The treatment process varies slightly depending on the referral source. If the employee is self-referred, the entire process takes place without feedback to supervisors, but if management refers the employee, treatment progress reports (leaving out personal details) are given to management (see Chapter Four).

There are advantages to EAPs, including the flexibility to offer specific services and the potential for greater control over mental health care resources. Programs can be customized to fit employees' needs. They have been found cost-effective not only by reducing absenteeism and accidents and improving productivity, but because services are often provided more economically than they are when the company offers traditional mental health benefits as part of an insurance policy. The location of an EAP within the corporation is more convenient for the employee and facilitates follow-up care.

Potential disadvantages of an EAP include use of gatekeepers and clinicians with limited training and with a financial bias not to refer employees for psychiatric care. As a result, EAP gatekeepers are often reluctant to refer employees for sophisticated psychotherapy or medication treatment (and in about half of all patients, medications are indicated for specific symptoms or syndromes).

Gatekeepers tend instead to refer to low-cost providers who may have limited training and often have less experience than other providers in the community, resulting in potentially suboptimal care.

Other disadvantages of EAPs include their inherently greater possibility for breach of confidentiality given their ties to management (although EAPs must follow strict confidentiality procedures), and the stigma that employees may feel in seeking, being sent for, or obtaining treatment at their place of work. The employee may feel that the company has a vested interest in his or her productivity that is of greater importance than the employee's health itself. The appearance of a potential conflict of interest or goals could lead to resentment.

The Public Sector

Employees who have no mental health benefits and cannot afford to pay for care out of pocket in the FFS system can seek care within the state or local mental health system. Due to a number of factors, psychiatric care has been funded by the public sector to a much greater extent than other types of medical care. A state hospital system for inpatient care is available to those without insurance or who run out of benefits. A system of local community mental health centers (CMHCs) provides a continuum of mental health care, including twenty-four-hour emergency services, inpatient care, partial hospitalization, rehabilitation, and other outpatient services. State-funded clinics have a similar structure.

CMHCs charge lower fees than the private sector and readily use sliding scales for reducing fees. They have the funding flexibility to care for those in lower socioeconomic classes, whom it is their mission to serve. They bill uninsured patients directly and third-party payers for clients with coverage.

Providers in CMHCs include psychiatrists, psychologists, social workers, and mental health counselors. The psychiatrist is usually in the position of supervising the rest of the team and prescribing medications as necessary. Psychotherapy is almost always provided by the nonphysician staff.

The overriding advantage of the public sector is its lower cost and ability to provide care for the uninsured or underinsured population. The potential disadvantage of care in the public sector is that due to government budget limitations, services may be inadequate in breadth or duration. However, this is highly variable, depending on geographical area and the particular problem facing the patient. For the troubled employee without private sector coverage, the public sector is a viable option.

The public mental health care sector includes a network of state hospitals for inpatient care. State and local clinics provide income-adjusted outpatient care to the population. In large cities, city hospital clinics provide low-fee care to the poor. Private agencies, often run by religious groups, are another low-fee alternative found in most urban areas. Additional sources of reduced-fee care include teaching clinics staffed by physicians in training, research clinics for persons with designated conditions, and psychoanalytic training institutes.

Managed Care

Managed care has had a profound effect on mental health care. In its broadest sense, managed care refers to any attempt to control the organizing, financing, and delivering of mental health services. Many employers today have made an arrangement with a managed care organization (MCO) to directly manage, under a capitated fee, their employees' mental health and substance abuse needs. In other instances, they rely on their HMO or PPO plans to carve out the gatekeeper function for mental health care to a separate managed behavioral health care (MBHC) company. Critics have argued that carve-outs impede coordination of psychiatric with general medical care and increase administrative costs while supporters assert benefits of more effective specialized management improves value and efficiency (Frank, Huskamp, McGuire, & Newhouse, 1996).

In 1998, over 162 million people were covered by private managed behavioral health care plans, up from 78 million in 1992 (Sturm, 1999). A 1997 survey of employee health plans sponsored by the Substance Abuse and Mental Health Services Administration found that 9 percent of small firms and 1 percent of large firms did not offer mental health or substance abuse benefits to their employees' most widely used plan. Most plans covered inpatient detoxification, and three-quarters of plans covered outpatient detoxification. Three-quarters or more of employer health plans restrict their behavioral health coverage more than their medical coverage. From 1993 to 1997, enrollment in traditional indemnity plans dropped by 48 percent to 15 percent, whereas enrollment in PPOs increased from 27 percent to 35 percent and point-of-service plans (POS) from 7 percent to 20 percent.

There have been an enormous number of mergers and acquisitions in the MCO industry since the late 1990s, a trend that is likely to continue, leaving only a few large players in the market. Already, Magellan Behavioral Health Services has 70 million covered lives, which is about 30 percent of the managed care market. The two largest companies combined have a more than 50 percent market share. Nearly every large company in the United States makes use of behavioral health plans. Some employers arrange contracts for a MBHC to provide specific functions such as EAPs and utilization review and case management (Manderscheid & Henderson, 1998; Manderscheid, Henderson, Witkin, & Atay, 2000). This Chinese menu approach of services has created new markets for MBHC while at the same time making it even more difficult to measure quality (see Chapter One).

The growth of managed care since the early 1980s was a direct result of efforts to control costs. Now that many costs have been cut as low as possible, the future role of what is left to be managed is less certain. As a result of these cost savings (achieved through practices such as limiting inpatient hospitalizations, reducing provider payments, increasing the use of nonphysician providers, and the use of drugs over talk therapy), many companies have saved millions of dollars (Zieman, 1998). One large employer had a 40 percent reduction in mental health costs with the introduction of managed care (Goldman, McCulloch, & Sturm, 1998). In a 1999 study of 1,043 employers, spending for behavioral health care in the private sector dropped from 6.1 percent of all health care costs in 1988 to 3.2 percent in 1998 and spending dropped from $151 per covered life to $69 (Jeffrey & Riley, 2000). Large employers now force plans to compete not only on the best price but also on proven outcomes. New data suggest that cost savings in mental health may not tell the whole story. One large company that decreased mental health spending by more than one-third over a two-year period was found to have a 37 percent increase in the use of non-mental health services and increased sick days among employees who use mental health care (Rosenheck, Druss, Stolar, Leslie, & Sledge, 1999).

The future of the MBHC industry is now. Increasing demands are currently being placed to measure quality (see Chapters One and Three). As they are beginning to do in other areas of medicine, employers know, as the purchasers of health plans for the majority of Americans, that if they require quality measures as benchmarks for their MBHC contract decisions, they can drive the outcomes field. And like any other service that is paid for, questions about return on investment are legitimate concerns; however, unlike the auto industry, measurements that take into account improved quality of life, enjoyment of one's family, days without depression, and job satisfaction, to name a few, have traditionally not made it into the equation. These sorts of measurements are infinitely more problematic and costly to study. It appears that psychiatry in general and managed care in particular will be forced to demonstrate what most people who have successfully received mental health treatment already know: that the early detection, proper diagnosis, and treatment of their illness gave them back their life.

As a result of the successes of managed care in reducing costs, the push toward parity (nondiscriminatory benefits for mental health and substance abuse care) has gathered new momentum. Thirty-five states have some form of parity legislation on the books, and the federal government passed a parity bill in 1996 that is being strengthened and renewed in 2002. Recognition of mental illness as a "no-fault" series of conditions, with roots in brain pathology, and of the effectiveness of early diagnosis and treatment has reinforced this expansion of coverage under insurance.

The major components of mental health care in the U.S. health care system and the variety of professionals available can make provider selection difficult. Although there are advantages and disadvantages in choosing particular health care providers, in most cases, psychiatric evaluation is the optimal initial evaluation for a troubled employee.

Employees may be treated in a number of different types of health care systems, including traditional FFS care, discounted fee for service such as PPOs, or managed care systems such as HMOs. Many corporations have established EAPs within their businesses to provide referral, and in some cases treatment, to employees who need psychiatric care or treatment for substance abuse. The public sector and a variety of reduced-fee private agencies are available for those who are uninsured or have no coverage for mental health care. Understanding the nuances of these programs and the characteristics of different types of professionals will enable employers to make the most appropriate referral.

References and Additional Sources

Frank, R., Salkever, D., & Sharfstein, S. (1991). A new look at rising mental health insurance costs. *Health Affairs, 10*(2), 116–123.

Friedman, H. S. (Ed).(1988). *Encyclopedia of mental health.* Orlando, FL: Academic Press.

Goldman, W., McCulloch, J., & Sturm, R. (1998). Costs and use of mental health services before and after managed care. *Health Affairs (Project Hope), 17*(2), 40–52.

Hoge, M. A., Davidson, L., Griffith, E.E.H., Sledge, W. H., Howenstine, R. (1994). Defining managed care in public sector psychiatry. *Hospital and Community Psychiatry, 45,* 1085–1089.

Jeffrey, M., & Riley, J. (2000). Managed behavioral healthcare in the private sector. *Administration and Policy in Mental Health, 28,* 37–50.

Manderscheid, R. W., & Henderson, M. J. (Eds.). (1998). *Mental health, United States, 1998.* Washington, DC: National Institute of Mental Health.

Manderscheid, R. W., Henderson, M. J., Witkin, M. J., & Atay J. E. (2000). The U.S. mental health system of the 1990s: The challenges of managed care. *International Journal of Law and Psychiatry, 23,* 245–259.

Rosenheck, R. A., Druss, B., Stolar, M., Leslie, D., & Sledge, W. (1999). Effect of declining mental health servicee use on employees of a large corporation. *Health Affairs (Project Hope), 81,* 193–203.

Scheidemandel, P. (Comp.). (1989). *The coverage catalog* (2nd ed.). Washington, DC: American Psychiatric Association Press.

Sharfstein, S., & Koran, L. (1990). Mental health services. In A. Kovner & S. Joans (Eds.), *Health care delivery in the United States* (4th ed.). New York: Springer.

Sturm R. (1999). Tracking changes in behavioral health services: How have carve-outs changed care? *Journal of Behavioral Health Services and Research, 26,* 360–371.

U.S. Department of Health and Human Services. (1986, December). *Standards and criteria for the development and evaluation of a comprehensive employee assistance program.* Washington, DC: U.S. Government Printing Office.

Zieman, G. L. (1998). *The handbook of managed behavioral healthcare.* San Francisco: Jossey-Bass.

CHAPTER THREE

Cost-Effectiveness, Cost Containment, and Worker Productivity

Alan M. Langlieb
Benjamin G. Druss
Robert Rosenheck

Two major forces have shaped the delivery of mental health treatment in the past decade: the availability of new medications that have advantages over their predecessors and the rise in managed behavioral health care, which has functioned to limit services at some cost to quality of care. Each of these factors plays an important role in determining the cost-effectiveness and quality of mental health in the United States today. Benefits covering treatment of psychiatric disorders are often poorly understood, and as the costs of specific services increase, so too does the need to know which treatments are considered most effective. As workers are beginning to pay a larger share of their medical costs, they are taking a more active role in issues related to health care costs and their reported benefits. In order to know how to improve both mental health status and the efficacy of mental health care service delivery, employers and employees need an understanding of basic factors such as medical costs and employee productivity.

The increasing cost of health care in the United States raises questions about returns on investment. Rather than measuring profit margins or stock prices, returns in the business of medicine take on new meaning when what is being considered is the value of a healthy, productive employee. Mental health is now recognized to be an important part of the equation, particularly since the surgeon general recently reported that one in five Americans suffers from a mental disorder over the course of a year (U.S. Surgeon General, 1999). Nearly half of private insurance spending on mental health care involves treatment for depression (DePaulo & Horvitz, 2002). Not surprisingly, it has also been the most extensively studied mental disorder in the workplace. The cost of depression to employers of this disorder is substantial (see Chapter Twenty-Two). Druss, Schlesinger, and Allen (2001) examined the health and employee files of 15,153 employees of a major U.S. corporation and compared mental health and medical costs, sick days, and total health and disability costs associated with depression, heart disease diabetes, hypertension, and back problems. They found that the cost to employers in lost workdays was greater than the cost of many other common medical illnesses. Ash and Goldstein (1995) found that the greatest predictor (84 percent) of employees not returning to work who were on short-term medical disability (mostly for musculo-skeletal injury) was the presence of moderate to severe depression.

Other common mental disorders may also have a major impact on worker productivity. Persons diagnosed with a panic disorder reported a significantly greater rate of complete disability and also a greater rate of reduced hours (Roy-Byrne et al., 1999). And several studies examining claims data found that patients with selected psychiatric disorders have excess absenteeism compared to persons without mental health insurance claims (Berndt, Bailit, Keller, Verner, & Finkelstein, 2000).

COST-BENEFIT AND COST-EFFECTIVENESS

Because resources available for health care are limited and disability and lost productivity due to mental illness are important to employers, decisions have to be made about where to invest resources. Cost-benefit and cost-effectiveness analyses (respectively, CBA and CEA) are tools that can be used to make such choices and are also commonly used to set public policy.

Cost-effectiveness analysis at its core poses a relatively straightforward question: What value are we getting for our money? However, conducting such analyses can be anything but simple when it comes to medicine. The answer to the question is highly dependent on the choice of measures and the perspective of the analysis, that is: How do we measure effectiveness, and whose costs and benefits are we considering? Most employers traditionally measure both investment and returns in dollars; this is the goal of CBA, which tries to quantify treatment outcomes in terms of monetary value. Although such analyses benefit from the ability to present results as a single bottom line, they rely greatly (some say too greatly) on economic assumptions, including the economic value of a human life.

A second issue is that CBA and CEA require time and money. Employers and benefits managers typically lack the skills to conduct such analyses on their own. Collaborative efforts between employers and academic researchers hold promise in studying these issues, but to date, difficulties in meshing the academic approach and corporate culture, along with issues of employee confidentiality, have hampered the full development of such working relationships.

The current contraction in the U.S. economy raises both the challenges and importance of understanding the impact of mental illness in the workplace.

Although employers and health managers may have fewer available resources to improve the scope of their benefits packages, this is a time when it is particularly important to allocate health resources effectively to maximize productivity and ensure retention of workers.

How CBA and CEA Work

In the mid-1960s, CBA and CEA began to be employed in the health field, and they have been increasingly used ever since. Today, every area of medical practice has received some form of this kind of analysis. CEA relates value to money, that is, a particular service is considered cost-effective if it is worth the outlay of resources required to perform it. The main distinction between CEA and CBA is how one values the consequences of programs. In CBA, all benefits are valued, like costs, in monetary terms. Because all costs and benefits are measured in monetary terms, this technique can be used more easily to compare programs that are different. Improving human capital (that is, people who are healthy are more productive over their lifetime and therefore contribute more to the economy) and willingness to pay are two of the most common ways health outcomes are given a dollar value. In CEA, some consequences are measured in nonmonetary units, such as days without illness. This allows comparison of costs per unit effectiveness among competing alternatives, each designed to address the same goal. These estimates are particularly important for examining treatments that are more expensive than standard care but that may also result in greater health benefits. For instance, the use of a combination of medication and psychotherapy to treat depression may be more expensive than the use of either treatment alone but may nonetheless be a good value since the added expenditures may result in higher rates of improvement of depression, reduced health care service use, and an increase in productivity. Often, CEA and CBA lead to similar conclusions. Examples of measurable health outcomes include reduction in disability days and days without depression.

The primary measurement used in CEA is the cost-effectiveness (C/E) ratio. Usually it compares two alternatives: providing a given treatment versus not providing the treatment. The C/E ratio is the difference in their costs divided by the difference in their effectiveness. The most desirable outcomes are those that result in net savings (that is, reduced cost and improved health). However, when both costs and health status increase, the most desirable alternatives are those with the lowest C/E ratio.

An important development in the evolution of CEA was measures of health outcomes that could be used to estimate the quality-adjusted years of life (QALYs) gained from an intervention. The QALY assigns a weight to each period of time, ranging from 0 to 1, where 1 is equivalent to perfect health and 0 corresponds to a health state equivalent to death. QALYs are a measurement of the number of healthy years of life that are valued equivalently to the actual outcome. They make it theoretically possible to capture the potentially diverse effects of one intervention (for example, QALYs gained from medication compliance for schizophrenia) and compare interventions with different outcomes. A particular type of CEA that uses QALYs is commonly referred to as cost-utility analysis.

Another measure is disability-adjusted life years (DALYs). DALYs measure lost years of healthy life regardless of whether the years were lost to premature death or disability. The disability component of this measure is weighted for severity of the disability. For example, disability caused by major depression is found to be equivalent to blindness or paraplegia. Using the DALYs measure, major depression ranks second only to ischemic heart disease in magnitude of disease burden. Researchers predict that depression will be ranked first by 2020 (Murray & Lopez, 1996). DALYs and other standardized methods cannot compare all interventions. For example, CEA can evaluate pharmacotherapy for treating panic attacks and for treating diabetes mellitus, but the health outcomes are so different that only by using a general health status measure that is applicable to both disorders, such as QALYs and DALYs, can a useful comparison be made.

In order to perform CEA, one must first have demonstrated effectiveness and then applied the intervention to an appropriate population. For example, a very inexpensive intervention will have a poor C/E ratio if it is used in a low-risk population that is unlikely to benefit from it. In contrast, an expensive technology can have an attractive C/E ratio if used in patients with a high probability of benefiting from it (Balas et al., 1998; Richardson & Detsky, 1995). In the workplace, it is essential to identify conditions that are prevalent, have a major impact, and for which there are effective treatments. Because depression meets all of these criteria (high prevalence, substantial impact on workplace function, and effective treatments), it has been offered as an example of an illness for which treatment can be highly cost-effective.

The purpose of any treatment for a mental disorder is to improve mental health or prevent or delay declines in mental health in the future. For example, when antidepressants and talk therapy are prescribed to treat major depressive disorder, the goal is to reduce the symptoms of depression (improve mood, appetite, energy, self-worth, concentration, and so forth; see Chapter Twenty-Two). In economic terms, such improvements in health status can be thought of as having three possible effects. First, health has its own value and can be measured indirectly as the most a person would pay to achieve a certain state of mental health. Second, improvements in health should lead to better performance at work (in terms of both quantity and quality). Third, early detection and treatment may result in a decrease in the subsequent use of other health resources, such as medical services for diabetes and heart disease. An example of delaying declines in future functioning is the continuation of antidepressants in an employee with a successfully treated depression.

Cost-Effectiveness and Mental Health

Because there has generally been a lack of consensus among experts in deciding on a standard method of performing CEA, individuals who benefit from these sorts of studies, such as policymakers and businesses, end up having to weigh conflicting, and sometimes confusing, data and therefore have had difficulty drawing explicit conclusions. Comparability among analyses, after all, is at the cornerstone of CEA methodology. Efforts to examine the cost-effectiveness of treatment for mental disorders have been increasing in numbers as all of the participants in the health care system, from payers to patients, have begun to question the value of their investments. Today, only a few randomized trials have examined the cost-effectiveness of mental health care in general, and even fewer have assessed employment outcomes.

Schoenbaum et al. (2001) performed a randomized control study in forty-six primary care clinics in six community-based managed care organizations and found that patients who received quality improvement interventions for depression reduced the individual suffering and economic consequences of the illness. Specifically, they found that employees in the intervention group had one additional month of employment over a two-year period and that point estimates for cost-effectiveness of the treatment were comparable with that of other accepted medical interventions. Relative to the marginal increase in health care costs associated with training the health providers to implement the interventions, the authors concluded that employers could reap the benefits of maintaining employment or reducing absenteeism, or both.

Observational studies have also demonstrated that long-term treatment with antidepressant therapy can improve self-reported workplace performance. Simon et al. (2000) performed a secondary analysis of health maintenance organization data on enrollees treated for mild to moderate depression. After adjusting for clinical severity and the association of a coexisting medical disorder, they found that patients with greater clinical improvement were more likely to maintain paid employment and also reported fewer sick days from work.

In part because there has been only one scientifically controlled trial demonstrating that treatment for depression improves work performance, as measured by a variety of subjective (self-report) and objective (absenteeism) ratings, it is difficult to fully document the general benefit of this or other treatments on employment. Kessler et al. (1999), using data from two national work populations, found that depressed workers had between 1.5 and 3.2 more short-term disability days per month than those without depression, resulting in a salary equivalent productivity loss of $182 to $395 per month. Using a systems cost-effectiveness approach, Frank, McGuire, Normand, and Goldman (1999) concluded that even under actual treatment conditions, the costs associated with producing a depression-free case ($6,031) is a good value when viewed alongside other health care problems. However, neither of these studies was based on definitive experimental methodology.

COST-OFFSET

The cost-offset hypothesis proposes that early detection and treatment of an illness may save a purchaser money (in other words, offset the costs of treatment) by reducing other medical expenditures or costs related to decreased productivity and absenteeism. Classically, cost-offsets were compared between mental health and other medical care, postulating that psychiatric symptoms led patients to use excess medical services and that effective mental health care could reduce these excess costs. Although these early expectations have not yet been fully documented, there is general agreement that from an insurance company's perspective, treatment for depression is an effective medical treatment, but it costs rather than saves money. From a corporate purchaser's perspective, though, such treatment may be an excellent value, that is, cost-effective, even if it does not result in complete medical cost-offset.

Case 1

Lynn Harcheck is a thirty-five-year-old executive of a food distribution company. She has been employed at the same company for the past ten years and has steadily risen through the ranks. She is considered instrumental in the company's success. Overseeing all operations on the West Coast, she is often under considerable stress: she is responsible for nearly 30 percent of the company's revenue and the livelihoods of one hundred employees and their families.

Lynn was diagnosed with Major Depression in her twenties while at college, and her symptoms have been well controlled with medication and supportive therapy since then, except for three periods, each requiring an average of seventeen days in the hospital. She also has numerous medical problems, including insulin-dependent diabetes mellitus and asthma.

Each time Lynn falls into a prolonged depressive episode, she begins to neglect her own care and becomes reclusive, prompting her coworkers to believe she has a substance abuse problem. Last year, her company sharply reduced its mental health benefits, forcing most of its workers who use these services, including Lynn, to undertake large out-of-pocket expenses. Rather than seek help from her psychiatrist during her most recent depression, she opted to tough it out. As Lynn's depression worsened, she stopped taking her insulin for several days, and by the time she was taken to the emergency department by a friend, her blood sugar and potassium levels were at dangerous levels; she had to be treated for seven days in a subacute medical bed before she could be safely transferred to the psychiatric service.

Because employers can consider both health expenditures and worker productivity in their bottom line, a cost-offset may be a more realistic possibility for this group than for health insurers. In terms of depression, one study estimated the monthly productivity loss of approximately $200 to $400 for each worker (Kessler et al., 1999). The only randomized study that addressed this issue specifically found savings, at least in the first year of treatment (Wells et al., 1989). Rosenheck, Druss, Stolar, Leslie, and Sledge (1999) examined claims data of 20,814 employees of a large corporation. As changed benefits led to a decline in mental health service use and costs by more than one-third over a two-year period, employees who used these services had a 37 percent increase in the use of other health services and increased sick days, thus eradicating any potential savings. The implication is that medical costs might have declined if those mental health services been provided. A recent estimate using results from several studies in the area suggests that between 45 and 98 percent of the incremental costs of depression treatment could be offset by resulting gains in work productivity. (Simon et al., 2001; Wells, Golding, & Burnam, 1988; Kessler & Frank, 1997; Leon, Walkup, & Portera, 2002). Recently, authors have argued that cost-effectiveness may be a more appropriate metric than cost-offset when thinking about the value of depression treatment (Sturm, 2001; Goldman, 1999).

Cost-offset does not even arise in arguments of whether or how generously to fund treatments for medical conditions such as diabetes or coronary artery disease. These treatments are funded not because they are expected to save money but because they improve health. Similarly, even if depression treatment does not offset medical or productivity costs, it has clearly been demonstrated to be a cost-effective use of health care dollars (Sturm, 2001).

COST CONTAINMENT

As noted in Chapter Two, managed care has played a significant role in reducing the costs of mental health care. The target of such efforts has primarily been decreasing inpatient admissions and length of stay, but they have also decreased clinicians' fees and outpatient visits. The central clinical and policy question in both the general medical and mental health literature has been the degree to which such cost cutting has had a detrimental effect on quality of care (see Chapter Two). Although the literature does not provide a definitive answer to this question, some studies have demonstrated a potential trade-off between reductions in services and quality of care. For instance, Wickizer and Lessler (1988) found that for every day of reduced length of stay in a hospital for psychiatric treatment, the odds of readmission within a sixty-day period increased by 3.1 percent. Thus, for a decrease of ten or more days in length of stay, which is not uncommon, the risk of readmission within two months was 37 percent higher than for patients whose days of care were not reduced. From the standpoint of the insurance carrier, shifting patients away from mental health specialists (to internists, for example) might decrease costs but worsens functional outcomes and thus has an impact on cost-effectiveness, leading Sturm and Wells (1995) to conclude that "the best strategy for making care for depression more cost-effective is through quality improvement" (p. 58).

Most people recognize that now that the cost cutting has occurred, the challenge for the future is to manage care better, not just cost (see Chapter Two). All this comes at a time when there is an expanding pipeline of new and more expensive medications that will surely make cost-containment strategies even more challenging to assess.

PRODUCTIVITY

Research has consistently found an association between depression, for example, and lost productivity due to illness, as well as between schizophrenia and profound disability. Less is written about anxiety and substance abuse, but one might logically conclude similar results. A large percentage of the costs of depression are not found in direct health care costs, but rather are found indirectly: absenteeism, decreased productivity, temporary worker costs, replacement and retraining costs, and the losses that might be encountered if the replacement employee is less effective. In two major community surveys, people with depression had a fivefold or greater increase in time lost from work compared to those without symptoms of depression (Broadhead, Blazer, George, & Tse, 1990; Kessler & Frank, 1997). In CEA, productivity costs arise from lost or impaired work function, which may result in short- or long-term disability payments or, in the more extreme case, lost potential economic productivity due to death, say, from suicide.

Case 2

Evan Lesh is the quintessential thirty-something dot-com millionaire who started his own software company right out of college. Eventually, an international multimedia company bought the company, and Evan has continued to work there ever since. Since he returned last year from a six-month trip abroad (helping to oversee a new plant in Malaysia), he has been missing an average of six days of work each month. His dress is more casual than in the past, and sometimes he attends important meetings unshaven. Coworkers who had worked closely with him in the past say he sometimes looks preoccupied, staring out his window at the Bay Bridge for long periods of time. His boss, through a series of tense but highly personal meetings, convinces him to seek help through the company's employee assistance program. Shortly after a comprehensive evaluation, he is diagnosed by a psychiatrist with cocaine and alcohol dependence and sent to a comprehensive inpatient rehabilitation facility for treatment. Following six months of outpatient follow-up and a commitment to stay clean, Evan is looking forward to returning to work and helping to update the backbone of the company's software platform in order to keep it competitive.

Two concepts have been used as direct measures of productivity: absenteeism and presenteeism. Absenteeism has been traditionally used as one measurement of recovery: it asks whether the person is able to return to work. Many studies have replicated the finding that absenteeism declines with successful diagnosis and treatment for depression (Claxton, Chawla, & Kennedy, 1999). Presenteeism perhaps recalls an old saying, "Ninety-nine percent of work is just showing up," that is, being present on the job (hence, *presenteeism*). Because simply showing up at work may not necessarily reflect actual functioning, new and more sophisticated metrics that reflect job function are being used (Burton, Conti, Chen, Shultz, & Edington, 1999). Several studies have found that depression—with symptoms that often include poor concentration, slowed thoughts, and lack of energy—in contrast to a general medical illness, might have a particularly large impact on presenteeism (Druss et al., 2001; Wells et al., 1989). In the same way that psychiatrists perform fitness-for-duty evaluations (see Chapter Seventeen) to examine an individual's job description and performance measures in order to assess readiness to begin or return to work, researchers can use specific objective measures of daily functioning on the job as measures of productivity. Measuring productivity objectively is a difficult issue. Whereas it can be fairly easily measured for keypunch workers or telephone operators, it becomes increasingly difficult when looking at people performing white-collar and other administrative jobs. Most current measures use worker reports because more objective measures are very hard to come by.

Even with the growing empirical research in this area, there is a great deal to learn about the allocation of available resources aimed at reducing the burden of mental illness in the workplace. Research published to date suggests the following conclusions:

- Mental illness in general, and depression in particular, poses substantial costs to employers.
- Effective treatments exist for these conditions.
- These treatments are cost-effective (they provide substantial health care value per dollar expended) when compared with other medical interventions.

- From an employer's perspective, some of these treatment costs may be offset by reducing worker absenteeism, general medical expenses, and increasing worker productivity. Many companies have already chosen to offer their workers expanded mental health benefits, and now the demand for better-quality health services is growing.

As cost-effectiveness and cost-benefit analyses for mental health treatment become more widespread and rigorous randomized effectiveness trials yield results, corporate decision makers will be in a better position to make allocation decisions. But until that time, human resource and benefits managers would be correct in concluding from the data that do exist that investment in the early detection of and treatment for mental illness is money well spent. Ultimately, the willingness of employers to invest in improved mental health treatment will depend in part on their experiences with their own employees at all levels of the company. Given some of the practical challenges in conducting these analyses, collaboration between employers and academic researchers, managed care, and the public sector may provide the most promising vehicle for measuring the costs of improving care in order to achieve maximum mental health benefits in the workplace and beyond (Wells, 1999).

References and Additional Sources

Ash, P., & Goldstein, S. L. (1995). Predictors of returning to work. *Bulletin of the American Academy of Psychiatry and Law, 23,* 205–210.

Balas, E. A., Kretschmer, R.A.C., Gnann, W., West, D. A., Boren, S. A., Dentor, R. M., Nerlich, M., Gupta, M., West, T. D., & Soderstrom, N. S. (1998). Interpreting cost analyses of clinical interventions. *Journal of the American Medical Association, 279,* 54–57.

Berndt, E. R., Bailit, H. L., Keller, M. B., Verner, J. C., & Finkelstein, S. N. (2000). Health care use and at-work productivity among employees with mental disorders. *Health Affairs (Project Hope), 9,* 244–256.

Borus, J. F., Barsky, A. J., Carbone, L. A., Fife, A., Fricchione, G. L., & Minden, S. L. (2000). Consultation-liaison cost offset: Searching for the wrong grail. *Psychosomatics, 41,* 285–288.

Broadhead, W. E., Blazer, D. G., George, L. K., & Tse, C. K. (1990). Depression, disability days and days lost from work in a prospective epidemiologic survey. *Journal of the American Medical Association, 264,* 2524–2528.

Burton, W. N., Conti, D. J., Chen, C. Y., Shultz, A. B., & Edington, D. W. (1999). The role of health risk factors and disease on worker productivity. *Journal of Occupational and Environmental Medicine, 41,* 863–877.

Claxton, A. J., Chawla, A. J., & Kennedy, S. (1999). Absenteeism among employees treated for depression. *Journal of Occupational and Environmental Medicine, 41,* 606–611.

DePaulo, J. R., & Horvitz, L. A. (2002). *Depression: What we know and what you can do about it.* New York: Wiley.

Druss, B. G., Schlesinger, M., & Allen, H. M. (2001). Depressive symptoms, satisfaction with health care, and two year work outcomes in an employed sample. *American Journal of Psychiatry, 158,* 731–734.

Frank, R. G., McGuire, T. G., Normand, S. L., & Goldman, H. H. (1999). The value of mental health care at the system level: The case of treating depression. *Health Affairs (Project Hope), 18*(5), 71–88.

Gold, M. R., Gold., S. R., & Weinstein, M. C. (Eds.). (1996). *Cost-effectiveness in health and medicine.* New York: Oxford University Press.

Goldman, H. H. (1999). Justifying mental health care costs. *Health Affairs (Project Hope), 18*(2), 94–95.

Institute for Healthcare Improvement. http://www.ihi.org/.

Kessler, R., Barber, C., Birnbaum, H. G., Frank, R. G., Greenberg, P. E., Rose, R. M., Simon, G. E., & Wang, P. (1999). Depression in the workplace: Effects on short-term disability. *Health Affairs, 18,* 163–171.

Kessler, R., & Frank, R. (1997). The impact of psychiatric disorders on work loss days. *Psychological Medicine, 27,* 861–873.

Leon, A. C., Walkup, J., & Portera, L. (2002). Assessment and treatment of depression in disability claimants: A cost-benefit simulation study. *Journal of Nervous and Mental Disease, 190,* 3–9.

Murray, C., & Lopez, A. (1996). *The global burden of disease and injury.* Cambridge, MA: Harvard University Press.

National Committee for Quality Assurance. http://www.ncqacalculator.com/Ncqa/Index.asp.

Richardson, W. S., & Detsky, A. S. (1995). Users' guides to the medical literature: VII. How to use a clinical decision analysis: A. Are the results of the study valid? Evidence-based Medicine Working Group. *Journal of the American Medical Association, 273,* 1292–1295.

Rosenheck, R. A., Druss, B., Stolar, M., Leslie, D., & Sledge, W. (1999). Effect of declining mental health service use on employees of a large corporation. *Health Affairs (Project Hope), 18*(5), 193–203.

Roy-Byrne, P. P., Stein, M. B., Russo, J., Mercier, E., Thomas, R., McQuaid, J., Katon, W. J., Craske, M. G., Bystritsky, A., & Sherbourne, C. D. (1999). Panic disorder in the primary care setting: Comorbidity, disability, service utilization, and treatment. *Journal of Clinical Psychiatry, 60,* 492–499.

Schoenbaum, M., Unutzer, J., Sherbourne, C., Duan, N., Rubenstein, L. V., Miranda, J., Meredith, L. S., Carney, M. F., & Wells, K. (2001). Cost-effectiveness of practice-initiated quality improvement for depression: Results of a randomized controlled trial. *Journal of the American Medical Association, 286,* 1325–1330.

Simon, G. E., Manning, W. G., Katzelnick, D. J., Pearson, S. D., Henk, H. J., & Helstad, C. S. (2001). Cost-effectiveness of systematic depression treatment for high utilizers of general medical care. *Archives of General Psychiatry, 58,* 181–187.

Simon, G. E., Revicki, D., Heiligenstein, J., Grothaus, L., Von Korff, M., Katon, W. J., Ludman, E., Grothaus, L., & Wagner, E. (2000). Recovery from depression, work productivity, and health care costs among primary care patients. *General Hospital Psychiatry, 22,* 153–162.

Sturm, R. (2001). Economic grand rounds: The myth of medical cost offset. *Psychiatric Services, 52,* 738–740.

Sturm, R., & Wells, K. B. (1995). How can care for depression become more cost-effective? *Journal of the American Medical Association, 273,* 51–58.

U.S. Surgeon General. (1999). *Mental health: A report of the surgeon general.* Rockville, MD: U.S. Department of health and Human Services.

Wells, K. B. (1999). Treatment research at the crossroads: The scientific interface of clinical trials and effectiveness research. *American Journal of Psychiatry, 156,* 5–10.

Wells, K. B., Golding, J. M., & Burnam, M. A. (1988). Psychiatric disorder and limitations in physical functioning in a sample of the Los Angeles general population. *American Journal of Psychiatry, 145,* 712–717.

Wells, K. B., Stewart, A., Hays, R. P., Burnam, M. A., Rogers, W., Daniels, M., Berry, S., Greenfield, S., & Ware, J. (1989). The functioning and well-being of depressed patients: Results from the medical outcomes study. *Journal of the American Medical Association, 262,* 914–919.

Wickizer, T. M., & Lessler, D. (1988). Do treatment restrictions imposed by utilization management increase the likelihood of readmission for psychiatric patients? *Medical Care, 36,* 844–850.

CHAPTER FOUR

Mental Health Ethics and Confidentiality in the Organization

Robert C. Larsen

Those who conduct occupational psychiatry consultations must always emphasize the importance of proper communication and adherence to ethical standards. The referral source, the patient, and the clinician must be fully informed about the nature and method of the consultation, the reporting requirements, and any limits on confidentiality. When communications take place between the employer and the clinician, the patient-employee must be informed before these take place. Inattention to ethical standards or to proper communication can result in breaches of confidentiality, lack of informed consent, conflict of interest, perceived conflict of interest, undue administrative influence, and concerns about access to medical records. Appropriate attention to these issues increases the chance of an effective consultation process.

Whether consulting with an attorney, accountant, or physician, people expect to be treated with respect and professional concern, and they do not want confidential information disclosed. Material contained within their file is considered privileged and can be released only under certain circumstances. The public expectations and the restraints of privilege are especially subtle and complex regarding mental health services.

Ethical conduct and respectful behavior are not easily taught. Formal seminars and individual supervision guide clinicians in training. They learn the proper steps in conducting an interview, maintaining a relationship with the patient, and disclosing information to third parties when appropriate. Supervised clinical hours are part of training before and after receiving one's clinical degree. Their goal is to ensure proper attention to the role that clinicians assume in dealing with emotional well-being. This chapter examines additional professional responsibilities related to communications and disclosures of which both the doctor and the referral source must be mindful.

MEDICAL ETHICS

The principles of medical ethics derive from the physician's duties and responsibility for patients' well-being. When physicians and other clinicians are not in the role of providing treatment, their responsibilities can be different from when they are in other medical roles. It is thus crucial to the referral source, the physician, and the referred employee that the purpose of the clinical encounter be completely clear to all parties. (The American College of Occupational and Environmental Medicine's code of ethical conduct, to which its members subscribe, is contained in the chapter appendix.)

When a company refers an employee into a traditional doctor-patient treatment relationship, even a helpful confirmation that the employee has come for consultation or has entered treatment is an inappropriate break in absolute confidentiality. There are permissible exceptions, though, as long as the employee-patient gives consent. For example, the individual employee must give consent to the physician to provide information to others about diagnosis, recommended treatment, fitness for duty, or the need for job modification. This consent should not be provided after the employee has already disclosed the information. Rather, early in the consultation, the clinician should advise the person that such disclosure will take place. This practice follows ethical guidelines and avoids legal issues that might be raised if the employee is not aware from the onset of possible third-party disclosure. Furthermore, the individual should be aware of what type of information will be disclosed and in what format. The release of medical information is governed by statute; California, for example, has specific provisions that are required of a written release. The reasons for this are illuminated by some sample situations. An employee's job might be affected if the employer learns that drug abuse is an active clinical issue. Candidacy for a managerial position might be affected if others learn of a personality disorder diagnosis. Having access to psychological test results does not give the practitioner the right to share that information with others. The person evaluated must agree to a release of the data if he or she is the holder of privilege. If there is another holder of the privilege, his consent must be obtained. Jonas Rappeport (1981), a prominent forensic psychiatrist, has emphasized the critical importance of obtaining fully informed consent. When employees present for evaluation purposes, any limitations on confidentiality between the physician and employee must be clarified.

ROLE OF THE PHYSICIAN

There are three different settings where the role of the physician alters the doctor-patient relationship.

The Traditional Doctor-Patient Relationship

Most people expect that the role of a physician, whether internist or psychiatrist, is to diagnose illness and institute treatment to improve their health. An employee referred for mental health services expects that the clinician will not disclose matters they discuss in the clinical setting. Nevertheless, limited reporting outside the office frequently takes place. For example, physicians must submit insurance forms with information about diagnosis, dates of visits, and fees. Alternative delivery systems such as health maintenance organizations and preferred provided organizations and managed care organizations often request even more information from the treating physician—perhaps a summary of the patient's history, clinical course, prognosis, and diagnosis. A treatment plan in writing may be required by a third party to authorize payment for services. Based on the diagnosis, treatment plan, or prognosis, a third-party reviewer may authorize treatment for the period requested or not. It is important to recognize the impact on treatment that this release of information can have. The clinician must share this recognition with the patient before releasing this information for there to be informed consent.

Commonly, patients looking for mental health treatment worry that others might learn that they are in therapy. Some people are so wary of this that they may choose to forgo insurance benefits or delay entering treatment. In companies where a fellow employee may be monitoring health claims, this becomes a particular area of patient concern. Those employers might be better off with an independent party monitoring mental health claims.

Psychiatrists are sensitive to their responsibility to maintain confidentiality. A psychiatrist who consults with a colleague about a particular case will typically disguise the patient's identity, for example. And patients in group psychotherapy commonly are instructed not to discuss anything that fellow group members say outside the therapy setting.

To summarize, when an employee enters a doctor-patient relationship, treatment is largely confidential. Physicians must tell their patients about any third party that will obtain clinical information. Human resource professionals should not expect feedback from the psychiatrist of an employee who is given a list of recommended clinicians. Patients can be comfortable discussing intimate details of their lives only when they have no concern about public disclosure.

The Occupational Psychiatry Consultation

When asked to assume the role of an evaluator, the psychiatrist's duties to the employee are quite different. Taking a history, making a diagnosis, and recommending treatment may seem very similar to traditional doctor-patient relationships. However, in circumstances of a medical-legal evaluation, the employee is not a patient, and treatment is not started. In this situation, an employer representative (perhaps an internal employee assistance program or the company's medical department) is requesting an employee evaluation to assess certain issues. The employee should be aware before arriving for the appointment that the employer expects feedback from the psychiatrist on the issues of concern. If this is not clear, confidentiality and perceived conflict of interest problems can arise.

Typically, the evaluator issues a formal report to the employer with comments on the employee's reported symptoms, observed signs and behavior in the interview, a review of medical and other records, psychological testing, and occasionally investigative reports. The examiner strives to be independent, neutral, and unbiased in this assessment.

Sometimes an employer is concerned about an employee's well-being and requests an evaluation. In these situations, the issue usually involves more than a benign concern of the employer for the employee. Perhaps a long-term employee is using undue amounts of sick leave and demonstrating erratic behavior at the workplace. This behavior disrupts an important work group and thus comes to the attention of management, which requests a mental health consultation of the individual. Proper attention to the release of information in such situations is exemplified in the case of *Pettus* v. *Cole et al.* (1996), where the California court found that a doctor-patient relationship existed for purposes of confidentiality of medical information despite no treatment relationship being present. The examining doctor was sued for releasing personal information in a disability report to a self-insured employer without obtaining a written consent from the employee. Forensic reports can also be required for cases of long-term disability or work-related injury. (See Chapter Eighteen.)

Case 1

Jane Smithers, a manager in her mid-forties, has had lengthy work absences because of gastrointestinal symptoms. After a five-week absence, her supervisor has referred her for a psychiatric evaluation. Over the course of the interview, Jane suggests that her symptoms began after a major company reorganization when her work volume increased at the same time that staff support fell. She does not complain of feelings of depression or anxiety and focuses instead on abdominal pain and the need for antacids. During the interview, Jane brings up some aspects of her work history that she misrepresented on her employment application when she was hired fifteen years earlier.

Only after the interview ends does Jane learn that a report will be issued to her company's medical department and that it will include her prior work history. She pleads with the examining physician to alter the record so that it will be consistent with her application. Fearing she will lose her job, Jane contacts her company's personnel department and says that she will be returning to her position. As a result, there is no need for any further assessment of disability, and the company cancels the reporting requirement without learning of Jane's misrepresentation. Had Jane known the purpose of the examination purpose and reporting arrangements ahead of time, she might have dealt with this sensitive topic in a different fashion. Both she and the company would then have been able to make the best use of the evaluation.

Most people are not aware that physicians acting in administrative roles or making administrative decisions operate under a different set of guidelines than they do in the typical physician-patient relationship. Instead, they expect the psychiatrist to be their advocate or at least a source of benevolent concern. Therefore, evaluating psychiatrists must make clear the purpose of the evaluation and that treatment will not be started.

Frequently, what is good for the employee is also good for the employer. For example, an employee who is appropriately placed on a leave of absence for chemical dependency treatment can return to work as a productive contributor. The leave may have resulted from an employee-mandated psychiatric evaluation. The resulting information was needed to make an administrative decision. However, the employee was required to cooperate with the evaluation process knowing that information would be released to specific persons in his company.

In other situations, employee and employer needs and desires may be at odds. For instance, when disability determinations are influenced by ongoing litigation, the clinical evaluation often becomes an adversarial process. The physician is asked to assess clinical issues associated with the employee's state of mind and associated disability and then reports to the insurer, the company representative, attorneys, or a judge. An employee's benefits might be curtailed as a result, or the employer might be obligated to provide assistance where it did not feel benefits were due.

The Limited Clinical Consultation

Employees are sometimes referred for a brief clinical assessment to a physician outside the company structure with the goal of helping the employee resolve certain personal issues. One to four visits may take place. The physician is acting in a treatment role, but referral was made because personal problems were suspected as a cause of the employee's deficient work performance. In this situation, a human resource officer or the employee's manager expects to receive confirmation that the consultation has been completed and the problem is being treated. For example, couples therapy, medication, or substance abuse treatment might be suggested to the employee. The physician is acting solely in the patient's interest here, but the employer may want at least an informal telephone report from the physician. Here, too, the employee must give consent to any breach of confidentiality. If a written report is needed, it is often prudent to give the employee a copy. The limited clinical consultation is generally less comprehensive and more confidential than the occupational psychiatry consultation.

MENTAL HEALTH REFERRAL SITUATIONS WITH POTENTIAL FOR MORAL CONFLICT

A variety of situations might lead to moral conflict, making attention to ethical guidelines even more critical.

Lack of Informed Consent

Employees must be told the reason for a consultation and give prior consent to any release of clinical information. In practical terms, employees often have little choice about going for evaluation. They do not have to comply, but if they do not, the organization may instead pursue disciplinary or legal action. Problems arise when the purpose of the evaluation process is misrepresented to the individual.

Case 2

Burt Jones, a company salesperson, is referred by his employer for evaluation of his erratic behavior with clients. The company suspects drug abuse, and Burt has attended company sales meetings while intoxicated with alcohol. Burt goes to the psychiatric consultation. He discloses that he has been drinking, taking cocaine daily, and sometimes using amphetamines. He has a family history of substance abuse. He has never sought treatment and is not certain that he wants treatment now. The psychiatrist recommends inpatient treatment, but Burt does not want to take a leave from work. Only late in the interview does he learn that his employer will be sent a report describing his substance abuse problem and his resistance to treatment. Burt responds by threatening the psychiatrist with legal action if his confidentiality is violated. Neither the employer nor the psychiatrist had told Burt to expect anything other than a confidential clinical consultation, solely for his own purposes.

This case emphasizes the importance of obtaining prior informed consent from employees. An even worse scenario can occur if the employee follows through on a recommended consultation and only later learns about telephone discussions between the consultant and company representatives. This kind of episode creates problems for that particular consultation and makes it less likely that the employee will obtain needed treatment. In addition, it can lead to widespread mistrust of management. Compliance with psychiatric referral is directly related to employee expectation of a professional and trustworthy referral and consultation process.

Conflict of Interest

The clinician and referral source must consider whether there are any real or potential conflicts of interest. This is particularly important when administrative or legal decisions are at issue. Here, medical evidence and opinion are used to determine if an employee is entitled to certain company benefits. A psychiatrist in this role has a potential conflict of interest if he is an employee or shareholder of the company.

Case 3

Tom Cameroon, M.D., is the salaried psychiatric consultant to a large microelectronics firm. Through a program provided for management, Sam Verde, an accountant with the firm, has come for short-term counseling. Over the course of the session, Sam reveals a planned corporate takeover and expectations of significant corporate change. He says that he revealed the information as a courtesy and asks that it be kept confidential; he thinks that his position with the company would be jeopardized if his role in the planned takeover were known. Dr. Cameroon finds himself in a quandary: he feels he must protect confidentiality and the doctor-patient relationship, but he is a member of management who has signed a sworn statement to reveal any evidence of fraud, embezzlement, and deleterious acts directed toward the company. He believes that the takeover would constitute such a deleterious act. The company's top management took great pains to fend off a similar hostile takeover attempt the previous year. A further complication is that Dr. Cameroon would lose his salaried consulting position in the aftermath of a takeover.

In this case, Dr. Cameroon is not only a treating physician; he is also an employee, administrator, and member of the management team and thus has conflicting obligations. He is faced with seemingly incompatible obligations to patient confidentiality and to managerial needs to protect the company against threats. If he were not a member of management, it would be clear that confidentiality would be due his patient. And if he were an evaluating physician functioning solely in an administrative role, he would have told Sam that the consultation was not confidential and could then disclose the information to the company.

Perceived Conflict of Interest

Conflict of interest problems are not always easy to anticipate. Even the appearance of a conflict can pose substantial practical, administrative, and clinical problems.

Case 4

Joyce Schwartz, a laboratory technician at a local university hospital, has been referred for disability consultation to a member of the medical center's faculty, John Wright, M.D. She has been on a leave of absence for three months. Her treating psychiatrist reports that she is suffering from symptoms of depression and anxiety that stem from conflict between Joyce and her immediate supervisor. The company wants to know if her leave, symptoms, and need for treatment are from a work-related condition. When Joyce goes to the consultation, she realizes that Dr. Wright has a faculty appointment and works in the same medical school department that she does. She says that she feels he cannot be unbiased and that she is uncomfortable revealing information to him. Joyce ends the interview convinced that she has been set up by management. She later contacts her union and is directed to legal counsel.

This case illustrates how referral sources and consultants must be sensitive to even the appearance or perception of a conflict of interest. Other clinicians in the community could have been used for the consultation. Had that occurred, the employee may have cooperated and an adversarial process might not have followed.

Criminal Conduct

Criminal activities are sometimes disclosed in a confidential clinical setting, and this information may threaten the continued viability of the treatment process. In such circumstances, the clinician might encourage the patient to confess to authorities if treatment is to continue. State laws generally require clinicians to breach confidentiality when there is a real and present danger to the patient or others. At other times, the clinician will feel torn between duty to the patient and other social obligations.

Case 5

Peter Argent, a ten-year veteran of the municipal police department's narcotics unit, has been referred to the department's psychiatrist, Tyler Evans, M.D. after a shooting incident. This is standard departmental procedure; Peter's conduct is not under investigation. However, during the short-term psychotherapy for posttraumatic symptoms, Dr. Evans learns that Peter is involved in drug dealing. He feels that he has a confidential relationship with Peter and so cannot reveal the drug sales to the commanding officer who made the referral. Instead, he works therapeutically to have Peter come to terms with his illegal actions. Dr. Evans does not think the criminal behavior poses any imminent dangers, and Peter does not turn himself in. Months later, evidence surfaces from an unrelated source, and Peter is arrested, convicted, and sentenced to a brief jail term.

Administrative Influence

Sometimes companies attempt to influence the outcome of a clinical evaluation. Perhaps they do not wish an employee who is being evaluated to return to work, or they think that the employee does not deserve disability benefits. When these matters arise, there is a danger that the clinician administrator may act in a way that is anything but unbiased.

Case 6

Kevin Harsch, M.D., a psychiatrist in charge of employee assistance services for a Fortune 500 corporation, decides to set up an outside evaluation of a middle-level manager. During a telephone conversation with the potential consultant, Dr. Harsch says that the manager has been on leave for a major depression, and senior management does not want him back, but the treating psychiatrist has released his patient for unrestricted return to his normal managerial duties. Dr. Harsch makes it clear to the potential consultant that he expects a report that will preclude the manager from ever returning to work with the company.

This case reflects the power and potential for abuse that can come from disregard for ethical issues in the mental health referral process. Political maneuverings may be commonplace in any organization and often include improper actions. In clinical practice, professional ethics and the need to maintain public confidence require a scrupulous avoidance of improper actions.

Access to Professional Opinion and Records

When a consultative report about an employee's condition and capacity to perform normal work duties is issued to a company, the employee often wants his own copy. Employees commonly assume that they have the ordinary rights to their medical records—all reports, doctor's notes, correspondence, and testing results. In these administrative consultations, however, employees do not have these rights. The employee might obtain a copy of the formal report with the consent of the company or through legal mechanisms. State law generally governs employee access to medical and psychiatric information that the employer and its consultant may maintain separate from the personnel file. It is incumbent on the company and its consultant to be aware of such laws within their jurisdiction.

Psychiatrists and other mental health clinicians have traditional responsibilities to patients and to confidentiality. When they are acting in administrative, legal, or consultative roles, they may have competing obligations as well. It is essential to make sure that referring sources, clinicians, and patients are all fully aware of the nature and obligations of every consultation. Confidentiality and its limits must be carefully discussed with referred employees. The purpose of the employee's meeting with a mental health practitioner should not be vague or misleading. Inattention to ethical guidelines or to proper communication can result in breaches of confidentiality, lack of informed consent, conflict of interest, perceived conflict of interest, undue administrative influence, and concerns about access to medical records. Appropriate attention to these issues increases the chance of beneficial results of the consultation process. (See Chapter Seventeen for further discussion of confidentiality and information exchange relative to those employer-initiated evaluations.)

References and Additional Sources

Committee on Medical Education. (1990). *Group for the Advancement of Psychiatry: A casebook in psychiatric ethics.* New York: Brunner/Mazel.

Larsen, R. C. (1988). Ethical issues in psychiatry and occupational medicine. In R. Larsen & J. Felton (Eds.), *Psychiatric injury in the workplace.* Philadelphia: Hanley and Belfus.

Pettus v. Cole et al. (1996). 49 Calif. App. 4th 402, 57 Calif. Rep. 2nd 46, rev. denied.

Rappeport, J. R. (1981). Ethics and forensic psychiatry. In S. Block & P. Chodoff (Eds.), *Psychiatric ethics.* New York: Oxford University Press.

Stone, A. A. (1987). *Law, psychiatry and morality.* Washington, DC: American Psychiatric Press.

APPENDIX

Code of Ethical Conduct of the American College of Occupational and Environmental Medicine

This code establishes standards of professional ethical conduct with which each member of the American College of Occupational and Environmental Medicine (ACOEM) is expected to comply. These standards are intended to guide occupational and environmental medicine physicians in their relationships with the individuals they serve, employers and workers' representatives, colleagues in the health professions, the public, and all levels of government including the judiciary.

Physicians should:

1. Accord the highest priority to the health and safety of individuals in both the workplace and the environment;

2. Practice on a scientific basis with integrity and strive to acquire and maintain adequate knowledge and expertise upon which to render professional service;

3. Relate honestly and ethically in all professional relationships;

4. Strive to expand and disseminate medical knowledge and participate in ethical research efforts as appropriate;

5. Keep confidential all individual medical information, releasing such information only when required by law or overriding public health considerations, or to other physicians according to accepted medical practice, or to others at the request of the individual;

6. Recognize that employers may be entitled to counsel about an individual's medical work fitness, but not to diagnoses or specific details, except in compliance with laws and regulations;

7. Communicate to individuals and/or groups any significant observations and recommendations concerning their health or safety; and

8. Recognize those medical impairments in oneself and others, including chemical dependency and abusive personal practices, which interfere with one's ability to follow the above principles, and take appropriate measures.

CHAPTER FIVE

Psychiatry, Productivity, and Health

A Brief History of Psychiatry in the Workplace

Len Sperry

Alan A. McLean

For nearly a century, psychiatry has addressed workplace issues, including those with an impact on individual and corporate health and productivity. Initially, the emphasis was primarily on distressed employees and mental health concerns. Since the 1980s, this role and the number of psychiatrists have expanded to encompass the impact of the corporation on the employee and the health and productivity of the organization itself. Specific activities include clinical work consulting with employee-patients, applied research, policy development, leadership development and executive consultation, and organizational consultation. Psychiatrists, as well as the psychiatric profession itself, have become increasingly focused on employee health and productivity issues, and workplace-oriented psychiatrists have broadened their role to include concern with mental health screening, cost-effectiveness studies, health and mental health policy and benefits, and related issues.

Corporations are increasingly sensitive to the link between productivity and health. For a long time, they have recognized that disease and disability have a negative impact on productivity and profit. They have become painfully aware of the impact that undiagnosed substance-related and mental disorders, as well as absenteeism and presenteeism (being present on the job but underproductive), have on productivity and employee commitment to the corporation.

Historically, concern for the mental health of workers has been the province of psychiatrists to a greater extent than any other discipline. In the same way that the occupational physician over the years has been mainly responsible for the physical well-being of workers, so too the medical arm of the mental health

---

The original chapter was prepared by Alan A. McLean, deceased, and revised for this edition by Len T. Sperry.

disciplines has pioneered and maintains a leadership role when it comes to clinical concerns for psychiatric aspects of health.

To be sure, the basic sciences have also made significant contributions to the understanding of physical and emotional aspects of individuals reacting to their work environments. Toxicologists, ergonomists, and industrial hygienists have provided specialized understanding of the potential threats of the physical work setting. Social psychologists and other behavioral scientists have given us tremendous knowledge of behavior in the workforce. But the primary responsibility for dealing with the impact of mental and physical disorders in the world of work and promoting healthy behavior, has fallen to physicians. Elmer Southard, M.D., chief of psychiatry for the U.S. Army during World War I, was one of the first physicians to respond to this need. Southard's roles as chief psychiatrist, faculty member at Harvard, consultant to the Engineering Foundation, and an author spoke to the importance of a psychiatric presence in the workplace. Not surprisingly, he is considered the father of industrial psychiatry.

Illustrative of one aspect of the practice of occupational psychiatry from its early days are situations that involve individual psychopathology and its interaction with the work organization. The clinical side of practice often involves evaluation of patients referred by medical department staff, management, and employees themselves. In one sense, this is the traditional role of the medical consultant in any setting. In the occupational setting, the focus of complaints is more often likely to be work related, and intervention strategies frequently enlist some aspect of the job.

Case 1

Some years ago, fifteen women worked in the secretarial pool of a large manufacturing plant, providing support for most of the supervisors and managers in the organization. Many considered their work stressful. The work flow entailed the transcription of dictation with little face-to-face contact with those whose work they processed. In fact, they often could not associate a face with the nameless voices, sometimes garbled, whose documents they transcribed. The main feedback to the transcribers was usually in the form of criticism of the final reports or letters that were sent anonymously back to the dictators. There was time pressure, with different voices asking why a document was not yet transcribed. The department was managed by a supervisor and two assistant supervisors, all of them women.

There was an excellent medical department at the location with two full-time physicians and several part-time consultants, including a half-time psychiatrist. Over the course of several weeks, twelve of the secretarial staff reported to the medical department with a variety of stress-related complaints. There were psychophysiological reactions and significant symptoms of anxiety and depression. A number of the women were referred to the psychiatric consultant, who, in addition to evaluating and often referring patients, made a detailed inquiry into the current work situation.

The secretarial pool was known to be a difficult place to work, but in the past, few employees had sought help from the medical department. "What might have changed?" wondered the consultant. This was the question he put to each secretary he saw.

The replies were invariably the same. The department supervisor had become increasingly short-tempered and demanding. She did not seem to be as much on top of the workload as she had been previously. Rather than serving as a buffer between secretaries and the "client" dictators, she simply relayed their frustrations and complaints, often siding with them and demanding that all their needs be met. (One of the patients said, "I can't satisfy thirty people every day in every way. I can't have thirty bosses!")

The supervisor had also been a recent visitor to the medical department. There were entries over the past few months in her medical file about serious personal problems (a potential marital breakup), menopausal symptoms, and mild depression. She had not been referred to the psychiatric consultant; it did not appear necessary to do so. She was apparently receiving good care from her own physician, with whom the local medical director had been in touch.

In a meeting between the consultant and medical director, the psychiatrist's observations were reviewed. He thought that the symptoms of the employees were related to those of the supervisor. The medical director, without breaching confidence, sought a meeting with the supervisor's manager. He noted an unusually large number of medical cases coming from the secretarial department and suggested that the manager look into the situation. Being a competent executive, the manager launched his own low-key investigation, visiting the department more often and talking with the employees and supervisor. He rapidly came to the same conclusion as the consultant.

In a matter of days, he arranged for the supervisor to receive a new temporary assignment, a staff project that was recognized as requiring her skills and that resulted in no loss of face for her. One of the assistant supervisors was appointed the new supervisor of the department. Within a short time, employee symptoms vanished, morale improved sharply, and productivity rose.

This rather classic combination of the application of clinical and managerial skills demonstrates the kind of effect an occupational psychiatric consultant can have on both individuals and organizations. Rather than suggesting treatment for the employees who presented with significant symptoms, he explored their work environment indirectly and effected the best health outcomes for both the subordinate employees and their supervisor.

During recent years, there has been a sharp increase in practitioners of nonmedical disciplines who have become concerned with the mental health of employees and their dependents. For a while in the 1950s in the Southeast, pastoral counselors outnumbered psychiatrists as consultants to employers and employees. The R. J. Reynolds Tobacco Company built a chapel in which employees were counseled by a minister. Of considerably greater significance, the employee assistance movement, originally staffed mainly by recovering alcoholics in the

1950s (starting at Du Pont and Mobil), burgeoned during the 1980s into a much more sophisticated group of employee counselors who are sometimes social workers or psychologists. There are now more than six thousand such professionals providing counseling and referral services to employees and their dependents. Some see this movement as a professional threat to occupational psychiatry, but in fact their role is much more limited than that of psychiatrists; their skills are largely confined to short-term clinical evaluation and referral of workers and their families and only sometimes with psychiatric supervision. The scope of employee assistance program activities is also expanding to encompass mental health case management, although that activity remains largely the province of firms specializing in such services.

At the same time, the role of psychiatrists has assumed a breadth unforeseen by Southard, even though the preventive, consultative responsibilities he suggested in 1920 remain the principal work in the field.

EARLY HISTORY

In the first issue of the journal *Mental Hygiene,* Herman Adler, chief of staff of the Boston Psychopathic Hospital, reported on the psychiatric symptoms of patients for whom the lack of a job had been a serious problem (Adler, 1917). These males, between the ages of twenty-five and fifty-five, were grouped into three classifications: paranoid personalities, inadequate personalities, and the emotionally unstable. Three years later, follow-up of this same group of patients repeated that 75 percent had become successfully adjusted from an occupational point of view (Jarrett, 1920). These were among the first articles appearing in the literature that could properly be included in an emerging field of occupational or industrial psychiatry.

Meanwhile, in England, starting at the time of World War I, the Industrial Fatigue Research Board began to focus attention on the psychological components of industrial accidents (Greenwood, 1918), on fatigue, and on psychiatric illness in the work setting (Culpin & Smith, 1930). Basic concepts of accident proneness and the first indications of the prevalence of psychiatric disorder in an industrial population came from this work.

1920s: PSYCHIATRISTS IN THE WORKPLACE

The first "Review of Industrial Psychiatry" in the *American Journal of Psychiatry* in April 1927 summarized the literature to date, defined the field, and traced its development. Mandel Sherman, the author, considered the psychiatrist's proper area of concern to be the "individual's adjustment to the situation as a whole." The psychiatrist, working in industry, was also portrayed as one who "attempts to forestall maladjustments by aiding in developing interests and incentives" (Sherman, 1927).

At the conclusion of his review of the field, Sherman said that among the various methods of industrial psychiatry, the most successful procedure used to aid the individual in adjusting to industry had been the analysis of the total situation: the patient's early life history, social situation, and motives and incentives, in addition to the immediate difficulties at work. His major appeal was for increased vocational guidance during the formative years to obviate many later industrial maladaptations. While the language may seem archaic, the meanings of Sherman's words seem remarkable contemporary some sixty-five years later: consider all aspects of the patient's situation, and focus preventive work on early exposure to work-related activities.

In 1922, the first full-time psychiatrist was employed by an American business organization. Lydia Giberson, M.D., joined the Metropolitan Life Insurance Company in New York. At first, she apparently focused on clinical work in the medical department, later moving to the personnel area with broader responsibilities, including involvement with organizational policy and practice (Giberson, 1936).

In 1924, a mental health service was introduced at the R. H. Macy department store in New York City. V. V. Anderson (1929) summarized this program in the first book on industrial psychiatry. He described modeling his activity after the child guidance clinics of the time: that is, with a psychiatrist, psychologist, and psychiatric social worker serving as staff.

In addition to clinical counseling of employees and consulting to management on problem behavior of employees, he became interested in several organizational problems, such as the high accident rate among delivery truck drivers. In the space of some two years, he implemented programs that reduced those rates by two-thirds. With the onset of the economic depression in 1930, Anderson's program was discontinued. In the late 1930s, Macy's again sought a psychiatrist to serve as a full-time organizational consultant. Temple Burling, M.D., who was hired, focused on morale issues, among others. In the process, he found the "executive elevator" and other status symbols to be disruptive, and his suggestions led to a less hierarchical administration (Burling, 1942).

1930s AND 1940s: WAR STRESS AND INITIAL ACADEMIC EFFORTS

After World War II, Burling went to Cornell University's School of Industrial and Labor Relations in Ithaca, New York, where he headed the program of two-year Carnegie Fellowships in Industrial Psychiatry for psychiatrists who had completed their formal clinical training. Some twelve fellows completed that training (Burling & Longaker, 1955). His distinguished academic career at Cornell provided leadership for nonpsychiatric graduate students, impressive behavioral research (Burling, Lentz, & Wilson, 1956), and active participation in the distinguished research and teaching of the human relations group on that campus. The group included psychiatrists Alexander and Dorothea Leighton, sociologist William Foote Whyte, and many other brilliant academicians.

Although Alexander Leighton would consider himself a social rather than an occupational psychiatrist, his research teams at Cornell often included industrial psychiatry fellows. His wide-ranging studies of behavior, mental health, and mental disorder in defined populations established methodologies equally applicable to the assessment of work populations. His students subsequently applied many of his concepts in understanding both healthy and disordered behavior in industry (Leighton, 1959).

The depression years were characterized by quiescence in the field; even the annual review of industrial psychiatry, which had appeared regularly in the *American Journal of Psychiatry* for several years, was dropped. (For an excellent summary of developments during the 1930s, see Rennie, Swackhamer, & Woodward, 1947.)

World War II exerted a remarkable impact on the clinical applications on psychiatry in the industrial setting. The expectations on the part of employers were high, perhaps unrealistically so, and to a certain extent psychiatry was oversold. Yet during the war years, greater and more sophisticated applications could be seen (Brody, 1945; Ling, 1945; Lott, 1946; McLean & Taylor, 1958).

Among the many mental health programs in wartime industry, those at the Oak Ridge, Tennessee, Industrial Community subsequently received much attention (Burlingame, 1946, 1947, 1948, 1949). With available psychiatric assistance, primarily through "emotional first aid stations," a minimum of on-the-job treatment led to conspicuous performance improvements among employees. As with the writings of psychiatrists before the war, those reporting their wartime experiences in civilian industry noted that stressors associated with psychiatric disabilities lay primarily in individual vulnerability or in the home or nonwork social surroundings rather than in the job situation.

In the armed forces, psychiatrists were called on to make significant clinical and research contributions that in many ways paralleled their pre- and postwar activities. Roy Grinker and John Spiegel, two psychiatrists in the Army Air Force, observed a large number of combat fliers in the European theater. Their careful observations of these men under stress included background details, personality characteristics, types of breakdown, and a description of the day-to-day existence of hundreds of fliers. This work provided valuable insight into reactions to major environmental stressors (Grinker & Spiegel, 1945). They concluded, "The stress of wars tries men as no other test that they may have encountered in civilized life. Like a crucial experiment it exposes the underlying physiological and psychological mechanisms of the human being. Cruel, destructive and wasteful though such as experiment may be, exceedingly valuable lessons can be learned from it regarding the methods by which men adapt themselves to all forms of stress, either in war or in peace." They went on to say, "If the stress is severe enough, if it strikes an exposed 'Achilles heel' and if the exposure is sufficiently prolonged, adverse psychological symptoms may develop in anyone." Their work helped to establish a baseline for the subsequent understanding of major stress reactions and such entities as posttraumatic stress disorders. In many ways, Grinker and Spiegel laid the groundwork for clinical methods of studying occupational stressors and psychosomatic reactions to them.

Following the war, with the sharp cutback in defense industries that had employed psychiatrists, many industrial mental health programs came to a halt. It is noteworthy that almost all occupational and military mental health activities before, during, and for some time after the war were headed by psychiatrists and firmly embedded in occupational health units.

A number of new postwar psychiatric programs, such as those at Eastman Kodak Company (led by Ralph Collins, M.D.) and American Cyanamid (led by Walter Woodward, M.D.), grew out of a corporate desire to assist returning veterans adapt successfully to their peacetime work. The federal government initiated the Vocational Rehabilitation Act Amendments of 1943 and established the Office of Vocational Rehabilitation. Stimulus was given to the training of clinical psychologists in greater numbers, primarily in programs of the Veterans Administration. Many were subsequently to work in industry.

1950s AND 1960s: INCREASING CLINICAL INVOLVEMENT

The decade following the war saw a rapidly growing interest in the field among psychiatrists and employers. The activities of Collins and Woodward may serve as examples of private sector programs. Ralph Collins was both a neurologist and psychiatrist who devoted half-time to the medical department at Eastman Kodak in Rochester, New York. The balance of his efforts was occupied with private practice. His concerns were for the most part clinical: evaluating patients referred to him by other physicians in the Medical Department and making recommendations about their psychiatric treatment and ability to work. Perhaps more important than his daily efforts at Kodak was his role as a spokesman for industrial psychiatry. During the 1950s and 1960s, he served as chairman of the Committee on Industrial Psychiatry of the American Psychiatric Association (APA) for more than a decade. In the same capacity at the Group for the Advancement of Psychiatry, Collins made these bodies the centers of professional interaction in the field. He was also influential in ensuring a place on the annual APA's program for speakers on topics relating to occupational psychiatry.

Worker compensation for disability arising out of the course of employment received increasing attention. By the 1950s, the courts had ruled a wide variety of illness and injury, including psychiatric, to be compensable. Coronary infarcts, occurring on the job following occupational stress, hypertension, cancer, and tuberculosis activated by employment, suicide caused by job-related depression, and "paralysis by fright" had all been ruled compensable (Lesser 1967). This trend continues to receive close attention as awards for work stress and psychiatric disability increase each year. Indeed, for several years during the late 1970s and early 1980s in Michigan, following a state supreme court case, a worker had only to "honestly believe" that his work was responsible for psychiatric disability to be eligible for worker compensation benefits. Now, disability awards for psychiatric injury are among the most common of worker compensation cases. Psychiatric evaluation and worker compensation court testimony, which started in the late 1940s, remains an increasingly important segment of occupational psychiatry (McLean, 1979).

Work in occupational psychiatry was not limited to the United States. From the Tavistock Clinic in London came the first volume of the seminal Glacier Metal Company studies, led by Elliot Jaques (1951). Both the methodology and the research results of this pioneering application of psychoanalytic concepts to the study of organizational behavior had considerable influence on the development of subsequent programs. Jaques's volume is a highly recommended landmark for psychiatrists interested in work organizations. His later concepts of equitable wage payment based on the time span of a job's responsibility were published in the 1960s but had their roots in earlier work (Jaques, 1956) and remain current today.

During the 1950s, Erland Mindus from Stockholm conducted a six-month study of industrial psychiatry in Great Britain, the United States, and Canada for the World Health Organization. He later developed his own concept of industrial psychiatry (Mindus, 1955). The survey resulted in an extensive report on occupational psychiatric programs in English-speaking countries. Mindus visited plants, universities, institutions, agencies, and union facilities, summarizing his observations and relating them to earlier experiences in the Scandinavian countries (Mindus, 1952).

By the 1960s, formal interest in and acceptance of the role of the psychiatrist in work organizations in Western Europe and North America was made clear at the Fourteenth International Congress of Occupational Health held in Madrid in 1963. More than forty presentations were concerned with the psychological problems of the work environment. The 1964 annual meeting of the World Federation for Mental Health (at the time a fairly powerful international force whose annual meetings brought together well over a thousand attendees) held in Berne, Switzerland, had its entire program devoted to mental health in industry. During that meeting, some twenty mental health professionals, mainly psychiatrists, formed the International Committee on Occupational Mental Health. This group was still active in the 1990s, with some four hundred members, most of them in Western Europe. The First International Congress on Social Psychiatry in London, also held in 1964, included many formal presentations on occupational psychiatry.

In the United States, APA surveys in the 1950s indicated that more than two hundred psychiatrists were active in work organizations. New professional organizations were created, including the Occupational Psychiatry Group in New York City, which remains an active part of the New York Occupational Medical Association. The Center for Occupational Mental Health sponsored seminars and published its proceedings, trained psychiatric fellows, produced *Occupational Mental Health Notes,* and published the journal *Occupational Mental Health* from 1970 to 1973. Alan McLean, M.D., started the center in 1963; it became part of the Department of Psychiatry at Cornell University Medical College in 1966 and remained an interdisciplinary communications center there until the early 1980s. It was the first postresidency training program for psychiatrists and during its tenure trained approximately sixty psychiatrists. Some of the conference publications are listed among the references (McLean, 1967, 1970, 1974, 1978).

Under the leadership of Harry Levinson, M.D., the Division of Industrial Mental Health of the Menninger Foundation conducted research on the relationship between people and the organization and operated a fellowship program in industrial psychiatry and educational programs for management personnel and occupational physicians. A variety of seminars and other mental health programs for managers and others continue to be made available at the Menninger Foundation. Levinson moved to the Harvard Business School and later started the Levinson Institute in Cambridge, Massachusetts, which remains an active psychoanalytically oriented center for consultation and education in the occupational mental health arena. Currently, psychiatrist Gerald Kraines, M.D., is chief executive officer of the Levinson Institute (see Chapter Twelve).

During these two decades, many new programs of psychiatric consultation got under way. Part-time consultants staffed the majority, although some full-time psychiatrists were also employed. Most were based in occupational medical departments, and a few reported to personnel and other management staffs. Their work might consist of straightforward clinical evaluation or treatment with varying regard to the circumstances of the work setting, of clinical consultation, education, training, policy consultation, research, or a combination of these; the last arrangement was most common for those spending a major part of their time in the work setting.

Publications of that period varied in their content from psychodynamic speculations to descriptions of occupational mental health programs. Many writers continued an earlier trend of exhorting and directing others to develop better mental health programs or to become interested in psychiatric problems in the world of work. Carefully executed clinical research was not often seen in the literature. Many clinical programs of fair sophistication were not published because of the belief of some employers that the conduct of mental health programs and the results of related research within organizations are properly proprietary.

Annual reviews of publications and activities in industrial psychiatry, reinstated by Burlingame (1946), continued in the *American Journal of Psychiatry* written by Collins and others (Collins, 1956). The publication of *Mental Health in Industry* received considerable publicity and led to invitations to both Graham Tayor and Alan McLean to provide interviews and make various presentations (McLean & Taylor, 1958). Business publications of the time contained fairly regular articles on occupational mental health issues, as well as quotations from psychiatric consultants to industry. Most, such as the *Wall Street Journal,* provided sound, objective reporting. Others made light of programs and psychiatric commentary. One example of the latter will serve to illustrate.

At a one-day seminar at the University of Santa Clara, one of the topics discussed was the impact of personality characteristics in career choices. It was pointed out that an individual with fairly deviant behaviors could be quite productive if properly placed in a work organization. Although the author had been told the press would not attend the program, the *San Francisco Examiner* the next morning carried a headline, "IBM HIRES NUTS!" (At the time, McLean was chief psychiatric consultant for the company.) More than two hundred papers around the country picked up the story.

1970s, 1980s, AND 1990s: EXPANDING PSYCHIATRIC HORIZONS

The practice of occupational psychiatry during the past two decades became increasingly concerned with three important concerns: educating psychiatrists about work-related issues, gaining organized psychiatry's support and commitment to a work-related focus, and establishing a partnership with corporate America.

Educational seminars and training experiences in workplace psychiatry proliferated beginning in the late 1980s and throughout the 1990s. It seemed that neither medical students nor psychiatry residents received much, if any, formal training. At least one formal study was undertaken to clarify what kind and how much formal training and experience with work-related concerns psychiatrists received or was available to them in their residency training. Directors of psychiatry residency and psychiatry fellowship programs were surveyed about the type and extent of their programs' required and elective training in occupational and organizational psychiatry. The results of this national survey indicated that only a few programs had any formal training in work-related issues. While these programs admitted that residents were asking for such training, only a handful of programs required courses or seminars on the topic. A few more programs offered only elective rotations. Although many residency directors were open to including workplace psychiatry training, most believed that there was no room in the curriculum for another seminar or course and that to incorporate workplace issues into existing courses would be at the expense of material they believed was more important (Sperry, 1995). It appears that neither medical students nor residents and fellows in nonpsychiatric specialties received much training in the impact of work-related issues on health. In large part, this reflects the fact that a brief work history is not an expected part of the medical history taken by medical students, residents, and graduate physicians.

Nevertheless, the need for such education and training led many recent graduates to attend APA courses and programs as well as to read more recently published books such as Kahn's *Mental Health in the Workplace* (1993) and Sperry's *Psychiatric Consultation in the Workplace* (1993). Providing educational seminars and training experiences in workplace psychiatry proliferated beginning in the late 1980s. The APA Committee on Occupational Psychiatry offered component workshops, and some half-day courses were offered at annual APA meetings. With Peter Brill as its first president, the Academy of Occupational and Organizational Psychiatry (AOOP) was founded in 1990 largely to provide psychiatrists who might be interested in expanding their scope of practice to obtain training and network with those already practicing this specialty. AOOP began conducting workshops and training sessions at its annual meetings. Throughout most of the 1990s, it also hosted events at annual APA meetings. For several years, there were no formal postresidency training programs in workplace psychiatry until a fellowship program in occupational and organizational psychiatry was established in the Department of Psychiatry and Behavioral Medicine at the Medical College of Wisconsin in 1991. Prior to this, the Door County Summer Institute, sponsored by the Medical College of Wisconsin, began offering week-long seminars on organizational psychiatry topics in 1989. These well-attended seminars continue today. For the past three years, Weill Medical College of Cornell University (in Manhattan) has had a ten-week residency course in occupational and organizational psychiatry.

Other notable local and regional professional activity includes the Occupational Psychiatry Group (OPG), which runs three seminars a year for business personnel. OPG is an arm of the New York Occupational Medicine Association, itself a branch of the American College of Occupational and Environmental Medicine (ACOEM). Jeffrey Kahn has chaired this group since 1995.

Workplace-focused psychiatry greatly expanded its organizational roots in the 1980s and early 1990s in both medicine and psychiatry and the professional organizations they represent. The APA Committee on Occupational Psychiatry remained active during this period, as did the Group for the Advancement of Psychiatry (GAP)–sponsored Committee on Occupational Psychiatry (recently renamed the Committee on Psychiatry in the Workplace). This GAP committee published a monograph in 1993 entitled *Psychiatry in the World of Work,* which described the wide range of practice patterns and settings of organizational and occupational psychiatry practice.

It was during the early and mid-1990s that the missions of these three groups began to be clarified. The mission of the APA Committee on Occupational Psychiatry was focused on the development of organizational and occupational psychiatry as a psychiatric discipline through the development, coordination and dissemination of knowledge about psychiatry and the world of work. The GAP committee's mission was to focus more on developing publications, while the mission of AOOP was to develop the field as a profession by establishing training and networking opportunities for psychiatrists interested in psychiatry in the workplace.

Throughout the 1980s and early 1990s, the APA committee maintained a close liaison with the American College of Occupational and Environmental Medicine (ACOEM) and the American Academy of Occupational Medicine. Although composed primarily of internists practicing in corporate medical departments a number of workplace psychiatrists are members of or fellows of ACOEM. Alan McLean was president of that organization in the early 1980s.

Workplace psychiatry continued to increase its impact on the APA in the late 1990s. Under the chairmanship of Len Sperry, M.D., Ph.D., the Committee on Occupational Psychiatry focused a great deal of energy on mainstreaming psychiatry in the workplace by building alliances with corporate America through engaging in dialogue with top corporate executives. To reflect this focus, the committee's name was changed to the Committee on Psychiatry in the Workplace in the fall of 1998. During 1998 and 1999, Sperry collaborated with Rod Munoz, M.D., then APA president, to establish a liaison with the Canadian Roundtable on Mental Health and Economics and, with Stephen Heidel, M.D., to entreat the APA board of directors to establish a formal mechanism in which American psychiatry could enter into an active partnership with the business community. The board of directors agreed to create a Task Force on Psychiatry and Business Relations, chaired by Albert Herzog, M.D. In its first six months, the task force developed an extensive proposal for establishing a formal link with the business community and plans for small pilot projects to study the link between productivity and health.

THE THIRD MILLENNIUM: NEW DIRECTIONS

The task force's proposal was approved and funded for a three-year period, and the Committee on Psychiatry/Business Relations was established to continue the work of the task force. One of the major aims of this committee was to educate corporate America about the value of psychiatric skills. Norman Clemens, M.D., was named chair of this new committee. It is noteworthy that three members of the board of directors were appointed as initial members of this committee along with three organizational and occupational psychiatrists: Robert Gordon, M.D., Jeffrey Kahn, M.D., and Len Sperry, M.D., Ph.D. Daniel Bornstein, M.D., was the APA president who approved the new committee; he was a member of the original task force and joined the committee when he completed his presidential term. The value and importance of this committee to the APA can be gauged by the substantial annual budget and the appointment of two full-time and one part-time staff members, including Lawrence Kraus, former chief operating office of the U.S. Chamber of Commerce. APA leadership has high expectations that this initiative will develop business's understanding of mental health and the role of psychiatry in the workplace.

This committee has begun collaborating with corporate leaders ranging from vice presidents of benefits and CEOs to employee assistance program health services researchers to offer its expertise in increasing health and productivity. Within the APA, the committee has focused on educating and supporting APA members and district branches in becoming more responsive to the work issues of their patients, as well as corporate concerns about fostering return to work and productivity. The committee also has supported the efforts of the Committee on Psychiatry in the Workplace to promote the use of work history in psychiatric residency training and the inclusion of work-related core competencies in the board certification examination process.

Since 1922, when Metropolitan Life Insurance Company employed a full-time psychiatrist, the role and stature of psychiatry in the workplace has alternatively risen and regressed. For much of this time, these changes in role and stature were a function of management's perception that psychiatry was primarily valued in resolving health issues and secondarily productivity issues. Recently, organized psychiatry has become increasingly proactive regarding its role and stature in the workplace.

Psychiatry's role in the workplace, originally referred to as industrial psychiatry, assumed considerable stature in the 1920s but regressed during the depression years largely because management turned to technological methods to resolve concerns about productivity. During World War II, the field surged ahead and then regressed in the postwar period. Since 1955, there has been a steady increase in the number of psychiatrists involved with workplace issues. Traditionally, psychiatrists have been associated with the corporate medical department, functioning as internal consultants at large corporations like IBM, U.S. Steel, and General Electric. Now it is more common for psychiatrists to function as external consultants to a variety of organizations. As internal consultants, psychiatrists initially provided psychiatric evaluations and clinical care to employees or through consulting with the personnel department or other members of the corporate medical staff. More recently, the roles of psychiatrists have expanded beyond the clinical domain to include consulting and organizational development issues, health care benefits, corporate mental health policy development and advocacy, and a variety of advisory and liaison functions with top management.

Organized psychiatry, particularly the APA, has influenced the role and stature of workplace psychiatry. Although Sigmund Freud insisted that mental health was a function of both love and work, organized psychiatry has not always been so supportive of efforts by psychiatrists in the workplace. As early as 1927, the *American Journal of Psychiatry* published articles and reviews on "Psychiatry in Industry," and the APA sponsored the Committee on Industrial Psychiatry whose pamphlet *Troubled People on the Job* sold 3 million copies; its *The Mentally Ill Employee* (1965) sold more than twenty-five thousand copies. It was not until 1981 that the APA created the Task Force on Psychiatry and Industry, which issued a landmark report in 1984, and the Committee on Occupational Psychiatry was formed. The APA has developed increasing awareness of the importance of work and workplace issues. Starting in 1998, that committee, which had focused on rather insular concerns, shifted its focus to mainstream psychiatry in the workplace and collaborated to convince the APA board of directors to form and develop partnerships with corporate leaders. The result of this endeavor was the formation and funding of the Committee on Psychiatry/Business Relations, entrusted with the mission of making the case for psychiatry's value in improving corporate health and productivity. This is a particularly challenging and exciting time for workplace psychiatry.

At least six trends are evident in the development of this specialty in psychiatry. First, the role of practicing workplace psychiatrists seems to have shifted from being an internal consultant, usually in a salaried position such as medical director, to being an external consultant to the organization. Second, there has been a major shift in the focus of treatment or intervention. Through the 1950s, the distressed employee was the patient. Beginning in the 1960s, the focus of treatment extended to individuals' disability, work teams, and the organization itself. The psychiatrist not only evaluated, referred, or treated individual employees, but now took on consultative responsibilities. Third, the focus shifted from primarily treatment and referral (tertiary prevention) to also screening employees for depression and substance-related issues (secondary prevention), and in some instances to modifying corporate structures and culture to reduce stress (primary prevention). Fourth, in the beginning, the specialty consisted of a rather small number of pioneering, and in many cases visionary, individual psychiatrists; now there appears to be a steadily increasingly number of psychiatrists. Whether workplace psychiatry can be declared mainstream psychiatry remains to be seen. Fifth, in the beginning, most psychiatrists practicing this specialty were self-trained; now it is possible to receive formal training. And sixth, productivity and health have in a sense been basic factors in workplace psychiatry from the beginning. Nevertheless, today both psychiatrists and corporate leaders are increasingly mindful of and intentional about the centrality of productivity and health for both the corporation and the partnership between psychiatry and the business community.

References and Additional Sources

Adler, H. (1917). Unemployment and personality. *Mental Hygiene, 1,* 16–24.

Anderson, V. V. (1929). *Psychiatry in industry.* New York: HarperCollins.

Brody, M. (1945). Dynamics of mental hygiene in industry. *Industrial Medicine and Surgery, 14,* 760.

Burling, T. (1942). The role of the professionally trained mental hygienist in business. *American Journal of Orthopsychiatry, 11,* 48.

Burling, T., Lentz, E., & Wilson, R. (1956). *The give and take in hospitals.* New York: Putnam.

Burling, T., & Longaker, W. (1955). Training for industrial psychiatry. *American Journal of Psychiatry, 111,* 493–496.

Burlingame, C. (1946). Psychiatry in industry. *American Journal of Psychiatry, 103,* 549–553.

Burlingame, C. (1947). Psychiatry in industry. *American Journal of Psychiatry, 104,* 493–495.

Burlingame, C. (1948). Psychiatry in industry. *American Journal of Psychiatry, 105,* 538.

Burlingame, C. (1949). Psychiatry in industry. *American Journal of Psychiatry, 106,* 520.

Collins, R. (1956). Industrial psychiatry. *American Journal of Psychiatry, 112,* 546.

Committee on Industrial Psychiatry of the American Psychiatric Association. (1965). *The mentally ill employee: His treatment and rehabilitation, a guide for management.* New York: HarperCollins.

Culpin, M., & Smith, M. (1930). *The nervous temperament.* London: His Majesty's Stationery Office.

Dickerson, O., & Kaminer, J. (Eds.). (1986). Special issue: The troubled employee. *Occupational Medicine: State of the Art Reviews.* Philadelphia: Hanley & Belfus.

Giberson, L. (1936). Psychiatry in industry. *Personnel Journal, 15,* 91.

Greenwood, L. (1918). *A report on the cause of wastage of labour in munitions factories.* London: His Majesty's Stationery Office.

Grinker, R., & Spiegel, J. (1945). *Men under stress.* Philadelphia: Blakiston.

Group for the Advancement of Psychiatry, Committee on Occupational Psychiatry. (1993). *Introduction to occupational psychiatry.* Washington, DC: American Psychiatric Press.

Jaques, E. (1951). *The changing culture of a factory.* New York: Dryden Press.

Jaques, E. (1956). *Measurement of responsibility.* Cambridge, MA: Harvard University Press.

Jarrett, M. (1920). The mental hygiene of industry: Report of progress on work undertaken under the Engineering Foundation of New York City. *Mental Hygiene, 4,* 867.

Kahn, J. (Ed.). (1993). *Mental health in the workplace: A practical psychiatric guide.* New York: Van Nostrand Reinhold.

Kahn, R., Hein, J., House, J., Kasl, S., & McLean, A. (1982). Report of stress in organizational settings. In G. Elliott & C. Eisdorfer (Eds.), *Stress and human health.* New York: Springer.

Leighton, A. (1959). *My name is legion.* New York: Basic Books.

Lesser, P. (1967). The legal viewpoint. In A. McLean (Ed.), *To work is human.* New York: HarperCollins.

Ling, T. (1945). Roffey Park Rehabilitation Centre. *Lancet, 1,* 283.

Lott, G. (1946). Emotional first-aid stations in industry. *Industrial Medicine and Surgery, 15,* 419.

McLean, A. (1967). *To work is human: Mental health and the business community.* New York: Macmillan.

McLean, A. (1970). *Mental health and work organizations.* Skokie, IL: Rand McNally.

McLean, A. (1974). *Occupational stress.* Springfield, IL: Charles C. Thomas.

McLean, A. (Ed.). (1978). *Reducing occupational stress.* Washington, DC: National Institute for Occupational Safety and Health.

McLean, A. (1979). *Work stress.* Reading, MA: Addison-Wesley.

McLean, A., & Taylor, G. (1958). *Mental health in industry.* New York: McGraw-Hill.

Mindus, E. (1952). *Industrial psychiatry in Great Britain, the United States, and Canada: A report to the World Health Organization.* Geneva: World Health Organization.

Mindus, E. (1955). Outlines of a concept of industrial psychiatry. *Bulletin of the World Health Organization, 13,* 561.

Quick, J., Bhagat, R., Dalton, J., & Quick, J. (1987). *Work stress.* New York: Praeger.

Rennie, T., Swackhamer, G., & Woodward, L. (1947). Toward industrial mental health: An historical review. *Mental Hygiene, 31,* 66.

Sherman, M. (1927). A review of industrial psychiatry. *American Journal of Psychiatry, 83,* 701–710.

Southard, E. (1920). The modern specialist in unrest: A place for the psychiatrist in industry. *Mental Hygiene, 4,* 550–563.

Sperry, L. (1993). *Psychiatric consultation in the workplace.* Washington, DC: American Psychiatric Press.

Sperry, L. (1995). Residency education, work-related issues and organizational and occupational psychiatry. *Academic Psychiatry, 19,* 44–45.

Sperry, L. (1996). *Corporate therapy and consulting.* New York: Brunner/Mazel.

Sperry, L. (2002). *The effective leader: Strategies for maximizing productivity and health.* New York: Brunner/Routledge.

PART TWO

COMMON
OCCUPATIONAL CONCERNS

This part begins with two chapters that take an in-depth look at occupational concerns of executives. A chapter on the role of the psychiatrist in executive skill assessment and development includes step-by-step guidance on effective techniques for maximizing executive effectiveness. When problems arise for top management, the stress can become overwhelming for even the most seasoned executive, and the effects can ripple through an organization unless the root of the problem is addressed. No book such as this would be complete without a discussion of job loss and its effects on the psyche, all the more important in times of economic change. A chapter on the mental health effects of sending employees and their families oversees will become an increasingly important topic in the expanding global economy. Part Two ends with an in-depth look at the ever-present but rarely examined topic of office politics. Lack of understanding of office politics can cast a dark cloud on an advancing career or an otherwise effective organization.

CHAPTER SIX

Executive Development

Assessment, Coaching, and Treatment

Jeffrey P. Kahn

Len Sperry

Executive skill is the lifeblood of any organization. It determines the shape and effectiveness of the organization, the productivity of its people, the ability to change and adapt, and ultimately the success of the enterprise. Many tools are useful in developing those skills. The process often starts with an assessment of executive skills, personality, and character. Both written tests and specialized interviews can be used. Management and leadership development programs can effect change through courses, mentors, and several styles of coaching. Personal treatment is sometimes the most effective and cost-effective approach to coaching. At other times, the organization as a whole can be studied for impediments to executive development.

What does it take to be an effective executive? Is it just skill and knowledge in technical areas like financial modeling, information technology, business strategy, sales technique, product design, and industry knowledge? Certainly, knowledge of technical skills is essential, but the most effective leaders use finely tuned relationship skills to organize and motivate the people around them.

Case 1

JoAnn Mettler is the director of northeastern operations for Acme Media. She has been a long, loyal, and highly effective Acme executive, with recognized technical expertise. After a thriving year in the small southwestern office, she has now been in charge of the crucial Northeast for the past month. Needless to say, the media sales world is a chaotic yet essential market, more so with the growth of Internet and cable outlets. Although JoAnn is off to a good start, Acme wants to be sure that she is fully prepared to stay on top of this market for both the short and long term. What does it take? Does JoAnn have it? What does she need?

Organizational skill is an important piece. Companies are complicated places, requiring the ability to organize people and work, navigate complex situations and competing agendas, and manage tasks through to completion. This involves highly refined people skills. Leadership, decisiveness, understanding, fairness, motivation, and empowerment are each important. Emotional intelligence (see Chapter Eleven) facilitates these goals and allows ongoing self-assessment and development. Leadership by benign hierarchy, directive command, or group consensus are useful at the right times. Strict reliance on benign hierarchy may not work well for urgent situations. Overuse of directive commands can impede morale and discourage useful feedback. And group consensus may not be appropriate for some mission-critical tasks. The most effective leaders have a flexible style that they can adapt to each employee personality and task requirement as needed. Companies and executives are increasingly aware of the essential value of cultivating the most effective management, executive, and leadership skills.

EXECUTIVE ASSESSMENT

Formal executive assessments are conducted for a variety of reasons. Most often, they are done as part of an ongoing executive development program. Combined with performance evaluations and other sources of information, a formal assessment describes workplace strengths and weaknesses that may benefit from developmental attention. Frequently, assessments are also done for executives who have known leadership problems, who have high technical skills but need help with management abilities, who have been a focus of employee complaints, or who have been or are about to be promoted. It is not always easy to recognize executives who need closer attention to their development. Recognition can be prompted by information from human resources, senior managers, peers, subordinates, clients, performance measures, and company medical departments.

Assessment procedures vary depending on the depth of information required, the specific skills needed for a given job, and the culture of the organization. It is important to start out with a careful definition of the assessment goals, the kinds of skills to be examined, and the procedures to be followed. Afterward, effective developmental follow-through is needed to ensure that the assessment leads to real change. One part of the assessment is often psychological testing.

Psychological Testing for Personality and Character

Psychological assessment methods have been traditionally used, along with intensive interviewing, in screening candidates for executive positions and, to a lesser extent, evaluating managers and other employees who are experiencing individual problems. In the job screening process, top management wants to know if a particular candidate has the requisite professional and interpersonal skills and personality to be a good fit with the company. This was the traditional focus of much of psychological assessment in the screening process.

Besides good fit with the company, company officers also need to know if the candidate's work performance will be consistent over time and demonstrate sound judgment when threatened, when tempted, or when doing the right thing may not be in his or her best interest. In other words, companies need to know about the character of these executive candidates. This second consideration can be addressed with psychological assessment methods that evaluate character. Leonard (1997) contends that of the two considerations, the second is probably the more important for companies in the long run. A number of psychological assessment methods are available for evaluating personality and character in executives.

Psychological Assessment of Executive Personality. Although there is no consensus on what constitutes a standardized protocol for the psychological assessment of an executive's personality and professional skills, several standard personality inventories are commercially available. These include the California Personality Inventory, the Sixteen PF Test (16-PF), and the NEO Personality Inventory (NEO-PI). The NEO Professional Development Report (NEO-PDR) is a derivation of the NEO-PI that addresses an individual's strengths and weaknesses in four critical job performance areas: problem-solving skills; planning, organizing, and implementation skills; styles of relating to others; and personal style. The NEO-PDR is one of the more promising psychological inventories for use in screening candidates.

Some psychological consultants may also use additional methods such as the Thematic Apperception Test (TAT). Despite some concerns about reliability and construct validity, the Myers-Briggs Type Indicator (MBTI) is often used with executives, particularly in leadership development programs and team-building contexts. For example, the MBTI is a basic assessment instrument in the leadership development program of the Army Management Staff College (Giber, Carter, & Goldsmith, 2000). Other psychological assessment methods are incomplete sentence forms, certain cards from the Rorschach test, and clinical personality assessment instruments such as the Minnesota Multiphasic Personality Inventory–Revised (MMPI–2) and the Millon Clinical Multiaxial Inventory, Version III (MCMI-III). MCMI-III is keyed to *Diagnostic and Statistical Manual of Mental Disorders,* Fourth Edition (DSM-IV) Axis I and II diagnoses. (Axis I diagnoses include specific anxiety and depression disorders, and Axis II diagnoses reflect personality disorders.) Since the MMPI and MCMI-III are instruments with norms for clinical populations, psychological and psychiatric consultants find them useful in evaluating psychopathology in executives.

However, evaluation of psychopathology in a work setting requires added caution about legal and ethical concerns.

Unlike traditional types of assessment instruments and surveys that provide unilateral or single-dimensional feedback, 360-degree surveys provide feedback from multiple sources. The surveys are called 360-degree because feedback comes from all directions: self, superior, peers, subordinates, and even customers. More accurately, 360-degree assessment is a multiple-feedback methodology rather than a special or new kind of survey or instrument. Nearly any survey or instrument that addresses job performance and interpersonal style of relating can be used. The methodology involves collecting data on identical surveys or instruments, from at least three different sources or directions of feedback, to assess the specified individual. This method of assessment is common in business today and has become an essential part of leadership assessment. This 360-degree methodology is typically used to assess overall leadership performance or effectiveness or specific skills and competencies.

Psychological Assessment of Executive Character. Character refers to good judgment, self-regulation, consistency, and acting in a responsible, cooperative, and self-transcendent fashion. Leonard (1997) suggests that the assessment of character in executive candidates essentially revolves around a single question: Will a manager be able to demonstrate sound judgment when under stress, when threatened, when tempted, or when doing the right things is not in his or her best interest? Character can be assessed through the use of inventories and interview, but the best assessment uses both.

Case 2

Teddy Donaldson had recently been hired as senior vice president for group sales. He was handsome, self-assured, articulate, and winsome in manner, and his ideas about expanding market share were novel and provocative. The chairman of the board, president, and top management team were deeply impressed by him during their interview process. His letters of recommendation were glowing, as was the psychological consultant's report. That report discussed the results of psychological instruments that included the NEO Personality Inventory (NEO-PI), the 16-PF, and selected cards from the TAT. He seemed to be an all-around fit for the company, including sharing the company's family-friendly culture and values. Two days after he started, Teddy took off for a three-day trip to visit the east coast regional office. While the president had expected to spend most of that first week orienting Teddy, he was not going to restrain Teddy's take-charge enthusiasm in getting out in the field. At least, that was his first thought. When Teddy returned, he immediately took on three key projects, but in each instance he delegated the projects to a key subordinate. Later, when asked to report on the progress of these projects to the management team, Teddy would defer to that subordinate, who would accompany him and give the report.

Teddy seemed to talk about his family constantly: his kids' soccer and tennis and the seemingly endless number of their games and tournaments that seemed to take up nearly all his free time. His office was a shrine to his family, with pictures of family members filling every available space. He would drop in to see the president and inevitably would steer the conversation to his family activities. Since the company was family friendly, the president was initially quite pleased by this. In hindsight, however, the president would conclude that this family talk was usually Teddy's excuse for a missed deadline, meeting, or appointment. Within six months, it became increasingly evident that Teddy was not living up to expectations. When he was at the company office, Teddy would defer to subordinates on nearly all his projects and duties, cancel meetings at the last minute, or leave early to deal with family issues or emergencies. The last straw was his failure to show up for the annual weekend retreat of the top management team. The CEO was furious, and within a week Teddy was terminated. The CEO was angry with both Teddy and the selection process. He wanted to know why had this character flaw not been picked up. From that point on, the psychological consulting firm incorporated the assessment of character through both inventories and corresponding interviews.

Some validated inventories purport to measure the construct of character. The Hogan Personality Inventory (Hogan & Hogan, 1995) is a measure of the "bright side" of personality. It includes three scales that reportedly describe how moral an individual appears to others. The Hogan Development Survey is a revision of the Hogan Profile and measures the "dark side" of personality (what individuals are like when no one is watching them). Individuals with high scores are described as selfish, deceitful, self-absorbed, and unable to garner the trust of others.

Cloninger's Temperament and Character Inventory (TCI; Cloninger, Svrakic, & Prybeck, 1993) is based on extensive research by Cloninger and colleagues and suggests that individuals with mature character structures tend to be self-reliant or responsible, cooperative, and self-transcendent. In contrast, those with immature character structures (also referred to as personality disorders) tend to have difficulty with self-acceptance, intolerance, and vengefulness, while feeling self-conscious and unfulfilled. Healthy personality or matured character reflects positive or elevated scores on the TCI; negative or low scores reflect the presence of character or personality disorders.

Interview Assessment of Executive Skills and Character

Interviews and psychological testing discover information in different ways. As a result, they yield two different kinds of information and complement each other in producing a thorough and thoughtful assessment. A well-designed interview looks at the executive in several ways.

Case 3

N. Ronaldo Carpe-Opes was a rising young star at Widgeco Industrial, well known for turning the small investment operation into a major profit center. He had used his bonuses to leverage such a luxurious lifestyle that some people silently wondered how he had been approved for so much debt. His unit was so successful that he had many starry-eyed admirers but no open complainers, even though turnover was three times the company average. Ron's boss realized one day that a lack of negative feedback might be limiting Ron's career development. He was sent for an executive assessment process that involved psychological testing and an interview.

The testing suggested a few limits in communication skill and some self-preoccupation, but not much more. The interview was more complex. Ron said that his turnover happened because he maintained morale partly by helping less talented employees to move on to better jobs. He did all of their exit interviews himself. He claimed to know nothing about the concept of hidden agendas in a company. But when pressed, he became irritated, before finally giving a detailed discussion with several good examples. The question of his own hidden agendas was thus implied. The interviewer also noted that while nearly all executives enjoy the interview, Ron was much more irritated by the process than anyone before him.

Assessment report in hand, the boss encouraged Ron to follow a developmental plan that would use 360-degree evaluation and other methods to increase employee feedback and improve retention rates. After Ron moved to another company three months later, company interviews with his unit's current and previous employees raised important questions about accounting methods and conflicts of interest.

The interview addresses the key skills that have been identified for a given job. Leadership, teamwork, communications, judgment, interpersonal and relationship approaches, planning, salesmanship, creativity, strategic thinking, and change management are just a few examples. To pick just one topic, questions can assess leadership skills by asking for a direct self-description, an example of a situation requiring leadership skill, comments on a leadership scenario, thoughts about an old boss or other role model, previous feedback, or even open-endedly asking for thoughts on leadership. Open-ended questions are especially useful in eliciting unrehearsed answers that offer insight into viewpoints and approaches. Asked open-endedly about creativity, one executive noted first that he had none, but then went on to describe a novel approach to a sales problem. Had he merely been asked if he were creative, he would have said no. Follow-up questions provide more detailed opinions and levels of understanding.

The interview also allows an opportunity to observe executives in person. Are they thoughtful or spontaneous? Have they thought through these topics before, and can they also think on their feet? Are they confident, anxious, or aggressive on interview? Do they seem to be direct or guarded, honest or shading the truth?

What do they show of their personal style? How do they relate to the interviewer and manage the interview situation? Do they act differently either before or after the formal interview? After the "final" question, one woman showed a softer side when she spoke openly about her anxieties as a boss.

Assessment of character relies on several kinds of interview information. Specific questions ask about ethical dilemmas, proper conduct, and the dark side of company politics (see Chapter Ten). Knowing the right answers is only part of the data. Attention is also paid to the tone of response, the depth of understanding, and the apparent sincerity of the executive. The assessment of character is also viewed in the context of such other personality traits as limited concern for others, exaggerated self-confidence, and excessive focus on personal success.

An executive assessment interview is not a clinical interview (see the sample assessment report in the chapter appendix). While everyday psychopathology can certainly influence business skills (and good treatment can improve them), no attempt is made to ask about or assess psychopathology. Keeping the content focused on work ability is important for ethical, confidentiality, interpersonal, and legal reasons.

Interviews and psychological testing often yield somewhat different information. While testing seems more standardized, it is not a perfect tool. For example, psychological tests may allow a description of leadership style that is based on basic character traits. Yet many executives have learned to be more flexible in their approaches. On interview, they frequently describe what they learned from mentors, training programs, or performance feedback and how they adjusted their style as a result. Often, this outwardly changed behavior goes uncomfortably against the grain of their personality. They see the clear performance advantages, but the new style continues to take emotional effort for a long time.

Importantly, these kinds of learned changes may not be reflected on testing. The same woman who mentioned her anxiety had test results that inaccurately suggested that she had problems showing concern for employees. In fact, with the help of a mentor, she had already fine-tuned her ability to show real concern, and it was this new-found skill that ironically left her with continuing anxiety.

LEADERSHIP DEVELOPMENT

Unlike many of the other executive development strategies whose focus is the individual executive, leadership development is a companywide initiative to identify and develop potential leaders for a company or to enhance the skills and competencies of existing executives. While theoretically leadership development is a separate and independent executive development strategy, practically speaking, leadership development is often combined with other executive development strategies.

Case 4

MathWorks is a global leader in developing and supplying technical computer software to universities, government research labs, financial institutions, and the technology sector.[1] Privately held and profitable every year since its inception in 1994, MathWorks employs five hundred people. Despite its innovative software products and profitability, the company had some major concerns, particularly with one unit.

Employees shared top management's concerns as well. An employee survey asked them to identify the company's biggest internal hassle, and employees overwhelmingly named the operations division. This division had the reputation of consistent delay in fulfilling orders and increasing customer complaints. Because of low productivity, poor customer satisfaction, and a culture that accepted poor performance as a norm, the president approved the proposal of the vice president of operations to institute a leadership development program. Aided by outside consultants, the vice president took the lead in planning and implementing the program.

A detailed analysis of the division's work flow and process undertaken at the outset of the program indicated that the work process was so fragmented and circuitous that any hope for a sense of ownership and pride in workmanship was unlikely. Lack of leadership ability within work teams compounded matters. What was needed was a new work structure and effective leadership that would transform the division's culture to one of teamwork, ownership, and pride. The program was to be a two-year experiment in transformation in which coaching was one of three critical components. Team development and training team leaders were the other two components. The goal was to establish cross-functional teamwork that would facilitate a more mature level of interaction and empowerment. The hope was that the newly formed culture would lead to better business results since each employee would see himself or herself as responsible for the unit's success or failure.

Because of turnover and other factors, many employees in this division were inexperienced and overly dependent on their managers for direction. At the same time, these employees resented being told what to do. Thus, the new leadership style needed to provide employees with the experience and support they would need to grow and mature in their work patterns. It was to be a collaborative form of leadership. Performance-based coaching is, of course, an excellent approach to redirecting employee work patterns. Using managers as a triage team provided the necessary support and reinforcement for the new way of working. Managers were able to observe ineffectual patterns as they happened and redirect them.

Because senior executives had framed the transformation as a systemic change for the division rather than as a leadership problem, there was minimal resistance and maximal ownership of the process by the division managers. Senior management also gave its full support to the expectation that division managers function as coaches and role models of the collaboration. Thus, managers were not simply talking about teamwork and collaboration; they were actually doing it. Not surprisingly, these managers began to communicate and interact differently than they did before, and employees responded by becoming more participative and proactive.

Managers spent considerable time coaching and teaching employees how to manage their emotions, foster effective two-way communication, and resolve conflict. Managers benefited from the parallel process of coaching each other. They attended leadership development conferences and learned firsthand from daily experiences about the competencies they needed for this new system to work. They began to view themselves not simply as managers but as change agents, coaches, and internal consultants. Interestingly, they agreed that a 360-degree review process was necessary for evaluating their performance, and they quickly implemented this initiative.

An early success of the coaching initiation was a weekly open-door initiative that provided employees an opportunity to contribute new ideas or vent their emotions in a safe, receptive forum. This initiative also permitted managers to introduce basic tools and analytical problem-solving skills that helped team members through some difficult roadblock early in the change process. As the new culture stabilized, it became clearer that managers who were resistant or incapable of functioning as coaches were eventually counseled to move on.

The two-year leadership development experiment at MathWorks succeeded. The culture of the operations division was permanently transformed and remains in place. Productivity, quality, and customer satisfaction have continually exceeded expectations, and turnover has been minimal.

U.S. corporations have spent approximately 1 percent of their total revenues for the training and development of their executives, amounting to about $40 billion annually (McCall, Lombardo, & Morrison, 1988). Of the fifteen major companies recently surveyed, half spent more than $1 million in 1999 on their formal leadership development programs (Giber et al., 2000). Traditionally, leadership development was classroom based and focused on building and upgrading a set of generic leadership competencies, such as interpersonal skills and financial analysis.

The underlying assumption was that course work fostered executive performance as it facilitated the executive's ability to gain technical knowledge, understand leadership models and theories, solve and frame problems, and develop self-confidence and judgment skills. But this assumption has been subject to intense scrutiny, largely because there are few data to justify its cost. Increasingly, top management has come to believe that the most effective and useful manner of learning about leadership is on the job rather than in the classroom.

This belief is based on their experience and mounting research evidence, such as that reported in McCall and colleagues' *The Lessons of Experience: How Successful Executives Develop on the Job* (1988). Based on their groundbreaking research, the authors concluded that the process of executive development occurs during the course of ten or twenty years of progressive job experience.

They described five sets of lessons successful executives learned on the job (setting and implementing agendas, handling relationships, basic values, executive temperament, and personal insight) and five developmental events that spawned these lessons.

The designation of leadership development as a system (Potts & Sykes, 1993) connotes that leadership development is a strategic initiative and not simply classroom instruction. In 1998, a study was launched to determine how the world's most successful organizations are developing their leaders. This study of 350 companies found that nearly all respondents recognized the need to develop stronger leaders, but less than 44 percent had a formal process for developing high-potential leaders. However, those companies that were successful in producing high-potential leaders used structured leadership development systems (Giber et al., 2000).

Best Practices

What are the best practices in leadership development today? Looking at fifteen of the most successful corporate leadership development programs provides some clues. In terms of essential components, the best programs emphasized 360-degree feedback, action learning, and exposure to senior executives that included coaching and mentoring programs. The leadership competencies with the most impact on the design of these leadership development systems were strengthening team building, business understanding, and conceptual thinking.

Despite increasing concern that executives lack the emotional capacity and maturity to lead organizations successfully, emotional intelligence was a low priority in these programs. Three critical factors with the most impact on the success of these leadership development systems were the support and involvement of senior executives, continuous evaluation, and linking leadership development with the company's strategic plan (Giber et al., 2000). In short, where the consultant's role in leadership development had been to teach or facilitate leadership seminars, now the consultant's role involves the design and implementation of learning experiences that are strategically focused and often use other executive development strategies such as executive profiling, executive policy development, and executive coaching or mentoring.

EXECUTIVE COACHING

In coaching, a coach works collaboratively with an executive to improve the executive's skill and effectiveness in communicating company vision and goals, facilitating team performance, organizational productivity, and personal development. It is usually of short duration (Sperry, 2002). Executive coaching is similar to but different from executive consultation, as well as psychotherapy with executives, with regard to roles, focus, and duration. Executive consultation is a form of organizational consultation in which a consultant, functioning as a sounding board, expert adviser, or evaluator, forms a collaborative relationship with an individual executive to address a broad range of professional and personal issues of concern to the executive. Unlike coaching, executive consultation tends to be an ongoing process and of a longer duration. Psychotherapy with executives is a process in which a psychotherapist and executive establish a close, collaborative relationship and use psychotherapeutic methods to achieve greater self-understanding and resolution of work-related problems or symptoms. This modality usually involves weekly sessions and is of short to long duration.

The Practice of Executive Coaching

Although there are a number of approaches to executive coaching, four basic models of coaching can be described. In the first model, the executive coach meets face-to-face with the client person being coached in a one-to-one format for a limited time frame. The coaching format is intensive, usually involving a few to several hours over the course of a day or two until the goal of coaching is reasonably achieved. Benton (1999) describes this approach.

In the second model, the executive coach meets face-to-face with the person being coached for scheduled sessions of one to one and a half hours, usually weekly for three to six months. The coaching sessions are scheduled at the executive's work site, but in a neutral office or meeting room. Stephenson (2000) typifies this pattern.

In the third model, the executive coach meets face-to-face with the person being coached in various formats: one-to-one, with a work team, with the person being coached and the work team, or in a one-to-one session with the executive and person being coached. Formal sessions are scheduled, but the duration and frequency of the sessions are a function of the format and goals to be achieved. O'Neill (2000) describes this approach.

In the fourth model, the executive coach meets primarily by telephone with the person being coached. Although the first meeting may be a one-hour face-to-face session, it can also be by telephone. A specific number of half-hour weekly telephone sessions are scheduled (usually four to six), as well as a final session to review progress and determine whether the coaching contract should be extended. This model seems to be less attractive to senior executives.

Case 5

Cindy Wong is the thirty-five-year-old manager of the product division of a recently merged financial institution. Her most recent performance review noted morale problems in her division. Fearful that she would be terminated, Cindy sought out the advice of an executive coach who was also a member of her country club. He reviewed her concerns and concluded that the primary source of disharmony in the division was an older secretary. Janice Davis was disgruntled with the recent merger and generally difficult to work with and for because of her almost incessant demands for special privileges. Cindy felt intimidated by Janice. Cindy believed that her problem managing the division and the difficult employee stemmed from her passive nature and domineering mother and thought she might need formal psychotherapy. The executive coach suggested framing the problem as one of skill deficits in assertive communication and negotiation and offered to provide some time-limited coaching. If the coaching were not sufficiently helpful, the matter of psychotherapy would be revisited.

In a one-to-one context, the coach used role playing to assess Cindy's communication and negotiation skills. The coach modeled both skills in the context of role playing and role reversal, first taking on the role of manager and then that of difficult employee. Throughout the remainder of the first two-hour session, the two worked on preparing Cindy for a forthcoming six-month performance review with Janice. Cindy practiced and reversed roles until she was confident she could reasonably handle the performance review. When they met the second time, Cindy reported that the review had gone reasonably well as compared to previous reviews. Specific expectations for the employee's attitude and productivity had been mutually negotiated. Nevertheless, Cindy was still somewhat intimidated by Janice. Skill building continued with role-playing focusing on typical encounters between both women. The coaching was also directed at replacing Cindy's denigrating self-talk with more positive self-talk when she anticipated dealing with the secretary.

By the time of the third coaching session, morale in the division was better, and Cindy felt more confidence as a manager.

In this example, coaching, rather than psychotherapy, appeared to be the initial intervention of choice and was effective. Had an adequate course of coaching been only partially successful, formal psychotherapy might then have been offered. These models of coaching practice are quite diverse and do not appear to reflect theory or research but rather seem to have evolved based on the coach's or the executive client's preferences or circumstances. They specify at least four phases of the coaching process (Sperry, 2002). Phase 1 involves establishing a viable relationship and some agreement about the nature of the coaching.

Many people consider establishing a collaborative relationship a necessary condition for success of the undertaking. The agreement or contract for coaching usually specifies the goal, methods, frequency and duration of meetings, and remuneration. Phase 2 includes some sort of assessment of the executive. This may be quite broad or narrow and might include an evaluation of job description, functions, and performance standards, skills, talents, and competencies, and reporting relationships. Phase 3 includes some sort of action planning that specifies the goal to be achieved (perhaps learning a new skill, improving performance, or better interpersonal relations) and articulates the methods and techniques for achieving it. Phase 4 is the implementation of the action plan: skills training, modeling, role playing, the use of executive resources, or whatever else is decided on. Monitoring and evaluating outcomes against goals are essential.

Performance-Based Coaching

Performance-based coaching is a strategy for increasing, correcting, or recalibrating the executive's overall performance and job effectiveness as a function of leadership competencies and personal style. "As a rule, coaching to correct performance involves interventions to remedy problems that interfere with an executive's job performance or that risk derailing a career" (Witherspoon, 2000, p. 169). In short, the primary purpose of this type of coaching is to reduce or eliminate impediments to higher-level executive performance.

Typically, an executive works collaboratively with a coach to achieve the following objectives. First, they assess the executive's overall competencies for his or her current position. Second, they clarify expectations, of both the executive and the executive's superior, for job performance. Third, they prioritize the executive's needs as they relate to current job performance. Fourth, they establish a plan for continuing improvement. And, finally, they implement that plan and periodically evaluate outcomes. Coaching for performance improvement tends to be an ongoing process that typically spans several months or quarters.

Skill-Based Coaching

Skill-based coaching is typically what most people associate with the term *coaching*. Distinct from teaching, which relies on one-way instruction, coaching relies on "observation, inquiry, dialogue and discovery. The essence of coaching executives is helping them learn, rather than training or tutoring them. To coach in this sense is less to instruct than to facilitate" (Witherspoon, 2000, p. 168). Skill-based coaching addresses deficits in the core leadership skill sets: technical and analytic, relational, strategic, financial and informational, and self-management skills. The primary purpose of skill-based coaching is to sharpen skills in one or more areas that will facilitate the executive's efforts with a current project or task.

PERSONAL TREATMENT

There is an inevitable interaction between life at work and life at home. A tough day at the office can cause fatigue, anxiety, or grouchiness that gets carried home. An argument with the family can lead to extra sensitivity to disagreement at work. If the notion of a relationship problem at home is too worrisome to think about, it sometimes appears as an exaggerated concern about someone at work, or vice versa. An employee with a child leaving for college may dwell on loss of a minor client at work. Perhaps most important, while someone's environment may shift in moving between work and home, the basic self does not. The same concerns that interfere with personal life will usually affect career as well.

Case 6

Joe Quiethawk is the senior vice president for Information Systems at InterPrize Industries. He is known for his outstanding management skill and rapidly progressive responsibility since he started as a junior programmer more than fifteen years ago. Joe is especially good at delegating work and generating enormous warmth and loyalty from his staff, but he has always accepted promotions reluctantly.

When the InterPrize CEO unexpectedly asks Joe to become the new executive vice president in charge of information services, human resources, and all support services, Joe not only declines but also takes an unplanned vacation week.

The CEO is perplexed, to say the least. After talking with his chief operating officer, he suggests that Joe seek a confidential opinion from their consulting psychiatrist. Joe agrees to follow through. During the evaluation, several issues start to emerge. Joe has always seen himself as no more than a lucky programmer: good with a line of code, he thinks, but woefully deficient in people and leadership skills. Actually, that perspective is a major part of what shapes his effective hands-off management style. It is not that Joe does not want the promotion and raise, but he feels overwhelmed and threatened. The way he sees it, the promotion is not only undeserved but also a set-up for embarrassing failure.

There are also issues at home. When he was growing up, Joe's parents always told him that his math and science skills would get him through despite his shy and quiet style. And while they halfheartedly celebrate Joe's success, they never fail to remind him of their modest means. Finally, although Joe speaks well in public, he is still terribly afraid that he will embarrass himself. Every time he even thinks of speaking, he is painfully aware of his flushed face, racing heart, and nearly overwhelming fear. As an executive vice president, there would be many more speeches, meetings, and cocktail parties to face.

Joe and the psychiatrist agree to begin weekly psychotherapy and to treat his social phobia with paroxetine. Early conversations focus on Joe's fears of embarrassment and soon expand to his concerns about work, with his parents, and at home. Two months later, Joe has his social phobia under better control and has started to realize the importance of better understanding the connections between his rational and emotional lives. He accepts the well-deserved promotion with new-found ease and contentedly wraps up psychotherapy five months after that.

Can psychiatric treatment help in developing business skills? Of course. Executives who enter treatment for personal reasons often find that there are substantial benefits for their business skills as well.

Compared to coaching and other forms of executive development, treatment has both disadvantages and advantages. First, while all genuine issues of work performance are legitimate concerns of an employer, personal life and everyday issues of psychopathology are not. It is important not to intrude on employees' personal lives, and not all employees will immediately see any connection between work and their emotional lives. For many, it will feel less intrusive and be nearly as helpful to focus solely on the workplace behaviors at issue. When employees are known to be in treatment, it is extremely important to protect both real and perceived confidentiality.

In appropriate circumstances, though, treatment has notable advantages over coaching. Looking at the full picture of the executive's life makes it easier to see all of the issues that she is struggling with and the important patterns of behavior that transcend circumstance. An executive who always strikes out in the last inning of a neighborhood baseball game may also have trouble in the final stages of closing a deal. This picture allows a better understanding of emotions that can get displaced from home to work (or the other way around). An executive who struggles with a domineering husband at home may respond with either submissiveness or domineering at work.

Most useful, treatment can also identify and address the root causes of problems. When the underlying causes of a problem are resolved, the surface-level problem tends to become much less of an issue. There can be many root causes—for example, family issues, personality traits, workplace relationships, and commonplace anxiety, depression, and substance abuse disorders. Although nearly everyone has one or several of these personal issues, such root causes are rarely evident in the workplace or even to the executive. It makes sense that treatment of marital problems, depression, or alcoholism can cause a major improvement in executive performance. Good treatment can bring about much greater and longer-lasting improvement than coaching and with much greater confidence and sense of well-being.

When is personal psychiatric treatment appropriate? Many executives seek help on their own, but there may also be times when a company suggestion is appropriate. For example, an executive who mentions personal problems, seems notably distressed at work, or shows a change in work habits can be informally reminded that treatment can help and that the company can suggest confidential resources in occupational psychiatry. Suggestion of work-life or work-focused treatment feels less threatening, even if it comes with the awareness that other issues will also be explored. Even so, care must be taken to point out that business performance will remain the focus of management attention. When the intellectual guidepost of a large company suddenly tried to resign, the CEO asked him to take a paid leave and see the company's consulting psychiatrist for confidential care. After a few weeks of treatment for panic disorder and for concerns about his children, he returned to work eager, at his best, and more relaxed than ever before.

Finding the best resources is not always easy (see Chapter Two), and resources should be identified in advance of potential problems. Providers available through managed care and employee assistance programs (EAPs) do not always have the broad range of training and skills in occupational psychiatry that these employees require. Guidelines issued by the Equal Employment Opportunity Commission in 1997 for reasonable accommodation of mental illness under the Americans with Disabilities Act are sometimes raised as an exaggerated concern for any referral for treatment, including EAPs (see Chapter Nineteen for a fuller discussion).

ORGANIZATIONAL INTERVENTION

Any discussion of executive development is incomplete without attention to the organization where the executive is trying to develop skills. Sometimes the organization itself gets in the way of individuals who are trying to develop their skills to the fullest. One sign is the appearance of many dissatisfied or poorly performing managers in one area of a company. Are there management, leadership, or communications problems? Are managers getting good feedback, training, and support? Or has weak management selected a weaker pool of executive talent? As the old saying goes, B people hire C people, but A people hire A+ people. (See Chapter Ten.) This is a useful aphorism when thinking about individuals as well. Especially talented executives sometimes feel threatening to some superiors. As a result, they may be offered fewer opportunities and rewards, especially at times of organizational change or other uncertainty.

In these situations, the focus needs to be more than just an individual's development. Careful attention must be paid to management structures, reward and recognition mechanisms, job design, and the underlying culture of the company.

Effective executives need a wide variety of skill sets. Beyond conventionally technical skills and industry knowledge, they need to have a thoughtful deftness with the people skills that motivate and manage people, enable strategic leadership, empower organizations, and allow self-awareness. Actually, these people skills are another kind of technical skill that can be assessed within company performance evaluations and by formal assessment methodology. They can be improved by experience, courses, mentors, and coaching. Where appropriate, the greater benefits of personal treatment will also spill over to other areas of an executive's life. Bringing about executive excellence is an essential task for any company that plans for ongoing success. The payoffs in productivity, effectiveness, retention, and subordinate morale are enormous. Here, as in so many things, the greatest value occurs when the process is done right the first time around.

Note

1. This case is adapted from Slobodnik, Slobodnik, and Haight (2000).

References and Additional Sources

Benton, D. (1999). *Secrets of a CEO coach.* New York: McGraw-Hill.

Cloninger, R., Svrakic, D., & Prybeck, T. (1993). A psychobiological model of temperament and character. *Archives of General Psychiatry, 50,* 975–990.

Giber, D., Carter, L., & Goldsmith, M. (2000). *Linkage, Inc.'s best practices in leadership development handbook.* San Francisco: Jossey-Bass.

Hogan, R., & Hogan, J. (1995). *Manual for the Hogan Personality Inventory.* Tulsa, OK: Hogan Assessment Systems.

Leonard, S. (1997). The many faces of character. *Consulting Psychology Journal, 49,* 235–245.

McCall, M., Lombardo, M., & Morrison, A. (1988). *The lessons of experience: How successful executives develop on the job.* San Francisco: New Lexington Press.

O'Neill, M. (2000). *Executive coaching with backbone and heart: A systems approach to engaging leaders with their challenges.* San Francisco: Jossey-Bass.

Potts, T., & Sykes, A. (1993). *Executive talent: How to identify and develop the best.* Homewood, IL: Business One Irwin.

Slobodnik, D., Slobodnik, A., & Haight, E. (2000). MathWorks. In D. Giber, L. Carter, & M. Goldsmith (Eds.), *Linkages Inc.'s best practices in leadership development handbook* (pp. 277–297). San Francisco: Jossey-Bass.

Sperry, L. (2002). *Effective leadership: Strategies for maximizing executive productivity and health.* New York: Brunner/Routledge.

Stephenson, P. (2000). *Executive coaching: Lead, develop, retain motivated talented people.* Frenchs Forest, NSW: Pearson Education Australia.

Witherspoon, R. (2000). Starting smart: Clarifying coaching goals and roles. In M. Goldsmith, L. Lyons, & A. Freas (Eds.), *Coaching for leadership: How the world's greatest coaches help leaders learn* (pp. 165–185). San Francisco: Jossey-Bass/Pfeiffer.

APPENDIX

ACME MEDIA

DEVELOPMENTAL ASSESSMENT OF:

DIRECTOR OF NORTHEASTERN OPERATIONS

WorkPsych Associates, Inc.
Jeffrey P. Kahn, M.D.
Charles L. Sodikoff, Ph.D.

INTRODUCTION

The recently promoted director of Northeastern Operations at Acme Media was presented for executive assessment. An initial discussion was held with Eric Santana, senior vice president for human resources, covering the key personality and behavioral characteristics needed for success in the position. The candidate appeared for a full-day battery of interviewing and psychological testing. The names of testing instruments used are listed at the end of this report.

This report is based solely on a condensation of test and interview information and is the interpretation of a licensed psychiatrist and psychologist. The conclusions contained in this report are made in good faith and with every care following ethical and technical standards set out by the American Psychological Association. It is intended that such standards be maintained in their use.

JOANN METTLER

JoAnn is friendly, even-tempered, highly sociable, and nurturing. Her executive effectiveness is primarily due to her ability to build strong personal relationships. On interview, she came across as relaxed, personable, thoughtful, and articulate. She values harmony and cooperation and looks to avoid or ignore conflict.

JoAnn is bright and uses a balance of logic and emotion in her decision making. On a test of her ability to solve abstract problems, she correctly solved fourteen out of fifteen items, placing her in the top 5 percent of the general population. On a second test, JoAnn demonstrated strong logic, the ability to make inferences and draw conclusions from complex material, and skill in evaluating arguments. She scored at the eighty-sixth percentile compared to a typical group of executives and above the average range (sixty-third percentile) of graduate business students. But JoAnn also relies heavily on her instincts in making decisions.

Although JoAnn tends not to be highly creative, she is a good listener and is open to the new ideas and approaches of others. "I'm inspired by creativity . . . creative people help me through difficulty." She will always weigh these ideas against practical standards. Her primary focus tends toward the most immediate and pragmatic issues, but she will include long-term, future-oriented considerations in planning.

JoAnn does not have a need to dominate others. She can take the lead if she feels that she is particularly competent in an area, but in most cases prefers to be an active team member. She respects authority and is loyal to her superiors. When in a supervisory role, JoAnn tends to give people lots of leeway. She will indicate her expectations but will not closely manage staff.

JoAnn has a typical need to achieve success. She sets moderate, attainable goals for herself. She does not have overly high expectations about others' level of performance. JoAnn is highly responsible and reliable and prides herself on being someone you can count on to see the job though to completion. She willingly takes on assignments and at times may become overloaded because she won't say no to new assignments, even when she should.

JoAnn is a strong cooperator. She does not play political games and willingly shares ideas and workload. JoAnn is likely to trust others initially and have them prove her wrong. She struggles, at times, with situations where her trust and openness have gone wrong, but likely has learned by now when to be a bit more cautious. She offered a keen analysis of a scenario with a hidden agenda, seeking to understand and address underlying issues and providing overall perspective at the same time.

JoAnn is not aggressive and will rarely initiate conflict. In her desire to achieve harmony, she can sometimes run the risk of not confronting important issues or of being overpowered by more aggressive and assertive people. She may have difficulty confronting others who are not performing up to standard. On occasion, she may increase her own workload to make up for inadequate efforts of others. JoAnn is not likely to complain about this overtly, but her resentment may build until it is expressed in ways that startle others, who are caught by surprise.

JoAnn is warm, friendly, and outgoing. She is quite approachable and reaches out easily to others. JoAnn is able to build solid relationships because people know that she cares about them and that she rarely will act solely out of self-interest. JoAnn trusts others and they trust her. After building a relationship with JoAnn, people tend to be persuaded by her because they believe that if she says something is good for them, it must be true. JoAnn's empathic skills are both intuitive and deliberate, and were a clear and consistent thread throughout the interview.

While JoAnn is a pleasant coworker, she does take a serious approach to work. She has a calm, relaxed, and self-assured temperament. She does not get riled or excited during crises. She keeps her head and attacks the problem rather than looking at others to place the blame. Many appreciate this in JoAnn, but some who manage her may wonder if she stays so calm because of lack of motivation or perhaps inability to assign responsibility.

JoAnn is quite open to change and is willing to try new methods or techniques. She is a steadying factor when changes are introduced into the organization, and while she has a strong respect for existing rules and structure, she is readily supportive when management restructures them. Also, she is probably highly supportive of management when changes are made.

JoAnn is not impulsive and is most effective when there is time to consider her response before acting. She prefers to have a plan of action thought through. She likes her work orderly and her day under control. Once she makes a judgment, it tends to be firm, and she does not like to change her decisions without overwhelming evidence that there is a need to do so.

COMMENTS AND DEVELOPMENT RECOMMENDATIONS FOR KEY SUCCESS FACTORS

1. Leadership Ability—JoAnn will take on management or supervisory responsibilities when asked to or when she feels sufficiently competent, but that is not her strongest inclination. JoAnn tends to be more interested in team participation than in command authority. She can influence and persuade by pulling people in her direction through trust and loyalty. As the formal leader, it may be difficult for JoAnn to discipline or deal with staff performance issues. In addition, while her nondirective tendencies may be well appreciated by some, there are others who expect or need more direction from management. As a leader, it is likely that JoAnn would be more successful with a mature, self-directing team than with less mature more dependent individuals.

   JoAnn should diversify her leadership style to include more directive approaches and also conflict management skills (note her suggestions in Factor 2 below). In particular, JoAnn needs to be comfortable with delegating individual responsibility, offering concise performance feedback, and asserting command authority. Combined with her existing abilities, she would then have a superb leader-manager skill set. Course work and reading could teach her basic concepts, and mentoring or coaching could then help her with application. In addition, she should reflect on any possible discomfort at appropriate use of these approaches. It might be useful for her to thoughtfully manage a project where she is not personally a member of the day-to-day team.

2. Communication Skills—JoAnn tends to be an open, straightforward communicator. She is outgoing, approachable, and easy to talk to. She speaks directly to people in a down-to-earth, direct, and empathic fashion. She is not political and may say things that leave her vulnerable at times, although she has probably become more guarded as her career has progressed. JoAnn is a good listener, and this helps her build trust with others because she pays attention to their needs. Asked to evaluate one workplace scenario as a manager advising a subordinate, she first offered some broadly general praise, but with some prompting then offered some reasonable guidance (explore and address seeming issues of office conflict and personal anger).

   JoAnn does need to be sure that she attends to the political aspects of communication and to communication about political issues. This is an issue that can be dealt with by a mentor or coach.

3. Team Oriented—Clearly, this is one of JoAnn's strongest characteristics. She is a believer in the effectiveness of teamwork and works hard to develop, solidify, and

reward her teams. She can also be a loyal follower and eager participant in team activity.

JoAnn's great strength in this area may make her overly dependent on her team, especially as she moves up organizationally. She may well benefit from taking on an independent special assignment that she performs without close team support.

4. Intellect and Sound Judgment—JoAnn is bright and deals with situations with sound, logical judgment. She is calm, unruffled, and mature and she deals with work as a serious endeavor. She will, at times, pay useful attention to her "gut" in making decisions, and most of the time her instincts are on target.

   This factor does not appear to need specific attention.

5. Interpersonal Skills/Relationship Building—JoAnn is warm and friendly. She works to build relationships with people and relies heavily on mutual trust. People truly like JoAnn as a friend. She is proud to stay as true to her word as possible, and most people appreciate that. She is a nurturer and truly cares about other people, and this allows her to maintain strong, long-lasting associations that likely carry through inside and outside business. She emphasizes the importance of managing different people differently and offered the novel observation that this offers her an opportunity to learn from each of them. She offered a concise but strong list of factors that differentiate employee styles. Asked to comment on two different hypothetical employees, JoAnn offered two distinct and empathic approaches to their career development.

   This factor does not appear to need specific attention.

6. Planning and Organizing—JoAnn tends to be orderly and organized and likes to work with a plan. She is sufficiently action oriented that she does not get frozen in the planning stage. Her implementation, however, tends to be more effective the more time she has to scope it out. At times, JoAnn might frustrate others by not being aware of their time pressures. JoAnn balances her primary interest in short-term tactical planning with some focus on more long-term strategic concerns.

   While this factor does not appear to need much specific attention, JoAnn should be sure to understand the sense of time urgency that others may sometimes have.

7. Creative Problem Solving—JoAnn can be creative on occasion, but more often she is open to and relies on the creativity of others. JoAnn is quite comfortable with new approaches, but they must ultimately meet the test of practicality.

   While this factor does not appear to need much specific attention, JoAnn might consider reading or course work on creative problem solving that might open up new opportunities for her.

8. Transition Skills/Advancement Potential—JoAnn should have little difficulty in making transitions. She is open to change and learning new areas and likely looks at each transition as an exciting new challenge. She handles success well, feeling recognized, relaxing, and celebrating with "people who are really close to me." With regard to her potential for advancement, she has a number of very strong suits, including intelligence and strong relationship-building skills. She should easily be able to expand her leadership skill set to include more directive approaches and greater command responsibility for others.

   This factor does not appear to need specific attention.

TESTS USED IN THIS ASSESSMENT

- Watson-Glaser Critical Thinking Appraisal, Psychological Corporation
- Myers-Briggs Type Indicator—Form F, Briggs & Myers, Consulting Psychologists Press
- Personality Research Form—Form F, Jackson Research Psychologists Press
- 16PF—Fifth Edition, Institute for Personality and Ability Testing

CHAPTER SEVEN

Executive Distress and Organizational Consequences

Jeffrey P. Kahn
Mark P. Unterberg

Leadership strengths and failings are central to organizational structure and function. Continued attention has focused on such problems as productivity, dishonesty, fostering creativity, and succession planning. Under the pressure of emotional distress, there is an increased potential for executive behavior with problematic organizational consequences. Problems arise for specific reasons, have specific solutions, and are always more complex than they seem. The underlying work, family, or intrapsychic causes are usually complex, and often hidden or subtle. Narcissistic-level personality problems, recreated family dynamics, personality styles under stress, and psychological defenses are all important constructs for understanding the mechanisms and organizational effects of distressed executives. Treatment must consider not only job issues themselves but also family concerns, specific psychodynamic and psychiatric diagnoses, and the possibility of medical illness. Careful consideration of underlying causes allows potential problems to be recognized, addressed, and ultimately avoided.

Executive leadership is the lifeblood of any organization. Leadership decisions, vision, and behavior set the tone for organizational structure, function, and culture. No organization can be better than the model that its leaders see or that they themselves demonstrate. The problem, of course, is that leaders are human beings. They have strengths and failings, and they are prone to the same emotional vagaries as everyone else. A public persona may be designed to hide away whatever emotional mechanisms lurk within, but under the pressure of emotional distress, the potential for organizational problems increases. The underlying work, family, or intrapsychic causes are usually complex, and often hidden or subtle. The solution is to understand the problems as much as possible in order to address and resolve them as they arise, and in order that organizational structures can be designed to counterbalance the vagaries of human emotion.

This chapter gives examples of some all-too-familiar organizational problems and corresponding psychodynamic concepts. The first two cases are about narcissistic-level personality problems (only under stress in the second case). The next two are about reenacted family dynamics (both cases are about aspects of intergenerational "oedipal" competition). The third pair describes two personality styles under stress (paranoid and obsessional). Finally, the last pair of cases is about psychological defenses against the experience of painful emotions (displacement and suppression). Notably, there are always overlapping mechanisms, and no one situation is ever a simple and discrete problem.

Organizations and managers should not feel obliged to address these issues themselves with any given employee. Rather, there should be an awareness that these problems arise for specific reasons, have specific solutions, and always are more complex than they seem. Psychotherapy pursues identification of the underlying causes, relief of distress, and future avoidance of problematic behavior. As the cases in this chapter show, treatment must not focus on job issues alone. Superficial efforts yield superficial results. Ignoring family concerns, specific psychodynamic and psychiatric diagnoses, and potential medical problems can severely limit psychotherapeutic value, and even allow problems to worsen.

NARCISSISM: PATCHING OVER THE UNCARING WORLD

Organizational leaders need to have a healthy and realistic appreciation of their own abilities. Such healthy narcissism contributes to effective leadership style and productive team efforts. Excessive narcissistic traits may reflect a relative incapacity for emotional intimacy. Under the pressure of intrapsychic, family, or organizational changes (often subtle or hidden), narcissistic individuals are vulnerable to episodes of heightened mental distress. With a thus intensified or altered emotional frame of reference, they have more difficulty than usual to perceive and address organizational circumstances realistically. Notably, there can be an intrapsychically determined assumption that the organization or its members are not supportive, and a consequent increased likelihood of depression, substance abuse, and other behaviors with adverse effects on the organization. Two adverse behaviors of particular concern are self-serving grandiosity, and dishonesty.

Grandiosity: Empire Building and Masters of the Universe

Successful managers like to feel that they are good at what they do and that they are wanted and needed by those around them. "Doing well by doing good" is the motto of healthy adult narcissism, and the manager with that approach is a benefit to subordinates, superiors, clients, shareholders, and the organization itself. In whole or in part, though, ambition is often a grandiose attempt to cover over inner distress. Excessive grandiosity can lead to unfeeling and self-destructive behavior. Grandiose plans are designed for their immediate emotional reassurance, not for the pleasures of success, and without real concern for others. And what looks on the outside like infantile behavior can make some people see only a desire to "have their cake and eat it too" rather than the hidden inner loneliness. Unfortunately, further feelings of rejection from the group are a common result.

Case 1

Wanda Boynton has been on the fast track since her first day in Selco Corporation's executive training program. From the start, people knew that she was someone who would rise to the very top. It was only a question of how fast. Wanda developed many ambitious and exciting projects. Many fell apart, but there were a few that she turned into big successes. She moved up the corporate ladder, took on increasing responsibility, and managed to build a bit of an empire for herself. Her department expanded in size and scope, and it appropriated some tasks from other departments. Even so, she traded favors with other executives and became known as a consummate corporate politician.

Recently, though, her career has run into some difficulty. Her superiors still seem pleased, but there have been increasing complaints from colleagues and from within her own department. Fellow department heads have noted that Wanda has become more intense and disagreeable at their weekly meetings. She continues to accept their help, but now often refuses to help in return. In one notable case, another department head needed to borrow five engineers. Wanda asked that her department be paid in advance for their time, but then assigned only three engineers for the project. Before, her good-natured style had made her the center of attention at business meetings and social gatherings. Now, though, there are frequent outbursts at employees who do not do their work precisely as she asked. Colleagues and subordinates feel increasingly estranged, and some have tried to talk with Wanda. She does not take all this criticism too seriously. She figures that her special talents entitle her to rise above ordinary rules and that her actions are really for the company's good anyway.

Curiously, Wanda's personality change has seemed to coincide with the continuing financial success of her department. Wanda has always kept an inner loneliness carefully hidden from herself and others, all the while searching for compensatory recognition. But despite her current success, Wanda is actually less happy than usual. She now spends long hours in her office, writing detailed memos to the CEO about her ideas for the company's future. Not a few of these ideas were taken, without credit, from eager subordinates. Wanda envisioned one or two of the ideas catapulting her up the corporate ladder, perhaps soon becoming special assistant to the CEO. Secretly, she thinks of replacing the current CEO, whom Wanda feels sure is not as competent as herself. She is aware of the danger of talking openly about such matters, so she discusses them only with her husband. He certainly seems to agree with her, although he pretty much agrees with all of Wanda's thoughts, comments, and demands. His passive adulation and praise have won him stability in their fifteen-year marriage. Even so, he and their three children have always felt that Wanda is emotionally detached, and they now worry about her increasing tirades at home.

Wanda also has become increasingly isolated from colleagues and departmental subordinates, and eventually is called to discuss "a matter of importance" with the CEO. Wanda is convinced that the CEO will offer her the special assistant position. No doubt the CEO has recognized the importance of her ideas for the future of the company and wants her in charge of their implementation. Anticipating the good news, Wanda arrives early for the meeting.

The usually lighthearted CEO looks worried. Concerned at first, Wanda quickly decides that the CEO is worried about the implications of selecting her for the promotion over more experienced senior managers. In fact, the CEO has a frank discussion with Wanda concerning the many complaints about her leadership and behavior. There have been several written statements from other department heads, who have been approached by employees afraid to talk directly to Wanda. The complaints focus primarily around Wanda's need for absolute control over everything within the department. People are feeling browbeaten and under the "dictatorship" of a "tyrant." They cite many specific examples of angry outbursts, unavailability, lack of rewards, and perceived dishonesty. The CEO thinks that Wanda is acting more like an *enfant terrible* than a mature leader. He points out that Wanda's department cannot continue its success with ever sinking morale and that someday one of Wanda's grandiose business plans will go badly wrong. He strongly advises her to seek psychiatric help before she finds her career in the company more seriously jeopardized.

The therapy does not start easily. Wanda at first sees herself undergoing an unwelcome and unnecessary business assignment. Eventually, though, she becomes more aware of her painful lack of emotional intimacy and consequent need for compensatory accomplishment and adulation. She comes to understand, too, that each success has brought with it fears of envy and embarrassment, and thus greater loneliness. Two months into treatment, masked symptoms of social anxiety disorder become apparent and are treated with paroxetine. Instead of increasing her distress as in the past, Wanda's new accomplishments could now bring her greater feelings of security, respect, and well-being.

Causes. There is always a tension between the emotionally self-protective need to seek accomplishment and attention, and the interpersonal demands of the real world. In the process of growing up, two environmental factors can impede the ability to develop an adaptive balance. In some families, affection or material needs are withheld or withdrawn. As a result, it is harder to see other people as a source of joy and security, and there is an increasing need for self-reliance. Such early deprivation leads to insulation against the vulnerability of relationships. More important, it leads to a need for ultimate control and mastery of the universe in order to make the world right at last. Surprisingly similar are families where the child is given too much superficial affection and material things. The child becomes an adult with an inflated narcissism and a sense of entitlement, but still an underlying failure of interpersonal security. Anger and righteous indignation result when others fail to go along with their perceived entitlement.

Effects. These individuals, however likeable, effective, and bright they are, can have devastating effects on an organization. Their self-protective "master of the universe" position ultimately goes against reality and causes difficulty among the other members of the group. Dissension within the group results from the ability of these individuals to seduce some members into supporting them against the attacking forces of the others. Playing people off against each other might seem useful in business but usually leads to serious morale problems. And judgment can be an issue of real concern. When grandiose plans take precedence over realistic ambition, failure is a common result. Even when the grandiose plans unexpectedly succeed, they can result in seemingly paradoxical despair, a heightening of interpersonal conflict, and subsequent detrimental actions that negate the success. Importantly, their behavior can set a bad example for some, leave others feeling cheated, usurped, or ignored, and can generally lead morale downhill.

Intervention and Prevention. Ideally, it would be nice to harness the energy and creativity of narcissistic grandiosity while still protecting against its adverse effects. This is not easy to do. A generally supportive and secure work environment is less likely to provoke needs for grandiose efforts. Specifically, care must be taken to recognize individuals and their contributions, and maintain an atmosphere of honesty and common cause. Problems will always arise anyway, and it is then important to remember the underlying distress. That distress cannot be solved in the workplace, but it can be substantially helped in a sophisticated psychoanalytic psychotherapy.

Understanding and resolving the problem ultimately involves recognition of the deep-seated lack of emotional trust and the compensatory needs for self-protection and dramatic accomplishment. As with any other patient in therapy, careful attention should be given to the possible specific benefits of medication for identifiable mild anxiety or depressive disorders. Even the most effective treatment is gradual, and it does help a subordinate to feel the continued support of a supervisor and others, particularly in assessing positive assets.

Prevention is more difficult. Grandiose job applicants are often desirable candidates, with substantial accomplishments that speak well for their future efforts. However, it is always important to assess both productivity and people skills carefully, as well as watching helpfully for signs of emotional distress. Evident support, unambiguous rules, clear feedback, and opportunity for self-reflection all promote the idea of doing well by doing good.

Dishonesty: Perceived Infantilization, Hidden Rage, and Rationalized Entitlement

Every week seems to bring new revelations about scandal and unethical conduct in business and government. The more obviously sociopathic or criminal employees may be easier to spot in advance and are thus less likely to catch an organization by surprise. The stories that get the most media attention are those that involve seemingly happy and successful individuals, apparently involved in significant dishonesty for the first time. Less dramatic examples are commonplace and a continuing concern for organizations.

Case 2

Tom Hardy is in charge of government sales at the Chicago Motor Company. His salesmanship has been instrumental in expanding this market fivefold for the company in only five years. Senior management has shown its appreciation with friendly approval, public awards, and ever increasing financial compensation. Tom has unsuccessfully sought broader management responsibilities, but has been absorbed by his sales position, lives quite well, and has a stable family life.

As Tom approaches his fiftieth birthday, his eldest son is accepted at a prestigious college, and Tom begins to feel more stressed at work. Although he has never before been preoccupied with sales quotas (nor had he needed to be), he now becomes obsessed with finally selling fifty thousand cars in the sales year. He spends his weekends working ever harder on sales proposals. Family fishing trips become fewer and fewer, and an emotional distance grows in his family. As the end of the sales year draws near, Tom is in final negotiations for a sale of three thousand cars to a state government that will put him over the top.

To be certain that he will win the contract for Chicago Motors, Tom calls an old friend at the state purchasing office. Reminding his friend of past favors, Tom finds out his competitor's bid and sets his own prices just a fraction lower. He reasons that Chicago Motors is entitled to the contract, since it does good work and is an established state supplier. He also figures that ensuring the sale will help Chicago Motors by boosting yearly sales numbers and help stockholders by increasing the share price. He knows that management would be concerned mostly with whether he could get away with it, and he thinks that no one outside the company will notice. While all this is going on, he starts a pattern of slipping one morning paper (the one with the funnies) inside another, thus saving fifty cents a day.

He boasts to friends about how closely he has underpriced the competition, but then begins to worry that he will be found out and disgraced. Soon, Tom is unable to sleep, begins to have daily episodes of shortness of breath, and starts to dread going to work. One day, he goes to the Medical Department to ask for sleeping pills. The doctor sees how troubled he is and refers him to the consulting psychiatrist. Tom is secretly relieved at this opportunity to talk about his plight.

The psychiatrist recognizes Tom's shortness of breath as panic disorder and prescribes clonazepam. With relief of his panic attacks and insomnia, Tom can now start talking through his situation. Over the course of many psychotherapy sessions, he comes to recognize that he has long felt kept down by authority figures. As a child, he felt obliged to underachieve in school in order to seek his parents' affection. Since he did not see his childhood money-making schemes as mature behavior, he felt free to excel there. Similarly, he felt free to succeed at sales as an adult, and his success was also an expression of defiance to those who would keep him down.

Management's failure to give him broader management responsibilities was its unwitting recognition of his uneasiness at a more authoritative role, as well as reluctance to lose its best salesman. But Tom reexperienced the hurt he had felt since childhood at being denied grown-up authority. His anger and frustration intensified as he approached his fiftieth birthday milestone, and at the same time he felt an unwitting envy of his son's acceptance into a prestigious college. Tom's intensified sales efforts had been his characteristic method of covering unpleasant feelings while also seeking the company's approval. This time, though, he felt angrily entitled to succeed, and his anger had colored his actions. The result was that he had set up an illegal government contract, at some risk to himself and his company. While at first Tom rationalized his behavior on business grounds, discussion of his indefensible newspaper thefts helped him to see his angry entitlement more clearly.

Causes. It is not always easy to see the causes of dishonest behavior among successful, and often generally honest, individuals. From one perspective, dishonesty is a form of narcissistic entitlement. In other words, the individual has a hidden basic mistrust of others and does not expect them to be on his side. Under certain emotional stresses, the underlying mistrust is heightened, along with fear and anger. Consciously, the individual comes to believe defiantly that he is entitled to break the rules because he cannot count on the system to reward or remember him. Often, this will progress to the notion of a competition with the system and an interest in breaking the rules just to get away with it.

These kinds of behaviors are encouraged by organizations that foster a culture of maximum income or power without a corresponding focus on principles, rules, and the inherent value of the work at hand. An employee who sees no real value in his company, colleagues, products, family, or self may look to income or power alone for gratification. Further encouragement is provided by organizational cultures that tolerate or lionize dishonesty of any kind. The well-publicized Wall Street, savings and loan, and Enron and WorldCom scandals were not a complete surprise to everyone at the companies involved. In many cases, knowing management gave implicit or active support to the dishonest conduct. In other cases, dishonest employees felt that dishonest behavior had been accepted in the past and would be in the future. Moreover, individuals who see others getting away with something may feel angry and be afraid of being left out of the benefits. They do not want to be chumps.

Effects. Dishonest behavior has some obvious ill effects, even when it is supposedly in the organization's interest. It can lead to criminal and civil legal actions, alienate customers and employees, and encourage other dishonesty within the organization. By its demoralizing effects, it can detract from accomplishment and productivity.

Intervention and Prevention. The most important preventative action is to establish an environment of respect for rules, principles, and the value of a company's employees and products. Employees must feel rewarded for their work and treated fairly within the organization. Without jeopardizing the organization, there should be a way that they can let their needs (financial and emotional) be known and seek to effect remedies for others' dishonesty. Rigid or unprincipled systems do not lend themselves to these purposes. Rule breaking and dishonesty must be dealt with fairly, clearly, and firmly when it does occur. In the extreme, remorseless sociopaths have no place in a healthy organization (see Chapters Twenty and Twenty-Three). Consultants on ethical conduct can offer helpful courses and advice, but by themselves are no cure for either a disaffected organizational culture or a dishonest employee. More definitive solutions lie in thoughtful and deliberate attention to organizational culture and the emotional outlook of employees involved.

COMPETITION GONE AWRY: INTERGENERATIONAL OEDIPAL CONFLICT

Organizations thrive on competition. Corporations compete with each other for customers, skilled employees, technological advances, and investment capital. Individuals within the organization compete for accomplishment, advancement, income, and status. By and large, healthy competition has healthy results. But problems arise when competition is tainted by hidden agendas or unrecognized fears and when competitive strivings are muffled instead of encouraged. Organizations are always concerned with the development of new leaders and ideas and with succession planning.

Promotion and Suppression of Creativity: Oedipus and Laius Go at It Again

Every organization looks to the development of new ideas and leaders for improving and maintaining its activities. The need for new ideas is particularly strong among companies where products, processes, or marketing change rapidly.

Inevitably, though, any new idea comes into conflict with established ideas, and interpersonal conflict can result. These conflicts are heightened when competitive individuals are involved, and they escalate even more when existing power structures let emotionally threatened managers maintain a rigid or unprincipled organization. The organization's purposes can suffer most of all. This age-old conflict is represented in Greek literature and psychoanalytic thought through the story of young Oedipus and his father, Laius.

Case 3

Ed Hararkis was fresh out of business school when he started to work at Oceanblue Entertainment. He had been very successful in graduate school and had impressed those who knew him with his hard work, intelligence, and creativity. Many companies had heavily recruited him. He chose to work for Oceanblue because he saw an opportunity to help renew an inactive section of a company that promoted creative accomplishment. With the encouragement of management, the section leader had specifically sought new creative input, and there seemed to be a creative vacuum for Ed to fill. It looked like a perfect fit.

Lee Kellogg was his section leader at Oceanblue. Lee had been with Oceanblue for some thirty years. Early in his career, he had risen rapidly in the company. He had made few innovative contributions but had run his small section effectively, had not sought strong subordinates, and had maintained his position through company politics. For many years, though, he had felt stuck in that position and had remained preoccupied with protecting his organizational turf. He would often sacrifice apparent business advantages (such as obtaining new computers with discretionary section funds) if they had a perceived political disadvantage (appearing weak in Oceanblue if his computers were not specifically funded by the company).

Ed started the new job full of plans and ideas. At first, he seemed to have Lee's support and encouragement. Soon, however, Ed realized that Lee's verbal support was not matched by actions. In fact, Lee was withholding managerial, secretarial, and material support, thus passively weakening Ed's efforts. Ed tried to talk with Lee, but their conversations went nowhere. Lee responded to these attempts at dialogue with avoidance and poorly hidden rage. He made it implicitly clear that Ed was not to succeed in his projects and explicitly clear that neither was he to seek employment elsewhere. Ed was confused. He did not realize how desperately Lee wanted to demonstrate his section's achievements to the company, all the while feeling hopelessly threatened by Ed's plans and accomplishments. Ed also did not know that Lee was yet again seeking a promotion after many years of frustrated efforts.

After many months, Ed was finally given approval for some projects. But to Ed's dismay, each time a project was started, Lee removed it from Ed's purview, and the project soon faded. One of Ed's projects was a collaborative effort with the Oceanblue film restoration section. When Lee tried to intervene there, the other section would not let the project be dropped. As Lee felt more endangered and enraged, he threatened the other section leader, and he accused Ed of trying to undermine him.

Ed felt increasingly frustrated, trapped, and demoralized. Although management seemed sympathetic to Ed, they also wanted to preserve the organizational status quo, especially since Lee might finally achieve his long-sought promotion. Lee did win his promotion, but his section continued as a small and low-performing unit of Oceanblue. Ed was unable to find a suitable job elsewhere but ultimately found a similar position, with diminished career potential, in another Oceanblue section. Much later, he found a position at a competing firm.

Causes. Almost by definition, creativity and leadership involve the development and advancement of novel ideas. These ideas will necessarily be at odds with established wisdom. As if this were not enough potential for discord within an organization, there is commonly a rather pronounced conflict of personalities as well. Established and senior members of the organization will feel an emotional and also practical investment in the status quo. They may feel that their positions are dependent on current methods and their past development of those methods and ideas. This applies to issues as diverse as organizational structure, technological and scientific knowledge, and marketing strategies. Although an organization will look to members for novel approaches, often newer members, it will always have mixed feelings about accepting and incorporating those ideas. Aggressively creative members may have more novel ideas and greater success at developing and implementing those ideas, but they will also find that they meet greater resistance. Their approach will be seen in a more threatening way from above. This sort of problem has many causes, which can be attributed to the individuals involved, as well as to the organizational structure.

Effects. Many of the effects of these problems are obvious: retarded creative development, weak leadership, discord and strife, loss of good workers, failure to adapt to changing markets, failure to rectify rigid and corrupt organizations, and substantial effort wasted on emotional interpersonal conflicts instead of smoother cooperative ventures.

Intervention and Prevention. Although there will always be tensions surrounding the promotion and acceptance of new ideas and leaders, efforts can be made to keep the process from self-destruction. Promotion of a work environment that allows and encourages creativity and accomplishment and rewards managers for the success of their subordinates and colleagues is essential, but often difficult to accomplish. When a system is awry, a consultant can play an essential role. As in this intensified case, effective interventions may require group seminars and brief psychotherapeutic interventions for the key individuals. Adapting management styles to prevent such problems requires the active attention of senior management and of human resources. Creativity must be both sponsored and protected from above, with considerable attention to the concerns and fears of employees and managers at all levels.

Problematic Succession Planning: Fear of Subordinates

Organizational success and growth depend on leadership strength, depth, and continuity. This is not always easy to accomplish. For example, leaders at the top may have risen there because of inner needs to control their circumstances and minimize their competition. As a result, they may feel threatened by subordinates with real leadership potential and prefer weak or deferential subordinates. Such self-protective behavior can weaken leadership strength, and it can be a particular impediment when leaders find themselves in the awkward position of developing or selecting their own successor.

Case 4

Jack Wisnewski has worked long and hard to become president of Alderwood Air Charter. The company is his life, and he thinks of himself as the very soul of Alderwood. That has not made it easy to develop the executive ranks. Talented junior executives would arrive at Alderwood with freshly minted credentials and eager career plans. Sometimes Jack thought they were not really so good and would push them toward the door. Other times, they just seemed to stay in the background until one day they were gone. Jack figured that they did not have what it takes for the rough and tumble of the air charter business. Every once in a while, though, he would be surprised when one of them made vice president at some competitor.

Then there were the ones Jack called troublemakers. They would arrive on the scene, and after only a few months or a few years, they would be coming up with all sorts of ideas for how things should be different. Jack always liked things his way, and the troublemakers did not last too long. As a consequence, the Alderwood executive ranks are filled mostly with loyal and steadfast plodders. They admire Jack's vision and approach, gladly follow his unchallenged leadership, and never take much initiative themselves. Alderwood is a stable company with a protected market niche, few big mistakes, and little significant growth.

Now that Jack is four years from mandatory retirement, he recognizes that he should plan for his succession. He understands too that the future will bring increasing competition to Alderwood's market niche. He knows that Tom Nabish, his right-hand man, expects to succeed him and that others would not mind his job either. But when Jack looks around the company, he does not see anyone he respects enough for the top job. Instead, he decides to mentor two talented new executives. One was president of a newly acquired fuel supplier, and the other was hired away from a major airline. Despite Jack's conscious intentions, they fare no better than the junior executives of years past. As Jack takes control, confrontations over strategy escalate with the fuel executive, and the fuel business starts to lose money. Finally, Jack asks him to move on. For the airline veteran, the lack of increasing recognition leads to demoralization and declining ambition. Jack seems to oppose every attempt at increasing market share or even improving efficiency. He feels grateful when the airline veteran leaves without confrontation, and reassures himself that neither of the two was really any good after all. Then Jack again realizes that he cannot stay on forever.

This conflict also shows itself at home, where Jack's need to be number one has always interfered in his relationship with his wife and children. There are particular strains between him and a son who has recently become the college football star that Jack never was. When the son refused to stop playing football to concentrate on his studies, Jack wouldn't talk to him for seven months.

When retirement finally arrives, Jack reluctantly turns over the president's title to Tom Nabish, who finds the company in surprising disarray. Productivity has fallen in the past three years, fledgling competition has eaten into Alderwood's traditional niche, and the fuel supply losses are mounting rapidly. He does not understand how Jack has let the company go to seed in his final years. But with Jack still watching over him, Tom is afraid to make strategic plans, and as a result the company employees view him as passive and ineffective. He does not know what to do. Jack, on the other hand, sees Alderwood's regrettable decline as the natural consequence of his own retirement. On a deeper level, he also feels reassured that he is indeed irreplaceable and that no one will ever overshadow his accomplishments.

Eventually, Jack's wife becomes quite concerned about the standoff between Jack and their son. She also sees the parallel to Jack's standoff with Tom at Alderwood. Despite Jack's anger and denial, she convinces him to see a psychiatrist for help. In therapy, Jack realizes that he has been keeping things paralyzed at home and at the company. And he fondly remembers that he had once been considered a bit of a troublemaker himself. With that recognition, he spends more time at his Palm Springs retirement home and gives more freedom to both Tom and his son. Tom hires an outside consultant, who helps formulate a new plan for Alderwood's future. Jack feels less threatened by the outsider's plans. That way, the succession process does not make him feel as if he has been defeated by his organizational son. Jack is ultimately pleased that Alderwood does well, but did not stay long enough in therapy to understand why the succession was so turbulent.

Causes. Competitive individuals often arrive at adulthood not only with drive and skill, but also with an acute awareness of the opposition. This obviously has some competitive advantages, but it can cause problems when it spills over into more cooperative relationships. Leaders who are unable to recognize or appreciate collaborative relationships may view them instead through a largely competitive focus. They are still fighting their incessant childhood battle for affection, respect, and recognition. Growing up in a family environment of emotional deprivation will increase the intensity of competition for what little affection or respect is available. And the competitive drive will be tinged with fears of competitive loss, emotional abandonment, and retributive opponents. At the organizational level, these problems are encouraged by an exaggerated focus on independent accomplishment, combined with inadequate attention to constraints on power and the responsibilities of leadership.

Effects. When leadership talent is squelched by the fears of those in power, the effects are not always immediate. There may be a period of increased stability, but with a growing stagnation of ideas and growth. Ultimately, the absence of sufficient leadership strength, depth, and consistency will result in impaired competitiveness for the organization as a whole. Belated attempts at compensation might then include reliance on new leaders from outside, but with risks of unnecessary turmoil and demoralization. In extreme cases, there can be catastrophic effects on performance, especially when a succession is finally necessary.

Intervention and Prevention. The individual who has difficulty with unresolved issues of rivalry may be difficult to help, as his rationalizations effectively counter the criticism directed at him. A deeper understanding of maladaptive competitive behavior is needed and can be addressed in psychoanalytic psychotherapy by understanding connections between present and past competitive circumstances. Ongoing treatment will bring increasing change as the patient gradually gains greater understanding of personality traits that had seemed self-protective. Clear organizational policies about the use and abuse of authority should be disseminated and enforced. Those few individuals who regularly impede the success of others need careful attention and might ultimately risk dismissal. Outside consultants, not entangled in organizational rivalries, can be valuable agents of change. Proper intervention can help bring about smooth and effective succession and can counsel both overly threatened leaders and younger talent in difficult competitive environments.

WHEN IT LOOKS LIKE CHARACTER IS DESTINY: RIGID PERSONALITIES UNDER STRESS

Everyone has a personality style and uses that style in adapting to stressful and changing circumstances. Rigid personalities, though, can have a tough time of it. Unable to recognize the hidden emotions that guide their behavior, they have little room for flexible adaptation to new demands. Old habits become burdened with mounting distress, and problematic consequences can keep growing until something gives way (see Chapters Six and Twenty-Three). Suspiciousness and compulsiveness can have some advantages, but can cause serious problems when exacerbated under stress.

Oversuspicion as Avoidance of Emotional Distress: Self-Reference and Paranoia

It is not uncommon to imagine what is going on in another person's mind. When a person's future depends on the undisclosed decisions or opinions of others, anxiety and speculation can run rampant. By projecting feelings, fears, and imagination onto another person, anxious uncertainty is replaced with seeming predictability. In effect, individuals will sometimes confidently believe that their own thoughts are what others have secretly in mind, all the while blissfully unaware of their projection. But there are problems for all involved when imagination merges with reality and unconfirmed fantasy is seen as fact. An especially confusing picture can emerge when good fortune develops for someone who has long avoided too much success.

Case 5

Maria Toth is a forty-five-year-old vice president for Yoshida Design Associates. Over twenty years, her cautious approach has earned her a respected but low-key role in the firm. She always plays her cards close to the vest, and she never seems comfortable with high-profile successes. Last year, though, the president asked Maria to assemble and manage a new team for computer equipment design. Apprehensively, Maria accepted. The president was pleased and surprised by the high quality of the resulting work, and rewarded Maria with a raise, a promotion, and invitations to his private club.

Maria was pleased, too, but she has begun to feel increasingly uneasy about work. She thinks that her current work is poorly received by her superiors and begins to talk about possible early retirement. She sees their reassurances as meaningless praise or even as an attempt to keep her off-track. More significant, she begins interpreting conversations, memos, and other communications within the firm in a negative and peculiar manner. Eventually, Maria becomes convinced that she will be let go through the efforts of certain top-level people whom she believes are "out to get her." At meetings, she becomes more aware of who speaks to whom and how things are phrased, and she becomes increasingly angry at what she perceives as subtle but consistent rejection.

Maria is angry, bitter, confused, and increasingly concerned about her professional and personal life. She is spending more time talking to other employees about senior people than doing her work. She frequently lashes out at others, and her comments about colleagues are a cause of concern within Yoshida Design. They seem off the mark in regard to others' perceptions of the senior people. Maria's personal life is in turmoil too. Five years divorced from a distant alcoholic husband, Maria has been dating a handsome, successful, and engaging sixty-year-old man for a year now. Although he has been pressing for marriage, Maria lately suspects him of secret sexual affairs. She sees his reassurances as an attempt to keep her in the dark until he is ready to leave.

One day, Maria becomes enraged over a miscalculated medical bill. She storms into her family doctor's office to complain. The doctor explains the bill to Maria, and convinces her that there was no error. Maria apologizes and sheepishly acknowledges her passing conviction that someone from Yoshida Design had manipulated the bill. The doctor does not challenge Maria's fears, but does get her to accept a discreet psychiatric referral.

In treatment, Maria does not need any medication and soon recognizes that her fearfulness seems to follow her successes at work and home. She has had milder such reactions to college graduation and to her marriage. Much later, continued psychotherapy uncovers the internal criticisms that Maria had developed in childhood and that she is now projecting onto others. At Yoshida Design, the president gradually senses the return of Maria's old style. Uncertain and a bit mystified, the president has hesitated before giving Maria another challenging new assignment, but decides to ask her over to the club again.

Causes. Paranoid personality traits have been a topic of much debate, particularly with regard to etiology. They are quite different from true psychotic illness. Some see them as exaggerated sensitivity to the emotions of others and a particular concern for their hostility. At the same time, paranoia may well represent unacceptable aggressive feelings that are placed outside the self and into another person. The other person thus becomes the perceived source of feelings that an individual does not want to recognize in himself or herself. This dilemma reflects a childhood inability to express natural aggressive thoughts and feelings and, instead, a felt need to keep those thoughts secret to prevent some frightening consequence. Other possible contributors to self-referential and paranoid personality traits can include anxiety and depressive disorders and insufficient social supports. Notably, paranoid traits can be substantially heightened by both emotional loss and emotional or material accomplishment. While severe paranoid behavior may reflect a real or incipient psychotic process (see Chapter Twenty-Six), it is also important not to mislabel more flexible personality traits. Organizational factors that can aggravate tendencies toward self-reference and projected aggressive feelings might include limited communication, limited availability of information essential for self-assessment, an unpredictable or changing work environment, and unethical or capricious management.

Effects. Sensitivity to the feelings and hostile intentions of others may offer some advantages, but oversensitivity helps no one. It is clearly detrimental to any organization when employees or managers are paranoid about coworkers, supervisors, or organizational intent. Left unaddressed, such situations often lead to emotional crisis or acrimonious departure. At the very least, it is less than productive for the organization to have employees who spend their energies pursuing figments of their imagination. At the level of the individual, there is also increased risk for serious depression, substance abuse, disruption of family relationships, performance impairment, and disgruntled employees. At the organizational level, there are substantial risks when management impairment has compounded effects on morale, ethics, communication, and leadership.

Intervention and Prevention. Since personality style colors the way people see the world and themselves, no one can fully understand how other people see them. And since paranoia lends itself to suspicion, such people can be uncomfortable to approach. Nonetheless, intervention is quite important. Documentation of unusual behavior is often a prerequisite for successful evaluation and diagnosis and should be obtained before recommending referral for professional consultation. Initial treatment emphasizes the need to distinguish between thoughts from the imagination and objective reality. This task can be especially difficult when the organizational climate is one of bona-fide hostility, intrigue, or uncertainty. Treatment works best in the company of a supportive organization and family.

Missing the Forest for the Trees: Counterproductive Compulsiveness

Compulsive personality style is nearly always a career advantage. It allows individuals to focus much of their attention on work and thus leads to career accomplishments. But compulsive traits may also diminish interpersonal skills at home and on the job, and even the advantages of the compulsive work orientation can become impediments at times of emotional stress. Top heavy with successful compulsive individuals, the organizational consequences can be serious.

Case 6

Frank Candelli is a very hard worker, and his job as director of marketing for Arden/Oak Data Services has always been more important to him than anything else. He is known around marketing for his marathon project efforts, his attention to organization and detail, his ability to clearly define business problems and solutions, and his dedication to Arden/Oak. Even so, many of his colleagues see him as perfectionistic, controlling, and emotionally distant. In particular, Frank is known for his procrastination.

Arden/Oak has been a successful regional company for many years, growing steadily during a period of economic expansion. Frank's contributions to company growth are legendary. Now, however, with a recession underway, the Arden/Oak CEO has decided to market company services in four new midwestern states, with marketing handled through a newly acquired midwestern competitor. Frank has been given a raise and a promotion and asked to focus on the essential task of retaining existing business.

Frank understands the business considerations, readily consents to the division of marketing into two sections, and outwardly is grateful for the recognition of his past contributions. Inside, though, Frank is enraged by what feels like a personal rejection, a loss of respect, and an insufficient reward. He has not been able to discuss these feelings with management, colleagues, family, or even himself. Instead, he feels more driven than ever before toward his work. Rather than just his assigned task, he also starts trying to expand existing accounts to new products. He is going to prove himself to management. He writes and rewrites a far-fetched business plan to sell high-priced on-line financial data services for high school economics classes. But no matter how much he reworks the details, he is not satisfied.

With all this effort, Frank is sleeping and eating less and with less inclination than usual to enjoy his family. Although he thinks of himself as determined to succeed in this project, others find themselves feeling vaguely irritated by his plans. And he keeps advancing the projected start date for the effort, making excuses, and saying that he is making the plan better still. With all this exertion, his departmental subordinates feel ignored, and his inattention to existing customers begins to take a toll. A new enhancement of existing data services was inadequately marketed, and some customers fall away.

Finally, management realizes that something is wrong and asks a psychiatric consultant for help. The consultant interviews Frank, his marketing colleagues, loyal customers, and the CEO. The consultant discovers the history above, and notes that Frank is also upset that his only daughter has just left for college. He suggests a psychiatric referral for the major depression that has recently aggravated Frank's compulsive personality traits. He also suggests a brief series of group seminars to refocus marketing on the task at hand. In therapy, and with the help of buproprion (an antidepressant medication), Frank begins to understand his reaction to the new assignment. Later, he also understands his pattern of working hard to seek emotional acceptance (originally from his distant and hard-working father, now also from management) but also as reflecting his defiant and angry perception that relationships can only disappoint him (the more he sought father's or management's acceptance, the more disappointed he felt, yet the harder still he worked). He is soon able to improve the morale and new function of his department, despite his working fewer hours. Similarly, he begins to forge a closer relationship with his wife.

Causes. Compulsive personality traits are presumably developed in childhood, but can be made worse under stressful circumstances. Faced with any change, but especially the loss of work roles important for self-esteem, a compulsive employee may feel rejected, angry, and unimportant. Consequently, he may attempt to repair his lot by even harder work, but with less benefit to himself or the organization. As in this case, the situation is compounded when a major depression develops. Although compulsive people are quite sensitive to rejection, they are less likely to realize that they are depressed and less likely to evidence it directly to others. They find it quite difficult, even in psychotherapy, to think or talk about feelings. This tendency is encouraged by social pressures to keep all feelings inside. Organizational cultures that are perceived as unsupportive will increase the risk of problematic functioning.

Effects. Compulsive personality traits can be a decided advantage, but they can cause problems as well. Successful organizations tend to attract and retain compulsive individuals. They are often very dedicated workers and able to focus on detailed analyses of organizational and business problems. These same employees, though, may have a detached emotional style, which can make them appear distant, unconcerned, angry, or controlling. In addition, their attention to detail is counterproductive when they put too much effort into minor concerns and essential matters are squeezed out as a result. Resulting inefficiencies and emotional stresses cause further problems at the workplace and also at home.

Intervention and Prevention. In general, organizations can try to head off this common problem by encouraging employees to maintain a balance between work and personal life. Specific attention should be given to employees who are known to work especially hard, display rigid managerial styles, or show signs of stress, depression, or excessive preoccupation with work. A careful and empathic psychiatric evaluation can then prevent the problems from worsening. Often, though, ambitious organizations and individuals will see such an approach as an impediment rather than a competitive advantage. Hours worked and reports completed are like trees in the forest. They can be easily mistaken for long-term accomplishment. The organizational culture should not mistake work hours or report pages for true effectiveness.

HIDING AWAY THOSE PESKY EMOTIONS: REPRESSION OF EMOTIONAL DISTRESS

Anxiety, fear, anger, and sadness are regrettably common emotions. They are not usually too severe and eventually diminish in intensity. Sometimes, though, there are such threatening hidden fears that even the feelings cannot be thought about. Instead, they are repressed from conscious awareness, yet remain potent covert determinants of mood and behavior. In that covert role, they can be handled through such mechanisms as displacement onto a less threatening perceived source. Or attempts at mere suppression of distress may cause a further intensification.

Emotions from Home Get Carried to Work: Displacement

When it comes right down to it, people are more concerned about other people than anything else, and they are concerned most of all about their families. For that reason, family worries are often the most troubling and thus the hardest to think openly about. Any real or potential change in the family environment will have emotional effects. If the thoughts are troubling enough, they may be attributed to some convenient focus other than their true source.

Case 7

Hank Smith has been with Pawlet Advertising for ten years, and his business achievements have helped him on a steady career track over that time. Although he works very hard, he does not usually feel stressed by the job. Hank is known for his dedication and independent mind, and also for his finesse at handling potential interpersonal conflict, thus avoiding consequent embarrassments for all concerned. From time to time, he has had found himself in difficult political situations, but he is always able to recognize the problems, think them through, and find diplomatic solutions for himself, his colleagues, and the company. Once, for example, he found himself reporting to a new boss with a very authoritarian management style. After a few difficult months, Hank was able to show his boss that he was a talented subordinate with a different approach. They recognized their differences, and Hank's boss was helpful in arranging a promotion to another department.

Some time later, Hank found himself working under Louise Riley. Louise could be abrasive, dictatorial, and unsympathetic, but not necessarily more than Hank's prior authoritarian boss. None of her employees was happy, but after many months, Hank was notably miserable. He began to feel trapped in a hopeless situation and was surprised to note that a particular animosity had developed between Louise and himself. He remained a first-rate team player, but unsettled Louise with a newly defiant aspect of his demeanor, and the office politics kept getting worse. He kept thinking about his situation and wondered whether he might have to leave Pawlet Advertising, but also whether he might be missing something.

In psychotherapy, Hank initially wanted to talk only about Louise but was intrigued to realize that his problems with Louise intensified at the same time that he had become engaged for marriage. Hank had always kept an emotional distance from women, but he thought it was time to settle down. As his thoughts evolved, he realized that he saw Louise, his mother, and his male psychiatrist as stern, controlling, and cold and that he particularly feared that his affectionate fiancé would ultimately leave him trapped in a cold and controlling marriage. This had been too frightening a thought for him to contemplate, so he had instead focused his fears and anger on Louise.

Once Hank understood that these new emotions had colored his usual style, he could more clearly assess his problems with Louise. He worked at defusing the situation with his usual diplomatic finesse. Although the office tensions were established by now, Louise eventually turned her attentions away from Hank, and she later left the company. Hank continued his steady career path at Pawlet, and his new marriage was a joy to him.

Causes. Hank's usual interpersonal office style was changed by his feelings about his upcoming marriage. With the onset of intense and hidden fear about being trapped in an intimate relationship, he was not able to realize where those intensified feelings had come from. Louise became an obvious substitute target. Because of her own personality and management style, the result was an escalating feud.

Effects. This common kind of underlying cause is rarely obvious, since the protagonists are themselves unaware of the external emotional fuel for their workplace distress. The potential organizational consequences are many and varied.

Since reactions to the work environment can become exaggerated or unrealistic, coping strategies become ineffective or counterproductive. Morale and productivity can be further impaired by the resulting emotional tension, conflict, and discord. Good workers may leave as they feel the emotional toll and see the indirect effects on their own families.

Intervention and Prevention. In the long run, management and human resource attention dedicated to observation of interpersonal dynamics can increase the likelihood of early detection, before problems get out of hand. This can be accomplished with ongoing group meetings, as well as with contact and assessment by unentangled human resource officers or outside consultants. Whenever workplace emotions intensify beyond a usual or reasonable level, care should be given to understanding all of the contributing factors, even when an obvious factor is present. Recognition of personality conflicts can lead to improvement through workplace interventions, as well as referrals for more sophisticated psychotherapy.

Problem and Solution Avoidance: Psychological Resistance to Change

All human beings have an inherent resistance to change. This is because change evokes two fears that most human beings attempt to avoid. The first is that change always requires loss. Dislike and fear are a natural response, particularly if the loss involves something familiar or comfortable. A second major resistance to change is the fear of the unknown. It is easier to stay with the familiar than it is to abandon it for something new and unmastered. As a result, many people actively avoid dealing with problems that may require them to change. They are left in a frustrating dilemma and are quick to decrease the frustration and conflict that they feel. Drugs, alcohol, and self-destructive behaviors often become means to that end. They become harmful self-treatment to decrease the pain of threatened change and unresolved problems.

Case 8

Susan Gold is a lawyer at the firm of Parette, McGuffey and Weldon. Three weeks after promotion to partnership, she marries her long-time boyfriend. She returns from her honeymoon refreshed, relaxed, and sporting a tan, convinced she can handle both marriage and partnership with ease. Despite her somewhat limited people skills, senior partners have long appreciated Susan's intelligence, dedication, and long hours and encourage her to think in terms of even senior or managing partner or group head, unusual for a woman at her firm. She understands that she is expected to start developing new clients for the firm. However, it soon becomes clear that her tremendous efforts are not producing new business. A short course on client development skills made intellectual sense to her, but has little real effect on her approach. Her husband is a consulting mechanical engineer, whose work hours are shorter and more flexible than hers. He had hoped marriage would lead to more time together, and he is more than eager to start having children. Their relationship starts to fray at the edges.

Susan becomes jealous of others who balance their work and personal lives with apparent ease. She sees her own problem as merely one of "stress," which needs to be suppressed. When her friends suggest practical changes or she reads about ideas in her many self-help books, she dismisses them quickly. She finds more than enough reasons to keep her patterns unchanged. Susan becomes increasingly short-tempered and loses her happy, enthusiastic disposition. An exercise program offers temporary relaxation, but she soon gives it up. While away on business, she flings herself into a brief sexual affair to renew her spirit, but ends up feeling mostly guilty. Susan starts to drink more at professional functions, and colleagues often notice alcohol on her breath at the office.

Finally, after weeks of working around the clock on a new project, Susan calls in sick. Her speech is slurred, and she says that she might need a leave of absence to take care of personal matters. At this point, the firm's psychiatrist is notified, and Susan is asked to attend a nonconfidential consultation to help determine whether she should seek treatment or leave employment. She points out that she has no problems worth mentioning, but reluctantly agrees to the evaluation and to subsequent referral. In treatment, Susan is able to stop drinking, and slowly starts to unravel the tightly hidden fears that lead her to her recent travail. She soon repairs some of the damage to her career and marriage. Changes in people skills on the job and at home come more gradually.

Causes. Innate fears of change become excessive when childhood experience does not leave expectations of ready parental approval and instead leaves fears of retribution for positive change. Safe and predictable environments at least allow familiar ground, and accustomed techniques for repressing and hiding emotional distress. Fears that change for the better will cause retribution or other problems are similarly kept under tight wraps.

Effects. The individual who struggles to ignore change will not have an easy time. Heightened and suppressed distress will manifest itself in problems at work or at home and can easily lead to more serious depression. There can also be ineffective and self-destructive attempts at anxiety reduction, including substance abuse, unethical behavior, and extramarital affairs. Lower-echelon employees struggling with significant resistance to change can significantly affect productivity and morale. Corporations are even more keenly aware of the effects of such resistance among those in positions of leadership. Many corporations have failed to succeed when key people had unwittingly maladaptive reactions to changes in organizational mission, circumstance, or structure.

Intervention and Prevention. For individual employees, it is essential to maintain awareness of the concomitants of both personal and professional changes. Any employee would be stressed by simultaneous marriage and promotion. Prompt professional discussion of changing roles, and recognition of the difficulties involved will improve the odds of successful adjustment. In psychotherapy, getting past emotional resistances to change is a gradual and continuing process.

Many individuals are affected when major organizational change occurs, and it is important to ease their concerns. A real crisis can develop if appropriate interventions are not instituted promptly (see Chapter Twelve). It is important not to confuse the temporary and limited benefits of stress management programs with improvements in individual or organizational adaptability. Stress management programs are a cost-effective approach to large-scale reactions to change, but are more useful for short-term crises than they are for lasting or substantial benefits.

The cases in this chapter reflect the complexity of motivational forces among leaders in distress. Executive and organizational problems are often the consequence of hidden work, family, or intrapsychic concerns. Problems arise for specific reasons, have specific solutions, and are always more complicated than they first appear. Awareness of such constructs as narcissistic-level personality problems, recreated family dynamics, personality styles under stress, and psychological defenses are essential for recognizing, addressing, and avoiding problems. Effective treatment considers not only job issues themselves, but also family concerns, specific psychodynamic, and psychiatric diagnoses, and the possibility of medical illness.

References and Additional Sources

Kets de Vries, M.F.R., and Associates. (1991). *Organizations on the couch: Clinical perspectives on organizational behavior and change.* San Francisco: Jossey-Bass.

MacKinnon, R. A., & Michels, R. (1971). *The psychiatric interview in clinical practice.* Philadelphia: Saunders.

Rohrlich, J. (1980). *Work and love: The crucial balance.* New York: Harmony Books.

Schwartz, H. S. (1990). *Narcissistic process and organizational decay: The theory of the organizational ideal.* New York: New York University Press.

Speller, J. L. (1989). *Executives in crisis: Recognizing and managing the alcoholic, drug-addicted, or mentally ill executive.* San Francisco: Jossey-Bass.

CHAPTER EIGHT

Job Loss and Employment Uncertainty

Nick Kates
Barrie Sanford Greiff
Duane Q. Hagen

*The downturn in the economy since early 2000, exacerbated by the consequences
of the terrorist attacks of September 11, 2001, has ushered in another era of
layoffs and job uncertainty as increasing numbers of workers from all walks
of life face the possibility of losing their jobs. Job loss has many consequences
for workers and their families. A number of interventions can take place
with individuals who are in danger of losing their jobs, and preventive programs
can be used in workplaces where layoffs or closures are pending.*

Layoffs, plant closures, business failures, and company mergers will continue
to be a fact of economic life. At least two out of three Americans will lose
their job at some time during their working life. For some, the effects will
be minimal, particularly if they possess marketable skills or live in areas where
there are plentiful work opportunities. For others, such as those with a strong
emotional investment in their work or limited financial resources, unemployment may have a major impact on activities, relationships, and physical and
emotional well-being.

To lose a job or to be excluded from the workforce can erode self-confidence
and create practical difficulties that can be overwhelming. Some people who
lose their job find alternate work quickly with little disruption of their daily routine. For others, continuing joblessness can lead to a sense of isolation and alienation, and eventually to helplessness and despair. Whatever the duration of the
period of unemployment, individuals who lose their job may develop physical
and psychological symptoms of varying degrees of severity.

The effects of losing a job are complex and can affect every aspect of a person's life. Although there is strong evidence of an association between job loss
and emotional problems, the nature of this link is complicated. Losing a job is
stressful in itself and can also set in motion a train of biological, psychosocial,
and family changes that can lead to further difficulties. It can also expose or

135

accentuate emotional, psychiatric, or family problems that predated the loss of the job.

Helping individuals who are about to lose their job presents many challenges for employers and clinicians. Clinicians need to appreciate the meaning a job can have, the changing effects of unemployment over time, and the relationship of work, family, and social activities. They must be able to take a systemic or ecological view of the impact of losing a job, respecting the uniqueness of each individual's problem, while being aware of common issues that may affect all jobless people. They must be familiar with appropriate community resources and possess additional skills in history taking and working collaboratively with social agencies. They must also recognize local, social, and political realities that can hinder the development of needed programs and social reintegration for the more chronically unemployed individuals.

When considering the impact of job loss, the clinician needs to bear in mind four recurring themes: what a job can mean to an individual; the interdependence of an individual's work, family, and social life; multiple, interconnected, and often preexisting factors that can affect the outcome of a period of unemployment; and the uniqueness of the experience for each individual who loses a job.

Case 1

Thomas O'Leary, a forty-nine-year-old steel worker, was referred to a psychiatric service for assessment of anxiety and depression. For as long as he could remember, he had always thrown himself into his work, and the activity had kept his chronic unhappiness under control. This time, though, he described a four-month history of anxiety, depression, insomnia, and anorexia. At first, he could not identify any cause for his distress, but questioning revealed that his plant was threatened with large layoffs.

He was sure he would not lose his job, but his work behavior had changed since news of the impending layoff leaked out. Trying to show that he was indispensable to the company, he had started to work overtime. But unlike his colleagues, he had made no attempt to find alternate work or to prepare for possible unemployment. He had not discussed these issues with his wife or children, not wanting to bother them over what he viewed as a minor concern. But he had noticed his work performance starting to deteriorate. His concentration had worsened, it took him longer to complete routine tasks, he was irritable with coworkers, and they were starting to ignore him.

Tom's rigid interpersonal style, his intense job commitment, and his difficulty in coping with emotions had led him into a depression. He had denied the reality of his situation, avoided planning for unpleasant contingencies, and alienated himself from potential sources of support. An interview with Tom's wife pointed out their increasing marital stress, as well as his wife's unawareness of the threat to his job.

In treatment, Tom's depression responded promptly to psychotherapy and an antidepressant. In therapy, Tom came to terms with the threat to his job and started to make appropriate preparations. He became more aware of the emotional and occupational support that was available from family and coworkers. He also talked about his fear of what might happen to his job, family, and himself and his anger about potentially losing a job in which he had invested so much of himself. When he eventually did lose his job, he adjusted quickly and found new employment within eight weeks. The feared financial impoverishment did not occur. But to fend off his long-term fears of rejection and emotional impoverishment again, Tom quickly became intensely dedicated to his new job.

THE IMPACT OF IMPENDING JOB LOSS

Most unemployed individuals eventually adjust to job loss, make necessary changes, and find new work. For some, however, despair and feelings of helplessness continue for months or years, with little optimism for the future. Emotional responses of the long-term unemployed change over time, as do the issues and problems that they confront (Harrison, 1976; Borgen & Amundsen, 1984; Kirsh, 1983). Of greatest concern to employers is the anticipatory stage of employment uncertainty before a job is lost.

This stage is important because it is when emotional changes begin, and especially because it is when appropriate preparation and intervention can effectively change job loss outcomes. In some situations, employees might receive a few months' warning about an impending layoff or plant closure. This allows them to make preparations for what may follow and to start a job search. In most instances, though, there is little advance warning or notice, particularly when only a small group of workers will be affected.

The anticipation stage can be a time of great anxiety and confusion, creating a sense of powerlessness or increased dependency. This can result in extra demands on family and friends, who may be unaware of what is taking place. Workers are often angry at what has happened to them but may have few outlets to ventilate this anger. The employer may be a remote or impersonal multinational corporation, immediate superiors may also be in danger of losing their jobs, and acting out may jeopardize opportunities for severance pay. For many workers, this period is also a time for self-recrimination and blame.

Some workers deal better with stress and uncertainty; they accept the inevitable and prepare for what they believe is to come. Some start to work harder, in the hope that they will make themselves indispensable to their employer, even volunteering for additional duties. And some, like Tom, choose to deny the reality of their situation by refusing to believe that their job is at risk or believing that they will have no trouble finding new work. A reluctance to begin short-term adjustment or practical preparation during this period can have serious consequences after the job is lost.

Even before a closure or layoff is announced, there may be other sources of stress. Rumors abound in many workplaces, generating fear and uncertainty among all who might eventually be affected. This can increase rivalry and reduce solidarity and support among the workforce, especially if some workers are privy to confidential information. It can also lead to a discrepancy within the workplace if upper management is aware of an impending closure and starts to plan for its own future while the rest of the workforce remains unaware of impending events.

HOW THE EFFECT OF JOB LOSS IS TRANSMITTED

Disparate but complementary hypotheses have been proposed about how job loss affects an individual.

Losses

When the many benefits that work offers are taken into consideration, it becomes apparent that job loss can lead to significant and substantive deprivations, which vary greatly from one situation to another. A full appreciation of the losses requires an understanding of what a job may have meant.

Economic Meaning. Remuneration from work pays for essentials for day-to-day survival such as food and shelter, as well as luxury items that can make life more comfortable. It also enables workers to purchase material possessions that symbolize social standing or status or allow participation in leisure and social activities. Often, work also provides long-term financial security through pensions, supplementary income after retirement, and savings programs.

Some authors have suggested that the greatest job loss hardships are loss of steady income, long-term career earnings, and long-term financial security (Aiken, Ferman, & Sheppard, 1969; Gordus, Jarley, & Ferman, 1981; Jacobsen, 1987; Howland, 1988; Gyanfi, Brooke-Gunn, & Jackson, 2001). Unemployed workers with access to additional material resources seem to cope better with job loss and feel better about themselves (Jacobsen, 1987; Rodriguez, Frongillo, & Chandra, 2001). For those without other resources, the loss of an income may lead to further deprivations when social activities must be curtailed or possessions sold.

Social Meaning. Work relationships offer opportunities for friendship, support, and social contact, and they can offer escape from a dissatisfying family or personal life. Work can also provide a sense of belonging and acceptance, as well as a clearly defined identity that extends beyond the workplace. In social settings, many people choose to define themselves by their job or work role. Talking about work can also establish fixed points or common ground in new relationships, especially at times when people feel unsure or vulnerable.

Work serves another function: it breaks up the hours in the day. If leisure is defined as the time spent not working, then there can be no leisure without work. And to a large extent, work and work behavior form the basis of societal organization.

Thus, the loss of a job can eliminate social contacts, friendships, and support from the workplace, as well as the daily structure that working brings. These losses cause feelings of sadness, anger, or guilt that create a sense of isolation or alienation. If a worker and his family are forced to relocate to find new work, they may have to leave behind friends, a local neighborhood, and a familiar environment where they may have spent many contented years.

Psychological Meaning. Psychologically, work serves many functions. It may offer opportunities to express creative abilities, develop competence and mastery, and achieve responsibility, recognition, and respect. These functions are all landmarks of healthy emotional development.

Especially when work roles have perceived purpose and value, work helps to form and preserve internal identity, self-worth, and a sense of personal continuity. Behaviors and interactions that are part of the work role are internalized and become an integral part of a self-image. Thus, a consistent after-effect of job loss can be reduced self-esteem.

Other psychological factors are also relevant. The work ethic is instilled from birth, and productive labor is held up as a social ideal. Work roles are modeled to children by parents and are consistently reinforced by educational and cultural experience.

Despite the advantages that work can bestow, not every job will meet an individual's psychological needs. Work can be stultifying, stressful, demeaning, and exploitative. In these cases, losing a job may be a relief or an escape. For some, being laid off provides an opportunity to pursue alternate career plans. It may challenge them to find a job that is better suited to their talents or previously untapped abilities. In general, though, loss of a job entails multiple material, social, and emotional losses. The greater the emotional investment is in a job, the greater are the losses. Someone who loses a job may face many deprivations. The overall impact is cumulative, and the full impact may not be fully apparent until many weeks after job loss.

Role Changes

Changes in roles and role behaviors can be a useful way of conceptualizing job loss effects. The work role can serve many different social and interpersonal functions. At one level, the employer designates clearly defined job description obligations. These may be accompanied by spoken or unspoken expectations about associated behavior. At another level, interpersonal contacts in a workplace offer opportunities to meet psychological needs. Self-esteem is enhanced by roles that allow personal growth, creativity, recognition, or respect. Those that are demeaning or stifling can have the opposite effect.

Change in Self-Esteem

However resilient or self-assured someone is, job loss or persistent unemployment can seriously undermine self-esteem and sense of personal continuity. This process can start with feelings of rejection and then be reinforced by rebuffs from unsympathetic employers and insensitive acquaintances. Negative comments from family members and other usual sources of support can increase feelings of inadequacy. Over time, such changes in self-esteem can lead to a perception of diminished personal value, with the status of a second-class citizen (Merrill, Taylor, & Kerr, 1998).

There is often a tendency for those who lose jobs to blame themselves, usually unnecessarily, for what has taken place. They portray their role in an uncontrollable unfolding of events in an ever worsening light. This self-blame further reduces self-esteem, already diminished by rejection and loss of a psychologically central work role and identity.

Increased Stress

Someone who has lost a job faces many sources of stress. It can emanate from external demands, which may exceed material resources or coping abilities, or from internal pressures, such as beliefs, values, and self-image. One of the most immediate pressures is the need to find a new job. Each of the steps in finding work (appraising one's personal skills and strengths, searching out opportunities, applying for jobs, and attending interviews) is potentially stressful. Pressures may mount as time passes, personal hardships increase, and the need to find work becomes more pressing. Many workers eventually reach a point where it seems futile to continue applying for jobs, risking inevitable disappointment, and so they give up the search.

Finding a new job may also involve additional expense or relocation to a new community. This is disruptive to family relationships, especially when other family members cannot move right away.

Unemployment can be stressful in other ways. It is often difficult to apply for unemployment benefits. The shame of dealing with a welfare agency may also prevent some from using available resources. If applying for social assistance becomes unavoidable, treatment with a lack of sensitivity or respect will reinforce feelings of inadequacy and failure.

Financial hardship is invariably a source of further stress, and budgetary adjustments may not be sufficient to make ends meet. Jobless workers are faced with the prospect of having to sell possessions or make major financial sacrifices in order to honor their daily commitments. This further reinforces feelings of failure and diminished self-worth, and consequently impairs coping abilities.

Change in Social Support

Social relationships and community support are frequently disrupted when a job is lost. In part, this results from the loss of support and social contacts that were previously available within the workplace. Other contributing factors include financially induced reduction in social activity, embarrassed avoidance of friends and former colleagues, and cessation of activities connected to the old job. The availability of community support and resources may also decrease at times of economic hardship or community disintegration. However, the perception of available support may be more significant in determining its use than the amount of support that is actually available.

Change in Family Relationships

The loss of a job affects every member of a worker's family. Changes in behavior of the unemployed worker will usually affect family relationships. Someone who is depressed may be short-tempered or withdrawn from other family members, and anxiety or stress may cause increased tension or reduced involvement in family activity.

Other changes, such as role adjustments, may be more subtle. Notably, families may need to adjust to increased amounts of time together. Every family member will be affected by financial cutbacks. A spouse may be forced to return to work or take on an extra job. Children may be aware that they can no longer afford to buy clothes or toys or continue to join their friends in certain social activities.

All family members may be confronted with the stigma of unemployment. There may be shame or embarrassment that a family member is out of work, especially if the local community is ambivalent or critical. Children may also become aware of differences between their parents and other working parents or may be subjected to ridicule by their peers.

Unemployment should not, though, be seen as a solely negative experience. It can bring members closer together to face the common threat and challenges. The additional time together can lead to greater intimacy and strengthened emotional bonds. And there can be a shared sense of accomplishment when the family overcomes adversity and resolves its difficulties.

Uncovering of Preexisting Emotional and Psychiatric Problems

Preexisting physical, systemic, interpersonal, emotional, or psychiatric problems can be uncovered or exacerbated by job loss. Physical problems may deteriorate and make it harder to return to work, especially for older workers. Workers who had adapted to physical disabilities may again be reminded of their impairments when looking for a new position. Impairments will also restrict the kinds of work that can be considered.

Preexisting psychological problems can include diminished confidence and self-esteem, poor coping skills, and more serious emotional, interpersonal, and psychiatric disturbances. These problems may not have been apparent in a previously secure job and predictable environment, but may become heightened in new or less tolerant work environments (Welch & Lewis, 1998).

Many people have chronic mild symptoms of depression, anxiety, and interpersonal dissatisfaction, to which they adapt through the emotional benefits of work and the work environment. Loss of this counterbalance will accentuate the underlying symptoms and may frequently lead to more pronounced psychiatric syndromes. The challenges of adjusting to job loss may also expose interpersonal weaknesses, exaggerate maladaptive personality traits, and aggravate preexisting marital and family problems. Concurrent personal stress can dramatically exaggerate the effects of job loss. It is essential to recognize emotional and psychiatric problems promptly and accurately.

AN INTEGRATED MODEL

The mechanisms described are not exclusive. Indeed, they can be integrated into a model that highlights their interrelationships and demonstrates how problems or weaknesses in one area can lead to further problems in other areas (Figure 8.1).

Protective factors reduce the impact of unemployment or support and strengthen the individual. Provoking factors increase the impact of unemployment by making an individual more vulnerable. These factors are closely interconnected and in a continuing state of flux. There are many ways of conceptualizing how these factors affect an individual, but changes in self-esteem are usually pivotal.

The stress and deprivation of unemployment threaten the ability to maintain a sense of personal continuity. Adjustments must be made to cope with stress, increase social support, manage change, and continue with day-to-day activities. If these adjustments are successful, they reinforce the positive (protective) factors, thereby increasing self-confidence and permitting adaptation until new work is found. If adjustments are unsuccessful, there can be diminished self-worth, restriction in role flexibility and range, leading to increased internal distress and further problems.

ASSESSING THE IMPACT OF IMPENDING JOB LOSS

The main goals of a clinical assessment are identification of risk for future problems and preparation for the consequences of unemployment. It is safe to assume that nearly everyone who loses a job will have at least some resulting problems.

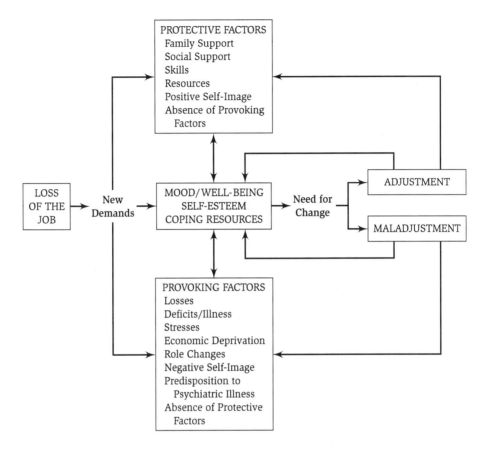

Figure 8.1. An Integrated Model of the Impact of Job Loss.

Source: Adapted from Kates, N., Greiff, B., & Hagen, D. (1990). *The psychosocial impact of job loss.* Washington, DC: American Psychiatric Press. Reprinted by permission of American Psychiatric Publishing, Inc., www.appi.org.

These problems often resolve spontaneously and require little more than support and information about available resources. Bringing the predicament into the open and confirming its reality can be a substantial benefit, even if little tangible help can be offered. Several areas must be addressed in a clinical assessment.

The clinician must recognize and understand the emotional response to job loss. Anger, anxiety, sadness, and fear are normal reactions that accompany the process of adapting to new realities. The clinician should be especially alert for more serious problems if the emotional event is out of proportion to the provoking event or if the distress fails to improve as the pressure eases. It is also essential to differentiate between actual and perceived impacts of job loss. Specific questions should elicit pertinent information on the accuracy of perceptions:

recrimination, self-blame, and guilt about essentially uncontrollable events and perceived loss of control.

The clinical assessment that follows is wide ranging but does not need to include all of the areas covered in a more in-depth clinical psychiatric evaluation. Some parts are appropriate only for some individuals. Each area or question included has been highlighted because it can unearth information that shows how the individual copes and provide guidance for developing a management plan. If other symptoms are present or the distress is severe, a more detailed and comprehensive consultation should be arranged.

Job- and Work-Related Factors

The first step is to assess the importance and meaning of the individual's job. Important questions include the length of the workday, amount of overtime, reasons for working, degree of long-term goal fulfillment, the attachment the individual has to coworkers or employer, stressors encountered on the job, and the extent to which work demands interfere with family and social activities. It is also worth asking about overall job satisfaction, attitudes toward the unemployed, impact of work role losses, and contingency plans already underway.

Personal Deficits and Preexisting Problems

An accurate assessment of preexisting problems or deficits is imperative for predicting emergent problems and highest-risk individuals. Problems that might hinder progress are limited coping skills; limited material resources; limited work skills; physical impairment; and prior depression, anxiety, personality, and other psychiatric disorders.

Limited Coping Skills. The ability to cope with the stress and problems of unemployment may be impaired by underlying psychological deficits. These deficits can include limited interpersonal skills, low self-confidence, reduced rejection tolerance, cognitive or intellectual impairment, and limited problem-solving skills. Although any of these can increase vulnerability, low self-confidence can be a particular handicap, because so many events associated with job loss can reinforce feelings of inadequacy.

Limited Material Resources. The relative contribution of economic deprivation to the emotional and occupational outcome of job loss varies. It is clear, though, that workers with fewer initial financial resources and those who must effect major economic cutbacks have more trouble coping with unemployment. It is worth asking about financial difficulties that predated and followed job loss. Meeting mortgages and other major financial commitments has symbolic as well as practical importance and may become increasingly difficult.

Limited Work Skills. Assessing work skills requires more than simply asking the individual what work he can do or would prefer. Specific skills and strengths need to be assessed and their value for local employers understood. The assessment should also cover job search skills and preparedness for possible retraining or relocation. Limitations in any of these areas can hinder the search for new work.

Physical Impairment. Physical impairment invariably impedes efforts at reemployment, especially for older workers. A physical ailment that had been untroublesome might now become a problem for the first time. For example, a knee injury would not have interfered with a sedentary job but becomes a handicap when considering manual labor. Sometimes a preexisting health problem can be downplayed or can become less consequential when the need for work becomes paramount. A realistic health appraisal or a new treatment approach may help guide an unemployed worker toward a more appropriate or manageable job.

Prior Anxiety, Depression, Personality, and Other Psychiatric Disorders. When workers have a predisposition to emotional problems, the stress of job loss can often trigger an exacerbation of symptoms (Goldberg et al., 2001). Common chronic predisposing syndromes include atypical depression, drug and alcohol abuse, panic disorder, and other anxiety disorders (see the other chapters in Part Four for details). Similarly, personality disorders and styles will make reemployment and readaptation more stressful and more problematic (see Chapter Twenty-Three). There might be a history of acute psychiatric illnesses such as depression or psychosis. Importantly, most prior emotional and psychiatric diagnoses will have been previously undiagnosed. Many will not have been specifically apparent to the worker before diagnosis. Workers might only have been aware of a vaguely distressful period or area of their life. Accurate psychiatric diagnosis requires substantial specific training and experience. It should not be attempted in the absence of proper qualifications or by self-report questionnaire.

Individual Strengths

Clinical assessment should include careful examination of personal strengths, resources, and supports. It can be extremely beneficial to ask the worker to list strengths and skills, pointing out how few have been affected by the job loss. This kind of approach contributes to a sense of personal continuity, while pointing to potential solutions for particular problems. The value of other useful resources, such as owning a car, personal contacts, and knowledge of community supports, should also be identified.

The clinician must recognize and understand the emotional response to job loss. Anger, anxiety, sadness, and fear are normal reactions that accompany the process of adapting to new realities. The clinician should be especially alert for more serious problems when the emotional response is out of proportion to the provoking event or the emotional distress fails to improve as pressures decrease. It is also essential to differentiate between actual and perceived impacts of job loss. Specific questions should elicit pertinent information on perceptual accuracy: recrimination, self-blame, and guilt about essentially uncontrollable events; and perceived loss of control.

Family Factors

The assessment should address the effects of job loss and consequent problems on family life and interaction. Areas to cover include family members' awareness of each other's problems; problems in the way the family unit manages functions such as communication, decision making, and problem solving; the stage of their life cycle the family has reached; family activities; the family's financial situation; and the presence and role of other wage earners.

Social Supports

The assessment should examine social support systems, including social activities, attitudes of social contacts, and knowledge of community resources. It is worth looking at whether changes are anticipated in social and community activities. Support network information can be gathered with a few key questions about principal social and professional relationships, their interpersonal roles, and their helpfulness. It is also important to find out what personal or organizational supports were previously available through the workplace.

An individual's perception of the availability and accessibility of support may differ from reality, but it is the perception that may more substantially determine whether supports are used. Large amounts of support may not compensate for a lack of quality. Friends and former colleagues who are perceived as critical or patronizingly sympathetic may be avoided or may even have destructive effects. Supportive relationships, like effective psychotherapy, require empathic concern, emotional attentiveness, and practical awareness.

Most communities have established such services as vocational counseling and recreational centers that can meet some needs of the unemployed. It is worth checking whether the worker is aware of these programs and knows how to use their services, especially if he or she is unemployed for the first time. Avoidance of these services might be influenced by embarrassment or the need to maintain a sense of independence. Different kinds of vocational services are appropriate for workers from different types and levels of previous employment. Assembly-line workers and accountants need different kinds of advice or retraining.

Attitude Toward Work

It is important to assess the effects of impending job loss on work attitudes, especially when residual anger interferes with the ability to find support or new work (Pernice, 1998). Some organizational cultures or specific circumstances will increase the chance that a newly unemployed worker will feel unexpected guilt, remorse, or self-blame. The clinician should ask about causes and effects of previous unemployment episodes. Someone who has been fired more than once may develop what Triandis (1975) has called "ecosystem distrust." A gradual reduction in the trust of authority figures and institutions will make it even harder to reintegrate this person into the workforce. It is also important to understand local views of unemployment and the unemployed and perceptions of local community attitudes by the unemployed. An appreciation of these attitudes can help the unemployed individual accept the reality of the predicament and take advantage of available support.

IMPACT ON THOSE WHO REMAIN AT WORK

Layoffs can also be exceedingly stressful for those who retain their jobs. Job survivors are often expected to do more work or pick up the tasks of those whose jobs have disappeared. Often, this effort goes unrecognized by supervisors, who may point to the good fortune of continuing employment.

Workers who remain employed may also have experienced a sense of loss of control or helplessness before learning they would retain their jobs. This can be accompanied by a sense of loss or guilt about those who were laid off. There may be bitterness, distrust of management, or fears of further employment problems. Ultimately, these individuals may emerge strengthened by the experience and more realistic about their long-term prospects. Nevertheless, some of the most emotionally distressed employees are among those who do retain their jobs.

INTERVENTION

There are three useful goals for clinicians who provide support or treatment to workers experiencing job loss or employment uncertainty:

- Provide support and advice about impending job loss
- Identify appropriate resources outside the workplace
- Identify emotional risk or distress requiring psychiatric referral

Helping an Individual Cope

Those who help others cope with job loss can address a number of areas.

Dealing with Deprivation. The ability to recognize, work through, and adapt to deprivations that follow job loss is very important. Although each of the losses may on its own have a limited impact, cumulative effects can be magnified, and the losses may continue for an extended period. The clinician can help recognize what has been lost, provide empathic support for emotional reactions, and help to focus on the specific adjustments needed. It is extremely helpful to put these reactions into a longitudinal time frame and emphasize that the impact of distressing events will diminish over time. This perspective can also help maintain a sense of continuity and stability despite ongoing social and financial disruptions.

Maintaining and Increasing Self-Esteem. Perhaps the most important therapeutic task is to ensure that blows to self-esteem are overcome and confidence restored. A clinician needs to be nonjudgmental and allow ventilation of anger and anxiety. These feelings can often be partially eased simply by a willingness to listen and accept them.

The emphasis should be on the preservation of a sense of personal continuity, encouraging the worker to recognize those parts of life that will not change. Putting these events into a longer-term time frame may be helpful. Personal and work-related strengths and skills should be identified and reinforced. Successes, however small, in any aspect of life should be pointed out and situations avoided where failure may be inevitable. Plans should be built on small, attainable targets rather than larger tasks that are less likely to be accomplished, however important they may seem.

Life situations, including the events that led up to the loss of the job, should be reviewed and reappraised. This exercise can show how there may have been uncontrollable events, thereby helping to dissipate inappropriate guilt. To offset feelings of helplessness, there should also be a focus on life areas where control and function are fully intact. Attention should also be given to understanding contributory personal deficits, thereby increasing future control of circumstances.

Managing the Stress. To cope with the stress of unemployment, the worker should focus on practical issues and handling immediate problems, particularly during the initial crisis. Although it is important to address longer-term issues, many can be left until the more pressing issues have been resolved. Problems that may arise can be predicted and management strategies developed.

A realistic approach to finances and budgeting is essential. Workers should be encouraged to make early adjustments before they deplete their savings and other reserves. They should be dissuaded from maintaining their lifestyle in order to keep up appearances or pretend that nothing has happened. Stress management and relaxation skills can offer some inexpensive temporary relief, often in support groups with others going through a similar experience. When needed and feasible, psychiatric consultation and psychotherapy can offer additional help.

Using Time Productively. Promptly establishing a new routine gives the day a focus, helps structure job-hunting activities, limits demoralization, and establishes continuity. Efforts also need to be made to maintain the continuity of relationships, social and religious activities, and memberships in organizations.

Mobilizing Available Resources. It is essential to ensure that embarrassment or guilt feelings do not prevent use of available supports. The earlier an individual facing job loss can discuss concerns openly with the family, the more helpful or understanding the family is likely to be. Engaging in this conversation can also give other family members a chance to talk about their own anxieties or needs. Individuals should take advantage of social supports or other networking contacts. Pride should not prevent asking for help or advice.

Exploring New Possibilities. Every encouragement should be provided to help find a new job. Job skills and options and long-term career plans should be reappraised before embarking on a job search. It is very helpful for workplace staff to have established active links with specialized community agencies that offer work programs.

The search for a new job should be taken as seriously as working itself, with sufficient time and energy devoted to the task. The clinician can offer simple tips such as how to put together a presentable resumé, how to prepare a personal information sheet that can be referred to when filling in job application forms, and how to build and take advantage of support networks and contacts. Personal tips or word-of-mouth produce many job leads. Workers may also find it helpful to read about the experiences of others who have coped with a period of unemployment, recounted in books such as *What Color Is Your Parachute?* (Bolles, 2002).

It may also be a time to look at different career options. For some workers, a review of skills and abilities may help them recognize that many of their skills are transferable to a new career. Other displaced workers may see unemployment as presenting a window of opportunity, although they may need support and encouragement to take a chance at something different. In these cases, the loss of a job may ultimately prove liberating.

Linking with Community Agencies or Supports

Many community agencies provide services for the unemployed and their families. There are advantages if they can work closely with workplace personnel. Most communities have established information centers or clearinghouses that offer practical advice, counseling, support, and information for the unemployed. Some communities have also established emergency hot lines or crisis centers, often staffed by individuals who themselves have been unemployed and have been trained and backed up by mental health workers.

Self-help or mutual support groups for unemployed workers can serve many functions, providing support, solidarity, a sense of purpose, and information for their members. However, they need not only serve a support function. Job clubs, for example, enable unemployed workers to gather regularly to share information and leads on potential jobs. Such initiatives need to be actively supported by social agencies and organized labor. And a few individuals may benefit from a psychiatric referral to help them adjust to the effects of losing their job.

Agency contacts can also stimulate the development of collaborative programs in which several agencies contribute resources and expertise. Interagency contacts and cooperation can help staff of different services provide each other with much-needed support and encouragement, as well as offering a forum for an exchange of ideas about solutions to common problems.

Identifying Those at Risk

Most of those who face job loss find sufficient support from workplace, family, and community. But some individuals experience more severe problems and may benefit from psychiatric referral. There are three situations where this is likely to arise.

The first are situations where the individual is experiencing an exaggerated response to the impending job loss. The person may be excessively anxious, depressed, or angry. In coping with excessive internal distress, he or she experiences a loss of perspective on the situation.

The second can occur when an individual has a preexisting vulnerability that may have required previous psychiatric attention—for example, a prior history of depression, anxiety, or other psychiatric disorders; difficulties in dealing with stress or change; problems in interpersonal relationships; or difficulties adjusting to previous job loss.

Third, it may be possible to recognize individuals who appear at risk because of social isolation, family dysfunction, limited coping skills, physical health problems, an excessive investment in the job, or other risk factors that suggest trouble coping with further change.

It can be useful for workplace staff to maintain working relationships with local psychiatric and mental health services. Their staff can often provide telephone advice or information if someone is in doubt as to whether psychiatric help is needed. This can then lead to a referral or suggestions for management.

PREVENTIVE INTERVENTIONS

Preventive interventions are feasible in situations where there is advance warning or a clear indication of the possibility of an imminent layoff or closure. The nature and speed of any response will depend on many specific local factors. These include the size of the community, the impact of the plant or business on a community's social and economic functioning, the attitude of the employer and the workforce, financial resources, local leadership, and political will.

Not all preventive interventions are applicable to each situation. Each community needs to choose the programs that best suit or can best be adapted to the local context. The greater the degree of local input is in designing flexible programs that reflect the characteristics and needs of a particular community or workplace, the greater is the chance of success. Cook (1987) reviewed early intervention programs in nine plants across the United States. In each case, the more the program planners could take local geography, demography, traditions, and culture into consideration, the more successful the reemployment outcomes were for participants.

The goals of preventive workplace interventions are to help workers understand their predicament, regain a sense of control, learn about available material and support resources, and make adequate preparations for future eventualities (Stone & Kieffer, 1984). Underlying this are the goals of strengthening the role of the workplace as a focus for these efforts and of building on existing strengths and resources. These interventions are much more likely to succeed if labor and management can collaborate to solve common problems.

Although interventions within the workplace before job loss can prevent some immediate problems of unemployment, many workers fail to take advantage of those programs (Cook, 1987; Gordus et al., 1981). Workers who do draw on these interventions may be those who are more likely to make preparations or take the impending job loss more seriously.

Interventions within the workplace mean that all affected workers can be reached. Problems can then be dealt with before they become disruptive. These interventions also provide a chance to identify workers who may require additional training or assistance, may be failing to make appropriate preparations, or are at risk of developing more serious problems.

The first, and perhaps the most crucial, intervention is to provide the workforce with as much forewarning of layoffs and redundancies as possible. The provision of practical information is essential. This can be achieved through the dissemination of written materials and resource guides, one-on-one interviews with affected workers, and educational workshops or seminars.

Written materials should be clear and contain practical information on worker entitlements, how to apply for benefits, free recreation activities for workers and their families, training and retraining opportunities, and possible problems that they may face. These materials can also provide information on community resources—for example, financial and budgeting services, legal services, accommodations, counseling programs, health services, leisure and recreation services, and activities for all family members.

Educational workshops, with contributions from staff of different agencies and services, can be an effective means of communicating this information. The content can focus on coping and dealing with the emotional and interpersonal aspects of losing a job or the practical aspects of finding new work. In the former, the problems likely to be encountered can be reviewed, and the preparations that workers can make to prevent these problems from happening can be discussed. Specific coping skills such as problem solving or stress management can also be taught. If relevant to participants, a workshop might choose to concentrate on a more specific issue, such as coping with early retirement.

Helping workers cope with the emotional responses generated by job loss is often best handled in a group setting, although workers may see this as having little personal relevance. A group run by someone who is not connected to the workplace may provide workers with more of an opportunity to vent their feelings and prepare themselves for what may come.

Workshops on finding alternative work should cover ways of looking for a new job and how to use vocational services. Job search information can include the local availability of work alternatives, retraining programs or relocation schemes, ways of looking for new jobs, techniques for appraising skills, and the intake criteria of community agencies that help with specific work-related problems.

The workplace should also support efforts by workers to find new jobs by providing sufficiently flexible workdays to permit them to look for other jobs or attend interviews. One option is the establishment of an employer or employer- and union-sponsored job counseling or outplacement program, by which outside agencies help displaced workers find alternative employment. Many private companies now contract to offer this service. Evidence from such programs across the United States stresses the need for flexibility in these initiatives. There is no one specific model or approach for every setting. Each community or workplace should develop programs that fit its own needs. Each should also assess efficacy as well as the implications of different forms of sponsorship (government, management, labor, private agencies, or a collaborative effort). And if workers at risk are identified through this process, they can then be referred for more specialized services.

Clinicians and workplace staff must remember that the psychological effects of job loss develop within a wider personal, social, and political context. Many interventions are unlikely to have any lasting impact unless the wider vulnerabilities are also addressed and social conditions that can exaggerate job loss stress are improved.

Workers who face employment uncertainty or job loss pass through several stages during their adjustment. Clinical interventions require awareness of those stages and the many meanings a job and its loss can have. Job loss can lead to increased stress, decreased emotional support, changes in family roles, and decreased self-esteem and can uncover preexisting individual or family problems. A thorough assessment should cover workplace, family, and environmental factors, as well as the skills and previous experiences of the worker faced with redundancy.

Preparatory intervention strategies can help people cope with the effects of job loss, link them with appropriate community resources, and identify those at high risk of developing emotional problems who may require a psychiatric referral. Preventive programs should be considered when job losses can be predicted, preferably months in advance. Collaborative efforts by government, management, labor, and community agencies can help prepare workers emotionally, assist them in looking for new work, and provide information and support in dealing with other practical problems.

References and Additional Sources

Aiken, M., Ferman, L., & Sheppard, H. (1969). *Economic failure, alienation and extremism.* Ann Arbor: University of Michigan Press.

Bolles, R. (2002). *What color is your parachute?* Berkeley, CA: Ten Speed Press.

Borgen, W., & Amundsen, N. (1984). *The experiences of unemployment.* Scarborough, Ontario: Nelson Canada.

Cook, R. (1987). *Worker dislocations: Case studies of causes and cures.* Kalamazoo, MI: W. E. Upjohn Institute for Employment Research.

Goldberg, R., Lucksted, A., McNary, S., Gold, J., Dixon, L., & Lehman, A. (2001). Correlates of long-term unemployment among inner-city adults with severe and persistent mental illness. *Psychiatric Service, 52,* 101–113.

Gordus, J., Jarley, P., & Ferman, L. (1981). *Plant closing and dislocation.* Kalamazoo, MI: W. E. Upjohn Institute for Unemployment Research.

Gyamfi, P., Brooke-Gunn, J., & Jackson, A. (2001). Associations between employment and financial and parental stress in low-income single black mothers. *Women's Health, 32,* 119–135.

Harrison, R. (1976). The demoralizing experience of prolonged unemployment. *Canadian Department of Employment Gazette,* pp. 339–348.

Howland, M. (1988). *Plant closings and worker displacement.* Kalamazoo, MI: W. E. Upjohn Institute for Unemployment Research.

Jacobsen, D. (1987). Models of stress and meanings of unemployment: Reactions to job loss among technical professionals. *Social Science in Medicine, 24,* 13–21.

Kates, N., Greiff, B., & Hagen, D. (1990). *The psychosocial impact of job loss.* Washington, DC: American Psychiatric Press.

Kirsh, S. (1983). *Unemployment: Its impact on body and soul.* Toronto: Canadian Mental Health Association.

Merrill, S., Taylor, R., & Kerr, C. (1998, Mar. 2). Jobless: Unemployment and young people's health. *Medical Journal of Australia,* 236–240.

Pernice, R. (1998). Association of work attitudes and mental health with level or type of income support received by unemployed people with disabilities. *International Journal of Rehabilitation, 21,* 93–96.

Rodriguez, E., Frongillo, E., & Chandra, P. (2001). Do social programmes contribute to mental well-being? The long-term impact of unemployment on depression in the United States. *International Journal of Epidemiology, 30,* 163–170.

Stone, J., & Kieffer, C. (1984). *Pre-layoff intervention: A response to unemployment.* Ann Arbor: Institute of Science and Technology, University of Michigan.

Triandis, H. (1975). Ecosystem distrust and the hard to employ. *Journal of Applied Psychology, 60,* 44–56.

Welch, S., & Lewis, G. (1998, July 11). Poverty, unemployment and common mental disorders: Population based cohort study. *British Medical Journal,* 115–119.

CHAPTER NINE

Sending Employees and Families Overseas

Mental Health in the Workplace Abroad

Thomas H. Valk

Many corporations and agencies assign employees and their families
overseas. Such assignments entail considerable direct and indirect costs.
An understanding of the mental health issues involved in such assignments
and the formulation and implementation of appropriate policies and procedures
to address them can help to ensure that assignments are completed and
productive and that returning employees are retained.

Working with expatriate populations and the organizations that sponsor them presents unique challenges to mental health practitioners. Because there may be few culturally compatible mental health services available in the overseas locality in question, the definition of the workplace by default is extended to include the families of expatriate employees to a much greater extent than encountered in domestic consultations. This extension frequently involves other expatriate community agencies, such as international schools and sometimes entire expatriate communities. Clinically, there are some novel issues, such as the culture shock and repatriation syndromes, that need to be well understood. There are psychosocial issues that are also present in domestic situations but can take on greater significance when they occur overseas.

The overseas practice environment can present special challenges as well. Expatriate community dynamics must be understood in order to deal effectively with emergent situations, such as threats of civil disturbance or the need to evacuate. Such dynamics also present unique challenges to clinicians living and practicing in overseas communities. Equally challenging is the wide variation in mental health and legal infrastructures encountered from country to country. In some countries, practicing overseas with expatriate populations can mean having no culturally compatible mental health system backup, possibly no access to a psychiatric hospital, and a legal system that may not well serve those needing commitment or special protection, such as abused children.

Consultants to organizations sponsoring expatriate families should also have a good understanding of the costs involved in overseas posting and the mental health and psychosocial issues that may lead to assignment failures and early curtailments. Consultants should understand what policies and procedures need to be in place to deal with these issues, as well as challenging clinical and situational events that occur overseas.

MENTAL HEALTH AND PSYCHOSOCIAL ISSUES IN EXPATRIATE POPULATIONS

Expatriate populations generally suffer from the same sorts of mental health disorders as do general populations, although the distribution of disorders differs in some aspects. Phenomena that may be unfamiliar to clinicians include the culture shock and repatriation syndromes. In addition, there are a number of psychosocial issues that affect families due primarily to the effects of frequent moves, separation from family or extended family members, and other factors. These issues should be understood in terms of the stressors with which families must deal and have implications for both the selection of families for overseas posting and the triggering of mental health difficulties in susceptible persons.

Culture Shock Syndrome

Culture shock and repatriation syndromes represent the collection of signs and symptoms over time that expatriates experience when they undergo the major stressor of an overseas move. Culture shock refers to the move from one's home country to the overseas post (or host country), and repatriation refers to the move home after an overseas assignment. For the most part, the signs and symptoms are the same, although the dynamics behind the syndromes differ.

Much has been written about culture shock since the term was coined by Oberg in 1954 to describe the reaction associated with contact with a foreign culture as experienced by expatriates after a move overseas. That there is a significant reaction should not be difficult to understand. Moving overseas to live is highly stressful. Families generally leave familiar work, home, and school environments behind, along with significant social and family support structures so ingrained in their lives that they are often taken for granted. Together, they must face the tasks of building new support systems and adapting to new workplaces, home settings, and schools in the context of a culture that may seem strange and incomprehensible, even threatening, at first.

In general, most authors have described culture shock as a series of stages through which an expatriate will proceed over the first year after arrival. The simplest is the U-curve hypothesis: an individual first experiences some degree of elation and optimism, followed by a downturn to frustration and feelings of depression, and completed by some form of longer-term resolution (Lysgaard, 1955). Elaboration of this hypothesis has been attempted, such as the **W**-curve of Gullahorn and Gullahorn (Gullahorn & Gullahorn, 1962), which represents the vicissitudes of self-esteem in students adapting to overseas study and back home, or the five stages of culture shock outlined by Pedersen (1995), which used critical incident methodology to study an international shipboard program. However, there is no clear empirical support in the literature for the **U**-curve hypothesis or its derivatives. Indeed, one study indicated that only 10 percent of workers overseas experience a **U**-curve type of adjustment (Kealey, 1989).

Given the lack of solid research support for the **U**-curve hypothesis and its derivatives and the degree of individual variation in adjusting to a new culture, it is better to think of culture shock in clinical terms. It thereby becomes a self-limited adjustment disorder, with a variety of potential symptoms, all of which will likely remit within the course of the first year overseas (DuPont, Valk, & Heltberg, 1997). This approach also has benefits in preparing families for overseas life. It avoids teaching a rigid, complex series of stages and time lines, which may serve only to set unrealistic expectations, and resulting in further stress.

Generally, symptoms of culture shock include disturbed sleep (an increased need or decreased amount), uneven appetite, and lower energy. Mood can be particularly affected, frequently being more changeable; some people experience depression or irritability. Sexual interest can also be more variable, and concentration and short-term memory are often decreased. Self-esteem can suffer, especially in the face of the loss of a sense of mastery over the environment. Tasks like food shopping that seemed simple in the home country have to be relearned. Interestingly, some people experience a significant change in attitude toward the host country culture. At some point, they may begin to dislike intensely the culture and the way things are done. Negative, derisive comments about the driving habits of the host country population are often a sign of this attitude change, although other habits may come in for their share of derision as well. Fortunately, this change usually resolves toward a better understanding and acceptance. Preschool and school-aged children and adolescents will react as well, and their reactions will be consistent with their age.

Most individuals do not suffer all of these symptoms. The degree of impairment that results is on the order of an adjustment disorder, and if problems persist for more than a year, there is usually some other problem occurring. A small fraction of individuals (probably less than 10 percent), especially those with predispositions, may move on to more serious mental disorders. Mental health interventions for this syndrome can be limited to accurate diagnosis, reassurance, education about the syndrome and the fact that it is entirely to be expected, and the occasional use of antianxiety medication for brief periods. Education in appropriate stress-reduction techniques can be helpful. Exercise; limiting of self-medication with caffeine, drugs, or alcohol; active attempts to learn about the new culture and its mores; and the fostering of a home and family environment that allows for appropriate expression of angst are often of benefit.

Repatriation Syndrome

Many families are unpleasantly surprised to go through a syndrome entirely similar to culture shock when they return home. In fact, the process has the same set of symptoms, degree of impairment, and time line as culture shock and has been referred to as reverse culture shock. For some people, reverse culture shock is more unpleasant than its outbound cousin (Werkman, 1986; Loewenthal & Snedden, 1986), in part because it is unexpected. Mental health interventions, however, are largely the same as with culture shock (Valk, 1998b).

Families reentering their home country must deal with a large number of changes (Loewenthal & Snedden, 1986; Mendenhal, Dunbar, & Oddou, 1987; Valk, 1998b). Reentering employees are likely to experience a significant downsizing of their scope of command and decision-making freedom in moving from a smaller overseas operation to headquarters. Sponsoring organizations frequently supply services or extra benefits to overseas families that home country employees do not get, and housing overseas, at least in some countries, can be palatial compared to affordable housing at home. Servants can be a large part of life overseas but not back home. Spouses, especially those who gave up careers to move overseas, must make yet another significant role change when they return. Almost all family members swiftly discover that their friends and peers who have not lived overseas are not interested in hearing about their overseas experiences, which were so important to them (Fontaine, 1986). As the result of living in a foreign country, most expatriates undergo significant changes concerning work habits, life priorities, or the importance of time and punctuality, and these may conflict with home country values. And when they get home, the country is no longer quite the same as it was when they left. Entertainment, social and political themes, fashions, and much more have all evolved.

The repatriation syndrome affects companies' bottom lines. The turnover among returning expatriate executives has been reported to be 28 percent over the first two years following return, versus a more normal 15 percent among nonexpatriate executives (Global Relocation Trends 2000 Survey Report, 2000). Such turnover costs companies a great deal in terms of lost talent and skills, especially those skills related to working in foreign cultures.

Mental Health Problems in Expatriate Groups

Good epidemiological or clinical data on expatriate mental health problems are rare (Foyle, Beer, & Watson, 1998). Nevertheless, when posted in Cairo, Egypt, with the U.S. Department of State, this author generated clinical data on all U.S. government employees, U.S. military personnel, and all family members posted in Cairo at the U.S. embassy (Valk, 1990). This population totaled about one thousand covered persons at any given time. In general, this was a screened population, with most all employees and family members having had a medical evaluation, with specialty consultation as adult patients; thirty were male (all were employees). Sixty percent of patients were employees as opposed to spouses or children.

Although the sample size was limited, there were some findings worth noting. Not too surprisingly, of disorders beyond life issue problems (DSM-IV Axis V) and adjustment disorders, which together accounted for 50.8 percent, depressive disorders and substance use disorders were the most frequently seen, at 17.5 percent and 12.7 percent, respectively. The findings concerning adjustment and depressive disorders are consistent with those of Foyle et al. (1998), who found a high incidence of affective and adjustment disorders among the 397 expatriates they examined during overseas service. Of some surprise was that only two patients (3.2 percent) had an anxiety disorder. This finding conflicts with data indicating that anxiety disorders were at least as prevalent in the general population as were substance use and affective disorders (Meyers et al., 1984). Data on use of mental health services also indicate that the combination of phobias and panic and obsessive-compulsive disorders outranks any other category of illness seen (Boyd, 1986). Given the limited sample size and the fact that it was compiled by a single clinician, such a discrepancy could be more apparent than real. If the findings are confirmed by future studies, one possible explanation could be self-selection: in general, those with a significant anxiety disorder do not elect to move and live overseas.

Other findings of interest included that prior tours had no obvious protective effect from being seen clinically overseas. Of patients seen, 78.4 percent had had prior overseas tours, although data were not available as to how many within the embassy population overall had prior tours. Also, there was a suggestion, when looking at both the population seen in Cairo and the patients seen in other Middle Eastern embassies covered, that a higher percentage of patients were seen in their first year at post and that they tended to be more ill. Such a finding, if replicated by future studies, would indicate that the first year at post, consistent with the culture shock syndrome, is uniquely stressful.

This author also collected data concerning the services provided to seventy adult patients of this expatriate population (Valk, 1991). Thirty percent of patients (n = 21) were treated with medications, with 48 percent of these receiving antidepressants, 33 percent receiving benzodiazepines (antianxiety medication), 9.5 percent lithium (antimania medication), and 4.8 percent receiving an antipsychotic. Despite best efforts, 8.6 percent (n = 6) of these patients were medically evacuated from post, with all but one requiring a medical or nonmedical attendant for assistance or behavioral control.

Finally, this author collected data collected covering all psychiatric evacuations from overseas from 1982 to 1986 within the U.S. Department of State and found an annual evacuation rate of 1.63 per 1,000 covered persons, using the estimate of covered persons prevalent at the time of 35,000 (Valk, 1987). In terms of broad diagnostic categories, alcohol use and depressive disorders were most prevalent, at 22.9 percent and 20 percent, respectively. Psychotic states were seen in 6.2 percent of evacuations, exclusive of manic or hypomanic states, which together accounted for 2.8 percent. Sixty percent of all patients evacuated were employees. Testifying to the seriousness of being evacuated, 57.7 percent were not allowed to return to the post.

Psychosocial Issues of Importance

A number of issues can affect an expatriate family overseas and can be important determinants of the quality, or even viability, of an overseas assignment. Dual-career couples is one such issue. In the most recent Global Relocations Trends survey, 37 percent of accompanying spouses were employed before the overseas assignment, but only 8 percent were employed while overseas (Global Relocation Trends 2000 Survey Report, 2000). These figures are down from the high noted in the 1996 survey of 57 percent and 20 percent, respectively (Global Relocation Trends 1996 Survey Report, 1996). The authors of the report speculated that either more potential assignees in the dual-career situation were turning down overseas postings or were not being asked as frequently. Either hypothesis would represent a serious diminution of the talent pool on which corporations or other sponsoring entities can draw for overseas assignments. Indeed, a 1992 survey that specifically addressed the dual-career issue found that participating companies had reached the same conclusion (Expatriate Dual Career Survey Report, 1992).

A spouse who gives up a career in order to move overseas and support that of the employee can be angry, resentful, and have feelings of loss, which can cause friction in the marriage. Such a large role change for the spouse must be addressed up front by both the organization and the couple as part of the decision-making process as to whether to take an assignment, and it certainly is a decision that is best made on a mutual basis. One solution is an unaccompanied tour: the employee goes overseas, and the spouse stays home. This decision can introduce significant strains in a relationship and should be approached with caution. The 2000 Global Relocation Trends Survey (2000) found that 23 percent of tours were unaccompanied, and comparisons to previous surveys established no clear trend.

The Global Relocation Trends 2000 Survey (2000) found that 60 percent of employees take children with them. Clearly, children's education is a major issue affecting tours. The critical issue is that overseas schools that cater to expatriate children vary widely in the extent to which they will accept or be able to handle children with special educational needs, and usually the issue of whether to accept a child is strictly up to the school. In the worst-case scenario, the family arrives at post only to find out that their child will not be accepted by the only school available. Certainly, any special needs should be addressed well ahead of the assignment, and if there is any doubt as to acceptance, it should be addressed ahead of time and in writing.

Other issues of importance may be summarized under the rubric of family life-cycle issues—for example, taking a teenage son or daughter overseas during the high school years, when peer relationships are at their most important and reactions are most likely to be strong. In some instances, it might be wiser not to take an adolescent out of the last two years of high school, a situation that can be particularly difficult for both parents and child. Another stressful family issue is the teenager who has graduated from high school while overseas and now must make the transition from home with family to the first year of college, typically back in the home country. Such separation can be difficult in any circumstances but can be worsened by extraordinary distance and fewer chances to return home or communicate easily with parents (although e-mail is now an option). Another issue that frequently comes up is the distress and guilt accompanying moving overseas and leaving aging parents in the home country.

Those who have been tapped for an overseas assignment should consider these issues carefully before accepting the assignment. The decision-making process as to whether to take the assignment should be a family affair as much as age and parental prerogatives will reasonably permit. To some extent, the sponsoring entity should make screening for and discussion of these issues part of the process leading up to the decision. These issues can produce significant difficulties for families overseas and, as a result, can contribute to assignment failure, an important bottom-line issue.

Expatriate Community Issues

Working and living in an expatriate community presents a number of challenges, especially for mental health professionals. It has been often noted that these communities are closely knit and living in one is akin to being in the proverbial fishbowl: everyone knows what is happening to everyone else, and there are few secrets. In addition, the pressures of living in a foreign land and culture can make for particularly intense and quickly made friendships between families, some of whom may later be patients. In this environment, drawing a clear line between professional and social lives can be very difficult, particularly for a mental health professional who may see a person one hour as a patient and work with him or her later on some community issue. Keeping careful track of hidden interpersonal feelings (transference and countertransference; see Chapter One) takes a high degree of maturity and professionalism and is not for the neophyte therapist. Obtaining supervision for difficult situations and patients in this environment becomes particularly important, although it may have to be conducted by telephone and should be with a senior practitioner who understands the community dynamics well.

The same fishbowl effect has consequences for organizational change during emergencies, such as the need to evacuate expatriates in times of political turmoil or civil unrest. Rumors tend to multiply swiftly, and high-visibility community leadership is essential. Community leaders need to be active and available to the community through frequent communications, sometimes through the vehicle of town meetings or other means. Emergency communications networks should be set up ahead of time, and it is frequently helpful to have a designated person for tracking down and verifying rumors swiftly. Such a rumor control mechanism can be essential and should be well publicized as part of any emergency plan. At the same time, rumor control can be an important tool in assessing what issues are foremost in the community so that the leadership can adequately address them.

Workplace consultations overseas can be particularly complex. Frequently, the workforce is truly cross-cultural, consisting of multiple nationalities, each with its own notion of the work ethic and relations to subordinates, peers, and superiors. Thus, in addition to the usual organizational dynamics, occupational mental health practitioners need to keep in mind that every problem can be compounded by startlingly different, culturally determined visions of what the workplace should be. A basic level of literature awareness concerning these cultural differences is important. Another tool would be to find a person who is a cultural bridge, that is, someone who has lived and worked in two or more of the cultures in question and can help interpret some of the circumstances.

COSTS OF OVERSEAS MOVES AND EARLY CURTAILMENT RATES

Placing an executive overseas is an expensive venture, with costs ranging over $500,000 per placement, depending on the circumstances (National Foreign Trade Council and SRI Selection Research International, 1995). Early curtailment rates range from less than 10 percent to 40 percent (Tung, 1981). The reasons for early curtailment are multiple and not always related directly to diagnosable mental health disorders. Nevertheless, some curtailments for personnel reasons are actually due to undiagnosed mental health problems. There has been a surprising consensus over the years as to the leading cause of failure: spousal inability to adapt or be satisfied. The executive's ability to adapt or other family-related problems are either second or third, depending on the report. The technical ability of the executive is usually fairly far down the list (Tung, 1981; Global Relocation Trends 2000 Survey Report, 2000). Thus, sending an executive overseas is a considerable investment, yet a significant percentage of tours are curtailed early, most frequently because of family issues, not competence. Clearly, sponsoring organizations should factor these facts into their overall expatriation process, beginning with selection.

MENTAL HEALTH SERVICES AND LEGAL ISSUES OVERSEAS

There is a large variation among countries in culturally compatible mental health services. Within the fifteen-country region this author covered from Cairo, Egypt, local availability ran from absolutely none in a number of countries to plenty of U.S.-trained mental health practitioners in one. Usable facilities for psychiatric hospitalization were relatively rare. In general, culturally compatible practitioners need to be sought out in each location and evaluated as to training, office facilities, language proficiency, and competence. In any country or city, practitioners may be host country citizens with compatible training and skills, spouses of expatriate employees who choose to set up private practices for expatriates, or individuals hired by English-speaking, expatriate-oriented mental health or community centers, which often operate under the umbrella of the U.S. embassy. Clearly, placing anyone overseas with a known (or knowable) mental health problem needs to be done with care and attention to what that individual's needs are likely to be and whether they can be met at the location in question.

Similar to the availability of practitioners and hospitalization facilities, medication availability and quality on the local market should be checked ahead of time. Some medications, such as methylphenidate, are not only unavailable in some countries but are also illegal. Although mental health practitioners can usually build a supply line for most patients needing medications, it certainly is an issue that must be investigated and arranged for ahead of time. The converse can also be true. That is, in some countries, medications requiring prescriptions in the United States are readily and legally available without prescription, which can lead to self-medication, with all its attendant problems. Laboratory facilities for monitoring blood levels and other necessary tests also need to be checked carefully because they are not always available or reliable.

There is a marked variation in the kinds of mental health–related legal and social agency supports from country to country. Unlike the United States, for example, some countries do not have a well-developed system to deal with child abuse. Indeed, what behaviors are regarded as abusive, especially in the realm of corporal punishment, and how they are dealt with can vary tremendously from country to country and culture to culture. In some countries, unless appropriate policy steps are taken in advance of assignments, practitioners may be faced with the unenviable dilemma of having a child abuse case on hand and no viable way of dealing with it.

How to deal with imminent danger to self or others can present an equivalent dilemma overseas. Civil commitment laws and procedures vary widely, from no laws at all, to laws with little in the way of due process, to those similar to those in the United States (Rodgers, 1990). Sponsoring organizations and the practitioners who consult to them need to be aware of this variation and should develop appropriate policies and procedures.

Finally, drug abuse and use is treated with wide variation from country to country. Some countries treat any drug use as a very serious crime, much more so than is true in the United States. At the same time, drugs may be fairly cheap and easily acquired. Adolescents who experiment with drugs with little risk in the United States may find themselves in serious legal trouble overseas. Clearly, families need to be forewarned of such situations, and sponsoring organizations and their mental health consultants should have done the necessary research beforehand. Equally clearly, screening procedures attempting to select employees for overseas service should also focus on possible substance abuse disorders for employee and family members.

POLICY AND PROCEDURES TO MINIMIZE DISRUPTION FROM MENTAL HEALTH ISSUES

Given the wide variability in the availability and quality of mental health services, medications, and facilities overseas, a sponsoring organization needs to pay some attention to the real possibility that persons could be placed in a situation in which they could not get adequate care for a known (or knowable) condition. Finally, some conditions or circumstances occurring overseas, such as child abuse and imminent danger, may not be easily handled in some overseas environments. Sponsoring organizations would do well to develop expatriation policies and procedures that address these realities and their variations, if for no other reason than as a bottom-line issue. These policies can be determined in terms of the phases of the expatriation process itself: predeparture, overseas, and repatriation.

Screening of Expatriate Employees and Families

Given the highly variable access to mental health care overseas, the fact that spousal adjustment is a key determinant of tour success, and the fact that some disorders may be quite dangerous in some overseas environments, appropriate screening of employees and their family members should be undertaken (Valk, 1998a). At a minimum, screening should seek to identify any mental health condition that, given the particular overseas assignment, would likely require more care than would be available, require medications or laboratory facilities not available, or would be a distinct danger to the individual in question. This screening requires both a detailed knowledge of the overseas post and the mental health disorder, its natural history, and the individual's treatment and response history. No list of prohibited disorders can be given, and, indeed, given the Americans with Disabilities Act in the United States, such a list would probably be taken as evidence of discrimination (Valk & Bunn, 1999). However, in general terms, disorders that involve a psychotic state, have required hospitalization or civil commitment in the past, have involved danger to self or others or may reasonably lead to such danger, or require medications or laboratory facilities unavailable overseas should be weighed carefully prior to posting. Bipolar disorders involving manic or hypomanic states should be considered very carefully. They can be spectacular in their effects and difficult to contain or treat. Any substance use disorder involving substances that are illegal in the country of assignment, especially where the laws carry heavy penalties, should also be weighed carefully with due regard to prior treatments, length of sobriety (if any), and stability, as well as the availability of appropriate self-help groups. Equally important, and yet another reason for screening family members, is to be sure that any special educational needs for children can be met in the overseas environment. Finally, it is important to screen for and address in predeparture counseling any of the psychosocial issues discussed above.

Any screening operation, especially when the overseas posting is particularly desirable, can become adversarial, with employees and families withholding information in order to obtain the transfer. One way to minimize this aspect is to educate both employee and family as to what works and what does not in any overseas environment. It is, after all, not in the family's or employee's interests to undergo a failed tour, and it is simply a fact that not all families are ready at all times for the stress of an overseas move. Ideally, the family would become partners in the screening process in order to ascertain if this posting is right for them.

The mechanics of the screening process can be flexible. Often, mental health screening is part of a general medical evaluation of family members for overseas posting. A fairly detailed mental health questionnaire, with a follow-up interview with a psychiatrist as needed, with or without psychological testing, would be adequate. Addressing the adversarial nature of the process and promoting a degree of education about overseas realities could be undertaken by knowledgeable personnel with a mental health background and may be accomplished as part of administering the questionnaire. It could be at this time that predeparture counseling about psychosocial issues could be carried out.

Screening on the basis of the personality traits and attitudinal factors most correlated to overseas success is also possible. A number of authors have reviewed or attempted to identify and measure such traits and attitudes (Hannigan, 1990; Kealey, 1989; Searle & Ward, 1990; Rath, 1995). These traits and attitudes include an ease of interacting with a variety of people, positive attitude for the host country culture, flexibility coupled with persistence, and an ability to deal with psychological stress, frustration, and change (Hannigan, 1990). Unfortunately, an adequate end-point measure has never been defined. That is, how does one define and measure a successful overseas tour beyond the gross measure of whether the employee stayed the course? If screening is to venture into this area, not only would accurate and reliable measurement of traits and attitudes have to be addressed but also what exactly they are correlated with. It is unclear how much of the variance between tour success and failure this kind of screening will catch, although it is done on a fairly regular basis.

Predeparture Training

Fifty-seven percent of corporate respondents in one recent survey provided at least a day-long cross-cultural training session prior to departure, but only 32 percent of respondents provided such training to the entire family (Global Relocation Trends 2000 Survey Report, 2000). Aspects of daily life, cultural dynamics, business culture, and host country background information were described as most useful. Other aspects that should be addressed in some detail are the culture shock and repatriation syndromes. A thorough briefing on health care, benefits, and how to stay healthy overseas is important and often of concern, as are general and specific safety concerns (such as crime, terrorism, street scams, and transportation). Although it is not clear that predeparture training correlates with improved overseas tours because outcome measures are poor, it is frequently delivered, frequently reported to be helpful (76 percent of respondent corporations indicated training had high value), and may improve the quality of life for families (Global Relocation Trends 2000 Survey Report, 2000).

Although legal liability has not been well established in the United States, at least not in court, it also makes sense to prepare families if they are going to be posted to areas with significantly higher or different health hazards from that with which they are familiar.

Delivering Mental Health Services to Expatriate Populations

There are a number of options available to deliver mental health services to expatriate populations (Valk & Heidel, 1996). To a large extent, how services are extended is contingent on the geographical distribution of families and the availability of culturally compatible services locally. The options are through a local mental health provider, telephonic or telepsychiatric delivery, "circuit riding" clinicians (a clinician is based in the home country and takes frequent scheduled or emergent trips to concentrations of families), or placement of a clinician overseas. Clearly, the first option, if available, is best, allowing for frequent face-to-face sessions. However, supervision and practice to specified standards may be difficult in the situation where the clinician is the only available practitioner. The second option, with telephonic sessions, is necessary if families are dispersed widely or in a number of countries. This author's opinion, based on experience, is that it should be limited to initial screening and triage, and follow-up support. To this author's knowledge, telepsychiatry, that is, live, two-way video teleconferencing based on telemedicine techniques with the potential of overcoming some of the disadvantages of telephone alone, is not in use for this purpose at this time. As for the "circuit-riding" option, clinicians who travel frequently suffer from considerable fatigue and the technique must be combined with telephone coverage between trips. The placement of a clinician overseas is expensive and suffers all the risks of expatriation. There can also be difficult licensure problems to be addressed and problems in supervising the clinician. Such an approach is usually undertaken only if there is a large group of families concentrated in one place or in only a few places in the same region. Given the percentage of patients needing medications, psychiatric supervision of service delivery is important. Since evacuations will occur, no matter what, organizations should be sure that adequate medical evacuation insurance is in place for each family member.

However services are delivered, sponsoring organizations must also look closely at the laws and practices in each country of assignment as they deal with child abuse and other situations of imminent danger. When the host country laws and practices are either inadequate or nonexistent, the organization should implement policies that aim at safely dealing with these events. Policies dealing with child abuse would likely have to have the leverage of immediate reassignment to the home country if the situation could not be effectively assessed and treated in place. Provisions to turn founded or undetermined cases over to the responsible home country agency on repatriation should also be included. Standards defining what constitutes child abuse would likely be based on home country standards. Imminent-danger policies would also likely have to have the leverage of immediate return to the home country should the situation not prove to be safe in the host country.

Dealing with Repatriation Syndrome

The best way to deal with the repatriation syndrome is during the predeparture training. Optimally, such education would be repeated before repatriation itself, before the family becomes subsumed with preparations for departure. This education process should be as interactive as possible and should begin with focusing on how families have changed while overseas and how this might affect their adjustment at home. After repatriation, a structured program of follow-up with families, perhaps set up through an employee assistance program (EAP), can be helpful, as well as reunions between families who have all repatriated at around the same time. The EAP follow-up can help catch those who are doing poorly and get them appropriate help, and the reunions can help ease the isolation that occurs when home country peers are not interested in hearing about the experiences overseas.

Corporations are increasingly allowing returning executives to use their acquired expatriate skills, which addresses the common complaint that skills acquired overseas simply are not regarded as valuable upon return. Corporations are also allowing a greater range of job options on return in order to address the "out of sight, out of mind" problem that occurs when an employee is overseas and as a result is not a party to networking, mentoring, or other career-advancing relationships that occur naturally at headquarters (Global Relocation Trends 2000 Survey Report, 2000). Some corporations are supporting or encouraging formal or informal mentoring programs for expatriates as well.

As with predeparture training, there are no formal studies that this author is aware of that correlate such programs with decrease in returning expatriate turnover, probably the most persuasive outcome measure. Thus, although such programs make sense on an intuitive level, it is not yet clear how much they accomplish.

Mental health practitioners seeking to work with expatriate groups encounter a number of differences compared to domestic workplace consultations. First and foremost, the definition of the workplace must be expanded to include the family members of employees to an extent not often encountered in domestic situations. Clinical issues are not frequently different, although the culture shock and repatriation syndromes need to be understood, as does a range of pertinent psychosocial issues that are uniquely stressful when encountered overseas. The focus of consultations frequently encompasses entire expatriate communities or key organizations within them, such as schools. An understanding of expatriate community dynamics is important. Practitioners must also recognize that the usual legal and social agency supports in many countries may not exist in overseas locales. Thus, issues of imminent danger to self or others, child abuse, or the need to medicate, have laboratory tests, or hospitalize are not trivial and must be considered carefully for each assignment location.

The sponsoring organizations need to address the lack of overseas mental health services and supporting legal and social agency systems. Policy and procedures addressing screening of families, predeparture training, delivery of services to families overseas, and repatriation need to be developed and implemented. Furthermore, policies and procedures to handle child abuse and imminent danger situations overseas may need to be developed depending on the laws and practices of the host countries.

References and Additional Sources

Boyd, J. H. (1986). Use of mental health services for the treatment of panic disorder. *American Journal of Psychiatry, 143,* 1569–1574.

DuPont, R. L., Valk, T. H., & Heltberg, J. (1997). Psychiatric illness and stress. In H. L. DuPont & R. Steffen (Eds.), *Textbook of travel medicine and health.* Hamilton, Ontario: B. C. Decker.

Expatriate dual career survey report. (1992). New York: GMAC Global Relocation Services/Windham International, National Foreign Trade Council, and SHRM Global Forum.

Fontaine, C. M. (1986). International relocation: A comprehensive psychosocial approach. In C. N. Austin (Ed.), *Cross-cultural reentry: A book of readings.* Abilene, TX: Abilene Christian University.

Foyle, M. F., Beer, M. D., & Watson, J. P. (1998). Expatriate mental health. *Acta Psychiatrica Scandinavica, 97,* 278–283.

Global relocation trends 1996 survey report. (1996). New York: GMAC Global Relocation Services/Windham International, National Foreign Trade Council, and SHRM Global Forum.

Global relocation trends 2000 survey report. (2000). New York: GMAC Global Relocation Services/Windham International, National Foreign Trade Council, and SHRM Global Forum.

Gullahorn, J. T., & Gullahorn, J. E. (1962, Sept.). *An extension of the U-curve hypothesis.* Paper presented at the American Psychological Association Meeting, St. Louis, MO.

Hannigan, T. P. (1990). Traits, attitudes, and skills that are related to intercultural effectiveness and their implications for cross-cultural training: A review of the literature. *International Journal of Intercultural Relations, 14,* 89–111.

Kealey, D. J. (1989). A study of cross-cultural effectiveness: Theoretical issues, practical applications. *International Journal of Intercultural Relations, 13,* 387–428.

Loewenthal, N. P., & Snedden, N. L. (1986). Managing the overseas assignment process. In C. N. Austin (Ed.), *Cross-cultural reentry: A book of readings.* Abilene, TX: Abilene Christian University.

Lysgaard, S. (1955). Adjustment in a foreign society: Norwegian Fulbright grantees visiting the United States. *International Social Science Bulletin, 7,* 45–51.

Mendenhal, M. D., Dunbar, E., & Oddou, G. R. (1987). Expatriate selection, training and career-pathing: A review and critique. *Human Resource Management, 26,* 331–345.

Meyers, J. K., Weissman, M. M., Tischler, G. L., Holzer, C. E. III, Leaf, P. J., Orvaschel, H., Anthony, J. C., Boyd, J. H., Burket, J. D. Jr., Kramer, M., et al. (1984). Six-month prevalence of psychiatric disorders in three communities. *Archives of General Psychiatry, 41,* 959–967.

National Foreign Trade Council and SRI Selection Research International. (1995). *International sourcing and selection practices.* New York: National Foreign Trade Council and SRI Selection Research International.

Oberg, K. (1954). *Culture shock.* Indianapolis: Bobbs-Merrill.

Pedersen, P. (1995). *The five stages of culture shock: Critical incidents around the world.* Westport, CT: Greenwood Press.

Rath, F. H., Jr. (1995). *Pre-employment screening: The MMPI, reliability risk and outcome.* Paper presented at the American Psychological Association Annual Convention, New York.

Rodgers, T. A. (1990). *Involuntary commitment of the mentally ill: The overseas experience.* Paper presented at the U.S. Department of State annual Continuing Medical Education meeting, New York.

Searle, W., & Ward, C. (1990). The prediction of psychological and sociocultural adjustment during cross-cultural transitions. *International Journal of Intercultural Relations, 14,* 449–464.

Tung, R. L. (1981, Spring). Selection and training of personnel for overseas assignments. *Columbia Journal of World Business,* 68–78.

Valk, T. H. (1987). Psychiatric medical evacuations within the foreign service. *Foreign Service Medical Bulletin, 268,* 9–11.

Valk, T. H. (1990). Psychiatric practice in the foreign service. *Foreign Service Medical Bulletin, 280,* 6–11.

Valk, T. H. (1991). Psychiatric service utilization in the foreign service. *Foreign Service Medical Bulletin, 283,* 20–22.

Valk, T. H. (1998a). Psychiatric and psychosocial counseling of the international traveler and expatriate family. *Shoreland's Travel Medicine Monthly, 2*(7), 1, 3–5, 10.

Valk, T. H. (1998b). Repatriation of expatriate employees and families: Pitfalls and solutions. *Shoreland's Travel Medicine Monthly, 2*(12), 1, 3–5, 10.

Valk, T. H., & Bunn, W. (1999). The ADA and employee screening for overseas travel. *Shoreland's Travel Medicine Monthly, 3*(3), 1, 3–6.

Valk, T. H., & Heidel, S. (1996). Americans abroad: Extending EAP services to the expatriate family. *EAPA Exchange, 26*(4), 20–21.

Werkman, S. L. (1986). Coming home: Adjustment of Americans to the United States after living abroad. In C. N. Austin (Ed.), *Cross-cultural reentry: A book of readings.* Abilene, TX: Abilene Christian University.

CHAPTER TEN

Office Politics

The Good, the Bad, and the Ugly

Roy H. Lubit
Robert P. Gordon

Organizational politics is unavoidable. In the process of promoting what they wish and what they think is best, managers need to confront the interests and personalities of others and the organization's culture. Being an effective manager and leader requires not only knowledge of the industry one is in, but the ability to understand other people's work styles and personalities and the ability to motivate them and interact profitably with them. Some people have particularly difficult personalities and are narcissistic or aggressive, and they can create great stress. Effective management and leadership also require being able to understand and work within a company's culture and dealing with hidden agendas and boundary issues. Being able to navigate the rapids of organizational politics is necessary to be an effective manager and leader.

Social scientists use the term *politics* to refer to the way in which decisions are made. Harold Lasswell defined politics as "who gets what, when and how" (1936). In organizations, it has come to have a decidedly pejorative connotation and refers to factors that interfere with decisions being made on merit. It concerns the impact of personal relationships on decision making and to people taking positions that further their personal power rather than the best interests of the company. Corporate politics also refers to the need to play the game and foster personal relationships in order to rise within an organization and to gather support for one's preferred policies. This chapter discusses why politics exists, how to understand political forces, and how to survive them.

Members of organizations are not perfect agents of the organization. People are motivated not only by the desire to do what is best for the organization but to advance their own career, to be able to work with people they like to work with, and to do things in the style they are accustomed to. Sometimes they consciously sacrifice the interests of the company in order to promote their own interests. Sometimes they are not aware that their own interests affect their decisions. Motivated bias is the tendency to believe that the option that furthers our own interests is also the best one for the organization we work in, although in reality it is not. Because of the human tendency to consciously and unwittingly let work decisions be affected by personal interests, office politics is constantly with us. Those who understand the elements of office politics are better able to complete work and foster their career, and by understanding leadership styles, personal styles, and organizational culture, they are better able to adjust their own style to work effectively with others and prosper.

Organizational politics also has a tremendous impact on the performance of business units. Problematic politics can interfere markedly with productivity, impair retention of workers, and lead to worker compensation cases (Collins & Porras, 1994; Ghoshal & Bartlett, 1997). By understanding organizational politics, leaders can improve performance and morale and avoid potential problems.

The politics in an office depends on broad organizational factors and the personalities of the people who work in it. Those who understand the variety of treacherous dynamics that can plague an organization and the various styles and interactive patterns of the people they work with have a much better chance of surviving and prospering.

KNOWING AND UNDERSTANDING PERSONALITY STYLES

There are many different ways to categorize personality styles. Different typologies focus on different factors, and each thereby contributes to our understanding of people. One of the most popular is the Myers-Briggs Type Indicator developed by Katherine Cook Briggs and Isabel Briggs Myers. The Myers-Briggs model, based in the work of Carl Jung, focuses on four dimensions of personality. Understanding where an individual fits along each of the four dimensions provides considerable information on aspects of his or her personality relevant to work style (see Table 10.1).

The first issue concerns whether an individual prefers—and is better energized by—private thinking time or interaction with others. Extroverts are energized by external factors (being with people), while introverts rejuvenate themselves by spending time alone. Both extroverts and introverts may enjoy being with people. After a long day, however, an extrovert is likely to choose to go to a party, while an introvert will more likely take the opportunity to go home and read or listen to music. In addition, extroverts tend to speak before they have thought a matter through, while introverts tend to gather their thoughts before speaking. Because of their tendency to talk a lot, extreme extroverts often make it hard for others to be heard, particularly introverts. When people are unsure of what to do, extroverts can be very helpful in getting the discussion going.

Table 10.1. Myers-Briggs Personality Dimensions.

Preference		
Energy: Source of motivation and energy	Extroversion • Energized by external • Involved with people, things • Expressive • Speaks to think • Act first, reflect later	Introversion • Energized by internal • Involved with ideas, thoughts • Reflective • Thinks to speak • Thinks it through
Information: Information focused on facts and figures versus gut feelings	Sensing • Focus on reality • Focus on what is (our five senses) • Likes concrete facts • Likes details and data • Focuses on the present	Intuition • Looks at possibilities • Focuses on what could be • Likes abstract theory • Sees the big picture • Concerned with meaning of data • Thinks about the future
Decision: Way decisions are made: head versus heart	Thinking • Logical and analytical • Detached • Impersonal	Feeling • Focus on relationships • Desire for harmony • Focus on impact on individuals
Lifestyle: Approach to life: organized or spontaneous	Judging • Desire for structure • Organized • Seeks closure • Likes to avoid surprises	Perceiving • Enjoys spontaneity • Keeps options open • Flexible • Enjoys surprises

The second issue concerns what type of information people focus on: facts and figures or intuition. Sensors focus on concrete facts and details. Intuitives are more concerned with the big picture and abstract theory. Intuitives will develop a company's vision of the future, and sensors will make sure that all of the details of planning and implementation are taken care of.

The third axis examines how concerned one is with the feelings of people versus getting the job done. Thinkers tend to make decisions based on careful, unemotional analysis and are generally described as tough minded. Feelers are more concerned with relationships and the well-being of individuals. Whereas thinkers often try to cover over their emotions, feelers are open to demonstrating them. They both play crucial, albeit different, roles in organizations. Thinkers provide the direction and drive for action to overcome obstacles (including the needs and desires of some people), and feelers provide the glue that holds the office together and the support to keep people engaged and motivated.

The fourth axis concerns lifestyle. Judges like order and structure. They want to come to closure on decisions and then carry them out. Perceivers prefer flexibility, spontaneity, and keeping their options open. Perceivers will keep their eyes open to new opportunities, be flexible about timetables, and head off in new directions that seem promising. Judges want to know in advance that everything is set and seek to avoid surprises.

Considerable tension can arise in organizations as a result of differences in people's work and perceptual styles and a failure to realize the value to an organization of having a variety of styles. For example, introverts may feel that extroverts are dominating the scene and not giving them a chance to participate. Sensors may feel that intuitives are careless and ignoring important details, while intuitives may complain that sensors are worried about trivia and do not understand what is really important. Feelers may argue that thinkers are cold-hearted and do not care about people, while thinkers may assess that feelers do not have the courage to make the tough decisions and will let the company fail in order not to offend someone's feelings. Judges and perceivers will fight over how much structure needs to be in place before moving ahead on a program and whether one can make midcourse corrections and changes in plans.

A manager who knows the styles of subordinates can see to it that a team has the appropriate mix of skills. A team designed to come up with new ideas, for example, should have several intuitives on it. A team focused on implementation should have sensors who will focus on details. Having some feelers is important to hold the team together. It is generally helpful for a team to have a combination of judgers (who help organize and structure the work) and perceivers (who can spot new opportunities and help with midcourse corrections).

Understanding your boss's style will help you to know how he or she likes things done and enable you to focus on those aspects of the work. For example, if your boss is a sensor, it is important to provide detailed information about why you want to do something. In contrast, if your boss is an intuitive, it is important to focus more on the overarching picture. If your boss is a thinker, a different argument is needed than when working with a feeler. Perceivers will be more tolerant of midcourse corrections and leaving things to be decided later than will a judger, who will want to see structure.

Just as it is important to know something about personality styles, it is important to know about difficult people.

Destructively Narcissistic Managers

Destructively narcissistic individuals are very common in organizations and cause considerable harm to morale and the work of teams. The defining characteristics of destructive narcissism are (1) grandiosity (an inflated sense of self-importance, arrogance, preoccupation with power and wealth, and excessive seeking of admiration); (2) a sense of entitlement to whatever they want, including a willingness to exploit others; and (3) lack of concern for and devaluation of others. Destructively narcissistic individuals generally do not realize that their behavior is problematic, and even if they do, they have little concern for its detrimental impact on others.

Narcissism can be healthy or destructive. Both provide outward self-confidence, but they are otherwise very different. The self-confidence of individuals with healthy narcissism comes from secure self-esteem, which helps them to function well in the face of stress. The grandiosity of destructively narcissistic individuals, in contrast, is frequently an attempt to seal over fragile self-esteem.

Certain traits commonly found in destructively narcissistic managers help them to rise within organizations: high levels of expressed self-confidence, magnetic enthusiasm, and unrelenting drive to attain prestige and power. They are frequently good at organizational politics and can charm superiors, manipulate people, and forge quick superficial relationships. Their ruthlessness, drive, ability to make tough decisions quickly, and ability to generate enthusiasm in others can help them climb the rungs of power and enable them to be effective in some aspects of leadership. They are willing to manipulate others to achieve their goals, steal credit for work, and scapegoat. Individuals with destructive narcissism may be able to assess whom they can manipulate and how to manipulate them. They can feign interest in others and play up to their bosses. Their driving ambition and lack of restraint can make them masters of organizational politics.

Damage to Coworkers. At the same time that destructively narcissistic individuals have skills that enable them to climb the rungs of power, certain personality traits undermine the organizations in which they work. These individuals lack empathy and are unable to understand other people in depth. Rather than relating to others as human beings with rights and needs, destructively narcissistic individuals are concerned only with how others serve their needs. Although they may transiently idealize individuals with power who support them, they generally deprecate and exploit others, including former idols. Constantly hungry and envious, they seek what is not theirs simply because someone else has it, rather than because it has intrinsic value for them. Preoccupied with reinforcing their self-esteem, they greedily extract admiration from others. They believe they deserve special treatment and are entitled to be served (Kets de Vries & Miller, 1985). They see nothing wrong with their behavior, since they feel they are special and are entitled to better treatment than they give to others.

Narcissistic individuals sometimes have a strong paranoid streak. They project their unacceptable motives and desires onto others and can become suspicious, mistrustful, hypersensitive, and argumentative. They look for signs of shameful conduct in others in order to support the projection of their own shameful self-image onto others. Since almost anyone placed under a microscope can be found to have faults, destructively narcissistic individuals can generally find reasons with a grain of truth for devaluing someone they dislike. Viewing the world as hostile and forbidding, they trust only a few chosen subordinates, cater to them to keep their loyalty, and demand total devotion in return. Lacking real connections to people, they often use new allies to betray old ones. They drive away the most talented people, divert people's energies from the real work of the unit, foster a problematic culture, and sometimes make reckless business decisions.

The aging process is particularly difficult for destructively narcissistic individuals. In middle age, they typically devalue things they once liked, since inevitably these things failed to bring the narcissistic gratification they had hoped for. They have no gratitude for the joys of younger years and resent that these pleasures are no longer available to them. There is aggression and rage over present and past frustrations. They also devalue the work of people who still have hopes and those things that they cannot have or be. They feel humiliation, suspicion, and anger toward people they depend on rather than gratitude. They tend to cling to power rather than hand it over to the next generation in a timely fashion (Kernberg, 1975).

Damage to the Organization. Destructively narcissistic leaders and managers are damaging to organizations in a number of ways. They tend to neglect the functional requirements of leadership, the needs of others, normal constraints, and value systems (Kernberg, 1998). Neglect of the needs of people who work for them is particularly destructive. If a task is easy or pleasant for them, they can often do nice things for others. But if they dislike a task, such as writing recommendations or responding to questions, they will fail to do so. As a result, their subordinates' morale flags, and their subordinates begin to focus their energy on political survival and dealing with their frustration with their manager rather than on doing their best work.

Destructively narcissistic managers also damage organizations by driving the most capable people away. They cannot tolerate the success of a subordinate who threatens to outshine them. Although possibly able to foster young colleagues for a while, in time they are likely to undercut them, especially if they show any signs of independence. Interested primarily in increasing the power they hold, they do not adequately delegate authority. Moreover, tending toward authoritarian leadership styles, these managers do not accept the real interchange of ideas needed for optimal decision making (Kets de Vries, 1993). Capable junior managers are unlikely to remain in a department headed by a destructively narcissistic manager since they will not obtain the authority, support, or ability to have input into decisions that they seek.

Another destructive aspect of narcissistic leaders is their tendency to focus their attention on increasing their own power and prestige rather than on the work of the organization. This leads subordinates to expend considerable energy feeding the manager's ego and dealing with the complex political situation and frustrations inherent in working under a destructively narcissistic manager. This massive drain on the energies of the manager and his subordinates can seriously compromise the work of the department.

Working with Narcissistic People. Working for a destructively narcissistic manager is very difficult, but there are several ways to contain the problem. One is to avoid narcissistic individuals when possible and be careful not to irritate them when contact occurs. It is also best to minimize any unnecessary information you provide them since almost anything can be used against you. Feeding their grandiosity when you do have contact will help to keep you on their good side. Finally, finding allies who can help to protect you if and when the narcissistic manager turns on you is important.

Organizations can take steps to make it harder for narcissistic individuals to rise in power. Many organizations focus overwhelmingly on short-term profits rather than a balanced scorecard and pay little or no attention to the human costs of how managers achieve this. Developing subordinates, teamwork, supporting morale, and treating others well may not be measured or even noticed by the hierarchy of the organization. Instead, making the numbers and political skill in grabbing credit for short-term profitability or sales increases are rewarded. When the culture, performance measurement and reward systems, and hiring and promotion criteria of a company are tolerant of destructively narcissistic behaviors, these individuals will rise within the company. The use of 360-degree feedback, a balanced scorecard, and hiring and promotion criteria designed to avoid the rise of destructively narcissistic individuals can make a significant contribution to limiting destructive organizational politics.

Despite the destructive aspects of their behavior, it can be very difficult to replace a destructively narcissistic manager who has critical knowledge and contacts. There are ways to ameliorate the most destructive aspects of their behavior. Consultants expert in working with narcissistic managers can be very helpful. Experts can assess the degree to which the destructive narcissism of the manager is learned, as opposed to psychodynamically based, and then apply a complex mix of emotional support, coaching and confrontation (Lubit, in press). Moreover, treating anxiety and depressive disorders that are fueling the narcissistic behavior can ameliorate the situation. Table 10.2 provides guidelines on coping with narcissistic managers.

Case 1

Ken Jonas had reached upper management through focused knowledge that was not widely held at the time of his rise. He was well paid, had considerable autonomy, and was bright. He often talked about his accomplishments, skill, and activities. He was friendly and helpful as long as someone was a good listener and made periodic comments about how good his ideas were and how helpful he was.

He was not particularly interested in others' activities. He could do nice things for people, such as sending flowers to someone who had a new baby. But if something was an effort, he simply did not do it. He chronically failed to write subordinates' yearly evaluations. Once when asked, he replied that people at his level were not expected to do such things. On projects, he liked to interact only with client executives, and he was very skilled with them. But his neglect of client managers often led to their considerable anger and compromise of projects. When people left his group out of frustration, he defensively told everyone how it had nothing to do with dissatisfaction with the group, and he would come up with various excuses for why the person chose to leave.

When an applicant for the position just below Ken's was interviewed, the four interviewers thought that he was capable and driven and should be hired. Ken, however, feeling threatened, said the applicant would get more out of the group than he would bring and turned down the recommendation of the four interviewers. Historically, almost every capable person who served just below Ken quit to go elsewhere out of frustration from working with him. Eventually, Ken's mediocre performance led to someone being placed over him in the hierarchy. He decided to leave the firm.

Aggressive Managers

Aggression, as opposed to assertiveness, is one of the most common ways in which work colleagues and superiors create a stressful work environment. Some aggressive people apply excess pressure to have their own way on a particular issue; others try to have everything their way. Sometimes people undercut or attack each other to prevail on a policy issue or gain more power.

People can be aggressive overtly, covertly, or passively. The overtly aggressive individual openly attacks others and their positions. Covertly aggressive individuals stab people in the back. The passive-aggressive individual quietly

Table 10.2. Coping with Narcissistic Managers.

Superiors	Peers	Subordinates
• Do not try and change their behavior.	• Avoid borrowing from them or gossiping with them.	• Set clear limits on their behavior.
• Avoid doing things that bother them.	• Don't share good ideas until you have told your boss in writing.	• Hire an executive coach skilled in working with narcissistic managers, or tell them they need to for their career to progress.
• Don't criticize them.		
• Flatter them.	• Set clear boundaries.	
• Be deferential.	• Avoid arguments.	
• Document your work.		
• Find a new position.		

sabotages what others want to do by failing to follow through on his or her part in a timely way or being constantly negative toward ideas and plans. What is common among these behaviors is the attempt (conscious or unconscious) to damage the work or reputation of others.

A variety of psychological and social factors may underlie aggressive behavior. Aggressive individuals are frequently narcissistic, focus overwhelmingly on their own well-being, and feel entitled to take whatever they can. Some have antisocial traits and feel no concern for the rights and well-being of others. Their personality traits lower restraints on behaving aggressively, since they serve to limit concern for the well-being of others and for rules (except when the rules help them).

Frustration, fear, and exhaustion can foster aggressive behavior and undercut concern for others and the ability to understand what actions might be unfair to others. Stress and frustration can lead to anger and a desire to hurt others. Frustration makes people feel weak, and anger is an antidote to that sense of weakness and vulnerability. Some individuals tend to feel chronically under threat and often behave aggressively as a result.

Whatever an individual's inner pressure is to behave in an aggressive way, aggression will occur only if the wishes overcome the individual's inhibitions against behaving aggressively. Both the organizational culture and an individual's own inner moral compass serve as brakes on aggressive behavior. These restraints will weaken under stress. In addition, most inhibitions dissolve with alcohol.

Damage to the Organization. Aggressive behavior can have serious negative consequences for an organization. As with destructively narcissistic managers, those behaving aggressively, rather than assertively, can undercut morale, increase tensions, decrease people's willingness to cooperate, undercut communication, and decrease retention. Table 10.3 offers some guidance for managing aggressive managers.

Working with Aggressive People or Behavior. In order to deal effectively with aggressive behavior, it is helpful to know what lies underneath it. People can behave aggressively from a sense of deprivation and failure to assess what is appropriate, from a failure to learn culturally appropriate social skills, from being perfectionistic and overly frustrated with work that does not meet their standards, or from a sense of narcissistic entitlement. Among the factors driving aggressive behavior are these:

Table 10.3. **Managing Aggressive Managers.**

		Drives to Aggression		
		Fear	*Frustration*	*Desire for power*
Lack of inhibition on actions	Not appreciating action (clueless)	Reassure them and educate them about the impact of their actions	Ease their stress and educate them about the impact of their actions	Set limits and educate them about the negative impact of their actions on the company and their career
	Lack of concern for hurting others (narcissistic/ antisocial)	Reassure them and set limits	Ease their stress and set limits	Set limits and educate them about the negative impact of their actions on the company and their career
	Exhaustion (burned out)	Reassure them and ease their stress	Ease their stress	Ease their stress and educate them about the negative impact of their actions on the company and their career '

- Personality disorder: ruthless desire for power and lack of concern for others
- Personality traits hardened by depression or anxiety
- Personality traits hardened by stress
- Firm culture allowing unbridled competition and ruthlessness
- Prior firm's culture and failure to learn how the new firm is different
- Immediate bosses' and colleagues' example
- Lack of appreciation of the effect of their actions on others

How to manage the situation depends on what is driving the aggressive style and not simply on what one sees on the surface. There are some key questions to consider in managing the situation:

- Does the aggressive person treat subordinates like this?
- Has he always behaved like this to others, and especially to reports?
- Is he under particular stress?
- Is a role model treating him or others like this?
- What is the firm's culture and bosses' behavior?
- What was his previous last firm's culture and bosses' behavior?
- How does he respond when confronted with the impact of his behavior?
- Does he seem completely unconcerned with the effect he is having on others, or does he seem only reluctantly concerned?

These questions will help you to assess why they are behaving in a problematic way and help you devise an effective plan for dealing with their behavior.

Case 2

Sally Moore, bright, hard working, and capable, was on the fast track at her company. She worked well with others as long as she was in charge, and she generally was. She was assigned to lead a new team. One of the managers on the team, Richard, was also very bright and had a greater knowledge of the team's project. Sally and Richard met the evening before the project kickoff and talked about the project. Trying to show Sally how helpful he could be, he showed off his knowledge. The next day at the project kickoff, every time Richard said something to the vice president who chaired the meeting, Sally interrupted and said he was wrong. When assignments were made for work, Sally handed them out without discussion. She did have some awareness of her controlling tendencies, and so joked about being a first-born child.

Sally's lack of knowledge of the project's subject area led her to overpromise what the team would do, and problems arose because she promised a work product that was almost impossible to deliver within budget. When the project went over budget, a team member needed to be released. She released Richard instead of Jen, a younger team member who had far less knowledge of the material than either Richard or Sally. When Richard asked Sally why she took him off the project, Sally said only that he should learn to be faster with Microsoft Office. He later found out that she had placed a destructive note in his file that referred to his delivery of the major work product.

Case 3

Eric Higgins had a tendency to yell. He yelled at his administrative assistants. He yelled at the managers under him. Even more painful to those under him than the number of decibels with which he spoke was the tendency to comment in a very disparaging way on their lack of intelligence. The turnover rate for those who worked under him was very high. Moreover, people who worked for him became stressed and irritable and often treated their reports less well than they had before having Eric as a boss.

To some extent, Eric was a perfectionist, and he became upset when things were not perfect. To a large extent, however, he was simply irritable and angry and took out his frustrations on others. He was able to get away with this behavior because of his power within the organization and because the organization's culture tolerated it. He was aware that people were often uncomfortable with his behavior but justified it by saying that this was the way things were done in business, that people deserved it, and that it helped to motivate them. He closed his eyes to the toll in terms of people leaving.

KNOWING AND UNDERSTANDING LEADERSHIP STYLES

Leaders of an organization have a profound impact on its politics and culture through a variety of channels, including serving as a role model, determining the measurement and reward systems, and making hiring and promotion decisions. Leadership also determines how decisions are made. Specifically, how people work to attain a promotion, obtain a bonus, and prevail in struggles depend on the expected reaction of leaders to potential courses of action.

Leadership styles can be divided into six categories (Goleman, 2000): coercive, authoritative, affiliative, democratic, pacesetting, and coaching. The leadership style that a manager uses depends on the manager's personality and the situation. Different styles have different long- and short-term effects on organizational productivity, development of the organization's culture, and how decisions are made.

Coercive leadership demands immediate compliance. The coercive leader expects people to do whatever they are told. At an extreme, it may include bullying and demeaning behavior. The assumption underlying the use of coercive leadership is that people respond to sticks and not carrots and that subordinates have little to offer other than carrying out their superiors' orders to the letter. Managers who use this as their preferred style are likely to have narcissistic or authoritarian personalities. They are very high on the thinking axis and low on feeling. Unless there is a crisis, those who work with them will generally resent the style. It damages initiative, discussion, gathering ideas from people, and communication. It can also impair morale and lead to alienation and loss of motivation.

Leaders using an authoritative style seek to motivate and inspire others with the power of their ideas and authority of their position. They tend to be intuitives rather than sensors and try to instill a sense of confidence in people that the leadership knows where to go and that all will be well if others follow. The style entails persuasion and respect for followers. The theory behind it is that providing a strong vision is the best way to motivate and coordinate people. Individuals are seen as having a lot to offer besides their obedience. The authoritative style is one of the most effective methods of leadership and is most likely to be used by individuals who are relatively self-confident and lack a desire to dominate others.

Affiliative leadership focuses on creating harmony and building emotional bonds within a company rather than on getting people to perform new tasks quickly. Leaders who use the affiliative approach are generally high on the feeling dimension. The underlying assumption for this style is that organizations prosper if people are given the support they need to do a good job. Moreover, people are internally motivated and will respond to support and good treatment if given a chance. Adequate support of workers leads to loyalty, commitment to the team, and hard work. Affiliative leadership can be effective when people are capable of significant self-motivation, teamwork is particularly important, and concrete reinforcements for work are hard to come by. This leadership style is also useful when trust has been broken and needs to be rebuilt, such as when the prior leader scapegoated people or stole credit for their work. Used exclusively, however, the affiliative style can leave people without adequate guidance. Some respond by producing sloppy work. It is generally good to combine this style with an authoritative approach.

Democratic leaders build cooperation and motivation by encouraging participation in decision making. The underlying assumption is that participation leads to greater buy-in, commitment, and hard work. Democratic leadership is the optimal style when achieving crucial cooperation depends on people participating in decision making. This arises in a variety of circumstances. For example, professionals often insist on being part of the decision-making process of their organizations. Moreover, when a new and painful direction needs to be set for an organization and the time line is not tight, democratic leadership is often best.

Pacesetters use their own hard work and excellent performance to set a high standard for what is expected. They are demanding of employees and replace those who do not meet their standards. Leaders who use this style are generally thinkers rather than feelers. This style works best with highly skilled and motivated workers such as those in research and development. When used in other situations, pacesetters may damage morale, since many people will be frustrated by not being clear on what their boss expects or by being unable to meet the boss's high levels of work and achievement.

Finally, a coaching leadership style focuses on developing people so that they can perform better and more independently in the future and be able to move to higher positions. Coaching involves thinking through problems with subordinates rather than telling them what to do and helping them to see the complexity of situations and new ways to view them. Coaching may entail sharing one's own managerial problems and decisions with subordinates, as well as thinking through the subordinate's problems together. Coaching is a useful style when there is adequate time to discuss problems in detail and the organization is concerned about developing leaders for the future. The foundation for the success of some companies is that they focus on building leaders at every level (Tichy, 1997). Coaching subordinates is the key to turning managers and workers at every level of the organization into leaders.

Regardless of the particular style of leadership employed, integrity, honesty, and honoring one's word are essential for allowing people to follow. Being a role model, that is, setting the example for how to act through one's own actions, encourages others to behave in a desired way. Possessing a vision and communication skills are also crucial. Leaders need empathy—the ability to realize what people's needs are—and willingness to support people's human needs and development needs (Bennis, 1994; Bennis & Goldsmith, 1997).

Understanding the leadership style that a potential superior uses can help indicate whether this workplace is the right fit. In addition, understanding the leadership style will help recognition of what is needed to do well. A coercive leader wants people to agree quickly without debate. A pacesetter wants people to work hard and show initiative. An affiliative leader will value the efforts of people to maintain an amicable and closely knit work environment. A coaching leader will want to see growth and development in reports. Democratic leaders want all to participate in decisions. An authoritative leader wants people to understand the vision and to act within the spirit of the vision.

Understanding leadership and personality styles can help to meet a superior's expectations. Adjusting to the stylistic desires of superiors is a crucial part of surviving the politics of an organization. Table 10.4 offers tips for working with the different leadership styles.

Table 10.4. Working with Different Leadership Styles.

Leadership Style	Prominent Traits	How to Work with Them
Coercive	Demands immediate compliance	Do things their way. Ask them how they want things done.
Authoritative	Mobilizes people toward a vision	Frame your efforts in terms of their expressed vision.
Affiliative	Builds emotional bonds and harmony	Show concern for others as people, be flexible, and work to maintain an amicable work environment. Don't make waves.
Democratic	Forges consensus through participation	Participate in group discussions and decision making.
Pacesetting	Sets high standards for performance	Let them know how diligently you are working, and show initiative.
Coaching	Develops people for the future	Try to develop your knowledge and skills.

ISSUES IN MANAGING YOUR BOSS

Managing your boss, like managing subordinates, takes thought. Effective managers are active about managing upward and downward. Management of people requires having knowledge of personal strengths and weaknesses and job needs, and the strengths and weaknesses and job needs, as well as their preferred work styles.

To succeed with a boss, it is important to understand the pressures and demands she faces. What are her personal goals and organizational goals? In assessing the boss's goals, do not take things at face value or make assumptions without information. Take steps to clarify the boss's objectives. For example, does she like to receive information in written form or verbally so she can ask questions? It is also important to assess how much information she needs to know and wants to know. Some bosses like to be highly involved and prefer that subordinates check in frequently on their progress. Others want to hear only about major problems or changes of direction. Managers frequently underestimate how much information their boss needs to know. To make the most of meetings, maximize the information communicated, and avoid confusion about communications. It is often helpful to send a background memo and agenda before a meeting and again after the meeting, covering the key points and agreed-on follow-up actions. Good bosses let their subordinates know what their wishes and expectations are. However, ultimately it is up to the subordinate to find out.

It is also important to assess the boss's preferred style of interacting. Does the boss like conflict or avoid it? Does he want to be challenged, or does he want things to be done his way? Avoid getting into fights with the boss. In general, he has more power, and higher-level management is likely to side with him.

Finally, it is important to communicate with the boss about what subordinates need and about what they want to be able to do, especially for developing a career track that is as fast as possible. In doing this, subordinates can be in a delicate situation with a boss who is less educated or less high powered. Someone who is on a faster track or is better educated can threaten bosses. Great care is needed to avoid provoking retaliation for real or imagined slights or attempts to disprove a subordinate's potential or skill.

UNDERSTANDING WHAT MOTIVATES LEADERS' BEHAVIOR

How leaders use their power within an organization is crucial to the success or failure of the business. Will the leader have an effective vision and the ability to communicate that vision to employees in a way that best serves the needs of the organization, or will the leader's power be used to maintain self-esteem? Equally problematic is the leader who feels uncomfortable with authority and therefore is never able to transform the authority into the power necessary to run the organization. Appreciating the psychology of the leader is essential to understanding the workings and politics of any business.

One way to understand the complex motivational structure of an executive is to look at it from both the conscious and unconscious points of view. From a conscious perspective, executives usually come to an assignment with an agenda that is congruent with a company's needs at a particular time. Sperry (2002) differentiates three styles that parallel stages of organizational growth. In their initial stage, companies need entrepreneurial types who are creative visionaries and risk takers. These people also tend to be very controlling. They have a way that they think things need to be and single-mindedly pursue their goal. As the company grows, specific tasks need to be accomplished, and at this point the appropriate manager is what Sperry calls a performer. When a company has settled into a more mature stage and is running smoothly, the chief executive's role is that of an administrator. The requirements of each situation thus tend to attract leaders with styles that parallel the needs of the company.

The unconscious motivation is far more complicated. Hidden agendas can significantly undercut conscious goals. Different character styles that appear to be appropriate for a situation may mask pathology. Several authors, including Kets de Vries and Miller (1984) and Kernberg (1998), have developed typologies of dysfunctional leaders whose psychopathology and unwitting agendas significantly interfere with appropriate management. Kets de Vries delineates three executive types: the idealizing type, who looks to others as ideals and cannot function alone; charismatic, narcissistic leaders, who require mirroring from others, overvalue their own talents and abilities, and lack empathy; and persecutory leaders, who need complete control and feel envious of and angry with others.

Kernberg underlines the centrality of how leaders handle aggression. Chief executives are at the center of powerful aggressive forces—both their own aggressive strivings and the aggression projected onto them by subordinates. These conditions can easily activate projective identification, where the internal world of the leader may be projected onto the organization. Kernberg's typology encompasses the leader who cannot say no, the leader who has to be admired and loved, the leader who needs to be in complete control, the absentee leader, the leader with affective unavailability, and the corrupt leader.

Executives who cannot say no have a fear of aggression that can promote compliant behavior. They use friendliness as a defense against sadism. Leaders who have to be admired and loved are similar to the charismatic, narcissistic type. In addition to their need to be admired, they are unable to assess individuals in depth and lack the capacity to truly listen. Authoritarian leaders need to be in complete control. They micromanage and are suspicious and resentful of decisions that others make. Their own devalued self may be projected onto others and serve as a rationalization of the need to be in complete control. Leaders who are emotionally unavailable have enormous difficulty in dealing with emotion in themselves and their employees. Consequently, they frustrate the dependency needs of those who work for them.

Zaleznik (1989) differentiates between managers and leaders: managers are narrowly engaged in maintaining their identity and self-esteem through others, whereas leaders have self-confidence growing out of an awareness of who they are and the visions that drive them to achieve. Leaders also have the capacity to let people depend on and identify with them (Zaleznik, 2001). This suggests that they need to be comfortable with the use of power and able to use it constructively. They need enough comfort with themselves to be simultaneously self-critical and self-confident, which calls for a sense of self strongly rooted in goals and ideals.

Organizations function best when employees feel that leaders have their interests in mind. Executives who are overly sensitive to corporate infighting will undermine their own effectiveness by attending less to substantive thinking and more to their own narcissistic needs. They must be able to be aggressive effectively and comfortably as well as handle the aggressive feelings of subordinates. Managing their own aggressive feelings and those of subordinates is crucial. Without this skill, leaders may become ineffective by inhibiting their forcefulness or projecting angry feelings onto subordinates with a consequent loss of reality testing.

Although office politics always presents a challenge, it can be particularly problematic in a family business, where issues of leadership and hierarchy often become blurred. Family problems become business problems, and leaders must attend to family dynamics at the same time that they attend to the business. A son taking over from a father may seek to make his mark by continuing unresolved intergenerational conflict struggles. Building a new plant may be based on a need to defeat the father rather than a sound business plan. The reverse may also be true. Sometimes a child who takes over a business will see it as a continuation of childhood imprisonment and rebel by trying to ruin the business. Guilt about using power is common, with a tendency to share control among siblings or relatives in a way that may provide peace in the family but ruin the business.

ATTITUDES TOWARD AUTHORITY

Attitudes toward authority within a business have considerable impact on its politics. Do people generally tend to follow the wishes of those with authority, try to get around those wishes, or pay them little heed? Attitudes toward authority arise from a combination of individual personality, the culture of the office, and the boss's reaction to actions that do not respect his authority.

A person's attitude toward the boss and colleagues is strongly colored by conscious and unconscious factors derived from childhood experience. This can make for paradoxical reactions. Someone who sees herself as noncompetitive and has fond memories of a large family may be unaware of long-standing feelings of jealousy and rivalry with siblings. This may manifest itself in the office by seeing herself as a team player yet promoting her own point of view to those in authority. This person is searching to satisfy an unfulfilled childhood wish. Others may seek to recreate the past. If the yearned-for wish is not fulfilled, hopeful expectations can easily turn into devaluation and disappointment.

Sigmund Freud (1955) proposed that people in mobs have an immediate sense of intimacy with one another that comes from the projection of their ego ideal (that is, their idealized self) onto the leader. There is also identification with the leader and the other members of the group. The projection of the ego ideal onto the leader eliminates moral constraints as well as self-critical functions. The sense of unity and belonging protects the members of the group from losing their identity. This giving over of responsibility to the leader is accompanied by the loss of individuality and initiative. Affective and intellectual functioning ceases to be on the adult level and becomes more like a child following a powerful adult. The leader holds sway. In the most extreme situation, citizens follow corrupt and immoral dictators. In more common situations, employees may lose their moral grounding as they follow a corrupt boss. Within a corporation, this can lead to subordinates' agreeing with unrealistic policies of a section chief and then to an us-versus-them relationship with other groups in the company. Organizational cooperation gives way to fighting and gamesmanship between parts of the company.

In *Treating the Self* (1988), based on the work of Heinz Kohut, who originated the psychoanalytic school of self-psychology, Ernest Wolf lists several character patterns that are applicable to hierarchical business situations. Mirror-hungry people need to display themselves to get admiring attention. An admiring response (a smile, a commendation from the boss) will combat their feeling of worthlessness. Ideal-hungry people will try to find someone whom they can look up to and admire. The sense that "I can be just like the boss" will boost their self-esteem. Sometimes they need to find someone who is just like themselves, an alter ego. People in each of these situations suffer from a weakness of self-structure and in their work situations will relate to those in authority as they might to an idealized authority figure, such as a treating psychoanalyst.

Czander's *The Psychodynamics of Work and Organizations* (1993) seeks to apply psychodynamic theory to the work situation. In his discussion of relationships to authority, he outlines three types. In the first, the employee wants to be subservient to an omniscient supervisor. Problems arise when the boss is no longer idealized because rebellion can ensue. In the second type, the superior is used as a maternal and nurturing figure. Here, problems may arise when the superior feels drained by the need to keep all reports happy and begins to feel burned out and angry. In this situation, the employee can become angry when he sees that the superior is pursuing her own goals. In the third situation, the relationship with the boss is seemingly friendly and egalitarian. Here, good cheer can cover up suspicion and fears of reprisal from the boss. In situations where employees become wary of bosses, there can be a reversal of normal dependency patterns. They can form power alliances with other subordinates, where organizational goals lose out to personal needs that undercut the work of the organization and an effective hierarchical structure.

ORGANIZATIONAL CULTURE

An organization's culture refers to its values, norms of behavior, and beliefs. It is the playing field, or in some cases the battlefield, on which office politics occurs. Culture proscribes and prescribes certain behaviors. A strong culture can be helpful to an organization as it helps to guide and coordinate employees' actions and thereby serves as an alternative to a costly, and sometimes stifling, level of bureaucratic controls (Nadler & Tushman, 1997). A strong culture also helps people to know what behavior is acceptable and what is not rather than leaving individuals to the mercy of a particular boss's whim.

Toxic Cultures versus Healthy Cultures

Certain cultures are particularly toxic and therefore difficult for individuals to survive in. The classic toxic cultures are noncooperative ones in which people refuse to help each other; nonsupportive ones in which the human needs of individuals are ignored and people feel alienated and dehumanized; intolerant ones in which ignorance and mistakes and alternative ways of doing things are met with marked derision; exclusive ones in which cliques replace a sense of community and newcomers are hazed; and rigid ones in which the boss is viewed as right even when he or she is not.

Each of these cultures violates the basic things that a company needs to do in order to foster high productivity. Research has shown six factors that are particularly crucial to high productivity (Buckingham & Coffman, 1999):

- Workers need to know what is expected of them.
- They need the materials and equipment to do the work right.
- They need an opportunity to do what they do best every day.
- They need to have at least weekly recognition or praise.
- They need to feel that someone at work, preferably their supervisor, cares about them as a person.
- There needs to be someone at work who encourages their development.

Cultures in which people do not receive support, or in which they are belittled and blamed for failures that are largely out of their control, or that are excessively competitive make it difficult to be kind and generous to others. In these environments, people become proprietary of what they know and tend not to share with others. These environments foster backstabbing and scapegoating. Exclusive cultures also limit cooperation and knowledge sharing, although less severely than nonsupportive and competitive ones do. Intolerant cultures breed fear. Hierarchical cultures limit creativity and innovation, hinder cooperation, and drive away the most talented employees. Cultures that embrace the not-invented-here syndrome markedly impede learning and performance improvements (Lubit, 2001).

Crafting the Environment

Cultures arise from several factors: the compensation system, the style of the leader, the myths and stories told in the company, the criteria used for hiring and promoting people, and the traditional behavioral norms and beliefs of people in the company. Some organizations are very careful about hiring people who are team players; they support those around them and focus on the team's goals and success rather than primarily on their own career enhancement and bonus. Other companies either fail to look at this quality or look for people who are individually oriented, and perhaps even ruthless. In some companies, the leader sets an example of ruthless behavior rather than cooperation. The leader may tell myths and stories of the success of the lone manager struggling for success or may talk about the value and potential of teams. Finally, the compensation system may reward the team's performance and helping and developing others, or it may ignore these. If the compensation system exclusively rewards individual productivity, workers will have a strong disincentive to cooperate and help others since time they spend helping others takes away from their personal productivity and thus undercuts their bonus and promotion opportunities. Moreover, in helping others, their performance in relation to others may weaken. Regardless of what is outwardly espoused by the leadership, if the compensation system fails to reward supporting and developing coworkers, it is unlikely that managers will make it a priority.

Cultures are not written in stone. Leaders and managers can change cultures by hiring and promoting the right people, rewarding the behavior they desire, telling fables and stories supporting the culture, and setting an example. By carefully crafting a culture, leaders can increase productivity and create an environment in which the best people will want to come and to stay.

Understanding the culture of the organization one works in is crucial. The culture has a tremendous impact on how things are actually done and what one needs to do to survive and prosper.

Howard Schwartz (1990) has argued for the "snake pit" model of organizational behavior in which people focus on getting ahead by catering to their superiors' vanity. He notes that his students find this to be the core of organizational dynamics in the real world rather than the "clockwork" model generally taught in business school organizational behavior classes. In the snake-pit model, promotions in organizations are frequently less a matter of capability than of not rocking the boat. Executives are often more concerned with how supportive a manager is of them than about how well the manager treats subordinates. As a result, a destructively narcissistic manager who lacks values, goes along with whatever is popular, and plays up to the boss can often progress rapidly despite poor treatment and development of subordinates.

Case 4

John Boudreux was excited about joining the new company. It had a reputation for having bright, industrious people. The frequent use of brainstorming and best idea sharing meetings indicated support for mutual growth. He was promised a mentor and two weeks of training each year. There was also money available for courses at the university and a fine compensation package.

On his first day at the job, he was set up with meetings with various people who were assigned to orient him to the company. It was very puzzling that almost all canceled, and those he did meet with cut their time with him short. In the end, he did not obtain the information he felt he needed. He reviewed manuals and documents and waited for his meeting with his boss and his first assignment.

In the weeks ahead, things were even more puzzling. He learned that people did not actually use the training time or college tuition program. Rather, they worked all the time because taking time off would seriously cut into their productivity, lower their bonus, and interfere with advancement. Knowledge-sharing meetings were either canceled or filled with sterile discussions in which no one revealed their own best ideas. The compensation system provided a strong incentive for not cooperating. People were ranked based on productivity, and place in the ranking determined compensation. Sharing information and helping each other was not recognized, measured, or compensated. In fact, people never got together to socialize or to share ideas outside of small cliques that were fairly exclusive and tightly knit. The leaders had grown up in this environment and thus did not cooperate among themselves. They neither provided a role model for cooperating nor told stories or fables supporting cooperating. Rather, they told stories of the lone worker putting in endless hours and coming up with a solution. All of the good processes and structures went unused. The culture won out.

HIDDEN AGENDAS

Offices and office politics are filled with hidden agendas. Understanding what those agendas are is crucial to surviving office politics and understanding why things are done in the way that they are done.

People seek to further their own power and interests, as well as the interests of the organization. Few of us are so committed to an organization that we would sacrifice our own opportunities for promotion and a year-end bonus in order to do what is best for the company. Hidden agendas arise when the interests of an individual differ from that of the organization and when proposing a course of action, the only politically acceptable way to promote it is to argue that it is for the organization's benefit.

An organization's measurement and compensation system are ideally designed to align the individual's interests with the company's strategy. Invariably, however, there is a gap between the two, and sometimes the gap is fairly large. The cost-benefit ratio for an endeavor may not be good for anyone in a given position, or it may be good for some individuals but not others. A new endeavor may be appealing as a result of the opportunity to be in charge, or terrifying because of the likelihood of being placed in charge. Identical events will have different meaning for and impact on different people.

Sometimes hidden agendas concern attempts to help someone, with the hope of obtaining their help in the future (or paying back an old debt). Once again, people will generally not advertise this. Rather, they will try to explain how their preferred policies and actions will help the business unit or the company. Because communication is neither open nor honest in these situations, it becomes very difficult to discuss the issues at hand and work together for an optimal solution.

Sometimes an individual has an agenda that he or she is not aware of. The human unconscious is very powerful. Why we like someone or do not like someone or why we like one agenda and not another is often based less on rational analysis than on what it unwittingly reminds us of from our past. Desires to help someone, hurt someone, or compete with someone are rich sources of hidden agendas, both conscious and unwitting. Similarly, a desire to be in the limelight, fear of being in the limelight, fear of competition, or ruthlessness in competition can all be markedly affected by unconscious factors.

Individuals are particularly susceptible to unwitting factors outside their control when there is high uncertainty about outcomes. Decisions in business are frequently judgment under uncertainty. Market size, development costs, relative strength of the competition, and who will perform best on a team can often be estimated only within an order of magnitude. Therefore, decisions are based as much on educated guesses as on careful analysis. When people need to make judgments under high uncertainty, they are particularly vulnerable to their own hidden agendas and the hidden agendas of those who provide them with information and advice. People often see what they wish to see (motivated bias) or what they fear as being a much greater threat than it really is. In both cases, the individual's assessment of the situation is skewed by unwitting factors, that is, a hidden agenda.

Case 5

Eric Toledo was managing director at a large company. The vice president of his division asked for his opinion on a new venture. The venture had considerable merit, and Eric's initial assessment was favorable. As he thought about it, however, Eric became increasingly uneasy. The project would link his business unit with that of another managing director with whom he did not get along and who had a reputation for being too good at organizational politics, particularly stealing credit when things went well and scapegoating when they went poorly. The project would necessitate a great deal of interaction between them. Eric feared that doing the project with this other manager could place his own career in danger. The more Eric thought about the potential implications for working together, the more he soured on the project. As he soured, he began to find more and more problems with it and gave a negative report to the vice president.

BOUNDARY ISSUES AND REGRESSION

The poet Robert Frost wrote that good fences make good neighbors. A slightly edited version of that might apply to groups and organizations: clear boundaries allow for the best functioning (and least regression). In the contemporary business world, new problems arise with the advent of the boundaryless organization and interdisciplinary approaches.

Regression

Regression is a common group phenomenon. Freud (1955) discussed the psychology of mobs and groups that fall under the sway of charismatic leaders. Members project their ego ideal onto the leader, which minimizes superego (conscience) and ego (self) functioning. Regression takes place, whereby ordinarily unwitting primitive emotional needs become dominant.

Another approach is suggested by Bion's work (1961) on shared fantasies that characterize the breakdown of healthy work groups. He described three types. In the dependency type, the members feel inadequate, and the leader is idealized and perceived as omnipotent—the source of knowledge, power, and goodness. If the leader fails to live up to this, denial is followed by devaluation, and the members look for a substitute.

In the fight-or-flight group, members are united against external enemies and expect the leader to both fight the enemy and protect the group from infighting. Since the group cannot tolerate opposition to their shared ideology, they easily split into subgroups that fight with one another. Characteristic features include the group's tendency to try to control the leader or experience itself as being controlled by the leader. Aggression may be projected onto an out-group. Splitting (playing people off against each other), projection of aggression, and projective identification prevail. The basic assumption of the third kind of group is pairing. The members focus on a couple that they see as being able to preserve its identity. This group sees intimacy and sexuality as a defense against dependency and aggressive conflicts that characterize the first two groups.

Case 6

Pat Kane, a consultant working with a financial services company, was asked to address communications problems between the owner and several key employees. The owner told Pat that in spite of the fact that he told his employees to act aggressively and with initiative, they had had not done so. When Pat talked to the employees, they said that when they did act independently, the owner was critical and took over their responsibilities. He would veer back and forth between treating them as equals and overpaid clerks. The owner, who was the same age as this group of employees, was unable to appreciate the psychological impact he had when he was critical. He was unable to accept his role as the leader with a clear boundary between him and the staff. All these factors blurred the line between the two. In addition, the owner would make assignments that he viewed as giving the staff more managerial work but the staff saw as busywork. Another important aspect was the increasing importance of computer-driven models in the work.

Although there were elements of regression on both sides, this would seem to be a clear example of a dependency based assumption group. The staff veered back and forth between an idealization of the owner, with fantasies that he was all-powerful and could protect them against any changes in the industry, and a feeling of de-idealization and a sense of abandonment. As Pat worked with the owner to be more comfortable with his role as a leader and to appreciate the impact that he had on his employees, things settled down as a clear boundary was established that allowed for communication and comfort on both sides.

Boundaries

Another interesting issue raised in this consultation was how the consultant set boundaries. Most consultants prefer to use a model with a clear delineation of the problem as the first step. Others prefer a process model that is closer to what happens in an analysis or psychodynamic therapy. In such a model, the consultant starts with the presumption that the openly stated problem is not the whole issue. The real problem will emerge only as the process unfolds. In the consultation at the financial services firm, the initial reason for the work had to do with circumscribed performance issues for two employees. As the process unfolded, the more basic issues came to the fore.

Traditional organizations were ideally organized with clear boundaries that allowed for optimal use of resources and minimal compromise of the designated task. In the modern corporate world, new models have appeared. Now there are corporations without boundaries, with an emphasis on horizontal rather than vertical integration, interfunctional teams, and strategic alliances. Hirshhorn and Gilmore (1992) suggest new kinds of boundaries for the flat organization and ways to identify problems. The authority issue is in play when the question is, "Who's in charge?" "Who does what" is the issue for the task boundary. A manager will ask, "What's in it for us?" with a political boundary, and identifying "who is and isn't us" is stirred up when identity is the boundary issue.

Elliot Jacques (1996) believes that consultants with psychological backgrounds overlook managerial and systematic organizational problems. He takes the position that consultants need to do a structural assessment of a company rather than just a psychological one. Over the years, he has developed a rigorous and systematic approach that allows the development of an optimal organizational structure for any organization. His approach should serve as a cautionary note to consultants interested in boundary issues that they must take into account both the psychological and the organizational.

MALE-FEMALE RELATIONSHIPS

With men and women holding similar positions in offices, and women no longer being relegated to the role of secretaries, a new set of dynamics has arisen. A world previously dominated by men has given way to a more complicated and heterogeneous environment with men and women working side by side and an increasing number of women in powerful positions. As a result, the twenty-first century workplace finds men and women struggling to develop effective and humane ways of working with one another.

Although the makeup of the new business team has a fresh look, old stereotypes persist. Women find that some of their male peers still see them as sisters or mothers and implicitly or explicitly relegate them to second-class status. They are condescended to, expected to behave in stereotypically feminine ways, excluded from important social networks, and criticized for being too sensitive if they complain. The higher that a woman gets in an organization, the more it may feel as if she is entering a male club with its own rules. Although stricter enforcement and greater awareness of sexual harassment laws have cut down on the most egregious offenses, women still find a world filled with many men who condescend to them and touch them inappropriately yet are surprised when women complain.

One high-ranking woman executive recounted numerous incidents where gender inappropriately and often uncomfortably came into play. After a busy and tense morning on an out-of-town sales trip, the chief executive of the client company gave her a tour of the company's impressive headquarters. At the same time, she was continuing to take a tough line in the negotiations involving the new program that she was trying to sell. They then went to the private dining room, where the discussion continued. At the end of the meal, a waiter passed around a box of cigars. She was offered a cigar, declined, and felt that she had been put in a difficult situation. Later that day in a meeting with two of the men who had been present at the lunch, she was told, "The difference between you and me, little lady, is that I would have taken a cigar." She felt attacked and put on the defensive.

Another common technique is to turn the conversation to a "guy" topic. At a dinner after a conference, the topic turned to hunting. The men seemed almost to delightfully anticipate that she and another woman would not have anything to say and would feel squeamish as well. She surprised them and joined in. They had not anticipated that she knew about hunting, but she had grown up in a rural area where she had learned how to shoot at the same time that she learned how to ride a bike.

In another situation, she was traveling with a colleague. They were to make a presentation the following day and talked about it over dinner. At the end of dinner, he asked her if she could come to his room to help him organize the materials for the presentation. Although she felt uncomfortable, she had traveled with this man before and felt that it was a legitimate request. Nevertheless, the colleague began to make advances and she rebuffed him. She recognized how unsafe she felt, knowing that she could have easily been overpowered. She thought about telling their boss about the incident but decided against it on two accounts. If the boss sided with her, he might fire the man, whom she needed for her project, or he might have thought that she had used poor judgment by placing herself in the situation. This is the kind of no-win situation that a woman can find herself in: she can be blamed for bringing on the problem, but bringing it up may interfere with getting important work done.

Communication and negotiation are two of the areas where both men and women fall into stereotypic expectations of one another. There are hidden, unfavorable agendas that can significantly compromise the effectiveness of the woman executive. Women are not expected to make waves. Generally, it is expected of them (and they may well expect of themselves) that they will keep the peace and, if necessary, make concessions. But in an aggressive business situation, women have to be self-protective and bargain effectively. Often socialized to make the other side happy, they may too easily undervalue their contribution and fall into the role of the so-called organizational wife. Women who fall into a mutual expectation pattern where they are seen as mother-sister-wife and feel that way about themselves are unlikely to be considered for leadership roles. They have to expect that conflict is inevitable in such situations and respond appropriately when men talk over them in patronizing or exclusionary ways. If speaking up is equated with being unfeminine, then a woman is in trouble. Although it is unfortunate that these stereotypes exist, they reflect powerful, though hopefully changing, cultural norms.

Although there are many generalizations about how men and women relate in the business world, organizational psychiatrists must look beyond these and recognize that every person is unique and will bring personal conscious and unconscious agendas to the workplace.

COMPETITION

Competition, present in one form or another throughout the life cycle, can be understood from a variety of perspectives, including familial, personal, organizational, and societal. To understand competition in any particular situation, including business, all these factors must be taken into account.

The roots of anyone's feelings about competition stem from both nature and nurture. We are all born with different temperamental dispositions, and these interact with our family environment to shape personality. Conscious attitudes and values concerning things such as aggression, winning, being fair, sharing, achievement, need for recognition, and material rewards interact with a host of unconscious factors. In one family, aggressiveness and winning may be highly valued, while in another, cooperation and sharing may be encouraged. These values learned in the family interact with cultural and societal norms. Some social groups and national cultures prize aggressiveness and individuality, while others value cooperation and group cohesion (think of the United States versus Japan). The complicated amalgam known as our personality thus also interacts with the social system.

Although conscious factors are of great importance, psychiatric consultants in the business world add a dimension by paying attention to unconscious issues as well. An adult may look to his colleagues at work as parents, siblings, or rivals to be defeated, as children to be nurtured, or as nonhuman objects to be cast aside on the road to personal glory. Often a consultant is called into a situation where conscious agendas hide far more complicated and duplicitous unwitting agendas. A corporate president who sees himself as a benign care-taker may call in a psychiatrist to help a key employee who is supposedly an alcoholic. Further investigation may prove that the real motivation is to find an excuse to fire the employee, though to acknowledge this consciously would be in conflict with the president's benevolent, noncompetitive self-image.

As adults, people relive competitive issues with parents and siblings that to a great extent remain unconscious. An office situation that in many ways recre-ates family dynamics will often bring latent agendas into play without some-one's full awareness. A person may recreate one set of competitive issues with a supervisor who is seen as a father, another with a colleague who is seen as a sister or a mother, and another with a supervisee who is seen as a child.

Equally important as knowing the dynamics of an individual and how that will influence competitive issues is the need to understand the culture of the organization or social system. There are tremendous variations in how systems deal with competition. In some situations, open and aggressive competition is central to the culture. Sales representatives compete openly to do the most deals in an office. A social service agency might pride itself on cooperation between employees and ostracize someone who is felt to be too competitive or aggres-sive. Dysfunctional groups are subject to regression, and competitive issues may be dealt with by idealizations of leaders followed by depreciation. It is extremely important that anyone new to a social system try to understand what the norms are in terms of competition. Without such knowledge, an employee can easily get into trouble.

Contemporary American business culture, perhaps paradoxically, seems to value both the super hardworking and competitive leader and the flat, non-hierarchical team. In the first, competition and aggression are lionized, while in the second, cooperation and harmonious respect are prized. In the first situation, one often finds the overly competitive individual or may lose sight of goals and ideals and instead find satisfaction only in winning. Here we see an example of competitiveness gone awry. With the so-called flat organization, the lack of a clear command structure may lead to complicated competitive issues. If normal competitiveness is not acknowledged, unwitting manifestations of aggression may severely impair group efficiency.

There are many ways to survive the politics of organizations. The first step is to be aware of politics. Politics is like potholes in the road: inconvenient and unwanted. If they are ignored, they will cause a very bumpy ride, if not actual injury. Awareness of the politics and culture of an organization helps to avoid inadvertently stepping into a pothole or onto a land mine.

When first entering an organization, it is important to study the politics and culture. Learn about the interests and views of those who wield power. Learn about the way things are done and what is not done. Learn about what is valued and what is not. Learn about what gets the attention of superiors, in both good and negative ways. Paying attention to political realities does not necessarily compromise personal integrity; it is an issue of understanding how organizations work, knowing how to be effective in organizations, and being tactful and diplomatic with those who wield power.

It is also important to build a network and find a mentor. Mentors and networks help us to learn about the culture and politics so that we become savvy. In addition, mentors and networks can help to protect us when and if we alienate someone with power or someone tries to scapegoat us.

In most organizations, it is also important to take steps to develop personal authority and power. There are several aspects. First, image control is important. People who carry themselves with confidence and style are much less likely to be targets for those who are aggressive than those who show their insecurity. Confidence is generally equated with competence. People are much more likely to attack an insecure person, just as sharks go after the wounded swimmer. It is also important to make a good first impression in a job. A good first impression will carry someone a long way. People develop an initial impression and then fit later data into that impression. When people are seen as careful and hard working, then discrepant data that arise later will often be ignored. People who develop a reputation for careful hard work are generally able to get away with mistakes or needing to take time off since others will see it as an aberration rather than the general pattern. An initial first impression of sloppiness or laziness can also persist despite how hard we work.

Developing expertise helps to increase one's power and protection. People seen as invaluable to the company are less likely to be attacked. If people do attack them, the company will need to protect them since they are not expendable.

Having patience is also important. It is frustrating to see a company take a wrong turn and waste money and resources. Nevertheless, if the direction is poor, in time, when the earlier path shows itself to be problematic, people will be open to new ideas. Fighting too hard when there is little chance of victory and no issue of morality or integrity is involved is like falling on one's sword or shooting oneself in the foot.

It is also important to know yourself and the culture of a company before accepting a position. People fit better into some cultures than into others. Some people can handle highly political situations, and others cannot. It is critical that you know where you will best fit in and what you can handle. This understanding will enable you to choose environments in which you can succeed and avoid those that are likely to be destructive to you. Everyone, however, should try to avoid snake pits.

It is not enough simply to make sure that your own power and position survives organizational politics. It is important that you survive and continue to be the sort of person you want to be. Therefore, it is important to maintain individual integrity. Ask what your own moral compass permits, and not simply fall into whatever set of behaviors you see those around you engaging in.

References and Additional Sources

Bennis, W. (1994). *On becoming a leader.* Reading, MA: Perseus.

Bennis W., & Goldsmith J. (1997). *Learning to lead: A workbook on becoming a leader.* Reading, MA: Perseus.

Bion, W. (1961). *Experiences in groups.* New York: Basic Books.

Buckingham, M., & Coffman, C. (1999). *First break all the rules.* New York: Simon & Schuster.

Collins, J., & Porras, J. (1994). *Built to last.* New York: HarperCollins.

Czander, W. (1993). *The psychodynamics of work and organizations.* New York: Guilford Press.

Freud, S. (1955). Group psychology and the analysis of the ego. In *The standard edition of the complete psychological works of Sigmund Freud* (Vol. 18, pp. 69–143). London: Hogarth Press. (Original work published 1921)

Ghoshal, S., & Bartlett, C. (1997). *The individualized corporation.* New York: Harper-Collins.

Goleman, D. (2000). Leadership that gets results. *Harvard Business Review, 78*(2), 126–132.

Hirshhorn, L., & Gilmore, T. (1992). The new boundaries of the "boundaryless" company. *Harvard Business Review, 70*(3), 104–115.

Jacques, E. (1996). *Requisite organization.* Easton, MD: Cason Hall.

Kernberg, O. (1975). Normal narcissism in middle age. In O. Kernberg (Ed.), *Borderline conditions and pathological narcissism.* Northvale, NJ: Aronson.

Kernberg, O. (1998). *Ideology, conflict and leadership in groups and organizations.* New Haven, CT: Yale University Press.

Kets de Vries, M. (1993). *Leaders, fools and imposters.* San Francisco: Jossey-Bass.

Kets de Vries, M., & Miller, D. (1984). *The neurotic organization.* San Francisco: Jossey-Bass.

Kets de Vries, M., & Miller, D. (1985). Narcissism and leadership: An object relations perspective. *Human Relations, 38*(6), 583–601.

Lasswell, H. (1936). *Politics: Who gets what, when and how.* New York: McGraw-Hill.

Lubit, R (2001). Tacit knowledge and knowledge management: The keys to sustainable competitive advantage. *Organizational Dynamics, 29,* 164–178.

Lubit, R. (in press). The long term impact of destructively narcissistic managers. *Academy of Management Review.*

Nadler, M., & Tushman, M. (1997). *Competing by design.* New York: Oxford University Press.

Schwartz, H. S. (1990). *Narcissistic process and corporate decay.* New York: New York University Press.

Sperry, L. (2002). *Becoming an effective leader: Strategies for maximizing executive productivity and health.* London: Taylor and Francis.

Tichy, N. (1997). *The leadership engine.* New York: HarperCollins.

Wolf, E. (1988). *Treating the self.* New York: Guilford Press.

Zaleznik, A. (1989). *Managerial mystique.* New York: HarperCollins.

Zaleznik, A. (2001). The discipline of building character. *Harvard Business Review, 79,* 56.

PART THREE

COMMON ORGANIZATIONAL ISSUES

The following ten chapters focus on a variety of important workplace issues where a psychiatric approach offers invaluable perspective. Anyone who has worked in an organization is familiar with these issues: corporate culture and change, the interface of personal and workplace problems, the role and mechanisms of evaluation for distressed, disabled, or violent employees, legal considerations, and the essential issue of corporate ethics.

The common thread among these chapters is that organizations have a unique set of characteristics that closely interact with the unique emotional characteristics of their employees. By making recognizable such factors as organizational culture and the ethics of a company, the chapters shed light on how employers and employees can maximize performance and avoid dysfunction. And by doing so, they also draw attention to the role that psychiatric professionals can play in achieving those goals.

CHAPTER ELEVEN

How Leadership and Organizational Structure Can Create a Winning Corporate Culture

Howard E. Book

The culture of any organization—the silent manner in which certain behaviors and attitudes are encouraged while others are forbidden—has a significant impact on whether that organization's objectives are met. As a result, culture affects profitability and market share. Although the culture remains invisible, it is profoundly affected by at least two major factors: the CEO's personality style and levels of emotional intelligence and the presence or absence of certain essential organizational structures. These two factors affect each other and together have an enormous impact on the organization's culture and success.

The culture of an organization is crucial to its success in the marketplace because it has a dominant effect on its productivity and profitability. What makes the culture so enigmatic is that despite its importance, it is often overlooked, and even when it is recognized, it is difficult to describe. Consider for a moment the organization within which you work. How would you describe its culture? What impact does it have on success? How often do members of the organization focus on the importance of culture? And when they do, are they talking about the same thing? What do we mean when we refer to an organization's culture?

This chapter answers these questions by offering a working definition of corporate culture, illustrating how some cultures are facilitative because they further the achievement of a company's performance and profitability, while others are obstructive and impede attaining these goals.

Managers should find it useful to identify the culture their organization expresses, whether it is a facilitative or obstructive culture, and to understand the dynamics that create and maintain it. With this understanding, they can approach their superiors or CEO to encourage them to address and resolve obstructive cultures.

Mental health professionals who understand organizational culture can see how their tools of observation are transferable to the business world. These tools can be used to assess culture and the interplay of a CEO's qualities with the organization's structures and then develop interventions that help shift these dynamics, so that the resulting culture is more facilitative, thereby promoting the organization's attaining a competitive edge in the marketplace.

WHAT IS CORPORATE CULTURE?

Culture refers to the unspoken beliefs, values, and traditions common to a group of people, expressed in silent but powerful rules and regulations that invisibly, yet firmly, control and reinforce which behaviors are encouraged and which are censored in that group (Stoner & Wankel, 1986). Corporate culture refers to this phenomenon as it exists and affects the organization.

Culture is often reflected through the "emotional climate," "psychological temperature," or "feeling state" that one experiences on first entering the organization (Czander, 1993). This state can be plumbed by introspectively attending to subtle feelings and transient thoughts (generally overlooked) that one experiences on initially entering that company.

Feeling states are evoked on one's entry into a company. They are first elicited by the physical qualities of the building itself. Consider for a moment the feelings of awe, stability, substance, and veneration that one frequently experiences on entering old, formal banks. Compare it to how differently one might feel and think on entering a Las Vegas casino with its flashy party lights, noisy excitement, and amplified sound of chinking coins, all of which speak to a culture of wealth beyond our wildest dreams infiltrated by transience and disappointment. As we spend time looking and listening, perhaps we may become aware of young frantic faces, the slow and resigned gait of elders, and the bored ritualized pulling of slot machine arms, all of which speak to an underlying culture of futile desperation.

These feeling states are also evoked in us by the attitudes and behaviors of the personnel. For example, one might feel overlooked and unattended in a shop where salespeople animatedly socialize and joke with each other while customers stand waiting and frustrated. This situation may lead to thoughts like: "Gee, people seem not to notice that I'm here." Or, "Aren't these people supposed to be waiting on me? Why are they standing around talking to each other as if I'm invisible? Am I dressed as if I can't afford to shop here?" These qualities are common to the elitist culture and characteristics of a number of upscale shops. Paying attention to and wondering about the meaning of these fleeting feelings and thoughts as we enter any company may offer clues to the organization's culture. In this example, it could be that the culture is chilly rather than embracing, aloof and elitist rather than engaging and welcoming, and disdainful rather than respectful.

The next time you enter your business, try to imagine you are entering it for the first time and attend to your feelings and fleeting thoughts. Do you feel welcomed or dismissed? Rejected or embraced? Confused or calmed? Scrutinized or ignored? And what is the net result, the overarching feeling state, with which you are left: anxious or calmed, depleted or energized, uneasy or relaxed? Because these feeling states may reflect which behaviors are allowed and which are disapproved, what do they say about behaviors that are discouraged or encouraged in your organization? Is input from customers encouraged? Are mistakes admitted? Or is blaming others the norm?

In addition to the challenge of describing an organization's culture, there is another common challenge: the authentic culture that exists may be directly opposite to that which the senior executives define it as being.

Case 1

At a financial institution, the CEO emphasized a new direction of customer-oriented relationship management by stating: "We cherish, embrace and exemplify sensitivity to our customers and their needs. That is our culture. And any insensitive behavior, by any employee, at any time, for any reason, to any customer, will be cause for immediate dismissal. Period."

Culture is not what is espoused; it is what is done, that is, how the organization functions and behaves (Kets de Vries, 2001). In the example, this CEO, although he is unaware of it, is behaving in (and modeling) an uncaring and insensitive manner to his employees. Such behavior by a leader puts the organization at risk for developing a culture characterized by disdainful dismissiveness to subordinates and fear and submission to superiors.

ORGANIZATIONAL CULTURES: THE TWO EXTREMES

Cultures that are obstructive lead to ineffective organizations; cultures that are facilitative give birth to highly productive and profitable companies. Each type is created by an interplay between the CEO's personality type and emotional intelligence and by the presence or absence of crucial organizational structures, and each has an effect on productivity.

Obstructive Cultures and the Ineffective Organization

Cultures that are obstructive ultimately lead to diminished productivity and profitability through the negative effect they have on morale, commitment, pride in workmanship, and efficiency. Obstructive cultures are identifiable by certain markers: these organizations recruit mediocre employees, lose high-quality workers, have a high turnover rate of workers throughout the organization, and do not achieve individual, divisional, and organizational objectives. The organization as a whole loses market share, misses business opportunities, and suffers from either generalized apathy or costly internecine turf wars.

In organizations with an obstructive culture, employees do not experience excitement about or commitment to their work. They feel isolated or alienated; there is little meaningful connection to their peers, superiors or subordinates; and no one is open with fellow employees. Very few in the workplace feel a sense of community, and little significant communication or spontaneity occurs. Often the overall feeling state is one of tension, depletion, unfairness, or fear.

In addition, workers do not feel acknowledged by their superiors for contributing to the organization's success. They see themselves as having no input in the decision-making processes and ultimately sense themselves as being merely replaceable cogs in the wheel. Compared to their industry standard, these companies are characterized by a workforce that shows an increase in absenteeism, more workplace accidents, high levels of staff turnover, low scores on quality-of-life scales, an increase in product turnaround times, and an increase in workplace errors. These companies are also at risk of losing market share and being less profitable.

Facilitative Cultures and the Productive Organization

The same benchmarks as for obstructive cultures can be used to identify a facilitative culture, that is, one that enhances profitability and productivity. Generally, in these organizations, employees with excellent technical skills and knowledge, as well as with strong interpersonal abilities, are recruited and retained; employees at all levels of the organization regard their quality of workplace life as excellent; the workforce turnover is lower than the standard for that industry; absenteeism and on-site accidents are lower than the industry average; and individual, divisional, and organizational objectives are achieved or superseded (Book, 2000).

Facilitative cultures give rise to organizations that are able to recruit, retain, and inspire high-quality employees who have the technical skills and knowledge necessary to get the job done and possess the personal and interpersonal skills that allow them to understand and manage themselves while building collaborative relationships with coworkers and customers.

The emotional climate in the facilitative culture is one of openness, fairness, genuine interest in workers as people, and an ongoing acknowledgment of their contributions. This culture also encourages ease of communication, criticism that motivates, and debate that is constructive. The general feeling state is devoid of tension, dread, or apathy.

The culture of highly successful companies encourages employees to let their subordinates, peers, and superiors know that they are important, make a difference, and contribute (Kanter, 2000; Ket de Vries, 2001). And they let them know not gratuitously but meaningfully. They let them know through simple measures such as, "Great job you did!" when, in fact, the job was executed very well. As a result, employees do not feel that they are merely replaceable cogs in the wheel. They feel that their supervisor knows them, knows a bit about their family, will ask them, "How's your wife doing? You mentioned yesterday that she was in hospital for a while. Are things going along okay now?"

This open, respectful, and acknowledging culture encourages workers' input in decision-making processes. They do not have to feel that their wishes or suggestions are followed; they only have to experience that their wishes and directions are sought and heard. In successful organizations, the culture also encourages transparency: an openness through which the CEO informs employees about what transpires at senior management levels in the day-to-day functioning of this organization.

A facilitative culture is built when an organization lets its workforce know they are valued by providing excellent physical facilities: pleasant offices, a day care center, an appealing cafeteria, and a gym. These facilities send the message that the company, through its CEO and senior executives, respects its employees by actively meeting their needs. Management's response to employees' needs also comes through by offering flexible hours, employee assistance programs, and appropriate pay.

A culture that demonstrates its appreciation of its workforce and of their contributions motivates and inspires its workers to be psychologically invested in their roles so that they do their jobs completely and efficiently. Harvard Business School professor John Kotter (2001) underlined this axiom when he wrote, "Motivation and inspiration energize people, not by pushing them in the right direction as control mechanisms do, but by satisfying basic human needs for achievement, a sense of belonging, recognition, self-esteem, a feeling of control over one's life, and the ability to live up to one's ideals."

What about pay as a motivator? Surprisingly, pay is less important than one might guess, because money is not a great motivator. Even when employees are paid significantly more than the industry standard, they will not work with commitment, motivation, and zest if the culture is such that they feel demeaned, verbally abused, or unacknowledged. If workers fear their superiors, consistently receive conflicting directives, are treated as if they and their contributions are not valued, or dread going to work each morning, no amount of money will inspire them to excellence (Goffee & Jones, 2000).

Although money is not a good motivator, it is a powerful demotivator. That is, even in a modern building with many perks, with management that seems to acknowledge and value them, employees will not work well if they are offered substandard pay. This not really surprising since substandard pay will be understandably experienced as management's disdain and lack of concern for its workforce. A disdained workforce passes this disdain on to how they carry out their roles, and a role carried out in a disdainful manner translates into errors, sloppiness, and inefficiencies.

Two major factors create and maintain a facilitative culture that attracts and retains the best workers and then inspires this workforce to experience their work as meaningful and carry out their roles with enthusiasm and efficiency. The first reflects certain personal attributes of the CEO (see Chapters Seven, Ten, and Twenty-Three); the second speaks to the presence of specific and critical elements in the organization's administrative structure.

HOW THE CEO's STYLE SHAPES CULTURE

Culture starts at the top. The personality type and emotional intelligence (EQ) of the CEO are two qualities that drive the culture.

Personality Type

Much has been written about how the CEO's personality type affects the organization's culture (Kets de Vries, 2001; Sperry, 1996; Stoner & Wankel, 1986). "Personality" refers to the individual's ingrained, constant, and characteristic ways of behaving, thinking, and feeling. It is the answer to the question, "What is the person like?" Personality tends to be consistent. If your high school buddy had an outgoing, gregarious, hail-fellow-well-met style as a teenager, chances are that at your high school's twenty-fifth reunion, whether or not he's gained weight or grown bald, he will still be that same gregarious, extroverted person.

A number of different models and tools describe personalities: the Myers-Briggs Type Indicator, the PA Preference Inventory, and the Sixteen PF Test, some of which are referred to in other chapters. This chapter relies on the fourth edition of the *Diagnostic and Statistical Manual of Mental Disorders* (DSM-IV; American Psychiatric Association, 1994), which describes thirteen personality types, as well as the book *Personality Self-Portrait* (Oldham & Morris, 1991), which offers a less academic elaboration of these styles. Although there are approximately thirteen personality types, only three tend to be commonly seen among CEOs. The other ten bring with them qualities that hamper an individual's capacity to move up the organizational ladder and reach the position of CEO.

Before focusing on these three personality types, it is important to differentiate personality types from personality disorders. All of us have personality types, but not all of us have personality disorders. Personality types are characterized by a flexibility that allows us to manage our environment adaptively. This flexibility is absent in those with personality disorders, who react in an ineffective or maladaptive manner in dealing with the environment (Oldham & Morris, 1991).

The personality type of a CEO influences the culture by the process of identification. That is, the leader's immediate subordinate unwittingly copies or identifies with the leader's personality type. For example, a vice president working closely with a president will unknowingly take on some of the behavior and attributes of the president in dealing with her immediate subordinate, say, the district manager. And the district manager will then unintentionally take on those qualities in his relationship with his subordinates, for example, the frontline salespeople.

To extend the example, a vice president with a meticulous, methodical, and cautious CEO often unwittingly takes on some of that methodical, tentative style. And in her relationship with this vice president to whom she reports, the general manager will also take on some of the methodical qualities that this vice president has recently adopted. Through this process of identification, these qualities are passed down organizationally as subordinates identify with superiors' attitudes and behavior in relationship to their subordinates, breeding a culture where meticulousness, thoroughness, and caution are prized, while spontaneity, risk taking, and innovation are subtly yet strongly discouraged. Certainly, thoroughness has its advantages, but when it becomes a pervasive characteristic of the organization, it can limit the business's success through inflexibility, overcautiousness, and fear of change.

Let us now consider three personality types that are commonly seen among CEOs.

The Irrepressibly Self-Confident CEO and the Slavish Organization. CEOs with an irrepressibly confident personality style bring with them a sense of enthusiasm, optimism, and energy (Oldham & Morris, 1991). Their charisma can attract and inspire workers around them. This CEO's capacity to excite and motivate others fuels the workforce to achieve the company's vision.

However, scratch the surface of irrepressibly self-confident leaders, and commonly you discover that their striking self-confidence cloaks a strong need to be admired. The energy and charisma that seem to reflect their boundless ego and self-certainty usually cover an easily activated inner core of self-doubt and insecurity. As a result, these CEOs commandeer the limelight, insatiably need to be admired, and cannot tolerate being wrong. This translates into needing to be the center of attention, difficulty admitting errors, an inability to tolerate excellence in others, and a failure to nurture and groom future leaders. Because they feel threatened by exemplary subordinates and colleagues, they tend to surround themselves with weaker colleagues and subordinates. Because they cannot brook criticism, they encircle themselves with yes people. The culture becomes one akin to "father [CEO] knows best" or "children [subordinates] should be seen but not heard."

Such CEOs play a pivotal role in creating a culture where the ordinary is rewarded, excellence is discouraged, open debate is silenced, constructive, healthy criticism to superiors is forbidden, and subordinates are blamed for errors that superiors make. Where excellence, openness, creativity, and competitiveness are inhibited, the organization is at risk of losing its competitive edge in the marketplace.

Irrepressible, self-confident leaders bring with them energy and enthusiasm that can create a fired-up, can-do culture, but in their need to be right, and thus surround themselves with mediocrity because excellence in others is a threat, they create a culture where the norm is obedience and supplication to superiors and disdain and contempt toward subordinates.

Case 2

Richard King left his position as senior vice president at Alliance Enterprises to launch Prophet Communications, a wireless communication company that provided superior-quality, real-time, audiovisual conferencing at minimal cost. Charismatic and visionary, Rich attracted and inspired a group of young and talented high-tech executives around him. A number left well-paying, stable positions for the opportunity to get in on the bottom floor of Rich's venture.

With his unbridled self-confidence, Rich instilled a terrific sense of optimism, excitement, and enthusiasm amongst staff. However, as the planning stage moved to the implementation stage, issues arose about financing, external competitors, and marketing. As these issues were brought up at weekly executive meetings by staff, Rich began to respond with increased irritation: "What we *don't* need is negativism. What we don't want is whiners, and you are whiners." Senior executives also discovered that the only acceptable ideas seemed to be Rich's. He dismissed concepts put forth by his executives with, "Yeah, I hear what you're saying, but my expertise tells me differently, and this is how we're going to do it." Staff became increasingly perturbed over Rich's quashing discussion about potential problems by labeling them as whiners and frustrated over his constant demeaning of any idea that didn't originate with him.

Given his supreme confidence, they were also bewildered and concerned over how surprisingly thin-skinned he could be at times. Once, when he noticed Keith Marsden and Barb Ickles glancing at each other while he was talking, he shouted: "Hey, I'm talking! Pay attention to *me* and what *I'm* saying. This is not the time to socialize." Many staff began to respond in an obsequious and solicitous manner. Others smarted under his pointed disdain.

Quite soon, the enthusiasm, excitement, and camaraderie that seemed to characterize the culture gave way to unsettling feelings that only Rich had the important ideas; that the rest of staff were inconsequential to him; that it was dangerous to bring up concerns and problems; and that the emerging culture was one of worshiping the chief and never suggesting that others' ideas were worthy or that his vision might have some flaws. To do so would be to risk his disdain.

With this culture, it is not surprising that morale fell, motivation dropped, productivity suffered, and staff resigned. Rich ultimately was forced to abandon Prophet, blaming his staff as losers.

The Overly Conscientious CEO and the Fossilized Culture. Overly conscientious CEOs tend to be dedicated, hard-working individuals who are uncomfortable with confrontations and strive to get along with others. They embrace order, precision, and routine and have an inordinate need for control. Their self-imposed high standards cause them to expect a lot of themselves and become quite self-blaming (unlike abundantly self-confident CEOs who blame others) when they or the organization fails to meet objectives. It is this dedication, thoroughness, and high standards that enable the conscientious manager to rise in the organization.

These personal characteristics are mirrored in their approach to the organization—ensuring clarity in the organizational chart, precision in job description, unambiguous lines of authority and accountability, updated policies and procedures, and detailed rules and regulations. Their need to avoid conflict discourages free-wheeling discourse and constructive debate. There is a cost to this orderly, methodical, routinized personality style.

Case 3

With a successful background as an accountant, Patricia Reynolds brought to her new position as CEO strong financial knowledge and an appreciation of clarity around role, responsibility, and policy that had been missing at Halojen Enterprises.

Vic Strauss, senior vice president, noted, "Before Pat's arrival, there seemed to be a lot of confusion about who was responsible for what. Communication between divisions wasn't streamlined, so that often the production people were not aware of what the sales force had generated, and customers complained that deliveries were not timely. The left hand didn't know what the right hand was doing. Sometimes it felt that the left hand didn't even realize that the right hand existed."

After the initial burst of enthusiasm over increased efficiencies as a result of Pat's clarification of roles and communication, staff began to experience a different mood that reflected a related side of Pat's push for definition, clarity, and accountability. David Oleano, a front-line worker, stated, "Since she arrived, there is this mood that no one trusts anyone else. My supervisor has started double-checking what I'm doing. Before, it was clear what I had to do, and I did it. But now he's breathing down my neck, questioning why I did this rather than that, and he's concerned about what seem to be insignificant and unimportant details. I feel I'm being treated as an incompetent."

David's experience was common to most of the workforce. Pat's need for control, inner pressure to check what others were doing, and fretting over insignificant details were unwittingly picked up by her senior vice presidents. Although they too complained about her overly detailed micromanagement, they nevertheless picked up the style with their own subordinates. So it went, down the organizational ladder. Under the burden of such constraints, there was no room for innovation, and only the tried and true was embraced.

Halojen began to lose market share as its loss of agility caused it to miss opportunities as the company, concerned with minutia, lost sight of the greater picture as old ways of doing things were no longer responsive to the changing marketplace.

Pat Reynolds became so mired in detail, out of a concern that she might miss something important, that she lost sight of the bigger picture. Her need to be in control made it almost impossible for her to delegate authority and subsequently pushed her to micromanage. Her vice presidents felt that she infantilized them, did not trust their decisions, and was constantly breathing down their necks. Although they behaved in identical ways to their subordinates, this experience with her left them feeling not trusted, constrained, frustrated, and eventually demoralized. But because the CEO, and therefore the culture, valued tranquility, control of contentious feelings, and an "if you can't say anything nice don't say anything at all" behavior, the vice presidents were unable to discuss their dissatisfactions or irritations, just as their subordinates, like David, could not discuss it with them. This unacknowledged hidden anger eroded their respect for the CEO and their dedication to and investment in their work. Ultimately, this led to a sense of apathy and futility that spread down the organizational chart and undermined the organization's capacity to maintain its market edge.

As if this were not enough, this CEO's prizing the routine and familiar made it difficult for her to embrace change. Her style created an inflexible organization where the culture eroded profitability because of the inability to spot, identify, and adapt to changing market needs. Pressure to value the routine and familiar also quashed any sense of creativity that was necessary for the organization to go forth in a changing business environment.

Leaders like Pat create a culture where everything is done by the book, creativity is inhibited, innovation is avoided, and change and risk are shunned. Such a culture puts the organization at risk because of missed opportunities, the need to remain the same when change is indicated, and the inhibition of open, meaningful and passionate dialogue.

The Hypervigilant CEO and the Persecuting/Persecuted Culture. Hypervigilant CEOs have a style of cautious and careful planning, a capacity to suss out threats, and an unobtrusive profile, all of which facilitates their rising up the organizational ladder. They are quite industrious, focused, and diligent—behaviors that they feel will keep them on the "good side" of superiors, that is, the board of directors and shareholders.

This carefulness, the skepticism, the capacity to sniff out threats, and the searching for hidden agendas, however, is often part of a more pervasive stance of a concealed hypervigilance that can erupt and be disastrous for the organization. Whereas healthy skepticism can be a strength that allows leaders to look beyond naively accepting situations at face value and encourages them to scan for complexities hidden below the surface, a hypervigilant individual is not only curious about hidden issues, but is often convinced that hidden threats exist in what objectively are ordinary behaviors, comments, or occurrences.

These CEOs have difficulty trusting the motives of others, and so they behave secretively, control information flow, see hidden agendas in ordinary occurrences, and are poised to overrespond vindictively to real or perceived threats. As CEO, they fear that others are envious of them, want their position, and may be conspiring to mount a palace revolt. This hypervigilance and pervasive mistrust make subordinates wary, prompt them to cover up even innocent errors, and instill caution concerning what they say lest the CEO misunderstand it as a betrayal. As this behavior spreads throughout the organization, it perpetuates a culture of suspicion, secrecy, withdrawal, and fear of vengeful retribution.

Case 4

Arnold Gunn rose to the top during a twenty-year employment with DataWays, a company specializing in background evaluation and searches for headhunters. Its database surveyed income, health, arrests and convictions, credit ratings, drug history, military history, and other covert personal databases. Arnold was a loyal, diligent, somewhat humorless man, slightly introverted yet with some valued friends. He brought with him a brilliance in developing highly sophisticated, computer-assisted databases of very personal information. His ascension reflected this dedication, diligence, and planning.

Once he became CEO, his usual sense of seriousness seemed to change into a sense of tension. Paradoxically, when other senior executives made suggestions that might benefit the company or when they did quite well on a project, Arnold responded as if he were being threatened. He expressed this view to Robert Baxter, one of his two confidants: "Can you believe Philip Dutton challenging me on my ideas about the Ur-Alias! Publicly! After all I've done for him! Do you think he would be promoted if it weren't for me? He owes me. Do you know what I'm thinking? Either he's jealous, or he's after my position. He always did envy me, and now he wants the board to see that they should have made him CEO."

A few days later, Robert was unprepared when Arnold stopped him in the hall and demanded: "I noticed you speaking to Philip the other day. What were you talking about? Me? Why were you talking to him? I thought you were on my side."

As stories spread through the workforce, staff became more cautious and circumspect about what they said and to whom, out of a fear of being branded disloyal or being seen as consorting with the enemy by their supervisor. Who knew with what side their supervisor was aligned, or how they were perceived by the CEO?

> Ultimately, suspicions about loyalty, concerns over being at risk, and fears of retribution permeated the organization, swamping the openness, ease of communication, and collaboration that had characterized the culture with their previous CEO. Such inhibitions and fears demoralized staff, inhibited open problem solving and idea sharing, and led to the ultimate demise of DataWays.

As this culture of wariness took hold, information sharing was inhibited, and the mutual trust necessary for team building was eroded. And as the organization ceased sharing information, pulling together, or collaborating, productivity and profitability fell—and so did DataWays.

Emotional Intelligence

In the past decade, research on how the culture of an organization is molded by the CEO's personality type has broadened to include how the culture is also shaped by the CEO's emotional intelligence (EQ).

Whereas personality type refers to the ingrained, habitual, lifelong style of behavior, thoughts, feelings, and attitudes with which one faces the world, EQ cuts through all personality types and refers to the presence and strength of specific competencies that allow one to overcome day-to-day pressures and challenges, regardless of one's personality types (George, 2000; Goleman, 1998; Cooper & Sawaf, 1996; Saarni, 1999; Stein & Book, 2000). These learnable competencies can be thought of as an array of social, personal, political, and survival skills that are critical for success in all of our day-to-day roles.

EQ is quite different from cognitive intelligence (IQ), as shown in Table 11.1. IQ refers to cognitive capacities of memory, analytical and rational thinking, mathematical ability, maintenance of a general fund of information, and certain spatial-motor capabilities. A high IQ shows itself in the ability to pass IQ tests, do well scholastically, and obtain admission to highly selective colleges and universities. IQ is also fixed, varying little after the age of twelve. It cannot be increased through learning.

EQ refers to noncognitive competencies or skills of a social, personal, political, and survival nature that are related to success in managing day-to-day expectations and pressures. It consists of five component types of skills: intrapersonal, interpersonal, adaptability, general mood, and stress management skills (see Table 11.2). Each of these building block skills is made up of approximately two to five components.

Unlike IQ, EQ increases with age, and its fifteen competencies are learnable. This is a crucial aspect of emotional intelligence, because if a CEO requires a significant competency to be stronger, that competency can be strengthened through coaching (Stein & Book, 2000).

Harvard Business School professor Rosabeth Moss Kanter (2000) speaks to these competencies when she notes the organization's need to be fluid, agile,

Table 11.1. Emotional Intelligence and Cognitive Intelligence: A Comparison.

	EQ	*IQ*
Skill sets	Noncognitive, social, emotional, and personal survival skills	Cognitive skills relating to logical and analytical thinking, memory, mathematical capacity, general fund of information, and spatial-motor capacities
Success prediction	Moderate to strong	Weak to moderate
Age of maximal skil1	Competencies increase with age until fifty and then level off—"older and wiser"	Fixed after the age of twelve
Learnable competencies	Yes	No
Everyday synonyms	"Street smarts," "savvy," "common sense," "survival skills"	"Book smarts"

Table 11.2. Components of Emotional Intelligence.

Intrapersonal Components	Interpersonal Components
Emotional self-awareness	Empathy
Assertiveness	Social responsibility
Self-regard	Interpersonal relationship
Self-actualization	Stress Management Components
Independence	Stress tolerance
Adaptability Components	Impulse control
Problem solving	
Reality testing	
Flexibility	
General Mood Components	
Happiness	
Optimism	

and responsive, for she is addressing the competency of flexibility. When she uses terms such as "building coalitions" and "involving people," she is identifying key components like relationship building and empathy. When she emphasizes the crucial capacity of "making everyone a hero," of recognizing and celebrating day-to-day accomplishments, she is again speaking of empathy and relationship building.

Successful CEOs—leaders who create a facilitative culture that recruits, retains, empowers, and inspires the workplace at all levels—are characterized by the presence of strong EQ components. Research strongly suggests that EQ may be more important than IQ in fueling the CEO's success and creating a culture that empowers the organization to attain its goals and maintain a competitive edge in the marketplace (Barling, Slater, & Kelloway, 2000; Book, 2000; Collins, 2001; Chrisman, Chua, & Sharma, 1998).

Although all fifteen components of emotional intelligence are important for the successful CEO, self-awareness, positive self-regard, empathy, assertiveness, and impulse control seem to be essential.

Self-Awareness. Self-awareness is the capacity to be aware of how you feel, why you are feeling that way, and the impact that the feeling may have on others. A CEO who is unaware of being angry, does not know what has provoked this anger, and is blind to the impact his angry attitude and sarcastic behavior have on others is always at risk for sabotaging relationships and alienating important internal or external stakeholders.

Case 5

After a disappointing performance review from her board, Lucille Perez strode into the weekly senior executives meeting. "Let's start now," she demanded—no "Good morning" or eye contact that characterized much of her usual style. Feeling perplexed and uncertain, Barry Coben, a senior executive inquired: "Is something the matter, Luce?"

"The matter is," she snapped, "that we should be focusing on last quarter instead of this small talk." Somewhat stung by this response, Barry replied: "You seem a little out of sorts."

"Look Barry, nothing is wrong with me. And this is not some kind of feel-good, new age, new wave group therapy. We're here to work, not socialize. Am I making myself clear?"

Lucille was unaware of how angry she was, blind to how her suppressed fury at the board was being redirected at her senior executives and unaware of the impact her barely concealed rage and sarcasm was having on them. She was also unaware of how her behavior alienated and caused caution among her senior people.

A CEO who is aware of being angry and knows why she is angry can use this knowledge to contain, tame, and diffuse this feeling. Recognizing the impact it may have on others, she can realign the relationship by saying something like, "I realize that I am irritable today; it has nothing to do with you or our relationship. I'll try to keep it from interfering with our working together."

Self-awareness is also a necessary ingredient in each of the other five key components. If you are unaware of how you are feeling or behaving, it is difficult to have healthy self-regard, to practice empathy, to recognize the difference between being assertive and being aggressive, or to recognize when you are reacting impulsively.

Positive Self-Regard. Lack of self-regard is a root cause in seriously limiting otherwise technically excellent workers from becoming star performers (Waldroop & Butler, 2000). CEOs with a positive self-regard are aware of their strengths, attributes, and abilities, as well as their shortcomings, foibles, and weaknesses yet nonetheless feel good about themselves. In other words, they like themselves warts and all, and they are aware of those warts. Self-regard is the ability to know one's strengths and weaknesses and feel confident with both. CEOs with low self-regard feel their strengths are not robust enough, cannot tolerate any foible whatsoever, or magnify the potency of their weaknesses.

CEOs who lack positive self-regard feel threatened by excellence in others, and so surround themselves with less competent colleagues and subordinates. Because criticism rattles their already shaky self-regard, they do not brook criticism well and tend to surround themselves with yes people. Since errors or wrong decisions shake their self-confidence further, they are unable to admit mistakes openly and tend to blame others when customers are lost or profits decline. This style creates a culture where blaming others is the norm and defensiveness replaces openness. A blaming and guarded culture undermines collaboration, innovation, and commitment.

Not surprisingly, some CEOs with an overabundance of self-confidence, like Richard King, the irrepressibly self-confident CEO described in case 2, can be understood as overcompensating for and keeping themselves unaware of their core feelings of low self-regard. They must deny the "warts" that all of us carry.

CEOs with healthy self-regard are able to be open about mistakes and do not blame others for their own errors. They show what British psychoanalyst and group specialist Michael Balint describes as "having the courage of one's own stupidity" (Balint, 1988). What Balint refers to is the capacity to be open and comfortable with being wrong. This capacity is crucial, because it allows the CEO to learn from mistakes, tolerate criticism, and be a role model for the workforce (Goffee & Jones, 2000). Rich was unable to do this.

This capacity also allows the CEO to tolerate the frustrations and anxieties associated with not knowing all the answers. Being comfortable in such a position gives them the ability to develop a reflective space, that is, an inner psychological sanctuary in which they can consider conflicting vistas, tolerate paradoxical perspectives, and creatively ponder and innovatively problem-solve to arrive at deeper and more meaningful solutions (Krantz, 1998).

Empathy. Empathy is the capacity to experience the world briefly from another person's perspective, even if you do not agree with these views, thoughts, and feelings. It is not what it would be like for *you* to be in their shoes, but rather knowing and appreciating what it is like for *them* to be in their shoes (Book, 1988). Empathy is a powerful, underused, and misunderstood interpersonal competency (Rogers & Roethlisberger, 1999; Stein & Book, 2000). It is the ability to read where the other person is coming from without commenting on the appropriateness or inappropriateness of the other person's perspective. Commonly, empathy is misunderstood to mean being "nice," "good," "compassionate," or "sympathetic." This is erroneous. Empathy is simply the capacity to know and briefly share another person's perspective, thoughts, and feelings.

When the CEO is listening empathically and putting into words his understanding of the other's perspective, thoughts, or feelings, the other person is left with an experience of having had the full and deep attention of the listener and being attended to and understood (Book, 1988; Goffee & Jones, 2000; Kruger, 1999; Stein & Book, 2000). This is what makes empathy such a powerful interpersonal tool: when the CEO puts into words his empathic understanding of the speaker's subjective experience, perspective, feelings, and beliefs, the speaker feels understood. And when people experience being understood in this manner, adversarial relationships are shifted to collaborative relationships, and already existing collaborative relationships are strengthened (Book, 1988; Stein & Book, 2000). Successful CEOs know that the key to having employees who actively want to follow and are inspired from within is based on strong, respectful relationships. The motto of respectful CEOs is, "People first, strategy second" (Charan & Colvin, 1999).

Case 6

The human resource manager, Shirley Duguid, was speaking to her HR vice president, Larry Manly. She was stating, somewhat irritably, "You've only been here for a short while, and I don't mean to seem complaining, but because you come from sales, I'm not sure you know how demanding this job can be. I'm reporting to you now, and I don't think you have any idea what HR is all about—the enormous demands and pressures we're under. You haven't been out in the field like we have. You're kind of a different breed. The previous VP of HR had worked herself up through HR, and so I just have concerns about how well you're going to understand what this job is like."

There are a number of responses Larry could have made. He might have said something like, "You're somewhat abrasive aren't you? I mean, I am your VP, and I feel you're being disrespectful." This may be true—the objective observer may agree that Shirley is being both irritable and disrespectful—but this is not an empathic comment, and truth or reality do not necessarily build strong relationships in all situations.

Larry might have stated, "Well, hold on a moment. Sales is a pretty demanding job too: lots of pressure and lots of politics. So how about giving me more of the benefit of the doubt?" This statement too is reality in that Larry had much pressure in his previous positions and perhaps he does deserve a chance. However, this reality is not a particularly helpful stance in a situation where an adversarial or conflictual relationship is starting to evolve.

Neither of these two statements is empathic. That is, although they may be true and an objective observer watching the exchange may state that Larry's response is truth or reality, neither is from Shirley's perspective. To be empathic, the statement must be from the position of the other. The power of empathic statements is that they allow the individual to whom they are directed to feel understood, calmed, and soothed. In feeling understood, the relationship shifts from adversarial to collaborative.

So what empathic statements might Larry say? Here are some statements that can be seen as empathic: "It sounds as if you're concerned about having to report to someone whom you see as having little knowledge or experience in your field," or "I guess you're wondering what good I'm going to be as a manager or supervisor because I come from a different division." In both statements, Larry is not agreeing that he is unable to understand the pressures and frustrations that Shirley faces, nor is he agreeing that he has nothing to offer her. He is simply putting into words his understanding of what Shirley is thinking and feeling from her perspective. As he does so, the prickliness that is beginning to emerge in the relationship is neutralized, and the unfolding of a more collaborative relationship takes place. This is quite different from what could have transpired had he responded with the unempathic first two statements.

Changing one's behavior, based on empathic understanding, can also strengthen contentious relationships, as the next case illustrates.

Case 7

In one of his coaching sessions with her, Dr. Errol Bright listened to Nancy Cutler, a thirty-two-year-old recently appointed senior manager, describe her beginning relationship with Eric Black, the sixty-one-year-old vice-president of marketing to whom she reported: "I can't stand that guy! He's got an ego as big as the ocean! Just because he's been in his position for twenty years, he thinks he knows everything! He has to have the last word. He's always right. His ideas are always the best. And

I'm left feeling that any ideas I come up with are useless! He is *so* impressed with himself he has no time to appreciate others!"

Errol responded, "It must be very frustrating to feel so belittled," an empathic statement that probably captured how Nancy was feeling. He went on to ask her a bit more about what she knew of Eric and then summarized back to her: "So, what I hear you saying is that Eric is sixty-one, hasn't had a promotion in the past twenty years, has retirement staring him in the face, and you're the third senior manager to come along in the past two years. And from what you told me, the other two women who previously held your position leapfrogged over Eric to become regional VPs. So from his perspective, how do you think he might be feeling?"

Nancy was silent for a moment and then replied, "When you put it that way, I guess he doesn't feel so good about himself. He probably feels overlooked, left behind, even envious of us younger, more successful women, and desperate for an acknowledgment that he has something to contribute."

Two weeks later when Errol met again with Nancy, she told him, "At our last couple of meetings, I've been asking Eric for his advice, talked about the amount of experience he's had, and have actually been able to let him know that I appreciate some of what he's told me. It's had a big impact on our relationship. My taking this new approach has resulted in his becoming more relaxed, less contentious, and able to listen to and even compliment me on a couple of occasions. And that's progress."

Nancy's new understanding that Eric's difficulty was not that he had a huge ego but rather that he had very little ego and felt undervalued and yearned for acknowledgment allowed her to change her behavior so that instead of confronting him, she could acknowledge him and some of his ideas and experience. This shifted their relationship from one of contention to one of collaboration and mutual respect. Feeling valued allowed Eric to cease having to have the last word, needing to prove that he was right, and allowed him to become an easier person with whom to work.

Assertiveness. Creating a culture that is facilitative also requires CEOs to have the capacity to be assertive. That is, they must have the ability to articulate clearly and defend their beliefs, wishes, desires, and vision while simultaneously taking into consideration the feelings of others. Assertive CEOs are unambivalently able to state their position and stand their ground in the face of opposing views. And they take this stand while simultaneously being sensitive to and respecting the views of others. In addition, because they listen to and assess differing perspectives, they also have the capacity to be flexible: to change their positions, views, and directions—not arbitrarily but because of new information from others or from the environment that they receive and evaluate. This capacity differentiates the assertive leader from an inflexible one.

CEOs who cannot clearly speak their mind and take a stand are being passive. And passive CEOs are at risk for giving in to the wishes, desires, and directions of others, so they cannot follow their own vision, stay the course, and ultimately lead. Without a strong (that is, assertive) leader, the organization flounders and is at risk of sinking.

CEOs who do not take into consideration the feelings of, and information from, others when pressing forth with their beliefs are being not assertive but rather authoritarian at best or aggressive at worst. Authoritarian CEOs are inflexible, controlling, and unreasonably demanding. Their inflexibility is costly because it means they are unable to change their stance despite incoming information that their direction is no longer viable. As leaders, they have difficulty tolerating change and are inept at shifting direction in response to a changing marketplace. As a result, they create a culture where opportunities are missed, innovation is avoided, and their competitive edge is blunted. Aggressive CEOs share these traits and in addition act and wield power in a tempestuous, uncaring, and destructive manner. When others experience this aggressiveness, they feel bulldozed and bullied. This communal experience creates a demoralized culture characterized by workers who passively underachieve or, worse, actively and vengefully sabotage the organization's objectives as a way of getting back at the aggressive CEO. This behavior undercuts their own personal goals as well as the organization's success.

Impulse Control. Successful CEOs have the capacity to rein in the temptation for immediate response. They look before they leap. They do not become overwhelmed with pressures or reflexively ride off in all directions at once. They are often described as calm under pressure, cool-headed during tense situations, and appropriately thoughtful while balancing intense demands. They can remain unperturbed by questions without immediate answers and can weigh options despite the pressure to react. Having the capacity to control the impulse to action and the ability to curtail reflexive responses allows these leaders to create a reflective space, essential for pondering crucial, complex issues and developing creative, sophisticated, meaningful—and therefore effective—solutions. In the immediate aftermath of the September 11, 2001, annihilation of the World Trade Center and the attack on the Pentagon, President George W. Bush showed admirable impulse control. He did not react reflexively through impulsive retaliation, but rather informed the world that there would be a substantial response, signaling that his stance would not be one of passivity and showing that he would not react with a simple, one-dimensional solution that did not consider the complex implications of such a response. As a result, he and his team were able to develop and implement a complex plan of response and retaliation while simultaneously maintaining a differentiation between terrorists presenting themselves as Muslims and the Muslim community at large.

Leaders who become quite busy through action deprive themselves of developing this psychological sanctuary that is necessary for pondering complex, multilayered solutions. CEOs without this capacity and are instead impulsive are often described as hot-tempered, tempestuous, reflexive, and not considered in their responses, and consequently they frequently miss the mark. Missing the mark translates to not achieving organizational objectives and marketplace presence.

Interventions

It is a daunting challenge for subordinates, even those who are seasoned senior executives, to approach CEOs about their personality types or EQ competencies. Often, they choose to hunker down and work around their CEO or look elsewhere for work opportunities. For those who decide to discuss style or EQ with the CEO, it is best to have a fairly positive relationship with the CEO, choose a time when the CEO seems least mired in difficulties, and then focus on the benefits such style brings to the organization before describing the cost that the style might be having on the bottom line. (More detailed information on how to address these issues is detailed in Chapters Six, Seven, Ten, and Twenty-Three.)

HOW ORGANIZATIONAL STRUCTURES AFFECT CULTURE

Although the personality type and EQ of the CEO are crucial in creating a facilitative culture, this in itself is not enough. To ensure that the organization develops a culture that fuels success requires the presence of clearly defined and well-communicated organizational structures: a mission; organizational chart; job titles, description, and activities (roles); authority and accountability inherent in those roles; and lines of authority and accountability up and down the organizational chart. Organizational structures also encompass formal, objective performance reviews and disseminated criteria on which those reviews are based; multidirectional channels of communication; and selection, orientation, and training programs.

These organizational structures provide standardization and clarity about who is accountable for doing what; who is accountable to whom; how, when, and by what criteria formal feedback about actual role performance is carried out; and how communication flows multidirectionally throughout the organization. These structures are critical for the ongoing success of the company since they ensure organizational stability and continuity. It is this stability that allows the organization to survive the comings and goings of its workforce and to coordinate dealings with its internal and external environment (Stoner & Wankel, 1986).

Such structures are too frequently wrongly viewed as rigid, hierarchical, and command-and-control relics (Book, 2000). They are also misperceived as obstacles to managing change, organizational flexibility, and innovative thinking. These are misconceptions (Drucker, 1998). In fact, it is only through such structures that communal understanding and clarity of mission, roles and reporting relationships, planning, implementation, benchmarking, and outcome monitoring can successfully take place. Clarity of role, authority, accountability, and communication allows the organization to be flexible without being impulsive, permits innovation without arbitrariness, and encourages appropriate bottom-up decision making without a risk of fragmentation.

When organizational structures are lacking, ambiguity over role, goal, authority, and accountability occurs, which is amplified by failure in multidirectional communication. With this degree of confusion, workers at all levels of the organization are at risk for experiencing significant anxiety and uncertainty.

When human beings experience ongoing feelings of anxiety and uncertainty, a peculiar psychological phenomenon begins to appear: employees begin to develop distorted views of even an emotionally intelligent CEO with a healthy personality type. Simultaneously, they develop a distorted view of themselves and their colleagues. This phenomenon puts the CEO at risk of having his or her behavior misinterpreted and motives misconstrued. For example, in such a situation, a CEO whom any objective third party would judge as dependable, honest, caring, and without guile is at risk of having his behavior misinterpreted as untrustworthy and their motives misconstrued as self-serving (Kernberg, 1998). At the same time, despite their own strengths and abilities, such workers may view themselves as being at risk and under attack by the CEO and his henchmen.

When only some organizational structures are absent, even the subliminal levels of anxiety and uncertainty that emerge can profoundly cloud workers' perceptions of their CEO and of themselves. According to Wilfred Bion, the British psychoanalyst and group scholar, this shift in perception tends to occur along two directions: the CEO is viewed as all-powerful while employees see themselves as inept (what Bion calls dependency basic assumption), or the CEO is viewed as vindictive and the workforce feels persecuted and at the mercy of the CEO and coworkers whom they perceive as "on his side" (the fight-or-flight basic assumption; Bion, 1968; de Board, 1978).

Dependency Basic Assumption

In this scenario, the lack of organizational structures leads to ambiguities, which stir up feelings of anxiety and uncertainty among the workforce. Swayed by these feelings, workers commonly begin to turn to their leader, the CEO, with the misperception that only he can remedy this ambiguity, save them from this uncertainty, look after them, and solve all workplace issues. Simultaneously, they begin to behave as if they are unable to affect any solutions and are without any personal resources. Ultimately, they abdicate more and more responsibility for solving any workplace issues to the CEO and believe that their salvation, and the organization's salvation, rests entirely on his shoulders, while behaving as if they are inept and inadequate.

Such groupthink, that is, uncritical acceptance of extreme beliefs by the full workforce, spreads among and affects employees at all levels of the organization. In the throes of groupthink, the workforce behaves as if the leader is omnipotent. He is experienced as a godlike figure who will take on all of their tasks, regardless of whether he is emotionally intelligent and of how they value delegation and decision sharing. Workers increasingly experience themselves as emotionally inept, and the culture becomes one where growing dependency replaces independence, passivity takes the place of assertiveness, and accurate perception of the CEO's role gives way to unrealistic rescue fantasies wherein the CEO solves all of their problems. In such a situation, the organization's effectiveness is severely undermined.

Case 8

Nina Svensen described her mounting irritation with her senior vice presidents: "They should be responsible people able to carry out and manage the process that all of us have agreed to embark on. But more and more, they come back to me asking questions, wanting directions, and behaving far more junior than they should. I just don't understand why they can't implement these things on their own without being baby-sat—or carried—by me. I'm beginning to feel like they're reverse-delegating everything!"

One of her vice presidents, Serge Laurent, had a different experience and perspective: "Nina doesn't have enough formal meetings with us or communications channels to us to communicate what she wants. So I've become somewhat cautious about what I'm doing and find myself checking with her more than I like just to make sure I'm on the right track. This checking undercuts my self-confidence, and *that* makes me turn to her even more!"

This scenario captures an ongoing process that had spread throughout the organization: subordinates turning to supervisors for answers that in fact they are able to accomplish, but doing so out of a pervasive sense of uncertainty that reflects the absence of structures that facilitate that they're doing it all wrong. This situation captures the essence of a work group functioning in a basic assumption mode. Subordinates feeling pressured out of a sense of uncertainty to turn to their superior for the go-ahead. This process undercuts subordinates' self-confidence, making it more difficult for them to make decisions on their own and causing them to turn even more frequently to their superiors to solve issues that they had the knowledge and skills to resolve.

The root of this difficulty lays not with the CEO's style or EQ but rather reflects the organization's response to the lack of formal two-way communication channels and formal biweekly meetings. Without such structures, little information concerning the progress and direction of projects could occur, and the uncertainty associated with this lack of vital information induced regression within the organization that resulted in individuals' feeling inept, while increasingly turning to their superiors to solve all problems. Once this root cause was discovered and formal communication channels and business meetings implemented, anxieties diminished, clarity emerged, and the workforce functioned in an appropriate, autonomous manner.

Fight-or-Flight Basic Assumption

An even more destructive form of groupthink takes hold in situations of anxiety and uncertainty when employees begin to view distortedly even an impeccable CEO with high EQ as deceptive, duplicitous, manipulative, and vindictive. Under the sway of their distorted perception, workers at all levels simultaneously experience themselves as helpless, unsafe, in danger, and at risk of the CEO's arbitrary vindictiveness. This groupthink spreads so that others in the workplace—perhaps those who have been seen talking to the CEO—are viewed as "on his side" and "one of the enemy."

Case 9

Reginald Tsu, the easy-going, amiable CEO of Work Wearables, a manufacturer of clothing for the construction industry, was a firm believer that workers gave their best on a level playing field. For him, hierarchical structures, with superiors and subordinates, inhibited creativity and fostered rigidity. To ensure a healthy sense of spontaneity and to offset bureaucratization, Reginald flattened the organizational chart, put in place peer and self-supervision, and created multitask roles so that each employee had a primary function but could also fill in and carry out two different roles.

Although this seemed democratic on paper, the loss of clarity, role ambiguity, lack of knowledgeable supervision, and absence of clear channels of communication resulted in confusion and anxiety. This state resulted in a lack of cohesion, increasing workplace errors, and escalating inefficiencies, all of which were responded to by mutual blaming and disorganization. These powerful feelings interfered with efficiencies and ultimately played a major dynamic in the collapse of Work Wearables.

Brenda Romero, senior sales manager, lamented, "We had such a great product, but communication was so poor I never knew whether the products our division sold got produced, let alone delivered. And then the customer would dump on us for not coming through with the product! All I heard was how badly we were performing. Then I discovered that at least a quarter of our sales personnel had been cross-trained to market, and the marketing VP thought she had ultimate authority over them. When I found that out, I became enraged. I told her to stop stealing my people and told my staff not to have anything to do with her whatsoever!"

Without appropriate lines of communication, one division had little idea of what was happening in other divisions on whom it relied. With no clarity around roles, workers did not know for what they were responsible. Multitasking led to managers' fighting with each other over which subordinates were accountable for what and to whom. And the escalating sense of confusion and tension led to angry accusations and irresponsible blaming. Soon, the intensity of suspicion reached such a level that a number of senior managers began to believe that Reginald had set this situation up purposefully to demoralize "weekend" managers whom he wanted to get rid of so that he could promote "certain" other managers. This lack of collaboration, the secretiveness, blame, and accusations that went on intradepartmentally and the view of Reginald as malevolent led to enormous inefficiencies and ultimately to the loss of significant market share for Work Wearables.

This phenomenon began to unfold with Brenda Romero. Recall that she stated, "I told her to stop stealing my people, and I told my staff not to have anything to do with her whatsoever!" With these statements, Brenda illustrates how she has developed a strong but faulty view of the marketing VP as a devious, underhanded woman, out to steal her workers. In fact, it was not this way at all. The marketing VP was neither devious nor underhanded. She was simply caught up in the same confusion and uncertainty that emerged from the lack of organizational structures as was Brenda herself.

In this situation, an obstructive culture emerges as suspicion replaces trust, secrecy swamps openness, closed cliques supplant team building, and a posture of defensive rigidity infiltrates adaptive flexibility.

How the Basic Assumption Group Weakens Even the Emotionally Intelligent Leader

The absence of organizational structures stirs up a sense of anxiety and uncertainty within the workforce, and this pervasive feeling gives rise to a distortion of how the workforce sees its CEO and how it also views itself. Its groupthink then results in a culture that seriously interferes with the efficiency of the organization. There is another linked phenomenon that may occur in either of these two situations. Ironically, and worse still, employees who view the CEO in a distorted way may unwittingly provoke the leader to behave just as they misperceive her to be (Kernberg, 1998). For example, a trustworthy CEO who is continuously misperceived as duplicitous is at risk of subliminally being pressed into behaving in such secretive and suspicious ways. Unfortunately, this further fosters organizational ineptitude.

Case 10

Candice Smithers had recently been recruited as CEO to replace Peter Kuchinski, who was let go in part for his duplicitous, secretive, and exclusive style that alienated most of the senior executives as they became increasingly aware of his untrustworthiness and lack of integrity. These senior executives, sensitive to any discrepancies between what Candice said and what she did, and understandably wary of her motives, scanned for evidence of untrustworthiness. Much of their behavior could be seen as the response of "once bitten, twice shy."

Initially inclusive and open, Candice began to smart from having her suggestions so scrutinized, explored, poked, and prodded. She began to feel irritated by the time she spent providing her executives with details, responding to their questions as to why she chose to do X rather than Y. Within a few months, she began to think that to work more efficiently and cut through the constant questioning of her motives, she would take it on herself to make a minor decision: renovating the cafeteria. She thought this was a benign decision and that the entire workforce would view her renovated, updated cafeteria as a reflection of her interest and concern for them.

When she sent out a memo of this decision and its implementation one week prior to the cafeteria's closing for renovations, all staff responded angrily to what they saw as her secretive, excluding action that so reminded them of the prior CEO's untrustworthy manipulativeness. They also worried about whose space would be abducted to enlarge the cafeteria and from whose budget monies would be ravished to pay for this undertaking.

Candice's motive was to illustrate how caring and giving she could be. But under the rain of the workforce's expectations that she might behave in secretive and therefore untrustworthy ways (and without knowing it), she was induced to behave the way staff feared: secretive and excluding, which further fueled their fears that she was behaving unilaterally and in ways that would cost them space and money.

Ineffective Organizational Structures

The existence of essential organizational structures is so crucial that in their absence, even the presence of an emotionally intelligent CEO will be insufficient to develop or sustain a facilitative culture. Lack of such structures stirs anxiety and uncertainty within the group. Under the influence of such effects, a regressive group process emerges whereby the workforce may distortedly view their CEO and themselves in highly unrealistic ways. Commonly, they see their CEO as a rescuer who will cure all their work problems while simultaneously viewing themselves as passive, unable, and inept. In this situation, the culture becomes one of worried dependency with the hope that some superior figure will be the answer to all workplace difficulties. Or they may misperceive the CEO as vindictively vengeful while viewing themselves as unfairly under attack. Here, the culture becomes one of secrecy, fear, and persecution.

When such a culture exists, it is essential to assess whether this reflects the absence of particular organizational structures—and if so, address that absence—before evaluating the role of the CEO's personality type and emotional intelligence.

OTHER FACTORS THAT INFLUENCE CULTURE

Some other factors also have an influence on culture and therefore organizational success (Kernberg, 1998).

Factors Affecting the CEO

The CEO may experience stress because of the unique characteristics of this role. First, the role requires that the CEO be friendly with senior managers but not have close personal friendships. A degree of separation is required if the CEO is to effectively and objectively fulfill the role of performance reviews or promoting and firing. This stance is captured by the expression, "The captain always dines alone." This characteristic potentially deprives the CEO of close, confidential relationships that many others in the workforce may experience. This state leaves the CEO at risk for feelings of loneliness that might affect her capacity to carry out her role effectively. Similarly, she may interpret the role of CEO as requiring that she must always present herself as independent, and therefore not requiring emotional support, and this may frustrate her dependency needs common to all human beings, further accentuating feelings of loneliness.

Because of the authority invested in their roles, CEOs may be experienced by others as formidable individuals, and senior managers may hesitate to give essential, open, and constructively critical feedback, regardless of how open, transparent, and eager for such feedback the CEO is. As a result, the CEO may be unsure how effectively she is functioning, and this uncertainty can obstruct her efficiency.

Factors Affecting the Organization

The culture of the organization is also affected by its resources. If resources are not available to carry out required activities successfully, the workforce will not only feel unsuccessful, they will also feel a sense of mounting frustration, anger, helplessness, or suspicion. It would be like informing the individual in the role of secretary that his work consists of word processing at sixty words per minute, yet not furnishing him with a word processor.

The product also influences the culture of any organization. The culture of an organization that markets machine guns is different, by virtue of that product, from an organization that markets dolls. The former might have a culture that is infiltrated by conflicts and issues about aggression, while the latter may have a culture that blends the importance of appearance with issues about femininity.

The culture of an organization is pivotal in defining what behaviors and attitudes are silently encouraged or forbidden. Organizations with a facilitative culture encourage innovation, spark interest, promote openness, and create a forum where constructive criticism or open debate is welcomed. These characteristics sharpen its competitive edge and promote success. Obstructive cultures discourage innovation, strangle communication, eschew openness, and fragment teamwork, all leading to a company that does not measure up to the competition and is at risk for failing.

Whether the culture fuels success or burdens the company toward failure is a reflection of two factors: the CEO, particularly this person's personality type and emotional intelligence, and the presence of pivotal organizational structures within the company itself. These factors affect each other and together mold a culture that encourages success or points toward failure.

References and Additional Sources

American Psychiatric Association. (1994). *Diagnostic criteria from DSM-IV.* Washington, DC: Author.

Balint, M. (1988). *The doctor, his patient and the illness.* Madison, CT: International Universities Press.

Barling, J., Slater, F., & Kelloway, E. K. (2000). Transformational leadership and emotional intelligence: An exploratory study. *Leadership and Organization Development Journal, 21,* 157–161.

Bion, W. (1968). *Experiences in groups.* New York: Tavistock.

Book, H. E. (1988). Empathy: Misconceptions and misuses in psychotherapy. *American Journal of Psychiatry, 145,* 420–424.

Book, H. E. (2000, Sept.–Oct.). The emotionally intelligent organization. *Ivey Business Journal,* pp. 44–47.

Charan, R., & Colvin, G. (1999). Why CEOs fail. *Fortune, 139*(12), 69–82.

Chrisman, J. J., Chua, J. H., & Sharma, P. (1998). Important attributes of successors in family businesses: An exploratory study. *Family Business Review, 11,* 19–34.

Collins, J. (2001). Level 5 leadership: The triumph of humility and fierce resolve. *Harvard Business Review, 79*(1), 67–76.

Cooper, R. K., & Sawaf, A. (1996). *Executive EQ: Emotional intelligence in leadership and organizations.* New York: Grosset/Putnam.

Czander, W. M. (1993). *The psychodynamics of work and organizations.* New York: Guilford Press.

de Board, R. (1978). *The psychoanalysis of organizations: A psychoanalytic approach to behaviour in groups and organizations.* New York: Tavistock.

Drucker, P. F. (1998). Management's new paradigms. *Forbes, 162*(7), 152–176.

George, J. (2000). Emotions and leadership: The role of emotional intelligence. *Human Relations, 53,* 1027–1055.

Goffee, R., & Jones, G. (2000). Why should anyone be led by you? *Harvard Business Review, 78*(5), 63–70.

Goleman, D. J. (1998). *Working with emotional intelligence.* New York: Bantam Books.

Kanter, R. M. (2000). The enduring skills of change leaders. *Ivey Business Journal, 64*(5), 31–36.

Kernberg, O. (1998). *Ideology, conflict, and leadership in groups and organizations.* New Haven, CT: Yale University Press.

Kets de Vries, M.F.R. (2001). *The leadership mystique: A user's manual for the human enterprise.* London: Financial Times/Prentice Hall.

Kotter, J. (2001). What leaders really do. *Harvard Business Review, 79*(11), 85–96.

Krantz, J. (1998). Anxiety and the new order. In E. Klein, F. Gabelnick, & P. Herr (Eds.), *The psychodynamics of leadership.* Madison, CT: Psychosocial Press.

Kruger, P. (1999, June). A leader's journey. *Fast Company,* pp. 116–129.

Oldham, J. M., & Morris, L. B. (1991). *Personality self-portrait: Why you think, work, love, and act the way you do.* New York: Bantam Books.

Rogers, C. R., & Roethlisberger, F. J. (1999). Barriers and gateways to communication. In F. Bartolome (Ed.), *The articulate executive: Orchestrating effective communication.* Boston: Harvard Business School Press.

Saarni, C. (1999). *The development of emotional competence.* New York: Guilford Press.

Sperry, L. (1996). *Corporate therapy and consulting.* New York: Brunner/Mazel.

Stein, S. J., & Book, H. E. (2000). *The EQ edge: Emotional intelligence and your success.* Toronto: Stoddart Publishing.

Stoner, J.A.F., & Wankel, C. (1986). *Management* (3rd ed.). Upper Saddle River, NJ: Prentice Hall.

Waldroop, J., & Butler, T. (2000, Sept.–Oct.). Managing away bad habits. *Harvard Business Review, 78*(5), 89–98.

CHAPTER TWELVE

A Comprehensive Overview
of Organizational Change

Gerald A. Kraines

*Leadership is about increasing the adaptive capacity of a business organization
and its people. To remain competitive, individuals and organizations must
adapt to rapidly changing events and environments. In order to do this, managers
need to understand the implicit expectations people bring to their organizations
and simultaneously address, understand, and renegotiate these changing
expectations. The most effective business leaders maintain an adaptive, rather
than a reactive, posture. They do more than manage organizational change;
they lead change. They are continually tuned in to what is coming next.*

It's a fact of business life today that organizations change. But there are many
ways that they change and many different ways that employees react. Understanding the forces at play are essential to effective change management.

Case 1

Francis Petro, a brilliant CEO and exemplary leader, was brought in to turn around an
international manufacturer of specialty metals. About six months into an organizational project with a management consulting firm, he asked the senior consultant to
go out on the shop floor to see how things were progressing. The consultant spoke
with a number of workers to ask how they viewed the recent changes. Here is what
the consultant heard from two machine operators.

The first operator was clearly bitter: "I'm gonna leave as soon as I can find another
job. It used to be fun coming to work. We'd catch up on the scores from the weekend
games for a while, talk about some of the great plays, and plan for our fishing trips.
Then we'd do some production until break. After coffee and some smokes, we'd do a
little more work, maybe break early for lunch. Now, with the new management, we've

---

Portions of this chapter are adapted from work by Gerald A. Kraines and the Levinson Institute
in Boston.

got to be at work at the machine when the bell rings, push hard all morning, maybe even miss the break, and have a shortened lunch if we encounter problems. Even with my seniority and great benefits, I'm leaving."

The second operator was more typical. "Boy, this place was going downhill. Most of the employees came to work to catch up on their sleep. I was afraid the plant would be shut down, and the whole town would be in trouble. Then Frank came in and shaped things up in a hurry. The supervisors got the message quickly after two were suspended and another one got fired for letting down on safety. Now the super meets with the whole team every Tuesday morning for thirty minutes at change of shift. He fills us in on the improvement projects and the new safety campaign, lets us know how our delivery performance targets are coming, and lists the new sales and the customer feedback. He asks for our ideas and listens carefully. He seems to really think we have something to contribute. He's on top of the problems and suggestions we raise; you can see how much better the equipment is running. Every time he walks by my station, he asks how I'm doing, if he can help with anything, and asks for my own ideas about how to make things work better. Last week, he asked if I'd be interested in taking some courses at the community college—at the company's expense—'cause he thinks I have the potential to move up. You know, it's really exciting what's happening around here!"

Notice the difference in the two responses. Despite what many people think, leading organizational change is not a popularity contest. It is about leveraging the full potential of people and other resources in order to deliver maximum value to shareholders and customers. The best leaders do not worry about whether people like them. It is much more important that their people respect the fact that they are performing serious work together. As Petro said quite prophetically, "We're engaged in economic warfare with the competition. My job is to make sure my troops are fit for battle, to keep them safe and in top fighting order. Those who only want to play can do so elsewhere; my troops respect me and love to win! I expect a lot, but I give a lot. I have a grand-daughter who loves me; I don't need my people to love me. When they deliver to standard, I let them know how good a job they're doing. When they surprise me, I give 'em hell. They all know it ain't personal."

The two machine operators described two vastly different perspectives on the changes Petro initiated in his company. The first operator felt betrayed. The second operator felt vindicated, relieved, and extremely positive about the company and its future. How can two people, working together in the same company and undergoing the same organizational transformation, experience things so differently? It has everything to do with changing the psychological contract and building a culture of adaptive readiness.

Employees in Petro's company who were comfortable and pleased with the existing contract, lasting over a generation and supporting an attitude of employee entitlement, were angered with a change based on accountability and genuine leadership. Those who were dismayed by the danger previous management had placed the company in welcomed the change. But no matter where people stand, change always represents loss coupled with new demands and that amounts to a violation of the psychological contract.

LEVERAGING A COMPANY'S POTENTIAL

Consider the kind of productivity a company could achieve if its leaders leveraged their employees' full potential and maintained it during a period of change. All senior managers fervently desire hard-working and committed employees, especially during times of change. We read articles about companies where people spend extraordinary numbers of hours in their attempt to develop a product in record time so as to beat out their competition. We hear stories about employees so consumed with turning around the performance of their companies that they appear to be thinking about how to improve company operations twenty-four hours a day, seven days a week. A few companies are legendary for their consistently superior levels of product quality and customer service that only a truly and extraordinarily committed staff can deliver. Legendary successes from companies such as L. L. Bean, Procter & Gamble, Southwest Airlines, and Toyota immediately come to mind.

Yet in many companies, one hears loud complaints from middle and senior managers about the lack of commitment, the low morale, and the strong cynicism among their employees. More and more companies are bemoaning their brain drain—the difficulty in attracting, engaging, and retaining top-quality talent. During the late 1990s, much of this problem was assigned to dot-com fever and the lure of fast money. Even in today's uncertain economy, people are becoming more aware of—and dissatisfied with—the working situations they find in their current positions. But is the issue really greener grass or a more fundamental lack of understanding of the basis for gaining employee commitment in the first place?

Most business school programs on management will tell their students that the principal task of a leader is to motivate people. Scan any Internet search engine for books on leadership, and you will find the five or ten or twenty sure-fire secrets for motivating a workforce. Read the promotional promises from consulting companies specializing in compensation, and they explain how to use rewards to motivate people, with complex formulas tied to strategic deliverables. Inherent in all of these assertions is the assumption that workers need to be motivated—that they are basically inert or motionless automatons waiting to be bribed or cajoled into action. And we all know what recalcitrant mammal is most commonly thought of as requiring carrots and sticks to get it moving. Do we really think of our employees as jackasses?

In 1973, Harry Levinson wrote *The Great Jackass Fallacy* to call attention to these superficial and mistaken notions about human motivation. People are not lifeless robots or computers. Rather, we are complex, multidimensional, intentional creatures. We are intrinsically motivated by universal basic human needs as well as by highly specific individual desires, drives, and aspirations. It is demeaning to say that managers must motivate their people.

Managers must instead create the working conditions and sense of transcendent purpose that will harness and focus the natural enthusiastic commitment that all people bring with them. Managers must forge psychological contracts with their people backed up by a lasting commitment to help them succeed in ways that matter to them.

Before managers can lead change, they need to explore various myths and misconceptions commonly held about what employees really want from their organizations and why they are self-limiting, at best, and self-defeating, at worst. Now the discussion shifts to the fundamental principles and applications that allow managers to negotiate, and continually renegotiate, healthy and meaningful psychological contracts with their people—contracts that will ensure their full and enthusiastic commitment to support the organization in succeeding in its goals.

MOVING TO ACTION

When you think back over all your days of getting up in the morning before going to work, do any stand out as brighter and more energizing than others? Have there been times when you not only got up without the usual dread but actually felt eager to rush to work and resume something exciting and challenging from the day before? When you look back at your years of working and reflect on some of the more memorable days, can you recall moments of satisfaction and accomplishment that made a major effort worthwhile? These questions are designed to help you zero in on the heart of human motivation, an essential concept for managing change.

Motivation literally means "moving to action." What are the specific forces within the human mind that move people to action? Although there are many schools of thought that have something to say about this question, a simple set of concepts is most instructive. For the most part, human motivation comes from within. Each of us has a unique personal and internal sense of what kind of existence is ideal, although we are rarely consciously aware of it. Where does it come from? Psychology has taught us that as young children, we readily identify some of the core traits, qualities, and aspirations of the adults who surround us and on whom we depend. We internalize these attributes (usually after idealizing these adults), and they begin to form our own web of goals and aspirations.

As we grow older, we begin to make choices and, without realizing it, compare the alternatives and their meanings against this growing sense of our ideal self. When we move in one direction and are successful, we feel good. If unsuccessful, we typically feel we have failed ourselves. This desire to live up to our own sense of what it means to be good, successful, or true to oneself is the most important motivator of all human needs. But it is not the only one.

We also have powerful needs to master, to be challenged, to grow, and to compete in addition to our needs to be liked, recognized, and admired. These basic human drives are largely innate, constituting the basic temperament we see in very young children. They are also significantly shaped by the people around us and by society in general. We learn early on how our own culture views these drives and offers strong incentives to modify their expression in ways that others will accept. Acceptance by adults is especially important to children, and acceptance by peers is especially important to adolescents.

We also learn quite early whether we experience people as reliable, secure, and trustworthy, especially when we are heavily dependent on them to meet our needs. Our capacity to trust, on the one hand, and our tendency to feel guilty, on the other, are strongly shaped during the first several years of life. All of this learning and the way it moves us to action come together in shaping our view of the world. It also comes together in the way people view us. Our personality, in the end, is the composite picture of all of these attitudes and behaviors. Our personality is who we are.

Managers who are about to lead significant organizational change must understand who their people really are. We cannot accurately know where someone is going unless we first know where that person is coming from. Forging strong, mutually successful psychological contracts with subordinates requires an understanding of how each one of them views becoming successful. This is because the psychological contract reflects a basic truth about human relationships: the degree to which an individual will commit to support another in becoming successful depends largely on how much the other individual demonstrates her commitment to making him successful.

FORGING PSYCHOLOGICAL CONTRACTS

What are the basic outlines of the psychological contract? How is it affected by organizational transformation? How should we examine the nature of the relationship between a manager and her subordinates and, at a higher level, between a company and its people? Harry Levinson et al. (1962), who introduced the term psychological contract in the 1950s, identified three dimensions of the company-employee and manager-subordinate relationship:

1. There must be a strong enough bond, built on common purpose and values, to want to work together.

2. There must be a constructive yet respectful distance between the two.

3. There must be a mutual commitment to support the legitimate needs of one another during times of change.

The first prerequisite is common purpose. This is what most companies are trying to define when they craft a statement of purpose and mission. It is an attempt to describe "goodness," a set of values and aspirations that will provide a large enough umbrella for people to want to huddle under together. How well does your company's mission statement speak to you? Is it specific enough to have personal meaning or so broad and filled with vague generalities that it might as well be motherhood and apple pie? As employees, we want to know what our company stands for and will not stand for, because we want to know whether it feels right to each of us. If you cannot relate to it at all or, worse, if you strongly disapprove of what your company stands for, no amount of forcing the engagement is going to correct for the misfit. Attempting to force a square peg into a round hole always creates pain and friction and never really yields a good fit.

Second, there is the mutual need for a healthy distance (control, recognition, and privacy) between the company and its employees. The employer has every right to decide on strategy, plans, and the specific assignments to meet those plans in order to meet shareholder expectations. Yet the employee, who has been hired to exercise judgment and add value while delivering on those assignments, properly wants to understand the bigger picture, to provide input into shaping it, and to have an active role in helping the manager define those assignments. And once accepting the assignment, the employee needs the resources and authority that were agreed on and proper processes and working conditions with which to meet his or her accountabilities. "If you [my manager] are going to decide on my accountabilities and are going to hold me accountable, then you must give me the necessary authority and control to meet them."

Similarly, every employer has the right to expect that its employees will attempt to represent its goals, means, and values well to others both inside and outside the company. Differences of opinions will be dealt with maturely, candidly, and openly, and employees will show respect for the diverse range of points of view of others. Employees will not speak ill of the company or people within the company, and they will not undermine others by going behind their backs. Employees have the right to know where they stand with the company, to have their contributions properly acknowledged and their legitimate needs for recognition, support, and development respected. It takes months and years to build trust and mutual respect, and only minutes to destroy it.

There must also be a reciprocal understanding of, and respect for, others' legitimate needs for privacy. Employers have trade secrets, confidential strategies, and even skeletons in the closet that they have a right to expect their employees will respect. Employees need to have a life of their own outside the company and a right to a certain measure of privacy inside the company. The recent wave of terrorist acts coupled with e-mail and Web-site-tracking initiatives have created a significant backlash of mistrust, resentment, and fear among employees. Although the appropriate solution for these problems is not yet clear, managers must realize that encroaching on their subordinates' privacy and sense of well-being profoundly strains the psychological contract.

The third dimension has to do with a mutual agreement to support the other during times requiring significant change. Employees should understand that the organization must respond accurately to changing environmental demands. They cannot expect that the organization will maintain the status quo just to support their personal comfort level. The organization's mandated role is to adapt and evolve in relationship to the business environment in order to support the shareholders, meet the needs of customers, ward off the competition, and support the long-term needs of its employees.

At the same time, there needs to be an understanding by management that as the organization changes and expects its people to change, the organization has a reciprocal obligation to support its people in addressing the change requirements: "If you want me to accept the changes, help me understand what's happened that forced this change, what alternatives you considered, why we'll be better off with this plan, and why we should see it as worthwhile to hang in there."

The psychological contract is a way of ensuring mutual and reciprocal trust and commitment. With solid psychological contracts, work provides people with meaning and purpose, the challenge and stimulation of purposeful activities, the support of others working on those activities, the potential of success, and the reward and good feeling of working well with others. Think of a psychological contract as the negotiation between two porcupines huddling together for warmth on a freezing winter night. The trick is for them to get close enough to share their body heat without getting so close as to hurt each other.

A violated psychological contract can occur whenever there is a significant organizational change, whether the violation was intended or not. When people and their organization are in sync, even with tremendous workloads, people feel good about themselves and the company. When the aspirations, values, and modes of behaving change, people not only experience loss but also a basic fracture of their sense of self and their sense of trust in the organizational relationship.

To forge a new psychological contract, managers need to know that this implicit psychological contract exists and remain aware of their peoples' unspoken (and often unwitting) expectations. They must be on the lookout for signs of a violated contract, such as betrayal, anger, hurt, and withdrawal. It is critical that they acknowledge the altered contract and its impact on people. Then they need to put forth, in active two-way discussion, their new assumptions, new expectations of what can and cannot be negotiated, and what can (and cannot) be changed. In order to recover the trust and confidence of their people, managers must convince them that proceeding down this new path is good, fair, and the best way to ensure employees' future success.

Psychological contracts exist between all people who find themselves in some ongoing mutually dependent relationship: husbands and wives, parents and children, teachers and students, teammates on a basketball team. It is also true in many kinds of work organizations other than managerial leadership systems. There are psychological contracts in partnerships, in churches, in universities, and among medical staff members in a hospital. What is unique about the psychological contracts between managers and their subordinates is that they are influenced strongly by the accountability relationship that exists between them.

Managers are inescapably accountable for what their subordinates do and how well they do it, and ensuring that they do it within defined boundaries. This is not true, for instance, between a managing partner of a law firm and another partner within the firm. Partners are the owners of the partnership; hence, they are also its shareholders and members of its governing body. The authority a managing partner has over any one partner is quite limited and principally consists of personal persuasion. The managing partner is elected by all of the partners and thus has political authority in relation to them, whereas a true manager (in a managerial hierarchy) is appointed into a role (by his own manager) that delegates authority to him over every subordinate and holds him accountable for those subordinates.

While the relationship between a manager and subordinate is intimate (the psychological contract requires an accurate understanding of each subordinate as an individual), it is not personal. Managers must accept that they are accountable for their people's effectiveness. If a subordinate cannot carry his own weight in the role, even after proper coaching, the manager must remove him from the role. As Michael Corleone says in *The Godfather,* "It's not personal, Sonny. It's strictly business."

MANAGING FOR CHANGING REALITIES

Managers and employees need to know that employment is not an entitlement; it is a privilege. This is especially important to remember during times of change. Changes can present the opportunity for people to gain a greater measure of security than they would have if working for themselves as entrepreneurs. They have a guaranteed salary, benefits, and opportunities to be challenged, to master, and to grow. In return, they must commit to add value to the organization at a level consistent with the size of role they are given and to honor their commitments with no surprises. They must continually earn the right to remain in their roles—even to remain employed. Again, it is a simple, mature accountability contract.

In addition, managers understand that people will fully invest themselves and their capabilities only when they see they can do good work, receive fair recognition for it, and develop their full potential. This then becomes the basis for negotiating a sound psychological contract.

There are four sets of working conditions that if fully achieved will ensure the full engagement of employee commitment to support any organizational change: personal security, personal value, effective leadership, and a culture of fairness.

Personal Security

Now, more than ever before, if the number one concern of the employing company were anything other than providing a safe and healthy working environment for its employees, those employees would feel like expendable commodities. "If you don't value my need to stay healthy, support my family, and continue to grow with the company, I guess I'll need to hold back some and look out for myself." Similarly, if the company appears to make only expedient change decisions (rather than well-conceived ones), not designed to ensure the long-term health and perpetuation of the organization, employees should rightly question whether to invest their mental capital and career aspirations there. "If I want a secure future for myself and my family, I better look elsewhere."

Personal Value

Since employees spend more than half of their waking hours in the workplace, they naturally prefer to work in roles and on assignments that have some personal meaning and that they consider on some level to be valuable work. In addition, people want to be challenged and to test and apply their capabilities. They want work that is sufficiently complex and that they can add value to when they solve its problems. Nothing disengages people more quickly than giving them boring assignments that have far less impact on the organization than they are capable of providing.

Employees know when they are not realizing their full potential. They become frustrated when they are not able to give the kinds of results and add the kinds of value they know they could. It makes sense to them that the organization would want their managers to work with them to identify areas that, if developed, could help them realize this potential. People want to know where they stand in their current role and in their career possibilities. Employees become significantly more engaged with their company when their managers work with them to enhance their effectiveness in a role and develop their capabilities to permit them to be promoted throughout their career in ways that are consistent with the maturation of their potential.

Finally, people receive significant value from having mature, constructive working relationships with others at work. Employees value working effectively with others to produce spectacular results and create a winning team. Their sense of self-worth grows significantly when they have given meaningful help to others and received it as well. When the organization manages for fantasy, it pits people against each other. When it fails to clarify who is accountable for what and in relationship to whom, it ensures unproductive conflict and strain between well-intentioned, responsible people. To ensure engagement not only upward but also with others across the organization, leaders need to get accountabilities clear, align accountabilities with authority, and set the context within which people know how best to support each other.

Effective Leadership

People want information and meaningful control over their lives, especially in times of change and uncertainty. Effective managers engage their people around open and direct discussions about reality: what reality the organization, the unit, the manager, and the team are up against. They create opportunities for employee input into addressing those realities and respond respectfully. Those that should be incorporated are so integrated, and with appropriate recognition. Those that cannot be incorporated obligate the manager to explain why, providing an opportunity to coach and develop subordinates further. In this way, employees have direct understanding, including immediate and recognizable input into what needs to be done to meet the challenge.

Above all, employees want to succeed. They want challenging assignments, but they also want to have the resources and capable processes that are necessary in order to succeed. Being set up to fail repeatedly breeds cynicism and disengagement.

Finally, people want recognition for their contributions, both public and private. Nothing discourages an employee more quickly than a manager who hogs the organizational limelight, taking credit for his own subordinates' good work. Although the most direct form of recognition is compensation, many employees today are extremely cynical about the manner in which their companies reward them. People view compensation as equitable only if it can meet three criteria:

- The range of pay is tied directly to an objective measure of the sizes of roles.
- The pay steps within such range are tied to a fair appraisal of the overall value an employee has contributed.

- The actual pay (base plus merit) is determined by the manager's assessment of the employee's unique efforts and contributions throughout the year.

Employees experience pay as equitable or fair when it is seen as reasonable in relation to what others are compensated. When people feel they have fairly earned and been fairly compensated for what they make, they trust the organization and become more amenable to change.

Culture of Fairness

The essence of the psychological contract is fairness, trust, respect, and reciprocity. People will never fully commit when they perceive their work relationship as unjust—and not just when they themselves are treated unfairly either. Consider how many organizational change efforts have stalled when the employees who survived the cuts feel that those who did not were treated badly? Most think, "If management can do this to them, why should I feel secure they won't do it to me next time?" Buying into organizational change is about entrusting your fate, to some degree, to others, so that all your creative efforts can be dedicated toward helping these others succeed now and into the future.

ADAPTING TO CHANGE

All living organisms struggle for survival and mastery in relationship to their environments. The process of struggling and succeeding is called adaptation. Many people think of adaptation as simply adjusting or coping, but at its core, adaptation is about increasing one's competitive advantage in relationship to the environment. This is true for microorganisms, for butterflies, for elephants, and for humans. It is also true for businesses and nations. The ultimate goal of any business organization is to fulfill its underlying purpose and perpetuate itself by adapting to the requirements of the marketplace.

The developments in human evolution that account for our greater adaptive capacity in relation to lower-order animals boil down to four uniquely human capabilities:

Cognition: The ability to process data and create new information, project future scenarios, and develop novel solutions for them

Communication: The ability to convey such newly developed information to others, using articulated language, and thereby enhance their knowledge

Mobilization: The ability to convert emotions into values, craft goals in common with others based on these values, and engage individual and collective commitment to deliver on those goals

Invention: The ability to create new tools and access information for solving problems and overcoming obstacles

These basic properties of human ingenuity explain the force underlying the power of what can be called the LEAD model (leverage, engagement, alignment, and development). Managerial leaders add value to their subordinates (and to the organization as a whole) in four ways:

- Understanding work complexities at a level higher than their subordinates and using that capability to leverage subordinate potential and effectiveness
- Communicating their aspirations and passions in order to engage subordinate commitment
- Communicating intentions, and means for achieving them, in order to align subordinate judgment and discretion
- Developing resources and subordinate capabilities to support their realizing their potential and meeting their accountabilities

Leadership, in other words, is the ultimate manifestation of human adaptive capacity. It is the primary vehicle in modern society through which human potential is fully realized. And it is the force necessary to create a culture of adaptive readiness in organizations.

At the core of adaptation is the ability of an organization to respond to, or anticipate, changes in the environment in such a way as to increase its leverage over the environment. Critical change carries with it tremendous vulnerability, for failure to adapt to this change means defeat. The Chinese people understood this double-edged sword eons ago when they created the word for crisis, *we che* (see Figure 12.1).

Inherent in all critical change is a threat to survival if new demands are not met, as well as an opportunity to prosper if the new demands are mastered. The way in which leaders present new change realities to their people, equip them to address those realities, and support them in learning and growing will determine whether those people will become optimists or pessimists about future change. Leaders can help their people master the new demands and come to realize that through change, they can better realize their potential. Demonstrating this creates a culture that not only welcomes but also seeks out change. When employees are scouring the environment for opportunities to improve an organization's competitive advantage, that company has created a culture of adaptive readiness.

Crisis = 危机   Danger + Opportunity

Figure 12.1. *We Che.*

Change and Loss

Harry Levinson's formulation of the psychological contract has been a major advance in understanding the force underlying employee identification with, and commitment to, an organization's leadership. He was also one of the earliest researchers to identify the sources of resistance to change and the nature of managerial leverage in overcoming that resistance.

Think of the way people form attachments in their lives as being similar to how a tree puts down roots (see Figure 12.2). Roots are necessary to both anchor and nurture a tree. Similarly, every individual is rooted in multiple attachments from which he or she derives identity and draws emotional and intellectual sustenance.

People come to depend on these attachments not only for a sense of permanence, but also for their sense of self. When a significant attachment is threatened in a physical or symbolic way, whether or not the threat is real or imagined, people recoil and turn inward. Levinson summarized it elegantly in 1986 in *Ready, Fire, Aim: Avoiding Management by Impulse.*

A critical change is a major impact, a threat, or a departure from the status quo. It immediately poses two types of threats to an individual's emotional, behavioral, and productive equilibrium: loss and new demands. Think of the uprooting as loss: loss of being anchored, loss of identity and familiarity, loss of control, loss of support, and loss of confidence and competence. Coping with loss consumes physical, intellectual, and emotional energy.

In order to free up that energy, managers need to help people carefully examine the meanings they have assigned to that severed attachment. Preserve the good things that can continue. Retain the good memories about good things that cannot continue. Celebrate the loss of bad things. This is, in essence, a kind of mourning.

Adaptive leaders help people to acknowledge the losses inherent in the changes they must contend with. Exercising this leverage helps to restore confidence in leadership and begins the process of renegotiating the psychological contract.

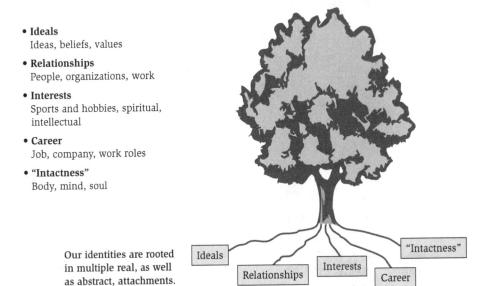

- **Ideals**
  Ideas, beliefs, values
- **Relationships**
  People, organizations, work
- **Interests**
  Sports and hobbies, spiritual, intellectual
- **Career**
  Job, company, work roles
- **"Intactness"**
  Body, mind, soul

Our identities are rooted in multiple real, as well as abstract, attachments.

Figure 12.2. Attachment and Change: Roots of Identification.

The second type of threat to an individual's equilibrium comes from the new demands inherent in forming new roots. We all struggle with feelings of inadequacy, which are perfectly human but painful nevertheless. Someone who has to start from scratch because of a critical change is filled with dread about being awkward, appearing ridiculous, and ultimately failing to meet the requirements of new demands.

Managers need to recognize the anxiety, fear, and stress that coping with these new demands places on their people—that this aspect of change also consumes considerable energy, requiring active managerial support. Leaders need to frame for their employees that the process of change is experimenting with new ways of thinking and performing and that experiments are really calculated risks—a kind of trial and error. Taking a reasonable, albeit radically new, approach is healthy, and an outcome other than the one intended should not be considered a mistake but a valuable point of learning. By helping people to get excited about learning, inventing, and creating, leaders create opportunities for growth and mastery. They help people to get a better sense of their own potential and how gratifying it can be to realize it.

Leaders need to see themselves as transitional anchors—sources of attachment during the transition from which employees can draw acknowledgment, support, encouragement, resources, information, and confidence. Managers need not be omniscient in order to serve as effective anchors. However, they need to be available, attentive, and aware. They need to maintain perspective about the transition, its dangers and opportunities, and its stages and pitfalls. They also need to help renegotiate the fractured psychological contracts.

Phases of Change

Each phase of critical change (see Figure 12.3) carries its own demands on the people going through it. The initial impact is inevitably a shock to the system. How many of us stared at the TV screen, observing the horror of the attack on the World Trade Center over and over again, trying to absorb what had happened?

When people first register a major change in their immediate environment and working conditions, their initial response is to feel overwhelmed. They cannot comprehend the enormity of what it will mean for them. For seconds, minutes, or even hours, people exist in a state of suspended disbelief. They focus on neither the past nor the future.

In order to avoid this kind of shock, managers should be setting the context on an ongoing basis about anticipated changes, so that people will be better prepared for whatever develops. But when managers must convey unexpected and potentially traumatic information to people, they should remember that people will begin to tune out after a few sentences of bad news once the enormity is registered. It is necessary to carefully script a concise, to-the-point message to be delivered simply and briefly. It should be followed up later with detail as people begin to assimilate new information.

Once the reality sets in, the second phase of critical change, disorganization, typically begins. Think of this period as a chaotic unleashing of unproductive energy. It can be understood as a state of heightened alarm, with thoughts and emotions racing and the body's fight-or-flight adrenaline response on alert. People feel quite ill at ease, anxious, and fearful. They cannot concentrate on the

Figure 12.3. Critical Change Sequence.

issues at hand. They do not eat or sleep normally. They feel out of sync with themselves and their surroundings.

This phase poses extreme challenges for managers because they need to ensure that everyone continues to do their day-to-day work while also focusing on understanding, formulating, and implementing new ways of doing things— during a time when they are less able to focus well on anything. Compounding this is the universal feeling among most employees during critical change of mistrust in and betrayal by their managers.

This is a critical time for leaders to act as anchors. They must speak with authoritative reassurance that the changes are real but manageable. Leaders need to address reality and simultaneously provide confidence.

During this phase, people often swing between being impulsive and indecisive. This also requires providing more direction than a leader would normally display. It is equally important to give people as much information and control as is practical in order to combat the normal feelings of helplessness during a crisis. Managers now need to support multiple forums for people to talk about the change: to acquire information, quell rumors, acknowledge fear and distress, clarify meanings, and receive encouragement.

During this phase, people tend to focus on themselves. "What will happen to me?" they worry. The focus is on what they had before and how they might recapture the old way of doing things. Energy is quickly depleted from dealing with the present and planning for the future. This phase ends when people tire of worrying and complaining, accept the reality of the loss, and have confidence that their leader will help them to succeed in mastering the new demands. If well managed, it should merge into the next phase in one to two months, as people begin to shift their focus from the past to the tasks now at hand.

The third phase of critical change, recovery, begins next. This is a period of experimentation, where people struggle to keep afloat in treacherous and uncharted waters. They are often hesitant, insecure, and afraid of failing. Managers need to be less directive and more Socratic, drawing out their subordinates' thinking about a problem and constructing a solution. Leaders must give their employees opportunities to try out new ways of working without knowing ahead of time if they will succeed. They must encourage risks without allowing recklessness. This is a time to help people find early successes in order to build confidence and momentum. It is vital to provide accurate, objective, and immediate feedback to ensure genuine learning. It is equally important to provide encouragement and praise for well-designed and well-executed plans.

Depending on the degree of change required and the amount and effectiveness of support given to employees, this phase may last another three to six months. The hope is to see people functioning reasonably well in their newly defined roles and accomplishing many aspects of the new processes by this time. They will have recovered much confidence in themselves and the organization and its leaders, but they are not yet fully acclimated to the new ways. Maintaining the gains still requires conscious effort and some emotional expenditure. At the point of the transit into the final phase, people begin to look forward to the future.

The fourth phase of critical change is reorganization. During the next six months, people attempt to assimilate their new skills, knowledge, and working relationships. During this phase, managerial leaders, who have earned the trust, respect, and confidence of their people in the previous phases, can exert the final leverage toward building a new culture, with a renegotiated psychological contract. This requires a great deal of communication but of a different sort from before. People need time to reflect on their journey, celebrate their successes, anchor their learning, and contemplate how much more adaptive they have proven themselves to be. In this manner, leaders can instill and reinforce a hunger for learning, growth, and mastery. They can point to the evidence of their employees' potential to move the organization forward. In this way, each individual comes to understand better his own potential, his own accountabilities and authorities, and his own role in supporting the team and the organization to survive and thrive. This becomes the foundation for a culture of adaptive readiness.

Employees learn that they can have a profound impact on the organization's success in the degree to which they value looking for change, adapting to change, and remaining flexible in the face of uncertainty and ambiguity.

THE CASUALTIES OF CHANGE

Following any critical organizational change, expect everyone to look and sound a little shell-shocked, crazed, and unbalanced for the first few weeks. Most people begin regaining their equilibrium by the second month. However, if you still see people heading downward and acting dysfunctionally beyond this time period, you need to assess the situation and act quickly. With these signs, you should probably consult with a middle manager.

When your company is going through a major change, look for the early warning signs (symptoms and behaviors) of three distinct groups of derailed employees:

• The adaptively challenged. You may have frightened people who resist change because they are incapable of dealing with new demands. Their new roles probably have been redefined from their previous ones. The complexities of these new roles may be greater than their capacities to handle them, they may not possess the requisite skilled knowledge, or they may be too rigid or insecure. They may need to be retrained or reassigned to some smaller position that they can handle. As a last resort, you have a moral obligation (in a humane and respectful way) to assist them in finding employment elsewhere.

• The psychologically challenged. You may have employees who become genuinely, but transiently, incapacitated by the change. These are the individuals predisposed to bouts of major depression, anxiety, panic, or posttraumatic stress disorder. They too need help, and urgently. This is the time to engage the organization's employee assistance plan professionals and mobilize whatever support is needed. A consulting psychiatrist can be especially helpful. Because you have not abandoned them, many of these people recover and become even more effective (and grateful and loyal) employees.

• The behaviorally challenged. This third group consists of those who are constitutionally oppositional. These are the people who have habitually sabotaged, undermined, or torpedoed your efforts in the past. According to the Hay Group, so-called recalcitrants are the 15 percent of workers in any company who for one reason or another actively resist change (*Wall Street Journal*, October 12, 1999). This is the appropriate time to show them the door—unless they decide for themselves that they are going to check their dysfunctional behaviors and maturely commit to supporting the current changes.

Part of the approach to take in organizational redesign or restructuring is that an organization must work to keep the people it needs and the people senior management predicts will succeed in the changed environment. The effectiveness of implementing a plan for change requires the acceptance and ownership of that plan by employees. But even with the best plan and best intentions, some employees will have difficulty accepting change.

SUCCESSFULLY LEADING CHANGE

Battle-weary employees want far more than bear hugs or small tokens of appreciation or vague promises. They want leaders to come up with viable plans and then help them to understand why they are doing what they are doing.

Successfully leading change in any managerial system takes time, focus, consistency, and commitment. For most organizations, it requires a significant adjustment in its culture. It needs to go from one based primarily on personal responsibility to one built on a foundation of accountability.

This transformation will inevitably create tremendous tension and uncertainty for the people undergoing it before it is successfully implemented. Some of the strain will be due to the significant shift in paradigm and required behaviors. However, some upheaval is due to the process of change itself.

The best organizational leaders adhere to the following sequence in order to implement organizational change:

1. They communicate and provide the necessary information that ensures everyone will understand that the change is both necessary and reasonable.

2. They provide clarification about the implications of the change decision in order to encourage trust. In effect, they renegotiate the psychological contract.

3. They model appropriate behavior, so that there will be greater identification with the immediate leader, management in general, and new organizational goals.

4. They seek employee input and advice in the tactical implementation of the change so that people will become fully committed and support a change in which they have personal ownership.

5. They set and maintain limits requiring appropriate adult behavior and mutual respect.

Using this perspective, the effectiveness of the organizational change implementation will depend on four closely related variables:

1. A good plan. The plan needs to be a good one. It must apply the essential principles of LEAD, ensuring that structure and process are fully aligned with strategy, that accountabilities are clear and fully aligned with authorities, and that people are accurately aligned with the requirements of their roles.

2. Acceptance. The people who will implement the plan must come to accept that the plan is necessary, good, and reasonable.

3. Ownership. They must come to a point of personal ownership of the plan. They need to be convinced it will help them to succeed.

4. Setting limits. Managers must set clear limits around what is acceptable and desirable behavior by employees during the change.

During times of change the leader's credo sometimes becomes, "You may not like these changes, but we must work and act constructively together to support them."

CHANGING TIMES: WHAT IS COMING NEXT?

A good hierarchy promotes the release of human potential where that potential is accountably applied to the work of an organization. Similarly, organizational change, soundly implemented, releases human potential by creating favorable conditions where people can become increasingly productive and effective.

No one can argue that the current rate of change is unprecedented. As a result, company structures and processes and systems may need to change dramatically as business objectives are adjusting and adapting to deteriorating economic realities and disturbing geopolitical events. Today's resources may be the wrong resources two years from now. The need for accountability and leadership has never before been stronger. If business leaders can fully leverage, engage, align, and develop today's resources and provide employees with the conditions in which they can be as successful as possible, companies and their people will be in the best possible position to manage now and well into the future.

The key to helping business organizations stay ahead of the pack during this uncertain time involves renegotiating the psychological contract and infusing the company with the value of adaptive capacity and the desirability of new challenges. Leaders also need to return to commonsense ways of managing accountably. This way, employees will be less likely to be resigned and defeated and constantly worrying about what is coming next.

Wise leaders understand the importance of leading change and renegotiating the psychological contract. They know that this understanding will not have a salutary effect only on a company's psychological health but on its bottom line as well. When well led, organizational change and a culture of adaptive readiness become ingrained in a company.

References and Additional Sources

Kraines, G. A. (1991, March 20). Stress in the workplace. *Directions in Psychiatry.*

Kraines, G. A. (1994). *Essential organization imperatives.* Boston: Levinson Institute.

Kraines, G. A. (1995). Requisite organization: Primary mental health promotion in the workplace. *Psychiatric Annals, 25,* 229–233.

Kraines, G. A. (1996, July-August). Hierarchy's bad rap. *Journal of Business Strategy, 2,* 32–39.

Kraines, G. A. (1997, July). *Maintaining mental health during organizational change.* Alexandria, VA: Society for Human Resource Management and Academy of Organizational and Occupational Psychiatry.

Kraines, G. A. (2001). *Accountability leadership: How to strengthen productivity through sound managerial leadership.* Franklin Lakes, NJ: Career Press,.

Levinson, H. (1973). *The great jackass fallacy.* Cambridge, MA: Harvard University Press.

Levinson, H. (1986). *Ready, fire, aim: Avoiding management by impulse.* Cambridge, MA: Levinson Institute.

Levinson, H., Price, C. R., Munden, K. J., Mandl, H. J., & Solley, C. M. (1962). *Men, management, and mental health.* Cambridge, MA: Harvard University Press.

CHAPTER THIRTEEN

Organizational Consequences of Family Problems

David E. Morrison
David A. Deacon

*An unfortunate aspect of these exciting times is the increase in personal emotional
problems. They beset everyone, and the frequency of maladaptive responses to
family problems keeps going up. The adverse effects of work problems on family
life are commonly discussed, but the equally common effects of family problems on
the workplace are not always so carefully considered. Divorce, serious family
illness, and the complexities of dual-career marriages are but a few examples.
These and other common problems can have subtle and insidious workplace
effects. More often than not, the relationship between family problems and
workplace effects is altogether hidden to employers, employees, and families.
As family problems increase and workplace change becomes a constant, effective
attention to the workplace effects of family problems becomes ever more important.
Sensitivity to these issues offers benefits for productivity, profitability, and
employee mental health. Systematic review of common family problems
offers a framework for understanding organizational consequences.*

Business and mental health professionals hear and talk a lot about bringing
work problems home from the office: exhausted employees with no energy
left over for their children or employees who spend so much time at work
or on the road that they barely see their children, for example. This chapter
looks at problems moving in the opposite direction, from the family to the workplace. Family problems can have adverse effects on productivity and morale or
trigger behavior that puts the organization at risk. Table 13.1 outlines four general categories of family problems, and their many corresponding consequences.

This chapter was originally written by David E. Morrison and David A. Deacon and has been
revised for this edition by David E. Morrison.

Table 13.1. Subtle Organizational Consequences of Family Problems.

Loss of Family Support

  Depleted emotional energy

  Emotional unavailability for important interpersonal relationships

  Less capacity for ambiguity, more need for structure

  Narrower focus of attention

  Impaired judgment

  Acting out of anger

  Cognitive preoccupation

  Susceptibility to accidents

  Active or passive resistance to change

  Deskilling: loss of competence

Family's Needs Interfering at Work

  Confusion among colleagues about changed attitudes to work

  Changes in what the workplace can expect from the affected employee

  Employee resists changes that could affect the family

  Employee doesn't fulfill potential or sabotages own advancement

  Employee's work is undermined by family member's behavior

  Inappropriately risky or risk averse behavior

  Exclusive focus on career advancement versus developing competence

  Vulnerability to burnout

  Ambivalence over employer values

  Deflated commitment

  Lack of self-confidence

  Grandiosity

The Workplace as a Substitute for Unmet Family Needs

  Demands of work subverted by personal needs

  Feelings of guilt or shame over behavior

  Damaged self-esteem spills over to workplace

  Eventual loss of employee

Motivation to Work Is Family Driven

  Discord with colleagues

  Flimsy commitment

  Potential unfulfilled

Much more is heard about work's impact on the family than the family's impact on work partly because the work ethic of the industrial world has changed some functions of the family. Under this view, people are valued in terms of what they can add to the gross national product as part of the workforce rather than for their functioning as mothers or fathers. A family (like a school) is evaluated for its ability to contribute to the nation's economy and thus is where one gets ready to go to work.

One of the implicit functions of the family becomes rejuvenation of individuals, so that they can give their all back at the office or shop. Family is then merely a setting where they can play out (both consciously and unconsciously) all of their problems—personal, family, or workplace—and all without getting in trouble with the boss. This is an expanded version of the "kicking the dog" syndrome, where the family becomes the frustration safety valve so that things do not explode at work.

If that was all there was to it, one would think there would be more research and clinical data about families' impact on work. In fact, there are other reasons that data have been limited. Companies do not measure people costs as much in depth as they measure other expenses. Costs of personal malfunction, if measured, are less likely to be broken down into those caused by family problems. Even such obvious problems as dual-career families and geographical transfers are examined only superficially in the literature. Among social scientists, psychiatrists, and other therapists who consider family problems, it is generally more acceptable to discuss work effects on families than family effects on work, so both companies and clinicians tend to look at only part of the problem. Except for the most obvious cases, the problems stay hidden until they are looked for carefully.

Work is the arena of discipline, performance, and accountability. People need those experiences and get paid for what they do at work; hence, they are obliged to put out effort to keep personal problems from getting in the way of productivity. If they do not, they affect people beyond their family. Others are counting on them to live up to their employment obligations: fellow workers, customers who buy the employer's goods and services, and the stakeholders (shareholders, creditors, taxpayers, and others) who invest. "We should leave family problems at home" may be unrealistic when enforced in the extreme, but it is not the same as callous indifference to people.

Most of the time, families do a rather good job of supporting individuals so that they can competently meet their workplace obligations. Still, families can sometimes be distracting, distressing, or even pathogenic, and thus problems are created for work. Try as they might, people cannot always leave their family problems behind when they punch in every morning.

An employee depressed about a poor marriage cannot come to work and say, "For now, I won't be depressed" (although the diversion of work might serve to brighten this person's spirit). An employee boiling over in anger after discovering a spouse's affair will certainly have moments of distraction and diminished clarity of thought and expression. Most of the ways that family problems invade the workplace, though, are subtler than these examples suggest. In fact, they are often altogether unconscious to employer, employee, and family alike. They may know something is wrong, but the whys and wherefores remain elusive.

Furthermore, it may be very difficult for people at work to discover the underlying problem. Consider an executive whose superiors are concerned that he has become aloof, risk averse, overly controlling, and too concerned with form at the expense of substance. Nothing in the workplace or his career path offers any explanation, nor has there been any apparent change in his personal life. Only in clinical consultation is it discovered that a daughter's four-year history of juvenile diabetes has taxed his psyche and finances. He fears that if people at work knew about his sadness, they would see him as weak and diminish his responsibilities. Moreover, the daughter's illness has also resurrected unconscious fears linked to his own mother's lengthy disability during his childhood. Referred by his company, he opens up in a confidential psychiatric consultation that looks at personal problems affecting his work. Because of his determination to keep coworkers in the dark, people at work had no way of knowing his distress. In fact, he was himself unaware of the emotional links to his own childhood.

LITERATURE AND RESEARCH

In the past ten years, there has been a large increase in articles, books and Web sites on work family conflict. Even so, there are essentially no writings on the impact of the family on work. The research is about the effects of work on family, family stress, gender roles, and how work family programs benefit work.

The benefits for work are measured in generalities of higher morale, more commitment to the organization, and less turnover. There is no indication, however, that the improvements relate to the impact of family on work or just the Hawthorne effect (any workplace change produces initially improved productivity). It is quite possible that morale improves simply because the people at work appreciate another benefit and not because of a positive effect from the family. Thus, the older literature for this topic is highly relevant, despite much additional work on work-family balance.

Interesting material on the organizational consequences of family problems can be found in both the popular and academic literature. The *Canadian Business Review* notes the now longstanding trend for women to want or need work and also the growing trend among men to take a larger role in the family. The general point is that worker expectations about total lifestyle are changing, with potential effects on both family and workplace.

Data from a survey of Canadian employees by the Conference Board of Canada (Bachman, 2000) indicate that 66 percent of the survey sample experienced at least some difficulty in balancing the demands of work and home, with 20 percent reporting that balancing these demands was "very difficult" or "difficult." Nearly 80 percent of the respondents reported some level of stress or anxiety over the balance issue, with more than 25 percent indicating "a lot" or a "moderate degree." And specifically for work consequences, over 50 percent reported experiencing problems caused by absenteeism from colleagues' family responsibilities. Ten percent said they had left a position because of work-family conflicts, and 14 percent said they were considering leaving for such reasons. Just over 30 percent said that child or other dependent-care responsibilities had limited their opportunities for advancement, a loss to the company as well as the individual.

In an article on the "daddy track" (that is, a more family-sensitive career track for fathers), McKenna (1990) reported on a Robert Half International survey that 78 percent of the male and female respondents indicated that given a choice, they would choose a slower career track with more flexible hours and more family time. The same article also cited a study done at AT&T. Seventy-three percent of men and 77 percent of women with children under age eighteen reported they had dealt with family issues while at work, with 25 percent of men and 48 percent of women reporting unproductive time at work because of child care issues in particular. In a companion piece in the same issue, *Industry Week*'s editor argued: "We need all the good people we can find, so we'd better find out what the best and brightest can do, let 'em do it when they can do it, and get out of the way. About all that this 'track' foolishness will do is distract quality employees, and send them down another track to some other organization that's smart enough to understand how the world of work is changing."

Kelly and Voydanoff (1985) consider the special problems of female single-parent earners and their high level of job tension. They point out that these women sometimes have the burden of being the sole earner for their family and tend to be concentrated in the low-paying sectors of the market. They often join or rejoin the labor force under such unfavorable circumstances as separation, desertion, or death of a spouse. The higher job tension they experience can lead to decreased well-being of both parent and children. Burden (1986), however, found that single parents showed high levels of job satisfaction and no differences in absenteeism or other negative performance factors relative to other groups, despite being at risk for high job-family role strain.

Black and Stephens (1989) looked at American expatriates assigned to Pacific Rim locations and the influence of the spouse on their adjustment and intent to stick with their assignments (see Chapter Nine). They found that a spouse's favorable opinion about an overseas assignment is positively related to the spouse's adjustment, and the novelty of the foreign culture is negatively related to the spouse's adjustment. Furthermore, the adjustment of the spouse is positively related to that of the employee, and the adjustments of the spouse and the employee are positively related to the intent of the employee to stay in the assignment. Although these results are not surprising, Black and Stephens point out that most employers consider the spouse to be an irrelevant factor in considering assignments and recommend soliciting the opinion of the spouse and providing training on living in the new culture to both spouse and employee. This recommendation for expatriate assignments could also be applied to domestic transfers and even such other job changes as promotions, where there can be a significant family impact that works to the ultimate disadvantage of the company.

Morrison (1976) described the problems of emotional spillover between work and family and of excessive separation between work, family, and self for city managers. Evans and Bartolome (1986) considered five relationships between work and nonwork spheres that help illustrate a broad perspective on the important issues:

- *Spillover:* Family satisfaction or dissatisfaction can have an impact on work satisfaction or dissatisfaction, and vice versa. Feelings about one can spill over and affect the other.

- *Independence:* The spheres of family and work are basically independent.

- *Conflict:* Work and family are in conflict. For example, a happy home life requires sacrifices with respect to career advancement.

- *Instrumentality:* One sphere is primarily a means by which to obtain something in the other sphere.

- *Compensation:* One sphere compensates for the other. For example, work accomplishment can be a substitute for dissatisfaction at home.

Although Evans and Bartolome caution that there is no definitive way to describe the relationships between work and family life, their five relationships help provide a structure for understanding the various ways in which family issues have positive and negative effects on work. Burke (1986) agrees with the need to refine paradigms and notes that empirical studies that get at the importance of nonwork factors as they affect work are limited. His comprehensive frame of reference for future research (see Table 13.2) includes both objective and subjective measures of family considerations and workplace effects.

The cases in this chapter, on loss of family support, family needs that interfere at work, the workplace as substitute for unmet family needs, and family-driven motivation to work, reflect some of the principles raised in the literature

Table 13.2. Family Impacts on Work.

	Critical Factors in Family (Independent Variables)	Outcome Measures at Work (Dependent Variables)
Objective	Financial need	Number of rejections of promotion, transfer
	Spouse's career position	
	Number of children, dependents	Absenteeism
	Recency of critical events (for example, divorce, separation, family death)	Level in hierarchy
		Performance and potential ratings
	Quality of neighborhood	
	Existence of child care facilities	
	Ethnic background and traditions	
	Family connections—social	
	Type of marriage, family	
	Stage in family life cycle	
Subjective	Degree of marital harmony, satisfaction	Job satisfaction
		Job involvement
	Spouse's career aspirations	Level of stress
	Degree of complementarity or conflict in couple's expectations, values, and job commitment	Work orientation
		Motivation
	Spouse's personal beliefs and attitudes regarding work	Level of energy
		Performance
	Family demands for time and energy	Turnover intentions
	Degree of social support	Willingness to travel, transfer
	Amount of emotional bonding and family adaptability	Demands for or expectations of raises, promotions
	Family satisfaction with job	
	Spouse's adjustment to job location, transfers, promotion	

Source: Adapted from Burke (1986).

and go beyond the more superficial analyses underlying issues found particularly in the popular literature.

FAMILY PROBLEMS: CASES AND DISCUSSION

The cases that follow highlight some of the more common ways that work is affected by family problems.

Loss of Family Support

Most individuals rely on their family to provide the support they need to function successfully at work. When that support is disrupted, job performance can suffer.

Case 1

Jim Williams went through a very painful divorce. His ex-wife demanded more and more as the proceedings went on and succeeded in cutting Jim off from his children. He felt financially strapped, lonely, and betrayed. Meanwhile, he took a new job with a different employer. Alone, he moved to a new and unfamiliar town. He needed the new job to go well in order to get back on his feet financially and renew his self-confidence. He started to get aggressive and impulsive. Eighteen months into the new job, his boss confronted Jim with complaints from his peers that he was too pushy, self-interested, and defensive. His style was interfering with the teamwork that was necessary for his company to compete in a demanding new market.

Jim's divorce proceedings had left him emotionally and financially drained. He had left most of his support behind when he moved to a new job and a new town. The family is one of the most important support structures people take with them in a move. Jim's personal upheaval left him unprepared to tackle a critical challenge of any new job: building interpersonal relationships with colleagues at work. Perhaps the most important problem was that the lack of support coupled with his emotional depletion narrowed his focus. He was usually keenly attuned to relationship issues. One of his strengths in the past had been understanding the impact of his personality on other people. Now he was so preoccupied with his own need to get his life in order that the only relationships he could competently address at work were those with his own subordinates.

Everyone knows that divorce has effects on people that can show up in the workplace. But people face differing circumstances and react differently even to similar circumstances. Jim's divorce left him devoid of emotional resources to make adequate investments in his peers. He had to give of himself to get things off on the right foot but had little left to give.

Case 2

Steve Johnson, a first-line supervisor in a manufacturing company, had problems getting along with several supervisors two years ago. He profitably used professional consultation services provided by the company and completely repaired the relationships. His manager said six months ago that he had made a turnaround. His improvement was so great that he was asked to serve on a management-union committee that included some senior managers.

Last month, Steve's wife divorced him against his wishes. He became depressed and then appeared inebriated at an important meeting of the management-union committee. In the middle of a discussion and with a company attorney present, he made a lewd remark to a woman on the union team. In retrospect, people realized they had seen some evidence of probable excessive drinking in the previous several months.

Steve's circumstances and problems are different from Jim's. Steve is more stressed than depleted from his divorce, and the added stress from mixing with his seniors was enough to impair his judgment critically. His anger at his wife was acted out at work. The act was so obviously self-destructive that it also served as an expression of his guilt. He humiliated himself and was fired.

The unfortunate thing about Steve's case is that he was a good investment, a good bet, for his company. He had shown the willingness and ability to work on his problems and to change. One wonders if the earlier personal changes he had made to repair relationships with his supervisors did not also change the equilibrium in his marriage. There had not been a problem in his marriage before then. Steve's work affected his marriage, which then affected his work. Had the company been quicker picking up the new signs of work and family problems, it might have saved a developing manager.

Case 3

Dick and Molly Black have always been mutually supportive. Recently, Molly became seriously ill, and the emotional support has been moving primarily in one direction. Dick, a semiskilled worker, has been preoccupied at work and suffered two minor injuries in two weeks.

Dick is worried about Molly and is not concentrating well on the job, even when he tries. His many concerns include financial resources; not showing his concern to Molly, the children, or other family members; and what will happen to Molly. In addition to his worries, he has lost his most important source of emotional sustenance while having to put out more himself. Accidents have been well documented as an unconscious way to get out of an untenable situation (Group for the Advancement of Psychiatry, 1977).

Case 4

Tamika James used to be able to use her husband, Pete, as a sounding board for problems at work, and he would help her put things in perspective. Pete liked her company and the people in it. He was one of those loyal spouses that companies want. However, recently Pete has become angry with his wife's company as it laid off people for the first time ever. Because of the tight economy, the company became leaner and demanded more time of its managers. Tamika has spent more and more time at work, and company politics has become more intense.

Now, when Tamika complains to Pete, he criticizes the company with a vengeance. Tamika ends up defending her organization, the last thing she really wants to do. Instead of venting her anger with Pete like she used to, Tamika now plays it out in the workplace in the form of passive resistance to organizational change.

This is a more subtle form of loss of support. Pete is not aware of the impact his anger is having on his wife: he has cut her off from the one safe place she had to vent her frustrations. Tamika is not hostile toward her company; she just needs help with all of her feelings about the tough changes at work. She expresses less of her feelings at work because she feels vulnerable in the new, riskier environment. Tamika does not realize she has become passively resistant at work. Her colleagues know it all too well, but they have no idea it has anything to do with Pete.

Families are part of the organizational culture. They will support or undermine important cultural changes, because those changes modify the identities of the employees and family members who care about the organization. If they can not understand why the organization made the changes, they feel betrayed. If the families are not supported at times of significant change. they will be less supportive of the employees doing the work of the organization.

Case 5

Betty Stillman, a skilled technician in a professional organization, has never been much of a people person. She has always been able to rely on her husband, Bill, for counsel on people issues, which has kept her out of hot water. Bill's mother recently died, and his own job is not going well. He complains that he lacks the energy to invest in Betty's work problems.

Lately, Betty has become "more like herself" at work, insensitive to other people's needs, ignoring organizational procedures to get what she wants, and turning her requests into demands. She has a short fuse and impulsively confronts anyone who stands in her way, even senior management. Betty has started going around her boss, who is becoming fed up with Betty's impact on morale.

Sometimes the support an individual receives from the family is more than emotional. In Betty's case, Bill filled in a specific work vulnerability. When she lost Bill's counsel, her poor understanding and management of people issues rose to the surface. Betty needed more than the usual amount of emotional support and now had no place to ventilate, put things in perspective, or learn alternative approaches to workplace problems. Thus, the problems evoked still further needs for support and started a destructive spiral.

Family's Needs Interfering at Work

In addition to providing support, family requires individuals' time, love, and support. When these demands increase, they can affect employees' work life as well.

Case 6

Ingrid and Sven Jakobson are a dual-career couple. Ingrid's not assuming the traditional housewife's role has caused some minor problems. For example, there are squabbles over who does the dishes or takes out the garbage. But they have been able to negotiate the division of labor at home to their mutual satisfaction, and none of the issues have affected work in any way.

The recent birth of their first child has complicated the issue considerably. Ingrid is anxious for Sven to assume an equal level of responsibility for dropping the baby off at day care and picking her up at the end of the day. Sven would like to see Ingrid be more of a traditional mother and make more of a sacrifice in her own work. Until they are able to renegotiate their psychological contract with each other, they have decided to both pull back to eight-hour days and curtail travel as much as they can. Besides, they want to enjoy their new daughter for a while, and they will worry about the parenting role later. Their respective employers are surprised at their sudden reduction in overtime hours and willingness to travel.

The issue is not that the employer does not understand, but that people have not had the time to adjust: peers, subordinates, and superiors alike. Ingrid and Sven's past behaviors have created a set of unspoken expectations among their colleagues about how they will behave in the future. These expectations are a structure for their colleagues, who depend on the psychological contracts that the expectations constitute. Ingrid and Sven have unilaterally broken these contracts as they renegotiate their own. Befuddlement and exasperation ensue on an emotional level even though everyone understands intellectually why they have changed. People at work will have to adjust to the new reality in their colleagues' lives.

Ingrid and Sven also need to appreciate their responsibilities to the other people at work. They must organize their time to accommodate the new baby and work. They need to let people at work know if and when they can be expected to carry a regular load again. People at work have their own families with needs, just as Ingrid and Sven do. A person does not just take away from "work" or the organization when they reduce their performance. Organizations are made up of people. When one person gives less to work, coworkers must spend less time and energy on their own family interests.

Case 7

Change is rampant in Lisa Greenwell's company, and she is expected to evolve out of her technical functions into a broader business development role. This will require more socializing and traveling, as well as a deepening of her knowledge about more ambiguous topics like politics and economics. In a word, Lisa has an opportunity to become a full-fledged business woman.

The problem is with her husband, John, a technical expert in the same industry. He likes Lisa the way she is. He is afraid she will find him wanting as she is exposed to more "successful" men. "Will she still be my partner?" he wonders. He also worries about changes in their historical patterns of taking care of the children, preparing meals, and housework. He tends to highlight the downside of Lisa's opportunity, and it is safe to say she would have accepted more promotions and progressed more quickly had it not been for his nay saying.

This case could be seen as just another anecdote describing a man threatened by a competent woman, but this problem occurs with both sexes: one member of a relationship growing beyond the other because of work opportunities. Certainly the psychological contracts between the couple are changing in terms of taking care of the children and the house. The problem, however, is John's emotional needs, not just the administrative needs of house and child management. The more important issue is his feeling of loss of his relative competence and the attendant shame. He fears that Lisa's support will change, for she is a part of his support system as he is for her. Furthermore, he loves her the way she is. What will she be like if she changes?

He does not talk about any of those reasons or his worry that he will not be good enough for her after all her changes. Even if he did, it is hard for anybody to discuss such things. He may not even know many of those reasons. Instead, he gets defensive about men and competent women, while his fear and envy undermine her chances to be as successful as possible at work.

Case 8

Raji Patel is a salesman who transferred from Boston to Cincinnati three years ago to develop new markets. When they were given the news, he and his wife, Phyllis, had just closed on the purchase of their dream house in Boston. Phyllis was a Boston native who thought of it as the sophisticated cultural center of the country. Upset and angry, she nevertheless reluctantly agreed to the move.

Phyllis has openly criticized Cincinnati and Raji's company in front of other employees and even customers. In the community where Raji is trying to develop relationships, she makes disparaging comments as she compares Cincinnati to Boston. Raji's boss has told him that Phyllis's behavior is a liability with customers and to "figure out how to manage her." Raji is afraid to confront her. The one time he broached the subject, there was a fight that took a week to get over. It was never resolved.

Here the problem is not just lack of emotional support but inappropriate behavior caused by a spouse's emotions. Some family members have unrealistic views about what work can do for them. They believe they have a right to live where they want and still have increasing income from the organization. When a couple does accept a promotion and transfer, their house may represent all that they are leaving behind. It becomes all the more valuable in their eyes when they leave behind important emotional ties.

A spouse who feels self-righteously angry about a broken organizational "contract" can be an intimidating partner. Emotions become even more complicated when the transferred employee feels ambivalent about the move and guilty about the family ordeal. Both employee and family often need help in understanding the realities of work and the sacrifices required to move up or even remain in an organization. Saying that family members should be realistic about what they expect from an organization could be misunderstood as suggesting that companies be callously indifferent to family needs. The company must be concerned about the demands it makes on the people doing the work, if only for its own survival. At the same time, family members need to understand the realities of an organization that is trying to survive in a competitive global environment. Uninformed decisions can be hard to live with. When a family cannot live with its decisions, help in understanding and working through the feelings can reduce the risk of losing an otherwise effective worker.

Case 9

Over the years, Carol Browder has earned more and more money in her job as a bond trader. In some years, her performance has been nothing less than spectacular. The problem is that her husband has adopted a more and more lavish lifestyle, and she has gone into more and more debt to support it. Carol now finds herself in a position where she has to make at least as much as she did last year (one of her best years), and even that may not be enough.

Recently, her behavior has been confusing to her boss and colleagues. She has alternated between aggressive and timid, animated and lethargic, outspoken and quiet. She is less articulate and confident in strategy meetings. She has missed obvious opportunities and pursued dubious ones. She seems to be having more trouble conceiving and sticking to her daily trading plans.

The family pressures here are obvious. Two somewhat subtle issues deserve comment. First, families that have a significant jump in income and no prior experience with such an income level may need support in personal financial planning. Even an employee who is a financial expert may have no experience with this level of personal finances. And there may be such intense work involvement that family concerns fall by the wayside. Work commitments and high incomes can be a way to avoid family conflicts, only to see the problems escalate. The company can help by offering personal financial planning and referral for therapy.

The second problem is the employee who puts the organization at risk. Often the best performers cause the most disastrous problems, because management does not watch them or does not want to (see Chapter Seven). Management is primarily concerned about keeping them happy and misses the early signs because they are not psychologically prepared to see problems in their top performers.

Case 10

Ernie Garmisch's wife, Anna, comes from a wealthy family with a long history of male family members' holding top government and corporate executive positions. Anna puts a lot of pressure on Ernie to succeed, and he is motivated as much by her expectations as he is by anything else. In a real sense, Ernie works for his wife, not for his company. At work, he has built a reputation for pushiness and taking excessive risk. The recognition he demands is considered well above what his achievements would suggest. Most of Ernie's colleagues regard him as a pain in the neck.

Human needs can be broken down into the spheres of work, family, and self. In Ernie's case, Anna's personal needs supersede whatever Ernie or his organization need. Ernie is constrained by Anna from following and developing his own abilities, aspirations, and career at a more realistic pace. She contributes to his own motivation to develop a false self. As he focuses only on upward advancement and ignores developing his true competence, he does not consider whether the work itself is personally gratifying.

Such people can cause severe problems for organizations, particularly if they are successful in their ambitions and advance to senior management. They will be more vulnerable to burnout because work has no gratification for them other than status and marital stability. They will provoke cynicism and distrust when they push others to be concerned about quality or commitment to the organization. Their own true values will be communicated by their behavior and mixed messages. As they focus on short-term gains on their way up the corporate ladder, others will have to clean up the longer-term consequences of their actions, for they are interested in what is best for their career (appearance of success), not what is best for the organization.

Case 11

Lynn Fox's career is on the brink of skyrocketing, but she is fearful of having a more successful career than her husband. He has told her that he is particularly sensitive to outperformance by a woman. It now seems that every time Lynn is about to get promoted, she heads it off with an uncharacteristically stupid mistake.

In this case, once again, the spouse's personal needs get in the way of setting appropriate goals in the workplace and maximal career fulfillment. Lynn's mistakes are not mistakes at all, but unconscious attempts at self-sabotage in the interest of protecting her marriage and her spouse's self-esteem.

Case 12

Mike Castelli is a highly successful investment banker who earns a lot of money and advises at the upper echelons of corporate decision making. Mike's wife, Heidi, is a psychologist who has always leaned to the left politically. She sees money as increasingly important to Mike and does not like what she perceives as the capitalist mindset of his clients. She has any number of complaints about them: "exploitation of the people doing the work," "interest in profits to the detriment of everything else important," and "environmental irresponsibility." She has never been interested in business and does not understand Mike's work, let alone what it does for society and people. Furthermore, she is not interested in learning anything about his work or business.

As a result, Mike starts to doubt the validity of his work and act defensively at home. That provokes Heidi to take an even more aggressive position and Mike to extreme arguments in return. As he has begun to second-guess his motives, he has become much more timid in his behavior and tentative in his decision making at work.

The issue here is a fundamental conflict in values between Heidi and Mike. These kinds of conflicts can be especially incendiary because they cut to the issue of basic identity. By taking a moralistic position, Heidi succeeds in shaming Mike. He adopts a moralistic defense of his work but begins to doubt his genuine moral values and the value of his dedication. His new uncertainties are reflected in declining performance at work.

This case also points out that work is implicitly and explicitly charged with values that employees do not necessarily accept. And when family members focus on seeing value conflicts for their own emotional reasons, there can be serious consequences for organizational function. The organization can help through genuine concern for the broader contexts of society and the environment and for the inherent value of its own goals. Leaders need to articulate the organizational contributions to larger societal concerns. When this understanding is communicated to families, the strain of apparent value conflicts may diminish, while underlying emotional tension is focused elsewhere.

Case 13

Neil Cassidy is a skilled laborer with little opportunity to move up. His wife has seen work only as a place where Neil gets a paycheck. For her, the church is where people should give all their true effort. Her own church has a particularly charismatic priest, and she has recently encouraged Neil to become heavily involved in church administration activities, which has provided him a heightened sense of mission and accomplishment. At work, Neil is in a greater rush to leave at night and has begun to cut some corners in his production.

Neil's company competes in an industry troubled by foreign competition and customer dissatisfaction with quality and cost. The organizations that survive will have to make dramatic changes. Industry analysts believe the companies that will be successful will be those that are able to change as the realities of technology and markets change. Neil, though, does not want to attend after-work courses and team meetings. He and his wife do not see how manufacturing techniques and quality control have any real meaning for them, and they do not want any limitations on their church work.

There is a more important problem for organizations in this case than just dealing with somebody who is not interested in his employer's work. Neil has been pulled away from seeing his work as personally meaningful at a time when he will be asked to intensify his efforts, change his approach, and develop new skills. Potentially, his work will become more meaningful for him, but it will at first feel like an intrusion into the things he really wants to do. He will resist needed changes unless he gets some help.

Nonwork activities (civic, church, or whatever else) are enriching experiences, and they often enhance workplace performance by energizing the employee or developing transferable skills. The problem for the organization occurs when nonwork activities compensate for what is missing at work (see Evans and Bartolome, 1986, for descriptions of different relationships between work and nonwork), because then they can detract from employees' emotional investment and commitment. There are particular stresses during times of change. Through his nonwork activities, Neil might develop attitudes and skills that would facilitate his ability to change and grow. The difference depends on whether his company can find a way to make his work meaningful to him again. It would also be helpful if his wife could see his work as more than just a paycheck.

Case 14

Lou Wilson's wife, Mary, idealizes him and encourages his grandiose and omnipotent fantasies and has raised their children to do the same. Lou has carried a "king-of-the-hill" attitude into the workplace, to the annoyance of his peers and the concern of his bosses. They have observed him skipping details where he should not, being insufficiently sensitive to customer needs, and acting in other ways that suggest his perceived superiority.

People are happiest in their families when they receive support from them and the family helps them be who they are. But overestimation of competence can be damaging to work just as underestimation can. In fact, it is more likely to cause problems for the organization. Such individuals can put the company in serious risk because they do not plan, cross-check, adequately prepare, or submit to policies and procedures. In this case, Lou's family is reinforcing his unrealistic evaluation of himself and his worth. That may be the main reason he married his wife. They can be expected to act to neutralize any required confrontations he receives at work. Any efforts at getting Lou to make changes in his personal behavior will also have to consider the role of his family.

The Workplace as a Substitute for Unmet Family Needs

When a family is not fulfilling its role as a support system, an individual may expect work to compensate for what is missing.

Case 15

Sue Hanson's marriage has been weak for some time now and keeps getting worse. Emotional intimacy is absent altogether, and the couple's sexual relations are hollow and perfunctory. Although her husband does not particularly care for her, he does not believe in divorce. As a result of her frustrated personal needs, Sue has started working longer hours. Soon the only people she really knew well were at work.

After several years, when more and more of her life became centered at work, she started an affair with a manager in another department. He cares for her and understands her work (something her husband never bothered to do). They spend most of their time together talking about personal matters. Sue has come to realize she never did much of that before, and it has given her something she only vaguely knew was missing. But it is not without its cost. Sue is starting to feel guilty, but more about breaking company fraternization policy than her commitment to a dead marriage. She is thinking about quitting her job.

This is another example of compensation. Sue is not getting her emotional and sexual needs met with her husband, and she has found a man at work who provides them. As more and more waking hours become work time, particularly for white-collar workers, needs for intimacy surface prominently in the workplace. Sexual intimacy is often part of the equation. It is not enough to set policies against such relationships and publicly punish those who transgress.

The issues are more complex than that. Individuals need to work through their own unique needs, frustrations, and interpersonal realities in a setting that contributes to sound decisions.

Old solutions often no longer work very well. Many people will need the confidential assistance of a professional who can help them look at the underlying psychological dynamics of their complex lives. When the employee feels caught in an unresolvable dilemma over emotional needs, the organization also suffers.

Case 16

Forrest Taylor is from a blue-collar background, but he has succeeded in making it well into middle management in his company. He is often self-conscious about his roots, though this has not cost him anything. At home, his relationships with his children seem to be falling apart on all fronts. He feels like a failure as a father, and his wife supplements the children's rebellions with plenty of her own criticism. She even taunts him about his newfound "uptown ways."

As his self-esteem has dropped, Forrest fears his colleagues will realize he is less competent than they are. As a result, he has been extra careful about the quality of his work, but his productivity has suffered.

Forrest's self-esteem is undermined by events at home, which exacerbates the insecurity that has always tugged at him at work and undermines his performance. This is another example of the back-and-forth pressures between work and family. It is not uncommon for upwardly mobile individuals to feel insecure when working with people from higher socioeconomic backgrounds. Even those with top-notch educations can be so concerned about their status that they focus exclusively on work. Thus, they do not develop themselves as spouses or parents and confront their anxieties about family intimacy. The developing incompetence in the family adds to their insecurity, and once again there is a downward spiral.

A spouse from a similar background may feel abandoned in the task of making the family work and intimidated about the new social circles. The spouse then expresses these worries by nagging and eventually angry attacks and also has difficulty understanding the demands of the work. One professional in a rather sophisticated service organization complained, "If I were a cab driver, my wife would know what I do. As it is, she thinks I don't have any real responsibilities and can't see why I won't take off in the middle of the day to pick up the laundry or do some errand for her."

Motivation to Work Is Family Driven

Sometimes the main motivation to work is family—to support a sick relative or a family or a family on a tight budget, for example.

Case 17

Maria Christina Rivera's parents are living at her home with her and her husband and require increasing time and energy. As a result, Maria Christina sees work not only as a source of funds for supporting her parents, but also as a haven where she can relax a bit. In a sense, she goes to work to get some rest.

Maria Christina's motivation in working is not to maintain her sense of mastery and self-esteem by playing out her aggressive and creative drives. Rather, it is to finance something outside work and to get away from it all. This is not necessarily a problem for the organization, but managers will need to be sensitive to the impact of any significant changes in her work demands. For example, Maria Christina may be talented enough to be considered for promotion or a transfer. In many organizations, if managers turn down such an opportunity, it is held against them. That would be a mistake in Maria Christina's case. Although the organization should give her a chance to say if she wants the promotion or transfer at this time, they should also understand her reasons if she says no. If there is another opportunity when her family life has changed, she can be asked again. The same points hold for a parent with very small children.

Case 18

Peggy Delaney is a nurse. Her colleagues call her the "leisure nurse" because she works primarily to finance expensive vacations with her husband, Norm. She would just as soon stay at home as a housewife, but both she and her husband, Norm, enjoy a little extravagance around vacation time, and Norm does not make quite enough money to do that. He has pressed Peggy to go back to work so they can keep taking the vacations, and she has reluctantly decided to take a job in her old profession. The other nurses at the clinic where Peggy works do not begrudge her working just for money, but they recognize Peggy's resentment and are bothered that she is not the "caring professional" that they are.

As in the case of Maria Christina, Peggy is motivated almost exclusively by family and self considerations. The clash that this causes with her peers is more dramatic than in the case of Maria Christina, where the consequences of her elder care responsibilities may not even be noticed in the workplace. In Peggy's case, the chances are greater that her motivation will bump up directly against the grain of the inherent key value of the organization: the professional health care of others.

Management needs to attend to the behavior of both Peggy and her work group, but not to Peggy's motivations. It is certainly legitimate for someone to work to finance vacations. The organizational concern is for personal behavior and effects on morale. Unnecessary comments or behavior that provoke coworker envy should be confronted. If Peggy is an adequate performer, her peers need to understand her contribution. Not going the extra mile will not get her promoted, but it also should not generate resentment.

INTERVENTIONS

To the same extent that businesses are sensitive to the impact in the workplace of medical problems, they need to become attuned to the usually more elusive impact of family problems and the other sorts of psychiatric problems covered in this book. Not only is it a good thing to do, it is also in their best economic interests.

Emotional problems are always more complex than they appear. Hence, it is a significant challenge for businesses to get where they ought to be on this issue. One temptation many managers and other leaders will have is to take a short-cut by merely trying to be more sensitive, relying solely on their own good instinct and becoming, in essence, amateur psychiatrists. Being more sensitive is certainly a necessity, but when potential effects are substantial, professionals need to be involved early on. Comprehensive diagnosis and appropriate treatment require not only special skills but also detachment from the workplace environment. Employers should focus on the quality of work, raising red flags early, and seeking outside consultation when the issue is more than just matters of workplace routine. Of course, employees often are not aware that a family problem is affecting their work.

Beyond globally increasing workplace sensitivity to early work symptoms, perhaps the best difference an employer can make is to provide an environment that encourages employees to come forward with emotional problems. That is not as easy as it sounds. Common wisdom dictates to employees that they keep their personal problems out of the workplace. In fact, it is precisely this attitude that often makes the consequences of the problem worse. The means by which business can begin to chip away at this attitude and turn it around is communication of its commitment to provide a helping hand. An effective method is face-to-face sessions conducted by informed bosses, whereby people can sense the dedication of the organization. The more people see that dedication, the safer they will feel in seeking help for their problems.

Communications should include more than just a stated commitment, however. They should also include the mechanics and procedures for people to follow when they have a problem and the kinds of services the company will be making available. With details like this, employees have a structure to follow that will make them feel less tentative about coming forward with particular issues.

Everyone does better when options are laid out for them, especially when addressing matters of particular concern.

Work is affected by family problems more frequently than most people realize. The psychiatrist William Menninger once said that the incidence of mental illness is one-in-one, and one can add that the incidence of family problems with an impact on work is also one-in-one. Sooner or later, family problems affect everyone at work. Most of the time, it is not significant, and only a few close coworkers even know of the difficulty. Yet there are times when the organizational consequences of family problems are significant and yet no one sees or looks for underlying causes. At these times, the family's impact on work becomes an excessive business cost that needs to be addressed like any other. Family problems of this dimension are a legitimate concern of employers.

When family-driven problems at work occur, they are, on average, more significant than the literature suggests because the nature of any emotional problem is always subtle. Some of these more subtle organizational consequences of family problems are summarized in Table 13.1. Because in the real world each case has its own unique twist, the table does not purport to be complete but only reflective of the cases presented.

Employers need to be sensitive to the many motivations underlying employees' work and the many implications for their commitment and sense of responsibility. Families affect those motivations in both positive and negative ways.

References and Additional Sources

Bachman, K. (2000). *Work-life balance.* Ottawa: Conference Board of Canada.

Black, J. S., & Stephens, K. G. (1989). The influence of the spouse on American expatriate adjustment and intent to stay in Pacific rim overseas assignments. *Journal of Management, 15,* 529–544.

Burden, D. S. (1986). Single parents and the work setting: The impact of multiple job and home life responsibilities. *Family Relations, 35,* 37–43.

Burke, R. J. (1986). Occupational and life stress and the family: Conceptual frameworks and research findings, *International Review of Applied Psychology, 35.*

Evans, P., & Bartolome, F. (1986). The dynamics of work-family relationships in managerial lives, *International Review of Applied Psychology, 35.*

Googins, B. K., & Pitt-Catsouphes, M. (Eds.). (1999, Mar.). The evolving world of work and family. *Annals of the American Academy of Political and Social Science, 562* [special issue].

Group for the Advancement of Psychiatry. Committee on Psychiatry in Industry. (1977, June). *What price compensation?* Washington, DC: American Psychiatric Press.

Hammonds, K. H. (1997, Sept. 15) Work and family. *Business Week,* 96–104.

Kelly, R. F., & Voydanoff, P. (1985). Work/family role strain among employed parents. *Family Relations, 34,* 367–374.

Lilly, T. A., Pitt-Catsouphes, M., & Googins, B. K. (Comps.). (1997). *Work-family research.* Westport, CT: Greenwood Press.

McKenna, J. F. (1990), Mar.). The daddy track. *Industry Week, 239,* 211–213.

Morris, B. (1997, Mar. 17). Is your family wrecking your career? *Fortune,* 70–90.

Morrison, D. E. (1976, Mar.). Focus on the family. *Public Management.*

Potter, J. M. (1989, Autumn). Family-related programs: Strategic issues. *Canadian Business Review.*

University of Minnesota, Children, Youth and Family Consortium, Bibliography: Work Family Issues. http://www.cyfc.umn.edu/Work/bib.htm.

Work Family Researches. Electronic Network, Work-Family Links: http://www.bc.edu/bc_org/avp/csom/cwf/links.html.

CHAPTER FOURTEEN

Psychiatric Causes of Workplace Problems

Accidents, Absenteeism, and More

Steven E. Pflanz
Stephen H. Heidel

*Absenteeism, accidents, interpersonal conflict, poor job performance, and
job dissatisfaction are challenging problems for all employers. The psychiatric
and psychosocial causes of these common work problems and their negative
effects on both the employee and the organization are important to understand.
A careful assessment process includes the identification of the workplace
problem, referral to and evaluation by a consulting psychiatrist, and proposed
interventions to correct the problem. Thoughtful planning can minimize
or prevent these problems from occurring in the future.*

Employers frequently experience absenteeism, accidents, interpersonal conflict, poor job performance, and job dissatisfaction in their employee populations. These issues often disrupt the work environment, leading to poor morale and decreased productivity among an entire work group. Addressing these behaviors with employees can be difficult and awkward. Supervisors are often concerned that discussing these issues openly may hurt the employee's feelings and exacerbate an already difficult situation. Even the most constructive criticism and kind-hearted feedback can be devastating to an individual struggling with a psychiatric illness or a personal problem. Employees may react with anger and denial or may burst into tears during these discussions. These reactions can be very uncomfortable for coworkers and supervisors alike. In addition, employers may be angry about the problem behavior and have difficulty approaching the discussion in a fair, calm, and supportive manner.

COMMON WORK PROBLEMS

Psychiatric illness or psychosocial problems may be either the cause of the problem or a significant aggravating factor. When an employee is suspected of having a psychiatric problem, someone in management should consult with a psychiatrist or other mental health professional to evaluate the problem behavior and implement solutions.

Absenteeism

Two major forms of problematic absenteeism exist. First, an employee may be out of work for an extended absence of weeks or months due to an identified illness or injury. Alternatively, an individual may miss work frequently due to multiple minor problems or recurring symptoms from a chronic illness. In each instance, the employee draws a paycheck but does not contribute to the organization's productivity during the absence. Coworkers may be forced to accept additional work to make up for their colleague's absence, creating additional stress for them and frequently breeding resentment toward the absent worker. This stress and resentment can erode the organization's productivity and the corporation's bottom line.

When an illness is clearly diagnosed and physical in nature, supervisors and coworkers tend to be much more tolerant of an employee's absences. Acceptance increases as the disorder becomes more severe and life threatening. Many absences are due to vague somatic complaints of unknown etiology or to explicitly diagnosed psychiatric illness. In contrast to physical illnesses, absences for unclear or psychiatric reasons can be especially difficult for employers to understand and accept.

Accidents

Accidents are especially troublesome in work settings due to the costs associated with injured employees and damaged equipment. These accidents involve potentially large losses in terms of severe injuries to employees, lost time due to injuries, damaged equipment, and lost material. More often than not, accidents are due not to equipment failure but to mistakes by human operators. The military has long recognized the critical role human factors play in accidents. The distractibility and poor judgment that cause human errors have multiple causes, including unresolved psychiatric illness and personal problems.

Interpersonal Conflict

Misunderstandings, lack of support, arguments, and hostility between coworkers can be especially difficult to manage. If staff do not get along and are unable to work together, projects are delayed, do not receive the collaborative input they require, and lead to a diminished quality of the final product. Conflict may be the result of one disgruntled employee with whom no one gets along. It may also result from personality clashes between two or more individuals who cannot find a way to work together. Work groups may disintegrate into factions with different agendas.

Productivity decreases for several reasons. Employees are angry about the hostilities, distracted by the tension created, and upset over real or imagined insults. Irritable employees who lose their temper with customers will cause the company to lose valued customers. Poor working relations among subordinates consume valuable time of supervisors, diverting energy from critical managerial issues. Efforts by third parties to mediate and resolve conflicts take additional time and resources. In each instance, the organization's productivity and profitability are compromised.

Poor Job Performance

Work inefficiency and poor job performance may result from lack of adequate job skills or may be due to other factors. When employees with strong work records begin to perform poorly, managers must look beyond job skills for the cause of their deteriorating performance. It is rare for previously high-performing employees to suddenly stop caring about their job. Loss of motivation and focus occur because some other factor is distracting them from their jobs. Psychiatric illnesses, such as depression and substance abuse, or personal problems are often the cause.

Job Dissatisfaction

If employees are unhappy with their job, their attitude about work will be negative. In some instances, the employee may have never liked the job. In other cases, the job may no longer be interesting or have become too stressful due to a change in working conditions. Difficult relations with a new supervisor or coworker may create frustration. The employee may have an illness or personal problem that is causing the dissatisfaction. The dissatisfaction of one worker can spread to others, with an impact on the whole work group, causing poor morale and leading to unwanted turnover.

CAUSES

Although each work problem is somewhat different, the underlying causes for each have a great deal in common. Throughout this chapter, these problems will be treated as a group when discussing their psychiatric and psychosocial causes, effects, and possible solutions.

Psychiatric Illness

Psychiatric illness has been shown to cause work problems and is much more common than most employers recognize, affecting 48 percent of Americans during their lifetime and nearly 30 percent of the U.S. population each year (Kessler et al., 1994). Given the prevalence of psychiatric disorders, it is not surprising that many employees are afflicted with mental illness. Although severe conditions such as schizophrenia may be uncommon in working populations, depression, anxiety, and substance abuse disorders are frequently encountered in employees. Employees with these psychiatric illnesses and other psychosocial problems exhibit a variety of symptoms, including irritability, anger, inattention, apathy, loss of motivation, disinterest, and fatigue. It is not surprising that employees with these symptoms have problems with absenteeism, accidents, interpersonal conflict, poor job performance, and job dissatisfaction.

Several studies document the impact of mental illness on absenteeism. In one, roughly 14 percent of all work absences were due to mental illness (Jenkins, 1993). This estimate makes no accounting for absences due to emotional symptoms that were attributed to physical causes, such as headaches or the flu. Mental illness, including anxiety and depression, costs industry an average of sixteen days of sick leave per year per worker with psychiatric illness (Dauer, 1989). In an industrial setting, 4.4 percent of illness absences were due to mental disorders (Tsai et al., 1997). This study examined illness absence in excess of five days, which represented 43 percent of the total days employees were absent from work. In this study, the average duration of absence per episode of depression (36.6 days) was nearly nine days longer than the average illness absence for all causes (27.7 days). This research also demonstrated that a small number of employees account for a substantial portion of total work absences. The 13 percent of workers who had three or more absences accounted for 63 percent of the total number of absence episodes and 62 percent of the total number of workdays lost to absences.

Depression is a major cause of absenteeism. Depressed employees are significantly more likely to be absent from work than nondepressed personnel (Druss et al., 2001). Depressed workers miss an average of 1.5 to 3.2 days of work per month more than other workers, costing employers $182 to $395 per month in salary (Kessler et al., 1999). In a prospective study of depression and disability, depression accounted for more than one-fifth (22 percent) of all days lost from work (Broadhead, Blazer, George, & Tsee, 1990). In 1990, absenteeism secondary to depression cost industry $11.7 billion, representing 27 percent of the total societal costs of depression (Greenberg et al., 1993). In a retrospective study, depressed workers missed 7.8 days of work in the past year compared to 1.3 days for workers without depression (Jenkins, 1985). Looking prospectively, these same depressed workers missed 5.1 days of work over the next year compared to 1.6 days in nondepressed employees.

Conti and Burton (1994) studied short-term disability (including absence durations of greater than five days up to six months) at a large corporation in Chicago and found that depression contributed heavily to illness absences. Mental disorders accounted for 11 percent of all medical plan costs, and depression accounted for 52 percent of all medical claims for mental disorders. Of those disability absences secondary to mental disorders at this company, depression was responsible for 52 percent of the diagnoses and 62 percent of the total days lost from work. Disability absences due to depression averaged 40 days, greater than disability absences due to low back pain (37 days), heart disease (37 days), all other mental disorders combined (32 days), high blood pressure (27 days), and diabetes (26 days). Upon return from disability absence for depression, 26 percent of workers experienced another episode of disability for depression in the following twelve months. This disability relapse rate was significantly greater than the relapse rates for high blood pressure (11 percent), low back pain (10 percent), heart disease (8 percent), and all other mental disorders combined (8 percent). Only diabetes had a similar rate of relapse (26 percent). Thus, Conti and Burton established that depression is associated with both longer and more frequent absences from work. Another recent study confirmed that depressed workers miss significantly more days of work per year (9.9 days) than workers suffering from heart disease (7.5 days), diabetes (7.2 days), back pain (7.2 days), hypertension (5.4 days), and all other illnesses (3.3 days) (Druss, Rosenheck, & Sledge, 2000).

Substance abuse is another group of psychiatric disorders with a large impact on workplace problems, including absenteeism and accidents. This is not surprising given the high prevalence of substance abuse in the workplace. Eight percent of full-time workers use illicit drugs, and another 8 percent of the workforce are heavy drinkers (Hoffman, Brittingham, & Larison, 1996). Drug-using employees at General Motors average 40 days of sick leave each year, compared with 4.5 days for nonusers (U.S. Department of Labor, 1998). After 1.3 years of employment at the U.S. Postal Service, employees who had tested positive for illicit drugs at the time of hiring had an absenteeism rate 59.3 percent higher than employees who tested negative (Normand, Salyards, & Mahoney, 1990). In a study at an industrial worksite in Australia, problem drinkers were 2.7 times more likely to have absences related to work injuries than were non–problem drinkers (Webb et al. 1994). Utah Power & Light found that employees who tested positive on preemployment drug tests were five times more likely to be involved in an accident at work as those who tested negative (U.S. Department of Labor, 1998). A study was performed to determine if construction workers with a substance abuse diagnosis were at a greater risk of work-related injuries. For workers in the age range of twenty-five to thirty-four, substance abusers were 1.93 times more likely to have a work-related injury (Pollack, Franklin, Fulton-Kehoe, & Chowdhury, 1998).

Decreased job performance is often due to mental illness or psychosocial problems. Depressed workers were significantly more likely to report decreased effectiveness at work than nondepressed workers (Druss et al., 2001). Lost productivity due to depression cost American corporations $12.1 billion in 1990, representing 28 percent of the total societal costs of depression (Greenberg et al.,

1993). Anxiety disorders cost industry $4.1 billion per year, 88 percent of it attributable to decreased productivity (Greenberg et al., 1999).

Depression and substance abuse each cause numerous problems in the workplace. Employees suffering from both a substance-related disorder and depression are especially likely to experience serious problems at work, as well as with most other areas of their lives.

Despite this research, the tremendous cost of depression and substance abuse is not well recognized by industry. The total costs to industry of depression ($23.8 billion) dwarf the costs exacted by anxiety disorders ($4.1 billion), another common group of psychiatric illnesses in working populations (Greenberg et al., 1993, 1999). Although the total societal costs of depression and anxiety disorders are nearly identical, workplace costs represent a much greater fraction of the total costs for depression (54 percent) than for anxiety disorders (10 percent). Any effort to reduce absenteeism and workplace accidents needs to understand the central role that these mental illnesses play in causing these problems.

Physical and mental illness often occur together. Medical illness, when present, may be the most easily identifiable cause of work problems. Often overlooked, however, is the employee who suffers from a medical and psychiatric illness at the same time. A significant number of medical conditions are strongly associated with depression, including chronic pain, heart disease, stroke, AIDS, chronic fatigue, fibromyalgia, thyroid disorders, and cancer (U.S. Public Health Service, 1993; Wells et al., 1989). Adequate treatment of both the medical and psychiatric illness is essential for an employee's maximum recovery, regardless of whether the psychiatric illness is the primary illness or secondary to a medical illness. Even if an individual with a serious medical illness does not have a comorbid psychiatric illness, it is important to remember that every serious medical illness carries with it stress and life changes with which the employee must cope. Difficulties adapting to the psychosocial problems associated with medical illness often lead to work problems, especially absenteeism.

Psychosocial Problems

In the absence of a psychiatric or medical illness, psychosocial issues alone, including financial difficulties, relationship issues, major life changes, and work-related problems, frequently translate into significant problems at work. Financial problems are very worrisome for many employees. Relationships are critical to human functioning, and problems with spouses, children, parents, or others are very disruptive. Life changes, both positive and negative, require adjustment and often cause a great deal of stress. Such events as death of a loved one, loss of a job, getting married, or the birth of a child are examples of life events that can absorb the focus and energy of employees. Work-related problems can also cause difficulties. Employees who are worrying about job loss, experiencing conflict with coworkers or supervisors, involved in unchallenging work, or facing excessive work demands are going to experience more absenteeism, less productivity, and decreased job satisfaction. Niemcryk, Jenkins, Rose, and Hurst (1987) found that work-related stress, type A behavior patterns, dissatisfaction with management, and lack of coworker support are associated with higher rates of physical illness, with risks increased between 38 and 69 percent. By implication, these results suggest that these four psychosocial variables are associated with higher rates of illness absence. This study also found that these four variables are associated with higher rates of injury, with risk increased between 80 and 252 percent. This study reveals the critical role the work climate plays in the health of employees and the potential contribution of negative work environments to absenteeism and accidents.

Costs of Psychiatric Illnesses and Psychosocial Problems

Psychiatric illnesses and psychosocial problems interfere with day-to-day work tasks, impairing an employee's attention span, motivation, energy, and ability to relate to coworkers and customers. Increasingly, they are unable to leave these problems at the door when they come to work each day. It becomes more difficult, if not impossible, to devote their full focus and energy to daily work assignments. This leads to behavioral and cognitive problems, such as irritability, conflict with coworkers, and poor concentration. As these problems escalate, the employee becomes more prone to mistakes, works less efficiently and more slowly, misses deadlines, and makes faulty decisions.

Case 1

Bill Morris, fifty-two years old, worked as a driver for a delivery service. Over the course of eighteen months, he had one vehicular accident and two injuries. The accident occurred when he fell out of his truck; the truck kept moving forward and hit a parked car. On another occasion, he fell while delivering a package, severely spraining his left ankle. Finally, Bill cut himself with a knife while opening a package. He was referred to an occupational physician for a fitness exam and was found to have a tremor, but was released back to work with no restrictions. The occupational nurse knew that Bill had a long history of depression and asked for a psychiatric evaluation. This was done and revealed that the employee was on lithium for his depression and was experiencing significant side effects from this medication. His medication was changed to one without side effects, and he was free of accidents and injuries for the year he was followed after the changes were made.

Case 2

Henry Angle, forty-one years old, worked in a warehouse where he stored incoming shipments and prepared orders. Part of the time he used a forklift. He had problems with excessive absenteeism and erratic job performance, including irritability toward his coworkers. His supervisor had confronted him, but his behavior did not improve. One day, Henry drove his forklift into the side of a parked car in the loading area. When his supervisor investigated the accident, Henry became angry, claiming the parked car was the problem. He said it was parked in the wrong place. The company had a preemployment drug testing policy, but did not test for cause. Therefore, no test for drug use was done at that time. Henry was referred to a psychiatrist, who determined that he was abusing methamphetamines, which Henry claimed he needed to keep up with the heavy workload. Henry agreed to enter a treatment program and agreed to random drug testing as a condition to keep his job.

Case 3

Janet Marshall, a thirty-eight-year-old single woman, worked as a secretary for several engineers. She had held this job for nine years, and her performance had always been adequate. When her mother, with whom she lived, died unexpectedly at the age of sixty-four, Janet was devastated. She initially took two weeks off but ultimately took a four-month leave of absence before returning to work. When she came back to work, she resumed her same job with the same female supervisor. She began to complain about her working conditions almost immediately, saying that no one appreciated her and that her supervisor "had it in for me." Her work performance was far below what she had previously been capable of doing. She was referred to a psychiatrist, who determined she was having an abnormal grief reaction that had developed into a clinical depression. Janet was placed on sick leave and treated intensively with psychotherapy and antidepressant medications. In six weeks, she resumed her old job and performed as she had in the past.

EFFECTS ON THE EMPLOYEE AND THE ORGANIZATION

The effects of absenteeism, accidents, poor job performance, interpersonal conflict, and job dissatisfaction are difficult to overestimate. These problems may start with one employee but quickly spread to reach coworkers, management, and perhaps the entire organization.

Employees with a psychiatric illness or psychosocial problems may exhibit a variety of effects—emotional, behavioral, cognitive, and physical. Emotional effects include anger, sadness, and irritability. Behavioral effects include poor sleep, inappropriate grooming, and missing work. Cognitive effects include poor concentration, making mistakes, and poor judgment. Physical effects include fatigue, palpitations, and excessive sweating. Employees with a combination of these symptoms may be unsure where to turn for help and hesitant to involve their supervisor for fear it will jeopardize their career. This environment can be incredibly stressful and may aggravate the psychosocial situation or psychiatric illness that caused the problem. This can potentially lead to increased problematic behavior, creating a downward spiral of increasing tension between the employee and the organization.

Coworkers will likely be asked to increase their workload to make up for absent or inefficient colleagues. If they feel overwhelmed by the additional workload, overall morale will suffer, and problems may spread to other employees in the work group. When injuries are involved, employees become hypersensitive to the safety of the work area. Anxiety about the possibility of future accidents and the resulting fears may actually increase the risk of future accidents. If a problem employee jeopardizes the safety of coworkers or causes significant injuries, the work group will likely become very angry at both the problem employee and management for not addressing the problem in a timely manner.

For supervisors, problem employees become a major preoccupation and an enormous time drain, drawing them away from the duties for which they are primarily responsible. Each problem needs to be investigated thoroughly, documented carefully, discussed with several people, and monitored closely. If supervisors are too tolerant or ignore the issue, coworkers may get the message that the behavior is acceptable and begin behaving in similar ways themselves. Alternatively, coworkers upset over the problems may feel hopeless when they see the problem being ignored, increasing their stress level. These employees may consider resigning their position or transferring to seek a more satisfying work environment. If supervisors adopt the opposite extreme and aggressively go after the problem employee, beleaguered coworkers tired of laboring alongside a colleague who has not been pulling his or her weight may greet it with enthusiasm. It may also be viewed as harsh and intolerant, creating an oppressive environment where employees are afraid to get sick or have an off-day. In fact, some employees may view the actions of a supervisor as too harsh, while others welcome this involvement. Clearly, these problems require sensitivity and tact on the part of the supervisors, as well as a great deal of time and patience.

At the organizational level, these problems represent financial losses. Absenteeism, inefficient working, arguments, injuries and work stoppages following accidents, and time spent by supervisors dealing with these various issues translate into salary costs. Accidents cost money to repair damaged equipment, medically treat resulting injuries, recruit and train replacement staff, and pay disability costs during the worker's convalescence. Workplaces that suffer from deteriorating morale are less productive and produce poorer-quality goods and services. Workers exhibiting problem behaviors are more likely to be fired, and job dissatisfaction among a work group may lead to an exodus of valued employees, resulting in increased recruitment and training costs for replacement workers. Departures by employees in whom the company invested a great deal of training are especially costly because of their knowledge and customer contacts. In addition, employees manifesting untreated psychiatric illness and psychosocial problems have increased medical utilization and medical costs. A study conducted to determine the risk factors associated with reporting acute back pain at work found that other than a recent history of back problems, job dissatisfaction was most predictive of an employee's reporting acute back pain (Bigos et al., 1991).

If these common work problems, so costly to the employee, coworker, supervisor, and organization, can be identified early, referred for evaluation and resolved, many costs can be avoided, and the overall health of the organization, in terms of both employee morale and productivity, benefits.

ASSESSMENT

The referral process often begins when an employee's problematic behavior is recognized and documented by the supervisor. A professional mental health evaluation will follow when the organization contacts a consulting psychiatrist. When the supervisor suspects a psychiatric illness or psychosocial problem is a contributing factor to the workplace problem, the organization may request a psychiatric consultation. The approach to evaluating each of the five common work problems (absenteeism, accidents, poor job performance, interpersonal conflict, and job dissatisfaction) is similar, regardless of the individual circumstances of the case. In each instance, the evaluating psychiatrist must carefully investigate and understand the problem, thoroughly evaluate the employee, and understand the organization.

Investigating and Understanding the Problem

When an employee exhibits job performance problems, it is the responsibility of the supervisor to address the situation. The supervisor first documents the problem and then discusses the issues with the employee. The focus of this conversation is the work-related problem and how to remedy it. In the course of these discussions or while trying to correct the problem, it may become apparent that the employee is having behavioral or personal problems that are causing or contributing to the work problem. The supervisor and the organization should not try to explore these psychiatric problems or solve an employee's personal problems. When problems of this nature become apparent, the supervisor should refer the individual to the employee assistance program or a psychiatrist who has knowledge of the workplace.

When the company decides to use a consulting psychiatrist, it should retain one who will work on behalf of the organization to evaluate the problem and make suggestions about interventions that will remedy the problem. It is important that the psychiatrist not be the problem employee's treating psychiatrist.

These psychiatrists are very strong patient advocates, which can cause a conflict of interest and may not serve the company's needs.

Before talking to the employee, it is essential for the psychiatrist to solicit information from a knowledgeable person in the company. Simply relying on an account of the situation by the employee leaves the evaluator vulnerable to erroneous conclusions because the employee will present an account with a perceptual bias. The employee may not be forthcoming with critical information necessary for an accurate assessment, and someone in the workplace will be necessary to provide knowledge of issues not disclosed by the employee. It is best to interview several individuals at the workplace in addition to the employee. Gathering information from multiple sources will help capture the full scope of the problem.

At the time of the referral, the psychiatrist should ask both the company contact and the employee about the nature of the problem. The psychiatrist should begin by asking a series of questions:

- Where does the employee work?
- What is the problem?
- Who are the key employees involved in the situation, including the problem employee, his or her supervisor, and coworkers?
- What is the employee's explanation for the problem behavior?
- How serious is the problem?
- Has it occurred more than once?
- What circumstances result in the problem behavior?
- What pattern does the problem behavior follow? For example, is the employee always absent on Monday, on days when assigned a particular duty, or only after receiving criticism?
- How well does the employee get along with supervisors and coworkers?
- How well does the supervisor get along with other employees?

Specific details are critical because vague descriptions of problem behavior are difficult to work with. For example, documentation of an employee's being absent for thirty out of the past ninety work days provides a much clearer description than a supervisor's verbal statement that the employee has been absent frequently in the past several months. Similarly, a supervisor who can describe specific missed deadlines and specific job tasks that have not been accomplished gives the evaluator a better understanding than the simple statement that work productivity has recently dropped dramatically.

Understanding the employee's specific job is necessary to evaluate the adequacy of the employee's performance. The employee's performance reports and personnel records should be reviewed, including the written job description and job qualifications. The evaluator needs to understand the job itself, including the type of work performed, the required training, productivity goals, assigned tasks and responsibilities, and specific time lines and deadlines. It is important to understand whether job requirements are formalized, very explicit and written down, or more general, verbal and implicit.

Evaluating the Employee

A full understanding of the employee and his or her current life circumstances is necessary to assess the problem. The evaluator must understand why this particular problem is occurring at this time in the employee's life. This will include a careful exploration of the employee's explanation of the behavior and understanding of the problem. It would be important to establish whether similar problem behaviors have occurred in the employee's past, what the precipitating factors were then, and what helped solve the problems before. All the questions that the company contact was asked should be asked of the employee. It is essential that the psychiatrist have a thorough understanding of the problem and its context.

In addition to a careful history of the current problem, an evaluation should inquire about the presence of psychiatric and medical illness and obtain a history of each. A family and social history is important to fully understand the employee, including any traumatic experiences and the quality of relationships with the family of origin and current family. The psychiatrist should find out what important events or stressors (financial, legal, interpersonal, life events, work problems) are occurring in the employee's life. What is the employee's educational background, and how successful was he or she in school socially and academically? A work history is very important. What types of work has the employee performed in the past? What did the employee enjoy doing, and what were the reasons for leaving each of the past jobs? Why did the employee choose the current job? What does he or she like and dislike about the position? What is the employee's perception of the quality of relationships and degree of psychosocial support received from coworkers and supervisors? It is important to assess the employee's understanding of how well he or she meets specified productivity goals and accomplishes assigned work tasks and responsibilities. The employee's job skills, knowledge, training, and qualifications should be reviewed. The employee's reasons for working, career aspirations, motivation, work ethic, and value system need to be explored.

Case 4

Tim Rosen, fifty-six years old, returned to work after a six-week medical leave following a heart attack. He worked as a customer service representative and was given a similar job when he returned. He became upset immediately and left to see his cardiologist before he had even begun working. Tim returned the next day with a note from his doctor limiting his hours of work and not requiring him to wear a necktie, which was part of his required uniform. With these restrictions, he could no longer perform his job.

A consulting psychiatrist was asked to clarify the situation. First, the psychiatrist spoke to Tim's supervisor. She said the Tim had been assigned a slightly different job because he had been due to rotate to that position before he got sick. She acknowledged that the new job was a little more stressful, but stated that Tim's turn to be assigned to that job was overdue. The psychiatrist next spoke to Tim, who was very upset. He felt the job he had been assigned was much more stressful than his previous assignment, and he was afraid that additional stress might literally kill him. He assumed his female supervisor "had it in for him" and had done this deliberately. Rather than talk to her directly, which Tim felt would be futile, he went straight to his doctor. With Tim's permission, the psychiatrist spoke with his cardiologist, who said that Tim had been very upset when he came to the office and had tried to calm him down by agreeing to write a note with the restrictions that Tim wanted. The doctor acknowledged that the restrictions were not medically necessary, but he also did not want his patient to be so upset.

It appeared to the psychiatrist that Tim had been assigned a more stressful job. He told the supervisor that Tim perceived the job as more stressful and asked if another assignment would be possible. The supervisor said no, stating that the job assigned was part of the normal job assignment. The psychiatrist then spoke to the supervisor's manager, who understood the issue and suggested he would intercede and ensure that Tim returned to a job that he perceived as no more stressful than his job prior to his heart attack. He also agreed to keep a close watch on the employee and his supervisor. The cardiologist agreed to remove the restrictions, and Tim was able to return to work without any further problems.

Understanding the Organization

As part of the evaluation, the psychiatrist should become familiar with the organization where the employee works. In particular, understanding the supervisor can help establish whether the referral stems from a personality conflict between the supervisor and employee. A brief assessment of the organizational climate, including its culture, structure, hierarchy, membership, goals, and values, can provide a valuable backdrop for understanding the problem behavior. This will clarify the environment the employee is returning to and what he or she will need to accept in order to be successful on return. Finally, corporate policies regarding medical care and medical disability need to be reviewed.

Integrating the Information

After the assessment is complete, the information gathered needs to be integrated into a coherent formulation of the problem that succinctly describes the problem, its causes, and proposed practical solutions. The problem behavior and the proposed remedy must be expressed in terms easily understood by both the employee and the employer. The use of complex psychiatric language will be of no use to either and will tend to alienate both.

Implicit to the discussion throughout this chapter has been the assumption that problem behavior often has emotional or psychiatric origins. Emotions and behavior are patterns of responding that have been learned through prior experiences dealing with people or situations. Individuals decide how to react to new situations based on these experiences. There is a powerful connection between past experiences and current emotions that drives behavior in ways that individuals do not always consciously understand. This is often not obvious to either the employee or the employer. Indeed, the employee frequently will be resistant to this suggestion. The psychiatrist is wise to use this insight to understand the problem, but must be careful to explain the findings in a manner that does not offend or confuse the employee or the employer.

Case 5

John Mitchell was a twenty-eight-year-old salesman struggling each month to meet his sales quota and facing possible dismissal. He considered going to his wife for support in dealing with this problem. However, his mother had neglected him during his childhood, and as he thought about talking to his wife, he imagined that she wouldn't care or listen. This was his learned expectation, based on his experiences with his mother. Expecting neglect, he behaved angrily toward his wife, as if she had already been neglectful. His angry behavior pushed his wife away, resulting in his receiving no support from her.

At the office, John's problem continued to manifest itself. Angry with his wife, he was irritable at work, leading to poor relations with coworkers and customers. He became increasingly isolated, angry, and depressed, and his sales performance steadily fell. John's expectation of neglect became fulfilled by his own angry behavior.

The relationship between past experiences and present behavior must be explained in simple and practical terms so that employers can understand the origins of problem behavior in employees. Rarely are workers suddenly deliberately neglectful of work responsibilities or calling in sick without cause. More often, these common work problems arise when a serious issue overwhelms a worker. If employers can recognize that psychological issues are at play and not attribute the behavior to misconduct, a more rapid referral to a mental health professional will result. A successfully treated employee will be more productive. Thus, resolving these problems benefits both the employee and the employer.

INTERVENTIONS

With the assessment completed, the employer and employee must attempt to resolve the problem. If this is to be successful, a series of agreements must first be reached between the supervisor and the worker. They must both agree that the problem exists and that the problem behavior needs to change in order for the employee to remain at this job. Both parties need to discuss and understand any relevant policies pertaining to the situation. This establishes the ground rules under which they will operate. Both must understand to some extent why the problem has arisen. Finally, they must agree on a plan for solving the problem and returning the employee to satisfactory work performance. The plan should identify specific proposed corrective actions, which may include psychiatric and medical treatment and any accommodations that are necessary, such as working half-time for several weeks or having time off to participate in treatment sessions. The plan will outline the parameters to be used to measure adequate job performance and the time line to accomplish the corrective actions and return to full duties, after which time the employee's performance will be measured by the same standards used for other employees.

The consulting psychiatrist is an invaluable resource to the company in designing this corrective plan. Psychiatric treatment, including psychotherapy and psychiatric medication, is often a key component to the intervention. The vast majority of psychiatric disorders can be successfully treated with medication or psychotherapy or a combination of both. Psychiatric care returns workers to the job, improves their job performance and satisfaction, decreases medical care use and costs, and prevents costly employee attrition. One study revealed that after two years of group therapy for employees suffering from work stress, researchers found that 75 percent reported increased job satisfaction, 73 percent were still working at the same job, 88 percent were still employed overall, and only 5 percent had filed workers' compensation claims (Lehmer & Bentley, 1997). Another study looked at career outcomes for employees referred to a consulting psychiatrist. Of those referred, 61.7 percent were still working for the company after two to three years, and 95 percent were rated as meeting or exceeding job requirements (Robbins, Kaminer, Schussler, & Pomper, 1976). Of eighty-three employees initially rated as unsatisfactory in job performance at the initial psychiatric referral, forty-nine (59 percent) remained with the company and exhibited satisfactory job performance. In summary, psychiatric interventions are effective and valuable aspects of programs designed to correct common work problems.

Consulting psychiatrists should be highly cognizant of the political ramifications of any suggestions they make regarding treatment. The primary role of the consulting psychiatrist is to provide objective assessments to help the employee and employer understand the reasons for the problem behavior and implement practical solutions. Any commentary on the emotional health of the organization or suggestions for broad-based preventive measures should be withheld unless specifically asked for by the employer. Many employers and organizations are not going to be interested in or able to change the organization to accommodate the employee. This may not be possible in large corporations. Policies are established at a national level, and problems may be occurring in a district office that has no ability to influence the corporate policy.

Organizations with proactive and progressive leadership may request the psychiatrist to conduct a more general analysis of the emotional functioning of a work group or department within the company. These corporations may offer the psychiatrist the unique opportunity to suggest programs for a large cross-section of workers. Occupational psychiatrists must recognize, however, that many employers will not welcome this feedback or be open to suggestions intended to improve the emotional climate of the organization. Therefore, they must be careful to offer this feedback only when the company specifically requests it.

To be effective, the psychiatrist needs to work within the corporate system. Treatment recommendations need to fit the realities of the workplace. The psychiatrist must be sensitive to both the cost and time duration of recommended treatments. The psychiatrist should work with both the employee and the employer to identify reasonable work restrictions and set a realistic date for returning to work. When working frequently with the same company, getting to know supervisors and senior leadership can enhance the psychiatrist's credibility. The more that corporate leadership respects a psychiatrist's professionalism, the more effective the psychiatrist will be in suggesting solutions. When working in the field of occupational and organizational psychiatry, blind allegiance to an employee patient will severely limit a psychiatrist's effectiveness. To be successful, the psychiatrist must effectively balance the client's needs against the organization's needs, striking a fair and equitable balance between the two. If both parties are not at least minimally satisfied, the intervention will fail.

PREVENTION

Preventing work problems from occurring is preferable to dealing with them after they occur. With psychiatric illness and psychosocial problems, identifying potential problems early and instituting prompt interventions best accomplish this. There are many reasons, however, that problem behavior is not always addressed quickly. Employees may minimize their problem or be hesitant to ask for help. Supervisors may hope the problem will go away without confronting it directly, or they may feel the employee should be given time to deal with the problem alone. Coworkers may be afraid to address the issue openly, fearing they will hurt the employee's feelings or create an angry outburst. Patience may wear thin while everyone silently looks the other way, hoping the situation will improve on its own.

These delays are often harmful because problems have a tendency to worsen with time and become more difficult to resolve. By the time the problem is too big to ignore, coworkers and supervisors may be impatient for a solution and are less likely to be tolerant of time delays while a plan for corrective action is implemented and carried out. Thus, it is essential to address issues of absenteeism, poor job performance, accidents, interpersonal conflict, and job dissatisfaction promptly.

Organizations should implement specific policies and programs to encourage early identification and intervention of workplace problems. These include a drug and alcohol policy, an employee assistance program, good mental health benefits, occupational medicine and psychiatric consultation, training programs, and an organizational audit.

A drug and alcohol policy should include preemployment drug and alcohol testing, testing for cause after a workplace incident, and random testing after a substance-abusing employee completes treatment and returns to work.

The employee assistance program should be promoted in the workplace so employees know how to access it voluntarily. Because the stigma associated with psychiatric illness is one of the main reasons employees delay seeking needed assistance, mental health promotion programs should attempt to destigmatize psychiatric illness and psychosocial problems. Periodic training should teach supervisors to recognize the warning signs of employees with problems and how to deal effectively with problem employees, including making referrals to the employee assistance program or a psychiatrist.

Mental health insurance must be affordable and easy to access. All health plans should have an adequate panel of psychiatrists and other mental health professionals to choose from. If access or quality problems arise, there should be easily understood avenues for employees to use to resolve them quickly.

Companies should have either an internal occupational medical department or an external one. These individuals (doctors or nurses, or both) should perform preemployment exams to ensure that new employees are well matched physically to their job. When employees seek treatment for illnesses and injuries, the medical evaluation should routinely screen for psychiatric illness and psychosocial problems. The occupational medical staff can refer these employees to a psychiatrist experienced in corporate settings.

Training programs should educate staff about common psychiatric problems and common workplace issues. Training about illicit drug use and alcohol abuse will be beneficial to both employees and the company. A training program on the recognition and treatment of depression will encourage early treatment of this disorder. Training programs on stress management, conflict management, and balancing work and family will be well received and lay the groundwork for early intervention of common workplace problems.

An organizational audit can be used to identify and eliminate sources of employee stress. The level of workplace stress can initially be assessed through the careful review of employee attitude surveys, attendance and illness records, and accident and injury reports. Individuals and departments with possible problems can then be targeted for closer examination and interventions planned to promote worker health and morale.

Case 6

Juanita Velasquez was a forty-year-old prison guard with an outstanding track record at work. Her husband of twenty years, Miguel, suffered from Huntington's disease and was increasingly disabled. His mother had died from the same illness in her forties, and Juanita knew that Miguel would die young as well. Due to concerns over symptoms of depression, the company referred Juanita to a psychiatrist. She was prescribed an antidepressant for depression and began psychotherapy to deal with his anxiety and grief over Miguel's illness.

Shortly after her husband's illness began to worsen, she was moved to the day shift, which began early in the morning. Miguel frequently suffered from bouts of weakness and dizziness in the early morning hours. On her old work schedule, Juanita was at home to care for him in the mornings when these symptoms occurred. His symptoms generally improved sufficiently through the day that she could go to work in the evening without worrying about him. With the new schedule, Juanita was now scheduled to work when Miguel felt the most ill. Juanita asked to be returned to the evening or night shift but was denied.

Within a few weeks of taking over the day shift, she began missing two to three shifts each week. She openly admitted to her supervisors that she was missing work to care for her husband. She became very unreliable regarding working scheduled shifts. In discussing the situation in therapy, she was clear that she felt she owed it to Miguel to be there for him when he was sick. In addition, she was angry with her work supervisors over changing her schedule during this time of crisis. After years of exemplary service, she felt the Corrections Department owed it to her to accommodate her scheduling needs. She felt entitled to take the time she needed, regardless of whether the department gave permission. As her therapy progressed, Juanita developed increasing insight into these issues.

After several months of weekly absences, her supervisor called Juanita into the office. They discussed the situation, and the supervisor made it clear to Juanita that her job was in jeopardy if the absences continued. This was the first time the absence issue was ever discussed, and the conversation threw Juanita into a panic. She went immediately to her psychiatrist's office, where they briefly discussed the situation. The psychiatrist suggested that Juanita contact her supervisors to set up a meeting to discuss the situation and attempt to work out a solution satisfactory to all parties.

The meeting occurred two days later. In attendance were Juanita, her supervisor, and the section supervisor. Her section supervisor was unequivocally supportive of Juanita during this meeting. He openly praised Juanita's work performance while on duty, which had remained outstanding. He said that he would continue to be tolerant of some variations in the work schedule on account of Miguel's illness. However, it was emphasized that Juanita would need to be much more reliable in reporting to work in order to keep her job. Throughout the meeting, Juanita felt that she was treated with respect, that she was being supported, and that she was considered a valuable employee. During the meeting, she freely acknowledged that she needed to cut down her absences. All three agreed to meet in one month to review the situation. Over the next three months, Juanita did not miss any work shifts, returning to her original baseline of high work performance.

This case illustrates several points. First, a number of complex psychological issues were involved in contributing to Juanita 's absences. It was not merely a case of her becoming deliberately irresponsible. Second, solving the problem required active collaboration between Juanita and her supervisors, with input from the psychiatrist. Problems do not usually go away by themselves and often cannot be fixed by one person alone. Third, the demeanor of the supervisors was critical. Juanita responded more favorably to the section supervisor's supportive posture than to her immediate supervisor's initially threatening approach. Fourth, supervisors need to state job expectations firmly in order for employees to be clear about performance goals. While the section supervisor was supportive, he also sent a clear message that Juanita needed to be more reliable about coming to work. Finally, psychotherapy played a key role in helping Juanita to understand the origin of her behavior, allowing her to work successfully with her supervisors on solving the problem.

Challenging yet common work problems are often caused by psychiatric illness or psychosocial problems. The problems of absenteeism, accidents, poor job performance, interpersonal conflict, and job dissatisfaction can be highly disruptive to the work environment. Through a careful assessment of the issues, effective interventions can be planned. The most successful results are achieved when the process involves collaboration among the employee, the employer, and the consulting psychiatrist. Vigilant supervisors can learn to recognize problem behavior promptly and quickly institute corrective actions to help minimize the severity of these issues. Psychiatric assessment and care play a central role in the resolution of these common work problems. This psychiatric care is relatively inexpensive and very cost-effective, considering the tremendous cost incurred by these work problems. Organizations can prevent or minimize these problems, to the benefit of both the employee and the employer.

References and Additional Sources

Bigos, S. J., Battie, M. C., Spengler, D. M., Fisher, L. D., Fordyce, W. E., Hansson, T. H., Nachemson, A. L., & Wortley, M. D. (1991). A prospective study of work perceptions and psychosocial factors affecting the report of back injury. *Spine, 16*, 1–5.

Broadhead, W. E., Blazer, D. G., George, L. K., & Tsee, C. K. (1990). Depression, disability days and days lost from work in a prospective epidemiologic survey. *Journal of the American Medical Association, 264,* 2524–2528.

Conti, D. J., & Burton, W. N. (1994). The economic impact of depression in a workplace. *Journal of Occupational Medicine, 36,* 983–988.

Dauer, C. (1989). Stress hits 25 percent of workforce. *National Underwriter, 93*(44), 49–58.

Druss, B. G., Rosenheck, R. A., & Sledge, W. H. (2000). Health and disability costs of depressive illness in a major U.S. corporation. *American Journal of Psychiatry, 157,* 1274–1278.

Druss, B. G., Schlesinger, M., & Allen, H. M. (2001). Depressive symptoms, satisfaction with health care and 2-year work outcomes in an employed population. *American Journal of Psychiatry, 158,* 731–734.

Greenberg, P. E., Sisitsky T., Kessler, R. C., Finkelstein, S. N., Berndt, E. R., Davidson, J. R., Ballenger, J. C., & Fyer A. J. (1999). The economic burden of anxiety disorders in the 1990s. *Journal of Clinical Psychiatry, 60,* 427–435.

Greenberg, P. E., Stiglin, L. E., Finkelstein, S. N., & Berndt, E. R. (1993). The economic burden of depression in 1990. *Journal of Clinical Psychiatry, 54,* 405–418.

Hoffman, J. P., Brittingham, A., & Larison, C. (1996). *Drug use among U.S. workers: Prevalence and trends by occupation and industry categories.* Rockville, MD: Substance Abuse and Mental Health Services Administration, Office of Applied Studies.

Jenkins, R. (1985). Minor psychiatric morbidity in employed young men and women and its contribution to sickness absence. *British Journal of Industrial Medicine, 42,* 147–154.

Jenkins, R. (1993). Mental health at work—Why is it so under-researched? *Occupational Medicine, 43,* 65–67.

Kessler, R. C., Barber C., Birnbaum H. G., Greenberg, P. E., Rose R. M., Simon, G. E., & Wang, P. (1999). Depression in the workplace: Effects on short-term disability. *Health Affairs, 18,* 163–171.

Kessler, R. C., McGonagle, K. A., Zhao, S., Nelson, C. B., Hughes, M., Eshleman, S., Wittchen, H., & Kendler, K. S. (1994). Lifetime and 12-month prevalence of DSM-III-R psychiatric disorders in the United States. *Archives of General Psychiatry, 51,* 8–19.

Lehmer, M., & Bentley, A. (1997). Treating work stress: An alternative to workers' compensation. *Journal of Occupational and Environmental Medicine, 39,* 63–67.

Niemcryk, S. J., Jenkins, C. D., Rose, R. M., & Hurst, M. W. (1987). The prospective impact of psychosocial variables on rates of illness and injury in professional employees. *Journal of Occupational Medicine, 29,* 645–652.

Normand, J., Salyards, S. D., & Mahoney, J. J. (1990). An evaluation of pre-employment drug testing. *Journal of Applied Psychology, 75,* 629–639.

Pollack, E. S., Franklin, G. M., Fulton-Kehoe, D., & Chowdhury, R. (1998). Risk of job-related injury among construction laborers with a diagnosis of substance abuse. *Journal of Occupational and Environmental Medicine, 40,* 573–577.

Robbins, D. B., Kaminer, A. J., Schussler, T., & Pomper, I. H. (1976). The psychiatric patient at work. *American Journal of Public Health, 66,* 655–659.

Tsai, S. P., Gilstrap, E. L., Colangelo, T. A., Menard, A. K., & Ross, C. E. (1997). Illness absence at an oil refinery and petrochemical plant. *Journal of Occupational and Environmental Medicine, 39,* 455–462.

U.S. Department of Labor. (1998). *Working partners for an alcohol- and drug-free American workplace.* Available on-line at: http://www.dol.gov/dol/asp.

U.S. Public Health Service. (1993). *Depression in primary care: Volume 1. Detection and diagnosis.* Rockville, MD: U.S. Department of Health and Human Services.

Webb, G. R., Redman, S., Hennrikus, D. J., Kelman, G. R., Gibberd, R. W., & Sanson-Fisher, R. W. (1994). The relationships between high-risk and problem drinking and the occurrence of work injuries and related absences. *Journal of Studies on Alcohol, 55,* 434–446.

Wells, K. B., Stewart, A., Hays, R. D., Burnam, M. A., Rogers, W., Danick, M., Berry, S., Greenfield, S., Ware, J. (1989). The functioning and well-being of depressed patients: Results from the Medical Outcomes Study. *Journal of the American Medical Association, 262*(7), 914–919.

CHAPTER FIFTEEN

Emotional Crises in the Workplace

Stephen H. Heidel

Emotional crises in the workplace may occur due to disasters, emotionally traumatic events at the work site, and psychiatric emergencies, including substance abuse, suicidal behavior, and acute psychotic illness. Crises may be caused by natural or human events, problems in the workplace, or employees' emotional problems. These disruptions have a dramatic impact on individual employees and work groups. Organizations should develop appropriate policies and procedures, and should have an inventory of internal and external resources available before an emergency occurs.

Emotional crises in the workplace are increasingly common and can include the following:

- Disasters, such as earthquakes, hurricanes, airplane crashes, school shootings, and terrorist acts

- Work site crises, such as accidents, fires, robberies, and loss of valued leaders

- Substance abuse, causing an unsafe or disruptive workplace for millions of workers

- Suicidal behavior

- Psychotic illnesses, causing peculiar or dangerous behavior

Despite the increasing frequency of emotional crises, companies often do not know how to recognize and respond when problems occur. Managers are often uncomfortable with emotional issues. Not knowing what to do and afraid to make the situation worse, they often avoid emotional problems, hoping the problems will eventually correct themselves. Employees may be equally uncomfortable with emotional crises; feeling awkward, they may find them hard to discuss or understand. They often react with silence. Employees who are themselves in crisis may be afraid of looking weak if they seek help. As a result, emotional crises are too often denied, minimized, and even ignored. The most constructive approach requires acknowledgment, discussion, and proper action.

Healthy organizations accept that emotional crises will affect them periodically and develop policies, procedures, and resources to help deal with problems as they occur. First, each organization needs to consider which emotional crises they may face. Second, each should determine what procedures should be adopted to address those potential crises. Third, they should identify internal resources and supports to deal with those situations. Finally, they should identify what external resources are necessary to supplement their internal supports.

DISASTER AND EMOTIONAL TRAUMA

An earthquake jolts San Francisco. A hurricane strikes Florida. The Mississippi River floods. A nuclear power plant destructs on Three Mile Island. A high school student comes on the school grounds with a rifle and begins shooting at students and teachers. A government building is bombed in Oklahoma City. The World Trade Towers and the Pentagon are struck by airplanes almost simultaneously. Anthrax is mailed to several prominent people. These are traumatic events—some natural, some accidental, and others caused by terrorists—that cause a loss of life and disruption for many people. Individuals who live through these events are victims just as much as those who are killed. The survivors have experienced a severe stress, beyond the range of normal human experience, and may well exhibit symptoms long after the incident has occurred.

Case 1

Employees of Alteer Chemical Company work in Edison, New Jersey, just across the Hudson River from Manhattan. On September 11, 2001, they watched two airplanes crash into the World Trade Center where some of their friends worked. After seeing the fire in the towers, they witnessed the collapse of the towers. The employees reacted with emotional shock. Stunned and overwhelmed by these events, they exhibited a wide variety of symptoms, including grief, uncontrollable anxiety, sadness, anger, crying spells, withdrawal, poor sleep, and diminished concentration. Some of their initial efforts to volunteer and to give blood met with frustration, because the Red Cross and other volunteer organizations were overwhelmed by an outpouring of support.

After several days of continued high emotions and chaos in the workplace, the manager of human resources called an occupational psychiatrist to ask for assistance. The psychiatrist recommended a debriefing for all employees who had witnessed the events of September 11. Employees who worked together met in groups of between ten and fifteen people to discuss what they witnessed and their reactions to it. The groups were filled with emotion as employees described the horror they felt when the attack occurred, their utter helplessness as they watched, their anger at the terrorists, their grief for those who lost friends, their feelings of vulnerability, and their inability to focus on their work. Toward the end of the groups, they discussed ways they could cope and volunteer to assist in the recovery process.

Case 2

Leslie Knotiss, an employee at a high-security facility on the West Coast, discovered a white powder on the floor of a rest room. She notified human resources, which contacted security. The decision was made to evacuate the building, causing four hundred people to leave work. The material was collected using appropriate precautions and taken to a laboratory for analysis. It turned out to be artificial sweetener.

Employees' reactions varied widely. Some seemed to take the incident in stride, recognizing that people were on edge and very hypervigilant. Others were scared and developed symptoms of mild anxiety. Still others were very angry. They thought the organization had overreacted, causing a huge disruption in their work schedule. They were also upset at the thought that one or more of their coworkers had deliberately put the white powder on the floor as a hoax. Because there was so much turmoil and disruption at work following this event, the decision was made to ask a mental health professional to conduct group debriefings. These sessions helped calm the employees and allowed them to return to a normal work schedule.

Case 3

In 1995, two terrorists bombed a federal building in Oklahoma City. Local employers who were interviewed some years after the bombing reported a variety of employee reactions that they observed for a year or more. Some employees exhibited impulsive behavior, such as unexpectedly quitting their jobs. Others had exaggerated fears of bombs and explosives. Some employees who had previously been stable began to exhibit reckless behavior. The reactions of managers and supervisors toward their employees varied. Some became kinder and gentler, while others were less tolerant and heavy-handed, only later feeling guilty about their behavior (Shellenbarger, 2001).

Effects

Individuals involved in a disaster may exhibit a wide range of reactions. These are usually normal reactions to abnormal events. Reactions include physical, behavioral, psychological, and cognitive effects. Physical effects include fatigue, palpitations, and sweating. Behavioral changes include withdrawal, outbursts, changes in sleep patterns and appetite, and increased use of alcohol. Psychological effects include denial, anger, sadness, anxiety, fear, and uncertainty. Cognitive changes include nightmares, confusion, poor concentration, and poor problem solving.

Although most people fully recover over time, others may have an acute stress disorder, a grief reaction, or an adjustment reaction, which will continue for weeks or months. Some may develop long-standing psychiatric illnesses, including depression, anxiety, posttraumatic stress, or substance abuse. They may also experience more physical symptoms or develop a physical illness as a result of being involved in a disaster (Norwood, Ursano, & Fullerton, 2001).

Assessment of the Stressors

Disasters cause traumatic stressors that put people at risk for psychiatric illness. It is important to assess the psychologically stressful aspects of a disaster when trying to determine which employees might be affected the most. These stressors include the threat of losing one's life, physical injury caused by a disaster, exposure to dead bodies and mutilation, loss of a loved one in a sudden or horrific manner, witnessing violence to a loved one, exposure or possible exposure to toxic substances such as radiation or anthrax, living with uncertainty, causing death or harm to other people, and knowing that pain was deliberately inflicted on other people.

The more severe the stressors are that the employee experienced, the more likely that person is to develop a psychiatric illness. Within an organization, employees who were in danger, lost loved ones and close colleagues, or witnessed the traumatic events should be targeted for interventions. Police, paramedics, and others who first respond to disasters and hospital staff involved in assisting the victims may need help as well. Another group at risk are those who are involved in the cleanup of the site of the tragic event (Norwood et al., 2001).

Intervention

A manager needs to respond in an appropriate manner to employee behavior following a disaster. An underreaction might appear as if the manager is not caring and may cause employees to think poorly of their employer. Each manager needs to be a good listener. Initial interventions should focus on educating managers about what to say to employees and giving them suggestions about what to do. They need to acknowledge everything that has happened, offer support, and try to restore order in the workplace (Heidel, 2001). They may need to assist employees in gaining access to insurance money and taking care of basic needs such as housing. Employees with children often want suggestions as to how they might discuss the tragic events with them. A psychiatrist should be able to help parents talk to their children in a manner that is appropriate to their age and development.

An early intervention for employees who have experienced a disaster or traumatic workplace event is a critical incident stress debriefing (CISD): group meetings led by a mental health professional for people who have experienced a traumatic event. An employer considering a CISD should think about the level of distress among the employees, the level of danger posed, the number of employees affected, and the difficulty returning the workplace to normal. Employees are brought together in their normal work groups to discuss what happened and what they experienced emotionally. These groups offer a proactive way to support employees and educate them. One of the main educational messages is to normalize their reactions to the events by telling them they are not crazy; rather, they are having normal reactions to abnormal events. Employees are given the opportunity to express painful emotions and receive emotional support at a time when they might otherwise become isolated and withdrawn. Good coping skills are elicited from the group and reinforced by the facilitator. Employees who appear to be at high risk, based on what they say or their behavior, are identified and offered further assistance after the group is over (Heidel, 1993; Mitchell & Everly, 1994).

Employees at risk should be identified and seen in follow-up on one or more occasions. Those who develop persistent psychiatric symptoms should be referred to the employee assistance program or directly to a psychiatrist for treatment.

TRAUMATIC EVENTS AT THE WORK SITE

A fire in a production plant kills three employees. A lineman with a local power company is accidentally electrocuted. An explosion in a munitions factory kills a machine operator. A well-liked chief operating officer unexpectedly dies in an automobile accident at age forty-one. A small business with forty-five employees lays off ten when the economy heads into a recession. Organizations experience a wide range of events that have a profound impact on the employees, the working environment, and the ability for the organization to conduct its normal business.

Case 4

A machine caught fire in a chemical plant. Ten employees were evacuated when their area filled with smoke. After they left the building, they realized that the machine operator was still inside. Two employees reentered the building and helped the operator out. His clothes were on fire until he was wrapped in a blanket in the parking lot. He was admitted to a burn unit in critical condition and died two days later.

Four days later, the company was still in disarray. Management did not know what to do. Many employees had still not come back to work, and production in the area had stopped. A psychiatrist was called in to meet with top management. He listened to management describe in detail the events of the fire, including their own reactions and those of the employees; described to the managers how people are affected by traumatic events; and outlined a strategy to meet with employees in a series of group meetings.

Two large group meetings were held for all interested employees, who were encouraged to discuss their reactions. The first meeting concluded with a discussion of feelings that would be expected after a disaster, symptoms to be on the lookout for, and healthy coping mechanisms. A second meeting, a follow-up to the first, was attended by a smaller number of employees. They talked more about their reactions to the event, going back to work, and how to cope. Two employees who were still overwhelmed were then identified and referred for individual treatment.

Nine people in the immediate work group had been affected by the fire. Three two-hour meetings were held with this group over a two-week period. These were confidential meetings, and participants were told not to share this information with outside coworkers, management, or friends. One employee had severe anxiety and was not able to enter the fire area. Another was drinking a quart of vodka every night to fall asleep. A third had recurring visual images of the fire and could not concentrate. Another had recently lost both his mother and a friend and had become very depressed. Finally, one employee thought that the company was trying to cover over its own mistakes and did not want to say anything at all. As a result of these meetings, symptoms subsided in all but one employee, who was then referred for individual treatment.

A final meeting was held with top management. By then, the company had become fully operational, and the meeting served as a final report on the employees' progress. In case further efforts were needed, management was given guidelines for detecting recurrent symptoms and workplace dysfunction. In a six-month follow-up, all of the immediate work groups were performing well. No one had quit their job, and management reported that the organization had been running smoothly for two months.

Case 5

George Kain, the chief executive officer of Eagleview Development Company, was a dynamic leader who was very well liked by his employees. Many of the employees had joined the company because they knew and respected him so much. Under his leadership, the organization and the employees had prospered. At the age of forty-eight, he had a massive heart attack and died immediately. Initially, the employees were in a state of shock and disbelief. Several decided to quit, and others felt they could not stay and began looking for another job. The general feeling was that the company would not be worth working for without their leader.

The board of directors met with top management to decide how to react to this crisis. They knew they had to act quickly to replace Kain with another dynamic leader. They were concerned their valued employees would leave and weaken the company. They retained a consulting psychiatrist to help deal with the morale of the staff and help them select the next CEO.

The psychiatrist met with staff individually and in groups, first to facilitate the grief process and then to involve key employees in the process of screening a new leader. This involvement in the process gave the employees renewed confidence in the company, and morale improved. A new CEO with excellent leadership skills was hired. After several months, the new leader was well accepted, and only two employees had left the organization.

Case 6

A man entered a Cielo Bank branch, pulled a gun from a bag, pointed it at a teller, and demanded all the money she had, which was approximately four thousand dollars. As a result of this incident, the individuals working in the bank were in a state of shock and fear. They felt a loss of control and felt violated by the bank robber. The teller who was robbed had a variety of emotional reactions: she felt incompetent because she should not have had so much money available, guilt for somehow not stopping the robber from being able to get the money, anxiety and fearfulness about what might have happened to her, anger at the individual for having done what he did, and relief that no one had been injured. A number of employees experienced poor sleep, nightmares, and increased anxiety as a result of the bank robbery.

The bank asked a psychiatrist to conduct a CISD. Following this intervention, work levels returned to normal, and there was no further emotional disruption. No employees left their jobs, and no workers' compensation claims were filed as a result of the robbery.

Response Determinants for a Traumatic Workplace Event

People who experience a traumatic event at their workplace have widely differing reactions to it. Individual reactions differ for the following reasons:

- *Severity of the event.* The more severe the event is, the greater is the reaction. For example, an accident in which a coworker is injured would precipitate a less severe reaction than if the same person was also injured in an accident where many people were killed and injured.

- *Previous trauma.* An individual who has experienced traumatic events in the past has a more severe reaction than if no previous trauma had been experienced. A bank teller who has experienced previous robberies, for instance, would be more vulnerable than one who has not. The recent trauma would be likely to cause a flooding of emotions from the previous event, as well as the recent one. In contrast, many people are immunized by a trauma and thus less distressed by subsequent events.

- *Previous psychiatric disorder.* Someone who suffers from or has a predisposition to a psychiatric disorder (such as anxiety, depression, or substance abuse) will have more difficulty coping with a traumatic event than someone who does not.

- *Social supports.* A person with a strong nuclear family, close friends, and other community supports (such as church) will be better able to deal with trauma than someone without those supports.

- *Major life changes.* A person who has sustained one or more major life changes (for example, death of a spouse or friend, loss of a job, a move from one location to another, or a major illness) in the past year will have more difficulty dealing with a traumatic event.

- *Self-esteem.* People who have high regard for themselves will be less dev-astated by a traumatic event than those who do not have a good self-image. They are better able to recognize the difference between themselves and their circumstances.

- *Protective role of a supportive and stable work environment.* Some work environments are more supportive and nurturing than others. When a traumatic event occurs at a company that is perceived as caring for its staff, employees may recover more easily because they feel the support from their employer. When support services are offered to employees in need, they and their less affected coworkers will be better able to resolve their problems instead of react-ing with anger or inappropriately blaming the organization.

Effects on the Workplace

Every traumatic event in the workplace will be disruptive to the workforce. At a minimum, it will cause downtime for a few involved employees, but it may destroy the effectiveness of an entire organization. In the case of the factory fire, it took four months for the company to regain its previous level of production. With the bank robbery, it took only a few days. If management does not offer the chance to work through these emotional reactions, employees will be more likely to retain symptoms, delay their recovery, and be more vulnerable to future events. They may harbor tension or resentment toward an employer they per-ceive as unsupportive.

Prevention and Intervention

Organizations that are at a low risk for traumatic incidents may only need to know where to find outside assistance in the unlikely event that it is needed. High-risk organizations include banks, retail stores, gas and electric compa-nies, police and fire departments, airlines, and hospitals. They should have a strategy to deal with traumatic events before they occur. They should develop policies, procedures, and training programs for selected employees. Staff with responsibilities in the event of a trauma might be from human resources, safety, security, the employee assistance program, and the medical depart-ment. They need to know when to respond to traumatic events, how to control their own reactions, how to interact with victims, how to recognize symptoms, and when to call for professional help. Management plays an essential prac-tical and symbolic role in organizing the response to circumstances and main-taining morale.

To the extent that external resources might be necessary, they should be identified in advance. There should be logical reasons for calling different re-sources. Resources might include police, fire department, paramedics, security, public health, the employee assistance program, and professionals trained to perform CISDs.

SUBSTANCE ABUSE EMERGENCIES

Drug and alcohol abuse are devastating problems (see Chapters Twenty-Four and Twenty-Five). Intoxication or drug withdrawal on the job is often an emergency that affects the workplace.

Case 7

Chuck Derossi, a fifty-three-year-old married bank senior vice president, had gone through an alcohol treatment program three and a half years ago. He said that he was then able to stop drinking alcohol. Now, though, he was not handling stress well and had trouble concentrating at work. He rambled, had temper tantrums, and lacked attention to detail. He appeared to have blackouts, since he could not recall recent conversations. Confronted by the president of the bank, Chuck admitted to drinking and said he would stop. He did stop, but without any medical or psychiatric assistance. Two days later while at work, he developed nausea, vomiting, profuse sweating, and severe abdominal pain. Paramedics rushed him to the emergency room, where he was found to be in alcoholic withdrawal. He was admitted to the hospital under psychiatric care and three days later transferred to an evening alcohol treatment program. Six months later, Chuck said that he would be dead if it was not for the bank president's intervention and subsequent alcoholism treatment.

Case 8

Doug Drover, a forty-four-year-old married manufacturing company supervisor, was known to spend extended lunch hours at a local bar. After lunch, he usually smelled of breath mints. It was well known within the production area that he would then be more belligerent. One day, he became verbally and physically abusive while reviewing problems with a finished product. In addition to swearing at several employees, he began throwing equipment. The personnel manager met with a consultant for advice about how to handle Doug and then referred him for help.

A meeting with Doug and his wife revealed a long history of alcohol abuse, including the consequent loss of a job ten years before, an automobile accident while drunk, and a citation for driving under the influence. Doug agreed he had an alcohol problem and entered an outpatient treatment program. Afterward, though, he refused to attend Alcoholics Anonymous meetings and agreed only not to drink during working hours. A one-year follow-up showed that Doug had an improved job performance and was no longer belligerent but presumably was still drinking alcohol.

Causes of Substance Abuse Workplace Problems

Alcohol and drug abusers often lose the ability to control the addictive substances they use. As a result, they may use the substances before coming to work or while at work. When this happens, they may become acutely intoxicated or be in a state of withdrawal, situations that can lead to a workplace crisis.

Effects on the Workplace

The effects of substance abuse in the workplace range from chronic to acute. Many substance-abusing employees seem to have a series of isolated incidents that are not emergencies and that coworkers do not recognize as a real problem. As an addiction progresses, employees and supervisors often deny the seriousness of the problem. Workers may be afraid to speak up, unsure if management will support them and fearing reprisals from addicted employees. This can be especially problematic when drug-abusing employees are involved in drug sales or otherwise enmeshed in the drug culture. Employees must be assured that any comments they make to a supervisor will be treated confidentially and with discretion.

Coworkers will make excuses or cover for an impaired employee. Supervisors will accept poor or erratic performance, delegate work assignments to coworkers, take on tasks themselves, and ultimately become frustrated and angry. After supervisors express their anger and frustration with an addicted employee's performance, the employee's job performance may improve temporarily but then deteriorate further. Later, the addicted employee may suddenly show serious misjudgment, outrageous behavior, or acute illness or incur serious accidents. Coworkers will become alarmed or fearful, especially in safety-sensitive areas. Ultimately, morale deteriorates, and the company is viewed as unwilling or unable to deal with the problem until an emergency arises. These events are clinical emergencies and can have major disruptive effects on the organization.

Intervention

Many companies anticipate drug and alcohol problems before they occur with preventive elements of a drug-free workplace that include policy development, drug testing, education for employees, training for supervisors, intervention, and treatment (see Chapters Twenty-Four and Twenty-Five for more detail).

When an employee is obviously intoxicated, action must be taken immediately. A supervisor should follow company protocol to document the problem, talk to the employee, and make an intervention. Other staff from the company may need to be involved, including another supervisor or manager, human resources, security, and the medical department. Intoxication severely impairs the capacity for rational discussion. If the employee is belligerent, security or the local police may be needed to keep control of the situation.

If an employee is mentally or physically impaired, it may be necessary to escort that person away from the workplace. Decisions must be made about whether the employee should be escorted home, sent to the medical department, referred to an outside physician, required to take a drug test, scheduled to see an employee assistance counselor, or scheduled for a psychiatric fitness-for-duty exam. An employee who is having difficulty breathing or is unresponsive may have overdosed on drugs or alcohol. Paramedics should be called, and the employee should be taken to a hospital as quickly as possible.

Prevention

Companies can minimize these problems. Every company should perform pre-employment drug and alcohol screening on all new employees and educate all employees about the use of alcohol and illicit drugs, including the consequences for using them at the workplace. They should monitor employees who are returning to work after substance abuse treatment by random urine tests for drugs and alcohol and careful documentation of their behavior and job performance. This will allow an organization to become aware of many drug and alcohol problems before they become an emergency.

SUICIDE

Depression, anxiety disorders, substance abuse, and psychotic disorders are risk factors for suicide. Suicidal threats, gestures, and actions are unfortunately commonplace in our society and occur in the workplace.

Case 9

An employee jumped from the roof of his office building. Denise Harimoto, a coworker with a long-standing depression, was the first person on the scene. Denise was flooded with emotions, felt angry and victimized by the event, and began talking about suicide. She was immediately taken to the medical department, assessed by a nurse, and referred to a psychiatrist. After one crisis intervention session, she no longer felt victimized or suicidal. Her depression fully resolved after a four-month period of treatment with supportive psychotherapy and an antidepressant.

Case 10

A female machinist who was an excellent employee committed suicide. Prior to the suicide, she had shot herself in the foot, reportedly while cleaning a gun at home. She also had had three industrial accidents in a one-month period, two of them on the same day. Several times, she told coworkers that it was very difficult for her to "go on." No one had ever directed her to the medical department or to a qualified professional.

Following the suicide, two support groups were held for coworkers. Some of these employees were not surprised when they learned of her suicide but felt guilty and responsible for its occurrence. Some were angry at her for abandoning her husband and children. Others spoke of how her death triggered thoughts of vulnerability and traumatic events in their own lives. Employees talked about previous social events and conversations with the deceased. One supervisor remembered her fondly for her diligent work on an important project. A close friend was left a note saying, "I am sorry, but I can't go on anymore." Employees in her work group reported that they were not functioning well on the job after the suicide. After the support meetings, there was a large employee turnout for the funeral and many offers to help the bereaved family. The company nurse made a visit to the family afterward and encouraged the husband to seek family therapy.

Case 11

Stella Groban, a twenty-nine-year-old computer technician, had been an average worker for four years. She was moody, had poor interpersonal skills, and often talked about suicide. Sometimes she showed coworkers a razor she carried in her pocketbook and then complained that nobody understood her. Twice she was out on medical leave, returning once with scars on her wrists and the other time with vague comments about "taking too many pills." Her coworkers had always found Stella difficult to deal with, and many had transferred to other work areas. Those who remained found themselves feeling constantly on guard, angry, and frightened whenever she was around. Morale and productivity were low.

This time, Stella had been loudly unhappy for two months, with uncontrollable crying, anger toward coworkers, and poor-quality work. Her coworkers stayed away from her, which made her feel even unhappier. One day, she left her razor on her desktop, put her head down, cried openly, and threatened to kill herself when coworkers did try to help. At the supervisor's insistence, she was referred for immediate psychiatric evaluation. The consultant noted symptoms of acute major depression, chronic atypical depression, and borderline personality disorder. After three weeks of an antidepressant medication and supportive psychotherapy, she returned to work. Although her severe depressive symptoms had subsided, her chaotic and angry interpersonal style was at first unchanged. Weekly psychotherapy, with continuing medication, brought about gradual change. Stella was later able to apologize to coworkers for her anger and gradually felt more accepted at work.

Causes

Suicide has the following risk factors (Barber, Marzuk, Leon, & Portera, 1998; Bostwick & Pankratz, 2000; Hall, Platt, & Hall, 1999; Harkavy-Friedman et al., 1999; Mann, Waternaux, Haas, & Malone, 1999; Radomsky, Haas, Mann, & Sweeney, 1999):

- Direct verbal suicide threats
- Subjective feelings of severe depression and hopelessness
- Previous suicide attempts or aborted attempts
- Previous hospitalization with expressions of suicidality

- History of aggressive and impulsive behavior
- Recent loss of a relationship (widowed, separated, divorced, bereaved)
- Family history of suicide
- Psychiatric illness (depression, anxiety, psychosis, substance abuse, severe personality disorder)
- Physical illness

Suicidal behavior usually results from the interplay of life stresses and predisposing psychiatric problems. Events at work can be among those stresses, especially when an employee loses his or her job for a humiliating reason, such as embezzlement. Major organizational changes, such as rapid growth, mergers, and reductions in force, cause a loss of control, uncertainty, and emotional distress for involved employees (see Chapters Eight and Twelve). These may all contribute to depression and anxiety, and thus suicide risk. Critical, unresponsive, or distressed managers increase employees' distress and their feeling of hopelessness.

Effects on the Workplace

The suicide of an employee leaves an emotional aftermath that should not be underestimated. Coworkers may feel grief, anger, and fear. They may feel guilty about the suicide and fearful for their own well-being. The effects on morale can be devastating. These effects are worsened still when the organizational culture does not allow recognition of the emotions and their disruptive potential.

Prevention and Intervention

Before managers or coworkers can recognize and help an employee at risk for suicide, they must first understand something about the nature of depression and anxiety symptoms and their workplace manifestations. Employees must know where to turn; supervisors must know how to talk to a distressed or dysfunctional employee.

Every company should identify sources of support for crisis or time of need. The human resource, medical, security, and training departments, as well as psychiatric consultants and employee assistance programs, may all be sources of support.

Key staff should be taught the symptoms of depression and how depression may manifest on the job. They must also be taught how to talk with an employee exhibiting job performance problems and steer the person to an appropriate resource for a thorough psychiatric assessment. It is not adequate simply to tell an employee to seek help or to refer the person to the family doctor. The chance that an employee would follow through on that kind of a referral is slight. An employee with an emotional problem should be seen by an employee assistance program or a psychiatric consultant for accurate diagnosis and appropriate referral.

Finally, when an employee commits suicide, group debriefings (CISDs) should be led by mental health professionals who understand suicide, diagnosis, and group process. This will allow employees to talk about the suicide, express their grief, support each other, and discuss how to help the surviving family. This supportive group process will help employees put the event behind them more quickly and refocus on their job.

PSYCHOTIC BEHAVIOR

Occasionally an employee will make little sense or appear to have lost contact with reality (see Chapter Twenty-Six). This is clearly a psychiatric emergency. Possible causes include psychosis of various kinds, medical illness, and substance abuse. Common symptoms of psychotic employees include incoherent speech or thought, grossly inappropriate emotions, paranoia (markedly unreasonable and unbending distrust), delusions (false beliefs maintained in the face of reason), and hallucinations (usually false voices). Employees who are psychotic are also at risk for suicide (Radomsky et al., 1999).

Case 12

Louis Spakos, a twenty-eight-year-old single aircraft assembler, had worked at his company for seven years. He had been an average employee until he began showing strange behavior. For several months, he was verbally aggressive and stared into space. He was paranoid, feeling that people at work and home were following him. Louis began talking about being Jesus Christ and commented to a coworker that he might kill his supervisor. He was taken to the medical department and referred for emergency psychiatric hospitalization. He responded well to a short inpatient stay and an antipsychotic medication. Back at work, Louis was somewhat withdrawn, but otherwise back to his old self.

Case 13

Molly Brooks, a thirty-five-year-old married flight attendant, developed a higher level of energy at work and tremendous enthusiasm for her company. She went to one of the company's directors to give him some ideas for promoting the airline. Consequently, she was offered a job in the marketing department. On her last flight before her transfer, she was inappropriately cheerful and sexually seductive, making passes at male passengers. While serving dessert, she shot whipped cream throughout the airplane. After the flight, Molly was referred for a psychiatric evaluation. She was euphoric, grandiose, and easily agitated. She said she had been talking to God and also that she had been drinking more alcohol than usual. She was diagnosed as having bipolar (manic depressive) illness, hospitalized, and treated with medication to normalize her mood and thought process. Molly successfully returned to work in the marketing department.

Case 14

Pat Scranton, forty-one years old and married, complained of hearing music through the air-conditioning vents. Although her manager could not hear the music, he had the vent boarded up to block the sound anyway. She continued to complain of music and was ultimately referred to a psychiatrist. Pat admitted to the psychiatrist that she was smoking crack cocaine every day. The cocaine was causing an auditory hallucination that went away when she stopped smoking. This psychiatric emergency was not initially recognized but was addressed before the psychosis worsened.

Case 15

Morse McCarron, a fifty-five-year-old separated senior executive for a defense contractor, was sent to a management training program for one week. During the group sessions, he was frequently unintelligible. He had a grandiose mood and felt that he was Jesus Christ. He was drinking six to ten martinis each evening during the conference. When he returned to work, he was seen in consultation and immediately hospitalized. He was gradually withdrawn from alcohol, at which point his mood stabilized and his delusions went away. Morse returned to work, stayed sober, and decided to try to reconcile with his wife.

Causes of Psychosis

Among the many causes of psychotic behavior, the most common are schizophrenia, mania, depression, alcohol, cocaine, amphetamines, hallucinogens, prescription drug side effects, and medical illness. Although workplace stress might indirectly worsen a psychotic illness, psychosis is not generally work related. Too often, employees with a psychotic illness are overlooked until there is a crisis.

Effects on the Workplace

When employees become psychotic, they disrupt the workplace and may pose a threat of injury. Reactions of coworkers vary a great deal, but many become very concerned. Most will be frightened or distressed and will usually not want to work or associate with psychotic employees. Other coworkers will take pity and try to help. Some may deny the significance of the situation and hope the problem will correct itself in time.

Prevention and Intervention

It is essential for employers to react quickly when emergencies of this nature occur. The internal and external resources must be mobilized immediately. When there is a risk of violence, security should be called. The employee with a psychotic disorder should be escorted from the workplace to an appropriate medical facility for an immediate psychiatric evaluation. There is a high likelihood that this employee will need hospitalization and treatment with psychiatric medications.

When the employee is stabilized and ready to return to work, a fitness-for-duty exam should be performed. This will give valuable information to the company about the nature of the problem and the employee's level of functioning. The prognosis of an employee who has been psychotic depends on the underlying cause of the psychotic illness. If the psychosis was caused by schizophrenia or a depressive illness, there may be a decline in occupational performance (Beiser et al., 1994). When the employee is released to work, a return-to-work meeting should specify job expectations and the employee's responsibilities for continued psychiatric treatment (see Chapter Seventeen). These might include medications, psychotherapy, and support groups. Side effects of prescribed medication should be specified. A release of information should be signed for the psychiatrist to contact the employer if the employee is noncompliant with treatment or there is a change in the employee's clinical condition. All of this information should be summarized in a return-to-work agreement. Employees who have suffered a psychotic episode should be reassured that they will be helped to stay in control. Managers and supervisors of these employees will need help to create a working environment that maximizes support and stability.

Organizations need to be prepared to deal with emotional crises at the workplace. They should first think about how they might inadvertently cause or contribute to emotional crises. Policies and procedures should be developed to guide organizations when a crisis occurs. Supervisors and managers should have training about their initial response to different situations and how to contact internal and external resources. Planning will ensure that employees are promptly directed to needed professional help and minimize the disruption to the workplace.

References and Additional Sources

Barber, M., Marzuk, P., Leon, A., & Portera, L. (1998). Aborted suicide attempts: A new classification of suicidal behavior. *American Journal of Psychiatry, 1*(55), 385–389.

Beiser, M., Bean, G., Erickson, D., Zhang, J., Iacono, W. G., & Rector, N. A. (1994). Biological and psychosocial predictors of job performance following a first episode of psychosis. *American Journal of Psychiatry, 151,* 857–863.

Bostwick, J. M., & Pankratz, S. (2000). Affective disorders and suicide risk: A reexamination. *American Journal of Psychiatry, 157,* 1925–1932.

Hall, R., Platt, D., & Hall, R. (1999). Suicide risk assessment: A review of risk factors for suicide in 100 patients who made severe suicide attempts: Evaluation of suicide risk in a time of managed care. *Psychosomatics, 40,* 18–27.

Harkavy-Friedman, J. M., Restifok, Malaspina, D., Kaufman, C. A., Amador, X. F., Yale, S. S., & Gorman, J. M. (1999). Suicidal behavior in schizophrenia: Characteristics of individuals who had and had not attempted suicide. *American Journal of Psychiatry, 156,* 1276–1278.

Heidel, S. (1993, July 15–16). Responding to emotionally traumatic workplace events. *Psychiatric Times.*

Heidel, S. (2001, October 24). Managing employees in turbulent times. *San Diego Daily Transcript,* p. 9A.

Mann, J., Waternaux, C., Haas, G., & Malone, K. (1999). Toward a clinical model of suicidal behavior in psychiatric patients. *American Journal of Psychiatry, 156,* 181–189.

Mitchell, J., & Everly, G. (1994). *Human elements training for emergency services, public safety and disaster personnel: An instructional guide to teaching debriefing, crisis intervention and stress management programs.* Ellicott City, MD: Chevron Publishing Corporation.

Norwood, A., Ursano, R., & Fullerton, C. (2001). Disaster psychiatry: Principles and practice. Available on-line at: http://www.psych.org/pract_of_psych/principles_and_practice3201.cfm.

Radomsky E. D., Haas, G. L., Mann, J. J., & Sweeney, J. A. (1999). Suicidal behavior in patients with schizophrenia and other psychotic disorders. *American Journal of Psychiatry, 156,* 1590–1595.

Shellenbarger, S. (2001, October 10). Oklahoma City bomb offers some insights into employee reaction. *Wall Street Journal,* p. B1.

CHAPTER SIXTEEN

Violence in the Workplace

Ronald Schouten

Workplace violence has become a focus of considerable concern for employers and employees. The actual scope of the workplace violence problem is more limited than is commonly believed. Nevertheless, the serious consequences of actual incidents and threats of violence require that employers pay attention to the issue and craft appropriate responses. Mental health professionals who possess the necessary skills and experience can play important and helpful roles as consultants in workplace threat and violence matters. Knowledge-based risk assessment, awareness of the limitations on certainty in this area, appropriate management of situations, and development of workable policies can help reduce the risk of these incidents.

The 1990s was the decade of workplace violence, not because of its frequency but because of the attention it received. A series of shootings at U.S. Postal Service facilities started a decade in which many began to believe that work had become an unsafe place and that gun-toting, disgruntled coworkers were stalking the locker rooms and cubicles of every workplace in the country. Reasonable concerns arising from a series of incidents were converted to widespread fear, fueled by the intense media coverage of the incidents, the availability of the Internet as a means of spreading often inaccurate information, and the entreaties of an army of newly hatched consultants offering their expertise and profiles of potential perpetrators of workplace violence.

DEFINING WORKPLACE VIOLENCE AND THREAT ASSESSMENT

There is no single, widely accepted definition of workplace violence. A recent review of the literature yielded a limited number of peer-reviewed articles using empirical research and original data analysis published from 1987 to 2001 (Schouten & Rothman, 2002). Of the twelve articles identified, three defined workplace aggression as including organizational obstructionism and verbal, emotional, and sexual abuse, as well as physical assault. Two others limited the definition of violence to physical assaults, and two used definitions of workplace violence that include threats, assaults, and harassment. Others included work slowdowns and other acts of nonviolent aggression against the organization. Workplace aggression is defined by one group of authors as "any form of behavior by individuals that is intended to harm previous or current coworkers or their organization" (Folger & Baron, 1996, p. 52).

For the purposes of this chapter, workplace violence will be broadly defined to include all hostile acts toward employees, customers and clients, and the organization, physical and verbal. This includes threats and defamatory statements communicated by letter, e-mail, voice mail, fax, or published in the print media or on the Internet. This definition is broad in order to capture the types of referrals that mental health professionals and others who work in this field receive.

POTENTIAL ROLES FOR MENTAL HEALTH PROFESSIONALS IN THREAT ASSESSMENT

Threats and acts of violence in the workplace constitute abnormal behavior. Perhaps that is why mental health professionals are often called on to assess the potential for danger and to help manage potential threats. Or perhaps it is because despite the research available, mental illness is frequently equated with violence (Monahan & Steadman, 1994). No matter the reason, mental health professionals are often presumed, with variable degrees of accuracy, to have a level of expertise in this area. Although nothing in the standard training of psychiatrists, psychologists, and social workers provides this specific knowledge, the clinical expertise and knowledge of human behavior that these professionals possess can be valuable additions to the threat assessment and management process. Additional education, training, and collaboration with professionals from other fields, such as law enforcement, private security, law, and human resources, can make the mental health professional a valuable member of the team.

Mental health professionals and other behavioral consultants in this area have four basic functions:

- Assess the likelihood, nature, and seriousness of a threat or act of violence. This can include the threat of physical injury to others, physical injury to the subject, damage to property, intentional injury to the reputation of other individuals or the company, and intentional injury to business operations.

- Develop strategies for managing a particular threatening situation in order to minimize or eliminate a specific risk and prevent a recurrence.

- Assist organizations in the development of violence policies.

- Serve as permanent or consulting members of organizational crisis management and threat management teams.

Ultimately, the most helpful role for mental health professionals in workplace threat and violence situations relates back to their clinical skills in two areas: the ability to understand behavioral responses and shape them and the ability to understand anxiety and manage it. Threats and acts of violence are problematic behavioral responses. Mental health professionals can use their understanding of mental disorders, especially personality disorders, to help interpret the physical and verbal behaviors of subjects and choose management strategies to resolve conflict and reduce risks. It is the anxiety of the client about those behavioral responses that usually drives the consultation request. The consultant who adds the most value is one who can use his or her knowledge and skill to calm the client who is overly anxious and encourage an appropriate level of concern in the client who refuses to recognize that some risk may exist.

KNOWLEDGE BASE FOR THREAT ASSESSMENT AND VIOLENCE IN THE WORKPLACE

The necessary information for understanding and addressing workplace violence begins with information about types of violence, motivations, categorization, problem magnitude, and methods for assessment and prediction.

Types and Motivations for Threatening Behavior

The term *threat* encompasses a number of behaviors that result in, or are likely to result in, fear on the part of the person who experiences them. Threats can be direct ("I'm going to kill you") or implied ("You know, a guy with an attitude like yours could find himself in a bad situation some day"). Threats may be made contingent on the occurrence, or nonoccurrence, of some other event, such as, "If I lose this grievance, someone's going to get hurt." In many cases, concern is generated because threats are inferred, such as where one individual perceives the completely unintentional and benign behavior of another as threatening.

Threats and acts of violence may occur for many reasons. Commonly, threats are made because the person making the threat is afraid of some action, real or imagined, on the part of the subject of the threat. Someone who is frightened of the financial consequences of a pay cut may make a threatening statement with the intention of dissuading management from taking such an action. Similarly, an individual may become violent in reaction to a real or perceived threat of harm from another. Threats and acts of violence can be used to create fear in others in order to manipulate decisions that may affect the threatener. Increasingly, such behavior is not tolerated and leads to suspension or termination. However, I have consulted on numerous cases where employers were hesitant to take disciplinary action against an employee who had made similar statements, for fear the employee would make good on the direct or implied threats. To a large extent, these employees used threats successfully, at least for a time. Another manipulative use of threats or violence is for political gain. Here, the violence or potential for violence is used to influence political decisions or to attract attention to a cause.

Threats and acts of violence toward people or property may also be used for revenge or to harass others. Mental health professionals can be helpful in identifying individuals who are acting out of rage or desire for revenge and offer strategies for defusing the situation.

Case 1

Alan Socary became enraged at his employer after his paycheck was shorted on three subsequent occasions. Generally perceived as an angry, hostile man, Alan's initial complaint after the first incident was aggressive but fairly restrained. The response from the payroll department was indifferent and unhelpful. After the third incident, which resulted in Alan's being unable to pay some of his bills, he became increasingly angry and began verbally harassing the payroll manager with hang-up phone calls and comments like, "What the payroll department needs is a couple of bullets." After hearing information about the incident and Alan's past interactions at work, the mental health consultant serving on the company's threat assessment team suggested that the problem was arising from the interplay between Alan's apparent personality traits and payroll's lack of respect and concern regarding his problem. An intervention was designed that included counseling the payroll department on handling this and other matters, as well as a referral for a fitness-for-duty evaluation.

In the evaluation, Alan explained his devotion to the company (confirmed by other informants) and his frustration at not being able to provide for his family, and he detailed the disrespectful attitude of the payroll manager (also confirmed by other informants). Following the fitness-for-duty evaluation, which found that he did not pose a significant risk of harm, the employer decided to place Alan on probation and allow him to return to work.

Finally, there are those who engage in threats, such as bomb threats or biochemical terrorism hoaxes, for fun. In response to the anthrax threats following the terrorist attacks of September 11, 2001, Congress passed legislation that makes it a felony to threaten harm with a weapon of mass destruction. A series of well-published indictments under this statute appeared to stem the rising tide of these disruptive and decidedly unamusing acts.

A Classification System for Workplace Violence

Workplace threats and violence can take many forms. One classification scheme for workplace violence events divides them into four groups (Peek-Asa, Howard, Vargas, & Kraus, 1997):

Type I: Events that are the result of criminal intent, such as robbery

Type II: Events perpetrated by customers or clients

Type III: Worker-on-worker violence

Type IV: Violence stemming from personal relationships, such as domestic violence spilling over into the workplace

While most media attention and public concern is focused on Type III violence, they account for a limited proportion of total workplace homicides.

Scope of Workplace Violence

The combination of media attention and the catastrophic nature of workplace homicides have resulted in an impression that there is an epidemic of workplace violence. The published literature is replete with references to this so-called epidemic. However, examination of the data gathered by the Bureau of Labor Statistics of the U.S. Department of Labor reveals the epidemic, and several other commonly held beliefs, to be inaccurate (U.S. Department of Labor, 2001b):

Belief: Workplace violence is on the increase.

Fact: There was a 34 percent drop in workplace homicides between the peak number in 1994 and 2000 (U.S Department of Labor, 2001b).

Belief: Workplace homicide is the leading cause of death at work.

Fact: Workplace homicide is the number three cause of death in the workplace, behind highway accidents and falls from high places (U.S. Department of Labor, 2001b). It has never been the leading cause of death in the workplace and has always been second to highway accidents.

Belief: When workplace homicides do occur, the perpetrators are primarily disgruntled coworkers or former coworkers.

Fact: The vast majority of workplace homicides are committed by outsiders in the course of robbery or attempts at other crimes (Type I). From 1993 to 2000, coworkers or former coworkers committed a minority of workplace homicides, varying between 5 and 11 percent (Type III). Thus, of the 677 workplace homicides in the United States in 2000, 74 (11 percent) were committed by coworkers or former coworkers. Customers or clients accounted for 2 to 6 percent of the workplace homicides from 1993 to 2000 (Type II). Personal acquaintances, primarily in domestic violence situations that spill into the workplace, were responsible for 4 to 7 percent (Type IV; U.S. Department of Labor, 2001a, 2001b).

A more pervasive problem than workplace homicides is nonfatal assaults at work. According to the Department of Labor (1998b), from 1992 to 1996, almost 2 million people were victims of violent crime in the workplace each year, with 23,225 such incidents in 1999 (U.S. Department of Justice, 2001) This number is certainly of concern, but should be compared to other types of injuries. For example, more people are harmed as a result of self-poisoning or insect stings in a year than are assaulted by coworkers (Office of Statistics and Programming, 2001). Yet a search of the Lexis-Nexis database, which includes articles from top-circulation English-language newspapers, revealed sixty-five articles on workplace violence published in 2001. Only five articles were published on self-poisoning or insect stings for this same year period.

In short, there is no epidemic of workplace violence in the United States, especially with regard to Type III events. Yet any incidence of violence, nonfatal or fatal, is too high. The consequences are devastating to the individual victims and the organization.

Assessing the Risk of Violence

Faced with a threat of potential violence, the typical individual or corporate victim has some basic questions and needs:

- How likely is the event to occur?
- What is the threatener's potential for violence?
- How significant is the harm threatened?
- What can be done to prevent it?

Analysis of any threat situation requires an acknowledgment that violence is not the product of a single factor. Rather, it is the product of the interaction between a number of variables, including the individual's traits, the environment in which he or she is functioning, and situational factors or triggers (Fein, Vossekuil, & Holden, 1995). Even a person with a high propensity for violence is not violent all the time. The challenge lies in determining what factors are likely to incite such a person to act and to intervene so that those factors are diminished or eliminated. Employee Alan Socary in case 1 represents just such a situation: someone with a propensity for aggressive behavior who is provoked by actions within the company.

Employers who are concerned that an employee may be predisposed to aggressive behavior may seek solutions that actually increase rather than decrease risks. For example, a client calls a consultant and states that he is worried because an employee has a history of violence. The client wants to terminate the employee on the basis that he may be violent at work in the future. Although the client may be justifiably concerned about the employee's history of violence, the use of termination as a means of dealing with the risk may in fact escalate it by creating a situation without which the risk might remain minimal.

Analysis of threat situations also requires acknowledging the limits on our ability to predict violent behavior. Mental health professionals should be familiar with the literature on prediction of violence. The most recent research suggests that when actuarial data and clinical judgment are combined, mental health professionals can predict violent behavior with a better-than-average rate of accuracy (Monahan & Steadman, 1994). Monahan et al. (2001), in their research as part of the MacArthur Study of Mental Illness and Violence, concluded that an actuarial model that uses iterative classification tree analysis can yield estimates of violence risk. They identified a number of risk factors for future violence among people with mental illness, including (but not limited to) the presence of psychopathy, history of serious child abuse, frequency of prior arrests, father's drug use, and psychotic symptoms associated with threat and control override symptoms. They conclude:

> Our data are most consistent with the view that the propensity for violence is the result of the accumulation of risk factors, no one of which is either necessary or sufficient for a person to behave aggressively toward others. People will be violent by virtue of the presence of different sets of risk factors. There is no single path in a person's life that leads to an act of violence [p. 137].

These studies and the risk factors they identify include many of the factors that mental health professionals have used clinically for years in assessing the potential for violence by mentally ill patients. There are two caveats for those who would attempt to adopt their findings wholesale as part of a workplace threat assessment consultation. First, these excellent studies were conducted on current and former psychiatric patients and so are of limited applicability in the majority of workplace violence and other threat assessments where there is no mental illness or, if there is an illness, the symptoms, diagnoses, and other relevant factors are not known. Second, the client who seeks consultation on a workplace threat situation is unlikely to be satisfied or comforted with the response, "The probability of violence for this type of individual is 'only' 55 percent."

Ultimately, the consultation provided in threat situations serves many purposes: identification of risk factors, assessment of degree of risk, identification of the need for protective measures, and management of threatening situations.

These can all be distilled into a single function: reassurance and anxiety management for the client.

What We Know (and Think We Know)
About Workplace Violence Risk Assessment

The degree of concern about workplace violence has resulted in a demand for information and certainty that has not yet been filled by scientific research. Under the best of circumstances, this demand is met by experience-based knowledge and clinical expertise. At worst, it is met by supposition and entrenched bias.

The most widely used technique for violence risk assessment in the workplace is the behavioral profile. The popularity of profiles is understandable. They answer the public's desire for a simple, understandable, and apparently accurate method of identifying employees and coworkers who are likely to be violent.

The study of workplace violence suffers from a number of statistical challenges. First, workplace violence is a low-incidence phenomenon. As such, even very accurate measures will result in a high rate of false positives, that is, over-prediction of violent behavior (Rosen, 1954). As a result, the instrument would identify as potentially violent, and subject to not hiring or termination, a high number of individuals who are unlikely to be violent. This has significant implications for manpower needs as well as legal liability (for example, wrongful termination and disability discrimination).

A second problem is the small number of workplace homicides results in a sample size that is too small to allow conclusions to be drawn and applied to the population at large.

Third, the problem of small sample size is compounded by the fact that few perpetrators of completed acts of workplace violence are available for study. In workplace homicides, a significant number of perpetrators are unavailable due to death at the time of the event (by suicide or in the course of apprehension), ongoing litigation, or unwillingness to speak with researchers. Those who do survive the event and agree to be interviewed are a self-selected group who may not be representative of the larger universe of violence perpetrators.

A fourth problem is that the sources of information come from less-than-complete sources. Common sources of information are anecdotes related by those who have experienced violent incidents or threats, newspaper and television accounts, and court records. Although court records could potentially contain the most complete accounts of perpetrators and the circumstances of an incident, the rules of evidence and legal strategies can result in an incomplete picture.

The factors assumed in workplace violence profiles have face validity, that is, each individual factor appears to be present in one or more perpetrators of Type III violence in known cases and is thus assumed to have some predictive value. But the profiles themselves have never been validated and have never been demonstrated to have any predictive value. Some authors have conducted empirical studies of individual factors in Type III violence. For the most part, however, the commonly accepted factors have not been empirically validated. Even when they have been validated as being present in perpetrators of workplace violence, none of the factors has been demonstrated to have predictive value.

The profiles offered most frequently tend to include factors such as these:

- White male between the ages of thirty and fifty
- Expects to lose job or has lost it
- Sense of identity closely tied to the job
- History of poor relationships with coworkers and supervisors
- Loner
- Difficulty with authority
- Tendency to blame others for problems
- Threats of and actual sexual harassment
- Substance abuse
- Preoccupation with weapons
- History of depression or paranoia
- History of violence
- History of encounters with violence
- Discusses past violence by others
- Works in a company with an authoritarian management style

A review of the literature generated a list of sixteen risk factors that had been found through empirical research to be present in employee-on-employee violence incidents (Schouten & Rothman, 2002). None of the studies reviewed covered workplace homicides, and methodological concerns, such as a lack of denominators, existed for many of the studies. In addition, they suffer from the same statistical problems as profiles. Therefore, caution must be exercised when interpreting and extrapolating from these data. The methodological flaws require that conclusions regarding the implications of any of these factors be questioned. The following factors were identified in these studies:

- Dissatisfaction with treatment by supervisor
- Younger age (in contrast to the ages thirty to fifty often suggested)
- Male gender
- Union membership
- Being laid off

- Trait anger
- Believing revenge is justified when wronged
- Tendency to blame others for problems
- Previous exposure to aggressive cultures
- History of antisocial behavior
- Alcohol abuse
- Criminal history

The literature review found no research establishing the validity of a number of widely accepted individual risk factors:

- History of violence
- High frustration level
- Negative affect
- Loner
- History of drug use
- Poor work history
- Psychological dysfunction
- Fascination with the military and weapons
- Inability to accept criticism or authority
- Irrational beliefs or ideas
- Length of job tenure
- Paranoid personality traits
- Mismanaged stress
- Marital and financial problems
- Rude remarks to others, harassment, and bigoted beliefs
- Being older than thirty-five years

That does not mean, however, that these factors are not relevant, have been disproved, or might not be validated in the future, merely that they have not been validated at the time of this writing.

A number of organizational risk factors for workplace violence have also been proposed. Fifteen organizational factors were identified in the literature search along with seven proposed protective factors that were unsubstantiated. The following studied risk factors correlated with the occurrence of workplace aggression:

- Pay cuts or pay freezes
- Use of part-time employees
- Changes in management
- Increased diversity of the workforce
- Use of computers to monitor employee performance
- Corporate reengineering
- Budget cuts
- Deteriorating physical environment
- Workplace located in the city
- High unemployment in the industry
- Low work group harmony
- Conducting terminations with more than one employee present
- Conducting terminations on a Monday or a Tuesday

The following factors are assumed to be protective but are unvalidated:

- Installing metal detectors and other hardware solutions
- Training employees to work with workplace bullies
- Creating early intervention plans
- Offering workplace workshops on nonviolent communication and conflict resolution
- Avoiding hiring applicants about whom managers have a bad instinctual feeling
- Time-of-day of termination

The lack of scientific research supporting or disproving commonly assumed risk and preventive factors is disturbing to those faced with the need to respond to threats and potentially violent situations. Nevertheless, employers and consultants should not adopt a nihilistic approach to workplace violence and assume that nothing is known simply because the research in the area is in its infancy. Rather, they should be aware as decisions are made that there is no certainty in this area and that much work remains to be done. Threat assessment and prevention of violence in the workplace are, like a good deal of medicine, more art than science. Therefore, an organization's response to threats and workplace violence incidents should be flexible and team based, and draw on the expertise of qualified individuals from a variety of fields.

RESPONDING TO WORKPLACE THREATS AND VIOLENCE

The following recommendations for assessing and managing threats and potential violence incidents are drawn from my experience as a consultant in this field, in collaboration with legal and security professionals. These include measures that have not been scientifically tested but have helped organizations respond to incidents in a timely and efficient fashion, develop confidence in their ability to respond, avoid legal liability, and contain the anxiety of individual employees and the organization as a whole:

- Every organization should have a workplace violence policy. This can be included as part of a respectful workplace program or other policies aimed at preventing sexual harassment and other misconduct. Many companies adopt a zero-tolerance policy toward workplace violence. When doing so, a decision must be made as to the exact meaning of *zero tolerance.* If it means that anyone who engages in an act of violence will be terminated, the organization may learn that this impact is overly inclusive when applied. Most companies find that an interpretation of zero tolerance that calls for a corporate response to all incidents but sanctions specific and appropriate to the circumstances works well. Whatever the interpretation is used, the rules must be applied to all members of the organization in a nondisparate fashion. Thus, zero tolerance for angry outbursts, if that is the standard, must be applied to managers as well as line workers. In addition, the rule cannot be applied to an employee who is perceived to have a disability such as mental illness or substance abuse but not to nondisabled employees, as this can result in liability under the Americans with Disabilities Act. (See Chapter Eighteen.)

The plan should define the behaviors it proscribes, clearly describe the mechanism for reporting concerns or incidents, and outline the procedures for handling reports or events. A major goal of the plan is to encourage reporting by those who observe an incident or hear information that raises concerns about violence. Assurance that any report and investigation will be handled professionally, through an established procedure, and with efforts to maintain confidentiality can help overcome some of the resistance to reporting shown by many employees.

- Every organization should have a crisis management plan that is practical, functional, and rehearsed at least annually. The plan should be designed to accommodate a variety of crises, including weather emergencies, utility failure, computer failure and sabotage, biological and chemical terrorism, and workplace threats and violence (including bombings). In the case of plans for biological and chemical terrorism, for example, it is important to develop the plan in coordination with local authorities that will ultimately control the scene, such as municipal hazardous materials response teams and law enforcement.

• A team of individuals from different fields should be organized and given responsibility for the crisis management plan, training exercises, coordinating with local law enforcement, and response to incidents. Different names, often reflecting the scope of their duties, are assigned to such teams—for example, threat assessment team, threat management team, crisis management team, or workplace response team. Whatever the name assigned to the team, the basic functions are the same.

• The size, resources, and needs of the organization will determine the size and composition of the team, including the number of internal versus external members. Basic members of the team should include representatives from human resources, security, and the legal department. Smaller organizations that do not have in-house security or legal staff may build a team around an in-house human resource professional or member of management. Other team members, who may also be internal or external, include a mental health consultant, occupational health, and a representative from the employee assistance program (EAP) if there is one. Some organizations choose to leave the EAP off the team in order to preserve its role as a support mechanism for employees who may become the object of concern.

The core team members, or their designees, should be available twenty-four hours a day, seven days a week, and prepared to respond to reports and concerns immediately. Pager or cell phone access is essential if the office is not continuously staffed. Procedures for reporting incidents, with the telephone number for the reporting line, should be prominently displayed in the workplace.

Once one member of the team receives a report, the other core team members should be contacted. After gathering initial information, a decision should be made about immediate next steps, for example, calling 911 if that has not been done and assembling the rest of the team. The team should then conduct an investigation of the incident in order to determine the nature and extent of the threat and necessary safety steps. Information from collateral sources, such as coworkers and supervisors, is an important part of the investigation. In addition, all written materials, including e-mail communications, Web sites visited, and recorded telephone messages should be reviewed. Depending on the nature and seriousness of the threat, a criminal background investigation may be warranted.

• Once the information has been gathered, the team reconvenes and determines if there has been a violation of the workplace violence policy. If so, a decision must be made about the action to take with regard to the offending employee. This decision is based on such factors as the seriousness of the offense, its impact on other employees and the organization, the employee's history with the organization, the need to deter similar behavior by others, and the manner in which these situations have been previously handled. Some possible responses include no action but with close monitoring, medical leave, leave of absence with referral for a fitness for duty evaluation, immediate termination, and discipline short of termination.

- Once the incident has concluded, the team should also be responsible for follow-up. Following up on an incident and how it was handled allows the organization to learn what did or did not work and provides ideas for improving the process.

Mental health professionals can make important contributions to the team in a variety of ways: analysis of behavior patterns and communications from anonymous threateners, treatment recommendations to employees suffering acute or chronic illness resulting in problematic behavior, and advice on managing threats from individuals with personality disorders.

Workplace violence is a complex problem that engenders significant anxiety in employees and employers. The degree of concern is significantly greater than the scientific knowledge in the field. While waiting for the science to catch up, employers are obligated to plan for and respond to these incidents. Policy development and a team approach, drawing on the experience and skills of different disciplines, increase the chances of preventing an incident and adequately handling any that do arise. Mental health professionals who possess the appropriate skills and experience can make an important contribution to the work of the team.

References and Additional Sources

Fein, R. A., Vossekuil, B., & Holden, G. A. (1995). *Threat assessment: An approach to prevent targeted violence.* Washington, DC: U.S. Department of Justice, National Institute of Justice.

Folger, R., & Baron, R. A. (1996). A model of reactions to perceived injustice. In G. R. VandenBos & E. Q. Bulato (Eds.), *Violence on the job: Identifying risks and developing solutions* (pp. 51–85). Washington, DC: American Psychological Association.

Monahan, J., & Steadman, H. J. (Eds.). (1994). *Violence and mental disorder.* Chicago: University of Chicago Press.

Monahan, J., Steadman, H. J., Silver, P. S., Appelbaum, P., Grisso, T., & Robbins, P. C. (2001). *Rethinking risk assessment.* New York: Oxford University Press.

Office of Statistics and Programming. National Center for Injury Prevention and Control. Centers for Disease Control. (2001). *Ten leading causes of violence-related injury, United States.* Available on-line at: http://webapp.cdc.gov/sasweb/ncipc/nfilead.html.

Peek-Asa, C., Howard, J., Vargas, L., & Kraus J. F. (1997). Incidence of non-fatal workplace assault injuries determined from employers' reports in California. *Journal of Occupational and Environmental Medicine, 39,* 44–50.

Rosen, A. (1954). Detection of suicidal patients: An example of some limitations in the reduction of infrequent events. *Journal of Consulting and Clinical Psychology, 18,* 397–403.

Schouten, R., & Rothman, E. F. (2002). *Perpetrators of coworker violence: A review of the literature.* Unpublished manuscript.

U.S. Department of Justice. (2001). [Bureau of Justice statistics.] Available on-line at: http://www.bls.gov/iif/oshwc/osh/case/ostb0943.pdf.

U.S. Department of Labor. Bureau of Labor Statistics. (1998a, April 22). *Lost-worktime injuries and illnesses (1999) characteristics and resulting time away from work, 1997.* [News release].

U.S. Department of Labor. Bureau of Labor Statistics. (1998b, April 4). *National census of fatal occupational injuries, 1998.* [News release].

U.S. Department of Labor. Bureau of Labor Statistics. (1999, December 16). *Workplace injuries and illnesses in 1998.* [News release].

U.S. Department of Labor. Bureau of Labor Statistics. (2000, August 17). *National census of fatal occupational injuries, 1998.* [News release].

U.S. Department of Labor. Bureau of Labor Statistics. (2001a, March 28). *Lost worktime injuries and illnesses: Characteristics and resulting time away from work, 1999.* Washington, DC: U.S. Department of Labor.

U.S. Department of Labor. Bureau of Labor Statistics. (2001b, August 14). National census of fatal occupational injuries in 2000. *News: United States Department of Labor.*

CHAPTER SEVENTEEN

Psychiatric Fitness-for-Duty Examinations

Robert C. Larsen

Psychiatric fitness-for-duty examinations can determine for an employer whether an employee is capable of performing in a particular job position based on his or her emotions, behavior, thoughts, and interactions with others. Psychiatric exams are governed by the same principles as medical exams, although the privacy of mental health records is typically more protected than medical information in general. Employee consent for the release of information between the examining psychiatrist and the employer representative must be obtained in accordance with local law. The fitness report should address functionality with respect to a written job description. If the examiner is experienced in performing such services, the information exchange will be pertinent, timely, and professional. Unnecessary exams should be avoided, yet delays in dealing with troubled employees can create disruption in the work group. The use of a skilled clinician can increase proper communications and allow for appropriate personnel decisions.

Just as there must be a reasonable fit between an employee's physical capacity and the demands of a particular job, so too must there be complementarity between an individual's psychological status and the characteristics of a particular position. Employers routinely consider a prospective employee's personality during the preemployment screening process. Punctuality, attire, makeup and jewelry, body language, and verbal response during interviews all provide valuable information about the individual. Once the individual has been employed by the company, his or her ability to handle deadlines, cope with irate clients, deal with conflicting information, and address a variety of other difficult or ambiguous situations provides cues about the person's character and resilience. Often, it is within the probationary period or initial training phase of employment that a potential high achiever stands out from one destined to become the troubled employee.

Mental health practitioners usually have little, if any, input into decisions concerning employee hiring or retention. However, when certain sets of circumstances exist, it behooves an employer to obtain psychiatric assessment of an employee's state of mind relative to the work context. For some employers and in particular industries, the use of psychiatric evaluations is rare; for others, it can be commonplace. The nexus between the need for such expert advice and the type of employment setting varies proportionately with the potential for adverse outcomes due to having a seriously disturbed individual in a position that exceeds the employee's resilience. For example, allowing a police officer with documented poor impulse control to continue to be assigned patrol duties without restrictions has associated public safety concerns. Ignoring signs of a clinical depression in a schoolteacher while not imposing similar liability can have untoward consequences for the employee and her charges.

When erratic behavior, potential dangerousness, and uncharacteristic emotional displays present themselves at work, expert opinion may be in order.

FITNESS-FOR-DUTY GUIDELINES

Psychiatric examinations and their results are governed by the same principles that apply to all other medical evaluations. A clinical examination at the request of a third party greatly differs from an assessment provided by a treating doctor. Not always is that difference apparent to the examinee, and thus, the examiner bears the responsibility of clearly establishing the purpose of the examination and the limits of confidentiality with that individual. Examiners and referral sources should be familiar with state and federal law that protects employees' rights relevant to privileged medical information. (See Chapter Four for more on this topic.)

Certain guidelines apply to all fitness evaluations. It is necessary that the examining physician understands the area of inquiry to be addressed by the examination. A written job description is crucial to consider when putting forth opinions about an employee's work capacity or limitations for a specific job position. The physician should also be attentive to what specific medical information is necessary rather than providing generalized or irrelevant data. Some clinicians might take the position that no information obtained in the course of a comprehensive psychiatric examination should be considered irrelevant or without purpose to the ultimate findings in a report. However, the courts, when considering the right to privacy, have tended to emphasize that only material that is necessary for implementing administrative decisions should be communicated. When a written release is obtained or litigation is pending, a more comprehensive report may be appropriate.

It is this author's practice to explain to the examinee the purpose of the examination and the materials reviewed prior to the assessment. At the end of the examination, once the employee has responded to the areas of inquiry, a written consent is then obtained. When addressing the procedure for work release evaluations, other clinicians have agreed with this method. It seems illogical to obtain a release before the examinee experiences the examination and knows what issues will be covered.

In order to comply with the Americans with Disabilities Act (ADA), medical examiners must be familiar with the essential and nonessential job functions of a given job position. An experienced clinician is best advised to have a protocol for assessing fitness for duty. Colledge, Johns, and Thomas (1999) have suggested a methodology that physicians and employers can use to determine an employee's performance capability. The guidelines they suggest are more applicable for musculoskeletal limitations than emotional and behavioral difficulties; however, they emphasize the physician's responsibility in safeguarding medical information beyond what is necessary in the personnel decisions about job assignments or reasonable accommodations. Common exceptions to the concept of protected medical information should be familiar to the employer, representatives, and physician's staff (Colledge et al., 1999):

- Supervisors must be informed about necessary work restrictions.
- First aid and safety personnel should be informed if a disabling condition may require emergency treatment.
- Government officials can investigate ADA compliance.
- Relevant information must be provided to state workers' compensation or second injury funds.
- Relevant information must be provided to insurers when a medical exam is required for health or life insurance provision.

The employer and clinician will avoid potential litigation by staying within the guidelines of the law in clinical practice relative to privacy. *Easterson* v. *Long Island Jewish Medical Center* (1989) represents an example of the principle of the employer's need to know versus the protection of an employee's medical records. In this case, an occupational health nurse was terminated from her employment at a New York medical center for refusing to disclose information concerning an employee's nonoccupational medical condition. The nurse brought suit against the medical center (though she lost). Smith (1994) has underscored that breaching confidentiality where a clinician-patient relationship exists must serve a legitimate concern. Without public safety issues, a pending workers' compensation claim, or another valid exception to an individual's medical privacy rights, it is clear that a medical professional can be held liable for divulging medical information. Obtaining a written consent to release information prior to any reporting should prevent even the appearance of breach of confidentiality.

The court in *Urbaniak* v. *Newton* (1991), involving disclosure of test results for human immunodeficiency virus, found in favor of the injured worker's right to confidentiality of highly sensitive data. Due to concerns that have come forth as a result of this and other cases, the Industrial Medical Council for the State of California has alerted physicians to situations where confidentiality varies in its applicability depending on the employer's, insurer's, or public's need to know about an employee's health status. The role of the physician relative to the employee ultimately governs in what manner the clinician may disclose information to the employer. Without proper attention to this relationship, there may be liability for medical malpractice, libel, and unauthorized release of information. An experienced, knowledgeable doctor taking the appropriate steps to obtain informed consent can avoid all of these potential pitfalls. The examination can then go forth, and relevant information needed for personnel decisions can be provided.

THE SENSITIVE NATURE OF PSYCHIATRIC INFORMATION

There is a general agreement that issues that surface in psychiatric assessments should be handled with extra care. The potential for the appearance of, or even the actual infringement on, privacy is a common concern when the examiner probes into personal history, daily activities, and patterns of behavior regarding social, home, and work settings. A comprehensive psychiatric examination delves into the employee's past, present, and projected future level of functioning. By its nature of being comprehensive, information that is very personal is obtained. Often, the examinee expresses strong emotion or displays strong affect (observed emotion) in recounting painful, disturbing events and negative feelings toward having to participate in the examination process. Skilled clinicians recognize this response on the part of the examinee and assist the individual through the process in a respectful manner. A thorough examination will cover a broad range of historical topics, with the protocol being amended given the issues particular to the examinee and the areas of inquiry. Regulatory bodies, psychiatric associations, and individual authors have addressed guidelines for such employment-related psychiatric examinations (see Chapter Eighteen).

APPROPRIATE SITUATIONS FOR PSYCHIATRIC EXAMINATIONS

Five situations typically trigger the possibility of a psychiatric examination: pre-employment assessment, a disruptive employee, postdisability leave status, a failure to return to work, and threat assessment. Management determines what situations justify an evaluation by a psychiatrist or psychologist.

Preemployment Psychiatric Screening

The expense of routinely assessing job candidates' psychological status is not justified for most employers. Obtaining such information also raises concerns about how the data will be used. Those who apply for jobs as police officers, sheriff's deputies, and corrections officers, however, are commonly asked to undergo a clinical interview and standardized psychometric testing. Public safety is clearly the main reason for a police agency to use clinicians in making personnel decisions. The information gleaned from that process is used to eliminate those with psychotic symptoms, impulsive behavior, conflict with authority, or an inability to act decisively.

Case 1

A psychological evaluation is routinely required of all candidates for an entry-level position in law enforcement with a large city in central California after an offer has been made. Steve Tackle is a twenty-three-year-old job candidate who has applied to the city's department and a number of other sheriff departments and law enforcement agencies. He has received an associate degree from a local junior college in the field of criminal justice. His history shows that he has had no problems with the law over the years. However, he was repeatedly counseled in high school related to physical confrontations with other students and was expelled from a parochial school for openly challenging teachers and cheating on a promotional examination. In addition to this historical information that was gleaned in the course of the psychological evaluation, Steve endorses standardized test items consistent with impulsivity, antisocial tendencies, and conflict with authority.

Although no obvious paranoia or psychotic symptoms came forth in the test data, Steve was not offered a position in the upcoming police academy class. The historical information along with the test results were found to be most consistent with an individual who was predicted to have conflicts with a command structure, demonstrate poor control of his anger, and likely disregard rules over time. These characteristics were felt to be enduring elements of Steve's personality and unlikely to be amenable to change as a result of standardized training and experience in command situations. When he learned of the department's decision, Steve repeatedly cursed at the employer representative and was escorted from the premises by two patrol officers.

The Disruptive Employee

It may be only after having been hired and employed for some time that forms of major mental illness become apparent. When an employee's behavior becomes disruptive of the work unit, there may be an underlying illness. Of course, certain maladaptive behavior such as passive-aggressive action, dishonesty, and unacceptable displays of anger need not be due to a psychiatric condition. It is when the behavior and thoughts of the employee are clearly unusual and bizarre that the employer may wish to consider obtaining a psychiatric consultation. If the employee is so disturbed as to be delusional, there may be some difficulty in convincing the individual of the need for the clinical assessment.

Case 2

Frank Aneiro is a forty-five-year-old computer programmer for a major telecommunications corporation where he has worked for a dozen years. He has always had acceptable, though not exceptional, job performance evaluations. His peers and managers have viewed him as somewhat of a loner. Over the past six months or so, Frank has repeatedly told his manager and the human resource staff that he is convinced that the company is the object of sabotage. Because the corporation recently fended off a hostile takeover, corporate security investigated Frank's allegations, but they found no substance to Frank's report that a computer hacker had inserted viruses in the software controlling the corporation's communications satellites.

A fitness evaluation was scheduled after Frank refused to turn over the results of a software compliance project to his manager. Frank now insists that the conspiracy to undermine the company involves his manager, those in human resources, and internal security. Nevertheless, he reluctantly agrees to the psychiatric evaluation. At the evaluation, he insists that portions of the interview be conducted in a foreign language so as to thwart any electronic eavesdroppers. As support for his conspiracy allegations, Frank points out that the directors of the Federal Bureau of Investigation and the Central Intelligence Agency had given public interviews in recent weeks broadcast on network news shows. The company's satellite network was used in part for those broadcasts, according to Frank, thus confirming his conviction that elements of law enforcement were attempting to take over the company's means of communication.

Frank appeared to have a highly elaborate scheme involving a paranoid delusional system. As a result of the evaluation process, he was placed on an administrative leave and referred for psychiatric treatment. Frank, however, did not believe he had a mental illness and began corresponding with the company's board of directors in an effort to inform them of the inevitability of the intelligence community's taking over the company's assets.

Second Opinions Related to Psychiatric Leaves

Once an employee who has been off work for a period of time while treated for a psychiatric disorder desires to return to work, the treating physician needs to provide a release for this person to assume normal duties, perhaps with some work restrictions or recommended job modifications. The treating physician, however, may not be fully aware of the employee's duties and responsibilities or may not consider the impact on the work unit of an employee only partially able to resume work activities. In these situations, a second opinion examination can be helpful in making personnel administrative decisions.

Case 3

Shirley Brown is a fifty-year-old middle manager for a savings and loan. She has been with the company for twenty years, having worked her way up through the ranks. Her most recent job position has been that of a branch manager, which was a demotion from her prior role as an assistant vice president with responsibilities as a regional manager. The demotion came about after her bank was acquired by a larger corporation. Many of Shirley's peer group were laid off, and she saw herself as having few options at that point in her career other than to accept the alternative position. She was given responsibility for a branch with an expanded product line and reduced staffing. The branch met its sales quotas for the next two years, although Shirley received no raises. She found herself regularly exhausted by her work schedule and job demands. Her regular physician placed her on a disability leave after her regional manager criticized her for becoming tearful once at work. Shirley has no prior history of psychiatric treatment. She took one week off work at the recommendation of her physician and did not follow through on a referral to a counselor for apparent job stress. When she returned to work, she again evidenced tearfulness and some confusion when meeting with a long-term business client of the branch. Her regular physician again placed her on a disability status. This time, her employer insisted that Shirley have a psychiatric fitness evaluation before she returned to her normal management duties. As a result of the examination, a recommendation was made for her to take a more extended leave, and during that time Shirley was referred for treatment of a major depression. She later successfully returned to work. She continued in outpatient treatment over the next six months, during which time increased staff support was provided related to new product lines.

Psychiatric Assessment Involving Failed Attempts at Return to Work

Evaluation of behavioral issues and motivation may be in order with an employee who has required multiple leaves from work. The employee may be perceived as acting out when repeatedly failing to remain at work upon returning from a medical leave, a Family Medical Leave Act leave, a sabbatical, or other approved work absence. There may be no indication that the individual is receiving mental health services, yet management becomes aware that others see the employee as emotionally fragile. These matters are often handled strictly as personnel issues. A management referral to the company's employee assistance program (EAP) can result in acknowledgment of active psychological distress, appropriate intervention, and an increased chance for successful work reentry.

Case 4

Mark White is a forty-year-old account executive for a major bottling corporation. He has sold products and services for a number of different corporations over the course of the past fifteen years and was recruited for his current position from a competitor three years ago. For the first two and one-half years, he was a high producer, consistently bringing in new accounts and expanding his territory. Over the past six months, however, there have been a number of reports of his not showing up for client contacts and sales meetings. Mark has missed four weeks of work during that same time period for illness and personal reasons. At a recent dinner meeting with colleagues, he appeared to be inebriated and when leaving the dinner fell down a flight of stairs and was taken to the emergency room at the local hospital. Mark was then referred to the company's EAP, which referred him for treatment. In the course of the evaluation, Mark admitted to having a pending charge for drunk driving and some financial problems associated with using alcohol and cocaine. Company policy allows for the employee to take a prolonged leave from work as long as he agrees to participate in an approved chemical dependency detoxification and treatment program.

Psychiatric Threat Assessment

Perhaps the most disturbing circumstances for the employer arise when an employee appears to be potentially dangerous. Violence is an extreme form of maladaptive aggression. Aggression is not necessarily a pathological state (in fact, successful businesses thrive on aggressive drives to meet goals and achieve objectives). Rather, it is the way in which aggression is expressed that determines its value or detriment to the organization. Maladaptive aggression has many forms of expression: procrastination, verbal assaults, nonproductive criticism, intimidation, spying, sabotage, and overt violence (see Chapter Sixteen).

Displays of workplace violence not uncommonly become the source for headlines in the media. According to the Bureau of Labor Statistics (Toscano & Weber, 1995), about a thousand employees are homicide victims each year, and another ten thousand are assaulted. A recent California study estimates that workplace assaults in that state alone number thirteen thousand annually. Homicide is the second leading cause of employee fatalities. Although any work group can be targeted by a troubled employee or disgruntled member of the public, taxi drivers, law enforcement officers, security guards, and retail clerks are at highest risk for work-related homicides.

The commonplace occurrence of violent traumatic events has resulted in a revision of the diagnostic criteria for posttraumatic stress disorder. According to the *Diagnostic and Statistical Manual of Mental Disorders* (American Psychiatric Association, 2000), a stressor outside the range of normal human experience is no longer required for the diagnosis. Assault, robbery, and hostage situations, while not typically everyday employment events, are not rare either. And beyond actual traumatic events, there is a widespread concern about workplace violence among many employees.

As with other social issues, the playing out of workplace violence has implications that are being addressed through the courts. Tort law, civil rights, the employment contract, and regulations may all be used to hold the employer responsible for violent acts that could have been foreseen or perhaps mitigated. For these reasons and in an effort to maintain a functional work site, management takes threats of violence seriously. A disgruntled worker found to have made verbal or written threats is likely to be referred for psychiatric assessment. Obviously, there are circumstances that result in the involvement of corporate security and law enforcement as well. Mental health practitioners with known expertise in threat assessment should be selected to evaluate employees viewed as a potential danger. Such professionals use protocols to assess specific risk factors such as personality, substance abuse, job loss, and a desire for retaliation. In these cases, the evaluating clinician must be provided with explicit details of the threat, the employee's personnel file, medical and psychiatric records, and direct communications with the examinee's manager.

Intervention in threat situations can involve a number of potential management actions, depending on the serious potential for destructive behavior. Job transfer and separation of employees may be the advised action in one set of circumstances, while in another situation, mandated psychiatric treatment may be required. A range of psychiatric syndromes can be associated with violent behavior (see Chapter Sixteen). Personnel action, including job termination coupled with the use of a restraining order, may be the appropriate intervention when dealing with a vindictive individual having a history of antisocial acts. Referral for drug detoxification and treatment of chemical dependency may be considered for an impulsive employee struggling with alcohol and amphetamine abuse.

Each instance of threat assessment requires an individualized examination and set of recommendations. Obviously, the examiner's findings and recommendations will vary, as will management's response, commensurate with the evaluation context. Usually, the clinical consultant will put forth recommendations directed toward minimizing the risk for the expression of violence, not a clinical opinion indicating that the employee is fit or not for work. Rather, the employer should receive information describing under what conditions the employee should be allowed to resume duties at the work site.

Case 5

Louie James, a stationary engineer who works at an international airport, has been placed on an involuntary leave as a potential danger to others. In fact, a year ago, the airport police took him into custody under similar circumstances: Louie was found ranting to members of the public about "homosexual perverts" who were taking over the community. And when he was taken for emergency psychiatric evaluation, he threatened to blow up the airport. At that time, a psychiatric consultant told his employer's medical director that he had a history of bipolar disorder (manic depression). Louie, who has an extensive gun collection and nearly unlimited access to the infrastructure of the airport given his job position, had been allowed to return to work to his regular duties under the stipulation that he would remain in outpatient psychiatric care and continue to cooperate with the use of psychotropic medication.

Within weeks of returning to work, Louie had dropped out of treatment and stopped taking the drugs. When the mania returned, evident by his exhibiting insistent speech, erratic behavior, and grandiose thought processes, he was once again referred to the employer's psychiatric consultant, who offered the opinion that Louie could not be trusted to remain on the prescribed treatment program and that it was entirely possible that Louie would act on his delusions. The psychiatric consultant provided a written report for Louie's employer after having obtained Louie's written release to issue it. Based on the consultant's opinion, the employer opted to discharge Louie from his position out of concern for public safety. Louie took his grievance to the union, but the public safety concerns were found to override his personal right to refuse treatment while remaining employed by a public agency.

WORK FUNCTION ASSESSMENT

An independent psychiatric examiner who is assessing an employee's fitness for duty should detail the employee's ability or deficiencies to perform the job functions for the individual's normal position. Typically, the psychiatric consultant, and even the treating mental health practitioner, address different areas of work function from those of concern to an orthopedist or internist. The employer should provide any reporting clinician regardless of the medical specialty with a written job description. The physician should obtain a verbal description from the examinee but should not rely entirely on that characterization. The absence of a written job description can result in the physician's making recommendations that are not tailored to the specific job.

The amount of interpersonal interchange, planning skills, attention to critical detail, and work pace varies by job, and even the same type of position may vary in regard to job functions from one employer or department to the next. A branch manager for one bank may be responsible for all training and supervision, while at another those same functions are shared or delegated to subordinates. An ironworker for one construction company may be required to work at high elevations, and at another place of employment there might be designated ground-level positions. The depressed bank manager with sufficient assistants might well return to work sooner from a psychiatric leave than one without such help. The phobic ironworker with ground-level positions available could return to duties but not if the examiner is unaware of that option.

The task of the psychiatric consultant concerning fitness for duty is to consider how the employee's clinical condition and its impact on cognition, mood, interpersonal relations, and executive functions would affect the individual's ability to perform particular duties. In California (1993), for example, psychiatrists and psychologists who are reporting on factors of psychiatric disability are expected to address an employee's ability in the following areas:

- Understanding and following instructions
- Performing simple and repetitive tasks
- Maintaining a work pace appropriate to the word load
- Relating to other people beyond giving and receiving instructions
- Influencing others
- Making generalizations, evaluations, and decisions without immediate supervision
- Accepting and carrying out responsibility for direction, control, and planning

Rather than merely reporting symptoms, the clinician is expected to explain how the symptoms will affect functionality. The work function categories are somewhat broad and have relevance for the open labor market. A particular position may have more need of certain work functions than others. For example, work functions having to do with interpersonal relations are more important to a salesperson than work functions having to do with executive duties such as planning and supervision. Although not every clinician will use this particular schema for identifying job limitations, the concept is one that should be followed when making a determination of job fitness relative to psychiatric issues.

Psychiatrists consider how mental disorders affect a wide range of tasks, most commonly those having to do with attention, concentration, memory, and the ability to perform simple tasks. All of these functions can be affected by dementias, serious depression, anxiety, and psychoses, although they may be relatively spared by mild psychological symptoms. Maintaining a work pace and performing complex tasks are usually more affected than the more basic functions by the same level of symptomatology. For example, a manager in the midst of a major depressive episode might have a slight impairment in attention but moderate difficulty maintaining a work pace due to fatigue and self-doubt. Virtually all jobs require some amount of interaction with others; some require dealing with the public, functioning as part of a team, or managing others. Whereas conditions that affect mentation, mood, and thought can have an impact on interpersonal functioning, the personality disorders clearly come into play in this area. Every individual has a range of personality traits and styles of coping. The compulsive individual is well suited to a role as an accountant. The person possessing a hysterical flair might do well as a designer or artist. It is when traits become inflexible or interfere with occupational and social functioning that a personality disorder is deemed present. A paranoid personality might be fine in the role of investigator but cause conflict in a work site where teamwork and trust are desired. A security guard working the night shift who has prominent schizoid characteristics might not be able to adapt when assigned to daytime duties requiring greater interchange with the public. Not uncommonly, personality is a central issue that results in the need for a psychiatric fitness exam.

Executive functions, which involve tasks such as decision making, planning, and the capacity to give and receive constructive criticism, are more crucial to performing the duties of a partner in a large law firm than to an employee assigned the task of a dedicated word processor. Both intelligence and personality come into play regarding one's predisposition to take on executive functions. Certainly, all jobs have some amount of these tasks, but some positions have minimal requirements and others emphasize such skills. Many forms of mental disorders that affect self-confidence and self-efficacy have an impact on these higher-level abilities. Anxiety states, depression, and maladaptive personality features adversely affect managerial tasks. The phobic researcher has difficulty presenting ideas. A depressed project manager is doubtful of his abilities to delegate or follow through. The pathologic narcissist cannot accept being anything other than the center of attention in a group planning session.

INFORMATION EXCHANGE

Selecting an examiner is an important responsibility of an employer considering a psychiatric fitness examination for an employee. The doctor should readily supply his or her curriculum vitae, publications and presentations list, a sample anonymous report, references, expected availability, and a fee schedule. An employer who makes initial inquiries early on in the process should have a larger choice of clinicians to perform the examination and have greater control over what information is made available. The clinician may assist the employer by suggesting that a limited consultation or no exam at all may be necessary. Sometimes administrative or personnel matters can be addressed without subjecting the employee to an exam by instead using already available sources of data. When an employer exam is deemed desirable, proper planning should allow for sufficient notice to the employee and the provision of agreed-on information to the examiner.

After appointment options have been addressed, usually the employer secures the employee's commitment to an appointment at a particular time and date. The examiner may send a separate notice to the employee confirming the appointment and providing some basic information about it. No-shows and late cancellations can be minimized through such simple measures, reducing costs and delays.

A referral letter confirming the appointment should be sent to the examiner in a timely manner, and an attorney familiar with employment law probably should review it. The employer's concerns about the employee's ability to perform particular job functions should be detailed in the written communications to the doctor, with a written job description detailing the essential and non-essential job functions. To the extent that the employee's tenure with the company is chronicled in the personnel file, it is a valuable source of information to the examiner as well. The employee's employment application, resumé, salary history, performance reviews, commendations, leaves, and personnel and disciplinary actions may be contained within the file and provide background information.

When the examiner is to be provided medical and psychiatric records as a result of the exam, the employer should secure appropriate written releases from the employee before the exam whenever possible. By reviewing these records prior to the exam, the doctor has the background necessary to explore the history of symptoms, stressors, and treatment response more specifically. If other records are deemed desirable to have, the examiner may obtain the employee's written consent at the time of the evaluation. It is this physician's practice to use a standardized release to obtain additional records as well as to document the employee's consent for reporting to designated parties, for example, the human resource officer or corporate medical director. (See Appendix A for a sample release.)

After the interview, the examiner may wish to confer with the employer concerning preliminary findings. The employer may desire a tentative verbal opinion about the employee's work capacity. A written report usually follows after any psychometric testing has been scored and interpreted. The completion of the report may also await the review of additional documents not available at the time of the clinical interview.

Depending on the situation, a discussion between the examiner and the employee's manager or supervisor may be in order to obtain information about the employee's behavior at work and provide recommendations concerning management strategies. Whether in verbal or written form, the recommendations from the psychiatric consultant should emphasize functionality over diagnosis. It is far more helpful to the employer to learn that an employee attempting a return to work after an extended psychiatric leave can do so with the provision that no overtime be required in the first three months than to indicate that the employee is partially recovered from a major depression, single episode of moderate severity. With sufficient information about functional ability or limitations, the employer can then consider under what circumstances the employee may be considered psychologically fit for work.

ADMINISTRATIVE MINEFIELDS

No employer should ever consider requesting that an employee undergo a psychiatric fitness examination on a whim. The phrase "appropriate and necessary" comes to mind. If management uses the psychiatric consultation judiciously, it can be a valuable administrative tool. The frequency by which psychiatric input is brought to bear varies across employers and employee populations. For most employers, the psychiatric fitness exam has its place in relationship to the worker potentially identified as troubled or disabled. The results of the clinical examination can then allow for personnel decisions to be made regarding the employee's status with the company.

Ignoring or denying the presence of an employee who is disturbed can lead to underuse of the exam process. In such instances, the workplace can become disrupted and coworkers made anxious by a lack of decisive action on the part of management. Unnecessarily long delays in referring an employee for assessment can create discomfort for the employee, coworkers, supervisory staff, and members of management involved in decisions concerning the employee's status. An employer who does not act decisively in this situation may be perceived as ineffectual.

At the polar extreme of the unduly deliberate employer is the manager who requests psychiatric input when it is not needed. There may already be enough information from the treating physician to accept an employee back to work following a stress leave. When a candidate's fit for a prospective position is being considered, clinical opinions may add nothing of value. Having more data that are duplicative and delays taking personnel action should be avoided.

When an examination is to take place, the most common mistakes occur in the area of communications. Whenever possible, correspondence, records, and a written job description should be provided to the psychiatric consultant before the exam takes place and certainly before a written report is issued. Obtaining the employee's cooperation is imperative, and to do so requires that the purpose and process of the exam be explained to the individual. Issues of privacy and consent must be addressed. Perhaps the most important responsibility of management, once having made the decision to request the psychiatric fitness exam, is selecting the examiner. Experienced clinicians have reputations with other human resource staffs and legal counsel. Using a doctor who is clinically competent but unfamiliar with legal parameters and generating timely reports is a set-up for disaster. Not all psychiatrists and psychologists are sufficiently familiar with or interested in the world of work. The proper clinician for the task has special expertise, just as the forensic doctors do who evaluate child custody or criminal responsibility matters.

Consider using an examiner who is a member of such professional organizations as the Academy of Organizational and Occupational Psychiatry, the American College of Occupational and Environmental Medicine, or the American Academy of Psychiatry and the Law. (See Appendix B for contact information.) Involvement in subspecialty associations relevant to occupational medicine and forensic psychiatry increases the likelihood that the doctor has the interest, skills and experience to perform the fitness exam desired and provide important information for these administrative matters.

The psychiatric fitness examination can provide valuable information regarding an employee's capacity to perform certain duties. Careful attention to its scheduling should prevent delays in taking personnel action, avoiding unnecessary exams, and protecting the employee's rights. A comprehensive program of services to minimize the consequences of mental disorders at the workplace is advised:

- Employee education
- Supervisor training
- Employee assistance programs
- Early intervention
- Mediation services
- Outpatient mental health benefit
- Comprehensive psychiatric examination
- Claims review
- Standardized personnel policy
- Executive consultation

Psychiatric examination is but one component of a larger structure involving behavioral health, personnel, and employee benefit matters.

References and Additional Sources

American Psychiatric Association. (2000). *Diagnostic and statistical manual of mental disorders* (4th ed. rev.).

Brakel, S. J. (1998). Legal liability and workplace violence. *Journal of the American Academy of Psychiatry and Law, 26,* 553–562.

California. Industrial Medical Council. (1993). *Method of measurement of psychiatric disability.* Sacramento: Department of Industrial Relations.

California. Industrial Medical Council. (1999). *Confidentiality of medical information: Information for physicians.* Sacramento: Department of Industrial Relations.

Castillo, D. N., & Jenkins, E. L. (1994). Industries and occupations at high risk for work-related homicide. *Journal of Occupational Medicine, 36,* 125–132.

Colledge, A. L., Johns, R. E., & Thomas, M. H. (1999). Functional ability assessment: Guidelines for the workplace. *Journal of Occupational and Environmental Medicine, 41,* 172–180.

Council on Ethical and Judicial Affairs. American Medical Association. (1989). *Principles of medical ethics.* Chicago: Author.

Easterson v. Long Island Jewish Medical Center. 549 N.Y.S.2d 135 (1989).

Group for the Advancement of Psychiatry. Committee on Occupational Psychiatry. (1994). *Introduction to occupational psychiatry.* Washington, DC: American Psychiatric Press.

Larsen, R. C. (1995). Workers' compensation stress claims: Workplace causes and prevention. *Psychiatric Annals, 25,* 234–237.

Larsen, R. C. (1998a). Psychiatric syndromes common to the workplace. In W. N. Rom (Ed.), *Environmental and occupational medicine* (3rd ed., pp. 881–889). Philadelphia: Lippincott-Raven.

Larsen, R. C. (1998b). Inappropriate workplace aggression: Case examples. *Psychiatric Annals, 28,* 253–258.

Morrison, D. E. (1998). Leadership and aggression: Affect, values, and defenses. *Psychiatric Annals, 28,* 271–276.

Peek-Asa, C., Howard, J., Vargas, L., & Kraus, J. F. (1997). Incidence of non-fatal workplace assault injuries determined from employers' reports in California. *Journal of Occupational and Environmental Medicine, 39,* 44–50.

Postal, L. P. (1989). Suing the doctor: Lawsuits by injured workers against the occupational physician. *Journal of Occupational Medicine, 31,* 891–896.

Resnick, P. J., & Kausch, O. (1995). Violence in the workplace: Role of the consultant. *Consulting Psychology Journal of Practice and Research, 47,* 213–222.

Rischitelli, D. G. (1995). The confidentiality of medical information in the workplace. *Journal of Occupational and Environmental Medicine, 37,* 583–593.

Smith, J. F. (1994). Occupational medical records. *American Academy of Occupational Health Nursing Journal, 42,* 18–22.

Toscano, G., & Weber, W. (1995). Patterns of fatal workplace assaults differ from those of non-fatal ones. In U.S. Bureau of Labor Statistics, *Fatal workplace injuries in 1993: A collection of data and analysis* (pp. 43–50). Washington, DC: U.S. Department of Labor, Bureau of Labor Statistics.

Urbaniak v. Newton. 277 California Reporter 354 (1991).

Warshaw, L. J., & Mossite, J. (1996). Workplace violence: Preventive and interventive strategies. *Journal of Occupational and Environmental Medicine, 38*(10), 993–1006.

APPENDIX A

Authorization for Release of Medical Information

By signing this form, you are giving permission for this physician and this medical group to release your confidential medical information. It is important to fill out the entire form to make clear what information you agree to release, to whom it may be released, the purpose(s) the person receiving the information may use it for, and how long this authorization to release your medical information will remain valid. If you do not sign an authorization such as this, the Confidentiality of Medical Information Act (and other statutes) requires the physician or medical group to keep your medical information confidential, unless they are required to disclose it by law.

I, _____ , authorize the following persons/entities:

_____

(print name and address of each person/entity)

to release the medical information listed below regarding myself to the following persons, who may use that medical information only for the purpose(s) stated:

a. workers' compensation benefit determination
b. long-term disability benefit determination
c. fitness for duty
d. medical consultation
e. civil litigation
f. other (specify)

_____
name and address   purposes designated by my initials

The types of medical information which I give permission to release include (circle and initial appropriate types):

A. mental health records
B. drug and/or alcohol monitoring and treatment records
C. HIV test results
D. all other records of treatment and/or evaluation made by the persons stated above
E. other specified information

This authorization to release medical information is effective now and will remain effective until _____ (enter specific date).

I understand that I have a right to receive a copy of this signed authorization.
Signed this _____ day of _____ , 200_ , at _____ (city & state)

_____ signature of patient/examinee
_____ signature of physician

APPENDIX B

Professional Societies for Fitness-for-Duty Examiners

Academy of Organizational and Occupational Psychiatry
717 Princess Street
Alexandra, VA 22314
(877) 789–2667
www.aoop.org

American College of Occupational and Environmental Medicine
1114 North Arlington Heights Road
Arlington Heights, IL 60004
(847) 818–1800
www.acoem.org

American Academy of Psychiatry and the Law
1 Regency Drive
Bloomfield, CT 06002
(860) 242–5450
www.aapl.org

CHAPTER EIGHTEEN

Disability and Workers' Compensation

Brian L. Grant
David B. Robbins

Disability is a legal and administrative concept and is distinct from the medical concept of impairment. There are important differences between treating physician and evaluating physician roles. Various types of disabling psychiatric injuries are found in the workplace, and barriers to accurate data collection complicate assessment. Therefore, causal impairment determination is a complex task with special challenges, somewhat unique among medical evaluation roles. Prevention of disability includes attention to factors both internal and external to the worker.

The social, human, and economic costs of disability are enormous. Determination of disability for administrative and legal bodies is a complex and unique task that differs from the usual practice of medicine. The legal determination of disability differs significantly from the appraisal of medical needs. The evaluation is typically done at the request of a third party rather than the patient, and the usual doctor-patient relationship is often absent. The disability determination evaluation includes the usual clinical data. Special attention to causality determination, including attribution of injury or condition to a particular event, requires specific techniques. Complicating factors make such determinations especially challenging.

Psychiatric injury in the workplace has many causes and manifestations. The psychiatric assessment requires specific attention to the disability process, disability prevention, workers' compensation systems, and fitness-for-duty determination. There is a special role for such screening techniques as drug and psychometric testing. Predictive value is enhanced by a careful history of past functioning in comparable or parallel settings.

WORKPLACE DISABILITY PROBLEMS AND DEFINITIONS

Medical and psychiatric conditions contribute significantly to disability, lost work, and productivity. In 1999, 5.7 million injuries and illnesses occurred in private industry workplaces, resulting in a rate of 6.3 cases for every 100 full-time workers. Of the total, 5.3 million were injuries, and the remainder was work-related illnesses. Sixty-six percent of these illnesses were disorders associated with repeated trauma. The direct cost of workplace injuries and illnesses in 1998, which includes medical costs and time-loss replacement, was $38.7 billion. The total costs, including indirect economic impact, are far greater, with estimates ranging between $125 billion and $155 billion. Moreover, these numbers represent only conditions directly related to work on a causal basis. The impact of non-work-related conditions on workplace productivity is also significant. One study in the telecommunications industry demonstrated that 8 percent of the total revenue for participating companies was lost due to employee time away from work. Workers' compensation claims accounted for only 15 percent of these absences. One-third of the lost time was from claims arising from short-term disability programs, sick leave or incidental absence represented about 25 percent, and 20 percent was represented by claims under the Family and Medical Leave Act (U.S. Occupational Safety and Health Administration, 2001). The numbers are even further understated because they do not account for the real value to society of volunteer and homemaker labor. Nor do the numbers include such nonquantifiable factors as psychological distress. Employers bear the economic and productivity impacts of disability regardless of its relationship to work when they provide optional and mandated benefits such as medical leave and disability policies. When an employee is no longer contributing to an organization, the benefits and costs associated with the hiring, training, and nurturing the experience and expertise of the worker are lost.

The impact on the self-concept and well-being of the absent worker, regardless of any wage replacement received, is profound. The costs associated with disability to the affected employees include pain and suffering, lost wages, and social disruption. Also affected are the family of a disabled wage earner, productivity losses to industry and society, and costs borne by employers and government for wages, health care, and disability benefits. Because most workers spend much of their waking hours at work and work demands can be stressful, commonly any impairment first makes itself evident in the workplace. This occurs whether the impairment is caused by, aggravated by, or even incidental to work.

It is important to remember that many physical impairments have prominent emotional components that can result from, exacerbate, or even cause disability. An employer should be concerned about conditions that impair employee ability to function in the workplace. Enhanced awareness enables appropriate screening of workers and applicants, workplace prevention, and treatment of affected employees, which may help decrease the incidence and severity of those conditions.

The Legal Meaning of Disability

Disability is a multifaceted concept with diverse connotations for the employee and society. It includes the legal meaning and definition, the individually experienced disability process, and the social implications. As a legal and administrative condition, a process that considers medical evidence and other criteria determines disability. According to the U.S. Social Security Administration definition (2002), disability is "the inability to engage in any gainful activity, by reason of any medically determinable physical or mental impairment, which can be expected to result in death, or has lasted or can be expected to last for a continuous period of not less than 12 months." This description essentially precludes any worker who can perform alternate work. Some other definitions have less stringent requirements.

Impairment

Disability occurs when medical impairment impedes an employee's ability to respond to external demands. Changes of either impairment or demand levels can initiate or eliminate disability. Physicians contribute to disability determination by establishing medical impairment.

Medical impairments are alterations in health status, medically measured as specific signs, symptoms, and laboratory findings that are attributable to bodily organ systems. Quantification efforts have resulted in impairment schedules that administrative bodies responsible for disability compensation determination have adopted. In addition to the Social Security Administration's guidelines, the American Medical Association (2001) has offered its *Guides to the Evaluation of Permanent Impairment*. In addition, some states have enacted their own guidelines for their workers' compensation systems. Each of these attempts to rate impairment on a graded scale of severity. The correlation of medical status to a corresponding impairment rating is a complex task that extends beyond the usual medical evaluation.

Impairment does not automatically constitute a disability, and an impairment that constitutes a disability at one job might not be significant elsewhere. For example, an employee unable to remain standing for prolonged periods might be disabled for a job as a clothing salesperson but not as a seated cashier. An employee's failure to function at work may be the result of many factors, which can include motivation and other voluntary elements. Impairment determination, though, should be based on objective medical and psychiatric data. Physicians who are asked to assist in disability determination should avoid offering opinions outside their expertise. It is the task of others to integrate the information from the physician with the appropriate definition of disability in a given context, along with other relevant information.

Disabilities

An individual who has an impairment or record of an impairment that substantially limits one or more life activities, including work, is considered disabled. In some settings, a person who is merely regarded as having such an impairment can be considered disabled, although this is a broad definition subject to legal interpretation. Operationally, disability status is assigned when a barrier to functional activity exists. Accommodation to such barriers can often be accomplished with assisting devices or modification of work or life environment and activities. An employee who cannot perform employment tasks even with accommodation is considered disabled.

Disability Evaluation

Because determination of medical impairment requires clinical evaluation, the physician has an integral role. At least three levels of physician involvement may take place: the treating physician, the consultative disability evaluation, and the administrative medical review.

THE TREATING PHYSICIAN'S ROLE

A patient may first present to a treating physician for clinical treatment with no expectation that impairment and disability might be at issue. Other patients, already pursuing a disability claim, may seek a treating physician with implicit or explicit expectations of medical evidence to support their claim. In both cases, the role of the treating physician should remain the same: to provide and record diagnosis and treatment. Not infrequently, the treating physician is placed in the untenable role of being asked to meet the perceived needs of patient, attorney, government, and employer. These several interests often have incompatible, or even antagonistic, needs.

In interaction with the patient, the treating physician has a special responsibility regarding diagnosis and treatment within accepted medical standards and adherence to the requirements of the doctor-patient relationship. The doctor-patient relationship is fragile and frequently challenged when disability is at issue. Tenets of this relationship include placing the interests of the patient first. Confidentiality can be broken only when waived by the patient, revoked by a court of law, or modified by predetermined administrative realities.

Legal revocation of confidentiality may occur when a patient makes a legal claim on a medical basis and declines to waive confidentiality voluntarily. Those defending a claim may have statutory rights to medical records of the person making the claim. For example, proper assessment of an employee who claims work-related psychiatric injury should include all past psychiatric history. The employee might be required to waive confidentiality of prior psychiatric evaluation and treatment. Legal revocation may also occur in criminal matters when medical history is felt to be relevant but the court has been denied access to medical records by the defendant. Confidentiality is regularly compromised in the normal course of medical practice by the requirements of financially responsible third parties. Medical records are obtained to process claims and determine medical necessity. Participation in insurance, reimbursement, and workers' compensation plans may imply a limited waiver of confidentiality as a condition of enrollment. Maintaining an effective doctor-patient relationship requires careful attention to the therapeutic relationship and to breaches of confidentiality for third-party needs (see Chapter Four).

The treating physician is not generally concerned with determination of illness causality unless causality affects treatment. For example, it is important for a physician who is treating a patient with back pain to learn if there is a fracture and how it occurred. A treating physician would be little concerned whether the fracture took place at work or in a backyard. However, this causal distinction is of utmost importance to an employer required to accept legal and financial responsibility for work-related injuries.

A treating physician must not become a patient advocate. It is essential to focus on proper diagnosis and treatment, while leaving advocacy to others. For example, physicians may be asked for statements of degree and cause of impairment. Reports should be limited to opinions of medical probability or certainty, regardless of the resulting legal or social effects on the patient.

As a general rule, physicians should not offer opinions about disability and should not be asked for or provide work absence authorizations. The physician is trained to address issues of injury, illness, and impairment but not to determine if an employee is disabled. The reason is that such a determination requires knowledge of the particular definition of disability that applies and nonmedical expertise on the actual requirements of a specific job. Common sense would dictate that an acutely impaired individual might have limitations in functioning that would preclude work activity; examples are a woman who is immediately postpartum, the postoperative patient, or an individual with a communicable respiratory infection. Frequently, physicians go beyond their expertise, offering opinions that an employee with chronic orthopedic complaints cannot work due to weakness or pain complaints. However, the physician should address only issues of impairment and what the patient can or cannot do; the employer can then determine if the worker can perform the requirements of their job or provide another job within the capacity of the worker. Similarly, the presence of a psychiatric disorder does not preclude employment, only the impairment that such a disorder would impose on necessary work functions, a determination best left to the employer.

Patients may become angry or seek care elsewhere when the physician's opinion is not consistent with their beliefs or wishes. Even so, the treating physician's obligation is clinical objectivity, despite any emotional or financial concerns. To protect medical objectivity and the doctor-patient relationship, the physician may suggest an independent consultative examination.

THE PSYCHIATRIC DISABILITY CONSULTATIVE EXAMINATION

An employee who claims disability may be asked to attend a consultative examination separate from any treatment. An administrative body may mandate the examination before considering or authorizing benefits or entitlements. Consultative examinations are most often conducted to resolve a medical question of concern to a third party—for example, employers, insurance companies, courts of law, and attorneys for claimants or defendants in injury claims.

Reasons for consultative examination include assessments of impairment, cause of injury, and appropriateness of treatment. Examination results help determine eligibility for social security and private disability coverage, workers' compensation, and benefits for work-related occupational disease (such as asbestosis and hearing loss claims) and also help determine the outcome of civil litigation of tort claims. Consultative examinations are also used to assess treatment for the treating physician or a third party (such as the surgical second opinion required by many insurance carriers).

Both consultative examinations and clinical treatment include a careful and comprehensive medical history, review of pertinent records, and examination of the patient before reaching a medical opinion. Consultative examinations should be conducted only by qualified physicians and should abide by the same professional standards expected for clinical treatment. The consultation examination is solely for medical opinion and should not include treatment. However, the resulting medical report can offer useful information to the treating physician. Confidentiality must be explicitly waived in advance, since a medical report will be provided to a third party (see Chapter Four). Because competing interests may result in an apparently adversarial situation, the doctor-patient relationship is not usually maintained after the examination.

The consulting physician generally should not subsequently provide clinical treatment for the claimant unless there are no alternate sources of medical care. Most consulting physicians will never treat anyone they have evaluated. Conflicts can arise between consulting physician and referral source or current treating physician. In particular, questions can arise about the consulting physician's objectivity if he provides treatment during continuing litigation or dispute resolution. Treatment under these circumstances might also be construed as a conflict of interest, potentially damaging the physician's reputation. Once retained for legal matters, the physician is generally precluded from being available to the patient (or representative) outside a formal legal setting such as an evaluation requested by the retaining client, deposition, or trial.

Regardless of purpose, any doctor-patient relationship must be compassionate, courteous, and respectful. The patient must be reminded at the outset that the examination is not for final diagnosis, is not for medical treatment, and is not confidential and that a written report will be provided to a third party. Although it is not uncommon for an examination to uncover new medical problems or details, the patient must not rely on this examination for comprehensive diagnosis or a substitute for his or her own medical care. A psychiatric examination, for instance, will not directly assess cardiac or neurological problems. Nevertheless, resulting medical information and opinion is of potential value to both the referring third party and the patient.

Conduct of the Examination

The following evaluation outline should not be used as a beginner's guide to a psychiatric interview. Effective interviewing requires specific prior knowledge, training, and experience. Moreover, while this discussion assumes a careful and comprehensive standard psychiatric approach, it emphasizes only the more specialized aspects of disability examinations. Although the conduct of the examination varies with every clinician, it is vital that examinations be careful and comprehensive and that reports include all necessary medical data and resulting conclusions. Reports should be easy to read and should avoid technical jargon because parties without medical training may need to understand the findings, logic, and conclusions of the report.

Who Should Be Present. Psychiatric interviews deal with personal experiences and feelings and are always potentially sensitive or uncomfortable. While patients should be protected from undue discomfort, their full and honest responses are necessary for accurate assessment. Patients sometimes request, or even demand, that they be accompanied during examination. Since refusal to allow an observer may lead to refusal of the examination, this issue is best discussed in advance.

Depending on local laws and the type of evaluation process, some patients may have a legal right to representation during examination. In these cases, the representative should not interfere, either by offering unrequested information or advising the patient not to respond to certain areas of inquiry. Any objections to particular questions should be saved for the subsequent administrative process.

Sometimes the physician may request the presence of an assistant to help with a severely impaired or potentially violent patient. When physician and patient do not share a common language, a professional interpreter, rather than family or friends, should translate. Language interpretation requires training and at times special certification. Family or friends may have personal interests in the examination outcome and could inadvertently or deliberately alter clinical data presented by the patient. Frequently, the patient will be unwilling to discuss intimate material in the presence of close companions, further compromising the evaluation quality and reliability.

Audio- or videotape recording by patients is beyond the scope of normal procedures and should be discouraged. It intrudes on the privacy and comfort of the physician, especially if there is no control over disposition of the recording. Exceptions should be made by prior agreement, and the recording should be maintained in a safe setting, and ideally performed by a professional trained in maintaining integrity of the process.

Medical Record and Collateral Information Review. The record review can be invaluable in determining the long-term and current functioning of the person being evaluated, especially when issues of causality are being addressed. The quality of the records depends on the quality of the observer. For example, are they offering their own observations based on objective data or merely repeating the statements of the claimant? The evaluating physician should review pertinent records for additional and independent information about the patient. In complex or prolonged cases, there may be many volumes of material. Record review should include past medical and psychiatric evaluation and treatment. The clinician who is assessing impairment can also use vocational reports, school records, employment records, and performance evaluations, which can provide data about level of functioning over time, especially before the onset of the claimed disability. The written report should concisely summarize the records reviewed and allow the reader to retrieve relevant material easily.

Presenting Problem. One way to start the interview is with a nontechnical and nonspecific question about the patient's view of the disability or problem. For example, when a psychiatric condition is claimed, it is better to ask, "How are your spirits?" rather than, "Do you have depression?" Psychiatric terms often have varied meanings, and a common definition should never be assumed. When patients have physical complaints that others feel have a significant emotional component, the physician might choose to avoid any initial reference to emotions. For example, a repeatedly disabled patient undergoing an evaluation for workers' compensation benefits might first be asked, "What situation keeps you from being able to work?"

Current, Past, and Family Psychiatric History. The next phase of the interview is commonly a psychiatric review of systems for potentially relevant psychiatric syndromes. Disability cases often involve affective (depressive) and anxiety disorders, psychosis, drug and alcohol abuse, organic mental disease, and personality disorders. A detailed psychiatric history includes a careful review of past symptoms, syndromes, diagnoses, and treatment. Counseling and psychotherapy for emotional distress can come from a wide variety of sources. Substance abuse and other emotional problems often lead to encounters with police, court, and prison. A careful history of legal problems and litigation is also needed. Family history of psychiatric illness, treatment, and disability helps in diagnosis and can be facilitated by drawing a simple pedigree chart. The assessment should include requested impairment ratings according to a standard scale, such as the AMA's guide (2001). Never assume that level of functioning has necessarily declined as much as patients believe. For example, a young parent might leave clerical employment yet continue to function well as the primary caretaker of several children and a home. An administrator might feel unable to sit at an office desk yet spend many hours reading at home.

Developmental, Current Social, and Employment History. Family and culture of origin are the primary sources of emotional outlook and define the framework of later interpersonal relationships. Early childhood experiences help mold adult personality and are important contributors to later problems, including psychiatric and medical disability. Adult experiences are more likely to shape existing structures than they are to induce entirely new problems. Knowledge of a patient's early life is essential for understanding the present circumstances. One approach is to ask about early relationships with family and friends. Recent interest in childhood emotional, physical, psychological, and sexual abuse and neglect has focused attention on later development of adult depression, anxiety, dependence, and somatization. It is also important to understand religious and socioeconomic background, early home environment (including nontraditional arrangements), and family occupations. Early family losses and separations can have lasting effects, especially if there is limited contact with parents living elsewhere.

The developmental social history leads into the current social history. Educational achievement reflects past functioning and occupational coping mechanisms. One might think of school as the work of children. Not surprisingly, those with problems in school, including high school dropouts, are at increased risk for problems adapting to and succeeding in the workplace and more likely to claim disability. This may reflect a decreased ability to cope with external academic and occupational demands, decreased social skills, a disruptive social environment, or diminished capacity for delay of gratification. High school dropouts also have fewer academic skills to compensate for changing work requirements or impaired physical abilities that would permit them to succeed in more intellectually challenging but less physically demanding employment.

Complete employment history is a primary goal. The job types, performance levels, lengths of employment, reason for leaving positions, history of related injuries, and job satisfaction are all important. Similarly, military history includes rejection for service, level of performance, highest rank, discharge type and reasons (honorable, general, or dishonorable; end of enlistment term or earlier), and service-connected disability. Special attention should be given to the most recent employment, including the job held at the time of injury or disability claim.

In the context of a workers' compensation claim, critical issues include duration of the implicated employment, work environment, job satisfaction, and quality of relationships with management, supervisors, and coworkers. Income from current employment, family employment, investments, time-loss compensation, and welfare or other public funds helps to clarify financial status and potential economic motivations. Future employment or training plans are similarly useful.

All past, current, and contemplated litigation should be explored. Claimants are routinely represented by counsel in some circumstances and may elect legal assistance in others. The use of legal assistance by a patient should not prejudice the examiner. As a piece of clinical data, it may reflect a thoughtful and adaptive response to a complex process or an adversarial stance. Legal strategies and clearly irrelevant factors (if any) may be considered privileged information. The patient's attorney ideally should facilitate the evaluation process and patient comfort by providing information about the administrative process to the client.

Personal relationships frequently contribute to and are affected by disability status. History should include important relationships, living arrangements, and changes over time. Past and present relationships with family and friends will parallel workplace relationships. Marital and other intimate relationships can profoundly interact with a disability claim. For example, occupational disability can be a powerful form of family communication and conflict resolution or a major cause of family discord. Quality and number of friends, hobbies and avocations, club or organizational involvement, and religious activities also reflect current relationships and adaptation.

These psychosocial factors are only a partial list of potential areas of inquiry. All data that help to understand the character and adaptation of the employee are relevant, although potential relevance may not always be apparent to patient or attorney. Such concerns can be answered with the explanation that it is important to understand the whole person and that emotional and social factors can both influence and be affected by a disability.

Past Medical History. When only psychiatric disability is claimed, the psychiatrist will usually perform the examination without other medical specialties. It is essential to obtain a complete standard medical history from the patient, questionnaires, other physicians, and medical records. Current medical problems, medications, and attending physician names should be reviewed. Prior specialty consultation or a preprinted general health questionnaire is not a substitute for a careful integrated evaluation, but it will reduce the time needed for medical review of systems and allow the psychiatrist to explore pertinent details further. The data can reveal other medical conditions of diagnostic importance and critical information about health beliefs and patterns.

This is also a second opportunity for psychiatric review of systems. For example, an unexplained neurological problem might represent psychologically caused physical symptoms, while chest pain or shortness of breath can be caused biologically by panic disorder. Past and existing medical conditions and diagnoses are often mistaken diagnoses and may represent masked psychiatric syndromes or somatic equivalents for psychologically based conditions.

Mental Status Examination. The mental status examination (MSE), the psychiatric equivalent of a physical examination, includes both structured and unstructured observations during the interview. The MSE addresses appearance, behavior, affect (outward emotions), mood (reported emotions), speech, thought content, preoccupations, and suicidal or homicidal thoughts. Cognitive and intellectual functioning is assessed through fund of knowledge; tests of short-, medium-, and long-term memory; capacity for abstract thinking; and orientation. The MSE is formally recorded to allow for assessment of changes over time.

Psychological Testing. Psychological tests are never an appropriate substitute for clinical evaluation. Although they are often useful and sometimes seductively elegant, standardized tests must be used with caution. The results are subject to influence by conscious and unwitting patient concerns; by social, testing, and legal environments; and by improper administration or interpretation. Certain kinds of tests can quantify such patient data as intelligence (IQ), personality traits, and organic impairment (neuropsychological testing). Psychological testing neither diagnoses nor determines cause. Rather, test results demonstrate only correlation of responses with response patterns of a normed group. Also, certain tests of clinical value may be less valid in a forensic setting, especially if the test does not include measures of compliance and reliability.

Summary, Assessment, and Recommendations. In contrast to a typical medical consultation, which concludes with diagnostic information and treatment recommendations, the consultative examination concludes with responses to specific third-party questions. The fourth edition of the *Diagnostic and Statistical Manual of Mental Disorders* (DSM-IV; American Psychiatric Association, 1994) represents the current standard for psychiatric diagnosis. DSM-IV provides a five-axis format—current psychiatric diagnoses, developmental and personality disorders, concurrent physical diagnoses, level of psychosocial stressors, and overall level of functioning—that offers a concise summary of health and social functioning. DSM-IV diagnoses reflect only observable signs and symptoms, and do not address etiology for either particular syndromes or individual patients.

In addition to a diagnosis, the summary may include an explanation of symptom development and pathogenesis. Common themes are early developmental issues, with their potential reenactment in current relationships and workplace; the timing between significant personal events and symptom onset; and the natural history of possible psychiatric diagnoses. It is critical to justify conclusions with documented clinical data and to avoid esoteric jargon and unnecessary complexity so that nontechnical readers can understand the report.

Opinions as to level of stability needed for specific treatment, further evaluation, and prognosis may be required. Sometimes the opinion may need to be tentative pending additional information, such as a need for more records or further testing. When this occurs, arrangements should be made to obtain the information as soon as possible to complete the evaluation.

When a psychiatric condition is suspected, treatment suggestions should include type of treatment (such as specific psychotherapies or medications), anticipated treatment intensity and duration, and selection of an optimal treating clinician. Depending on the circumstances of the evaluation, the consultant might suggest several qualified local practitioners with specific expertise.

DETERMINATION OF CAUSALITY

Clinical medicine is concerned with the origination and development of disease whenever it affects diagnosis and treatment. Causality is also important for benefit determination, but may not be important for social security or other disability insurance benefits. The legal standard for opinions of cause in civil proceedings is "on a more probable than not basis." This is equivalent to a 51 percent or greater chance that a particular circumstance has caused the reported medical condition or disorder.

The determination should consider whether the disorder would likely have occurred in the absence of the particular circumstance. Because most psychiatric disorders are multiply determined, they cannot easily be attributed to a single circumstance or event. Even a traumatic triggering event will generally require other concurrent circumstances, as well as social or genetic vulnerability, for emergence of overt psychiatric symptoms (see Chapter Fifteen). Unequivocal determination of cause is frequently not possible. It is important not to allow a particular event to be considered a cause by default in the absence of clear data that would support this opinion.

Case 1

Jane Wylie, a thirty-five-year-old single accountant sought disability leave for anxiety that kept her from working. Jane reported she had gotten along well with her male supervisor for seven years, but that he had been increasingly critical and overbearing during the past three months. She started to have panic attacks and severe anxiety. Since she was too nervous to work, she sought a disability leave. A human resource memo said that coworkers had not noticed any change in the supervisor's behavior or management style. The psychiatric consultation elicited a ten-year history of panic disorder, exacerbated for three months. Jane and her boyfriend had been growing closer lately. At the boyfriend's insistence, they had moved in together last year, and he had proposed marriage three months ago. As a result of her panic disorder, he was taking time off from his job to take care of her.

Jane was referred to a psychiatrist for brief psychoanalytic psychotherapy and medication treatment. After four weeks of treatment, she was back at work. After ten weeks, she was able to recognize that she had fears of intimacy and that the marriage proposal had worsened her existing panic disorder. She did not yet know what all of those fears were, but she did make amends with her supervisor, and she returned to her usual high level of professional performance and interpersonal skill.

Causality determination always involves understanding the diagnostic basis and emotional meaning of symptoms. Patients, lawyers, and treating physicians often misattribute cause to recent external events while not considering developmental, personality, and genetic factors. There are many causes of misattribution, including the following ones:

- *Primary gain:* The symptom creates relief from unconscious internal emotional conflict. It is useful in reducing the interpersonal conflicts or other external threats that triggered the internal conflict.

- *Secondary gain:* The symptom improves relationships or life circumstances through real or symbolic emotional support evoked from others. These advantages might not have been sought or foreseen when symptoms first occurred.

- *Denial of psychiatric illness:* The employee is emotionally unable to accept the existence of psychiatric illness (for instance, to preserve an image of self-reliance) and therefore seeks an alternative explanation of symptoms.

- *Ignorance or confusion:* Misattribution is inadvertent, without any obvious psychological intent.

- *Malingering:* Conscious goal-directed behavior is designed to derive inappropriate financial or other advantage through false representation of symptoms.

Case 2

Marshall Frampton, a twenty-year-old single man, was employed as a countertop installer for five months and claimed that he was poisoned by chemical solvents used for plastic laminate installation. Although both he and his family internist said that the solvents had caused auditory hallucinations, the solvents were always used with industry ventilation standards, there was no scientific literature describing psychiatric effects, and none of his coworkers reported any problems despite similar exposure.

The evaluating psychiatrist noted that Marshall had flat affect (that is, no emotional depth) and a fearful expression. Moreover, it turned out that the marked deterioration in his function had started after his mother's death ten months earlier. Always a loner, he had become even more socially withdrawn, no longer attended church, and had stopped cleaning his apartment. Marshall knew that his older sister had been chronically hospitalized for agitated behavior in another state, but since that thought made him nervous, he had never told his internist. The medical data strongly suggested a diagnosis of schizophrenia, and the work-related disability claim was denied. Marshall disagreed, and he declined a referral for treatment until emergency hospitalization a year later.

By their very nature, psychiatric symptoms are defenses that protect patients from underlying emotional discomfort. Patients thus are usually unable to provide full and correct explanations of true emotional causality. They may be unaware that they are misattributing personal concerns or psychiatric symptoms to the workplace setting. Until they benefit from appropriate treatment, the underlying emotional discomfort will prevent them from recognizing misattribution of cause.

Superficial assessment will often mistakenly assume a causal role for prior apparent stressors (*post hoc, ergo propter hoc:* it preceded, therefore it caused). But complex psychiatric conditions are typically caused by many factors, which usually include unapparent emotional issues, but sometimes do not include seemingly obvious external circumstances. Depression is one such complex disorder. One employee might experience a major depression after a traumatic workplace event, while his coworkers do not. That same employee might have a later recurrence with no obvious workplace stressor. Differing risk for depression could be due to increased genetic susceptibility, early childhood neglect, recent marital stress, or undetected onset of thyroid disease.

There are also many barriers to correct causal attribution by the consulting psychiatrist. Objective physicians offer medical opinions without bias toward either the referral source or the wish of their patient. But when subtly influenced by conscious or unconscious feelings, evaluating physicians can deviate from intended medical objectivity. This response is known as countertransference. Broadly defined, countertransference includes patient-induced physician emotions such as anger, boredom, sexual attraction, or nurturing. The narrower definition of countertransference refers only to unresolved internal conflicts of the clinician, nonspecifically evoked by patient attributes. For example, a patient who resembles a physician's intrusive parent may evoke feelings of hostility that color clinical judgment. Psychiatrists in all settings must recognize and understand these feelings to preserve their objectivity. Countertransference feelings can also provide clinical data. A patient who engenders certain feelings in the psychiatrist may have similar effects on other people, which could provide a clue to the source of conflict in the patient's life.

Confusing differences of opinion can occur when clinicians selectively focus on limited aspects of the medical data and fail to integrate symptoms, recent events, and developmental factors comprehensively. The assessment and formulation in the disability report should reflect an integrated view and indicate which factors are emphasized in reaching an opinion. Failure to do so may reflect countertransference, deficient or ideologically rigid theoretical beliefs, inadequate medical data collection, or patient misrepresentation.

Health care costs can also impede honest assessment. Despite clinical detachment, the physician will feel some responsibility for consultation patients. Financial coverage for treatment is sometimes available only through litigation or administrative process. Workers' compensation insurance usually covers treatment cost only for work-related conditions. A depressed patient without medical insurance may want to claim employment injury falsely in order to afford treatment. A treating physician who is involved in the process faces the difficult dilemma of either leaving the patient untreated (or not charging, with consequent transference and countertransference problems) or misstating his opinion and attributing the condition to the workplace (also with serious transference and countertransference implications).

The most disturbing barrier to objectivity can be physician concern for maintaining friendly relations with patients, families, and referral sources and avoiding uncomfortable conflict and challenge. He may be reluctant to alienate those who do not share his assessment of impairment level or causation. Patients and referral sources gravitate toward physicians with similar views of illness and health. However, professional, ethical, and societal considerations mandate unbiased opinions. Referral sources should seek proper evaluation but must respect adverse determinations. Patients should try to benefit from a comprehensive review of their condition and treatment. Evaluating physicians should insist on their right to integrity. Mutual respect for the truth is essential for maintaining integrity of the disability determination and impairment rating process, and of medical consultation and treatment in general.

Malingering is the intentional representation of false or exaggerated symptoms. It is seen in medical treatment settings and is especially common in settings where apparent illness can produce personal economic or social benefit. Malingering is always difficult to determine since there may be skillful efforts at falsifying symptoms. Physicians are often reluctant to believe that a patient might deliberately mislead them. Evidence can surface through markedly inconsistent data from the patient or contradictory information from collateral sources and medical records. Malingering can also be confused with factitious disorder, where intentional falsification of symptoms meets a psychological need to assume the sick role and external incentives appear to be absent. Somaticization differs from malingering and factitious disorder because reported symptoms are produced by unconscious mechanisms rather than conscious intent.

ADMINISTRATIVE MEDICAL REVIEW

In certain administrative proceedings, a medical reviewer is an additional physician in the evaluation process. The reviewer examines the medical evidence and then interprets the findings according to administrative rules. The reviewer does not usually meet the patient directly, but may issue the actual disability determination. Further administrative, adjudicative, or appellate processes are often available when involved parties challenge a determination made by review.

ADOPTING THE DISABILITY ROLE: A PSYCHOLOGICAL PROCESS

When an employee suffers physical injury and impairment, the level of disability very much depends on personality and circumstances. Adoption of the disability role, before or after an illness or disability claim has been made, is a psychological process that can transform vulnerable employees. The employee may perceive and present himself or herself as helpless and dependent. The illness may, in turn, allow unacceptable preexisting distress out of conscious awareness to be converted into a conscious physical condition. Overt expression of psychological distress is often not acceptable if it is felt to suggest weakness in the face of a hostile world or triggers unconscious fears of overwhelming emotion. Somatic symptoms can be used to protect self-esteem and provide more socially accepted models to explain personal, economic, and occupational dysfunction. This process is supported by cultural influences, disability programs, and sometimes by legal, medical, and mental health professionals. For example, it is often easier to present a claim for physical conditions than for psychiatric diagnoses, with the latter meeting more resistance by administrative entities or at times being outright prohibited by law. Furthermore, attributing conditions to external factors can avoid the emotional discomfort of accepting personal responsibility, while concurrently benefiting from greater social acceptance, psychological relief, compensation, and caring. It is not uncommon for an employee to pursue a disability claim out of a psychological need to misattribute an actual psychiatric disorder. For example, an employee with panic disorder might be unable to see his anxiety and social avoidance as internally derived. Instead, he might be more comfortable seeing an external cause of impairment and resulting disability. This kind of emotional solution allows for a more comfortable conscious adaptation to symptoms, but makes acceptance of effective treatment difficult. As the employee adapts to a lifestyle dependent on the sick role, he becomes still more resistant to insight and treatment.

Case 3

Four months after June McGraw, a thirty-seven-year-old divorced aircraft manufacturing employee, started work, she hit her thumb with a hammer. She did not seek medical treatment until several weeks later, when she also started having arguments with her supervisor and coworkers and described her workplace as psychologically intolerable. June entered treatment with a mental health professional who sympathized with her unhappiness and concluded that she suffered a disabling posttraumatic stress disorder as a result of her thumb injury. June then sought compensation for posttraumatic stress disorder. However, psychiatric consultation, requested by the employer, did not show that symptoms set out by DSM-IV for posttraumatic stress disorder were present and did reveal that June had suffered from sexual molestation in childhood. She subsequently had developed a chaotic school, employment, and marital history. She had never held any job for more than six months and had been relying on her parents for financial support. Her father, a long-term employee for the same employer, had arranged the job for her and told her that she was now old enough to fend for herself. Her previous brief attempts at emotional independence had always led to extreme dependence on nonfamily members, followed by an angry return to family dependence. June complained that her supervisor, like her father, was argumentative and unsupportive. She also complained that her male therapist would not accept more than one telephone call per day from her and asked the psychiatrist to offer her a more supportive treatment.

PREVENTION OF DISABILITY

Causes of workplace disability can be broadly divided into factors external and internal to the employee. External factors include psychological and physical demands of the workplace. Of prime importance is organizational culture and management style. Employees who feel supported and in control of significant aspects of their working lives will be more satisfied and less disability prone. Rigid and authoritarian environments may promote feelings of powerlessness and contribute to illness and disability. Employment uncertainty and unwillingness to accommodate individual needs will also increase disability risk. The physical work environment has an important role with regard to overall physical safety and accident prevention. Areas of concern that bear attention include such details as lighting, noise level, ergonomic design of workstations, and physical arrangement of desks and personnel. However, there is a lack of consensus on the ultimate importance of the physical environment in prevention of many chronic disability and injury claims.

When an injury has taken place or an impairment is present, efforts should be made to prevent disability. Genuine concern and a firm but supportive approach will encourage employees to readapt to the workplace. A modified or light duty position is preferable to sending an employee home. The claims review and management process should focus on claimants whose course suggests greater risk for disability resulting in the absence of active and ongoing intervention.

Internal determinants of disability include both long-standing personality factors and acutely stressful personal events. A worker with a troubled past, adversarial relationships, failure in school and prior jobs, and difficulty with everyday demands may have reduced intellectual and psychological resources and be at increased risk for disability. Careful and attentive management and training can partially address the issues, but there may be little that an organization can do to resolve an employee's internal deficits. Psychosocial support and psychotherapy may be helpful, but are not always able to make a real difference. Employees with chronic problems may be especially resistant to intervention. Since anxiety, affective, and substance abuse problems are commonplace, ensuring the availability of optimal psychiatric diagnosis and treatment also enhances prevention and intervention. It is the job of management to manage the hiring process so as to minimize the likelihood of hiring those who will fail due to factors outside the control of the workplace. Successful hiring should include assessing prior functioning in work and school settings, capacity to relate to others, and the ability to perform the requirements of the job through simulation and observation in the screening process.

WORK-RELATED IMPAIRMENTS AND WORKERS' COMPENSATION

Workers' compensation includes an evolving system of laws, health care, and vocational training designed to assist workers injured on the job. Benefits are available on a no-fault basis, without regard to injury cause, as long as the injury is considered work related. Injured workers usually cannot sue their employer for financial compensation but can seek recourse through civil litigation against an involved third party. For example, an employee who became depressed after injury by faulty equipment could benefit through workers' compensation and also bring tort action against the equipment manufacturer. When third-party recovery does occur, some of the recovered funds are used to reimburse workers' compensation costs.

Most employers in the United States are part of a workers' compensation system (exceptions include railroad workers, longshoremen, and those employed at sea) with the following basic benefits:

- Income replacement while unable to work
- Medical benefits for work-related injuries
- Disability payments or pensions for permanent work-related impairments
- Death benefits to survivors of a worker killed on the job
- Rehabilitation benefits to restore stable physical functioning
- Vocational rehabilitation to permit new employment with added skills
- Compensation for certain job specific occupational diseases

Prior to the creation of workers' compensation benefits, workers disabled on the job often had little recourse to secure medical care or economic support.

Employers typically provide workers' compensation benefits through commercial or government insurance policies. Some large employers self-insure. Premium costs are based on factors including type of employment, workforce incomes, and loss experience over time. Per worker hourly premiums can range from a few cents in sedentary low-risk jobs to many dollars in such high-risk industries as logging and construction.

Case 4

James Watkins, a twenty-two-year-old married construction laborer, was injured when scaffolding collapsed underneath him. He fell twenty-five feet on his back, causing the rupture of a cyst in his back that had been present from birth, with subsequent damage to the sacral nerves, causing impotence and incontinence. These impairments caused a marked reduction of his self-confidence and functional capacity. When evaluated, he had a major depression with depressed mood, anhedonia, insomnia, anorexia, and impaired concentration. He had been previously happy and well adapted, and there had been little change in his personal life before the injury. He and his wife of three years had planned to have children in a few years. His depression was apparently induced by his reaction to injury-induced physical impairment.

Case 5

Franklin Cowlitz, a thirty-two-year-old married police officer, shot and killed a robbery suspect who had drawn a gun and threatened bystanders and himself. Frank was cleared by routine police inquest and was quickly returned to the field without psychiatric intervention. Over the next three years, he gradually became distant from others, avoided entering stores that reminded him of the shooting, and became anxious around people who looked like the robbery suspect. He was jittery and couldn't sleep. When his captain finally referred Frank for psychiatric evaluation, posttraumatic stress disorder was identified. Several months of intensive psychotherapy allowed him to discuss feelings about the shooting and other issues, with a gradual remission of symptoms and return to his usual self.

Most employees with psychiatric conditions are fully functioning and unimpaired. Others, usually with more severe illness, are able to function well with careful accommodation to their psychiatric impairment. A few chronic psychiatric disorders may be fully disabling in all settings depending on the specific impact on the individual patient. It must be stressed that a diagnosis is not an impairment.

Prediction of disability from psychiatric impairment is difficult and imprecise. The best predictor of future functioning is past functioning in similar settings. Even so, people often do change for both better and worse, and a psychiatric illness can either improve or deteriorate. Because most chronic psychiatric disturbances are of developmental or biological origin, one should never assume that long-term psychiatric impairment is caused by the workplace. More typical is a short-term reaction with improvement over time, with or without treatment. Sometimes a workplace injury may cause a person predisposed by background to suffer a long-term condition, but alternative hypotheses should be considered in such events.

As reflected in Cases 4 and 5, work-related psychiatric injuries can be broadly placed in two categories: physical injury causing emotional impairment (physical-emotional, as in Case 4) and emotional injury causing emotional impairment (emotional-emotional, as in Case 5). Less often encountered is emotional injury causing physical impairment (emotional-physical). An example might be a bank teller's heart attack reportedly triggered by the stress of a bank robbery (see Chapter Twenty-Seven). Although physical injury causing physical impairment does not seem to involve psychiatric issues, these issues are among the most important determinants of disability criteria.

Optimal management of any emotional injury includes competent psychiatric evaluation and treatment. Most true psychiatric disabilities respond promptly to appropriate psychotherapy or medication, or both. Chronic personality disorders and other psychiatric conditions might be worsened under stress but are usually well ingrained and are less likely to show prompt response to treatment. Careful attention to preinjury functioning will usually help identify these patients.

Workers' compensation standards hold that impairments are work related whenever they are caused or worsened by work-related injury, even if the employee is predisposed to the impairment. This reductionistic legal construct is often at odds with the multidetermined psychiatric model of causality. Nonetheless, the compensation system mandates assignment of responsibility for work-related conditions.

Employees who experience work-related impairment or economic displacement may suffer emotional and financial consequences. Normal emotional response and social tragedy must not be confused with psychiatric illness. Most people emotionally adjust to adverse circumstances, although some develop significant psychiatric symptoms.

Work-related psychiatric illness may not always respond fully to treatment. A standardized rating scale to determine financial compensation may then assess residual psychiatric impairment. If impairment is sufficiently severe to preclude employment, a permanent pension may be awarded through workers' compensation, social security, or private disability insurance.

Impairment assessment and disability determination are challenging clinical tasks that differ from psychiatric treatment. Disability is multidetermined, with contributions from the employee, society, and the workplace. Because employers and employees and their representatives are often reluctant to consider complex causal models and interventions, understanding and reducing disability is an enormous challenge. Disability costs affect everyone: employees, coworkers, families, employers, and society. Ongoing efforts at disability management should emphasize proper understanding of the distinction between impairment and disability, the proper role of the treating and evaluating physician, accurate diagnosis, prevention, and early intervention.

References and Additional Sources

American Medical Association. (2001). *Guides to the evaluation of permanent impairment* (5th ed.). Chicago: Author.

American Psychiatric Association. (1994). *Diagnostic and statistical manual of mental disorders* (4th ed.). Washington, DC: Author.

Diorio, P. G., & Fallon, L. F., Jr. (1989). Workers' compensation, impairment and disability. In L. F. Fallon, Jr., O. B. Dickerson, & P. W. Brandt-Rauf (Eds.), *The management perspective: Occupational medicine* (pp. 145–152). Philadelphia: Hanley & Belfus.

Egdell, F. A., Horrocks, F. A., Lee, K., & Warburton, J. W. (1988). Psychiatric disorders, alcohol, and drug abuse. In F. C. Edwards, R. I. McCallum, & P. J. Taylor (Eds.), *Fitness for work: The medical aspect* (pp. 382–423). New York: Oxford University Press.

Harlan, L. C., Harlan, W. R., & Parsons, P. E. (1990). The economic impact of injuries: A major source of medical costs. *American Journal of Public Health, 80,* 453–459.

Integrated Benefits Institute. (2000, June). *Benchmarking study finds productivity loss dwarfs direct benefits costs.* Available on-line at: http:www.ibiweb.org.

Liberty Mutual Insurance Research Center. (2001, October). *Liberty Mutual Workplace Safety Index.* Available on-line at: http://www.libertymutual.com/research/news/releases/press_workplace.html.

Pannzarella, J. P. (1991). The nature of work, job loss, and the diagnostic complexities of the psychologically injured worker. *Psychosomatics, 21,* 10–15.

Robbins, D. B. (1988). Psychiatric conditions in worker fitness and risk evaluation. In J. S. Hillelstein & G. S. Pransky (Eds.), *Worker fitness and risk evaluations* (pp. 309–321). Philadelphia: Hanley & Belfus.

U.S. Department of Health and Human Services. (1986). *Disability evaluation under social security.* Washington, DC: U.S. Government Printing Office.

U.S. Occupational Safety and Health Administration. (2001, November). [Data.] Available on-line at: http://www.osha.gov/oshstats/work.html.

U.S. Social Security Administration. (2002). *Disability evaluation under social security.* Washington, DC: U.S. Government Printing Office.

Weinstein, M. R. (1978). The concept of the disability process. *Psychosomatics, 19*(2), 94–97.

CHAPTER NINETEEN

Workplace Forensic Psychiatry

The Americans with Disabilities Act and the Family and Medical Leave Act

Sara Eddy
Ronald Schouten

The Americans with Disabilities Act (ADA), passed by Congress in 1990 and effective for all employers with fifteen or more employees, affects nearly 50 million disabled employees. Human resource professionals must have a thorough working knowledge of the ADA as they interview job applicants, make hiring decisions, and consider the termination of employees with disabilities. Many of the persons protected under the ADA have psychiatric disorders; consequently, human resource and mental health professionals frequently must work together to ensure that workplaces are safe and employees are productive, while accommodating disabilities and complying with various statutory requirements and regulatory guidelines. It is essential to balance an effective approach to the mental health needs of employees with careful attention to potential legal concerns.

The Family and Medical Leave Act of 1993 (FMLA) is a statute that Congress passed with the hope of giving employees job security when they need to be away from the workplace for family and health-related matters.

The ADA arguably has had a greater impact on the workplace than any other legislation since the Civil Rights Act of 1964. It establishes a clear and comprehensive federal prohibition of discrimination on the basis of disability in employment, public services (especially transportation), public accommodations and services operated by private entities, and telecommunications. Title I of the ADA applies to employment and prohibits discrimination by employers on the basis of physical or mental disabilities. In other words, it protects individuals who are qualified to perform the job in question and disabled. This prohibition against discrimination is tempered somewhat by the concept of hardship to the employer and potential risk of harm to or by the employee. The employer can defend itself against a claim of an adverse employment action by showing that the individual is unable to perform the essential functions of the job, with or without accommodation, or that the employee presents a threat to the safety of the workplace and its employees. The Family and Medical Leave Act (FMLA) provides further employment protection for employees who need leave from work for health-related matters. It is essential to balance an effective approach to the mental health needs of employers and employees with careful attention to potential legal concerns.

Although the federal statute sets forth the broad terms of the ADA, Congress charged the Equal Employment Opportunity Commission (EEOC) with developing regulations to govern the ADA and enforcing them.

Between July 1992 and September 1996, persons claiming mental illness as a disability accounted for nearly 12.7 percent of all ADA charges filed with the EEOC. This figure is probably low because it does not include charges filed with state or local equal employment opportunity offices. Individuals with anxiety disorders, depression, bipolar disorder, schizophrenia, and other disturbances claimed they were subject to employment discrimination because of their psychiatric conditions. Employers struggled to comprehend and deal with persons with mental disabilities in the workplace. Commonly held but false beliefs that mental illness is untreatable and that the mentally ill are unable to be productive members of the workforce added to employers' concerns that the ADA would require them to employ individuals who were unemployable but protected by the statute.

In response, the EEOC provided enforcement guidance with respect to individuals with psychiatric disabilities in its *Enforcement Guidance on the Americans with Disabilities Act and Psychiatric Disabilities* (commonly referred to as the *Guidance*) in March 1997. This *Guidance* is just what its name suggests: courts may accept its provisions or not, but they serve to inform and direct courts and litigants. The *Guidance* aimed to clarify how the ADA might be applied to psychiatric conditions and attempted not only to combat discrimination aimed at mentally ill individuals but also to dispel some of the myths, stereotypes, and fears on which such discrimination is based. Although the *Guidance* was designed for use by EEOC investigators in responding to charges filed by persons with mental disabilities, it also has been of use to employers. Nevertheless, attempts to educate employers and employees about mental disabilities in the workplace have been only moderately successful. Physical disabilities are concrete, sometimes visible, and often easy to understand and evaluate; mental disabilities cannot be seen, are often discomfiting, and can be difficult to assess and monitor. Some employers continue to argue that employees who seek its protection when they are hostile, tardy, irritable, unproductive, or socially inappropriate are undermining the policies of the ADA. Employees with mental disabilities may also complain that their disabilities are the sole cause of poor performance and that they are entitled to a variety of accommodations and protection from discipline or discharge.

States also have the ability to create laws, establish regulatory and enforcement bodies, and establish agencies where complaints of discrimination can be adjudicated. States have prohibitions against disability discrimination in the employment context, and most state laws closely track the language of the federal law. In addition, states have their own equal employment opportunity commissions to regulate and enforce these laws, and most have state agencies to which individuals may complain if they believe they have been the victim of discrimination. Massachusetts, for example, has the Massachusetts Commission Against Discrimination.

Even with abundant guidance from statutes, regulations, and state agencies, however, the ADA is in a state of constant evolution because of its interpretation by the courts. The ADA and the EEOC regulations have been the subject of considerable litigation and interpretation by bodies ranging from the U.S. Supreme Court to state commissions against discrimination, with state and federal courts hearing such cases as well; however, not all questions are raised in all courts, and decisions made by various bodies are not necessarily consistent. As a result, this complex statute is made even more difficult to understand because it is constantly changing as employers attempt to strike a balance between their duty to the workplace as a whole and their responsibilities to potential or current employees with disabilities. (See the chapter appendix for resources.)

UNDERSTANDING THE ADA

Understanding the definition of many specific terms is the key to understanding the ADA.

"Disability"

A disability is said to exist if an individual has a physical or mental impairment that substantially limits one or more of the individual's major life activities; a record of an impairment that substantially limited an individual in the performance of major life activities in the past, from which the individual has recovered in full or in part; or is regarded as having an impairment that substantially limits major life activities.

The ADA standards for disability therefore clearly apply to persons with psychiatric disabilities. Although the definition seems quite explicit, the *Guidance* clarified other terms within the definition as well: *impairment, substantially limits, major life activities, record of,* and *regarded as.*

"Impairment." An impairment can be any mental or psychological disorder, such as mental retardation, organic brain syndrome, emotional or mental illness, and specific learning disabilities. Some examples of emotional or mental illness are major depression, bipolar disorder, anxiety disorders (including panic disorder, obsessive compulsive disorder, and posttraumatic stress disorder), schizophrenia, and personality disorders. The *Guidance* suggests that the American Psychiatric Association's *Diagnostic and Statistical Manual of Mental Disorders* (DSM-IV; 1994) is relevant for identifying these disorders.

That a condition is delineated in DSM-IV does not mean that it is considered an impairment under the ADA and therefore a "covered" disability offering protection to an individual suffering from the condition. Even if a condition is an impairment, it is not automatically a disability. A disability depends not on a specific diagnosis but evidence that the condition substantially limits a major life activity.

The *Guidance* explicitly excludes certain conditions from inclusion in the definition of disability or impairment under the ADA, even though they are included in the DSM-IV. For example, compulsive gamblers, persons with psychoactive substance use disorders resulting from the use of illegal drugs, voyeurs, persons with certain gender identity disorders and other sexual behavior disorders, and persons with kleptomania or pyromania are all excluded from the definition of disability. The DSM-IV also includes conditions for which one might seek treatment (such as difficulties with a child or a spouse), but these conditions are not disorders and therefore are not impairments under the ADA. Traits such as irritability, chronic lateness, and poor judgment are not impairments either, although any of these may be linked to mental impairments.

Courts have determined that some conditions are not covered disabilities under the ADA. Stress and personality disorders are two conditions about which there has been some disagreement regarding their status as impairments. Although the broad definition of impairment offered by the *Guidance* includes stress-related and personality disorders, case law suggests that individuals who are experiencing stress in their attempts to cope with common family or workplace difficulties do not have impairments and therefore do not have disabilities under the ADA. For example, in *Weiler* v. *Household Finance Corp.* (1996), temporomandibular joint syndrome and stress were judged not to be covered disabilities where the plaintiff proved only that she had a personality conflict with one supervisor; in *Daley* v. *Koch* (1989), poor impulse control, irresponsible behavior, and poor judgment were judged as not constituting covered disabilities; and in *Bunevitch* v. *CVS/Pharmacy* (1996), depression was not a disability where it only lasted two and a half months.

"Substantially Limits." For an impairment to rise to the level of a disability, it must substantially limit a major life activity. A determination of whether an impairment is substantially limiting considers the severity of the limitation and the length of time it restricts the activity. Furthermore, the determination of substantial limitation must be based on the particular condition, and not generalizations about the condition.

To be a severe limitation, the impairment must either prevent or significantly restrict the condition, manner, or duration under which the individual can perform a major life activity; mild limitations are not sufficient. The impairment must last more than several months, and chronic episodic disorders (bipolar disorder, major depression, and schizophrenia, for example) may be substantially limiting if they are substantially limiting when active. In *Glowacki* v. *Buffalo General Hospital* (1998), a bipolar affective disorder was not judged a covered disability because it was sporadic and did not limit plaintiff's employment generally. In *Soileau* v. *Guilford of Maine, Inc.* (1997), the plaintiff's condition of chronic depressive disorder, which included periods of depression rendering him "unable to get along with others," was judged not a covered disability. Although Soileau was unable to get along with others in one job, he was not substantially limited in his ability to get along in a class of jobs.

In 2002, the U.S. Supreme Court made clear in *Toyota Motor Manufacturing* v. *Williams* that in order to claim a disability under the ADA, an employee must show more than a medical condition that impairs the ability to perform a class of jobs. In this case, an automobile assembly line worker's carpal tunnel syndrome was judged not a covered disability because it did not result in substantial impairment of a major life activity; the proper inquiry, said the Court, is whether the impairment prevents or restricts the performance of tasks of central importance to most people's daily lives. The Court noted that the ability to perform particular job functions, using hand tools in this case, is not necessarily an important part of the individual's life, and it distinguished the inability to perform certain manual tasks from the fundamental activities of life, such as walking, breathing, or caring for oneself.

Courts have looked at the likelihood that some illnesses seem more treatable than others, going to the issue of whether a limitation is severe. Two recent cases examined the issue of leaves of absence as reasonable accommodations. In *Evans* v. *Federal Express Corp.* (1998), the court ruled that the Massachusetts disability statute did not require an employer to provide an alcoholic employee with a second leave of absence to treat his alcoholism because the leave would probably not be effective in treating the problem. In contrast, in *Criado* v. *IBM* (1998), the court sustained a jury verdict for an employee who was terminated after she had asked for and been denied an extension of a leave for treatment of depression. The Court took note of the fact that there was evidence that an extended leave would have been both temporary and effective in producing a recovery.

The *Guidance* took the position that the existence of an impairment is generally determined without regard to whether its effects can be mitigated with the help of medication. For example, an individual with a psychiatric illness that affected her ability to work in a range of jobs would be considered to have an impairment even if the symptoms of her mental illness could be mitigated or eliminated by medication. There was a sharp division among the circuit courts of appeal on this point, and in 1999 the U.S. Supreme Court rejected the position of the EEOC *Guidance* and limited its scope on the question of whether mitigating measures should be considered when determining whether an individual has a disability. The Court concluded that the EEOC approach of evaluating individuals in their untreated state "is an impermissible interpretation of the ADA" in *Sutton* v. *United Airlines* (1999). *Sutton* held that persons are not disabled if their impairments are largely corrected by medication or other devices. In the case of mental and emotional difficulties, a person would therefore not be disabled under the ADA if his or her condition might be reasonably controlled by medication.

Individual states may interpret their own disability discrimination statutes in a way that leads to conclusions different from those of the federal courts. For example, the Massachusetts Commission Against Discrimination has stated that it will not follow *Sutton* when interpreting the Massachusetts statute prohibiting discrimination, and the Massachusetts Supreme Judicial Court has upheld this position in *Dahill* v. *Police Department of Boston et al.* (2001). In *Dahill,* the court determined that a police officer candidate who required a hearing aid was covered under Chapter 151B of the General Laws of Massachusetts, the state version of the ADA. In an advisory opinion, the court ruled that a corrective device to alleviate a disability is not relevant under the state's disability law. The highest state court thus made a clear break from federal law in allowing a mitigating device such as a hearing aid to be taken into account. Dahill was allowed to attempt to demonstrate that his hearing was adequate with a hearing aid. Readers are advised to be aware of the different rules among state and federal jurisdictions on this and other issues and, when in doubt, to consult legal counsel.

"Major Life Activities." Early regulations provided that caring for oneself, performing manual tasks, walking, seeing, hearing, speaking, breathing, learning, and working were major life activities. The *Guidance* expanded this list to include such mental and emotional processes as thinking, concentrating, and interacting with others.

"Record of." An individual who does not actually have a disability is protected under the ADA if he can establish that he has a history of an impairment that substantially limits one or more major life activities. The employer must be aware of the history, and some courts have not been persuaded that protection is due the individual unless the history of an impairment is lengthy or substantial.

"Regarded as." Under this provision of the ADA, an individual who does not actually have a disability and has no record of a disability may be protected by establishing that her employer perceives or regards her as being disabled. Some cases based on this premise have been unsuccessful; however, the employer must take care not to act in such a way as to create a "regarded as" status, especially where such a response arises from concerns rooted in bias against the mentally ill. In *Holihan* v. *Lucky Stores* (1997), a plaintiff was entitled to a jury trial on his "regarded as" status because the employer asked the employee whether he was having any problems, encouraged him to seek counseling through the employer's employee assistance program, and received doctors' reports diagnosing the employee's depression, anxiety, and stress.

The potential for litigation arising from the "regarded as" provision has given pause to many employers and human resource professionals who fear that the act of expressing appropriate concern for an employee's well-being may set the stage for an ADA claim. When an employee manifests evidence of a medical or psychiatric illness, employers must think carefully about how to assist employees without creating this "regarded as" status. Consider, for example, an employee whose productivity has declined, who comes to work disheveled and malodorous, and who is observed weeping in his office. How an individual company approaches such a situation often is a function of company culture and atmosphere. The company that places a priority on avoiding any possibility of ADA litigation may choose to avoid any intervention whatsoever in this situation and allow the employee to continue in this manner until he is no longer functional. This approach minimizes the risk of a "regarded as" ADA claim but creates many other risks: the individual's low productivity, possible disruption of the workplace and impact on the productivity of other employees, the risk of further deterioration, and the potential expense of a long-term disability claim when treatment is not obtained or a claim under the Occupational Safety and Health Administration for failure to correct an unsafe situation if an injury results from allowing the person to remain on the job.

ADA litigation remains a possibility in this situation if the depressed employee is ultimately terminated and returns to claim that he was dismissed because he suffered from major depression. In such cases, the ongoing tolerance of his poor performance while his depression was being ignored may be used as evidence that the employee was terminated only when the employer learned of the diagnosis. In other words, his termination was pretextual and not based on his actual performance. In addition, where the depressive symptoms are so apparent, the employee may be able to mount a "regarded as" claim successfully, regardless of efforts to ignore this condition. The employer choosing to intervene in such a situation may slightly increase the risk of a "regarded as" claim, but may also limit the other risks and find a defense in having done the right thing by expressing compassion for the depressed employee. Moreover, a reasonable inquiry based on concern for the well-being of the employee and a referral for appropriate care can often prevent the loss of a valuable employee and the employer's investment in this worker. In these extremely complicated situations, the employer's human resource personnel should discuss the various options with counsel before deciding how to proceed.

Qualified Individual with a Disability

The ADA requires that the individual simultaneously be disabled but also able to perform the essential functions of the job in question (with or without accommodation). An individual who is totally disabled may not be qualified for any job, regardless of accommodation.

"Qualified Individual." Requirements having to do with qualification come up most frequently in the hiring phase, although they are also relevant when employees suffer from progressive disabilities. The ADA establishes broad standards with respect to qualification; most often, an individual may be qualified by educational background, work experience, license, or interpersonal skills. As a general rule, prospective employers may not ask whether an individual has ever received treatment for a mental or emotional condition or been hospitalized for such a condition, although under certain very specific circumstances, the employer may inquire further—for example, if the applicant requests an accommodation in order to participate in the application process or voluntarily reveals the existence of a medical condition or if the medical condition is obvious to the employer.

The ADA (and state laws as well) not only restricts disability-related questions at the preemployment stage, but also restricts medical testing. Human resource professionals should be alert to the dangers inherent in preemployment testing and should satisfy themselves that any tests not be construed as medical testing. If the tests are administered or interpreted by health care professionals or conducted in a medical setting, they may be construed as medical testing. Similarly, a test designed to reveal the individual's psychological health may well be regarded as medical testing. In general, it would be prudent not to administer any so-called personality tests at the preemployment stage.

"Essential Functions." Determining whether a function is essential is a fact-based inquiry, is established on a case-by-case basis, and consequently is much litigated. In brief, the inquiry appears to turn on whether the employer actually requires the function to be performed and, if so, whether removing the function would fundamentally alter the position. A job description can be of great help in outlining the essential functions of a position, and human resource professionals should be certain to set forth in some detail the essential functions of job categories and particular jobs, where necessary, and always before an issue about a disability arises. Courts view with some suspicion job descriptions that are written after concerns develop about the job performance of an individual with a disability.

"Reasonable Accommodation"

A modification or an adjustment to the job application process, the work environment, or the conditions under which the work is performed is referred to as a reasonable accommodation. Its purpose is to enable an otherwise qualified individual with a disability to perform the essential functions of the job and experience the same terms and conditions, as well as benefits, of employment as nondisabled individuals.

Because there were many questions and controversies about what constituted reasonable accommodation, the EEOC issued *Enforcement Guidance: Reasonable Accommodation and Undue Hardship Under the Americans with Disabilities Act* in March 1999. That document sets forth in a question-and-answer format the expectation that the development of a reasonable accommodation be an interactive process. An employer must provide a reasonable accommodation only if it is aware that there is a disability requiring accommodation. In most cases, the individual with a disability (or a third party with knowledge of that individual) must both disclose the nature of the disability to be accommodated and request an accommodation. Without knowledge of the nature of the disability, the employer cannot be expected to, and is under no obligation to, accommodate it. Furthermore, the employee should work with the employer to arrive at a satisfactory accommodation. The employer need not provide the best accommodation available or the one that the employee requests, but it must provide an accommodation that is effective for its purpose. Let's say that an employee requests a flexible time schedule because she has difficulty awakening due to required antidepressant medication. The employer has an obligation to consider the requested accommodation to determine if it would be reasonable and to discuss it with the employee but is not required to provide the accommodation if it would be unduly burdensome.

Some individuals with mental or emotional disabilities request changes in work assignments to avoid perceived "stress." Courts have rejected such claims and have held that employers are not under an obligation to provide a stress-free environment (*Gaul* v. *AT&T,* 1997). Common accommodations include making job facilities accessible, modifying work schedules, reassigning nonessential job functions, permitting performance of job functions at alternative locations, and allowing temporary leaves of absence.

Although the courts may not impose an affirmative obligation on an employer to engage in an interactive process with the employee, case law suggests that the duty of the employer in this regard is higher when the employee suffers from a mental disability. A federal court of appeals noted that an employee's request for an accommodation requires "a great deal of communication between the employee and employer" and suggested that an employer's participation is particularly relevant where an employee is suffering from a mental disability (*Criado* v. *IBM,* 1998). Another federal court of appeals indicated that when dealing with individuals with psychiatric problems, employers must make an extra effort to communicate and assist the employee to identify necessary accommodations. In one case, submitting a letter from a psychiatrist who suggested assignment to a less stressful position for a custodial employee who was unable, due to his psychiatric difficulty, to make a request for an accommodation constituted a request for such an accommodation (*Bultemeyer* v. *Fort Wayne Community Schools,* 1996).

At this point in the dialogue between an employer and an employee with a psychiatric disability, the human resource professional and the mental health professional have an opportunity to work together to identify an accommodation that meets the needs of the workplace and the individual. Complications that sometimes arise during the interactive process may convince employers (and their attorneys) that involving medical or mental health professionals is more likely to create problems than to solve them. For example, the employer may see consulting a mental health professional as an opportunity to expose a malingering employee; the employee may view it as an opportunity to provide evidence of a disability. The employer may fear that consulting with a mental health professional will cause the employer to lose control of the process, and result in an exaggeration of the disability and thus the need for an accommodation. From the point of view of the employee, having his employer consult with his doctor might jettison his disability claim or accommodation request, not to mention result in a loss of confidentiality. Thoughtful information sharing, however, with informed consent as to clearly delineated material to be disclosed can produce significant benefits to the employee.

A typical situation is one in which an employee encounters difficulty performing some of the essential functions of her job and, in conversations with managers or human resource professionals, discloses the existence of a disability. The disclosure is often accompanied by a request for an accommodation—usually a leave of absence.

This may be the first time the employer has known of the existence of a disability and now must determine whether there is a relationship between performance problems and a disability and, if there is a disability, must enter into a dialogue with the employee about the disability and how to accommodate it in the workplace. The employer may inquire into the medical condition of an employee and request a medical examination if the request is job related and consistent with business necessity—in other words, learn whether an employee is able to perform the essential functions of the job or determine what might be a reasonable accommodation. Often the employer begins the interactive process by asking for information from the employee's doctor about whether the employee has a physical or mental impairment and, if so, what the impairment is; whether the employee can perform the essential functions of the job without an accommodation; if she is unable to perform the essential functions of her job without an accommodation, whether there are accommodations that would enable her to perform those functions and, if so, what those accommodations are; and how long she will require any accommodations. On receiving this information, the employer may want to arrange a fitness-for-duty evaluation with a psychiatrist or other health care professional of the employer's choosing. In that event, the employer should pay all of the expenses related to that evaluation; in most cases, employee participation in such an evaluation is a condition of continued employment.

The decision of whether to arrange a fitness-for-duty evaluation turns largely on the extent to which the employer is satisfied that the treating clinician has conducted an objective, complete clinical assessment. Employers should keep in mind that often the treating clinicians will act as an advocate for the employee-patient. Employers should understand that the treating clinician can be biased and should view the clinician's report accordingly. Nevertheless, if the disability is limited, the facts are well known, and the employer is familiar with the employee and the disability, the fitness-for-duty evaluation may not be necessary. Better results may be obtained in such situations by helping the employee obtain appropriate treatment if she is not already receiving it. If the employer has reason to doubt the veracity of the clinician's report or believes the treatment the employee is receiving is unsatisfactory, a fitness-for-duty evaluation will help to determine an appropriate next course of action.

A more difficult situation arises when the employer suspects that an employee is having performance difficulties that seem related to a serious mental illness but the employee has not disclosed any difficulty. Despite the general rule that normally the employee has the obligation to disclose a disability and request an accommodation, the *Guidance* suggests that under the following circumstances, the employer should initiate the interactive process, thus suggesting that under some circumstances, the employer may ignore its "regarded as" liability concerns:

- The employer knows of the disability.

- The employer knows or has reason to know that the employee is experiencing workplace problems because of the disability.

- The employer knows or has reason to know that the disability prevents the employee from requesting a reasonable accommodation.

If the employee responds to an inquiry appropriately raised by the employer by stating that he or she does not need an accommodation, the employer will have fulfilled its obligation.

At times, the human resource professional who suspects that an employee has a psychiatric difficulty will be tempted to make a referral to an employee assistance program or a mental health professional without having engaged in the interactive process. No matter how well meaning the human resource professional may be, to make such a referral runs the risk of creating a "regarded as" disabled status by his or her actions or attitude. If there are clear performance problems that seem related to psychiatric difficulties, the human resource professional should instead focus on performance and ask the employee in an open-ended fashion whether there are actions the employer might take to help the employee perform successfully. This can, and should, be done without asking the employee whether he or she has an illness or disability, for example, "Bob, you seem to be having some performance problems. Is there anything we can do to make it easier for you to get this work done?" rather than, "Bob, you seem to be having some performance problems. Are you depressed?" If the employee discloses the existence of a disability, the employer then may obtain information through a fitness-for-duty evaluation in order to provide an appropriate accommodation. Often the outcome of such an evaluation will be a recommendation for counseling or other psychiatric treatment. If the employee does not disclose a disability, it would be prudent for the human resource professional to defer any action until the employee or others offer more information. Consultation with an employment attorney familiar with these issues can often allay anxieties and help the employer chart an appropriate course that protects the company and ensures that the employee gets necessary treatment.

A fitness-for-duty evaluation done by an independent evaluator, as opposed to that done by a therapist or other mental health caregiver of the employee, gives the employer an opportunity to obtain information that might or might not substantiate a disability requiring accommodation and might assist in the provision of a reasonable accommodation. Information obtained by an independent evaluator will not be protected by the privilege running between doctor and patient, allowing critical information to be shared with the employer. Employers should furnish the evaluator with a description of the job held by the employee and specific questions that need to be answered. The examination cannot be a fishing expedition, however, and its scope should be limited to the effect of the condition on the employee's ability, with or without accommodation, to perform essential job functions. Inquiries about the employee's entire psychiatric history or details of psychotherapy would exceed the scope of the permissible inquiry. (See Chapter Seventeen.)

Employers must keep information with respect to psychiatric disabilities on separate forms and in separate medical files, apart from the usual personnel files. The information may be disclosed only when necessary, and then only to the employee's supervisor, first aid and safety personnel, and, under some circumstances, government officials.

Although the courts and the EEOC *Guidance* with respect to accommodations make it clear that the employer has an ongoing duty to provide reasonable accommodation, there is less information about the obligations of the employer to the person who becomes progressively more disabled from medical or psychiatric conditions. Although each situation requires analysis, there are certain considerations for an employer to keep in mind when balancing the needs of the progressively disabled employee against the needs of the workplace: having a clear and specific job description, providing leaves of absence when appropriate, considering periodic fitness-for-duty evaluations, analyzing reasonable accommodation versus undue hardship with fluctuations in the employee's condition, and determining at each stage whether the employee can perform the essential functions of the job. The employer may always enlist other resources to aid in developing suitable accommodations; consultations from specialists including physicians, physical therapists, occupational therapists, nurses, rehabilitation counselors, and engineers have all been of assistance to employers in providing accommodations.

Permissible Termination

The ADA does not suggest that it is never possible to terminate an employee with a disability. Employers may, of course, terminate disabled employees for legitimate, nondiscriminatory reasons. What the ADA prohibits is disciplinary action against an employee with a disability when no such action would be taken against a nondisabled employee who engaged in similar behavior.

Misconduct, absenteeism, and poor performance are all grounds for termination. The employer may defend itself against a claim that it failed to reasonably accommodate an employee by showing that to do so would constitute an undue hardship to the employer or that the employee posed a direct threat to his own health and safety or that of others in the workplace.

Misconduct. Employers need not accommodate an employee who is or has engaged in serious misconduct; employees with disabilities are to be held to the same standard of conduct as other employees. Even when the misconduct is related to a disability, courts have found in favor of employers that terminated employees who engaged in serious misconduct. In *Garrity* v. *United Air Lines* (1995), for example, the court granted summary judgment (pretrial resolution of a case) to an employer that terminated a flight attendant who claimed to be an alcoholic, stole free drink coupons, and became intoxicated on a flight on her employer's airline where she was a passenger. In *Bunevitch* v. *CVS/Pharmacy,* the court upheld the right of an employer to terminate an employee for repeatedly violating the employer's sexual harassment policies, and in *Palmer* v. *Circuit Court of Cook County* (1997), the court upheld the right of an employer to dismiss an employee who suffered from major depression after she made a telephone call threatening to kill her supervisor.

Absenteeism. An employer does not need to accommodate indefinite or unpredictable absences and may terminate those who regularly fail to come to work or who regularly arrive late (*Ward* v. *MHRI,* 1999). Put more simply, showing up for work is likely to be an essential function of a job.

Poor Performance. Employers are not required to give special treatment to disabled employees and may hold them to the same standards of performance that they expect of nondisabled individuals. Disabled employees are subject to the same disciplinary actions, including termination, to which nondisabled employees are subject.

Undue Hardship. An employer is not required to provide an accommodation that would be significantly difficult or expensive in relation to the size of its business, the resources it has available to it, and the nature of its operation. Therefore, an accommodation that is unduly costly, extensive, substantial, or disruptive or would fundamentally alter the nature or operation of the business constitutes an undue hardship to the employer. The ADA does not require an employer to restructure its operation or the position at issue. At issue in *EEOC* v. *Amego* (1997) was a behavior therapist who had attempted to overdose twice and whose job included dispensing medications to individuals. To reconfigure the job so that this employee had no access to medication would require the employer to hire an additional therapist or supervisor or restructure the position so that the employee worked only with clients not requiring medicine. The court determined that to do so would require the employer to exceed reasonable accommodation.

Direct Threat. Employers need not accommodate individuals who might pose a threat of harm to themselves or to others at the workplace; however, speculation or conjecture about the potential risk is not enough to exclude an individual. The employer must assess risk on a case-by-case basis, looking at the duration of the risk, the nature and severity of the potential harm, the probability that harm will occur, and the imminence of the potential harm. The *Guidance* suggests that information about potential risk may come from the employee, doctors, rehabilitation counselors, or other experts who may have information about the individual. As is the case where employers are confronted with potential risk situations in the workplace, employers often find it appropriate to insist on a fitness-for-duty evaluation for the employee. Some persons have attempted to argue that their violent behavior is a result of their disability and that employers should accommodate them. The *Guidance* makes it clear that an individual who threatens violence to self or others is not a qualified individual.

Thoughtful Application of ADA

Although the ADA prohibits discrimination against qualified individuals with handicaps, employers have a greater challenge when some of their employees have mental disabilities. These handicaps may be familiar or unsettling, distinct or amorphous, annoying or benign, but employers still must struggle to respond to mentally disabled employees in ways that are both fair and reasonable. Employers should not act unilaterally or be dismissive with respect to a request for an accommodation. Those with workplace policies, uniformly applied, that outline procedures and guidelines for responses to requests for accommodation will be most likely to enjoy productive relations with employees with disabilities, thereby reducing their possible exposure under the ADA.

FAMILY AND MEDICAL LEAVE ACT

Human resource and mental health professionals also have an opportunity to collaborate on matters involving the FMLA. With this legislation, Congress hoped to give employees job security when they need to be away from the workplace for health-related matters (either that of their own or that of a family member, or to care for a newborn, adopted, or foster child).

At its most basic, the FMLA requires employers with fifty or more employees to do the following:

- Provide up to twelve weeks of unpaid leave to employees on the birth, adoption, or foster placement of a child, and to subsequently care for that child; take care of a child, spouse, or parent with a serious health condition; or if the employee has a serious health condition.

- Restore the employee to the same or an equivalent position at the expiration of the leave.

- Keep the employee's health insurance benefits in effect during the leave.

Human resource professionals are intimately familiar with the details of this apparently simple but technically complicated statute. An employer may require an employee who is taking leave because of a serious mental health condition, for example, to justify the need for the leave and provide medical certification in writing (including details about the date the health condition originated, its probable duration, appropriate information about the condition, and information about why the condition makes the individual unable to perform the functions of his position). The FMLA permits the employer to obtain only limited information through this medical certification process; the employer is not permitted to make an independent assessment of the condition, only to judge whether it is indeed a serious health condition. The employer may, however, contact the health provider for clarification of the information provided and can require a second opinion under certain circumstances where it questions the validity of the certification submitted by the employee. As with medical information obtained through the ADA, employers must keep FMLA medical certification in separate files and treat it as confidential medical information.

The employer may also require the employee to provide medical certification that she or he can return to work, although it may be limited to a simple statement by the health care provider that the employee is able to resume work. In some jurisdictions, employers are able to require an employee returning from FMLA leave to submit to a fitness-for-duty medical examination if it can show that it would have required such an examination even if the employee had not taken FMLA leave (*Albert* v. *Runyon,* 1998).

References and Additional Sources

Albert v. Runyon, 6 F. Supp. 2d at 57 (D. Mass. 1998).

American Psychiatric Association. (1994). *Diagnostic and statistical manual of mental disorders* (4th ed.). Washington, DC: Author.

Arterton, J., Phelan, G., & Swords, K. (2002). *Disability discrimination in the workplace.* Deerfield, IL: Clark Boardman Callaghan.

Bonnie, R. J., & Monahan, J. (1997). *Mental disorder, work disability, and the law.* Chicago: University of Chicago Press.

Bultemeyer v. Ft. Wayne Community Schools, 100 F.3d 1281 (7th Cir. 1996).

Bunevitch v. CVS/Pharmacy, 925 F. Supp. 89 (D. Mass. 1996).

Criado v. IBM Corp., 145 F.3d 437 (1st Cir. 1998).

Dahill v. Police Department of Boston et al., 434 Mass. 233 (2001).

Daley v. Koch, 892 F.2d 212, 215 (2d Cir. 1989).

EEOC v. Amego, 110 F.3d, 147–149 (1st Cir. 1997).

Evans v. Federal Express Corp., 133 F.3d 137 (1st Cir. 1998).

Garrity v. United Air Lines, 421 Mass. 55, 63, N.E.2d 173–178 (1995).

Gaul v. AT&T, Inc., 955 F. Supp. 346, 351–352 (D.N.J. 1997).

Glowacki v. Buffalo General Hospital, 2 F. Supp. 2d 346 (W.D.N.Y. 1998).

Holihan v. Lucky Stores, 87 F.3d 362 (9th Cir. 1996), 117 S. Ct. 1349 (1997).

Palmer v. Circuit Court of Cook County, Illinois, 117 F.3d 351 (7th Cir. 1997).

Soileau v. Guilford of Maine, 105 F.3d 12 (1st Cir. 1997).

Sutton v. United Airlines, 119 S. Ct. 2139, 2146 (1999).

Toyota Motor Manufacturing v. Williams, 122 S. Ct. 681, 151 L. Ed. 2d 615 (U.S. 2002).

Ward v. MHRI, WL 289360 (D. Mass.) (1999).

Weiler v. Household Finance Corp., 101 F.3d 519 (7th Cir. 1996).

APPENDIX

Resources

ADA Document Center, http://janweb.icdi.wvu.edu/kinder: Contains copies of the ADA and its regulations, technical assistance manuals prepared by the EEOC, and links to other Internet sources of information concerning disability matters.

ADA Technical Assistance, http://www.adata.org: Provides information, training, and technical assistance to businesses and agencies with duties and responsibilities under the ADA and to people with disabilities with rights under the ADA.

Disability Law Reporter, http://www.abanet.org/disability/home.html: The nation's longest-running and most comprehensive source of disability law.

Equal Employment Opportunity Commission, http://www.eeoc.gov: The body charged with enforcing Title I of the ADA.

Job Accommodation Network, http://janweb.icdi.wvu.edu/: A consulting service providing information about job accommodations and the employability of people with disabilities.

U.S. Department of Labor, http://www.dol.gov/dol/compliance/comp-fmla.htm: Provides detailed information about the FMLA and its regulations and offers compliance assistance materials.

CHAPTER TWENTY

Organizational Ethics in the Company

Beyond Personal, Professional, and Business Ethics

Len Sperry

*Organizational ethics is an emerging ethical perspective that accounts
for organizational dynamics with an impact on ethical decision making.
Although there is yet to be a defined approach to organizational ethics, internal
moral values and ethical behavior between individuals and groups provide
a useful framework for effective ethical decision making in organizational
settings. An executive who has a good character and uses a covenantal
perspective can be expected to foster healthy relationships, make good
ethical decisions, and act with integrity. In addition to the resolution of
specific ethical concerns, an organizational ethics perspective can serve as
the basis for strategically designing organizational restructuring and
corporate culture transformation efforts. Although it does not replace personal,
professional, or business ethics, organizational ethics does significantly
expand these perspectives to include organizational factors and dynamics.*

Although there is general agreement that corporations should act ethically, some have yet to be convinced that ethics actually has a place in business. The reason offered is that profit-oriented thinking seems contrary to any good intentions an executive may have to act with integrity. At a time when productivity and health are increasingly important factors in achieving organizational well-being, integrity and ethical decision making cannot be ignored, since integrity and organizational health are integrally related. Accordingly, executives, and those consulting with executives, need to become knowledgeable and proficient in ethical decision making in organizational settings.

Organizational ethics is in its formative stages and lacks a solid conceptual framework for adequately encompassing ethical concerns in an organizational context (Worthley, 1999). This chapter proposes a conceptual framework for organizational ethics that combines the perspectives of virtue ethics and covenantal ethics.

ETHICS: DEFINITIONS, CLASSIFICATION SYSTEM, AND ETHICAL PERSPECTIVES

Ethics can be defined as the "philosophical study of moral behavior, of moral decision making, or how to lead a good life" (Brincat & Wike, 2000, p. 33). Ethics is distinguished from morality. Morality is understood as the activity of making choices and deciding, judging, justifying, and defending those actions or behaviors; ethics is the activity that studies how these choices were made or should be made. It is also useful to distinguish between good and bad and right and wrong. "Right and wrong apply only to actions, while good and bad describe not actions but motives, intentions, persons, means, ends, goals and so on" (Brincat & Wike, 2000, p. 33). Table 20.1 provides definitions of key terms for this chapter.

Classification System

The field of ethics is conceptualized as consisting of general ethics and applied ethics. General ethics aims to provide a moral framework for all individuals and focuses on universal ethical issues and concerns. It starts from a conceptual framework that typically is rooted in the abstract rather than the concrete. In other words, it usually begins with rules and theories and then applies them to cases. This contrasts with applied ethics, which begins with cases or situations and uses them to understand or develop rules and theories. General ethics includes meta ethics, prescriptive ethics, and descriptive ethics.

Applied ethics refers to the areas in which ethics comes out to meet the world. Thus, ethics that comes out of concern for the professions is called professional ethics, the ethics that comes out of concern for the environment is called environmental ethics, and so on. Applied ethics is typically subdivided into professional ethics, organizational ethics, business ethics, environmental ethics, and social and political ethics (Brincat & Wike, 2000).

Organizational and business ethics are commonly considered synonymous; in fact, they are quite different. Business ethics has been defined as "the study of how personal moral norms apply to the activities and goals of a commercial enterprise. It is not a separate moral standard, but the study of how the business context poses its own unique problems for the moral person who acts as an agent of this system" (Nash, 1993, p. 8). "Business ethics focuses on the choices of the individual *in* an organization whereas organizational ethics focuses on the choices of the individual *and* the organization" (Boyle, DuBose, Ellingson, Guinn, & McCurdy, 2001, p. 16). In other words, organizational ethics studies both personal moral norms and organizational moral norms applicable to the activities and goals of an organization. Such norms are reflected in corporate strategy, structure, codes of conduct, contracts with employees and users of services, and corporate culture.

Table 20.1. Definitions of Terms.

Ethics	The philosophical study of moral behavior, of moral decision making, or how to lead a good life.
Professional ethics	The form of applied ethics that endeavors to help professionals decide what to do when they are confronted with a case or situation that raises an ethical question or moral problem; it considers the morality of one's professional choices.
Organizational ethics	The form of applied ethics that recognizes the impact of organizational factors and involves the intentional use of values to guide decision making in organizational systems. Unlike business ethics and professional ethics, which characteristically view a given ethical concern from an individual perspective, organizational ethics views the same ethical concerns from a systems perspective.
Virtue ethics	The ethical theory that defines traits of character or virtues understood to make one a morally good person. From this perspective, ethics and morality are understood primarily in terms of a person's internal dispositions and character rather than in terms of an individual's external behavior or actions.
Covenantal ethics	An approach to ethical decision making blending the profit motive with other-oriented values to create trust and cooperation. Because it involves values and attitudes that are not accounted for in legal contracts, it represents a covenant between and among individuals.
Virtu	Machiavelli's counterpoint to virtue ethics, which emphasizes the traits (for example, shrewdness or boldness), needed to be a successful person as opposed to a good person.

Organizational ethics is also distinct from professional ethics, which endeavors to help professionals decide what to do when they are confronted with a case or situation that raises an ethical question or moral problem. Some cases and situations raise concerns that confront members of only select professions, such as business executives or organizational consultants, and others deal with issues confronting all professionals. Professional ethics is subdivided into legal ethics, medical ethics, business ethics, and engineering ethics. In short, professional ethics considers the morality of one's professional choices. Typically, most professions have established codes of ethics to guide the ethical practice of members of that profession.

Unlike professional ethics, which focuses on a professional and his or her ethical concerns in practicing that profession, organizational ethics focuses as much on the organizational context as it does on the professional manager or executive who is considering an ethical matter. Organizational ethics emphasizes the impact of organizational dynamics, such as the mission of the organization, its responsibilities to clients and the large community, its relation to associated institutions and professional organizations, and the ways in which it provides leadership in order to meet these responsibilities. In short, it involves the intentional use of values to guide decision making in organizational systems (Worthley, 1999).

Akin to codes of professional ethics adopted by most professions or professional groups, one might expect a corresponding code of organizational ethics. But with the exception of the Joint Commission on the Accreditation of Hospitals and Health Care Organizations (JCAHO), which requires health care organizations to meet and maintain certain organizational ethical standards for JCAHO accreditation, there is no industrywide code of organizational ethics. Nevertheless, some corporations have established codes of conduct that attempt to provide guidelines for the ethical behavior of its employees.

Furthermore, although professional ethics can be differentiated from organizational ethics, it does not follow that ethical issues are automatically classifiable as either professional or organizational ethical issues. Confidentiality, for example, has been traditionally considered to be a professional ethical issue (Sperry, 1993), but it also can and should be viewed from an organizational perspective (Worthley, 1999). Similarly, although much has been written on the ethics of managed care (Worthley, 1999; Sperry & Prosen, 1998), little has addressed it from an organizational ethics perspective. This is most unfortunate because issues such as provider-patient relations, access of care, and conflict of interests are considerably broader than an analysis from a professional ethics perspective permits. In other words, it may be more appropriate and advantageous to consider and analyze ethical issues from both ethical perspectives: professional and organizational.

Ethical Perspectives

Although this classification of ethics is logical, it is not particularly useful in the real world. In the real world, an executive with certain values and ethical standards enters a profession with its unique values and ethical code and takes a position with a corporation that has certain values and ethical standards. In other words, there are three perspectives that are operative whenever that executive confronts an ethical matter in the workplace: his own, the profession's, and the corporation's. In the best of circumstances, all three sets of values and ethical standards are similar or compatible. In the worst of circumstances, all three are in conflict. For example, two senior executives in a corporation face the same ethical dilemma. For one, the pressure to ignore an obvious conflict of interests is extremely distressing, while it seemingly is nonproblematic for the other executive. From the perspective of the first executive, there appears to be an incompatibility or conflict between personal ethics and organizational ethics, which is presumably not the case for the second executive. The first executive might also feel the tug of his professional code of ethics, that is, the professional perspective. The point is that these three perspectives can and do exert influence on the many ethical considerations that executives regularly encounter in the workplace, with one of these perspectives exerting more influence than the other two. For many individuals, because of the nature of organizational dynamics, there is significant pressure or influence on executives to adopt the ethical perspective of their peers.

COMMONLY ENCOUNTERED ETHICAL ISSUES IN CORPORATIONS

When the public is asked to identify common ethical problems in the workplace, they typically identify false advertising, misleading product or service claims, lying, and conflict of interests. When Nash (1993) surveyed executives about the ethical issues and quandaries they regularly face, she compiled a list of thirty items—for example:

- Greed
- Cover-ups and misrepresentations in reporting and control procedures
- Reneging or cheating on negotiated terms
- Establishing policy that is likely to cause others to lie to get the job done
- Poor quality
- Favoritism
- Price fixing
- Neglecting one's family or personal needs
- Courting organizational hierarchy versus doing the job well
- Promoting the destructive go-getter who outruns his or her mistakes
- Humiliating individuals at work
- Suppression of basic rights such as freedom of speech, choice and personal relationships
- Lying by omission to employees for the sake of the business

What is surprising about this survey is that these ethical issues are not academic considerations that arise only once or twice in an executive's career. Rather, a corporation "has at least twenty on the table every day. A manager has at least twenty on his or her desk every year" (Nash, 1993, p. 10). Such ethical issues are at the core of every executive's job, and their resolution resides in both the executive's own conscience and foundation of values as well as on the corporation structure and culture. It is this amalgam of personal and organizational dynamics that provides organizational ethics with its unique identity.

ORGANIZATIONAL ETHICS IN ACTION

A basic premise of organizational ethics is that executives make decisions and engage in behaviors that reflect both organizational values and their own values. The Tylenol crisis provides an excellent example of how executives in one corporation made a major ethical decision that reflected both organizational values and the personal values of its CEO and top management.

Case 1

In 1982, executives at Johnson & Johnson, the manufacturer of Tylenol, recalled all Tylenol products after confirming that some Tylenol capsules in the Chicago area had been laced with cyanide. Although it would turn out to be a single case of product tampering, James Burke, then CEO of Johnson & Johnson, citing the company's Credo (its formal statement of beliefs), held that a total recall was ordered because the company's primary concern was the health of its customers. It is noteworthy that Burke personally shared this organizational value. From a purely economic or public relations perspective, Johnson & Johnson could have made the case for keeping the product in the market or ordering only a partial recall, such as in the Chicago area, but the organization stood by its decision for a total recall of a product that represented a market share of $100 million annually.

The company's widely publicized response to the crisis was met with public approval. When Tylenol was later reintroduced with a tamper-proof wrap, toll-free hot line, and certificates for free replacements, the product regained nearly all its lost market share within eighteen months.

This case contrasts markedly with the stance that the Exxon Corporation took following the 1989 *Exxon Valdez* crisis. Unlike Johnson & Johnson's quick response of assuming responsibility for the Tylenol poisonings, executives at Exxon initially refused to accept responsibility for the vast oil spill off the Alaska coast. Not only did its relationship with the public suffer, but so did market share. To date, Exxon has already paid out more than $3 billion in costs, and civil litigation continues nearly thirteen years later.

TWO ETHICAL PERSPECTIVES
GERMANE TO ORGANIZATIONAL ETHICS

Unlike business ethics and professional ethics, which characteristically view a given ethical concern from an individual perspective, organizational ethics views the same ethical concerns from a systems perspective. Since organizational ethics is relatively new, there is no ethical system or approach to it that has yet gained widespread acceptance. A combined approach that draws on both internal moral values, referred to as virtue ethics, and ethical behavior among individuals and groups, referred to as covenantal ethics, provides different perspectives but complements each other. This complementarity is illustrated in the deliberations and actions of the board of directors and James Burke during the Tylenol crisis.

Leadership Character and Virtue Ethics

The relationship of character and leadership is complex and has been described in various ways. In describing the connection between leadership and character, Bennis (1989) notes that effective leaders manifest vision and a strong sense of purpose, inspire trust, and accomplish change; then he defines leadership as "character in action" (p. 144).

Character is the dimension of personality that describes how individuals conduct themselves in interpersonal and organizational situations and is shaped through the simultaneous development of self-identity and self-regulation. When this learning or socialization process is reasonably adequate and without significant developmental arrests, adaptive, creative, and socially responsible or virtuous behavior (called "good character") can be expected.

Character reflects an enduring and consistent way of functioning in both private and public sphere. However, there are hidden aspects of it that tend to emerge under stress, fatigue, or temptation. Usually, executives attempt to hide or disown their dark side (the more unflattering aspects of their character) and instead emphasize their "bright side" (their personality or persona). This phenomenon of impression management, or the ability to manifest different personas in response to the press of circumstances, has been called "postmodern identity" (Gergen, 1991). Unfortunately, success in the art of impression management is highly regarded by some in corporate America. The trade-off for this success is diminished or absent personal integrity and difficulty establishing and maintaining the trust of peers and superiors. Presumably, an individual with a mature character would not be a master of impression management but instead would present a consistent style of being. "Leaders have vision and a strongly defined sense of purpose, they inspire trust, and they work for change. Thus, one way to define leadership is character in action" (Bennis, 1989, p. 142).

For an executive, developing an ethical perspective involves not only learning ethical theories and principles but also incorporating such principles in one's own philosophy of life and then acting on these principles in daily personal and professional life. It means becoming a person of good character, someone who acts virtuously. In other words, developing an ethical perspective means becoming a "virtuous" executive.

The ethical theory that emphasizes character and virtue is virtue ethics. Virtue ethics defines certain traits of character that are understood to make a person morally good. From this perspective, ethics and morality are understood primarily in terms of a person's internal dispositions and character rather than external behavior. While other ethical approaches focus on morally good actions, virtue ethics focuses on morally good character. For virtue ethics, the question is not, Is this action moral? but rather, What kind of person am I becoming by doing this or that action? According to virtue ethics, moral virtues are states of character concerned with controlling and directing not only one's thoughts and rational processes but also one's emotions and feeling. The repeated performance of virtuous actions leads to the acquisition of virtue. The morally virtuous person aims at morally good ends rather than at being clever and goal oriented.

Virtuous executives are individuals of good moral character whose actions reflect both the practice of virtue and the ability to incorporate ethical standards in daily practice. They practice virtue and model it in their personal and organizational lives. James Burke is a good example of a virtuous executive. His capacity to inspire ethical thinking and action throughout a large Fortune 500 corporation reflects his virtuous character.

Four character traits comprise the "portrait of the kind of leadership that is critical to the fulfillment of ethical standards in large organizations today": (1) the ability to recognize and articulate the ethics of a problem, (2) the personal courage not to rationalize away bad ethics, (3) an innate respect for others, and (4) personal worth from ethical behavior (Nash, 1993, pp. 43–48). Although she does expressly acknowledge the virtue ethics approach, Nash describes other attributes of the executive of good character: "honesty, empathy, caring, respect, trustworthiness, fairness and developing the competency to deliver on one's state or implied promises in the marketplace" (p. 110).

The idea of the virtuous executive is not universally accepted in the corporate world. Similar but distinct from virtue ethics is the ethical approach described by Machiavelli and called *virtu*, "a combination of vigor, confidence, imagination, shrewdness, boldness, practical skill, personal force, determination, and self-discipline" (Badaracco, 1997, p. 108). Machiavelli believed that successful leaders must follow a special ethical code that differs from their private virtue: "At times, a person in a position of responsibility must do one right thing and leave another undone. At other times, a person must do something wrong, such as engaging in deception, in order to meet an important ethical obligation. Success and *virtu* sometimes demand what virtue discourages. . . . There is no final reconciliation of virtue and *virtu*. They remain in permanent tension" (pp. 118–119). Like Machiavelli, Joseph Baldaracco, a professor of business ethics at the Harvard Business School, contends that executives inhabit two worlds simultaneously: "One is a web of responsibilities, commitments and ethical aspirations. The best guides to this world are the search for balance and the practice of virtue; the other world is the arena of intense sometimes brutal competition. Here success demands *virtu*" (p. 120). Not surprisingly, the notion of a virtuous executive is so impractical it is "little more than greeting card sentiment" (p. 81) to those who share such a bifurcated view of life and work.

Organizational Factors and Covenantal Ethics

Covenantal ethics "reflects the idea that capitalism is at heart a voluntary social contract between the public and business to fulfill certain mutually beneficial obligations" (Nash, 1993, p. vi). It is an approach to ethical decision making that blends the profit motive with other-oriented values that help create trust and cooperation between and among individuals. It "is a covenant because it involves values and attitudes which cannot be totally accounted for in legal contracts" (p. 92). This ethical approach consists of three essential components: "(1) It sees value-creation in its many forms as the primary objective; (2) it sees profits and other social returns as a result of other goals rather than the overriding objective; and (3) it approaches business problems more in terms of relationships than tangible products" (p. 20).

A basic tenet of this approach is the belief that all individuals are worthy of respect and service rather than their worth being dependent on their performance or profitability. Another tenet is that a long-term ethical perspective is necessary since relationships tend to be ongoing. "It becomes easier to draw on values that support not just the short-term sale, but also the long-term well-being of both parties. . . . In other words, in a covenantal perspective, private norms are integrated into managerial thinking"(p. 110). For instance, Johnson & Johnson's Credo is basically a covenantal statement with its stakeholders, first and foremost being its customers and their health and well-being. The deliberations and forthright actions that Johnson & Johnson's board of directors and its CEO took provide a striking illustration of covenantal ethics.

In short, the purpose of covenantal ethics is to create delivered value in order to receive a beneficial return in exchange. It emphasizes service to others and accomplishes its purpose by means of creating mutually beneficial relationships. This approach appears to have considerable value for those working as executives in organizational settings as well as those consulting to those executives.

SYSTEMIC FACTORS WITH AN IMPACT ON ORGANIZATIONAL ETHICS

By their very structure and culture, corporations can undermine the executive perspective needed to function ethically in the workplace. "The inventive systems we create, the goals we set, the language we speak, the way in which information is gathered, and the channels through which it is communicated all contribute to any individual's ability to distinguish right from wrong" (Nash, 1993, p. 121). Nash identifies four systemic factors or organizational dynamics that appear to be major contributing causes to unethical organizational behaviors: (1) the inarguable importance of the bottom line, (2) an overemphasis on short-term efficiency or expediency, (3) the seductive power of ego incentives, and (4) the difficulties of personally representing the organizational polity.

Bottom-Line Preoccupation

It is not unfair to say that corporations are preoccupied with the bottom line because it is a quantitative indicator of organizational performance and success. But this indicator is limited and in some instances an inaccurate measure of qualitative factors such as client or patient satisfaction, teamwork, and critical aspects of managerial functioning such as ethical behavior. In theory, the bottom line is morally neutral. Yet in practice, high standards of conduct may be "linked to the bottom line for motivational and assessment purposes. . . . Ethical conduct is motivated through the promise of a dollar reward" (Nash, 1993, p. 134).

A preoccupation with the bottom line can lead to a limited definition of an executive's goals, as well as to an indifference to the means used to pursue those goals. When a corporation is preoccupied by bottom-line thinking, a manager's moral muscle may give way to the scalpel of a cost-cutting agenda. Moral obligations such as honesty and reliability are sacrificed at the altar of success. Accordingly, lying is justified as necessary in certain circumstances.

Research on the correspondence between an executive's sensitivity to unethical practices and preoccupation with the bottom line is quite telling. An American Management Association study of three thousand managers indicated that a majority felt pressured to compromise personal standards in order to meet organizational profit projections. Another study found that while 70 percent of executives would report serious safety violations to the government, only 25 percent would report illegal kickbacks or price fixing (Nash, 1993). In short, bottom-line thinking tends to trap executives in viewing ethical dilemmas as a choice between profitability and morality. A preoccupation with bottom-line thinking can limit awareness of other motivations that may be inconsistent with the corporation's best interest.

Case 2

Tony Kuless, the new purchasing manager for a high-tech manufacturing corporation, is invited to a two-day seminar on recent technology advances at a Florida resort in January. The seminar is formally scheduled to meet for three hours each morning, with the rest of the day designated as "personal time." Tony feels some ambivalence about accepting the invitation. On the one hand, he could use this time to network with other participants and discuss specific concerns with the expert presenters. On the other hand, he wonders how his boss and peers will view his winter escape knowing that Tony has relatives living in that resort community or to the sponsoring software company, which may assume he will feel obligated to give them some business. He wonders if it is a bad precedent to accept the invitation.

To the extent that an executive measures a decision solely in terms of tangible contributions to each party's bottom line, it is difficult to be sensitive to the ethical issues, and an ethical impasse may appear. Whereas it would be unlikely that Tony would succumb to conflict-of-interest pressures by accepting money directly from a software company, the enticement to escape the cold of winter or to visit relatives at the expense of a software representative could be tempting. To break this impasse, it is helpful to consider personal motivations. Nash contends that the true test of one's organizational ethics is to change scenarios and ask, What if the seminar was being held in Chicago or Minneapolis? The sponsor might also consider the change-in-scenario test. Granted that their overt motivation is to make money for the company, but does the invitation represent an exploitive tactic for influencing purchasing decisions at the invited corporations? Bottom-line rationales are routinely employed to legitimize promotional incentives. Asking what other intentions might be driving the choice of promotions is a good test of organizational ethics.

Executives who allow the bottom line to dominate their thinking become captive to a reductionistic approach to problem solving. "This can lead to a disregard, even disrespect for others as empathic and relationship thinking are abandoned. As a long as the bottom line is in the driver's seat, other ethics norms will be either decorative or suppressed" (Nash, 1993, p. 158).

Overemphasis on Efficiency and Expediency

Besides financial pitfalls, expediency is also a source of ethical problems. Short-term pressures can effectively silence moral reasoning because executives have less time for considering the complex, time-consuming ramifications of ethical decision making. According to Nash (1993), short-term thinking is a twofold moral failure of vision and reckoning. First, it is a failure "to adopt a vision of business purpose that adequately encompasses the dynamics of value-creation and relationship-enabling activities" (p. 166). Second, it is a failure of reckoning because by failing to look either far forward enough or far enough back, an executive has "few tangible anchor-points for conscience to attach itself to decision making in an integrated, productive way" (p. 166). Nash reports that in a survey of several hundred managers, she found that "a short-term frame for performance was consistently cited as the single greatest stress factor on personal ethics" (p. 166). She notes that hostile takeovers, insider trading, cheating on the futures exchange, and the stampede to flood the market with generic drugs as patents expire are examples of financial wrongdoing that occur when the time frame for decision making is extremely constricted.

Expediency tends to corrupt an executive's moral capacity in three ways. First, when expediency is the norm, there is little incentive for critically considering moral issues. Second, "Short-term mindsets encourage self-delusion. . . . Only a long-term view of career and performance can provide an antidote to the heady live-for-the-present high that success can encourage" (p. 167). Third, expediency invites greediness. Ethical rules are suspended, and having no future perspective suggesting the possibility of being caught down the line, executives "encourage this mindset in order to make people work harder and obey more unquestioningly. What is a survival scenario but a justification of short-term greediness at other's expense?" (p. 168).

Subsequently, when legitimate pressures for efficiency and expediency dominate one's thinking and communications, there is an ever-present danger of becoming shortsighted. Values such as integrity, compassion, and honesty require an expanded time frame. Short-term perspectives create both analytical and psychological barriers to such analyses. For the corporation, preoccupation with the short term precludes a consideration of long-term negative consequences and here-and-now process issues involving honesty and credibility, and it unfittingly fosters an ethos of greed and underhanded organizational practices. For the individual, the short-term perspective suppresses awareness of cause and effect and fosters delusion-like thinking, which inevitably corrupts good leadership values.

Case 3

During the U.S. Senate hearing following the *Challenger* space shuttle tragedy, Morton Thiokol engineers were questioned about the recommendation to proceed with the launch the morning of the crash. They testified that they had originally recommended a "no go" because of the unexpected cold snap that hit the Florida coast the night before. But National Aeronautics and Space Administration (NASA) officials experiencing the press of time feared that a launch delay would have an impact on the entire launch schedule for the next eighteen months. Prior to this launch, every systems recommendation was tested against the standard: "Can you prove it is safe?" However, in the early hours before the scheduled *Challenger* launch, the engineers received a new standard from senior NASA management: "Can you prove it [the decision to launch] is not safe?" Changing the operating standard of safety, the engineers came to an entirely different decision about the launch, with tragic consequences. Adopting a win-or-lose-all perspective, which is characteristic of expediency and short-term thinking, caused NASA to change a standard for safety that had been in place for years.

The Seductive Power of Ego Incentives

Incentives are another systemic factor that fosters ethical dilemmas for executives in corporations. That is because corporations provide a variety of status symbols and perks to executives for the purpose of increasing their commitment and productivity. Although such incentives may appear to be effective and efficient motivators, they can be problematic. Not only is it difficult to attribute an individual executive's specific contribution to a corporation's overall performance, but the assessment of one's contribution is particularly vulnerable to inflated claims (an unintended, but not surprising, result of an incentive system that fosters self-adulation and concern for one's own needs over the needs and welfare of others).

To the extent that ego is reified, the capacity for empathy is diminished. Ego-oriented incentives "prevent a manager from keeping the 'feel' for others alive, that other-orientation which is at the heart of achieving business integrity and market success. When self-motivation and ingenuity cross the line to ego, they prevent a person from seeing other points of view, and therefore from gathering relevant factors and objectively assessing information" (Nash, 1993, p. 190).

Corporations with incentive systems that reify and reinforce the ego foster a self-centered orientation that is alien to the other-oriented, service-driven, value-creation ethic that Nash and others who advocate covenantal ethics believe is a contract for good and prosperous leadership. In the extreme, this self-orientation cultivates the attitudes that "I [or the corporation] deserve everything I desire," and "I [or the corporation] am so smart that I am above the law and any other rules." These attitudes leave the executive "highly susceptible to inaccurate, hence unethical, judgments and complacent in the face of immoral acts of greed and exploitation" (p. 191).

In short, these incentives reinforce values and virtues such as pride, arrogance, and overconfidence over compassion, courage, and service. Nash (1993) contends that an executive's strength of character is his or her first resource in problem solving and decision making. Accordingly, any "occasion on which one's way of doing business or one's ego gratification dominates thinking is ultimately a moral failure to fulfill the fiduciary trust which a manager assumes. These occasions can quickly become face saving exercises in dishonesty and bombast as well" (pp. 210–211).

Case 4

Jerod Jensen, known by his coworkers as Jensen, is a software genius who has been with a software firm for two years. Almost from his first day at the firm, Jensen has demonstrated a remarkable degree of creativity and technical acumen in finding software solutions for clients when everyone else in the firm had given up. Jensen knew he was good and expected to be rewarded monetarily for his competence. He quite openly admitted that money was his only motivator. The CEO and president who had personally hired Jensen as manager of the software solutions team was Jensen's chief advocate in this firm of forty employees. Although the CEO was somewhat uneasy about Jensen's materialistic attitude, his only complaint was Jensen's rudeness and impatience with fellow members of the software solutions team. Other members of the team complained that Jensen often took sole credit for ideas that were jointly developed and that he often held back ideas. He cooperated only to the extent necessary to avoid making waves. Finally, team members were angry that the team project reports that Jensen wrote routinely failed to include long-term problems that the team had discussed. When confronted with his rudeness and lack of team spirit, Jensen shrugged these observations off, telling the CEO that he had no problems with individuals who did their job well and were competent. He said, "It basically comes down to this. Those who aren't pulling their weight take away from *my* bottom line, and I don't think that's fair." Consistent with his ego-oriented leadership style, Jensen lacked respect for anyone who didn't play into his ego needs. His egotism was loosely disguised by his "good of the company" rhetoric, a quality that the CEO admired and rewarded.

As a manager and ethical person, Jensen's main drawback was his efficiency focus and assessment of performance solely in terms of product output and revenue generation. With this narrow focus, he is unaware of his other management responsibilities and the destructiveness of his leadership behavior and its impact on team cohesiveness and functioning. The prescription for change in this and similar cases is for the executive to adopt a more relationship-oriented approach to management. Whether Jensen is capable of and agreeable to this change, which invariably means that the CEO must sanction and reward that new focus, is another matter.

Conflict Between Personal Conscience and Organizational Policy

Every executive wears several hats in fulfilling his or her organizational duties as well as personal and family matters. Executives routinely assume the roles of superior, coach, friends, counselor, subordinate, loyal supporter, parent, and spouse. They also embody personal values that may or may not match actual (as contrasted with stated or written) organizational values. Business problems arise when there is a conflict between the executive's personal roles and values and organizational roles and values. Matters of personal conscience inevitably become involved. Executives continually face internal conflicts between what they would do as a loyal representative of the corporation and what they as a private individual or citizen might think is the right thing to do.

Organizational influence on employees, particularly executives, is great indeed. Among other things, executives are expected to protect and promote the corporation's image. This obligation is germane to moral dilemmas involving personal conscience and organizational policy, that is, wearing two hats. In her research with organizational executives, Nash (1993) found that "'creating a good company image' was the most frequently cited organizational expectation after 'making money.' Interviewees viewed the morality of this goal with great ambiguity" (p. 216). Executives noted that while organizational loyalty may foster a "sweep-it-under-the rug" climate, they also believed that "not airing dirty linen in public" is a sentiment widely shared by members of a corporation. Nevertheless, deference to the organizational viewpoint, while not necessarily bad, can and does influence ethical decision making. That is because the motivational power of a corporation's image is analogous to the influence of charismatic leadership. Just as employees tend to idealize charismatic leaders and defer to their directives, "the more charismatic the organizational image, the stronger is employee loyalty and commitment to the company's interest. . . . Organizational charisma can prompt managers to put on their 'organizational hats' and never take them off" (p. 217). As a result, they are unlikely to consider their own values and viewpoints or judge issues from a broader perspective. In psychological terms, an executive may then "confuse company loyalty, which is a reasonable duty, with *unquestioning* loyalty, which is not" (p. 217).

Case 5

Jeanne Quimby goes to her boss and friend Ed Frank for advice. Because of a recent promotion, Jeanne now reports to Ed. She has been offered a position with a competitor and wants Ed's advice on the matter. Ed has just learned that his unit has been given only one more quarter to improve its performance or it will be eliminated. No one else in the unit is aware of this organizational mandate. Jeanne's part in the turnaround is critical, and Ed can't imagine getting through this without her. However, if he tells her that the unit may fold in three months, there is a good chance he will lose her immediately. Even if she passes up the other position and stays, word may leak out and demoralize the rest of the team. The ethical dilemma is whether Ed tells Jeanne about the top management decision. If he tells her, she may respect his honesty and risk staying to work with him to bolster performance. Or she may leave and divulge the information to the rest of the team, causing a major morale problem.

However, if Ed conceals the information, he contributes to a culture of deception in employee relations that may be destructive or beneficial in the short run, but will inevitably catch up with him over the long term.

From a covenantal ethics perspective, Ed should consider more than the personal relationship between Jeanne and himself. He should consider his relationship with other unit members, as well as with the corporation itself. There are implied obligations to each relationship, which can be boiled down to the organizational covenant: to provide value and receive a fair return in the process. According to Nash (1993), Ed must provide value to the friend, to other employees, and to the corporation itself, and he has a right to expect a return from all three.

From this perspective, the problem would be framed differently. The initial issue would be not secrecy but rather the welfare of others. The interview or conversation would be viewed as an opportunity to provide value for all parties. Thus, without revealing the corporation's recent decision, the executive would view this valued colleague's request as a source of information about her motivation, contributions to the team, and how well her needs are served by the corporation. Directing the discussion more broadly to the reasons that she is job searching can offer both the corporation and the friend valuable insights. Rather than sidestepping the secrecy issue, the nature of secret and closely held information and their attendant responsibilities for all parties can be discussed. Just as the friend is asking the executive to keep her job search confidential, the executive can set the stage for the agreement that both have secrets that they are obligated and trusted to keep. He should tell her that he cannot tell her about job security but can expand the discussion as suggested.

This solution does not force the abandonment of the dual roles of friend and superior. It takes a long-term view of the problem at hand rather than restricting the ethical analysis of the issue to a single decision. In this case, in developing relationships on the job and long before this issue arose, the executive would have been careful to avoiding switching hats, being a special friend to the employee on some days to the exclusion of his organizational role as executive on other days.

Dealing with Causes of Unethical Organizational Behaviors

There are three strategies for dealing with these conflicts. The first is straightforward: separate personal conscience from organizational roles and values, and endorse the organizational view. The second strategy is to change roles and values as situations change. Well-intentioned executives might be a friend one moment and a spokesperson for the corporation the next moment. The third strategy is to strive for an integrative approach to personal ethics in the workplace rather than in either-or terms. Accordingly, instead of seeing organizational profits as the first value and goal of an executive, the executive focuses on service to others and relationship thinking in pursuit of productivity and profit. Admittedly, the third strategy is easier to achieve in a corporation that has adopted some or all of the covenantal ethics perspective.

Organizational ethics has been described as a subdivision of applied ethics that accounts for organizational dynamics that have an impact on ethical decision making in organizational contexts. It significantly expands the ethical perspective to include organizational factors and dynamics. Accordingly, effective organizational consultants must become conversant with this broader organizational ethics perspective.

Both virtue ethics and covenantal ethics appear to be essential and integrally related to effective ethical decision making in organizational settings. An executive who has a good character and uses a covenantal perspective can be expected to foster healthy relationships, make good ethical decisions, and act with integrity.

Combining the covenantal and virtue ethics approaches may offer a useful framework for addressing organizational ethics, as the Tylenol case illustrated. Beyond the resolution of specific ethical concerns, the combined approach could also serve as the basis for strategically designing organizational restructuring and corporate culture transformation efforts to increase productivity, health, and integrity.

References and Additional Sources

Badaracco, J. (1997). *Defining moments: When managers must choose between right and right.* Boston: Harvard Business School Press.

Bennis, W. G. (1989). *The unconscious conspiracy: Why leaders can't lead.* San Francisco: Jossey-Bass.

Boyle, P., DuBose, E., Ellingson, S., Guinn, D. & McCurdy, D. (2001). *Organizational ethics in health care: Principles, cases and practical solutions.* San Francisco: Jossey-Bass.

Brincat, C., & Wike, V. (2000). *Morality and the professional life: Values at work.* Upper Saddle River, NJ: Prentice Hall.

Gergen, K. (1991). *The saturated self: Dilemmas of identity in contemporary life.* New York: Basic Books.

Nash, L. (1993). *Good intentions aside: A manager's guide to resolving ethical problems.* Boston: Harvard Business School Press.

Sperry, L. (1993). *Psychiatric consultation in the workplace.* Washington, DC: American Psychiatric Press.

Sperry, L., & Prosen, L. (1998). Contemporary ethical dilemmas in psychotherapy: Cosmetic psychopharmacology and managed care. *American Journal of Psychotherapy, 52,* 54–63.

Worthley, A. (1999). *Organizational ethics in the compliance context.* Chicago: Health Administration Press.

PART FOUR

COMMON EMPLOYEE PROBLEMS

Part Four provides a detailed overview of the most common mental health problems and their manifestations in the workplace setting. Individuals with emotional problems, like those with general medical illness, can be productive members of the workforce. Employers can play an invaluable role in helping their employees recognize the need for help and the benefits of appropriate treatment. The benefits can be greater for the employer than for the employee, even when employees seek treatment without company awareness.

The chapters that follow address problems common to or especially important among employees, so not all disorders are covered. Each chapter is designed to inform managers, individuals, and clinicians about the nature, diagnosis, and treatment of mental disorders from a workplace perspective. The chapters also look at return to work and reasonable accommodation to the Americans with Disabilities Act (ADA), which requires employers with more than fifteen employees to make reasonable accommodation to employ people with disabilities who would otherwise be qualified for the job. Under the ADA, individuals who choose to disclose to their employer that they have been diagnosed with a mental disorder are entitled to accommodations in the workplace that help them continue to work despite symptoms and illness-related impairments.

Included for each diagnosis are the standard diagnostic criteria from the *Diagnostic and Statistical Manual of Mental Disorders.* Although these chapters cover essential material for professionals in human resources, management, benefits, and clinical care, no one should play armchair psychiatrist. The workplace perspective offers understanding of how mental illness can affect the workplace and how the workplace can affect individuals. Special attention is given to the importance of early diagnosis and prompt referral for evaluation and treatment by an appropriate mental health professional. Although specific diagnosis, medications, and likely treatment outcomes are described in detail, medical decision making for any specific individual should always be made after a careful evaluation by a medical professional.

CHAPTER TWENTY-ONE

Anxiety and Stress

Dan J. Stein
Eric Hollander

Psychiatric knowledge of the anxiety disorders has increased rapidly in recent decades. This chapter reviews these conditions and how they manifest themselves in the workplace. The differences between ordinary anxiety and the anxiety disorders are outlined, and each of the most important anxiety disorders is then discussed. Adjustment disorder with anxiety, generalized anxiety disorder (tension), panic disorder (intense anxiety and phobias), social anxiety disorder (stage fright and shyness), obsessive-compulsive disorder (rituals), and posttraumatic stress disorder are each considered in turn. These disorders are seen commonly in the workplace and may be profoundly disabling. Appropriate psychiatric evaluation and intervention usually results in prompt and robust improvement in symptoms, with benefits for both worker and the workplace.

Few workers will argue with the idea that the workplace is a source of stress and anxiety. Work is performed in accordance with particular goals; there are time deadlines to be met and productivity standards to be maintained. Work also involves relationships that have particular requirements; interactions with employers, employees, coworkers, and clients can all constitute a source of stress.

A good argument can be made that some degree of stress and anxiety in the workplace is not only inevitable but also beneficial insofar as it constitutes a source of motivation. The goal of stress management, then, is not to eliminate stress but rather to foster positive and constructive responses to stress.

This commonsense notion of stress and anxiety and their management has been found useful and is widely held. Nevertheless, there are anxious workers who may conceive of themselves as suffering from stress, but for whom anxiety leads in fact to unbearable subjective distress or substantial impairment of work. The commonsense model may be unsuitable for such workers, and ordinary stress management programs may be ineffective.

Dan Stein is supported by the Medical Research Council of South Africa.

Instead, such workers may benefit from a more clinical perspective. When anxiety at work leads to unbearable subjective distress or substantial impairment of work, then workers may not merely be suffering from stress, but may instead have an anxiety disorder. The anxiety disorders are extremely common and include the panic and anxiety disorders (panic disorder, generalized anxiety disorder, and adjustment disorder with anxious mood), the phobic disorders (agoraphobia, social anxiety disorder, and specific phobia), obsessive-compulsive disorder, and posttraumatic stress disorder.

Each anxiety disorder has specific characteristics that allow it to be diagnosed, and each has particular causes that are addressed in treatment. Thus, a clinical perspective replaces the all-embracing notion of stress and its optimization with the concept that there are different kinds of anxiety syndromes, each of which responds to specific interventions.

Many of the most important advances in clinical knowledge have occurred in the area of the anxiety disorders, and a range of new treatment options has become available.

ADJUSTMENT DISORDER WITH ANXIETY, GENERALIZED ANXIETY DISORDER, AND OTHER TENSION STATES

Diagnostic Overview

Case 1

Bob Woodrow is a forty-two-year-old teacher who has had an outstanding record for many years. His students have consistently performed well on standardized examinations, and fellow staff have thought of him as someone who is able to instill a love for learning. In the most recent examinations, however, Bob's students did fairly poorly. Soon after learning these results, Bob began feeling increasingly anxious about his teaching. He worried continuously about whether he had prepared adequately for class, about whether he had any ability as a teacher, and about how his students would do on the next examination.

Other teachers began to notice Bob's perpetual jitteriness. At times, his worries kept Bob awake, and on the following days he was too exhausted to teach. Bob's difficulties came to the attention of the headmaster, who hinted that perhaps Bob needed a vacation. Bob took this suggestion, but his absence from the school only made him feel more anxious. When he returned from his vacation, he elected to seek professional help.

Bob was diagnosed as having adjustment disorder with anxiety. He was given a brief course of cognitive therapy to help change his overly negative thoughts. At the beginning of the therapy, when Bob was having difficulty falling asleep, he elected to take medication for a few nights.

Case 2

Fred Fassi is a thirty-two-year-old printer who has considered himself a worrier as long as he can remember. If he isn't worried about the standard of his work (which is good), then he worries about his children (who are all doing fine) or about his finances (which are in reasonable shape). He feels keyed up and tense from the time he wakes up, and at night he has difficulty falling asleep. Furthermore, he often has muscle aches, he gets tired easily, and he has difficulty concentrating. He feels sad at times, but can be cheered up.

Although Fred gets his work done, at times he is so worried about this, that, or the other thing that he is unable to focus on his projects. In addition, he is reluctant to accept challenging assignments because these only increase his worry load and give him even more trouble falling asleep.

During an evaluation session with his supervisor, the two agreed that Fred's ability far exceeded his performance. His supervisor suggested that a psychiatrist might be able to help him understand why this was the case.

Fred was diagnosed as having generalized anxiety disorder. His psychiatrist suggested a combined treatment of insight-oriented psychotherapy and a course of antianxiety medication.

Although stress and anxiety may be considered universal, there are times when the distress of anxiety, or its effect on social and occupational functioning, leads the sufferer of anxiety to seek help. The presentation of anxiety may be either acute or chronic.

Adjustment disorder with anxiety may be considered an acute form of anxiety. The diagnosis of adjustment disorder with anxiety according to the fourth edition of the *Diagnostic and Statistical Manual of Mental Disorders* (DSM-IV; American Psychiatric Association, 1994) is made when a reaction to an identifiable psychosocial stressor or stressors occurs within three months of onset of the stressor and the response of nervousness, worry, or jitteriness is clinically significant, as indicated by marked distress in excess of an expectable reaction to the stressor or by significant social or occupational impairment. When the symptoms are thought expectable or do not interfere with functioning, the diagnostician may use a DSM-IV code such as "Partner Relational Problem" or "Occupational Problem."

⁘ Diagnostic Criteria for Adjustment Disorders

A. The development of emotional or behavioral symptoms in response to an identifiable stressor(s) occurring within 3 months of the onset of the stressor(s).

B. These symptoms or behaviors are clinically significant as evidenced by either of the following:

  1. marked distress that is in excess of what would be expected from exposure to the stressor

  2. significant impairment in social or occupational (academic) functioning

C. The stress-related disturbance does not meet the criteria for another specific Axis I disorder and is not merely an exacerbation of a preexisting Axis I or Axis II disorder.

D. The symptoms do not represent Bereavement.

E. Once the stressor (or its consequences) has terminated, the symptoms do not persist for more than an additional 6 months.

Specify if:

Acute: if the disturbance lasts less than 6 months
Chronic: if the disturbance lasts for 6 months or longer

Adjustment Disorders are coded based on the subtype, which is selected according to the predominant symptoms. The specific stressor(s) can be specified on Axis IV.

With Depressed Mood
With Anxiety
With Mixed Anxiety and Depressed Mood
With Disturbance of Conduct
With Mixed Disturbance of Emotions and Conduct
Unspecified

Reprinted with permission from the Diagnostic and Statistical Manual of Mental Disorders, Fourth Edition, Text Revision. *Copyright 2000 American Psychiatric Association.*

Generalized anxiety disorder (GAD) may be considered a chronic and severe form of anxiety. The DSM-IV diagnosis of generalized anxiety disorder is made when there is excessive anxiety and worry occurring more days than not for at least six months about a number of events or activities (usually family, work, money, or illness), when the person finds it difficult to control the worry, and when the anxiety and worry are associated with a number of other specific symptoms (such as restlessness, being easily tired, and difficulty concentrating). The diagnosis should not be made when the worries are secondary to another DSM-IV axis I (clinical) disorder, to a substance, or to a general medical disorder. GAD needs to be differentiated from a variety of psychiatric disorders with anxiety symptoms, including mood disorders (especially anxious depression with morbid ruminations), somatoform disorders (such as hypochondriasis), eating disorders, and other anxiety disorders (such as obsessive-compulsive disorder). Excessive use of substances such as caffeine and general medical conditions such as hyperthyroidism can mimic GAD.

❧ Diagnostic Criteria for Generalized Anxiety Disorder

A. Excessive anxiety and worry (apprehensive expectation), occurring more days than not for at least 6 months, about a number of events or activities (such as work or school performance).

B. The person finds it difficult to control the worry.

C. The anxiety and worry are associated with three (or more) of the following six symptoms (with at least some symptoms present for more days than not for the past 6 months). Note: Only one item is required in children.
1. restlessness or feeling keyed up or on edge
2. being easily fatigued
3. difficulty concentrating or mind going blank
4. irritability
5. muscle tension
6. sleep disturbance (difficulty falling or staying asleep, or restless unsatisfying sleep)

D. The focus of the anxiety and worry is not confined to features of an Axis I disorder, e.g., the anxiety or worry is not about having a Panic Attack (as in Panic Disorder), being embarrassed in public (as in Social Phobia), being contaminated (as in Obsessive-Compulsive Disorder), being away from home or close relatives (as in Separation Anxiety Disorder), gaining weight (as in Anorexia Nervosa), having multiple physical complaints (as in Somatization Disorder), or having a serious illness (as in Hypochondriasis), and the anxiety and worry do not occur exclusively during Posttraumatic Stress Disorder.

E. The anxiety, worry, or physical symptoms cause clinically significant distress or impairment in social, occupational, or other important areas of functioning.

F. The disturbance is not due to the direct physiological effects of a substance (e.g., a drug of abuse, a medication) or a general medical condition (e.g., hyperthyroidism) and does not occur exclusively during a Mood Disorder, a Psychotic Disorder, or a Pervasive Developmental Disorder.

Causes

A number of factors—social, psychological, and biological—may be involved in the etiology of acute and chronic anxiety.

A variety of social stressors can initiate and exacerbate anxiety, and among these are the stressors of the workplace. One classification divides crises into the situational, which originate in material or environmental problems, personal or physical problems, and interpersonal or social problems, and the transitional, which originate in life cycle or developmental transitions and in shifts in social status.

In addition, psychological factors contribute to the initiation and maintenance of anxiety. Freud's psychoanalytic theory gave a central role to anxiety, which he conceived in terms of the forces of the mind. In this model, unconscious mental conflicts can result in hidden fears, and thus anxiety. A subsequent behavioral model also centralized anxiety, which was conceived of as conditioned by fear of environmental stimuli. In this model, particular learning experiences also lead to hidden fears and anxiety. Although there are some differences in the way psychodynamically oriented and behaviorally oriented practitioners think about anxiety, there is an increasing convergence of these models. Notably, most clinicians would agree that people learn to think and feel about themselves and others in particular ways during childhood. These patterns of mental processing continue to be important in adulthood, but they may take place outside of awareness. Exploration of these kinds of mental processes may lead to an understanding of the person's anxiety.

Finally, a number of biological systems have been shown to contribute to the etiology of anxiety. The amygdala is an almond-shaped structure in the brain that appears to play a crucial role in orchestrating the psychological and somatic response to fear. Many other brain structures and chemicals (such as neurotransmitters, the natural biochemicals that allow brain cells to communicate with each other) interact with the amygdala circuits and may also play a crucial role in mediating the anxiety disorders. For example, there is evidence that both the serotonergic and noradrenergic neurotransmitter systems are involved in the production of anxiety. Medications that act on these different neurotransmitters may be effective in relieving such symptoms.

Effects and Workplace Recognition

A worker with adjustment disorder with anxiety or from GAD may not only suffer from subjective distress but may also be unable to perform at an optimal level. In GAD in particular, restlessness, fatigability, and difficulty concentrating may interfere with productivity. The worker may attempt to relieve these symptoms by using a variety of medications. But self-medication can often make symptoms worse and even lead to substance abuse (see Chapters Twenty-Four and Twenty-Five). Finally, symptoms of depression may set in and exacerbate the situation.

At the workplace, an employee with adjustment disorder with anxiety or GAD may be thought of as a worrier who requires a great deal of reassurance. At times, all that others notice is a certain preoccupation or "spaciness." In some instances, irritability, physical symptoms, or impaired performance will be the first indication of the disorder. If coworkers identify the relevant stressors, they may extend more support.

Workplace Management and Referral

As always, prevention is preferable to treatment. The workplace can help in the early identification of stressors and the provision of programs to help with anxiety management. These may include the teaching of relaxation techniques and skills training and coping. Ongoing identification of stressors at work may lead to valuable changes in the workplace.

Once adjustment disorder with anxiety and GAD develop, they will be detected at work if the worker is open about his or her worries, if irritability or bodily symptoms are obvious, or if there is interference with performance. The workplace may offer reassurance and a system of social supports and may offer referral to a mental health professional.

Psychiatric Management

Psychiatric management of adjustment disorder with anxiety and GAD may entail the use of relaxation techniques, such as relaxation tapes, hypnosis, biofeedback, and meditation. Psychotherapy may be helpful in exploring mental processes that contribute to the anxiety, and there is strong evidence that a cognitive-behavioral approach (one that focuses on recording and monitoring thoughts with graded task assignments and self-reliance training) in particular is helpful for people with GAD.

Finally, the use of medication can prove invaluable in the management of GAD. Antidepressants are in fact very effective for the treatment of many anxiety disorders. Furthermore, more recently introduced antidepressants are particularly well tolerated. Although these agents may take several weeks to begin working, they show no potential for dependence. Thus, newer antidepressants, such as the selective serotonin reuptake inhibitors (SSRIs) and also venlafaxine (Effexor), are increasingly seen as the medications of choice for the treatment of GAD.

Return to Work and ADA Reasonable Accommodation

Both an adjustment disorder and GAD may lead to significant work impairment. Nevertheless, adjustment disorder is by definition an acute disorder, so that is not associated with long-term disability. Occasionally, the person may need or may benefit from some time away from work, but the expectation should be a rapid return to full function.

In contrast, GAD is typically a chronic disorder. During periods of exacerbation or during the development of comorbid disorders such as depression, the person may not be able to work. Given that such disorders are typically amenable to treatment, however, the expectation should be a return to work once treatment has resulted in symptom reduction.

PANIC DISORDER: INTENSE ANXIETY AND PHOBIAS

Diagnostic Overview

Case 3

Gail Dresden is a successful insurance salesperson who recently turned thirty-six. She has always considered herself in excellent physical and mental health. Last fall, she was given a new and potentially lucrative sales district. On the day she drove there, while speeding along the interstate, she suddenly felt as if her heart was pounding. She pulled over, but her heart continued to race. In addition, she felt short of breath and had chest pain and palpitations. She thought she was about to die or go crazy. After about ten minutes, the symptoms had diminished enough to allow her to drive to a nearby hospital. The doctor assured her that she had not suffered a heart attack, and she felt relieved and reassured.

Nevertheless, in subsequent weeks, Gail had a similar attack every other day. She began to feel nervous about going on long trips where there was no access to medical help and requested that she be reassigned to an office sales job. She became fearful of leaving her apartment and preferred to travel with others rather than alone.

It was not always possible to arrange for someone to accompany her, and at such times Gail stayed at home and made excuses. Her sales numbers plummeted, and she appeared in imminent danger of losing her job. Fortunately, one afternoon, Gail was watching television when she came across a program on panic disorder and diagnosed herself as having this condition.

Gail's psychiatrist confirmed this diagnosis. When she questioned Gail in more detail about her life, Gail recalled that she had great difficulty in separating from her mother on first going to nursery school. Gail knew from the television program that antidepressants were often helpful for panic disorder, and she elected to begin medication and psychotherapy.

Thanks to the efforts of psychiatric researchers, panic disorder has become recognized as a specific psychiatric disorder, with a particular biological substrate that responds to medication. The disorder is now also recognized as fairly common, with a six-month prevalence of at least 0.6 to 1.0 percent. Panic disorder typically begins in the patient's late twenties.

The person may be performing any one of his daily activities when suddenly is overcome with a sense of intense anxiety and impending doom. A number of bodily symptoms are also present, including shortness of breath, dizziness or faintness, palpitations or fast heart beat, trembling or shaking, sweating, choking, nausea, and chest pain. Attacks usually last from a few seconds to twenty minutes.

Although the first attack often occurs during a routine activity, attacks are also associated with a number of events, including life-threatening illness, an accident, separation from home (for example, going to college, getting married, or moving away to a new job), and the real or symbolic loss of an important relationship. Attacks may also begin with the use of mind-altering drugs, especially marijuana, LSD, sedatives, cocaine, and amphetamines. These stressors may act as triggers to provoke the onset of panic disorder in predisposed patients.

Individuals experiencing their first panic attack often interpret it as a heart attack or stroke. But physicians in the emergency room find nothing other than perhaps a fast heart beat. The person may receive an extensive medical workup or be summarily dismissed with the advice that it is all merely "in the mind."

If the panic attacks continue, the person may begin to dread the experience of having attacks and to develop what is called anticipatory anxiety, which may lead to phobic avoidance or agoraphobic fears of leaving home, of being alone, or of being trapped with no escape and no available help. Typical fears are of using public transportation or being in crowded places. The severity of these fears may range from mild distress over solo travel to severe incapacitation with an inability to leave home.

The diagnosis of panic disorder by DSM-IV criteria is made when panic attacks or the fear of them persist and when at least four somatic symptoms are present during a panic attack. This diagnosis should not be made when the panic attacks are secondary to a physical disorder such as pheochromocytoma (an epinephrine-producing tumor), hypo- or hyperthyroidism, or a substance abuse problem with cocaine or amphetamines. Certain disorders such as agitated depression, depersonalization disorders, and substance withdrawal can mimic panic disorder. Similarly, fear of leaving home and avoidance of being alone may be seen in paranoid and psychotic states, depressive disorders, and posttraumatic stress disorder.

❖ Diagnostic Criteria for Panic Attack

A discrete period of intense fear or discomfort, in which four (or more) of the following symptoms developed abruptly and reached a peak within 10 minutes:

1. palpitations, pounding heart, or accelerated heart rate
2. sweating
3. trembling or shaking
4. sensations of shortness of breath or smothering
5. feeling of choking
6. chest pain or discomfort
7. nausea or abdominal distress
8. feeling dizzy, unsteady, lightheaded, or faint
9. derealization (feelings of unreality) or depersonalization (being detached from oneself)
10. fear of losing control or going crazy
11. fear of dying
12. paresthesias (numbness or tingling sensations)
13. chills or hot flushes

Reprinted with permission from the Diagnostic and Statistical Manual of Mental Disorders, Fourth Edition, Text Revision. *Copyright 2000 American Psychiatric Association.*

❖ Diagnostic Criteria for Agoraphobia

A. Anxiety about being in places or situations from which escape might be difficult (or embarrassing) or in which help may not be available in the event of having an unexpected or situationally predisposed Panic Attack or panic-like symptoms. Agoraphobic fears typically involve characteristic clusters of situations that include being outside the home alone; being in a crowd or standing in a line; being on a bridge; and traveling in a bus, train, or automobile.

Note: Consider the diagnosis of Specific Phobia if the avoidance is limited to one or only a few specific situations, or Social Phobia if the avoidance is limited to social situations.

B. The situations are avoided (e.g., travel is restricted) or else are endured with marked distress or with anxiety about having a Panic Attack or panic-like symptoms, or require the presence of a companion.

C. The anxiety or phobic avoidance is not better accounted for by another mental disorder, such as Social Phobia (e.g., avoidance limited to social situations because of fear of embarrassment), Specific Phobia (e.g., avoidance limited to a single situation like elevators), Obsessive-Compulsive Disorder (e.g., avoidance of dirt in someone with an obsession about contamination), Posttraumatic Stress Disorder (e.g., avoidance of stimuli associated with a severe stressor), or Separation Anxiety Disorder (e.g., avoidance of leaving home or relatives).

⁂ Diagnostic Criteria for Panic Disorder Without Agoraphobia

A. Both (1) and (2):
    1. recurrent unexpected Panic Attacks
    2. at least one of the attacks has been followed by 1 month (or more) of one (or more) of the following:
        a. persistent concern about having additional attacks
        b. worry about the implications of the attack or its consequences (e.g., losing control, having a heart attack, "going crazy")
        c. a significant change in behavior related to the attacks

B. Absence of Agoraphobia.

C. The Panic Attacks are not due to the direct physiological effects of a substance (e.g., a drug of abuse, a medication) or a general medical condition (e.g., hyperthyroidism).

D. The Panic Attacks are not better accounted for by another mental disorder, such as Social Phobia (e.g., occurring on exposure to feared social situations), Specific Phobia (e.g., on exposure to a specific phobic situation), Obsessive-Compulsive Disorder (e.g., on exposure to dirt in someone with an obsession about contamination), Posttraumatic Stress Disorder (e.g., in response to stimuli associated with a severe stressor), or Separation Anxiety Disorder (e.g., in response to being away from home or close relatives).

⁂ Diagnostic Criteria for Panic Disorder with Agoraphobia

A. Both (1) and (2):
    1. recurrent unexpected Panic Attacks
    2. at least one of the attacks has been followed by 1 month (or more) of one (or more) of the following:

a. persistent concern about having additional attacks
b. worry about the implications of the attack or its consequences (e.g., losing control, having a heart attack, "going crazy")
c. a significant change in behavior related to the attacks
B. The presence of Agoraphobia.
C. The Panic Attacks are not due to the direct physiological effects of a substance (e.g., a drug of abuse, a medication) or a general medical condition (e.g., hyperthyroidism).
D. The Panic Attacks are not better accounted for by another mental disorder, such as Social Phobia (e.g., occurring on exposure to feared social situations), Specific Phobia (e.g., on exposure to a specific phobic situation), Obsessive-Compulsive Disorder (e.g., on exposure to dirt in someone with an obsession about contamination), Posttraumatic Stress Disorder (e.g., in response to stimuli associated with a severe stressor), or Separation Anxiety Disorder (e.g., in response to being away from home or close relatives).

Reprinted with permission from the Diagnostic and Statistical Manual of Mental Disorders, Fourth Edition, Text Revision. *Copyright 2000 American Psychiatric Association.*

Causes

The finding that people with panic disorder can have attacks provoked by specific agents under laboratory conditions has allowed researchers to understand the neurobiology of panic better. Lactate infusions and carbon dioxide inhalations, for example, provoke panic attacks in people with panic disorder but not in people without panic disorder. These agents are thought to stimulate a general fear circuit, which includes limbic areas (such as the amygdala) as well as brainstem regions (such as the locus ceruleus, which contains more than half the noradrenergic neurons of the brain).

Psychoanalysts have emphasized the connection between separation issues and subsequent panic. Researchers have indeed found that a large percentage of patients with panic disorder recall having separation anxiety as children. Furthermore, the initial panic attack is sometimes preceded by real or threatened loss of a significant relationship. These phenomena may also fit with biological findings, insofar as the changes in the brain for normal separation anxiety may similarly be altered in panic disorder patients.

Freud also noted the connection between agoraphobia and anxiety attacks. While conditioning does not appear to account for the initiation of panic disorders, learning theory is useful in explaining the anticipatory anxiety that develops in panic disorder.

Certain events at the workplace may involve separation issues and so trigger panic attacks. These include job transfers, promotion or demotion, the employment of new workers, or layoffs. Later, certain situations at work may come to be particularly feared by the worker. These include airline travel, commuting to work, and meetings in which the worker feels physically or emotionally trapped.

Effects and Workplace Recognition

The panic attacks themselves may be extremely uncomfortable; moreover, the development of anticipatory anxiety inevitably leads to poor work function and personal distress. In many panic disorder patients, agoraphobia develops. Fear of flying or travel, for example, may become overwhelming. Severe disability often results. Such symptoms frequently lead to demoralization, and workers may begin to use substances such as alcohol in an attempt to obtain relief. People with this disorder may be sufficiently distressed to be driven to suicide.

Although workers with panic attacks often feel that their symptoms are conspicuous, their coworkers usually are unaware of the occurrence of such attacks. Occasionally, a period of muscular stiffening followed by relaxation is observed. As anticipatory anxiety increases, work may suffer. With the development of agoraphobic concerns, the worker may turn down assignments that involve traveling or feelings of being trapped.

Workplace Management and Referral

Panic disorder is usually detected only when anticipatory anxiety distracts the worker or when agoraphobic concerns become incapacitating. Management in the workplace comprises education about the disorder and reassurance that the prognosis is excellent with appropriate treatment. While treatment is initiated, the workplace can help diminish avoidance behaviors, for example, by assisting the worker with travel arrangements.

Psychiatric Management

Workers with panic disorder can benefit from a combination of pharmacological and psychotherapeutic interventions. A number of medications block panic attacks, including several classes of antidepressant medications and alprazolam and clonazepam (Xanax and Klonopin, two high-potency benzodiazepines). The presence of depressed mood is not a requirement for antidepressants to be effective. Treatment of panic disorder with antidepressants should be initiated at low doses, since these patients may initially experience paradoxical anxiety or jitteriness and are sensitive to side effects of medication. It is helpful to inform patients of potential side effects so they don't think that these are symptoms of imminent panic attacks. Blocking panic attacks will not necessarily lead to immediate diminution in the intervening anticipatory anxiety or phobic avoidance. A daily diary of anxiety and panic symptoms may help the patient learn this differentiation.

Anticipatory anxiety may be helped by a benzodiazepine. Phobic avoidance may respond to firm encouragement to face the feared situations. It is helpful to point out that the medications will block panic and lessen anxiety but not diminish phobic avoidance. Many patients may need additional psychotherapy or behavioral therapy. Behavioral techniques include learning to relax during exposure to feared situations and cognitive restructuring to give physical symptoms a more benign interpretation. Psychodynamic treatment may focus on possible relationships between the exacerbation of panic disorder and real, threatened, or symbolic separations.

Medication is usually given for about a year before a taper is begun. High-potency benzodiazepines work quickly, but there is a risk of withdrawal symptoms if they are discontinued too quickly.

Return to Work and ADA Reasonable Accommodation

When panic attacks have their first onset once the person is already at work, it is possible that the person will take time off work in order to obtain a diagnosis and begin treatment. Treatment is typically very effective, so that a relatively rapid return to work should be expected and encouraged.

When agoraphobia interferes with work, the situation may be more complex. On the one hand, agoraphobic fears may interfere with commuting to work or with certain kinds of work situations (such as travel). On the other hand, part of the behavioral treatment of panic disorder involves exposure to feared situations. It may therefore be reasonable to attempt to negotiate a gradual return to facing feared situations.

SOCIAL ANXIETY DISORDER: STAGE FRIGHT AND SHYNESS

Case 4

James Storch is a forty-two-year-old accountant who is occasionally required to make presentations to his department. Since high school, this kind of public speaking has made James anxious, but he has forced himself to do his job. Recently, however, James was asked to give a series of talks to representatives from another company.

During the week before the first presentation, he was so worried by the thought of embarrassing himself while giving the talk that he was unable to sleep. On the day of the presentation, he found himself feeling extremely anxious, sweating, and trembling. His mouth was so dry during the first talk that he frequently had to take sips of water. Although he succeeded in answering most of the questions from the audience, just before the second presentation, James called work to say that he had laryngitis and arranged for a colleague to present for him.

Although this excuse provided him with great relief, James knew that this was a short-term answer to a long-standing problem and asked human resources for the name of a psychiatrist. The psychiatrist found that James had social anxiety disorder, advised a course of an SSRI (a class of antidepressants effective for social anxiety disorder), and suggested a series of behavioral strategies to decrease his anxiety.

Diagnostic Overview

A phobia is defined as a persistent, irrational fear of a specific object, activity, or situation that results in a compelling desire to avoid the dreaded object, activity, or situation (the phobic stimulus). Most commonly, the person does avoid the object, activity, or situation, while recognizing that the fear is out of proportion to the danger.

In social anxiety disorder, or social phobia, the person's central fear is of acting in front of others in a way that will be humiliating or embarrassing. Typical situations that people with social anxiety disorder fear or avoid are performance situations (speaking, eating, or writing in public) and social interaction (attending parties, group discussion, or giving interviews).

When forced or surprised into the feared situation, the person feels intense anxiety, accompanied by a variety of somatic symptoms. While these may often be similar to the symptoms of a spontaneous panic attack, they differ in that blushing and tremor are common in social anxiety disorder. Furthermore, sudden onset is characteristic of panic disorder but not of social anxiety disorder.

Phobias are also fairly common disorders, with a six-month prevalence of 1.2 to 2.2 percent for social anxiety disorder and of 4.5 to 4.7 percent for simple phobia.

There appear to be two types of social anxiety disorder: discrete, which involves anxiety and avoidance only in performance situations, and generalized, which involves anxiety and avoidance in most social situations. Social anxiety disorder may be differentiated from simple phobias (circumscribed fears of specific objects, situations, or activities) in which humiliation and embarrassment are not involved. Avoidance of certain social situations is seen as a part of avoidant and paranoid personalities, agoraphobia and obsessive-compulsive disorder, depressive disorders, schizophrenia, and paranoid disorders. The well-trained diagnostician can usually distinguish such disorders from social anxiety disorder.

⁂ Diagnostic Criteria for Social Phobia

A. A marked and persistent fear of one or more social or performance situations in which the person is exposed to unfamiliar people or to possible scrutiny by others. The individual fears that he or she will act in a way (or show anxiety symptoms) that will be humiliating or embarrassing. *Note:* In children, there must be evidence of the capacity for age-appropriate social relationships with familiar people and the anxiety must occur in peer settings, not just in interactions with adults.

B. Exposure to the feared social situation almost invariably provokes anxiety, which may take the form of a situationally bound or situationally predisposed Panic Attack. *Note:* In children, the anxiety may be expressed by crying, tantrums, freezing, or shrinking from social situations with unfamiliar people.

C. The person recognizes that the fear is excessive or unreasonable. *Note:* In children, this feature may be absent.

D. The feared social or performance situations are avoided or else are endured with intense anxiety or distress.

E. The avoidance, anxious anticipation, or distress in the feared social or performance situation(s) interferes significantly with the person's normal routine, occupational (academic) functioning, or social activities or relationships, or there is marked distress about having the phobia.

F. In individuals under age 18 years, the duration is at least 6 months.

G. The fear or avoidance is not due to the direct physiological effects of a substance (e.g., a drug of abuse, a medication) or a general medical condition and is not better accounted for by another mental disorder (e.g., Panic Disorder With or Without Agoraphobia, Separation Anxiety Disorder, Body Dysmorphic Disorder, a Pervasive Developmental Disorder, or Schizoid Personality Disorder).

H. If a general medical condition or another mental disorder is present, the fear in Criterion A is unrelated to it, e.g., the fear is not of Stuttering, trembling in Parkinson's disease, or exhibiting abnormal eating behavior in Anorexia Nervosa or Bulimia Nervosa.

Specify if:

Generalized: if the fears include most social situations (also consider the additional diagnosis of Avoidant Personality Disorder)

Reprinted with permission from the Diagnostic and Statistical Manual of Mental Disorders, Fourth Edition, Text Revision. Copyright 2000 American Psychiatric Association.

❖ Diagnostic Criteria for Specific Phobia

A. Marked and persistent fear that is excessive or unreasonable, cued by the presence or anticipation of a specific object or situation (e.g., flying, heights, animals, receiving an injection, seeing blood).

B. Exposure to the phobic stimulus almost invariably provokes an immediate anxiety response, which may take the form of a situationally bound or situationally predisposed Panic Attack. *Note:* In children, the anxiety may be expressed by crying, tantrums, freezing, or clinging.

C. The person recognizes that the fear is excessive or unreasonable. *Note:* In children, this feature may be absent.

D. The phobic situation(s) is avoided or else is endured with intense anxiety or distress.

E. The avoidance, anxious anticipation, or distress in the feared situation(s) interferes significantly with the person's normal routine, occupational (or academic) functioning, or social activities or relationships, or there is marked distress about having the phobia.

F. In individuals under age 18 years, the duration is at least 6 months.

G. The anxiety, Panic Attacks, or phobic avoidance associated with the specific object or situation are not better accounted for by another mental disorder, such as Obsessive-Compulsive Disorder (e.g., fear of dirt in someone with an obsession about contamination), Posttraumatic Stress Disorder (e.g., avoidance of stimuli associated with a severe stressor), Separation Anxiety Disorder (e.g., avoidance of school), Social Phobia (e.g., avoidance of social situations because of fear of embarrassment), Panic Disorder With Agoraphobia, or Agoraphobia Without History of Panic Disorder.

Specify type:

Animal Type
Natural Environment Type (e.g., heights, storms, water)
Blood-Injection-Injury Type
Situational Type (e.g., airplanes, elevators, enclosed places)
Other Type (e.g., fear of choking, vomiting, or contracting an illness; in children, fear of loud sounds or costumed characters)

Reprinted with permission from the Diagnostic and Statistical Manual of Mental Disorders, Fourth Edition, Text Revision. *Copyright 2000 American Psychiatric Association.*

Causes

Children with behavioral inhibition seem particularly prone to develop later social anxiety disorder; this appears to be an inherited biological trait. In addition, ethologically minded theorists have suggested that phobias are an example of evolutionarily prepared learning and have adaptive value. Nevertheless, behaviorists have also indicated that it is possible to create and treat a phobia through conditioning and deconditioning techniques. Gradually, an integrated psychobiological model is emerging that includes an understanding of the underlying neuronal circuits that mediate social anxiety disorder and their response to environmental influences.

The workplace is unlikely to cause social anxiety disorder, but certain tasks at work, such as giving presentations or interacting with a group, may be feared and avoided by the person with this disorder. Organizational environments that are either overtly critical or superficially friendly can exacerbate social anxiety disorder.

Effects and Workplace Recognition

Some people with social anxiety disorder may be asymptomatic until they face their feared situation, and then they may experience intense anticipatory anxiety. Others develop a fear that people will sense their anxiety in a social situation and ridicule them. A vicious cycle may be set up, with fear leading to anxiety that impairs performance. Such developments may lead to social isolation, severe impairment, and abuse of alcohol or sedatives to self-medicate these symptoms.

In the workplace, social anxiety disorder may lead to few difficulties if the feared situation is avoidable. The worker with social anxiety disorder may simply be considered shy by coworkers. Avoidance may, however, limit career advancement, and indeed there is a growing research demonstrating an association between social anxiety disorder and occupational underachievement. If the worker has multiple fears, anxiety and avoidance may make impossible any work requiring social interaction.

Workplace Management and Referral

Social anxiety disorder may be seen initially during job interviews, and it can be detected if a worker avoids an important work-related social situation, if anticipatory anxiety is sufficiently high to interfere with performance, or an employee shows marked shyness. Programs that prepare these workers for performance and speaking situations can be very helpful. A time-limited diminution in overt criticism by workers may be helpful as part of such a program. Education about the disorder and reassurance that the prognosis is good with treatment are appropriate.

Psychiatric Management

Both psychotherapy and pharmacotherapy can be extremely helpful for social anxiety disorder. The SSRIs are the first-line medications for the medication treatment of this disorder. Beta blockers (such as propranolol and atenolol) can be used for rapid short-term management of discrete performance anxiety. Systematic desensitization, cognitive restructuring, and social skills training are also helpful.

Return to Work and ADA Reasonable Accommodation

Social anxiety disorder is a chronic disorder with early onset, so that it typically is present prior to employment. Changes in job description may well precipitate social anxiety disorder symptoms. In such cases, it is often to the benefit of both employer and employee if symptoms receive prompt professional treatment. Part of the treatment will involve exposure to feared situations, and the timing of this progress can be negotiated to suit the circumstances.

OBSESSIVE-COMPULSIVE DISORDER

Case 5

Milly Schmidt is a twenty-eight-year-old secretary for a partner in a law firm. Since adolescence, she has felt compelled to do certain things in a repetitive fashion. At one point, she went through a stage of door checking: spending much of her day wondering whether she had locked her apartment door, fearing that someone had robbed her apartment, and having to return home, often more than once a day, in order to check that the door was locked.

Over the past year or so, Milly noticed that her repetitive behaviors were appearing at work. Before beginning work, she felt compelled to arrange the stationery on her desk in a particular orderly and symmetrical fashion. Initially, this kept her desk tidy, but now this ritual was occupying far more time than it was worth. In addition, she felt an absolute urge to check the letters that she wrote at least six or seven times. Although this meant that her letters never had any mistakes, she knew that it was senseless to spend so much time doing this, and her efficiency had gradually but steadily deteriorated.

The partner became increasingly concerned. He had become quite aware of her inefficiency, and besides, Milly seemed a little "off" to him. An important legal contract was not submitted on time, and three more barely made it. The partner considered the options with the firm's human resource department. Rather than just dismissing Milly, he gave Milly the name of a psychiatrist he knew.

Once a diagnosis of obsessive-compulsive disorder had been made, Milly began treatment with an antiobsessional medication and cognitive-behavioral psychotherapy. Some weeks later, the worst symptoms had improved, and soon after there was a notable improvement in her work performance.

Diagnostic Overview

Obsessions are defined as recurrent, persistent ideas, thoughts, impulses, or images that are experienced, at least initially, as intrusive and senseless. The person who suffers from obsessions attempts to ignore or suppress them or neutralize them with some other thought or action. Compulsions are repetitive, purposeful, and intentional behaviors that are performed in response to an obsession, or according to certain rules, or in a stereotyped fashion. The behavior is designed to neutralize or to prevent discomfort of some dreaded event or situation, but either the activity is not connected in a realistic way with that which it is designed to prevent, or it is excessive, and, at least at first, this is recognized by the person.

A patient with obsessive-compulsive disorder (OCD) may suffer from either obsessions or compulsions. There are several commonly found symptom subtypes: obsessions about dirt and contamination leading to compulsions of ritual washing, intrusive thoughts with aggressive or sexual themes and subsequent checking compulsions, orderliness and symmetry behaviors, and hoarding. Often these groups of symptoms overlap or develop sequentially.

The phrase *obsessive-compulsive* may conjure up an image of a worker who is a perfectionist, overly neat, and overly rigid. Such a person is, however, unlikely to have OCD and is more likely to have an obsessional personality disorder (see Chapter Twenty-Three).

OCD itself has only recently been recognized as quite a common psychiatric disorder. It is now thought to have a six-month prevalence of 1 to 2 percent.

The diagnosis of OCD is made when obsessions and compulsions cause significant distress, are time-consuming, or significantly interfere with social or occupational functioning. Although activities such as eating, sexual behavior, gambling, or drinking may be performed excessively, or "compulsively," these are experienced as pleasurable by the person and are more akin to addictions than to true compulsions. The morbid ruminations or preoccupations frequently found in depression are unpleasant, but the person regards them as meaningful, whereas the obsessions of OCD are viewed as senseless. OCD should be differentiated from obsessive-compulsive personality disorder, which is characterized by perfectionism, orderliness, and inflexibility. These traits are egosyntonic (acceptable to the ego); they are regarded as realistic and not resisted or struggled against. It is also necessary to differentiate OCD from schizophrenia and phobia.

⁂ Diagnostic Criteria for Obsessive-Compulsive Disorder

A. Either obsessions or compulsions:

Obsessions as defined by (1), (2), (3), and (4):
1. recurrent and persistent thoughts, impulses, or images that are experienced, at some time during the disturbance, as intrusive and inappropriate and that cause marked anxiety or distress
2. the thoughts, impulses, or images are not simply excessive worries about real-life problems
3. the person attempts to ignore or suppress such thoughts, impulses, or images, or to neutralize them with some other thought or action
4. the person recognizes that the obsessional thoughts, impulses, or images are a product of his or her own mind (not imposed from without as in thought insertion)

Compulsions as defined by (1) and (2):
1. repetitive behaviors (e.g., hand washing, ordering, checking) or mental acts (e.g., praying, counting, repeating words silently) that the person feels driven to perform in response to an obsession, or according to rules that must be applied rigidly
2. the behaviors or mental acts are aimed at preventing or reducing distress or preventing some dreaded event or situation; however, these behaviors or mental acts either are not connected in a realistic way with what they are designed to neutralize or prevent or are clearly excessive

B. At some point during the course of the disorder, the person has recognized that the obsessions or compulsions are excessive or unreasonable. *Note:* This does not apply to children.

C. The obsessions or compulsions cause marked distress, are time consuming (take more than 1 hour a day), or significantly interfere with the person's normal routine, occupational (or academic) functioning, or usual social activities or relationships.

D. If another Axis I disorder is present, the content of the obsessions or compulsions is not restricted to it (e.g., preoccupation with food in the presence of an Eating Disorder; hair pulling in the presence of Trichotillomania; concern with appearance in the presence of Body Dysmorphic Disorder; preoccupation with drugs in the presence of a Substance Use Disorder; preoccupation with having a serious illness in the presence of Hypochondriasis; preoccupation with sexual urges or fantasies in the presence of a Paraphilia; or guilty ruminations in the presence of Major Depressive Disorder).

E. The disturbance is not due to the direct physiological effects of a substance (e.g., a drug of abuse, a medication) or a general medical condition.

Specify if:
> *With Poor Insight:* if, for most of the time during the current episode, the person does not recognize that the obsessions and compulsions are excessive or unreasonable

Reprinted with permission from the Diagnostic and Statistical Manual of Mental Disorders, Fourth Edition, Text Revision. *Copyright 2000 American Psychiatric Association.*

Causes

Contemporary researchers have made progress in delineating the neurobiology of OCD. There is growing evidence that specific brain circuits mediate the symptoms of this disorder. Evidence includes the association between brain lesions and the subsequent development of OCD symptoms, and the demonstration that particular brain regions are dysfunctional in brain imaging studies of OCD patients. Furthermore, there have been important advances in understanding the neurogenetics and neurochemistry of these circuits. The serotonin system in particular projects to regions of the brain involved in OCD, and by altering this system in specific ways, OCD symptoms can be exacerbated or reduced. Interestingly, cognitive-behavioral interventions are also able to normalize dysfunctional brain circuitry in OCD.

OCD is unlikely to be caused by the workplace. However, obsessive-compulsive symptoms fluctuate and may be exacerbated by both personal and workplace stresses. In some cases, OCD affects work only indirectly; for example, having to check at home may make the person late for work. In other cases, symptoms are more directly related to job description; for example, a person may check her work over and over.

Effects and Workplace Recognition

OCD often begins in childhood or early adolescence, although in women it sometimes also begins during or after pregnancy. OCD is one of the most disabling of all medical disorders. People with OCD may experience significant impairment in their overall quality of life. Nevertheless, new developments in pharmacological and psychotherapeutic treatments have led to vastly improved prognosis.

Compulsions may be recognized at the workplace in the form of ritualistic behavior or impaired performance. Repetitive obsessive thoughts can also impair attention and concentration. Workers with OCD may have rigid ideas or approaches that persist inappropriately. Although some obsessive-compulsive personality traits may be useful in some jobs, OCD is most likely to be dysfunctional.

Workplace Management and Referral

OCD can be detected if ritualistic behavior is observed or if obsessions and compulsions lead to impaired functioning. Management in the workplace may comprise education about the medical nature of the disorder and reassurance that workers with OCD are not "crazy" and it is not all in their head. Appropriate referral to a psychiatrist skilled in the treatment of OCD is essential.

Psychiatric Management

Both pharmacotherapy and psychotherapy are useful in the treatment of OCD. The SSRIs are again the first-line medication treatment of choice. Patients need to build up to higher doses than for other anxiety or depressive disorders and remain on the medication for as long as twelve weeks before a full effect is seen. If the patient is partially improved, these medications are often augmented with agents from a different class; low doses of the new generation of antipsychotics may be particularly helpful in this context.

Cognitive-behavioral treatment comprises exposure procedures that aim to expose patients to their feared objects (such as exposure to dirt) until they see that their discomfort does not last but eventually ceases, and response prevention techniques (such as prevention of washing) that aim to decrease the frequency of compulsive rituals. It is often useful to involve the family in such work. More psychodynamic therapy may also use cognitive-behavioral approaches, while also understanding issues of anger that may emerge after medication response.

Return to Work and ADA Reasonable Accommodation

OCD is increasingly viewed as a medical disorder. Nevertheless, as is the case in other anxiety disorders, exposure to fears is an important component of psychotherapy. In many cases, it is reasonable to expect the person with OCD to continue to perform at an optimal level. However, there are also some cases of OCD where treatment is ineffective and disability remains chronic.

POSTTRAUMATIC STRESS DISORDER

Case 6

Jane Segal is a twenty-six-year-old insurance broker. Two months ago, she and her four-year-old daughter, Susan, had a terrifying experience. On the way home from the grocery, a man sprang out from behind a tree, held a gun to Susan's head, and demanded Jane's purse. When Jane gave him the purse, he opened it, was disappointed by how little money there was, and made several more threats before finally taking off.

Afterward, thoughts of the episode kept intruding into Jane's mind. At night, she had difficulty sleeping and had nightmares about being held up. During the day, she was on edge, lost her usual cheerfulness, and would not walk along the route of the hold-up. She became demoralized and started drinking heavily to help her sleep. Some of her clients sensed that something was wrong, and Jane couldn't be as dedicated to her work as she wanted. A broker who was close to Jane advised her to seek help at a local health center. Jane was diagnosed as having posttraumatic stress disorder, and her psychiatrist encouraged her to talk about the traumatic experience. The psychiatrist also prescribed an SSRI.

Diagnostic Overview

Posttraumatic stress disorder (PTSD) comprises a characteristic set of symptoms that occurs after a psychologically distressing event. The stressor involves actual or threatened bodily harm, and the immediate response involves feelings of fear or helplessness. The characteristic symptoms include reexperiencing the event, avoidance of stimuli associated with the event or psychic numbing, and increased arousal.

Stressors that cause PTSD include participating in combat, physical or sexual assault, and environmental disasters such as hurricanes or tornadoes. The trauma is reexperienced in the form of recurrent painful, intrusive recollections, daydreams, or nightmares. Occasionally, the event is relived. Psychic numbing or emotional anesthesia is manifest by diminished responsiveness to the external world, with feelings of being detached from others, loss of interest in usual activities and in the future, and inability to feel such emotions as tenderness or love. The person may suppress thoughts and feelings associated with the event or avoid activities or situations that lead to remembering the event. Symptoms of excessive arousal include difficulty sleeping, irritability and explosive anger, difficulty concentrating, hypervigilance, and an exaggerated startle response. Other symptoms may include guilt at having survived, depression, anxiety, panic attacks, shame, and rage. The disorder may be complicated by substance abuse or suicidal actions. The onset of PTSD may be delayed until some months following the event.

Diagnosis is made when symptoms following a severely distressing event last for longer than a month. In adjustment disorder, the stressor is within the range of common experience, and the characteristic symptoms of PTSD are absent. Some researchers hold that even stressors within the range of usual human experience, such as bereavement, may lead to a syndrome of reexperiencing the trauma. Various psychiatric disorders secondary to brain injury or to substances may mimic PTSD. PTSD may mimic phobia and panic disorder, and indeed has been considered a variant of the latter condition. Major depression and generalized anxiety disorder may develop secondary to PTSD. Especially where there are existing or potential legal issues or entitlements, factitious disorder and malingering (conscious deception and feigning of illness; see Chapter Twenty-Seven) should be ruled out.

❊ Diagnostic Criteria for Posttraumatic Stress Disorder

A. The person has been exposed to a traumatic event in which both of the following were present:
   1. the person experienced, witnessed, or was confronted with an event or events that involved actual or threatened death or serious injury, or a threat to the physical integrity of self or others
   2. the person's response involved intense fear, helplessness, or horror. *Note:* In children, this may be expressed instead by disorganized or agitated behavior

B. The traumatic event is persistently reexperienced in one (or more) of the following ways:
   1. recurrent and intrusive distressing recollections of the event, including images, thoughts, or perceptions. *Note:* In young children, repetitive play may occur in which themes or aspects of the trauma are expressed.
   2. recurrent distressing dreams of the event. *Note:* In children, there may be frightening dreams without recognizable content.
   3. acting or feeling as if the traumatic event were recurring (includes a sense of reliving the experience, illusions, hallucinations, and dissociative flashback episodes, including those that occur on awakening or when intoxicated). *Note:* In young children, trauma-specific reenactment may occur.
   4. intense psychological distress at exposure to internal or external cues that symbolize or resemble an aspect of the traumatic event
   5. physiological reactivity on exposure to internal or external cues that symbolize or resemble an aspect of the traumatic event

C. Persistent avoidance of stimuli associated with the trauma and numbing of general responsiveness (not present before the trauma), as indicated by three (or more) of the following:
   1. efforts to avoid thoughts, feelings, or conversations associated with the trauma
   2. efforts to avoid activities, places, or people that arouse recollections of the trauma
   3. inability to recall an important aspect of the trauma
   4. markedly diminished interest or participation in significant activities
   5. feeling of detachment or estrangement from others
   6. restricted range of affect (e.g., unable to have loving feelings)
   7. sense of a foreshortened future (e.g., does not expect to have a career, marriage, children, or a normal life span)

D. Persistent symptoms of increased arousal (not present before the trauma), as indicated by two (or more) of the following:
   1. difficulty falling or staying asleep
   2. irritability or outbursts of anger
   3. difficulty concentrating

4. hypervigilance
5. exaggerated startle response

E. Duration of the disturbance (symptoms in Criteria B, C, and D) is more than 1 month.

F. The disturbance causes clinically significant distress or impairment in social, occupational, or other important areas of functioning.

Specify if:

Acute: if duration of symptoms is less than 3 months
Chronic: if duration of symptoms is 3 months or more

Specify if:

With Delayed Onset: if onset of symptoms is at least 6 months after the stressor

Reprinted with permission from the Diagnostic and Statistical Manual of Mental Disorders, Fourth Edition, Text Revision. *Copyright 2000 American Psychiatric Association.*

Causes

Individuals show marked differences in how they react to stress. It has been argued that the more previous trauma the person has experienced, the more likely he or she is to develop symptoms following a stressful event. People with high premorbid anxiety levels may be more likely to respond with pathological anxiety. When stressors become extreme, however, even in the absence of pre-existing conditions, the rate of morbidity increases significantly. A disruptive recovery environment may further increase the level of impairment.

PTSD may be modeled using biological and ethological constructs. Animals prevented from escaping from acute stress develop a syndrome of learned helplessness, which parallels the symptoms of PTSD. There is growing understanding of the specific brain circuits that mediate fear conditioning in animals and PTSD in humans; dysfunction in limbic structures such as the amygdala and the hippocampus may be particularly important in this disorder. There is also growing appreciation of the neurochemical and neuroendocrinological dysfunctions seen in PTSD.

In general, whereas PTSD was once seen as a normal response to abnormal events, it is increasingly viewed as a pathological condition mediated by specific psychobiological dysfunctions.

Effects and Workplace Recognition

The clinical course of PTSD may involve three stages. Stage I is the response to trauma. Nonsusceptible persons may experience symptoms immediately after the trauma, but these gradually diminish. Predisposed people with high anxiety levels may have an exaggerated response and continue to ruminate about the event. If symptoms persist past four to six weeks, stage II, or acute PTSD, is present. Feelings of helplessness and loss of control, symptoms of arousal, and reliving of the trauma occur. The person's life becomes centered around the trauma, leading to changes in personality, interpersonal relations, and occupational functioning. In stage III, chronic PTSD develops, with disability, demoralization, and despondency. The person is now preoccupied with the physical disability resulting from the trauma. Somatic symptoms, anxiety and depression, substance abuse, disturbed relations, and unemployment may occur.

The symptoms of posttraumatic stress disorder may affect many areas. Not only may there be intense subjective distress from recollections of the event, but the combination of excessive arousal and psychic numbing may lead to difficulties in concentration and performance and to strained interpersonal relations.

PTSD is commonly presented as a cause for disability claims and lawsuits. This has resulted in high costs for employers and insurance carriers, as well as expensive litigation and disruptive workplace effects. It is essential to ensure that preexisting conditions have been fully and accurately assessed, that diagnostic criteria for PTSD are met, that malingering is not present, that any associated panic or depressive symptoms have been addressed, and that optimal treatment has been conducted with full patient compliance. Both sophisticated psychotherapy and medication are often needed.

Workplace Management and Referral

After an intensely stressful event, it is important to provide a supportive environment, including the opportunity for consultation with a professional. Nevertheless, there is surprisingly little evidence that routine debriefing is useful in such contexts. Once symptoms of PTSD are present, referral to a professional is clearly indicated.

Psychiatric Management

Symptomatic management may involve psychotherapy and psychopharmacological intervention. Psychotherapeutic approaches include review of the traumatic event, understanding the emotional response, and understanding both the emotional antecedents and consequences. Various cognitive-behavioral techniques have been shown helpful in PTSD. Furthermore, there is growing evidence for the value of medication in PTSD; once again, the SSRIs are viewed as the first-line medications of choice in this disorder.

Return to Work and ADA Reasonable Accommodation

There is a complex relationship between PTSD and disability claims. Many people with PTSD are able to continue working, and indeed view the continued exposure to feared situations as part of their own psychotherapy. But in severe cases of PTSD, it may be unreasonable to expect an early return to full occupational function. Careful evaluation by an expert is indicated.

The symptoms of the anxiety disorders manifest in specific ways at the workplace. They may be exacerbated by work-related stress and may also lead to substantial interference with work performance. Early recognition of these specific disorders at the workplace, with appropriate workplace and psychiatric management, may be of significant benefit in reducing their occupational impact and lead to a greatly improved prognosis.

References and Additional Sources

American Psychiatric Association. (1988). Practice guideline for the treatment of patients with panic disorder. *American Journal of Psychiatry, 155*, 1–34.

Anxiety Disorders Association of America, www.adaa.org, www.nih.nimh.gov.

Ballenger, J. C., Davidson, J. A., Lecrubier, Y., et al. (1998a). Consensus statement on social anxiety disorder from the International Consensus Group on Depression and Anxiety. *Journal of Clinical Psychiatry, 59*, 54–60.

Ballenger, J. C., Davidson, J. R., Lecrubier, Y., et al. (2001). Consensus statement on generalized anxiety disorder from the International Consensus Group on Depression and Anxiety. *Journal of Clinical Psychiatry, 62* (Suppl. 11), 53–58.

Ballenger, J. C., Davidson, J. R., Lecruber, Y., et al. (2001). Consensus statement on posttraumatic stress disorder from the International Consensus Group on Depression and Anxiety. *Journal of Clinical Psychiatry, 61* (Suppl. 5), 60–66.

Dupont, R. L., DuPont, C. M., & Rice, D. P. (2002). Economic costs of anxiety disorders. In D. J. Stein & E. Hollander (Eds.), *Textbook of anxiety disorders.* Washington, DC: American Psychiatric Press.

Greenberg, P. E., Sisitsky, T., Kessler, R. C., et al. (1999). The economic burden of the anxiety disorders in the 1990s. *Journal of Clinical Psychiatry, 60*, 427–435.

National Institute for Mental Health, www.nimh.nih.gov/anxiety.

Obsessive-Compulsive Foundation, www.ocfoundation.org.

Stein, D. J., & Hollander, E. (2002). *Textbook of anxiety disorders.* Washington, DC: American Psychiatric Press.

CHAPTER TWENTY-TWO

Depression and Burnout

Philip M. Liu
David A. Van Liew

*A distinction is made between the normal mood of feeling down
and the four clinical depressions that are the focus of this chapter and
the leading cause of disability worldwide. In any given year, 9.5 percent
of Americans will suffer a clinical depression, and almost 20 percent of
people will suffer such a clinical depression in a lifetime. Clinical depressions
are primarily considered to be a medical illness. The complex interplay
of genetics, childhood experiences, and current psychosocial stresses
leads to a disturbance of certain neurotransmitters. Treatment is
very effective in a relatively short period of time when compared to other
chronic medical conditions. The combination of medications and
psychotherapy can restore normal functioning and prevent relapse.*

*D*epression is a word that is used commonly in daily banter and means different things to different people. When used loosely, it often refers to passing phases of sadness or difficult life experiences. When psychiatrists diagnose depressions, they mean particular disorders with specific signs and symptoms that are sufficiently prolonged to impair daily functioning. A distinction must be made between clinical depressions and the ordinary lows of everyday life. It is possible to feel very unhappy as one moves along a normal continuum of moods. Everyone experiences a depressed mood from time to time in the form of feeling sad or feeling down, and such moods are normal in that the experience is mild and transient. However, in this chapter, depression refers to specific clinical conditions that are defined by psychiatrists and mental health professionals. One of these disorders is an adjustment disorder with depressed mood, which is mild and transient and is often treatable with counseling and relatively minimal professional help. The other three disorders to be considered—major depressive disorder, dysthymia (and atypical depression), and bipolar disorder—are medical illnesses that can exact terrible costs in the quality of one's life and in the workplace. Decades of medical research have provided a better understanding of these disorders that has led to highly effective medical interventions.

The term *burnout* is used so frequently that it has lost much of its original meaning. As originally used, *burnout* meant a mild degree of stress-induced unhappiness. The solutions ranged from a vacation to a sabbatical. Ultimately, it was used to describe everything from fatigue to a major depression and now seems to have become an alternative word for *depression,* but with a less serious significance. When the term *burnout* is used in this chapter, it is equated with an adjustment disorder with depressed mood.

Depression is so common that some experts would say it is an epidemic. It is the leading cause of disability in the world (Murray & Lopez, 1996). Almost 20 percent of people will suffer a clinical depression sometime in their lifetime. In any given year, about 19 million people, or 9.5 percent of American adults, will suffer from depression (Regier et al., 1993). At any given time, one in twenty adults are clinically depressed. The RAND Corporation states that depression accounts for more days in bed than most other medical ailments, such as ulcers, diabetes, high blood pressure, and arthritis ((U.S. Surgeon General, 1999). Estimates of the annual cost of depression to the nation in 1990 range from $30 to $44 billion. The National Institute of Mental Health (NIMH) states that of the $44 billion, depression accounts for close to $12 billion in lost workdays and an estimated $11 billion in other costs associated with decreased productivity (see Chapter Three).

In the midst of these facts, there is good news. Tremendous advances have been made in the understanding and treatment of depression. Consequently, the 1990s have been recognized as the Decade of the Brain. There is now a National Depression Screening Day that is held annually in recognition of the magnitude of the disorder and to promote the advances made in the treatment of the more severe depressions. The proportion of the population that received outpatient treatment for depression from 1987 to 1997 increased threefold as a result of changing attitudes toward depression (Offson et al., 2002). Adjustment disorder with depressed mood continues to be seen as a relatively mild disorder that occurs in reaction to an event. The more severe depressions (major depression, dysthymia, and bipolar disorder) are now seen as primarily medical illnesses: a chemical imbalance in the brain leads to disturbances in mood, behavior, thinking, and physical functioning. We now have new and effective tools that affect biochemistry in combating the more severe depressions, and these treatments are highly effective in a relatively short period of time for medical illnesses. The NIMH estimates that at least 80 percent of people suffering from the more severe depressions will significantly improve with treatment. This means that many people return to a full and normal level of functioning. Successful treatment often occurs within one to three months.

ADJUSTMENT DISORDER WITH DEPRESSED MOOD

Case 1

Jody McDermott is a twenty-eight-year-old woman who has been an excellent administrative assistant for the past three years. However, recently, she was discovered crying uncontrollably in the rest room. It turns out that she had broken up with her boyfriend about two months ago, and her father had recently declared bankruptcy. Normally, Jody is perky and enthusiastic about her work, but coworkers had noticed that she seemed depressed and withdrawn. She also had taken a number of days off for sick leave because she had no desire to get out of bed, but she would then return to work and function, although her productivity fell. She continued to enjoy meeting friends after work for dinner most of the time, and she found relief with her yoga classes that she attended every other day.

Diagnostic Overview

An adjustment disorder with depressed mood means that there is a depressive adjustment to specific, identifiable psychosocial stressors. Typically, the depressed mood is transient. The nature of the adjustment disorder assumes that the disturbance will remit after the stressor ceases or when individual adaptations are made. The stressor—single or multiple, periodic or continuous—often occurs in a family or workplace setting. A stressor may affect only a particular individual or a group or community. Some stressors may accompany specific developmental events such as going to school, leaving the parental home, getting married, becoming a parent, failing to attain occupational goals, and retiring from the workforce. It is estimated that between 5 and 20 percent of the population suffers from this disorder from time to time (American Psychiatric Association, 1994). Women and men seem to be equally affected.

Bereavement is distinguished by the specific stressor of the loss of a loved one and has symptoms similar to an adjustment disorder with depressed mood or to a major depressive disorder. Because the reaction to the death of a loved one is so common and universal, the ensuing bereavement is considered a normal reaction (see Table 22.1). Survivors may have thoughts that they would be better off dead or that they should have died instead of the loved one. Bereavement may be delayed. Duration varies considerably, with the acute phase resolving in four to six weeks, and the overall bereavement lasting six months to two years. A full-blown depressive syndrome can develop from the depressed mood of bereavement, but this would then involve more complicated symptoms, such as a persistently poor appetite, weight loss, insomnia, pervasive guilt and self-blame, and no sense of resolution.

Table 22.1. Comparison of Depression and Bereavement.

Index	Depression	Bereavement
Timing	About six to twelve months following a loss	About one to twenty-four months following a loss
Depressive vegetative signs	Typical: insomnia, loss of appetite, lethargy	Less common
Thought	Guilt, self-deprecation	Thoughts, hallucinations of deceased relative are sometimes normal
Guilt	Pervasive guilt and self-blame	Limited to feelings about what patient should have done differently or about having survived when another person has not
Self-esteem	Lowered self-esteem and self-confidence	Intact self-esteem except for anxiety about living without the lost person or thing
Resolution	No sense of resolution	Feeling of acceptance
Abatement	Spontaneous improvement often takes six to twelve months but can be chronic	Acute phase abates in four to six weeks
Recurrences	Becomes more severe and longer lasting with time	Primarily at important holidays and anniversaries

Causes

A distinguishing feature of this disorder is the presence of an identifiable stressor. This disorder is primarily viewed as a psychosocial disorder. Certain changes in life that are considered to be almost universal can increase one's vulnerability. Such normal developmental tasks include leaving home, going to school, starting work, getting married, having a child, or retiring. However, in most cases, employee vulnerability is a more significant contributor than the stressor itself. Why some people respond to a stressor with the symptoms of an adjustment disorder remains unclear. As any parent would attest, each child is born with a certain temperament and sensitivity. Everyone also has a unique childhood experience that may predispose that person to certain stressors. Seemingly uneventful occurrences in the workplace may cause a reawakening of a painful past conflict. The intensity and duration of the stressor, combined with the unique vulnerability of that person, might eventually give way to helplessness such that depression and dysfunctional behavior set in.

Effects and Workplace Recognition

Both positive and negative changes call for psychological adjustment. Because the underlying problem can be intimate or interpersonal, direct consideration of the problem can be uncomfortable for the employee, coworkers, and supervisors alike. Accurate prediction of impairment magnitude, duration, or consequences is not always possible. Direct observation of employee emotions, moods, attitudes, conduct, and productivity, combined with support and direct feedback, is the most effective way to deal with adjustment disorders.

From a workplace perspective, corporate changes that obviously lead to stress are a red flag for the possible occurrence of an adjustment disorder. Examples are the threat of an impending layoff, a change in upper-level management, merger with another company, or a downturn in the economy. On a more immediate level, identifiable stressors include interpersonal conflicts, interdepartmental conflicts, or personal losses.

The greatest effects on worker and workplace occur when adjustment reactions take place without anyone's awareness. When the underlying disorder remains hidden, the problem becomes externalized. Tensions increase, sides are chosen, and both employees and employer start pointing fingers. A stressor may lead to a feeling of hurt to one's self-esteem that is then defended by an angry reaction. Sometimes the best defense can be a good offense. The behavioral symptoms of the transient depression usually become the focus of the problem. When the affected employee has difficulty setting agendas or problem solving, a supervisor can inadvertently worsen matters by focusing on the shortcomings. Ideally, when a worker has difficulty with focus, teamwork, and productive effort, a supervisor needs to consider underlying causes for the outward changes in behavior. In practice, however, tensions often rise, and there is a tendency toward either inaction or overreaction on both sides.

Workplace Management and Referral

Employees with possible adjustment disorders should be referred for professional evaluation as soon as severe symptoms become evident. Strong encouragement may be needed. Often the employee will think that he or she should be able to handle life's challenges without outside help. Psychiatrists are helpful in distinguishing between the psychological and biological causes. Mental health professionals also are adept at understanding the nuances and consequences of personal change and will take the necessary time to understand both the uniqueness and the universality of the problem at hand.

Adjustment disorders have a good prognosis, since the symptoms go away after the stressor ceases or after a new level of adaptation is reached. Extensive loss of work time is not usual. When work is missed, it is usually for patching up relationships, dealing with parental concerns, or working on legal or financial matters. Regular Monday absences, extended breaks, and other time-loss issues do need to be addressed. Emotional adaptation takes time. It is helpful to clarify employer expectations, foster resolution of the stressors, and sometimes allow time off to effect prompt solutions. Since some limited dysfunction can occur for a short time, special care should be taken in work situations that involve major responsibilities or physical risk. Decisions may have to be postponed and safety protocols followed with particular care. Expectations and communications should be extremely clear. They should be conveyed verbally first and followed up with written reminders if needed.

Psychiatric Management

For employees requiring help, individual psychotherapy is the treatment of choice. Typically, such treatment is brief, with effective help rendered in most cases in one to ten sessions. The focus of the treatment would first be on providing a safe and trusting relationship where support and empathy are provided. One would then better understand how the symptoms of an adjustment disorder might make sense in the light of that employee's vulnerability. It may be connected to the past or to some current event in that person's life. It may be that there is a distorted form of thinking or maladaptive behavior that contributes to the reaction to the stressor. Sometimes understanding the cause of the reaction in terms of one's unique psychology can be enough to alleviate the symptoms. Empathy can go a long way in providing relief and allowing for a new self-determined direction in adapting to the stressor. Therapy can also provide new coping skills such that helplessness is no longer felt and self-esteem is bolstered. Antidepressants are not usually required, but sometimes a psychiatrist may briefly provide medications for insomnia or anxiety.

Return to Work and ADA Reasonable Accommodation

An adjustment disorder with depressed mood does not generally lead to a medical leave. When such a leave is granted by a physician or psychiatrist, it is generally from a few days to possibly a couple of weeks. Reasonable accommodation might include providing the employee with time off for counseling and stress management support groups.

MAJOR DEPRESSION

Case 2

Karl Jensen was sixty-two years old when he learned that his wife had breast cancer, shortly before they left for a long-anticipated Caribbean cruise. Two months after their return, Karl's wife died. In the next seven months, Karl had increasing trouble keeping up with his work schedule despite overtime work and his experience as a machinist for thirty-five years. His physical movements were noticeably slower. Although he repeatedly checked his figures, he made several costly mistakes and took excessive time in making decisions. Karl was normally very friendly but was now given to sudden bursts of impatient anger toward his fellow workers. He lost interest in his outside activities. Instead of joining his buddies for lunch, he spent lunch hours sleeping in his car. Noticing that Karl looked worried, thin, and very tired, a coworker asked about his health. Although Karl said he felt all right, he admitted that he was not sleeping well; he would awaken at four o'clock in the morning worrying about work. He also complained of stomach problems that kept him from focusing on his work, and he thought that this stomach problem caused him to lose his appetite such that he had lost eighteen pounds. Several days later, the supervisor smelled beer on Karl's breath.

Diagnostic Overview

Major depressive disorder (MDD) is the best-known form of depression. Variously called clinical, endogenous, or biochemical depression, there are also subtypes including melancholia, seasonal affective disorder, postpartum depression, and depressive psychoses. MDD is popularly described as a "nervous breakdown" or "chemical imbalance."

External stresses may or may not lead to an episode of a major depression in contrast with an adjustment disorder. There is evidence that the initial episodes of a major depression are more likely to be triggered by an external stressor. However, recurrences may have no obvious stressor. For many people, there may be further recurrences during the course of a lifetime if left untreated. Also, a diagnosis of depression cannot be made with a laboratory test. The diagnosis is determined from the patient's history.

⁜ Diagnostic Criteria for Major Depressive Episode

A. Five (or more) of the following symptoms have been present during the same 2-week period and represent a change from previous functioning; at least one of the symptoms is either (1) depressed mood or (2) loss of interest or pleasure. *Note:* Do not include symptoms that are clearly due to a general medical condition, or mood-incongruent delusions or hallucinations.

  1. depressed mood most of the day, nearly every day, as indicated by either subjective report (e.g., feels sad or empty) or observation made by others (e.g., appears tearful). *Note:* In children and adolescents, can be irritable mood.

  2. markedly diminished interest or pleasure in all, or almost all, activities most of the day, nearly every day (as indicated by either subjective account or observation made by others)

  3. significant weight loss when not dieting or weight gain (e.g., a change of more than 5% of body weight in a month), or decrease or increase in appetite

nearly every day. *Note:* In children, consider failure to make expected weight gains.

4. insomnia or hypersomnia nearly every day

5. psychomotor agitation or retardation nearly every day (observable by others, not merely subjective feelings of restlessness or being slowed down)

6. fatigue or loss of energy nearly every day

7. feelings of worthlessness or excessive or inappropriate guilt (which may be delusional) nearly every day (not merely self-reproach or guilt about being sick)

8. diminished ability to think or concentrate, or indecisiveness, nearly every day (either by subjective account or as observed by others)

9. recurrent thoughts of death (not just fear of dying), recurrent suicidal ideation without a specific plan, or a suicide attempt or a specific plan for committing suicide

B. The symptoms do not meet criteria for a Mixed Episode.

C. The symptoms cause clinically significant distress or impairment in social, occupational, or other important areas of functioning.

D. The symptoms are not due to the direct physiological effects of a substance (e.g., a drug of abuse, a medication) or a general medical condition (e.g., hypothyroidism).

E. The symptoms are not better accounted for by Bereavement, i.e., after the loss of a loved one, the symptoms persist for longer than 2 months or are characterized by marked functional impairment, morbid preoccupation with worthlessness, suicidal ideation, psychotic symptoms, or psychomotor retardation.

Reprinted with permission from the Diagnostic and Statistical Manual of Mental Disorders, Fourth Edition, Text Revision. *Copyright 2000 American Psychiatric Association.*

The essential feature of this depression is that there is at least a two-week history of a depressed mood or the loss of interest or pleasure in nearly all activities that leads to significant impairment in occupational or social functioning. These disturbances are associated with at least five of the following symptoms as described in the DSM-IV criteria for a major depressive disorder in the fourth edition of the *Diagnostic and Statistical Manual of Mental Disorders* (DSM-IV; American Psychiatric Association, 1994). Typically, individuals sleep fitfully and have difficulty returning to sleep after they awaken in the middle of the night. Less commonly, they sleep too much. There is often loss of appetite with possible weight loss, but sometimes an increased appetite with weight gain. A markedly diminished interest or pleasure in almost all activities may be experienced as a loss of sexual desire, social withdrawal, or disinterest in hobbies. Commonly, a depressed person just doesn't care about anything. Fatigue or loss of energy may be described as having a hard time getting out of bed or feeling exhausted with minimal activity. Disrupted thinking in the form of poor concentration or indecisiveness may lead individuals to fear that they are becoming demented. They might just stare at the TV or computer or complain of poor memory. Others might observe an agitation or slowness in activity. Individuals may pace, wring their hands or seem to others slower in their thinking and talking. An excessive sense of guilt or worthlessness may lead to an exaggerated sense of responsibility for a failed project or rumination over past failings. Finally, recurrent thoughts of death or suicide may be present. The acute danger of depression is that individuals may start to feel hopeless and become preoccupied with thoughts of suicide. This preoccupation may take the form of not caring about dying. It may be fleeting. The danger of suicide is markedly increased if the person ruminates continuously about suicide and establishes a plan. Suicide is most often caused by a mood disorder, often in association with panic disorder.

Bereavement is a normal reaction that may have similar symptoms to a major depression. However, a diagnosis of a major depression is generally not made until at least two months after the loss. There are also certain symptoms that are not typical of a normal grief reaction that may help in distinguishing bereavement from a major depression. As described in DSM-IV, these unusual symptoms that suggest a major depression include "1) guilt about things other than actions taken or not taken by the survivor at the time of the death: 2) thoughts of death other than the survivor feeling that he or she would be better off dead or should have died with the deceased person; 3) morbid preoccupation with worthlessness; 4) marked psychomotor retardation; 5) prolonged and marked functional impairment; 6) hallucinatory experiences other than thinking that he or she bears the voice of, or transiently sees the image of, the deceased person."

Causes

Depression is caused by a complex interplay of factors: genetic predisposition, early childhood experiences when the developing brain is still being formulated, coping mechanisms that may have been adaptive in childhood but are now maladaptive, external events that trigger symptoms, and unconscious, unresolved conflicts that may be awakened by a current experience. Every individual has a unique pattern of biological, psychological, and environmental or circumstantial factors that together make a depression more or less likely to occur. In this sense, the causes of depression follow the typical factors that result in many chronic medical illnesses. Based on our family history, we all have certain medical conditions that we are more vulnerable to, especially when we are unduly stressed. The triggering of a depression can follow this medical paradigm.

Biological. All roads that cause a major depression lead to alterations in biochemical processes. Medical research has contributed a great deal to our understanding of the biochemistry underlying depression. Depression is thought to reflect an imbalance of neurotransmitters, the natural brain chemicals that allow brain cells to communicate with each other. A lack of bioavailability in these chemicals may cause a wide variety of psychological and physical changes.

Hence, there is the popular coining of the term *chemical imbalance* to describe depression. Among numerous neurotransmitters, an imbalance of serotonin, norepinephrine, and perhaps dopamine have been implicated as leading to depression.

Included in a biological cause of depression is evidence that major depression can be connected to a genetic predisposition. For this reason, a family history of medical illnesses is elicited in an initial evaluation. The incidence of genetic transmission is unclear, but it is clear that a family history of depression does not necessarily mean that descendants will develop depression. Again, other factors in one's life contribute to the likelihood of developing this medical disorder.

Alcohol, marijuana, narcotics, sedatives, and tranquilizers can cause or considerably worsen depression. Depression also typically follows withdrawal from cocaine, amphetamines, and even nicotine. Prescription medications (including antihypertensives, steroids, body-building steroids, and birth control pills), as well as many medical illnesses (such as hepatitis, infectious mononucleosis, cancer, or abnormal thyroid hormone levels), can also cause or complicate depression.

Psychosocial. Psychosocial causes of depression are many and varied. Why some people become depressed based on these factors is not entirely clear. Suffice it to say that the state-of-the-art view is that clinical depressions are medical illnesses. However, everyone has psychological issues that must be reworked in one's lifetime. These psychological conflicts may or may not have a causal relationship to depression. Any comprehensive evaluation of depression should consider these factors as well.

Effects and Workplace Recognition

Major depression has far greater effects on employees and organizations than are usually recognized. Depression is common and commonly unrecognized. Workplace recognition involves an appreciation for the official symptoms and time course for the depressive disorders. Additional symptoms can also alert the employees or the company that a coworker may be suffering a depression. Anxiety with a pervasive sense of dread can often accompany depression. Indeed, this sense of nervousness and agitation can sometimes mask depression. A preoccupation with physical symptoms and aches and pains can often be the predominant symptoms of depression, and depression is a major reason for visits to a primary care physician. Irritability and angry outbursts may be a prominent symptom of depression. Although alcohol and drug abuse can lead to depression, it is also possible that depression causes one to seek alcohol to self-medicate. Isolation from coworkers and avoiding office gatherings creates an atmosphere of discomfort and distrust. Overall behavior is less productive, less purposeful, and less helpful. Perhaps most significant, unrecognized depression can impair judgment, engender poor decisions, or produce ineffective management style. Tardiness, absenteeism, and accidents affect the morale of the whole workplace.

Sympathy for a person suffering from a major depressive disorder does not necessarily lead to effective referral and treatment. Well-meaning coworkers and managers may want to "protect" the employee from recognition of a serious illness or from treatments perceived as intrusive. Major depressive disorder can thus escape recognition or be addressed with minimal treatment approaches. Depression often comes on so slowly or surreptitiously that the employee remains unaware of the problem until crisis, confrontation, suicide, or accident supervenes. Major depression demands early detection and prompt referral.

Workplace Management and Referral

An initial intervention must always involve an underlying background of respect without a sense of patronizing. Establish a connection. If possible, talk to that person in a private surrounding. Explain that you've noticed a change in his work habits or his mood and that you are concerned. It is also important to acknowledge that you are not qualified to make a diagnosis of a depression, so expert advice is ultimately required. Discuss what you do know. Mention that depression is a medical illness just like high blood pressure or diabetes and is not looked on as a weakness of character. Depression is not that person's fault. It is also a mood that one cannot just "snap out of it." Explain that he or she is not alone in that depression is so common. Offer reading materials such as the NIMH brochure on depression or suggest Web sites that can answer questions. Finally, suggest that the coworker seek a confidential consultation with a psychiatrist. Some people feel that consulting a psychiatrist carries a stigma. Such a misperception is unfortunate, as a depression is considered to be a medical illness, and many psychiatrists treat emotional disturbances that are mild. A direct evaluation with a psychiatrist offers the advantage of seeking the expertise of a specialist who can provide comprehensive evaluation and treatment.

The organization itself can take several actions to help manage workplace stress and depression. Managers and supervisors can be trained and educated to identify people with depressive symptoms. They could also be provided with awareness training on managing employees with emotional disabilities.

During treatment and after recovery, it is helpful to talk directly to the affected employee about symptoms, medications, medical leave, time for medical appointments, and any workplace restrictions. Care must be taken to avoid intrusiveness. Suggestions or instructions should be simple and direct. Clearly defined work tasks, objectives, and report-back systems are also helpful during this adjustment time. Frequently, a reduced initial work schedule will ease readjustment to the workplace and demonstrate the employer's concern and support.

Psychiatric Management

The initial evaluation of a patient for depression begins with a full psychiatric medical examination. A history is taken, along with a full battery of laboratory tests. Medical illnesses as well as drugs and medications can contribute to or cause depression, and these causes must be ruled out.

Mood disorders are highly treatable. Most symptoms can be relieved in a few weeks, with more complete psychological recovery in four to twelve months. Milder forms of depression can sometimes be treated by psychotherapy alone. The most effective treatment for most clinical depressions is a combination of psychotherapy and antidepressant medication. There is good evidence that the combination of therapy and medications is more reliable and more effective in preventing relapse than when either treatment modality is used alone.

Medications. Antidepressants, available since the 1950s, have revolutionized the treatment for the clinical depressions. The early drugs were difficult to use because they affected a number of neurotransmitters in the brain and consequently had numerous undesirable side effects, such as dry mouth, dizziness, constipation, urinary hesitancy, sedation, heart palpitations, and weight gain. A relatively small dose that is ingested can also be lethal.

The new generation of antidepressants starting with fluoxetine (Prozac) in 1988 heralded a marked evolution in the treatment of depression. Science had developed the knowledge and tools to design drugs that are highly specific in their effects on serotonin and norepinephrine, two specific neurotransmitters in the brain that are implicated in depression. This newer generation of antidepressants became an instantaneous success; they were just as effective as the older antidepressants and with fewer and milder side effects because only specific neurotransmitters were affected. They were also much safer to use. Included in this newer generation are the selective serotonin reuptake inhibitors: fluoxetine (Prozac), sertraline (Zoloft), paroxetine (Paxil), and citalopram (Celexa). Other drugs with different mechanisms of action include buproprion (Wellbutrin), venlafaxine (Effexor), nefazadone (Serzone), and mirtazapine (Remeron). These drugs are among the most highly prescribed medications in the world, and all are considered to be effective. A doctor's recommendation of these drugs depends on the kind of depression, side effects, drug interactions, a doctor's familiarity with the drug, the effectiveness of a drug when used previously by the patient or the family, and the drug's availability on an insurance formulary. The older antidepressants are used with increasing rarity.

Antidepressants must be taken daily. In general, the gradual alleviation of depression begins in two to four weeks, although positive effects may sometimes take up to six to eight weeks. Symptom reduction includes a decrease in anxiety and obsessive rumination, improved sleep, a normalizing of appetite, increased energy, a return to normal interest, motivation, pleasure, improved concentration, and an erosion of negative thinking, and increased self-esteem and less guilt. Most people fully recover. Side effects are sometimes absent or are generally mild and transient, typically lasting up to two weeks. Depending on the type of drug, side effects can include headache, abdominal discomfort or nausea, lightheadedness, agitation, daytime sedation, insomnia, sweating, and weight loss. Sexual dysfunction can occur with certain drugs and is alleviated by a reduction in dose or change in medication. These drugs are not considered to be addictive. They do not provide the reinforcement of a high. A common statement is, "I don't feel I'm on a drug; I just feel better." The length of treatment varies from six months to years. There is no evidence of specific long-term deleterious side effects or medical disorders associated with antidepressants.

Some patients do not respond to the first antidepressant. A treatment strategy might then involve a switch to another antidepressant. Another option would be augmentation therapy, with the addition of another antidepressant, thyroid hormone, or lithium, or a stimulant such as dextroamphetamine. A monoamine oxidase inhibitor (MAOI) can be highly effective, but this class of drug requires extensive education regarding dietary and drug restrictions. When the label on an over-the-counter drug has a warning about the concomitant use of antidepressants, it is referring to MAOIs.

Psychotherapies. There is evidence that the combination of antidepressants and psychotherapy is more effective for preventing relapse than when either medication or psychotherapy is used alone. Effective psychotherapy can be relatively short term. Its purpose is to provide an education about depression, correct the distorted thinking that is present in depression, develop new coping mechanisms for future stressful events, and improve self-esteem by knowing and becoming more accepting of self.

The initial role of the psychiatrist is to give helpful guidance in understanding and dealing with depression. Psychotherapy then addresses prevention of recurrent depression by looking at coping skills and behavior patterns. Psychotherapeutic support is always beneficial during the suffering of depression. There is a variety of psychotherapies, but in the treatment of depression, most kinds fall under three categories: psychodynamic (insight oriented) therapy, cognitive-behavioral therapy, and interpersonal therapy:

- *Psychodynamic psychotherapy.* This insight-oriented form of therapy assumes that there is an unconscious self that powerfully affects one's daily life. The basic tenet is that one's unique biology and temperament, combined with the unique experiences of childhood and the resolution of universal developmental tasks, lead to some unresolved and unwitting ways of coping with internal conflicts. This compromised resolution was more or less adaptive in the past, but could now be maladaptive and lead to anxiety and depression. It aims for resolution of underlying issues by uncovering and understanding the unconscious conflict (conflicting hidden emotions) and emotionally resolving through these conflicts. One can then choose a more adaptive response to life and prevent a relapse of depression. A common misunderstanding of this form of therapy is that the focus is primarily focused on the past. In fact, the focus is more on linking the present with repeating patterns of the past. For instance, how a patient relates to the therapist in the waiting room may be related to an underlying theme in the session that day, interactions at work, and an unresolved interpersonal conflict with a parent. Such an insight allows for a clearer understanding of unconscious forces that affect one's daily life.

- *Cognitive-behavioral therapy.* The focus of this therapy emphasizes learning new ways of thinking to replace habitual negativity. The basic tenet is that by changing thinking, feelings change. The assumption is that the unconscious does not matter. The therapy involves identifying and categorizing various automatic distortions of thinking and doing exercises that will eventually lead to an equally valid way of thinking that will alleviate depression. Behavioral therapy focuses on specific goals to increase the depressed person's activity level, capacity for enjoyment, and ability to relax using specific relaxation techniques. Cognitive-behavioral therapy is a highly structured and directive approach.

- *Interpersonal psychotherapy.* The assumption is that disturbances in interpersonal relationships are a central cause of depression. The general goal is to improve social adjustment. This form of therapy, structured and directive in approach, is relatively new.

Many therapists combine these techniques in the treatment of depression. It is important that a prospective patient look for the right fit in choosing a psychotherapist. While seeing a therapist can sometimes feel intimidating at first, patients should start to feel more comfortable or better understood within a few sessions. Otherwise, another therapist might be considered. Although psychiatrists specialize in the medical treatment of depression, they are also well trained in the art of psychotherapy. With psychiatric psychotherapists, treatment can be combined so that both medication and therapy can be monitored closely and adjustments made quickly. Some depressed patients and therapists may prefer to use psychotherapy as a means of exploring deeper issues, while others may prefer to just seek more advice and exercises.

In the initial consultation with the therapist, a patient should inquire about the therapist's preferred approach to therapy and educational background. How much therapy a psychodynamic insight-oriented therapist has undergone is useful to determine. This kind of therapy requires more self-awareness from the therapist so as to be more objective in the therapeutic interaction.

Return to Work and ADA Reasonable Accommodation

Return to work and reasonable accommodation are linked to the severity and impairment of functionality, not to the diagnosis. In a severe major depressive disorder, medical leave may be two to four weeks or longer. When such a leave occurs, a return to work may initially involve a schedule of part-time work for one to two weeks. Reasonable accommodations may include providing time off for counseling and stress management groups, providing a mentor, providing additional training to learn new skills and responsibilities, scheduling regular meetings with the supervisor to discuss workplace issues, and parceling a large task into smaller ones so tasks do not seem so overwhelming.

Organizationally, return-to-work programs for employees can be developed with the assistance of mental health professionals. Employee assistance programs could also be expanded to help employees find solutions to non-work-related stressful situations.

DYSTHYMIA AND ATYPICAL DEPRESSION

Case 3

Joseph Carpino is a thirty-five-year-old aerospace engineer with an M.B.A. who was promoted to middle management three years ago. Although his performance was adequate, both he and his managers felt that his potential had not been optimized. Joe actually harbors a secret fantasy and expectation that he could become the CEO of the company someday. He holds himself to a very high standard and is continually disappointed. When he is complimented, he is typically dismissive and does not believe that the compliment is true. Joe has always been perceived as an under-achiever. Despite a high degree of intelligence as well as budding people skills, he always sells himself short. His friends often find themselves coaxing him to do more because of how inadequate he seems to feel. His demeanor is primarily serious and sometimes borders on the depressed. He can have a wry sense of humor if he is relaxed. The increased demands of his new role have made him increasingly fatigued. As soon as he gets home, he falls asleep in front of the television but then can't fall asleep in bed.

Diagnostic Overview

Dysthymia, roughly translated from the Greek as "ill humored," describes a chronic, intermittent, low-grade depressive mood disorder that frequently recurs or never completely disappears. The essential feature of dysthymia is that it is a low-grade chronic depression for much of most days that lasts for at least two years. There is evidence that the most common symptoms may be feelings of inadequacy, generalized loss of interest or pleasure, social withdrawal, feelings of guilt or brooding about the past, subjective feelings of irritability or excessive anger, and decreased activity, effectiveness, or productivity. The onset is often early and insidious. The low self-esteem and disinterest may be so chronic that the assumption is that these qualities are just part of one's personality. Also, there is often only mild impairment. Consequently, dysthymia can be difficult to diagnose, and there is a greater likelihood of recurrences. Dysthymia is a risk factor for developing a major depression in the future. Women are two to three times more likely to develop this disorder than men.

❧ Diagnostic Criteria for Dysthymic Disorder

A. Depressed mood for most of the day, for more days than not, as indicated either by subjective account or observation by others, for at least 2 years. *Note:* In children and adolescents, mood can be irritable and duration must be at least 1 year.
B. Presence, while depressed, of two (or more) of the following:
   1. poor appetite or overeating
   2. insomnia or hypersomnia
   3. low energy or fatigue
   4. low self-esteem
   5. poor concentration or difficulty making decisions
   6. feelings of hopelessness
C. During the 2-year period (1 year for children or adolescents) of the disturbance, the person has never been without the symptoms in Criteria A and B for more than 2 months at a time.
D. No Major Depressive Episode . . . has been present during the first 2 years of the disturbance (1 year for children and adolescents); i.e., the disturbance is not better accounted for by chronic Major Depressive Disorder, or Major Depressive Disorder, In Partial Remission.

Note: There may have been a previous Major Depressive Episode provided there was a full remission (no significant signs or symptoms for 2 months) before development of the Dysthymic Disorder. In addition, after the initial 2 years (1 year in children or adolescents) of Dysthymic Disorder, there may be superimposed episodes of Major Depressive Disorder, in which case both diagnoses may be given when the criteria are met for a Major Depressive Episode.

E. There has never been a Manic Episode . . . , a Mixed Episode . . . , or a Hypomanic Episode . . . , and criteria have never been met for Cyclothymic Disorder.
F. The disturbance does not occur exclusively during the course of a chronic Psychotic Disorder, such as Schizophrenia or Delusional Disorder.

G. The symptoms are not due to the direct physiological effects of a substance (e.g., a drug of abuse, a medication) or a general medical condition (e.g., hypothyroidism).
H. The symptoms cause clinically significant distress or impairment in social, occupational, or other important areas of functioning.

Specify if:

Early Onset: if onset is before age 21 years
Late Onset: if onset is age 21 years or older

Specify (for most recent 2 years of Dysthymic Disorder):

With Atypical Features

Reprinted with permission from the Diagnostic and Statistical Manual of Mental Disorders, Fourth Edition, Text Revision. *Copyright 2000 American Psychiatric Association.*

Atypical depression is an especially common and more specific form of dysthymia. Symptoms include a pattern of frequently depressed mood throughout adulthood, although the severity may be mild or moderate. During the depressive phases, patients commonly have increased appetite (often with cravings for sweets or chocolates), increased need for sleep, decreased energy (often feeling physically lethargic), and an ability to cheer up (temporarily) when something good happens. At all times, there is an increased sensitivity to interpersonal rejection and criticism, although this may not be evident to others.

Causes

In general, the causes for dysthymic disorder are biological and psychosocial, as in major depression. The biological causes are not as well studied but must be present since this disorder can be treated by antidepressant medications. An identifiable stressor is often not present because of its insidious and chronic nature. There is an increased incidence of dysthymia among biological relatives.

Effects and Workplace Recognition

Recognition of this disorder can be difficult. Dysthymic symptoms and behavioral patterns become viewed as a normal way of life for that person. Consequently, dysthymia in the workplace might be recognized in hindsight after other associated conditions have occurred. A severe depression may be the initial presentation in the workplace since dysthymic individuals are more prone to a major depressive disorder. Alcoholism or substance abuse symptoms might initially bring the dysthymic individual to the attention of the organization. Other indirect symptoms might be excessive physical ailments and medical leave. Often, the individual suffering from dysthymia is perceived as having a personality that is "always" lazy, underachieving, withdrawn, irritable, disinterested, or negative.

Such a person might be excessively sensitive to rejection and criticism. This exquisite sensitivity might result in a withdrawal from fellow workers or a passive lack of cooperation. Alternatively, there may be overcompensation from the hurt and lack of self-worth by repeated confrontations with fellow workers, excessive complaining about work assignments, or misperceptions about perceived discrimination in the workplace.

Workplace Management and Referral

The general principles for workplace management described for major depression apply for interventions involving those with dysthymia. It would be even more important to emphasize that this low-grade depression is not a weakness of character and can be treated by psychiatric intervention. When self-blame can already be prominent, it may be helpful to suggest that one seek "counseling" rather than "psychotherapy." Mentoring could be offered to provide support and clarify expectations. Clarifying accountability in a consistent and supportive manner can be particularly helpful for the dysthymic individual.

Psychiatric Management

Psychiatric treatment is similar for the treatment of major depression. Antidepressant medications can be very effective for the treatment of dysthymia, but the percentage of those responsive to medications is somewhat less when compared to a major depression. However, those with the atypical depression subtype are highly responsive to the SSRI antidepressants. Accompanying anxiety disorders may also need specific treatment. Psychotherapy is as essential for major depression, and for an additional reason as well. Because of chronic maladaptive patterns and the recurrent nature of the disorder, psychotherapy needs to address the novel feeling of well-being that comes with medication response, and a longer treatment is often appropriate.

Return to Work and ADA Reasonable Accommodation

Treatment for dysthymia does not generally require a medical leave. A reasonable accommodation may be a more flexible work schedule where an allowance is made for the treatment time. For instance, the person could be allowed to attend weekly psychotherapy sessions or stress management classes and then make up for the missed work time.

BIPOLAR DISORDER

Case 4

Jim Braithwaite was the thirty-two-year-old co-owner of a highly successful insurance agency. He was the most effective salesperson and the resident business genius. One day, he startled his partners by announcing that he had found the key to their future success. Without their knowledge, he had bought a failing business. He assured them that he could turn it around quickly, and with intense work, the new acquisition was profitable in four weeks. Buoyed by this success, Jim decided he could save his city from slow deterioration. He abruptly donated half of his savings to charity and announced plans to run for mayor. He put intense pressure on his best clients to "give until it hurts," and many of them left the agency. He became furious when his partners questioned his activities, and they quickly forced him out of the company. Feeling angry, discouraged, and victimized, Jim left his wife behind and moved to Washington, D.C. He spent most of the next month sleeping in a seedy motel room. After a short time, he felt a familiar surge of energy and began looking up lobbyists and senators. He began visiting hot singles' bars. Hearing the voice of God, he decided to run for Congress to save the world. He called everyone he knew for political support. Many of the calls were late at night, and he sounded incoherent. He was always turned down, and each time he would hurl insults before hanging up in midsentence. One evening at a singles bar, Jim started dancing on a table. When he started stripping off his clothes, the police were called and took him to a hospital.

Diagnostic Overview

The essential feature of bipolar disorder is a history of an episode of mania. Mania, a mood of euphoria or expansiveness, is the opposite of depression. Most people with bipolar disorder also have episodes of a major depression. Hence, this illness is often called manic-depressive disorder. Bipolar disorder is considered a recurrent disorder; 90 percent of those diagnosed as having a manic episode have future occurrences of either mania or depression. Without treatment, it is expected that on average there are about four episodes of either mania or depression in a ten-year period. Also, the interval between episodes tends to shorten with aging. There are many variations of bipolar disorder. Bipolar I disorder requires the classic symptoms of mania. Bipolar II disorder requires a history of an episode of hypomania (a milder form of mania) and an episode of major depression. Another variation may be a mixture of manic and depressed symptoms at the same time. Others may experience a variant of rapid cycling, characterized as having four separate episodes of mania or depression in one year. Most often, there is a recurrence of the illness if left untreated. In the depressed state, there is evidence that the suicide rate may be higher than for the suicidal patient who has a major depression.

❖ Diagnostic Criteria for Bipolar I Disorder, Single Manic Episode
A.   Presence of only one Manic Episode and no past Major Depressive Episodes.

Note: Recurrence is defined as either a change in polarity from depression or an interval of at least 2 months without manic symptoms.

B. The Manic Episode is not better accounted for by Schizoaffective Disorder and is not superimposed on Schizophrenia, Schizophreniform Disorder, Delusional Disorder, or Psychotic Disorder Not Otherwise Specified.

Specify if:

Mixed: if symptoms meet criteria for a Mixed Episode

If the full criteria are currently met for a Manic, Mixed, or Major Depressive Episode, specify its current clinical status and/or features:

Mild, Moderate, Severe Without Psychotic Features/Severe With Psychotic Features
With Catatonic Features
With Postpartum Onset

If the full criteria are not currently met for a Manic, Mixed, or Major Depressive Episode, specify the current clinical status of the Bipolar I Disorder or features of the most recent episode:

In Partial Remission, In Full Remission
With Catatonic Features
With Postpartum Onset

Reprinted with permission from the Diagnostic and Statistical Manual of Mental Disorders, Fourth Edition, Text Revision. *Copyright 2000 American Psychiatric Association.*

❧ Diagnostic Criteria for Bipolar I Disorder, Most Recent Episode Hypomanic

A. Currently (or most recently) in a Hypomanic Episode.
B. There has previously been at least one Manic Episode or Mixed Episode.
C. The mood symptoms cause clinically significant distress or impairment in social, occupational, or other important areas of functioning.
D. The mood episodes in Criteria A and B are not better accounted for by Schizoaffective Disorder and are not superimposed on Schizophrenia, Schizophreniform Disorder, Delusional Disorder, or Psychotic Disorder Not Otherwise Specified.

Specify:

Longitudinal Course Specifiers (With and Without Interepisode Recovery)
With Seasonal Pattern (applies only to the pattern of Major Depressive Episodes)
With Rapid Cycling

Reprinted with permission from the Diagnostic and Statistical Manual of Mental Disorders, Fourth Edition, Text Revision. *Copyright 2000 American Psychiatric Association.*

❖ Diagnostic Criteria for Bipolar I Disorder, Most Recent Episode Manic

A. Currently (or most recently) in a Manic Episode.

B. There has previously been at least one Major Depressive Episode, Manic Episode, or Mixed Episode

C. The mood episodes in Criteria A and B are not better accounted for by Schizoaffective Disorder and are not superimposed on Schizophrenia, Schizophreniform Disorder, Delusional Disorder, or Psychotic Disorder Not Otherwise Specified.

If the full criteria are currently met for a Manic Episode, specify its current clinical status and/or features:

Mild, Moderate, Severe Without Psychotic Features/Severe With Psychotic Features
With Catatonic Features
With Postpartum Onset

If the full criteria are not currently met for a Manic Episode, specify the current clinical status of the Bipolar I Disorder and/or features of the most recent Manic Episode:

In Partial Remission, In Full Remission
With Catatonic Features
With Postpartum Onset

Specify:

Longitudinal Course Specifiers (With and Without Interepisode Recovery)
With Seasonal Pattern (applies only to the pattern of Major Depressive Episodes)
With Rapid Cycling

Reprinted with permission from the Diagnostic and Statistical Manual of Mental Disorders, Fourth Edition, Text Revision. *Copyright 2000 American Psychiatric Association.*

Causes

There is strong evidence for a genetic influence as a cause for a bipolar I disorder. However, genes are only one causal factor that results in some family members suffering from this medical disorder while others are unscathed. Like the other mood disorders, individual vulnerability is influenced by a complex combination of childhood experiences, maladaptive responses, and external stresses. Again, all roads lead to alterations in biochemistry in the brain, but less is known about what actually occurs that results in the symptoms of mania. There is some evidence that sleep deprivation or changes in time zone can not only disrupt sleep but can also cause manic symptoms. Medical illnesses can mimic manic symptoms. Medications such as cortisone can also cause manic symptoms. As is true for all other medical illnesses, psychosocial factors can also be a major cause in triggering bipolar disorder.

Effects and Workplace Recognition

Nothing else stirs up the workplace like a case of full-blown mania. At best, it is disturbing; at worst, it is extremely disruptive. If the person with mania is mixed, with moods changing every few hours or days, the accompanying behavior will leave fellow employees bewildered and scared. Even if mania abates and a period of normalcy follows, a depressive phase will soon begin. Without treatment, mania can last for months, and over that time the manic individual can do irreparable physical, mental, social, and financial damage to self and to others. By the time mania is detected, there may be extreme grandiosity and rejection of normal rules of behavior. It may be impossible to convince the individual of the seriousness of the situation and the need for treatment.

Organizations can appear to benefit from the first stage of mania. The affected individual is still coherent enough to be effective, and the characteristic optimism and high energy can even increase the enthusiasm of other employees. However, things soon begin to fall apart. Mistakes and misjudgments appear; the manic individual becomes increasingly irritable, stubborn, and aggressive; and what had seemed to be shared productive activity becomes a loud, frantic nightmare. Sometimes the manic worker is the first one to try to put on the brakes, sensing that the situation has gotten out of control. Nevertheless, there may be sudden resentment, rage, or paranoia, often from thoughts of being denied sufficient credit for the productivity boom, or else from feeling misunderstood.

Bipolar II disorder with hypomania can be much more difficult to discern, even by a psychiatrist. In this milder state, behavior may viewed as part of one's personality. The person who suffers a bipolar II disorder may initially be perceived as likable and charismatic because of an uncritical self-confidence, outspokenness, and lack of doubt. Productivity and efficiency may be increased. Indeed, many of these people may be leaders in the organization or outstanding performers in their field. However, their performance could also be erratic because of depressive episodes where they have disappeared or their performance has noticeably waned. Eventually, such people can become annoying, overbearing, demanding, and impulsive with poor judgment.

The depressive phase can also have a significant effect on coworkers. The worker's depressed mood can be as infectious as the emphatically upbeat mood that preceded it, and a generally lower morale and diminished level of productivity may ensue. The effects of bipolar disorder in the workplace are confusing and potentially pervasive and disturbing. They must be dealt with promptly and frankly.

Workplace Management and Referral

In the depressed phase of the individual with a bipolar disorder, the anguish that is felt can be a motivating factor in obtaining help. However, when that person is in a manic or hypomanic phase, there is less motivation. Even mental health professionals can have difficulty convincing the person that a bipolar disorder is present and that the consequences could be dire. There is very little motivation to change if you are feeling great, you are supremely confident, you find yourself thinking faster and more creatively than others, and you are the center of attention and adoration. The thought of having a medical disorder that is limiting does not make sense.

The basic principles of intervening with an employee with a mood disorder apply here too. Consultation with a psychiatrist is especially important with these potentially difficult cases. A bipolar disorder is first and foremost a medical illness and requires the expertise of psychiatrists who are trained in the medical and psychotherapy aspects of treatment. When an employee's performance is erratic, the company may require an intervention. Such an intervention should be based on the erratic behavior in the work setting.

A medical leave is usually required for the initial treatment of a bipolar disorder, but a return to work is often possible within several weeks. Restoring the worker's immediate work environment and coworker relationships to a smoothly functioning state can take longer. Following a manic episode, self-esteem and quality of interpersonal relationships are often at an unprecedented low. Moreover, there may have been behavior that resulted in disastrous consequences for relationships, finances, and work. Even so, bipolar patients are characteristically highly motivated and productive employees who enjoy their work. They generally readjust to the workplace quickly and appropriately.

Management should minimize stress and stimulation, streamline responsibilities wherever possible, and check to make sure that psychiatric medication and therapy are continuing. Responsibilities should be increased as soon as reasonably possible.

Psychiatric Management

Although it can be difficult to establish a therapeutic alliance with the bipolar patient, the vast majority of patients respond well to the combined support of medication and psychotherapy. An extensive medical, psychotherapeutic, and psychopharmacological background is essential. Mood stabilizers are the foundation of treatment.

Lithium carbonate was the first mood stabilizer discovered and remains the gold standard to which other mood stabilizers are compared. Lithium is highly effective for treating the acute manic phase and preventing relapse and can also prevent repeated episodes of depression for many people. It requires psychiatric supervision to monitor blood levels and side effects. Blood tests are done infrequently after the stabilization of mood.

Numerous other drugs are also available as effective medications for the acute and maintenance treatment of bipolar disorder. Valproic acid (Depakote) is now considered a first-line treatment along with lithium, especially for a mixed type of bipolar disorder where one has both manic and depressed symptoms. Another anticonvulsant medication that has been highly effective is carbamazepine (Tegretol). Recently, additional anticonvulsants used include gabapentin (Neurontin), lamotrigine (Lamictal), and topiramate (Topamax). Also, the Food and Drug Administration has recently approved olanzapine (Zyprexa) for the treatment of bipolar disorder.

As with all other medications, mood stabilizers can also have side effects, but they are generally benign and transient, and the benefits far outweigh the risks. Frequently, a combination of medications is needed to treat the depression and anxiety and other symptoms. In addition to one or even two mood stabilizers, an antidepressant or an antianxiety medication might be added.

Psychotherapy might initially involve support and education regarding the illness and the use of medications. When the person has become stable, therapy may take the form of the psychotherapies used in the treatment of major depression. Family members may be involved. Bipolar disorders vary markedly in severity. On rare occasion, a brief hospitalization may be required.

Return to Work and ADA Reasonable Accommodation

Medical leave and reasonable accommodation is more a reflection of severity and not diagnosis. However, for those suffering from a bipolar I disorder in the manic or mixed state, a medical leave of absence is often required for four to six weeks. The initial return to work may be in the form of half-time work for one to two weeks to help with the readjustment to the workplace. Since a bipolar disorder is a chronic medical disorder requiring indefinite psychiatric treatment, a reasonable accommodation would be a more flexible work schedule to allow for time off for psychiatric treatment. The missed time off could then be made up. The principles described for reasonable accommodation for a major depression apply as well for a bipolar disorder.

Throughout human history, depression has inspired passionately waged debates regarding the separation of mind and body. Until recently, depression has been seen as a weakness of the mind. The debate has now been laid to rest. The mind and body are intimately entwined. How we feel about ourselves and perceive the world leads to changes in our brain chemistry, which can lead to changes in how we feel. Biochemistry can be changed by medications and by psychotherapy. Clinical depressions are among the most common medical disorders that plague people. Medical science now has much more effective tools in combating these debilitating disorders and restoring one to a full life. Many advances have been made in the understanding and treatment of the mood disorders, and many more advances are on the way.

References and Additional Sources

American Psychiatric Association. (1994). *Diagnostic and statistical manual of mental disorders* (4th ed.). Washington, DC: Author.

Bloomfield, H., & McWilliams, P. (1995). *How to heal depression.* Bundall Queensland, Australia: Prelude.

Burns, D. (1990) *The feeling good handbook.* New York: Plume.

Burns, D. (1999). *Feeling good, the new mood therapy.* New York: MassMarket.

DePaulo, J. R., & Horvitz, L. A. (2001). *Understanding depression: What we know and what you can do about it.* New York: Wiley.

Greist, J. (1994). *Depression and its treatment.* New York: Warner Books.

Jamison, K. (1997). *An unquiet mind.* New York: Random House.

Kramer, P. (1994). *Listening to Prozac.* New York: Penguin.

Murray, C.J.L., & Lopez, A. D. (Eds.). (1996). *Summary: The global burden of disease: A comprehensive assessment of mortality and disability from diseases, injuries, and risk factors in 1990 and projected to 2020.* Cambridge, MA: Harvard University Press.

Offson, M., Marcus, S. C., Druss, B., Elinson, L., Tanielian, T., & Pincus, H. A. (2002). National trends in the outpatient treatment of depression. *Journal of the American Medical Association, 287,* 203–209.

Regier, D. A., Narrow, W. E., Rae, D. S., Manderscheid, R. W., Locke, B. Z., & Goodwin, F. K. (1993). The de facto mental and addictive disorders service system: Epidemiologic catchment area prospective one-year prevalence rates of disorders and services. *Archives of General Psychiatry, 50*(2), 85–94.

Strock, M. (2000). *Plain talk about depression.* Rockville, MD: National Institutes of Health.

U.S. Surgeon General. (1999). *Mental health: A report of the surgeon general.* Available on-line at: http://www.surgeongeneral.gov/library/mentalhealth/chapter2/sec2_1html#epidemiology.

CHAPTER TWENTY-THREE

Personality

Personalities, Personal Style, and
Trouble Getting Along

Mark P. Unterberg

Of all the psychiatric problems that face organizations today, one of the most
insidious can be the otherwise high-functioning individual with a severe
personality disorder. These individuals create multilevel problems that defy
easy detection and definition due to the intermingling of their health and
pathology. They are usually much harder to recognize than the obvious
depressive or alcoholic. Their personality causes repeated but subtle
disruption in the workforce and in decision-making processes.

All business is personal. Whether on the assembly line or in the corporate boardroom, the workplace is made up of people with complex combinations of personality traits. Success in the workplace requires technical abilities as well as professional presence, but it is most profoundly determined by personality. Other than computers talking with each other, there is no workplace situation that does not involve personal and subjective aspects between individuals. The common expression "It's nothing personal, just business," is interesting just because it attempts to deny the significant contribution of personality to the workplace.

Decisions are constantly made out of a personal frame of reference that determines workplace perceptions. No matter how hard the effort, even the most determinedly objective decisions are ultimately affected by personality style. Productive organizations and good employee mental health require careful attention to individual personality traits and difficulties.

This chapter focuses primarily on maladaptive personality traits in otherwise reasonably or even exceptionally competent individuals. The consequent effects on both themselves and their workplace environment always have a significant impact. There is a subtle interplay between the environment and with both the

458

adaptive and maladaptive traits. As circumstances and individuals change, the personality assets and strengths of a relatively healthy employee can become destructive to the team effort. Employees who suffer from more recognizable depression, psychosis, and even substance abuse may create more obvious problems for the organization. But personality traits that become problematic under stress can create insidious and slowly progressive havoc. Even senior mental health professionals will sometimes leave maladaptive personality traits unrecognized. It is essential to maintain business and mental health professionals' awareness of the subtle and sometimes destructive effects of personality in the organizational setting.

There is no way to avoid bringing personality traits to the workplace. The psychological structures that define unique and separate individuals can be neither eliminated nor avoided. Personality is a reflection of emotional defenses (ways of operating) that individuals develop in reaction to interpersonal circumstances over the years. These defenses, called compromise formations, derive from the survival instinct to create a balance between internal emotional needs and the demands of external reality. There are always needs and instinctual desires to be gratified. Under ideal circumstances, personality is a complex set of psychological decisions that helps ensure a balance and calmness that foster maximal productivity, creativity, and enjoyment.

Established patterns of emotional defenses form personality traits that seek the most harmonious possible adaptation to external realities and present the unique individual to the world. We are like psychological fingerprints with no other identical in the world. Initially formed in childhood, defenses can be modified by experience. The most adaptive personalities are flexible in response to changing internal and external circumstances. Loss, growth, distress, pleasure, and change are ever present. While much has been written about interpersonal relationships in the social arena, there has been far less attention to personality adaptation at work.

Personality disorders represent defects in emotional defenses and resultant compromise formations. The psychological structure set in place to help the individual achieve maximum potential in a given environment is poorly adapted to newer circumstances. Perceptions and decisions become nonproductive and even repetitively self-destructive. Unwittingly, maladaptive personality traits now prevent attainment of desired goals. It is important to remember the difference between personality traits and disorders. Pronounced personality traits can exist without a personality disorder. Personality disorders exist when there is a distinct pattern of excessive, inflexible, and consistently self-destructive personality traits.

Adaptive individuals can modify their personality traits through experience. Actions lead to consequences, and assessment of those consequences is used to modify responses to similar problems in the future. In varying degrees, this process goes on throughout life and allows a high degree of balance and well-being. Life in both social and work arenas goes pretty well. But when there is a personality disorder, actions are unresponsive to their consequences. Faced with adverse feedback from the environment, the same behaviors are still repeated over and over. There is a defect in the feedback loop. Adverse consequences are either ignored or not perceived, or else there is an inability to modify behavior. There is something wrong in the old trial-and-error method. Most people with personality disorders tend to think that the problem resides with others or in the environment and not within themselves. This allows us to see workplace problems from a psychological perspective. Employees with personality disorders always have positive personality traits and characteristics. Otherwise, they would not have been hired in the first place. However, the maladaptive and inflexible patterns can emerge under stress.

Figuring out what to do requires good clinical data and judgment to assess personality issues in the workplace and help the employee make necessary changes to become a productive worker. More sophisticated understanding of underlying mechanisms allows the clinical information to be organized into useful and understandable findings and recommendations.

OBSESSIVE COMPULSIVE: OVERINVOLVED, UNDERACHIEVING EMPLOYEES

Case 1

Herbert Kroft is a thirty-four-year-old single man who was hired to head up the accounting section of a medium-sized firm. He replaced a recently retired, popular department head and was assigned the task of revamping the accounting department's collection methods. He dressed impeccably and spoke in an articulate, clear, and precise manner. After six months, four out of nine employees in his department had tendered their resignations. They complained that Herbert was impossible to work with and that no matter what they did, it was never good enough for him. Management and Herbert's supervisor found that their own interactions usually went well and that a major overhaul of the department was proceeding quickly and precisely.

In the next six months, three more people left. Two of them complained that the office atmosphere was oppressive. Although Herbert surprised management by his marathon work hours, his leadership reputation continued to suffer. His accusers called him moralistic, judgmental, and almost tyrannically perfectionistic. They felt that his only concern was for the production of his section, with little concern for employee morale. He would cancel vacations on short notice and be clearly irritated by leave requests for personal problems. Despite Herbert's long work hours, over the next year, more and more of his reports and projects were late. Herbert also started a pattern of frequent visits to his supervisor's office to discuss minute details of accounting system flaws, sometimes in heated terms. Herbert was starting to miss the big picture.

Events came to a head on the day his entire department threatened to resign en masse if the supervisor didn't do something about Herbert's effect on department morale. The supervisor called Herbert to his office, and as usual, Herbert didn't budge. He figured that his subordinates were only trying to shirk their responsibilities. He couldn't see their point of view or even acknowledge that they might have some legitimate grievances. After talking with the CEO, the supervisor recommended that Herbert see a consulting psychiatrist or accept suspension until the situation was reviewed.

In treatment, Herbert began to understand that he had a problem. With much work, he was able to start changing his usual approaches to people at work. Gradually, his behavior became more appropriate and less of a problem for his supervisor. He was still more concerned with fine details than others, but therapy helped him to use this skill for productive work. Herbert also learned to recognize that even his less obsessional subordinates could do a first-rate job if only he let them. Although his workers gradually noticed the change in him, his reputation lingered. Herbert stayed in individual therapy for a year and a half. He was happy enough with his experience that he went on to recommend treatment to others.

Diagnosis

Obsessive-compulsive personality style is usually an asset to a business, because of the intense dedication to work that it may entail, often to the exclusion of family and other outside life. When the traits become excessive, however, there can be a detrimental increase in inflexibility and perfectionism and an emotional need to make the world conform to a personal perception. Since obsessional traits make it hard to see what went wrong, further difficulties can result from confrontation, isolation, or termination.

❖ Diagnostic Criteria for Obsessive-Compulsive Personality Disorder

A pervasive pattern of preoccupation with orderliness, perfectionism, and mental and interpersonal control, at the expense of flexibility, openness, and efficiency, beginning by early adulthood and present in a variety of contexts, as indicated by four (or more) of the following:

1. is preoccupied with details, rules, lists, order, organization, or schedules to the extent that the major point of the activity is lost
2. shows perfectionism that interferes with task completion (e.g., is unable to complete a project because his or her own overly strict standards are not met)
3. is excessively devoted to work and productivity to the exclusion of leisure activities and friendships (not accounted for by obvious economic necessity)

4. is overconscientious, scrupulous, and inflexible about matters of morality, ethics, or values (not accounted for by cultural or religious identification)

5. is unable to discard worn-out or worthless objects even when they have no sentimental value

6. is reluctant to delegate tasks or to work with others unless they submit to exactly his or her way of doing things

7. adopts a miserly spending style toward both self and others; money is viewed as something to be hoarded for future catastrophes

8. shows rigidity and stubbornness

Reprinted with permission from the Diagnostic and Statistical Manual of Mental Disorders, Fourth Edition, Text Revision. *Copyright 2000 American Psychiatric Association.*

Obsessive-compulsive personality is not the same as obsessive-compulsive disorder (OCD; see Chapter Twenty-One). Obsessive-compulsive personality traits do not grossly interfere with functioning and are not accompanied by intense anxiety. In fact, the personality style is felt as quite appropriate, while others are blamed for any problems.

The etiology of obsessive-compulsive personality disorder is uncertain, but is thought to derive primarily from early difficulties in dealing with the emotional environment. In the workplace, traits can be exacerbated by increasing intensity, complexity, or importance of work or by a perceived decrease in support from superiors. There is always a push for perfection, and with more variables it gets harder to achieve that end. Perhaps more important, a perceived loss of support intensifies inner emotions and need for perfection. Too often, the forest can't be seen for the trees. Increasing brittleness and tension begins to have a strong effect on coworkers, who then see a humorless, difficult, moralistic, or aggressive colleague.

Workplace Management and Referral

Obsessive-compulsive employees are difficult to recognize in the workplace. They usually work hard, see themselves as productive and appropriate, and blame others whom they see as less than perfect. Problems are most commonly pointed out by coworkers and subordinates, and less often are immediately recognizable in the obsessive-compulsive employee by their superiors. And it is not always easy to discuss the problems with someone who sees the causes lying elsewhere. When usual performance evaluation and management approaches are not sufficient, referral for psychiatric evaluation may be helpful.

The prognosis for introspective employees is good. The ability to recognize their contribution to the problems is essential to their understanding and then modifying their counterproductive behavior. In fact, modification of personality defenses will often permit a higher level of productivity and personableness than before. Recognition of change requires careful supervisory awareness, as well as attention to possible future problems.

Psychiatric Management

The initial consultation reviews the current problem and past history and looks for associated life events and mood disorders that may have made things worse. Once a need for psychotherapy has been established, the initial phase of therapy is used to establish a nonthreatening atmosphere. Obsessive-compulsive traits have typically been used for emotional self-protection since childhood. The early phase of treatment also allows initial recognition of counterproductive behaviors and associated emotions. The counterproductive traits are often intensely driven psychological defenses against threatening hidden emotions and fears. A central goal of psychotherapy is to uncover fears of what would happen if behavior is modified and if a more balanced life is then attempted. In particular, therapy focuses on interactions with other people.

HISTRIONIC: OVEREMOTIONAL, OVERREACTIVE EMPLOYEES

Case 2

Sandra Green is a twenty-seven-year-old single woman who was hired for a middle management position in the marketing department. She came with excellent references and had impressed the head of marketing with her intelligence, quick wit, and extremely attractive appearance. Sandra quickly became part of the group. Within days, she had personally sought out each of her colleagues, introducing herself and winning them over with her humor, personality, style, and helpfulness to the department. She dressed better than anyone else at the office, and her male coworkers particularly liked her. Despite her recent arrival, she quickly established herself at meetings by presenting novel ideas that needed lengthy discussion. Even so, Sandra didn't actually seem to get much done.

Over the next few months, it became increasingly clear to some coworkers that she needed inordinate amounts of attention. Sandra kept finding ways to put herself on center stage. She started to date three male coworkers simultaneously, while at the same time her female colleagues found her increasingly competitive, uncooperative, and unsympathetic. A crisis developed when Sandra complained hysterically to her male supervisor that the other women in the office had not invited her to a Friday evening happy hour. She angrily decried how badly she was treated by the other women in the department, despite her own unusually considerate efforts. In dramatic terms, Sandra said she was a helpless victim of "jealous and competitive" female colleagues. She was very convincing.

The supervisor called an office meeting. Sandra subtly castigated some other employees for not appreciating her work. Several people asked her not to monopolize discussion time at business meetings. Some also complained that she spent more time at coffee breaks with men than on group projects. After the meeting was over, Sandra stormed into the supervisor's office. She demanded that a couple of people be threatened with termination if they tried to interfere with her performance or social life. She also suggested that a closer relationship with the supervisor could help them both and suggested continuing the discussion over lunch or dinner. Flattered at first, the supervisor suddenly became aware of Sandra's seductiveness and her effects on morale. He realized too that her work lacked the quality and depth that her references and initial plans had seemed to predict. The next week, he asked her to seek a consultation.

In consultation, the psychiatrist recognized the full spectrum of histrionic personality traits, as well as symptoms of a chronic mild atypical depression (see Chapter Twenty-Two). Importantly, he also discovered that she had left her previous job after a failed long-term romance with a colleague there. Although that relationship had always been rocky, she felt devastated by the breakup and increasingly despondent about her future social prospects. Sandra was referred for individual and group psychotherapy and started on phenelzine, an antidepressant. When her mood started to improve within three weeks, there was a marked reduction in office tensions.

Even so, Sandra had great difficulty recognizing and accepting that she played a significant role in her problems. When she was able to see this as a product of early childhood fears and wishes, though, she gradually began to make corrections. Her dress became more appropriate, and she no longer needed quite so much attention. She became increasingly aware of her oversensitivity to others and was able to respond appropriately.

In less than a year, coworkers were well aware of the changes that Sandra had made. Her work improved, and her romantic life was conducted outside the office. Although she still took up a lot of meeting time, she could catch the hint to finish and would often end a speech with humor.

Diagnosis

Employees with histrionic traits may initially come across as particularly attractive or seductive. Their dress, behavior, and demeanor all contribute to an emotional, even sexual, allure. Without awareness, they often use their attractiveness to achieve other goals or wishes. Coworkers often perceive an immature or infantile inability to recognize failings or even to acknowledge the potential validity of other people's observations. Instead, there appears to be an insatiable appetite for attention and a dramatically embellished manner of speaking. More problems arise in the workplace when exaggerated emotions bother other employees, stir up competitive and jealous feelings, lead to excessive controversy, or contribute to overblown promises and incomplete assignments.

❖ Diagnostic Criteria for Histrionic Personality Disorder

A pervasive pattern of excessive emotionality and attention seeking, beginning by early adulthood and present in a variety of contexts, as indicated by five (or more) of the following:

1. is uncomfortable in situations in which he or she is not the center of attention
2. interaction with others is often characterized by inappropriate sexually seductive or provocative behavior
3. displays rapidly shifting and shallow expression of emotions
4. consistently uses physical appearance to draw attention to self
5. has a style of speech that is excessively impressionistic and lacking in detail
6. shows self-dramatization, theatricality, and exaggerated expression of emotion
7. is suggestible, i.e., easily influenced by others or circumstances
8. considers relationships to be more intimate than they actually are

Reprinted with permission from the Diagnostic and Statistical Manual of Mental Disorders, Fourth Edition, Text Revision. *Copyright 2000 American Psychiatric Association.*

Histrionic personality traits are commonly demonstrated through overly emotional reactions to everyday situations. Tension and emotional excitability are combined with inappropriate exaggeration of relatively normal happy, sad, or angry feelings. Histrionic traits are commonly exaggerated under the stress of personal or work problems or if there is a concurrent depression or anxiety disorder. In particular, atypical depression can be associated with exacerbated histrionic traits. Nevertheless, these two syndromes are thought to have differing causes and treatments.

Workplace Management and Referral

Histrionic personality traits give an appearance of immaturity. An employee may feel that his attractive qualities entitle him to special treatment and may feel angry at a more emotionally stable supervisor. That anger can lead to unwitting manipulations designed to attract attention from those in authority.

Initially, management should help to set boundaries by providing the employee with clear rules, expectations, feedback, and modeling. Here, too, referral for consultation can be useful when problems persist. As with other personality disorders, histrionic employees may take the stance that their problems are caused by other people. It may be especially difficult in the workplace to address any problems of inappropriate relationships, personal dress, or seductive style. The prognosis is quite good when there are strengths that can enhance social and work activities and a capacity to develop introspection and change.

Psychiatric Management

When therapy begins, the patient often feels upset about undeserved criticisms or losses. There may be substantial, if partially unwitting, attempts to convince the therapist to offer sympathy for the perceived victimization. Unprovoked, behaviors and perceptions from outside soon start to appear within the therapy itself. Drawing a parallel to behaviors at work and at home, the patient can now begin to recognize counterproductive behaviors and painful underlying emotions. It is important for the therapist to remain empathic with the patient's distress yet not be unduly influenced by the intensely expressed emotions. In fact, therapist awareness of some of the feelings generated will provide information about how others react to the patient outside the therapeutic setting. Gradually, by using observation of behaviors along with exploration of how these may be connected with the past, the therapist can eventually help address the self-destructive traits, while recognizing the positive and engaging elements.

ANTISOCIAL: CRIMINAL OR AGGRESSIVE EMPLOYEES

Case 3

Phil Dixon is a thirty-five-year-old recently divorced shipping department employee who had impressed the job interviewer with his intelligence and style. Phil worked hard at first and impressed his supervisor. However, within several months, he started a pattern of calling in sick and taking family leave days. Sometimes when a personal crisis pulled him away in midday, his job assignments got fouled up or had to be completed by someone else. There were increasing reports to the supervisor about Phil's lack of consideration for coworkers. The complaints were mostly that Phil was avoiding work. And since his arrival, several expensive items had disappeared from the shipping department. Although Phil was a likeable man who socialized with the others, he sometimes became irritable and aggressive. Because this would happen when people disagreed with him or crossed him, he found it easy to get personal loans from coworkers, as well as advances on his salary.

Phil's difficulties culminated when housekeeping discovered some of the missing items in his locker during routine cleaning. When Phil was confronted, he claimed that someone must have planted the items there in order to sabotage his job status. His explanation was so tearful and convincing that the supervisor thought he was telling the truth. But coworkers had long suspected Phil and had not had much luck getting their money back from him. Some of their own things were missing too. When Phil met with the supervisor again, he became irate and threatened to walk off the job immediately.

Feeling confused and threatened and recognizing a significant personality problem, the supervisor asked Phil to see a psychiatric consultant. Phil said that he was going for therapy, but it was nearly a month before the supervisor realized that Phil never even went for the consultation.

Case 4

At age forty-six, Tom Newman was a senior vice president of the Zeilig Manufacturing Company. The busy CEO had recognized his adroit accomplishments, and Tom had risen rapidly through the ranks. Although there had long been quiet rumors about Tom's engaging in possibly improper activities, the stories, most of which came from disgruntled former subordinates, were passed off by a CEO preoccupied with other concerns. Eventually, a former female employee filed suit against Tom and the company, claiming he had intimidated her into a sexual relationship. The director of human resources was then surprised to hear similar stories from four other past and current employees.

Further investigation included review of Tom's extravagant travel expenses. Despite some records that disappeared, it appeared that he had padded as much as $80,000 over four years. Careful review of Tom's initial job application revealed that he had been suspended twice from college for cheating and theft, that he hadn't actually gone to graduate school at all, and that he had failed to acknowledge a conviction for tax evasion in his twenties. When confronted with some of these allegations, Tom denied any impropriety. When his explanations were questioned, he became irate and implored the CEO to fire the individuals who had confronted him. He attempted to fire a few of them himself but was blocked by human resources. As the information file grew on Tom grew, the CEO put Tom on leave and considered whether to bring legal action.

Diagnosis

Sociopaths in an organization want to beat the system. They will try to satisfy their own sense of entitlement, with little concern for the personal or professional effects on others. Notably, there is an apparent absence of guilt about these behaviors.

Assessment of antisocial personality must consider past history, as well as recent events. The pattern begins in adolescence and typically encompasses all spheres of activity. Antisocial patterns are likely to be present from school, other employers, and at home. It is important not to confuse isolated dishonest behavior under emotional stress (see Chapter Seven) with the more pervasive and intractable behaviors of antisocial personality.

❦ Diagnostic Criteria for Antisocial Personality Disorder

A. There is a pervasive pattern of disregard for and violation of the rights of others occurring since age 15 years, as indicated by three (or more) of the following:
   1. failure to conform to social norms with respect to lawful behaviors as indicated by repeatedly performing acts that are grounds for arrest
   2. deceitfulness, as indicated by repeated lying, use of aliases, or conning others for personal profit or pleasure
   3. impulsivity or failure to plan ahead
   4. irritability and aggressiveness, as indicated by repeated physical fights or assaults
   5. reckless disregard for safety of self or others
   6. consistent irresponsibility, as indicated by repeated failure to sustain consistent work behavior or honor financial obligations
   7. lack of remorse, as indicated by being indifferent to or rationalizing having hurt, mistreated, or stolen from another

B. The individual is at least age 18 years.
C. There is evidence of Conduct Disorder ... with onset before age 15 years.
D. The occurrence of antisocial behavior is not exclusively during the course of Schizophrenia or a Manic Episode.

Reprinted with permission from the Diagnostic and Statistical Manual of Mental Disorders, Fourth Edition, Text Revision. *Copyright 2000 American Psychiatric Association.*

Causes for antisocial personality disorder are uncertain. Antisocial patterns may partially reflect maladaptive adult role models from childhood or adverse socioeconomic factors. They may also be an extreme variant of narcissistic personality traits, with cold detachment from other people and feelings of angry entitlement. An inherited component has been suggested, possibly associated with somatization disorder (Briquet's syndrome; see Chapter Twenty-Seven).

Workplace Management and Referral

Antisocial personality traits wreak havoc in the workplace. Not only are the antisocial behaviors themselves destructive, but their occurrence can insidiously undermine morale. Manipulations, cons, and improper conduct are hidden at first, then earnestly denied. The apparent lack of guilt about harm to others can be especially destructive. Workplace recognition usually follows the overt association of a problem or pattern of problems with the responsible party. When the responsibility does become clear, management must be quite firm and set clearly defined rules of conduct. If the employee stays with the organization, close supervision and carefully structured work responsibilities are a necessity. In particular, the employee should not be allowed to make unsupervised decisions that could hurt other employees or the organization. Significant antisocial personality traits are an indication for prompt referral for nonjudgmental treatment.

Without treatment and careful reinforcement of workplace rules, there is little hope for change in antisocial personality disorder. Even so, prognosis is always guarded, since there is limited ability for those with these traits even to recognize that a problem exists and few internal safeguards to prevent manipulation of the treatment itself. Return to work is possible only when the damage done is minor and future risk is small. Otherwise, morale can be seriously affected by the anger of coworkers and supervisors over past behaviors and ongoing concern about continuing lack of concern and betrayal of others. Prognosis is far better when there has been only an isolated episode of dishonesty, in the absence of true antisocial personality.

Psychiatric Management

True antisocial traits present a problem for psychotherapy. Employees may agree to therapy solely because it is less painful than losing a job or going to jail. Characteristically, these employees present with pseudocompliance as a conscious resistance to treatment. It is important, then, to have as much clinical information as possible from outside sources (which does not necessarily mean breaching patient confidentiality). Because antisocial individuals do not always share the same emotional and behavioral monitoring system as others, they can quite readily agree with any interpretations and comments about their behavior. This thus gives the appearance of participation in therapy but without true introspection, insight, or change. Ultimately, change requires that the patient realize intellectually that existing behavior patterns will lead to dreadful pain and suffering. Antisocial patients are far more likely to be concerned about their own pain than they are the pain they cause others. At least a year of consistent therapy is usually needed for any chance of deep emotional change. Ideally, treatment also enables the patient to incorporate some of the psychiatrist's values through emotional attachment and emulation.

PARANOID: ISOLATED OR LITIGIOUS EMPLOYEES

Case 5

Ethan Waterman is a thirty-four-year-old married man who was recently elected union shop steward after seven years at his firm. Ethan had been known as a good worker, but had always seemed quiet, humorless, and a bit discontent. Although he was cordial to his superiors, he tended to keep his distance and was more comfortable talking to one or two people than in a larger group. Even before his election, Ethan would get angry about management and occasionally raise questions that imputed prejudiced motivations. After he became enraged during a meeting with company managers, he was referred for a confidential consultation.

After several interviews, it was clear that Ethan harbored tremendous resentment of authorities at work, within his union, in politics, and in his family. His questions of the psychiatrist were at first belligerent and accusatory. He felt that there was no relationship between his intensified anger, on the one hand, and the near simultaneous arrival of elective office and of a first child, on the other. He said that his anger had increased because of a new realization about the depth of company efforts against him. Ethan saw no reason to continue in treatment.

Even without specific information, Ethan was convinced that the company exploited and harmed union employees. He often used the power of the union shop to deliver attacks without any real basis in reality. Much of his angry fire was directed at managers who had previously offered him advice, helpful supervision, or constructive criticism. He was also spending far more time rallying workers against the company than trying to resolve the perceived problems. He spent even less time completing his work assignments. Finally, Ethan angrily threatened to sue the vice president for human resources. In front of other people, he also made obscene comments and appeared physically intimidating.

Faced with the prospect of termination and aware now that something was troubling him, Ethan agreed to enter treatment. Discussions of his earlier combativeness with the psychiatrist led to some awareness of his adversarial view of authority figures. He realized that his view of management had been colored by emotions from his personal life and upbringing. Gradually, he became better able to separate his emotions from his perceptions of the company. Although Ethan remained more suspicious of company motivations than others did, he could now assess each situation individually.

Diagnosis

Paranoid personality traits are more commonly heightened by accomplishments than by criticisms. The newly elevated role feels more precarious and more subject to the malevolence of others. To a limited extent, this can be a realistic consideration. For example, managers and leaders draw more attention than employees with less authority. But a paranoid perception can make newly found attention feel like attack.

⁂ Diagnostic Criteria for Paranoid Personality Disorder

A. A pervasive distrust and suspiciousness of others such that their motives are interpreted as malevolent, beginning by early adulthood and present in a variety of contexts, as indicated by four (or more) of the following:

1. suspects, without sufficient basis, that others are exploiting, harming, or deceiving him or her
2. is preoccupied with unjustified doubts about the loyalty or trustworthiness of friends or associates
3. is reluctant to confide in others because of unwarranted fear that the information will be used maliciously against him or her
4. reads hidden demeaning or threatening meanings into benign remarks or events
5. persistently bears grudges, i.e., is unforgiving of insults, injuries, or slights
6. perceives attacks on his or her character or reputation that are not apparent to others and is quick to react angrily or to counterattack
7. has recurrent suspicions, without justification, regarding fidelity of spouse or sexual partner

B. Does not occur exclusively during the course of Schizophrenia, a Mood Disorder With Psychotic Features, or another Psychotic Disorder and is not due to the direct physiological effects of a general medical condition.

Note: If criteria are met prior to the onset of Schizophrenia, add "Premorbid," e.g., "Paranoid Personality Disorder (Premorbid)."

Reprinted with permission from the Diagnostic and Statistical Manual of Mental Disorders, Fourth Edition, Text Revision. *Copyright 2000 American Psychiatric Association.*

Paranoid personality disorder is different from paranoid psychosis (see Chapter Twenty-Six). Psychotic disorders allow little capacity for reality testing, are more likely to appear bizarre, pose a greater risk of danger, and usually need medication or hospitalization. A psychotic employee, who talks to others solely through his own fantasies, is often recognizable to everyone.

Paranoid personality traits, which lead to constant concern about potentially harmful environments and people, are thought to derive from early failure of emotionally intimate relationships. Rather than feel abandoned by other people, an individual with paranoid traits allows substitution of an adversarial attachment. But there is an ongoing mistrust of friends, colleagues, and family. Feelings are strongly projected onto others, with the possibility of hair-trigger reactions to perceived anger or harm. Since the anger can be palpable to others, it can lead unwittingly to adversarial relationships, and thus become a self-fulfilling prophecy. Paranoid personality traits make some appear like "lone wolves." Kindness and a soft underside beneath the angry exterior can invite friendship and helpfulness. Unfortunately, paranoid traits carry a deeply felt fear of hostile intentions, and friendly efforts sometimes stir up an angry reaction.

Hypervigilance and self-protective data gathering can also be a major asset. High-functioning employees with paranoid traits are often able to make accurate observations about other individuals. These are commonly critical observations, perceived from a hostile position, conveyed as objective truth, and designed for self-protection. Colleagues may find it difficult to determine the frame of reference, especially of someone in a position of power. And apprehensiveness about people in general can include particular mistrust of those who are more trusting.

Workplace Management and Referral

People with paranoid traits are often most comfortable in a relationship that is supportive, consistent, fair, and emotionally nonintimate. That kind of anchoring relationship offers a degree of emotional stability and reality testing. Although a treating psychiatrist can fill that role, treatment also involves ultimate discussion of deeper emotional concerns. In the workplace, a manager can set up periodic brief meetings to discuss ongoing projects and organizational concerns. Those meetings also serve as a safe place to express grievances confidentially without fear of reprisal. Unlike a therapy session, the focus is entirely on work projects, without consideration of emotional relationships at home or in the workplace. Objective data collection and feedback is often reassuring. This kind of process can be effective only if the paranoid employee has sufficient trust in the supervisor to tolerate a differing opinion. Care must be taken not to get caught up in paranoid beliefs. Although optimal treatment and management may still leave some continuing fears of persecution, consistent reality testing can keep them in check and minimize effects on workplace relationships.

Psychiatric Management

As with any other personality style, the initial task of treatment is formation of a treatment alliance, based on the therapist's ability to instill a sense of trust, stability, and reliability in the relationship. The task is complicated because the general mistrust of others applies to therapists too, though careful perseverance can allow even this obstacle to be minimized. It is helpful to acknowledge how real the mistrustful perceptions are, but without challenging their accuracy. After an alliance has been formed, work can begin on recognizing the general mistrust of others and the reality that not everyone is actually hostile or even paying attention. A focus is also placed on learning to differentiate between reality and fearful perceptions. Greater change is accomplished through further understanding of hidden emotions and their childhood origins. Not infrequently, concurrent depressive or anxiety disorders require use of medication as well.

BORDERLINE: IMPULSIVE OR DIVISIVE EMPLOYEES

Case 6

Jane Tryen is a thirty-seven-year-old somewhat overweight former sales clerk, who joined Paycash Stores at an entry-level management position. She had always been an underachiever, but got this new job through hard work and intelligence and because of a company effort to have well-seasoned sales personnel in lower management. A few months later, her office seemed to be struggling with morale. Projects that required teamwork and collaboration were falling behind. When employees were interviewed individually about the problems, they kept mentioning Jane.

Jane would take provocative and angry positions against opposing views, while at the same time gathering passionate supporters for her side. In effect, she played people off against each other. Even in social interactions, coworkers would sometimes feel angry at each other until they realized that Jane had somehow set up their disagreement. Jane liked to gossip about people but was pretty much unaware of her effects on them or the extent of their discussion about her. She did feel that there were coworkers who were causing problems for her but would laugh and gossip with them, even while campaigning secretly for their dismissal.

Jane felt that any criticism of her was unfair, especially considering her current personal crises. After her recent third divorce, her ex-husband was not making alimony payments. They would sometimes argue late into the night, and Jane would be tired and tense the next day at work. Actually, she had always had a complicated personal life. Her emotions would shift from one extreme to the other, it took little to provoke her anger, and there was always the desperate loneliness. Increasingly estranged from coworkers and spending her limited funds on appropriate business attire, Jane now felt both emotionally and financially impoverished. Eventually, she became so enraged that she abruptly threw some of her files across the room. Later that week, she stormed out of a meeting with her supervisor and left for home.

The supervisor realized that Jane had become an increasing liability and a cause of other employees' dissatisfaction. Coworkers were spending enormous amounts of time and energy dealing with Jane and with the results of her actions. Even so, the company had invested considerable time and energy in her training, and she had completed some successful projects. When Jane was referred for consultation, she loudly ridiculed the idea to anyone in the office who would listen.

Diagnosis

Borderline personality traits can cause seriously disruptive effects in the workplace. Intense emotions, impulsive behavior, subtle divisiveness, and disaffection all contribute to discord and disunity. Causes of borderline personality are thought to include unstable or disruptive early childhood relationships, as well as comorbid anxiety and depressive disorders (see Chapters Twenty-One and Twenty-Two). Panic disorder is especially common.

⁂ Diagnostic Criteria for Borderline Personality Disorder

A pervasive pattern of instability of interpersonal relationships, self-image, and affects, and marked impulsivity beginning by early adulthood and present in a variety of contexts, as indicated by five (or more) of the following:

1. frantic efforts to avoid real or imagined abandonment. *Note:* Do not include suicidal or self-mutilating behavior covered in Criterion 5.
2. a pattern of unstable and intense interpersonal relationships characterized by alternating between extremes of idealization and devaluation
3. identity disturbance: markedly and persistently unstable self-image or sense of self
4. impulsivity in at least two areas that are potentially self-damaging (e.g., spending, sex, substance abuse, reckless driving, binge eating). *Note:* Do not include suicidal or self-mutilating behavior covered in Criterion 5.
5. recurrent suicidal behavior, gestures, or threats, or self-mutilating behavior
6. affective instability due to a marked reactivity of mood (e.g., intense episodic dysphoria, irritability, or anxiety usually lasting a few hours and only rarely more than a few days)
7. chronic feelings of emptiness
8. inappropriate, intense anger or difficulty controlling anger (e.g., frequent displays of temper, constant anger, recurrent physical fights)
9. transient, stress-related paranoid ideation or severe dissociative symptoms

Reprinted with permission from the Diagnostic and Statistical Manual of Mental Disorders, Fourth Edition, Text Revision. *Copyright 2000 American Psychiatric Association.*

Theorists have also pointed out that borderline personality disorder is associated with certain characteristic styles of emotional defenses. For instance, hidden anger at expectations of emotional rejection and despair is diffused through such mechanisms as splitting (divisiveness) and over idealization and devaluation (seeing people as all good or all bad).

Workplace Management and Referral

Employees with borderline personality traits are challenging for management. Although there can sometimes be overt evidence of impulsive or disruptive behavior, the problems are more often manifest in more subtle ways. Unwittingly, the employee can have a divisive influence on coworkers—for instance, by persuasive and emphatic expression about how other people have been either always helpful or always harmful to them. Appropriate limit setting is essential, with a focus on proper workplace conduct, completion of assigned tasks, and due consideration of coworker feelings. The supervisor must also be ready for angry protests and even tolerant of the possibility that the employee will be angry at him or her. Problems and complaints should be discussed specifically and with specific suggestions for improvement. Supervisory meetings should not deteriorate into arguments.

Psychiatric Management

Treatment of borderline personality disorder is always a complex process. Because circumstances and other people tend to be seen in all good or all bad terms, there can be difficulty in recognizing that most people have both strengths and weaknesses. Impulsive and angry behaviors are also common complications. Intense emotions combine with inner despair and limited self-control of behavior to make for behavioral problems in all relationships, and the therapeutic relationship will similarly follow a stormy course. The psychiatrist will be seen alternately in idealized and highly critical ways. One early goal of therapy is to foster a therapeutic alliance and point out that other people should be viewed in a more realistic way. Ultimately, the underlying mistrust of relationships and consequent anger at other people must be explored. It should be noted that depressive and anxiety disorders are extremely common in these patients but usually unrecognized. Psychotherapy without appropriate medication for those syndromes will usually have quite limited benefits.

NARCISSISTIC: GRANDIOSE OR DEMANDING EMPLOYEES

Case 7

Bill Chang is a forty-one-year-old vice president of manufacturing operations. He had been promoted over several other managers after only ten years with the company. More than a few colleagues had the feeling that Bill's prestigious position came more through office politics and ingratiation of the president than it did from significant personal accomplishment. Although a few people were resentful, most were impressed by his looks, bearing, charm, and achievement. Bill's wife is extremely attractive, well positioned in society, and the mother of their two beautiful children.

Rumor has it that his expensive cars, showy house, and exclusive country club were paid for more by his wife's family than by his own income or investments.

Gradually, there were increasing complaints from Bill's subordinates. They thought that Bill was unconcerned about their well-being. They also thought that their assignments seemed mostly designed to advance Bill's position in the organization and that he was sacrificing production quality and efficiency for his own short-term benefit. Bill sometimes used departmental meetings as a platform for his grandiose ideas or even for outright discussions of his personal power, brilliance, and future success. And despite his dazzling success, he was hypersensitive to criticism. Almost everyone agreed that he was intolerant of even the most constructive advice. Still, Bill had quite a following. He sought out those in positions of power. Although he tolerated subordinates who might be useful to him, he had little apparent concern for anyone beneath him. Those who would feel appreciated for a while would eventually end up feeling used.

After several months of growing complaints, the president realized that some of Bill's character traits had been exaggerated by the promotion. Besides the obvious impairment of departmental enthusiasm and morale, there were questions about management style and direction. He shared his concerns with Bill and referred him to a consulting psychiatrist. Although the president figured that Bill needed work on some superficial behaviors, his overall respect for him was undiminished. Bill, though, felt rejected and a bit humiliated at first. Later, he realized the importance of the president's referral. In the near term, he was able to start paying more deliberate attention to his subordinates' concerns and to long-term planning for his department. Only much later did he start to understand how his emotional sensitivity had made him seek admiration as a substitute for affection.

Diagnosis

Narcissistic individuals can have strongly detrimental effects on the workplace. Through charm, intelligence, and very real contributions, they can advance a highly personal agenda that precludes actual concern for others or for organizational goals. Recognition of the problem can be difficult, especially of narcissistic traits in powerful individuals. Ultimately, destructive self-serving behavior creates significant adverse consequences, so it is usually better to handle the problems sooner than later. At the same time, it is important to remember that the significant difference between ambition and healthy self-advancement on the one hand and destructive self-aggrandizement on the other.

❖ Diagnostic Criteria for Narcissistic Personality Disorder

A pervasive pattern of grandiosity (in fantasy or behavior), need for admiration, and lack of empathy, beginning by early adulthood and present in a variety of contexts, as indicated by five (or more) of the following:

1. has a grandiose sense of self-importance (e.g., exaggerates achievements and talents, expects to be recognized as superior without commensurate achievements)

2. is preoccupied with fantasies of unlimited success, power, brilliance, beauty, or ideal love
3. believes that he or she is "special" and unique and can only be understood by, or should associate with, other special or high-status people (or institutions)
4. requires excessive admiration
5. has a sense of entitlement, i.e., unreasonable expectations of especially favorable treatment or automatic compliance with his or her expectations
6. is interpersonally exploitative, i.e., takes advantage of others to achieve his or her own ends
7. lacks empathy: is unwilling to recognize or identify with the feelings and needs of others
8. is often envious of others or believes that others are envious of him or her
9. shows arrogant, haughty behaviors or attitudes

Reprinted with permission from the Diagnostic and Statistical Manual of Mental Disorders, Fourth Edition, Text Revision. *Copyright 2000 American Psychiatric Association.*

Narcissism is best thought of as a reflection of an underlying inability to find or tolerate emotional intimacy. Instead, narcissistic traits develop as protection against underlying loneliness, fear, and anger. At the same time, they offer means of finding substitutes for the missing affection. The replacements can range from preoccupation with power, wealth, or material things or with such personal assets as intelligence, beauty, or physical strength. These reassurances offer a fragile stability, but are subject to disruption by their loss or by almost any manner of life changes. Major depression and self-destructive behavior are common consequences.

Workplace Management and Referral

Narcissistic individuals often present organizations with a real dilemma. They can be very motivated and creative, and have much to contribute to the organization. But ultimately, whatever they do, it is really for themselves. They may see themselves as indispensable and others as unimportant. They may feel such a need to appear perfect that they can't let themselves seek help. The narcissistic employee needs to be approached in a gentle, nonthreatening manner to prevent further blows to his ego and avoid further reaction. Correction should be put in a constructive light and must be balanced by positive input from the supervisor. It is always important to leave this individual with something positive, particularly self-respect.

Psychiatric Management

Psychotherapy initially fosters a therapeutic alliance and then focuses on developing a fuller lifestyle. The narcissistic preoccupations are not challenged directly. Rather, they ultimately fade in importance as the quality of emotional relationships improves. At the same time, though, initial reality testing is often important. Helping patients see that their behaviors and emotional distancing have effects on other people, and that those effects can hurt them in turn, is essential for their future success. Frequently, it can be helpful to point out conscious conflicts of narcissistically related behaviors with personal moral or religious beliefs.

PASSIVE-AGGRESSIVE: COMPLIANT OR UNDERACHIEVING EMPLOYEES

Case 8

Richard Sanders is a forty-five-year-old heavy-set man who has been with the company for over twenty years. He has held the same secure clerical position for the past ten years, and his career advancement has probably already peaked. His section, which had fallen behind in a changing business environment, needed to be turned around. After fifteen years on the job, the old supervisor was terminated for poor departmental productivity and because of his inability to recruit fresh talent.

Richard was not getting along well with the new supervisor, who was trying to reorganize the department and complained to human resources that Richard was one of the main impediments to change. He felt frustrated by Richard's apparent avoidance of work and even more frustrated because he couldn't really document the details. Richard would be quite agreeable to efforts at supervisory advice, but there was always a slackening of his output afterward.

On the surface, Richard got along fairly well with others in the department. He had even evolved into a kind of leadership position, although it was unclear exactly where he was leading everyone else. His inactivity seemed to inspire it in others. He had little investment in initiating and completing his assigned tasks. Richard seemed to take longer with his work and turn it in later than anyone else, although always with a plausible explanation. At times, he could be difficult to deal with, coming in late to work or leaving essential papers at home. And his computer had many more destructive hard disk crashes than anyone else's in the office. But because of his positions at both the company and the union, extra information would be needed to terminate him. So far, it had been difficult to document that he was avoiding or resisting work. Mostly, he just left people feeling angry at him.

Recently, the supervisor proposed a new and potentially exciting direction for the department. Richard's silent opposition to these changes made it difficult to maintain enthusiasm and excitement from everyone else. Moreover, the supervisor noticed that Richard's activities were focusing more and more on gathering support for his resentment and oppositionalism. When Richard was eventually referred for counseling, he had to be pushed for weeks before he made an appointment.

Diagnosis

Passive-aggressive traits are difficult to recognize, since most of the resistance is hidden. A key characteristic is the increasing frustration of coworkers and supervisors who try to encourage more productive activity. Meanwhile, the passive-aggressive employee seems to move calmly on, apparently unaffected by the surrounding inefficiency and irritation. The employee will seem unaware of creating anger or expressing aggression by passivity and will be surprised by any confrontation about his or her behavior.

⁂ Diagnostic Criteria for Passive-Aggressive Personality Disorder

A. A pervasive pattern of negativistic attitudes and passive resistance to demands for adequate performance, beginning by early adulthood and present in a variety of contexts, as indicated by four (or more) of the following:
1. passively resists fulfilling routine social and occupational tasks
2. complains of being misunderstood and unappreciated by others
3. is sullen and argumentative
4. unreasonably criticizes and scorns authority
5. expresses envy and resentment toward those apparently more fortunate
6. voices exaggerated and persistent complaints of personal misfortune
7. alternates between hostile defiance and contrition

B. Does not occur exclusively during Major Depressive Episodes and is not better accounted for by Dysthymic Disorder.

Reprinted with permission from the Diagnostic and Statistical Manual of Mental Disorders, Fourth Edition, Text Revision. *Copyright 2000 American Psychiatric Association.*

Workplace Management and Referral

Employees with passive-aggressive traits can be difficult to manage. The harder you try to push them, the less they seem to get done. There may be very reasonable explanations for individual episodes, but in the long run, the supervisory process feels more and more frustrating. To make matters more complicated, the employee is usually unaware of the subtle aggression in his or her inactivity. Documentation of complaints, low productivity, effects on coworkers, and resistance to change is important. In particular, this information is useful in giving feedback to the employee on his or her behavior and its effects. It is also essential when further action is indicated, such as referral for treatment or probationary work periods. Sometimes it is easier for an employee to understand the problem if there is similar feedback from coworkers. At other times, this can also lead to greater feelings of resentment and passivity.

Psychiatric Management

Although all personality styles tend to be self-perpetuating, passive-aggressive traits may lead to particularly heightened passive resistance in response to advice or initial psychotherapeutic efforts. Since passive-aggressive personality traits are usually positively self-perceived, the impetus for change does not originate inside the patient. As a result, the best way to initiate therapy is to point out behaviors that will lead to difficulties and suffering. Appealing to concern for others is usually fruitless. As long as other people are seen as uncaring or hostile, it is hard to elicit sincere empathic behavior. Eventually, though, intelligence and self-preservation allow most to seek more flexible and adaptive personality traits.

Objective data about maladaptive behavior are especially important early in treatment. Otherwise, the patient will try to rationalize away the details, minimize the nature of the problem, and justify a lack of commitment to treatment and change. Genuine change is no small feat. Childlike emotional defenses need to be discussed in a clear and unembarrassing manner, pointing out when current problems are a reenactment of early childhood relationships. In varying degree, the difficulties tend to occur in all relationships: at work, socially, and at home. Effective psychotherapy will be a gradual process, sometimes over an extended period. Changes in passive-aggressive behavior are significant for both the organization and the employee.

Each of the personality disorders includes at least three elements. First, the behavior patterns are both inappropriate and painful to the self or to others. Second, the maladaptive patterns are substantially unaffected by external inducements to change. And third, little by little, the patterns create problems for the organization and for coworkers. The workplace effects of personality disorders and styles are initially more subtle than the effects of such more overt problems as depression or alcoholism.

References and Additional Sources

American Psychiatric Association. (1994). *Diagnostic and statistical manual of mental disorders* (4th ed.). Washington, DC: Author.

Bellak, L., & Faithorn, P. (1981). *Crises and special problems in psychoanalysis and psychotherapy.* New York: Brunner/Mazel.

Colarusso, C. A., & Nemiroff, R. A. (1981). *Adult development.* New York: Plenum Press.

Freud, S. (1954). *The standard edition of the complete psychological works of Sigmund Freud.* London: Hogarth Press.

Gabbard, G. O. (1994). *Psychodynamic psychiatry in clinical practice: The DSM-IV edition.* Washington, DC: American Psychiatric Press.

Kaplan, H. I., & Sadock, B. J. (1997). *Synopsis of psychiatry* (8th ed.). New York: Lippincott Williams & Wilkins.

Kernberg, O. F. (1975). *Borderline conditions and pathological narcissism:* New York: Jason Aronson.

Kernberg, O. (1984). *Severe personality disorders: Psychotherapeutic strategies.* New Haven, CT: Yale University Press.

Levinson, D. J. (1978). *The seasons of a man's life.* New York: Ballantine Books.

Nicholi, A. M. Jr. (1988). *The new Harvard guide to modern psychiatry.* Cambridge, MA: Belknap Press.

Vaillant, G. E. (1977). *Adaptation to life.* New York: Little, Brown.

CHAPTER TWENTY-FOUR

Drugs

Abuse and Dependence

Avram H. Mack
Jeffrey S. Rosecan
Richard J. Frances

Drug abuse is a major problem in the American workplace. In this chapter, the terms drug abuse, drug dependence, and drug addiction are defined, and guidelines for identifying and managing drug abuse in the workplace are reviewed. Individual drug abuse syndromes are described and illustrated with case studies. Guidelines for urine testing are provided, as is a sample corporate substance abuse policy.

Drug abuse is a major social problem in the United States. Fifteen million Americans are current users of illicit drugs, and almost one-third of such individuals are dependent on the substance (Substance Abuse and Mental Health Services Administration, 2002). Seventy-five percent of drug users are employed; 8 million workers abuse drugs and many more experiment; 16 million have alcohol dependence; and 60 percent of adults have used marijuana once, 28 percent have tried cocaine once, 12 percent used drugs the previous year, and 19 percent of employed used them in the past month. With the stresses of international terrorism and disasters, the social environment conditions are present for another epidemic outbreak of addictions.

Seventy-nine percent of Fortune 1000 CEOs see addiction as a prominent problem in the workplace (Substance Abuse and Mental Health Services Administration, 2002). The cost to the U.S. economy related to increased health care costs, absenteeism, increased disability costs, and decreased productivity is estimated to be more than $275 billion, and estimates are that the direct costs to industry are close to $80 billion per year. Aside from the staggering cost to business, drug abuse is directly responsible for problems including injury, accidents (recall the *Exxon Valdez* disaster; an ounce of prevention may have been cheaper and might have prevented environmental catastrophe as well as litigation extending into the year 2001), disability, lateness, absenteeism, theft, embezzlement, and overall reduction in performance and morale. Coworkers who do not use drugs, employers, and the general public all pay the price for these consequences of drug abuse in the workplace. Drug abuse has also been linked to other major societal problems, including AIDS, homelessness, and crime.

POSSIBLE CAUSES OF WORKPLACE DRUG ABUSE

Drug abuse is common in the workplace for several reasons. Many drug-abusing employees may have liberal attitudes toward the use of illicit drugs, especially marijuana. As cocaine increased in popularity in the 1970s and 1980s, it too became acceptable as a recreational drug, and many thought it was safe and nonaddicting. Waves of use of opiates, opioids (such as heroin), club drugs, and amphetamines have occurred more recently. Many employees erroneously assume that the use of these substances outside the workplace (at home or on weekends) will not affect their performance on the job; they believe that it is their choice or right to use drugs socially or recreationally in their private time. "Club drugs" have grown in popularity among young adults in urban areas. Many businesses have developed drug abuse and urine testing policies. This is a controversial area and reflects the difficulty of differentiating an individual's rights from his workplace responsibilities.

WORKPLACE MANAGEMENT AND REFERRAL

The response of business to the use of drugs increasingly has been the development of employee assistance programs (EAPs), where the overall approach is to identify and treat rather than fire drug-abusing employees. EAPs provide job-based evaluation and referrals, and some also provide substance abuse treatment, increasing job retention and lowering complications. EAPs are valuable for workers in that they provide a nonthreatening place to obtain alcohol and drug abuse information and counseling, as well as early diagnosis and treatment. In some companies, up to 40 percent of employees use EAPs, with approximately 17 percent of these for substance abuse. EAPs give employees the message that their companies would rather help them with their problems than fire them. Approximately thirty thousand EAP programs exist in the United States, although their number has been falling as managed care has grown.

By definition, EAPs are in a difficult position. They are the advocate of the employee yet must simultaneously protect the interests of the employer, and they often serve as the intermediary between the two during the period of substance abuse treatment. And although patient confidentiality must be preserved in all types of mental health treatment (see Chapter Four), there must be some communication with the employee's supervisor, union, or personnel office in order for the EAP to be effective. It is important that the guidelines for communication of this type be clear at the beginning of treatment. Cooperation between labor and management in terms of addictions has been more strained as companies have increasingly pared the treatment opportunities. In most programs, the employer communicates with the EAP regarding job performance, and the EAP provides the employer with periodic progress reports without divulging confidential information.

Employers are generally in favor of the EAP system since they feel that in the long run, it is more cost-effective to treat employees than to fire them and hire and retrain replacements. It is also helpful for company morale to see recovering alcoholics and drug abusers return to work happier and more productive. Insurance companies too are generally in favor of EAPs because successful substance abuse treatment has been shown to reduce overall medical costs. Company EAPs vary in demeanor from stern to forgiving and also from a moral to a medical model (which most EAPs now encourage). Education about the EAP is essential, and a clear written policy indicating that drug use will not be tolerated is helpful as well. The elements of a drug-free company policy are as follows: an explanation of reasons such as safety, improving cost-effectiveness, and compliance with regulatory agencies; a clear description of prohibited behaviors; a clear explanation of policy violations; and elements of the program's drug testing policy.

Supervisors need to be trained in the use of EAPs in understanding their role in implementing the policy, observing and documenting job performance problems, confronting employees who are unsatisfactory in job performance, understanding the effects of substances in the workplace, and knowing how to refer employees with suspected problems to the EAP or other mental health professional.

Employee training should include the dangers of alcohol and drug abuse to the employee and his or her family; the negative effects of substances on job performance, health, and safety; company policy and consequences of violating it; the presence of the EAP; drug testing policy; confidentiality; and the ways in which employees can get help.

There are important limitations to EAPs. First, many executives, upper-level managers, and company presidents do not seek treatment for substance abuse through their EAPs. They often prefer off-site treatment programs or clinicians since their substance abuse may involve an illicit drug rather than alcohol, company morale would probably suffer if it became known, for example, that the CEO was a cocaine addict, and it is difficult to be treated by someone they employ. Moreover, the EAP focus on substance abuse often means less broadly trained clinicians and less careful attention to other emotional and psychiatric problems. Many of these patients will benefit from consultation with an occupational psychiatrist.

DRUG USE, DRUG ABUSE, AND ADDICTION

All drug use is not abuse. The terms *abuse, dependence,* and *addiction* are often used interchangeably in the context of drugs and alcohol, but there are important technical differences among them. The scientific community would prefer not to use the term *addiction,* but it is widely used to imply severe drug dependence.

Among the substance use disorders (SUDs), the American Psychiatric Association's text revision of the fourth edition of the *Diagnostic and Statistical Manual of Mental Disorders* (DSM-IV-TR, 2000) differentiates among substance abuse, substance dependence, and the immediate complications of substances (intoxication, withdrawal, or psychiatric features). In DSM-IV-TR, substance dependence is a constellation of cognitive, behavioral, and physiological features that together signify continued use despite significant substance-related problems. It is a pattern of repeated self-administration that can result in tolerance, withdrawal, and compulsive drug-taking behavior. According to DSM-IV-TR, the patient must, over a twelve-month period, exhibit three behaviors from a seven-item criteria set. The presence of tolerance, the need for increased amounts of the substance to achieve the same effect, or a lessening of effect at the same amount of the substance indicates that the individual is in need of timely help, and it predicts withdrawal in some cases.

❖ Diagnostic Criteria for Substance Dependence

A maladaptive pattern of substance use, leading to clinically significant impairment or distress, as manifested by three (or more) of the following, occurring at any time in the same 12-month period:

1. tolerance, as defined by either of the following:
   a. a need for markedly increased amounts of the substance to achieve intoxication or desired effect
   b. markedly diminished effect with continued use of the same amount of the substance
2. withdrawal, as manifested by either of the following:
   a. the characteristic withdrawal syndrome for the substance . . .
   b. the same (or a closely related) substance is taken to relieve or avoid withdrawal symptoms
3. the substance is often taken in larger amounts or over a longer period than was intended
4. there is a persistent desire or unsuccessful efforts to cut down or control substance use
5. a great deal of time is spent in activities necessary to obtain the substance (e.g., visiting multiple doctors or driving long distances), use the substance (e.g., chain-smoking), or recover from its effects

6. important social, occupational, or recreational activities are given up or reduced because of substance use
7. the substance use is continued despite knowledge of having a persistent or recurrent physical or psychological problem that is likely to have been caused or exacerbated by the substance (e.g., current cocaine use despite recognition of cocaine-induced depression, or continued drinking despite recognition that an ulcer was made worse by alcohol consumption)

Specify if:

With Physiological Dependence: evidence of tolerance or withdrawal (i.e., either Item 1 or 2 is present)
Without Physiological Dependence: no evidence of tolerance or withdrawal (i.e., neither Item 1 nor 2 is present)

Reprinted with permission from the Diagnostic and Statistical Manual of Mental Disorders, Fourth Edition, Text Revision. *Copyright 2000 American Psychiatric Association.*

Substance abuse is a less severe form of substance dependence in which there is neither tolerance nor withdrawal. It describes a continued twelve-month maladaptive pattern. A critical criterion in the diagnosis is "failure to fulfill major role obligations": this cannot be used regarding caffeine or nicotine, and it is not a blanket term to connote any use at all.

Another important factor to note is that it is rare to find an abuser of just one drug. Dependence on legal or medically prescribed drugs is nonetheless dependence, and DSM-IV-TR wisely does not make this distinction in its diagnostic criteria. Of note, the majority of substance abusers are polysubstance abusers. Common drug combinations include stimulants (such as cocaine, amphetamines, or diet pills) with depressants (such as alcohol or tranquilizers), although there are drug combinations of all types. Even psychiatric medications can be abused: there is an increasing degree of abuse of topiramate (Topamax), a new medication used in epilepsy and bipolar disorder. It is abused for its appetite-suppressing side effect and can produce serious toxicity when taken in large doses, especially in thin people.

A more practical definition, which is widely used, looks at four main criteria for drug addiction: compulsion, continued use despite adverse consequences, loss of control, and denial. Compulsion is defined as a preoccupation with the drug. Addicts spend most of their time thinking about the drug (where to obtain it, how to buy it, how to conceal it, where to use it), using the drug, and withdrawing from the drug. Clearly, this preoccupation leaves little time for work or anything else. Many addicts in the workplace are able to conceal their drug use for years and can appear to be functional. It is only when they are confronted with their drug abuse and forced to enter treatment that the full extent of their compulsion to use drug is revealed.

Another cardinal feature of drug addiction is continued use despite adverse consequences. Addicts are unwilling (usually earlier in the course of the addiction) or unable (in the later stages) to stop drug use. Despite threats to the marriage, financial losses directly attributable to drugs, or medical complications of drug abuse, addicts continuing drug use. Spouses can threaten divorce, creditors can sue or take away credit cards, and doctors can warn their drug-abusing patients. Ironically, it is the employer, who can say, "Get help or you're fired," who often has the greatest leverage. Denial of a problem is a challenge, and confrontation is often part of the intervention. The first steps to recovery are recognition of a problem and agreeing to a need for help.

Loss of control is an important criterion for drug addiction and one of the more confusing for employers to comprehend. If the addict can show up and work reliably some of the time, why not all of the time? Why can some drug abusers appear to be conscientious employees Mondays through Fridays and binge nonstop on drugs throughout the weekend? Why doesn't the addict have the willpower not to use drugs? The problem is that once the addict starts using drugs, it becomes increasingly difficult to stop. Loss of control may not be apparent until a period of time has passed, because of the principle of progression of the addiction. Over time, untreated drug use progresses from social and recreational use, to more problematic heavy use, and finally to out-of-control addiction. In order to understand the loss of control the addict experiences, addiction must be looked at as a progressive, not static, illness.

Denial of the problem is a related symptom of the addiction. If the addict was able to control drug use in the past (that is, early in the progression), why not at present? If a person has apparent control over the drug use for a period of time, it is difficult to accept the eventual loss of control. Addicts at first minimize the damage the drug abuse has caused in their marriage and relationships with family and friends. They typically blame others or circumstances outside their control (for example, "My wife doesn't understand me," or "My boss passed me over unfairly for a promotion") as justification for their continued drug abuse. They become quite adept at rationalizing their behavior (for example, "Cocaine isn't addictive anyway") and minimizing the problem.

The first step toward successful treatment of alcohol or drug addiction in the workplace is the direct confrontation of the denial. The employer or partners often have more leverage and more emotional neutrality than a family member. Drug abusers are usually unwilling to seek help on their own and must be made to see the adverse consequences of not stopping drug use (such as loss of job or a broken marriage). The employee is given the choice of treatment or termination, and the usual result is a referral to an EAP.

A helpful way to conceptualize addiction to any substance is to view it as an interaction of the individual, the environment, and the substance. All three factors are important, but in certain situations, one factor outweighs the others.

This approach is related to the biopsychosocial approach to illness, where biological, psychological, and social factors are all important in the etiology and treatment of human illness (see Figure 24.1):

• *The individual.* Certain individuals have psychological traits that leave them predisposed to addiction. Many employees use drugs as self-medication for such painful emotional states as the breakup of a marriage, a family crisis, or a financial loss. Alcohol, marijuana, cocaine, prescription analgesics, and tranquilizers are the drugs most commonly used to medicate life's stresses and anxieties. Over time, susceptible individuals can develop an addiction. It is important to note that many employees become psychologically dependent on legal or illegal drugs before the physical dependence sets in.

Other individuals are at risk for the development of drug dependence because of their biochemical or psychiatric predisposition. Employees with strong family histories of alcoholism or depression may be at higher risk, although the data are not definitive. Because alcoholism and drug abuse often coexist with anxiety and depression, a comprehensive psychiatric examination is necessary for accurate diagnosis and successful treatment.

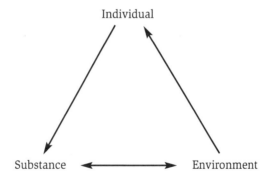

INDIVIDUAL	ENVIRONMENT	SUBSTANCE
• Psychological predisposition	• Family factors	• Individual substance
• Constitutional predisposition (biochemical or psychiatric)	• Cultural factors	• Route of administration

Figure 24.1. Factors Involved in the Development of an Addiction

- *The environment.* The workplace, whether it is the boardroom or the mailroom, is where the employee's drug attitudes meet the employer's. Each workplace has its own personality and its own view of drug use. Some are militantly antidrug, with mandatory urine testing policies, active EAP programs, and employee outreach services (see the chapter appendix). Others are relatively laissez-faire; soft drug use (such as marijuana) and drinking are openly tolerated.

The family is the mediator between the individual and his culture, and the family environment is where attitudes toward drugs are first learned. Family factors are important in the development and treatment of drug dependence. For example, an employee who was brought up in a family where it was grown and smoked openly may honestly feel that marijuana is safe and nonaddicting. Drug dependence may be one of the indicators of family dysfunction; hence, treatment will not be successful without active involvement of the family.

For adolescents and younger adults in the workforce, the peer group supplants the family as the primary determinant of attitudes toward alcohol and drug usage. It is understandably difficult for these young adults to abstain from drugs if all of their friends are users. An important principle of drug abuse treatment is for the abuser to avoid the people, places, and things associated with drugs. In order to do this successfully, most employees need to form new friendships and new support systems through treatment programs and twelve-step programs like Alcoholics Anonymous, Narcotics Anonymous, and Cocaine Anonymous.

- *The substance.* The individual substance and its route of administration are important determinants of the progression of social drug use to drug dependence. Alcohol is a drug with a relatively low potential for dependence, yet alcoholism remains by far the major substance abuse problem in the United States, responsible for tens of thousands of deaths per year (see Chapter Twenty-Five). Only 10 to 15 percent of alcohol users progress to alcoholism, while an estimated 75 to 90 percent of freebase cocaine and crack users become addicts (the number is significantly lower for nasal users). With freebase cocaine or crack, the addiction triangle is weighted heavily to the left. Individual factors and the environment are less important than the substance itself in determining the development of the addiction. With alcohol, familial, cultural, and genetic factors appear to be more important than the drug.

INDIVIDUAL DRUG-DEPENDENCE SYNDROMES

The nature of drug addiction differs for each substance and perhaps for each individual user. Some authors have theorized that the choice of drug (or alcohol) reflects an underlying psychological condition that the individual is trying to "self-medicate" (the self-medication hypothesis; see Khantzian, 1997). Nevertheless, it seems more likely that it is the substance that promotes certain maladaptive behaviors (Vaillant, 1995). Either way, there are important aspects of each type of addiction that must be recognized when thinking about the individual's problem with drugs.

Stimulants: Cocaine, Amphetamines, and Diet Pills

Stimulants and cocaine are different substances, and different populations have historically abused them in different manners. Nonetheless, recent studies have shown that they act for different lengths of time at the same places in the brain, and this may explain their similar presentations in the eyes of observers.

Stimulant dependence, like most other forms of drug dependence, is difficult to detect in the workplace. Unlike alcohol or marijuana, there is no odor or hangover. Stimulants are often used as appetite suppressants or "pep pills," and initially a loss in weight and an improvement in mood or energy level are seen. Many women who develop stimulant dependence started using these substances for their appetite-suppressant effects.

Cocaine abuse is the most common form of stimulant abuse, and there are several clinical features to watch for. Personality changes are commonly seen in cocaine abusers. They become depressed, irritable, and sometimes quite paranoid (see Chapter Twenty-Six). Mood swings and temper outbursts can occur for no apparent reason. Users of cocaine initially can report euphoria and an increased sense of well-being, well described by Sigmund Freud in 1884: "The psychic effect of cocaine . . . consists of exhilaration and lasting euphoria, which does not differ in any way from the normal euphoria of a healthy person. . . . One senses an increase of self-control and feels more vigorous and more capable of work. . . . One is simply normal, and soon finds it difficult to believe that one is under the influence of any drug at all" (p. 291).

Although the initial effects of stimulants are positive for some individuals, with chronic use there are invariable personality changes and adverse psychological effects. Stimulant abusers can gain or lose weight and can become trapped in a cycle of insomnia at night and oversleeping during the day. Abusers of stimulants commonly use depressants such as alcohol, tranquilizers, or marijuana to counteract overstimulation. This often leads to cross addiction, where there is dependence on both a stimulant and a depressant. People who were once industrious workers find that they have difficulty concentrating and staying alert. With cocaine abuse, nosebleeds, sore throats, chronic sinusitis, skin excoriations, shortness of breath, and chronic cough (especially in freebase or crack users) are common. All of the stimulants dilate the pupils, raise the pulse and blood pressure, and can cause palpitations and profuse sweating. Frequent unexplained absences, lateness, inability to sit still, and excessive trips to the rest room, along with the physical and psychological symptoms, should lead the employer to suspect stimulant, especially cocaine, abuse.

Case 1

David Homansky is a twenty-six-year-old attorney who was seen in consultation with a senior partner from his law firm and his mother. David had a relatively normal suburban upper-middle-class childhood and adolescence. He had many friends and outside interests. By the time he was in high school, he knew that he wanted to be a lawyer like his father and was soon working for his father's firm in the summers. David experimented with marijuana, but like his father preferred to "wind down with several beers" after tennis or at a party. In David's last year of law school, his father died suddenly of a heart attack. Although David applied for a prestigious position at a federal agency, he withdrew his application and after the funeral asked his father's partners if he could join the firm.

David's first year at the firm was a disappointment. He worked constantly but never seemed to catch up. He became anxious and lonely and lost touch with his college and law school friends. One day after work, he snorted a few lines of cocaine he was offered by a colleague. He felt relaxed and euphoric and was able to work all night. He was surprised at how effortlessly he completed his project. David bought a gram of cocaine for himself and began to use it regularly. His mood was much better, he was talkative and outgoing, and he found his confidence and sense of humor returning.

After several months, he began a romantic relationship with Susan Wheeling, a twenty-five-year-old lawyer from another firm, and began to socialize with her friends. Many of these new friends used cocaine socially, and Susan always seemed to have it around. David began using it several times a week, and after several months he found he needed it to wake up and get to work on time. He began having trouble sleeping and would smoke marijuana or have a few beers every night to get to sleep. Susan noticed that he became irritated easily, and they began to argue. When she suspected that David was more interested in using cocaine than having sex, she insisted that they both stop using cocaine "until things are better." Susan was able to stop easily, but David found the first week without cocaine terrible. He was depressed and lethargic and called in sick twice because he couldn't get out of bed. Finally, he bought more cocaine and used it every morning, deceiving Susan. One evening, Susan found a vial of cocaine in his pocket and confronted him. David broke down in tears and promised to seek professional help if he ever used cocaine again.

Over the next few days, David craved cocaine. He felt tense and exhausted. He suspected that Susan was watching him constantly and believed she was talking behind his back at his firm. When he angrily confronted her, she denied everything, told him he was paranoid, and said she wanted to end their relationship. David was crushed. He felt numb but was unable to cry. He bought a quarter-ounce of cocaine and snorted it continuously alone; he called in sick three days in a row. He was despondent, he hadn't eaten or slept in days, and he had lost fifteen pounds. He called a senior partner at work, one of his father's closest friends, and said he was quitting. Then he locked himself in his apartment, took the telephone off the hook, and began to think that suicide would be better than facing his family or colleagues again. Several hours later, the partner and David's mother arrived.

David entered a private psychiatric outpatient abuse program and was started on imipramine, an antidepressant medication. He was seen in individual, group, and family therapy and began to improve after several weeks. He became involved in Cocaine Anonymous and began to attend meetings regularly. His performance at work also improved, and after several months David decided to leave the firm and reapply to the agency in which he was originally interested.

In David's case, one problem was that he joined the firm for the wrong reasons (guilt over his father's death). He was lucky that his relationship with his superiors was such that he wasn't fired when his cocaine dependence was discovered. His performance at work was certainly improved by cocaine initially, but eight months later, he was nonfunctional. David's firm has since decided to set up an EAP to deal with problems of alcohol and drug abuse among employees.

Marijuana

Around the world, marijuana is the most commonly used illicit drug. It not usually smoked openly in the workplace because of its pungent odor, but its use is widespread. The active metabolite of marijuana is delta-9-tetrahydrocannabinol (THC). The THC content of illicit marijuana has increased dramatically in recent years, reaching 10 to 15 percent, from 1 to 5 percent in the late 1960s. This is the presumed reason that there are now more cannabis-dependent individuals than in the past, although few people own up to using the drug in national surveys. THC is lipid soluble, meaning that it accumulates in the fatty tissue or the body, including the brain. For this reason, THC can be measured in the urine up to several months after cessation of chronic use. In occasional users (less than once a week), urine can still test positive for THC for extended periods, although these users may show no social or occupational impairment.

Case 2

Melvin Garrison is a forty-two-year-old bus driver who has been working for the county for nineteen years. He is married, has two children, is a model company employee, and is an active volunteer for local charities. Since his graduation from high school, Melvin has been a social drinker and marijuana user. Although his wife of fifteen years initially objected to the marijuana ("it's illegal"), she now occasionally smokes it with him. Five years ago, Melvin's union agreed to a drug testing policy where county employees have their urine tested for drugs during the annual physical examination. Melvin's tests have all been negative, since he stops smoking marijuana several weeks before the urine test each year.

Recently, Melvin was involved in an accident where he seriously injured an eleven-year-old girl who had chased a ball in front of his bus. Melvin was unable to stop in time. Because of a state law requiring testing for alcohol and drugs at the time of a bus accident, Melvin was tested and found to have traces of marijuana in his blood and urine. He was arrested and after a lengthy public trial was fined, had his driver's license revoked, and was reassigned to a desk job at the bus company. The girl recovered after a lengthy hospital stay.

Melvin does not appear to fit DSM-IV-TR criteria for marijuana dependence, though it is unclear just how impaired he was at the time of the accident. Perhaps if he were drug free, his reflexes would have been milliseconds faster, allowing him to brake before hitting the girl.

Marijuana-dependent individuals who smoke daily have deficits in vocational, social, and psychological functioning. Common findings include inability to concentrate, difficulty with judgment and fine motor coordination, memory impairment, and social withdrawal. Lethargy, depression, and a loss of goal-directed behavior are common. In the workplace, the results can be dangerous to the individual user, coworkers, and the general public, depending on the occupation. A marijuana-dependent bus driver, security guard, factory worker, or air traffic controller can endanger the health and even lives of coworkers and the public. If nothing else, it opens the employer up to additional, avoidable legal liability.

Physical signs of marijuana dependency include red eyes with a glazed stare, dry mouth and throat with a chronic hoarse cough, a rapid pulse, and occasional weight gain (because of increased appetite for sweets). These signs in combination with the psychological changes should lead the employer to suspect marijuana dependence. An analysis of the urine or blood is necessary to confirm the suspicion.

Opiate Narcotics and Opioids

The opiate narcotics can be arbitrarily divided into two classes: the illicit and the medically prescribed. The pharmacological effects and potential for abuse and dependence are independent of this arbitrary division, and both are major problems in the workplace. Heroin is the major illicit opiate narcotic in the United States. It is predominantly injected intravenously, although it can also be inhaled nasally or smoked. Heroin produces a rapid and powerful physiological dependence with tolerance (increasing amounts needed to achieve the desired euphoria) and a withdrawal syndrome (when supplies are interrupted). The withdrawal syndrome includes nausea, vomiting, diarrhea, muscle aches, abdominal cramps, and cravings for more heroin, which will alleviate the withdrawal. Although overdose is frequently fatal, withdrawal from these drugs is almost never fatal. Once the heroin dependence is established, procuring the drug becomes the focus of the addict's life. There are a host of medical complications of intravenous heroin dependence, most notably overdose with respiratory arrest, infections from contaminated needles and nonsterile conditions, and human immunodeficiency virus infection from shared needles.

In the workplace, heroin addicts are frequently absent and late. They are prone to accidents because of heroin intoxication (lethargy, somnolence, difficulty concentrating, impaired motor coordination and judgment) or withdrawal. Injuries resulting in disability and theft or embezzlement to support the dependence are common.

The legally prescribed opiates, such as codeine, hydromorphine, meperidine, oxycodone, oxycontin, and morphine, are also abused in the workplace. The abuse of these substances has increasingly been portrayed in the lay press. They are more difficult to detect because they are usually taken in pill form (the analgesics) or in syrups (the cough suppressants). Regular use of these substances leads to a high level of tolerance and to withdrawal syndrome identical to that of heroin. Dependence on illicit opiates is difficult to evaluate and treat when there is a medical disorder requiring analgesia or cough suppression. The employee initially obtains the opioid by prescription from a physician, but gradually increases the dose because of tolerance. Eventually, the employee makes procurement of medication the focus of his life and frequently obtains prescriptions from multiple doctors or illicit sources.

Optimal psychiatric evaluation and treatment of these individuals require familiarity with drug dependence and pain control and careful coordination with other treating physicians. One approach is to make the psychiatrist solely responsible for prescribing appropriate narcotic medication.

Case 3

Sylvia Kim is a thirty-five-year-old single nurse anesthetist at a local hospital. She was brought to the employee health office after passing out in the operating room while at work. Review of her personnel record showed a pattern of lateness and excessive absenteeism, and a supervisor had filed incident reports indicating missing narcotics from Sylvia's nursing station during the past year. When confronted with these findings, Sylvia admitted addiction to intravenous meperidine (Demerol), which she had taken from the narcotics cabinet. The director of the anesthesia service at the hospital consulted with the personnel director and the employee health director, who suggested that Sylvia be hospitalized at another hospital for a twenty-eight-day detoxification and rehabilitation program. If she refused hospitalization, her employment would be terminated. In addition, the legal department felt that the hospital was obliged to notify the state nursing board.

Sylvia agreed to be hospitalized and did well in the inpatient chemical-dependency program. She entered the outpatient program after discharge, began individual and group therapy, was urine drug-tested twice a week, and went to frequent Narcotics Anonymous meetings. At a hearing where she appeared before the nursing board, Sylvia was ordered to remain in the outpatient program for two years, with twice-weekly urine testing. If she failed any drug tests, her license to practice nursing would be suspended.

Sylvia did well, and after her two years were completed, she entered a certified alcoholism counselor degree program. She is now the director of nursing at the same hospital where she had been a patient.

What is important about this case is that the patient recovered and was given a second chance. Use of hard drugs such as heroin or opiates has stigmatized many individuals in the past. For those who are motivated to quit, compassion and support in the workplace can make a big difference in successful abstinence.

Tranquilizers: Sedative, Hypnotic, and Antianxiety Drugs

Minor tranquilizers are the most commonly prescribed psychoactive medications. Benzodiazepines are approved for the treatment of insomnia and anxiety and, in the case of alprazolam, panic disorder. As is the case with the prescription opioids, employees become adept at concealing their dependence on these medications. They are taken orally as pills and are usually legally prescribed by physicians. The intoxication syndrome consists of oversedation, lethargy, and impaired coordination, which can be quite dangerous if the employee is required to drive, operate equipment, or perform complex tasks in a pressured work environment. Another factor is that these medications are commonly combined with alcohol, another central nervous system depressant, potentiating the adverse effects. The withdrawal syndrome typically begins within hours to days on abrupt discontinuation and consists of extreme anxiety, agitation, insomnia, nausea, tremors, and, in extreme cases, seizures. The pulse and blood pressure are elevated, and the employee is clearly in distress. Urgent medical treatment is advised.

The recent terrorist attacks against the United States resulted in an increase in the cases of acute stress disorder and posttraumatic stress disorder, and previous research has found that these states often lead to increased impulsive use of substances, including relapse in recovering individuals (Vlahov et al., 2002). They may cause new dependency on sedatives that might begin as prescribed medicine but can lead to development of an addiction.

Sedative-hypnotic dependence is similar to medically prescribed opioid dependence, in that there is usually an initially valid medical or psychiatric indication for the medications. The employee gradually increases the dose on his own because of tolerance and the need to prevent withdrawal. When dependence finally develops, pill-seeking behavior becomes prominent. A psychiatrist experienced in treating anxiety and depression and familiar with substance dependence should coordinate treatment of the employee in these cases.

Case 4

Maureen McGuire is a thirty-two-year-old secretary for a suburban bank who went to the employee health service complaining of insomnia. The doctor's questioning revealed that she was agitated and upset over a recent breakup with her boyfriend. She had lost ten pounds in the past month and was complaining of abdominal pain and bloating. The doctor ordered laboratory tests and x-rays, including an upper gastrointestinal series. She was given prescriptions for several ulcer medications and for alprazolam at bedtime and as needed during the day for anxiety.

Within days, Maureen began to feel better physically. She was also sleeping better and feeling calmer during the day. Although she was still hesitant to date or attend singles events, she began to socialize with coworkers and twice a week had several drinks after work. At this point, she was taking a small dosage of alprazolam, without adverse effects. After unexpectedly running into her ex-boyfriend at the bar one evening, she became agitated, went home, and took several extra alprazolam. Over the next week, she doubled the dose of alprazolam that she was taking. When she ran out of medication, her doctor telephoned in a prescription with five refills.

Over the next few months, Maureen continued to do well at work. Her ulcer apparently healed. When she ran out of medication this time, she decided she was feeling much better and no longer needed it. Within a day, Maureen became extremely shaky and jittery. She was nauseous and light-headed and felt her heart racing. When she woke up in the emergency room that evening, she was told that she had had a seizure due to alprazolam withdrawal.

Although Maureen does not fit criteria for DSM-IV-TR sedative dependence, she experienced a severe withdrawal syndrome because of physical dependence on alprazolam. Maureen was admitted to the hospital and gradually detoxified. Her company's employee health department then referred her for continuing psychiatric treatment. She was seen in weekly psychotherapy, and her psychiatrist coordinated treatment with her internist.

TESTING FOR DRUG USE

Preemployment and periodic mandatory urine testing for illicit drugs, has become a controversial topic in recent years. Table 24.1 summarizes some pros and cons of mandatory workplace urine testing. The main argument in favor of mandatory urine testing is deterrence of illicit drug use, at both work and home. Drug-using employees are required to stop, and employees unable to stop are identified and referred for evaluation and treatment.

Table 24.1. Pros and Cons of Mandatory Urine Testing for Illicit Drugs.

Pros	Cons
Deterrent to drug use	Might be unconstitutional
Permits early identification of abusers	Urine tests can be inaccurate
Drug-free workplace is safer and more productive	Does not differentiate drug use from abuse
Drug-free high-risk occupations (such as airline pilot) promote the public safety	Job performance, not drug use, should govern employment

Both employees and organizations increasingly view a safe and drug-free workplace as a right. Employees feel that substance-abusing coworkers jeopardize everyone's safety and invite criminal behavior in the workplace (see Chapter Fifteen). Companies are aware of the enormous financial losses from drug-related absenteeism, pilferage, poor performance, and accidents. Many would like to see a drug-free workplace as the first step toward a drug-free society. Feasibility and even desirability are questions that society as a whole must answer.

Those who are opposed to mandatory urine testing say that it is a violation of constitutional rights to privacy. What an individual does in his or her private time, including illicit drug use, should not concern an employer. They feel that job performance is what matters, not the presence or absence of drugs in the urine. Even with safeguards, concerns are also raised about reporting errors and potential breaches of confidentiality.

An employee's right to privacy, however, must be balanced with society's best interests. If public safety is involved, should certain professions or occupations be subject to mandatory drug testing? For example, should airline pilots, air traffic controllers, or anesthesiologists be required to have mandatory urine testing? Society, through its legal and judicial system, will answer these questions.

An additional concern is the accuracy of the urine tests themselves. There are always limitations on accuracy, and an employee's career, reputation, and livelihood can be mistakenly jeopardized. Although it is possible to repeat all positive urine tests and then confirm them with more accurate blood tests, there is no guarantee that this will be done.

Urine tests do not distinguish drug use from drug abuse or dependence, which can be done only with a comprehensive medical and psychiatric history and a physical examination. At best, laboratory tests are adjunctive and provide diagnostic confirmation. It is accepted in the treatment community that urine testing is a useful adjunct in the treatment of the drug-dependent individual, but not all drug users are abusers.

PUBLIC POLICY AND LAW

The rights and responsibilities of patients with addictions is another important workplace issue. The Americans with Disabilities Act covers alcohol but not the illegal drugs discussed in this chapter. If disability is present for a recovering alcoholic, the law requires the individual to receive the same job as anyone else, but with accommodations that are appropriate. The Family and Medical Leave Act gives up to twelve weeks of leave. It is important that employees are aware that any company can hire or fire for drug use but not for alcoholism, especially if the patient is in recovery, although the consequences of alcoholism can lead to job action when needed.

PSYCHIATRIC MANAGEMENT

The best goal for treatment of a substance use disorder is abstinence: the cessation of all use. When attained, this provides the user with the best long-term prognosis. Recovery occurs when the abstinent individual has found alternative ways than substance abuse as a way to cope with life. (For a brief description of the types of treatment, see Chapter Twenty-Five.)

Each user has specific problems, life situations, cultural issues, and perhaps psychiatric disorders that require consideration in order to match patients with treatments. And patients almost always benefit from the application of more than one treatment at one time. Not every patient needs medication as treatment, but under the supervision of a physician, a comprehensive treatment plan often includes some phase of medication and perhaps hospitalization (for overdoses on opiates and opioids; for detoxification from alcohol, benzodiazepines, and opioids; and for cases in which there are comorbid psychiatric disorders) in concert with psychotherapy and other interventions. Data show that treatment of addictions with both psychotherapy and medication is more efficacious than either alone.

Psychotherapies

There are a number of specific psychotherapeutic approaches that are applied by trained professionals with individuals, families, network approaches, and groups. The individual therapies with proven efficacy for substance use disorders include cognitive-behavioral therapy and dialectical behavioral therapy. Traditional psychotherapy is probably just as helpful. Alcoholics Anonymous is a self-help group that is an immensely helpful activity, and its format has been applied to drugs of abuse other than alcohol. Many patients early in the recovery process are encouraged to go to ninety meetings in ninety days. Al-Anon and other groups for family members are helpful as well.

Medications

One of the most important scientific advances of this century was the delineation of the nerve receptors that are associated with pain and medications that treat pain, such as morphine. A number of medications for addiction have built upon these discoveries. Methadone, levo-alpha-acetyl-methadol, and buprenorphine act like opioid drugs of abuse, but last much longer and are given in controlled doses that do not cause intoxication, ideally reducing the dangerous behaviors associated with addiction. Naltrexone is a well-known medication that blocks these receptors, reducing the craving for opiates, opioids, and even alcohol, and for opiate addicts it can block intoxication when taken regularly. Antabuse is used for alcoholism. Acamprosate is a promising experimental drug for reducing alcohol craving. A variety of psychiatric medications are useful in treating the psychiatric comorbidity of addiction. There has been no success in finding a medication that diminishes the craving for cocaine or stimulants. Clonidine (Catapres) is often prescribed for opioid abusers who are detoxifying.

It may be very difficult for employers to have compassion for workers or colleagues who abuse or are dependent on drugs of abuse. Such use certainly may place productivity, property, or even lives at risk, untenable conditions that need attention when they are discovered. For those who resist help, the threat of loss of job or discipline may be realistic alternatives. We urge supervisors to be firm about the need for treatment and to have compassion for those who make the changes needed. Addiction treatment, even with the risk for relapse, is cost-effective for the individual, the employer, and, when applicable, the union, and all parties should cooperate in offering this benefit. It will pay in the long run.

References and Additional Sources

American Psychiatric Association. (2000). *Diagnostic and statistical manual of mental disorders* (4th ed. rev.). Washington, DC: Author.

Beck, A. T., Wright, F. D., Newman, C. F., & Liese, B. S. (2001). *Cognitive therapy of substance use.* New York: Guilford Press.

Frances, R. J., & Miller, S. (1998). *Clinical textbook of addiction psychiatry.* New York: Guilford Press.

Freud, S. (1884). Uber koka. *Wiener Zentralblatt für die Gesamte Therapie, 2,* 289–313.

Group for the Advancement of Psychiatry. Committee on Alcoholism and the Addictions. (1991). Substance abuse disorders: A psychiatric priority. *American Journal of Psychiatry, 148,* 1291–1300.

Khantzian, E. J. (1997). The self medication hypothesis of substance use disorders: A reconsideration and recent applications. *Harvard Review of Psychiatry, 4,* 287–289.

Mack, A., Franklin, J. E., & Frances, R. J. (2001). *Concise guide to the treatment of alcoholism and addictions.* Washington, DC: American Psychiatric Press.

Schukit, M. (1989). *Drug and alcohol abuse: A clinical guide to diagnosis and treatment* (3rd ed.). New York: Plenum.

Spitz, H., & Rosecan, J. (Eds.). (1987). *Cocaine abuse: New directions in treatment and research.* New York: Brunner-Mazel.

Substance Abuse and Mental Health Services Administration. (2002). [Substance abuse and mental health statistics]. Available on-line at: http://www.drugabusestatistics. samhsa.gov/.

Vaillant, G. E. (1995). *The natural history of alcoholism revisited.* Cambridge, MA: Harvard University Press.

Vlahov, D., Galea, S., Resnick, H., Ahern, J., Boscarino, J. A., Bucuvalas, M., Gold, J., Kilpatrick, D. (2002). Increased use of cigarettes, alcohol, and marijuana among Manhattan, New York, residents after the September 11th terrorist attacks. *American Journal of Epidemiology, 155*(11), 988–996.

APPENDIX

Sample Corporate Substance Abuse Policy

The company is committed to providing a safe and productive work environment for all employees. Substance abuse by an employee can adversely affect the employee's productivity, jeopardize the safety of the employee and others, and damage the reputation of the company. The company developed this substance abuse policy to maintain a workforce free from the use of illegal drugs and controlled substances and to ensure the elimination of drugs and drug-related activities in the workplace. The company will apply the terms of this policy strictly to all covered employees and applicants. Employees and applicants are provided a copy of this policy and copies of the attached consent forms for urine (and/or blood) testing and for release of medical information.

Policy

The company strictly prohibits the unlawful manufacture, distribution, possession, or sale of controlled substances, or the use of controlled substances in a manner not medically authorized, on company premises, or while engaged in company business, or during work hours. The presence of an illegal drug or its metabolite in an employee's system while on company premises, while engaged on company business or during work hours, is also strictly prohibited.

Use of prescribed drugs in accordance with a physician is not prohibited under company policy; however, employees taking prescribed drugs are responsible for any effect the medication may have on their performance.

The company recognizes that drug dependency is an illness and that early recognition and treatment is the key to successful rehabilitation. The company maintains an employee assistance program (EAP) to assist employees with substance abuse problems by making referrals to appropriate treatment programs, and employees who feel they need help with substance abuse problems should contact the director of human resources. Employees voluntarily seeking assistance for a substance abuse problem through the EAP or a qualified outside professional resource will not be disciplined for seeking such assistance, and the treatment will be handled in confidence. Employees who request a leave of absence to participate in a treatment program will be given favorable consideration. However, if an employee has not volunteered for treatment and is found to have violated company policy, he or she may not avoid discipline by volunteering to participate in a treatment program. Moreover, participation in a voluntary treatment program will not excuse violation of the company's policy.

The company will provide education for supervisory personnel to assist in identifying and addressing substance abuse by employees. Supervisors will be provided with guidelines for maintaining confidentiality of all substance abuse–related information and for referring employees to our EAP or appropriate treatment.

Drug testing

All applicants for employment are subject to testing for drug abuse. Any job offer made by the company is contingent on the applicant's consenting to take and passing the test. Refusal of the applicant to comply with the testing procedure will disqualify the applicant from consideration for employment.

Current employees may be required to submit to drug testing if in the opinion of their supervisor there is a strong suspicion of drug abuse or other breach of this policy. If this is the case, the supervisor notifies the director of human resources, who then notifies our EAP. Our EAP and its medical director will then decide if a drug test is warranted. Any employee who refuses to submit to testing may be subject to immediate discharge. If the drug test is positive, our EAP and its medical director, in consultation with the director of human resources, will decide on a recommended course of action. If the employee refuses to comply with this course of action (such as drug abuse treatment), this may be grounds for immediate dismissal.

Testing Procedures

Specimen collection for a drug test will be accomplished in a dignified and private matter. Collection will take place at the company medical facility, and in the case of urine testing, will be observed by same-sex medical facility personnel. Appropriate chain-of-custody procedures will be employed, and a laboratory satisfying forensic standards will conduct the tests. The laboratory will preserve for six months an aliquot of specimen sufficient to permit independent confirmatory testing at the request of the applicant. The laboratory will endeavor to notify the company of positive test results within two days after receipt of the specimen. An applicant or employee may request a retest within three days from notice of positive test results.

I hereby acknowledge that I have received the company's drug abuse policy, have read and understood it, and consent to drug testing for substance abuse as outlined in the policy.

Date: Signature: Witness:

CHAPTER TWENTY-FIVE

Alcohol

Abuse and Dependence

Carlotta Lief Schuster

When alcohol abuse and dependence occur in the workplace, the cost to productivity, health, and morale is tremendous. This chapter offers guidelines for workplace recognition, referral, and management. Treatment approaches and choice of treatment setting are discussed because knowledge of alcohol abuse recognition must be combined with awareness of optimal treatment techniques.

The total cost to the nation of alcohol abuse and dependence increased 12.5 percent between 1992 and 1995. This includes the costs incurred from lost earnings due to premature death or illness, as well as vehicular crashes, crime, and incarceration (Harwood, Fountain, & Livermore, 1998).

To date, no specific gene or group of genes has been identified as involved in the transmission of alcoholism. Nevertheless, certain individuals may be at greater risk for developing alcohol than others. For example, alcoholic fathers whose alcoholism developed at an early age, with histories of antisocial behavior preceding the onset of alcoholism, seem more likely to produce alcoholic sons than fathers without such a pattern (Cloninger 1987, 1999). Sons of law-abiding and risk-avoidant fathers, whose alcoholism developed later in life, are more heavily influenced by environmental factors, such as family dynamics, peer pressure, and stress (Cloninger 1987).

Most studies of women reflect a greater influence of environmental than genetic factors on the development of alcoholism. In recent years, gender differences in alcohol disorders are receiving more attention among researchers. Women metabolize alcohol more slowly and develop alcoholic cirrhosis more rapidly than men. In the 1950s, the age at which women began to drink was later than their male counterparts, with a drinking initiation ratio of four to one. In the 1990s, it became one to one. The gender differences in metabolism of alcohol and the increased vulnerability to alcohol-related medical illness among women suggest a need for early detection and treatment. However, women seek treatment specifically for their alcoholism less often than do men. They tend to seek help in mental health or primary care settings instead (Greenfield, 2002).

The fourth edition, revised, of the American Psychiatric Association's *Diagnostic and Statistical Manual of Mental Disorders* (2000), links alcoholism with other drugs and makes a distinction between drug abuse and dependence. Operationally, the difference between the two is of little importance in the workplace. Therefore, this chapter will be referring to both as if they were one. Regardless of whether the alcoholic employee suffers from alcohol abuse or dependence, the consequences seen in the workplace can be one or more of the following: absenteeism, lateness, impaired decision making, temper tantrums, accidents, carelessness, failure to complete assignments on time (often accompanied by myriad excuses), sexual harassment of fellow workers, irritability with clients, and reduced employee morale.

WORKPLACE RECOGNITION AND REFERRAL

Case 1

When Tom Hayes graduated from law school, he was offered a position with a prestigious law firm. He advanced mercurially in the liquidation department and was in the running for junior partner within a year. His heavy drinking in law school continued into his legal career. Drinking had not interfered with his work before, but business lunches with clients steadily increased his daily alcohol intake. Tom developed considerable tolerance to alcohol; he could drink more than the average person without appearing intoxicated. However, by the time he arrived home, he had usually consumed two scotches and two glasses of wine with lunch. With more drinks to unwind, wine with dinner, and a brandy or two afterward, Tom was drunk by bedtime.

Gradually, his job performance began to show the effects of his drinking. He would arrive at the office pale and slightly nauseated. Clients complained because of his forgetfulness, especially after lunch. The head of the liquidation department asked him to improve his job performance and suggested that Tom had been drinking excessively.

Tom's physician evaluated him at the insistence of his partners. His liver function studies were abnormally elevated, and he suffered from shaking and nausea each morning after being separated from alcohol for several hours. These findings suggested that he needed to be detoxified from alcohol in a medically monitored setting to prevent life-threatening rapid pulse and convulsions from occurring. After a three-day hospitalization on a detoxification unit, an outpatient alcohol rehabilitation day program was recommended, and his law firm gave him a month's leave of absence.

Psychiatric evaluation there revealed no underlying anxiety or depressive disorder. He seemed immune to attempts at psychotherapy. When Tom returned to work, he attended Alcoholics Anonymous faithfully for several months and was soon offered a junior partnership in the firm. Within months, he forgot that drinking had caused his recent career setback. Proud of his newly bestowed partnership, Tom lulled himself into thinking that drinking had no adverse effect on his life. After maintaining abstinence, he considered himself "normal" and decided that a controlled approach to drinking would be better than complete abstinence. He started one evening with two glasses of wine at dinner. Since he did not find himself wanting more on that night, he tried drinking wine with dinner again. The habit continued for several weeks, until Tom convinced himself that before-dinner drinks would be okay too. His drinking increased steadily, and he again began to sabotage his work performance. A major case was transferred to another partner, and Tom was sent back for treatment. He was told that any further relapses would result in loss of his position with the firm.

Psychotherapy was now more helpful for Tom. His therapist stipulated that for treatment to proceed, Tom must remain sober and attend Alcoholics Anonymous (AA) meetings regularly. Tom did remain abstinent from alcohol and maintained a high performance level at work while he worked toward uncovering the conflicts that had thwarted his recovery and career.

In discussions with his therapist, Tom gradually learned that he suffered from guilt surrounding chronic, unconscious anger at his father, who had died shortly after Tom graduated from law school. Tom remembered his father as domineering, cold, and impossible to please. His father's education was limited, and at his career peak, he became a factory foreman. Although Tom's father always urged him to press for success, achieving greater success than his father felt like angry retaliation. Tom revealed a fantasy that his law school graduation was his father's death blow. Tom realized that each time he reached a new level of success at work, his anxiety increased. He drank more to cover it, and he sabotaged his career as a result. His drinking and unreliability also caused discomfort and resentment among coworkers. So without any conscious awareness, Tom had set up defeat with the aid of alcohol to "take back" his success, and thus reduce his anxiety.

The more he understood the roots of his problem, the more Tom learned how to adapt. When he no longer perceived achievement as an aggressive act, he could accept praise, promotion, and increased responsibility. His work became reliable and productive. With the help of AA and psychotherapy, he maintained abstinence from alcohol.

When to Refer for Treatment

Although an odor of alcohol on the breath of a worker might heighten suspicion, confrontation at that point would be premature. One key to effective intervention is timing. A clear pattern of decline in job performance must be documented. Several weeks of lateness or absenteeism or months of diminished productivity need to be on record. There are some exceptions to deciding when to refer for treatment: omissions of procedure that endanger others (particularly in the cases of pilots, train engineers, or physicians) and obvious intoxication at work or work-related events.

Although laboratory studies including liver function tests and complete blood counts may suggest alcoholism, the abnormalities are not specific and can be due to a variety of other causes.

Referral Strategy

Confrontation should proceed gradually, initially with a private verbal warning about behavior. This first warning can be empathic—for example, "You seem to be having trouble arriving on time for work. It's a problem for us, and I wonder if you could improve on this." The worker's immediate supervisor makes the warning. If the behavior does not change, a written warning is issued and placed in the worker's confidential file. Human resource departments usually have a policy stipulating a set number of warnings about a given behavior before taking a next step. For example, three written warnings about failure to arrive at work on time would justify mandating that the worker consult the human resource department, consulting psychiatrist, or employee assistance program (EAP). Workers are referred for treatment when their behavior at work, poor attendance, or impaired performance is intolerable to management or to the worker.

After the required number of warnings, the worker should be informed unequivocally that his or her job is on the line unless he or she is willing to accept treatment. The employee is given to understand that the job will remain available until treatment is completed. Often, it is useful to enlist the aid of family members in confronting the employee regarding the need for treatment. Spouses and children often mistakenly protect alcoholism through a conspiracy of silence. Empathic support from mental health professionals can ultimately lead to treatment intervention for the family, as well as for the alcoholic worker.

Case 2

Sam Janus was head of sales for the northeast region of his company. For ten years, he had been a superb salesperson and an excellent manager of the other sales representatives in his division. For the past year, though, he was less attentive, often arrived at the office two hours late, and took very long lunch breaks. In the afternoons, he was less alert and often forgot transactions. After one three-hour lunch, he had a telephone conversation with an important business contact and completely forgot the details of a contract. The client reported this to the company president. There had also been two incidents where his brusque manner had reduced his secretary to tears.

The vice president in charge of sales had noticed a sharp profit drop for Sam's region. He called Sam in for a conference, thought that Sam looked seedy, and found him remarkably defensive about the decline in profits. The vice president also talked with the human resource department. Sam's job performance had been evaluated not only by interviewing Sam, but also through confidential discussions with his directly reporting subordinates. There was a major decline in office morale, coinciding with the changes in Sam's behavior. Sam's boss concluded that action was needed. He and the human resource director called Sam in for an interview. The director gave Sam two options: get help or look for work elsewhere. Clear point-by-point documentation had been available about Sam's absenteeism, lateness, forgetfulness, irritability, and profit decline.

Sam was initially resentful, but he agreed to enter a rehabilitation program. He was treated as an inpatient because he had shakiness, perspiration, and nausea whenever a few hours elapsed between drinks. Sam thus needed twenty-four-hour monitoring to prevent alcohol withdrawal seizures. In addition, his behavior had alienated his office staff to the point that they didn't really want him back in the office. Removal from the work environment seemed the best option. Because insurance would not cover inpatient rehabilitation for several weeks, he was referred to a halfway house for recovering substance abusers that had an attached day program and AA meetings on the premises. While completing the outpatient portion of treatment, the vice president and the human resource director met with Sam, his alcoholism counselor, and the psychiatrist member of the treatment team. Gradually, the team saw that Sam's initial defensiveness changed to refreshing candor and a deep commitment to continued sobriety with the help of AA.

Sam was given a second chance with the company, but it entailed a lateral move to a smaller division in a new geographical location. Still sober and in treatment three years later, he had turned that division around and was commended for excellent leadership.

Case 3

Steve Harris was a welder at a factory that manufactured home appliance parts. Although a reliable worker, he spent much of his weekly paycheck on alcohol. Every Friday when his shift was over, he and his buddies converged on the local tavern.

Although Steve arrived home intoxicated and verbally abusive, he said he didn't understand why his marriage was strained. He felt that his wife was nit-picking about alcohol and that she didn't understand how men relaxed. For a long while, his binges were short-lived, and he showed up for work on time every Monday morning. Steve's two young sons watched plenty of screaming between their mother and father. Their four year old was having trouble playing with the other children in nursery school. Steve saw no connection to his drinking.

Steadily, the interval between binges became shorter. Steve started drinking all weekend and then began again midweek. He started to stay out all night and show up at work still drunk. His welding precision deteriorated, and his defective output was increasingly returned to the factory. Eventually, the defects were traced to Steve. His supervisor called him in and pointed out that the change in his performance was endangering the company's reputation. Steve promised to improve, but mostly just called in sick when his hands were too shaky or his mind too cloudy. He had always been proud of his welding skills, and he was alarmed at his work problem.

Steve became less vehement in his denial of alcoholism. He saw an EAP counselor and accepted referral to the medical department for medical assessment and treatment selection. It was decided that Steve didn't require inpatient detoxification. Because he worked the day shift and drank at night, he was referred to a six-week, five-day-a-week intensive evening program.

The peer pressure and support of group therapy and chemical dependency education paid off. He began attending AA meetings daily and enthusiastically. After his return to work, he attended an evening aftercare program, and stayed in AA.

Steve's family behavior was different now. In sobriety, he was a more sensitive and attentive father and husband. With the help of the EAP department, Steve and his family were referred to family therapy. His wife attended Al-Anon, a self-help organization for adult relatives of alcoholics. Steve and his wife increased their understanding of normal growth and development and corrected their earlier disciplinary mistakes with their children. With the guidance of the family therapist, the children could discuss their father's alcoholism openly. The level of communication among all family members improved, and the children started to recover from the emotional trauma of their father's drinking days. His sons' social and academic adjustment improved. Steve remained sober, a masterful welder, and a happier family man.

CAUSES AND EFFECTS OF ALCOHOLISM IN THE WORKPLACE

There is a reciprocal relationship between the worker and the workplace. Alcoholic behavior jars and demoralizes coworkers. Workers who show up late or cannot finish their work on time increase the workload of more conscientious coworkers. Intoxication on the job causes personal conflict and sometimes physical risk. Coworkers become resentful, tense, and fatigued. When they think that the problem will not be addressed, they may feel considerably less motivated to arrive on time or to finish their own work. And their resentment feeds their colleague's alcoholism. Alcoholic workers cause problems for everyone.

Insecure or unpleasant working environments often trigger depression and anxiety. Some workers might respond with a drink or two to unwind. The susceptible worker might develop accelerating alcohol intake and problematic behavior. Growth, mergers, and layoffs produce anxiety and depression (see Chapter Fourteen). Overly critical, irritable supervisors or coworkers are another source of workplace tension. Hypercritical supervisors are often guilty of lambasting a worker in front of others and never praising work well done. Workplace change, work relationships, and individual traits can lead to a sense of futility. Workers perceive that no matter how hard they try, they will not please the boss. Some become angry and depressed, stop trying to excel, and frequently overstay the tavern on their way home.

Alcohol abuse and alcohol withdrawal produce depression and anxiety states. Just one or two drinks can lead to a pleasant euphoria and an easing of inhibitions. But as more and more alcohol is consumed, the central nervous system depressant effect of alcohol predominates, and feelings of pessimism and hopelessness are exacerbated. Severe depression can result, with a corresponding high risk for suicide. Whereas alcohol initially calms the nervous system, its removal has the opposite effect. If there is physical dependence on alcohol, then even a brief abstinence can produce withdrawal anxiety, palpitations, sweating, and tremor.

Most suicide attempts occur while intoxicated, and withdrawal anxiety can also increase suicide risk. For these reasons, careful psychiatric management should include evaluation for underlying depression and anxiety symptoms when the worker is in an alcohol-free, detoxified state.

Situations that promote drinking with coworkers and clients can permit the development of alcoholism in susceptible workers. In many businesses, the worker perceives an expectation of alcohol consumption at business meals. Office parties, business conventions, on-the-job alcoholic refreshment, and business air travel are other opportunities to drink and behave inappropriately on the job. The susceptible worker may drink too much at lunch, reducing afternoon performance. Afternoons are often the time that supervisory sexual harassment takes place. The intoxicated supervisor is disinhibited and perhaps in an alcoholic blackout as well and the next day may not recollect what happened. Staff will often cover for an alcoholic boss by making excuses and ensuring the work gets done. This tense, demoralizing, unproductive situation is typically ignored until a crisis supervenes.

PSYCHIATRIC MANAGEMENT

As with any other illness, management of alcoholism starts with a careful diagnosis of the syndrome, consideration of related and complicating problems, and thoughtful treatment selection for the individual patient.

Diagnosis of Alcoholism

There are nine symptoms in the criteria for alcohol dependence, and an individual must suffer from at least three of them for diagnosis of alcohol dependence (DSM-IV alcohol and drug criteria are identical; see the Diagnostic Criteria for Substance Dependence in Chapter Twenty-Four). The alcohol-dependent person may suffer from physical dependence, consisting of withdrawal symptoms such as elevated pulse, sweating, shaking, nausea, hallucinations, and a sensation that one's skin is crawling. Untreated alcohol dependence can lead to convulsions, extremely rapid heart rate, and death. Another sign of physical dependence is tolerance, that is, progressively needing more alcohol in a drinking episode to produce the same effect. Other signs of alcohol dependence are spending a great deal of time scheming to be near a supply of alcohol (a bottle in one's desk drawer, for example) and drinking more than one is expected to on a given occasion (losing control of one's drinking.)

Alcohol abuse consists of drinking in spite of knowing that it will jeopardize one's job, health, or psychological well-being. An additional criterion is drinking in situations where doing so could endanger self or others, such as driving while intoxicated. With both abuse and dependence, the symptoms must have been present for at least a month.

Often, chronic maladaptive use of alcohol cannot be determined by laboratory tests. Urine screens are reliable only within a day of alcohol use; they may detect no alcohol in a binge drinker who did not imbibe alcohol within the previous twelve hours. In addition to impaired work performance, alcoholism can be suggested by such characteristics of alcohol intoxication as slurred speech, unsteady gait, red face, trembling, and an odor of alcohol on the breath.

Dual Diagnosis

It is not at all uncommon for alcoholics to abuse another substance at the same time or to have a psychiatric diagnosis as well. Commonly, alcoholics suffer from an anxiety or depressive disorder.

Polydrug Dependence. Alcoholics are often dependent on sedative-hypnotics (classes of addictive sleeping pills or tranquilizers) like diazepam (Valium) and alprazolam (Xanax), barbiturates like pentobarbital (Nembutal), or uppers like cocaine or Ecstasy. Urine tests for sedatives are often equivocal. Sedative-hypnotics typically remain positive in urine for two to four weeks after the last use. Occasional or regular prescription use for insomnia or a diagnosed anxiety disorder can also produce a positive urine test. Heroin, which is also sedating, can be detected by urine screen for four days after use. Cocaine and amphetamines are used for stimulation rather than sedation. Cocaine remains positive in the urine for at least four days after use. Beginning in the early 1990s, heroin and cannabis abuse became frequent companions of alcoholism.

Employees who abuse sedative-hypnotics and stimulants in alternation present a confusing clinical picture. Although a urine screen is not definitive for alcoholism, the presence of heroin or cocaine in the urine of a person suspected of alcoholism suggests dual or polysubstance use.

Comorbidity with Other Psychiatric Disorders. Certain psychiatric disorders occur quite commonly among alcoholics and can contribute to alcoholic behavior, emotional distress, and failure of alcoholism treatment. Proper psychiatric diagnosis and treatment are essential. The more common dually occurring conditions are affective disorders, consisting of depression and mood swings, as well as generalized anxiety, social phobia, and panic disorder. Personality disorders are also encountered often (see the other chapters in Part Four).

Central nervous system effects of alcohol and alcohol withdrawal mimic such psychiatric disorders as depression and anxiety. As a result, accurate diagnosis of coexisting psychiatric problems is nearly impossible during active drinking or detoxification. While taking a detailed history, a psychiatrist can make an educated guess. If symptoms of other illnesses predated the onset of alcohol dependence or were clearly present during a dry period, a coexisting diagnosis should always be suspected. It would be a mistake to treat alcoholism separately since the likelihood of relapse to both conditions is greater if one condition is ignored at the expense of the other. If there is any suggestion of comorbidity, referral should be made to a psychiatrist with expertise in evaluating and treating substance abuse.

Detoxification

Most commonly, withdrawal occurs within seventy-two hours after the last drink. Objective signs of withdrawal include increased elevated blood pressure, pulse, respiration rate, and temperature. Other symptoms include shaking, nervousness, nausea, and visual, auditory, or tactile (skin crawling) hallucinations. The hallucinations are an extreme manifestation of withdrawal, called delirium tremens. If not promptly treated, delirium tremens can lead to convulsions, coma, and death.

Alcoholics usually have mild withdrawal symptoms, which can be controlled with two or three doses of chlordiazepoxide (Librium) over a twenty-four-hour period. Binge drinkers, who can have intervals of days or months when they do not drink, often have no withdrawal symptoms at all. If patients have been drinking daily for months or years, have experienced nausea or shaking hours after the previous drink, have a history of hypertension, or have had withdrawal seizures in the past, hospitalization is advisable. Any one of these factors is potentially significant. Both hypertension and history of a previous withdrawal seizure merit around-the-clock monitoring.

Alcohol withdrawal symptoms are the mirror image of alcohol's effect on the nervous system. Initially, alcohol has a calming effect, lowers inhibition, and in overdose depresses heartbeat and respirations. After the body's nervous system has become accustomed to alcohol, abrupt removal leads to withdrawal symptoms. Benzodiazepines cross-react with alcohol and thus have a similar effect on the nervous system. Some benzodiazepines, such as chlordiazepoxide and diazepam, have a long half-life. A single dose remains active for forty-eight to seventy-two hours before it is metabolized (broken down into components and eliminated). Because alcohol is metabolized much faster, the longer-acting benzodiazepines are used for detoxification. They prevent convulsions and lower the blood pressure and pulse. When liver function tests are abnormal or if the liver is enlarged on physical examination, oxazepam (Serax) is often preferred for detoxification. Since oxazepam is not metabolized by the liver, it is less likely than alprazolam to cause additional liver damage.

Medical Complications

Although screening blood tests are not specific for alcoholism, certain findings suggest some common medical complications. For example, the blood count might indicate anemia. This may reflect alcohol's toxic effect on bone marrow production of red blood cells. Alternately, alcoholism can lead to anemia from dietary deficiencies of iron, vitamin B_{12} or folate, or from alcohol-related bleeding disorders. With anemia and depressed white cells, the alcoholic has a poor immune system for fighting infections, including hepatitis B and C and human immunodeficiency virus.

Unless the alcoholic is in liver failure, mildly abnormal liver function tests are best managed by total abstinence from alcohol. Advanced cirrhosis, pancreatitis (inflamed pancreas), peptic ulcer, and esophageal varices (dilated veins around the esophagus, which frequently bleed) are complications that should be treated in conjunction with an internist, gastroenterologist, or liver specialist. Alcoholic cardiomyopathy (flabby, damaged heart muscle) and diabetes are other frequent complications.

Common nervous system manifestations of alcoholism include memory loss and peripheral neuropathy (nerve and muscle damage causing loss of such sensations as pain and temperature sensitivity, or causing muscle weakness). Peripheral neuropathy represents local damage to muscles and nerves of the hands, feet, or eyes. Although complete paralysis of an arm or leg does not occur, the neuropathy often causes a wide-based gait. Loss of sensation limits spatial awareness, and thus walking with legs close together would cause loss of balance. Memory loss and peripheral neuropathy can be prevented with large doses of thiamine (vitamin B_1). Thiamine should be added to the admission order sheet whenever the neurological or mental status examination suggests cortical damage or peripheral neuropathy. A third type of nervous system damage is cerebellar atrophy. The two cerebellar hemispheres govern eye and arm movement. Intoxication induces a temporary cerebellar malfunction and consequent inability to walk in a straight line. When chronic alcohol exposure produces cerebellar atrophy (wasting), the lack of coordination becomes permanent. Nevertheless, neurological symptoms should never be automatically attributed to alcohol. Unsuspected alternate causes must also be considered. Similarly, what appear to be alcohol withdrawal symptoms can have such other causes as thyroid disease.

Inpatient Versus Outpatient Treatment

The possible increased efficacy of inpatient versus outpatient treatment programs has been the subject of some controversy. Many patients can be readily treated as outpatients, but inpatient treatment is necessary in situations that would make treatment outside a hospital dangerous or ineffective:

Inpatient Treatment	*Outpatient Treatment*
Risk of withdrawal seizure	No risk of withdrawal seizure
Severe medical complications	Healthy or medically stable
Severe coexisting psychiatric problem	Not psychotic or suicidal
Pathological environment at home or work	Supportive environment

There are many variations of both inpatient and outpatient treatment models and wide variations in treatment quality. Outpatient treatment in particular can range from simple brief counseling to comprehensive medical, psychiatric, and psychotherapeutic evaluation and treatment. The American Society of Addiction Medicine's patient placement criteria (Mee-Lee, Shulman, Fishman, Gastfriend, & Griffith, 2001) provide guidelines for determining the correct setting in which to place patients according to medical necessity with consideration given to treatment intensity. The recent revision of the criteria has individualized the treatment recommendations.

Case 4

Millicent Green, a forty-two-year-old single woman, is the adult child of two verbally and physically abusive alcoholic parents. Until she finished high school, Millicent was the designated caretaker of her younger sister. More than once, she stopped an intoxicated parent from beating her sister. Her father was fired from job after job, and the family was often on welfare. Millicent vowed that she was never going to drink.

Despite her chaotic home life, Millicent excelled academically, obtained full scholarship support at an elite private college, and was then immediately hired by a large accounting firm. She earned her CPA by studying at night and advanced to a high-level position. Millicent avoided emotional commitments. She devoted herself to her work and to her younger sister, now an alcoholic. When many of her company's clients left the metropolitan area, the company merged with another. Millicent was kept on, but she no longer reported directly to the CEO. Her new boss was uncomfortable working with women above the level of secretary and did not agree with Millicent's approach to client relationships.

Millicent depended solely on her work for emotional stability. She had no other sources of support to offset her reduced prestige and increased interpersonal stress. Since she had learned in childhood to keep feelings inside and her parents' behavior kept her from inviting friends to her home, her adult social life was not much different.

After the merger, walking into her empty apartment at night became a dreary experience. In the past, she had brought projects home, knowing that her efforts would be recognized. Now there was nothing to do except eat frozen dinners and watch television. She dreaded each workday, barely had the energy to get through her diminishing assignments, and had little hope for the future. She developed insomnia, with early morning awakening, and lost ten pounds without dieting. Although Millicent had no specific suicidal plans, she wondered why she was alive.

One day was particularly stressful. Her boss vetoed her proposal at a breakfast meeting and clearly put her down. She decided to try some wine with dinner to relieve the tension. She felt a little better and decided that one or two glasses of wine with dinner would do no harm. Soon, Millicent nipped wine all day on weekends, with four glasses with dinner, and a bit more in the middle of the night. Counting the hours until she could return home and start drinking, she began to drink wine at lunch. The local café opened at 11:30, and Millicent was soon the first customer each day.

It was the 10:00 A.M. shaking that frightened Millicent out of her doldrums. When it kept her from signing documents, she remembered how her mother's hands would shake in the morning. Although she had suppressed any concerns about alcoholism previously, she now made an appointment with the EAP department.

Because her shaking and rapid pulse rate suggested that she might risk seizure without medical supervision, inpatient treatment was considered. Moreover, her insomnia, weight loss, lethargy, decreased pleasure in her work, and passive suicidal ideation suggested the probability of a coexisting depression that would need attention. The depression, her work environment, and her lack of social supports all pointed to risk of relapse in outpatient treatment. Millicent was referred to the dual diagnosis unit of a psychiatric hospital that merged psychiatric expertise with a deep respect for AA.

On admission, Millicent had high blood pressure and a fast pulse. Her last drink had worn off, and she clearly needed detoxification. On physical examination, her liver was enlarged. Blood tests confirmed moderate but reversible liver damage, as well as dietary iron and folate (a vitamin) deficiencies. Iron and folate were added to Millicent's daily orders.

Millicent's depression was still there after a three-day detoxification. Moreover, she admitted that she was not just thinking about suicide. She was planning it by overdosing on over-the-counter Tylenol. Her psychiatrist started her on antidepressant medication. Now that detoxification was complete, she was not given benzodiazepines or barbiturates for insomnia because of their addictive potential. Medication response was not expected for at least two and a half weeks. She attended daily group therapy and educational groups that taught her how AA works and stressed relapse prevention. Her substance abuse counselor and her psychiatrist also sent her to an Adult Children of Alcoholics (ACOA) educational group. Because of her depression, it was difficult for Millicent to concentrate, and she was feeling hopeless about her ability to stay sober. But as the antidepressant started to work, she began to derive comfort from AA meetings, group therapy, and ACOA.

Millicent had an on-site meeting with her EAP counselor, her psychiatrist, and her hospital alcohol counselor. Together, they suggested that a lateral move to another department of her firm would take her out of the environment that had triggered her depression and alcoholism. Human resources staff agreed, and Millicent returned to work. Her hospitalization had lasted one month.

She began to use AA instead of her job to compensate for her lack of affectionate support. She enjoyed the new relationships she developed with her sponsor and other women in AA, and she learned to take criticism better at work. She continued to see a psychiatrist monthly for medication monitoring and supportive psychotherapy and to watch for reemergence of depressive symptoms. Within a few months, Millicent's job performance matched her earlier level, and she was even a bit better with clients.

This case demonstrates the importance of combining medical, psychiatric, and AA approaches. An inpatient dual diagnosis unit is designed to combine these approaches and to allow for close cooperation with outside EAP and human resource departments. Had she not been suicidal, Millicent would have been discharged to partial hospitalization (a day program) that would also have combined these approaches. Millicent's alcoholism, depression, medical problems, alcohol withdrawal, and emotional concerns were assessed, monitored, and treated in a safe, coordinated, and effective way.

Merging Psychiatric Treatment with AA Philosophy

AA is not incompatible with psychiatric treatment. Historically, AA had been suspicious of all psychoactive medications. This was not helped by psychiatrists who dismissed AA as a cult and prescribed tranquilizers and sedatives. Most psychiatrists now recognize the value of AA for maintaining sobriety and are leery of prescribing any medication with addictive potential. Correspondingly, most AA members have come to appreciate the value of appropriately prescribed medication. Should a sponsor advise a patient not to listen to his or her psychiatrist regarding medication, the psychiatrist can educate both patient and sponsor about the medication's action and properties.

No psychiatric condition can be treated successfully unless the patient is abstinent. Even today, the benefits of medication and psychotherapy can be blocked or hidden by the effects of alcohol. AA can be viewed as an ally in protecting abstinence and promoting socialization for the recovering alcoholic.

RETURN TO WORK

Newly recovering alcoholics are advised to place a moratorium on out-of-town business trips for several reasons. One is that establishing a new habit of AA meeting attendance provides a foundation for a solid support network. This habit is easily broken when it has not become second nature and even more so if interrupted by travel. Even if the employee is diligent in finding and attending AA meetings out of town, local group members know the employee best and are more likely to notice the subtle changes in attitude that lead to relapse. The histories of relapsed patients show a pattern of complacency about meetings that precedes a return to drinking. When the employee returns from a business trip, he or she may be less attentive to recovery and rationalize that AA attendance is not really essential for sobriety. Second, business- and first-class airline seats are almost like a flying bar. The temptation worsens when flights are lengthy or delayed. Finally, it is not easy for the newly sober alcoholic to be alone in a strange city. No matter how motivated the person, the craving for alcohol can become intense. And with craving comes the unconscious rationalization that "I'm out of town, so no one will know."

It is also important to address workplace factors that can trigger alcohol craving. The most significant stressors are often problematic interpersonal tensions that can be heightened by employee, peer, superior, and subordinate personality traits, by organizational change and stress, and by the lingering relationship effects of alcohol abuse. Sometimes a lateral job transfer can remove the employee from a difficult set of relationships. Human resource departments play a pivotal role here and should always keep in mind the employee's highest level of past performance. It is counterproductive and far too simplistic to overlook true career potential or to fire the sober alcoholic outright. But offering promotions too early in recovery can trigger relapse. Inadvertently, it sends the message that the employee has somehow gotten away with drinking.

Returning employees are apprehensive about coworkers' knowledge of their problem. It is of vital importance that management, human resource, and mental health professionals respect employee confidentiality. Treatment centers typically advise patients to offer very little information about their absence to nonintimate acquaintances and coworkers. Excuses and lies compound themselves into ever more elaborate and unconvincing stories. The resulting atmosphere of deception not only creates mistrust but also encourages rationalization, denial, and thus relapses. Recovery should be accompanied by complete honesty. This does not mean that the returning employee should say he or she has been detoxified. "I'm fine. Thanks for asking" is more than enough information. More open discussion is reserved for family, therapy, AA, and supportive intimates at work.

Clients with psychiatric comorbidity should be followed by a psychiatrist, with continuation of appropriate medication for at least several months. Many depressive and anxiety disorders have long-term intermittent courses and often recur eventually. If an employee has a history of recurrent symptoms prior to alcohol treatment or if symptoms recur when the medication dosage is reduced, follow-up should continue for an extended period of time. Periodic psychiatric assessment helps to prevent relapse and preserve high-level job performance. It is likely to save far more money than it costs.

This chapter has discussed diagnosis, workplace detection, and management of alcoholism. Case examples have been used to illustrate how and when to refer patients and how to select the correct treatment. Return-to-work strategies for preventing relapse have been outlined and have also been illustrated with case examples.

Although most of the coexisting psychiatric diagnoses commonly found among alcoholics have been discussed, some diagnoses were not included, particularly, bipolar disorder, atypical depression, generalized anxiety, psychosis, and personality disorders other than antisocial personality (see other chapters for details).

References and Additional Sources

American Psychiatric Association. (2000). *Diagnostic and statistical manual of mental disorders* (4th ed. rev.). Washington, DC: Author.

Cloninger, C. R. (1987). Neurogenetic adaptive mechanisms in alcoholism. *Science, 236,* 410–416.

Cloninger, C. R. (1999). Genetics of substance abuse. In M. Galanter & H. D. Kleber (Eds.), *Textbook of substance abuse treatment.* Washington, DC: American Psychiatric Press.

Greenfield, S. F. (2002). Women and alcohol use disorders. *Harvard Review of Psychiatry, 10*(2), 76–85.

Harwood, H. J., Fountain, D., & Livermore, G. (1998). Economic costs of alcohol abuse and alcoholism. In M. Galanter, F. J. Chaloupka, M. Grossman, & H. Saffer (Eds.), *Recent developments in alcoholism: The consequences of alcoholism.* New York: Plenum.

Mee-Lee, D., Shulman, G. R., Fishman, M., Gastfriend, D. R., & Griffith, J. H. (Eds.). (2001). *ASAM patient placement criteria for the treatment of substance-related disorders* (2nd ed. rev.). Chevy Chase, MD: American Society of Addiction Medicine.

CHAPTER TWENTY-SIX

Psychosis

Peculiar Behaviors and Inflexible Bizarre Beliefs

Corinne Cather
Kim T. Mueser
Donald C. Goff

Psychotic symptoms refer to experiences that reflect being out of touch with reality, such as perceiving sensory stimuli that others do not perceive (hallucination) or holding a false and often bizarre belief tenaciously (delusion). The presence of a psychotic symptom may be a sign of a psychological disorder, drug or alcohol intoxication, or a medical condition. Although early recognition, referral, and treatment are extremely important, the recognition of psychotic symptoms by persons in the workplace may be difficult because psychotic experiences are often concealed from others. Psychotic symptoms are frequently both distressing and distracting to the individual and therefore can impair work performance. Moreover, they may be associated with bizarre social behavior, impaired judgment, and affective (mood) symptoms. Work colleagues may have difficulty making sense of the behavioral and mood changes apparent in an individual experiencing an exacerbation of a preexisting psychotic disorder or new-onset psychosis. Early recognition and treatment of psychotic disorders can offset functional disability and may improve the course of the illness. The vast majority of psychotic disorders respond well to treatment, and there is reason to be optimistic about the capability of sustained employment for individuals with psychotic disorders.

Workplaces that elect to be educated about psychotic disorders can expect benefits from increased understanding of their colleagues with psychotic disorders. Moreover, only through education can workplaces become equipped to recognize symptoms of psychotic disorders, make appropriate referrals to mental health professionals, understand what constitutes reasonable

---

The same chapter title was used in the previous edition of this book for a chapter on this subject written by Richard H. Gabel.

accommodation under the Americans with Disabilities Act, and contribute to the worthy aim of destigmatizing mental illness.

DELUSIONAL DISORDERS

Several features differentiate delusional disorder from schizophrenia. Delusional disorder typically has its onset in middle age, whereas schizophrenia is usually diagnosed in early adulthood, although symptoms may start in adolescence. Unlike schizophrenia, delusional disorder is typically not accompanied by prominent hallucinations. Moreover, whereas delusional beliefs in schizophrenia may be broad and involve bizarre themes, in delusional disorder the beliefs tend to be nonbizarre or even plausible (for example, the belief that the Internal Revenue Service is tracking an individual's finances). Delusional disorders are categorized by the thematic content of the delusional beliefs.

Although delusional disorder can have devastating effects on particular aspects of an individual's functional status, the associated global functional deficits are typically more limited than in schizophrenia. Delusional disorder is fairly uncommon, with an estimated population prevalence of only .03 percent.

❧ Diagnostic Criteria for Delusional Disorder

A. Nonbizarre delusions (i.e., involving situations that occur in real life, such as being followed, poisoned, infected, loved at a distance, or deceived by spouse or lover, or having a disease) of at least 1 month's duration.

B. Criterion A for Schizophrenia has never been met. *Note:* Tactile and olfactory hallucinations may be present in Delusional Disorder if they are related to the delusional theme.

C. Apart from the impact of the delusion(s) or its ramifications, functioning is not markedly impaired and behavior is not obviously odd or bizarre.

D. If mood episodes have occurred concurrently with delusions, their total duration has been brief relative to the duration of the delusional periods.

E. The disturbance is not due to the direct physiological effects of a substance (e.g., a drug of abuse, a medication) or a general medical condition.

Specify type (the following types are assigned based on the predominant delusional theme):

Erotomanic Type: delusions that another person, usually of higher status, is in love with the individual

Grandiose Type: delusions of inflated worth, power, knowledge, identity, or special relationship to a deity or famous person

Jealous Type: delusions that the individual's sexual partner is unfaithful

Persecutory Type: delusions that the person (or someone to whom the person is close) is being malevolently treated in some way

Somatic Type: delusions that the person has some physical defect or general medical condition

Mixed Type: delusions characteristic of more than one of the above types but no one theme predominates

Unspecified Type

Reprinted with permission from the Diagnostic and Statistical Manual of Mental Disorders, Fourth Edition, Text Revision. *Copyright 2000 American Psychiatric Association.*

Case 1

Eric Delacroix, a fifty-two-year-old civil servant, became suddenly convinced that his wife of twenty-five years was cheating on him while he was at work, so he would leave work early some days to try to "catch her in the act." Despite her protestations that this was not occurring and his lack of any hard evidence to the contrary, Eric believed that she was cheating on him with other men and refused to believe otherwise. Eric did not share his beliefs with anyone at the workplace. However, his tendency to leave work early at times was reflected in poorer evaluations by his supervisors. Eric was contemplating early retirement so that he could keep a closer eye on his wife. When his colleagues questioned him about why he wanted to retire early, he finally admitted his suspicions. At first, his colleagues were sympathetic, but they were confused when he was unable to provide any details as to how he was aware of her infidelity.

One day, his wife came into work, and when she left, Eric accused a coworker of being overly friendly to her. This unfounded accusation prompted his coworker to report his odd behavior to a supervisor, who referred Eric to the employee assistance program (EAP). The counselor arranged a meeting with a psychiatrist, who started Eric on an antipsychotic medication. After six weeks, Eric's conviction in the belief that his wife was being unfaithful greatly diminished, and he no longer left work early to check on her.

Causes

The causes of delusional disorder are largely not understood. The stress vulnerability model (reviewed in the section on schizophrenia later in the chapter) is a broad paradigm for the multifactorial causes of any psychotic disorder. Based on the finding that delusional disorder is a more common diagnosis among immigrants, cultural stress has been identified as playing a role in the formation of a delusional disorder. Furthermore, it has been suggested that individuals who move to another country as adults may be unfamiliar with the social practices and customs of a country and therefore more likely to misinterpret social interactions, which places them at risk for the development of a delusional disorder.

Workplace Recognition and Referral

Delusional disorders can be difficult to detect because the individual is likely to be motivated to hide his delusional beliefs from others; and even if he does disclose them, the belief will sound plausible and will likely elicit empathy from colleagues rather than alert them to the presence of a psychological disorder. Individuals diagnosed with persecutory-type delusional disorder are often litigious, and in some cases, it will be the individual's discussion of seeking legal action that might alert coworkers to the presence of delusional beliefs. In other cases, colleagues may be struck by the incongruity of their experience of a person with what the individual reports to be the case (for example, the idea that others want him to leave town) or by the perception that a particular injustice is unlikely in the current legal system (for example, that the Division of Social Services broke into one's home and took custody of an individual's son without cause).

Effects of Symptoms in the Workplace

Individuals with a delusional disorder may have encapsulated delusional beliefs that do not revolve around the work setting and therefore may not have a direct effect on their work performance. Delusional disorder may be more apparent when an individual develops erroneous beliefs about a coworker (perhaps the belief that a coworker is in love with him) or a supervisor (that the supervisor is endeavoring to get him fired). Indirect effects on work performance may be seen when individuals are so distressed by their delusional beliefs that they are no longer able to work efficiently.

Psychiatric Management

Individuals with a delusional disorder are usually prescribed antipsychotic medication. Poor insight is typically a feature of delusional disorder, so poor adherence with medication is common. Individuals with delusional disorder may be motivated to take antipsychotic medication for its antianxiety rather than its antipsychotic effects. Although delusional disorder is associated with less functional impairment than schizophrenia, delusional beliefs are often not completely remediated by antipsychotic medication. There are no data on the efficacy of psychotherapy for the treatment of delusional disorder, although the promising results of cognitive-behavioral therapy (CBT) in schizophrenia suggest potential benefits of this approach in delusional disorder.

Return to Work and ADA Reasonable Accommodation

Individuals with delusional disorder may require psychiatric hospitalization to stabilize symptoms and thus may require a flexible policy with regard to returning to their workplace. Because adherence to medication may be an issue, it may be beneficial to make continued employment contingent on keeping regular psychiatric visits.

AFFECTIVE DISORDERS WITH PSYCHOTIC FEATURES

Psychotic symptoms can be part of an affective disorder, as in bipolar disorder (manic-depressive disorder) with psychotic features or major depressive disorder with psychotic features. These disorders are characterized by disruptions in mood that are accompanied by psychotic symptoms. Affective disorders with psychotic features differ from schizoaffective disorder insofar as psychotic symptoms are intertwined with the mood disturbance in the former; thus, as mood normalizes, the psychotic symptoms also remit. In contrast, schizoaffective disorders are characterized by the persistence of psychotic symptoms even when mood is normal.

Case 2

Kira Roth was a twenty-five-year-old eighth-grade history teacher and co-chair of the drama department at a public school. When the chair of the drama department went on maternity leave, the bulk of the responsibility for the school's musical fell on Kira. Prior to the demands of single-handedly running the musical, Kira had observed a strict regimen of getting eight hours of sleep each night, regular meals, and a rigorous exercise routine. Kira had religiously followed this routine following treatment for a major depressive disorder during her first year of college. The musical disrupted her schedule, and she started staying at work for twelve- and fifteen-hour days and sleeping very little. She began hearing flattering voices saying, "You are a true artist" and "One in a thousand." She began to contemplate a change in career and told her colleagues that she had been invited to attend a prestigious drama school. Kira started to behave as if the rules did not apply to her; she spent more than double the budget allotted to her for costumes and scenery and stopped observing the dress code of the school, dressing less conservatively and applying more makeup.

Her colleagues began to notice that Kira was speaking very quickly and that she seemed "hyper" and self-important. Kira's temper was short with the students in the musical, and when one of the parents called to complain, Kira told the parent that he needed to stop "babying" his son and face facts that his son was a "liar." This parent called the principal, who summoned Kira for a meeting with her at which time she revealed that many parents had issued complaints about Kira in recent weeks. Kira began to cry and told the principal that she wasn't sure what was going on, but that she had not felt herself recently. The principal recommended that she speak to a mental health professional as a condition of her continued employment.

Kira was diagnosed with bipolar I disorder, most recent episode manic, severe with mood-congruent psychotic features and treated with a combination of an antipsychotic medication and a mood stabilizer. When she returned to work two weeks later, she no longer had any psychotic symptoms, but her mood continued to be somewhat elevated. Five months later, Kira's mood had returned to normal, and the antipsychotic medication was discontinued.

Causes

There is no clear explanation as to why some individuals with affective disorders develop psychotic features and others do not. It has been suggested that some individuals are more prone to develop psychotic symptoms than others as a result of their environment, stress level, and biological factors.

Workplace Recognition and Referral

As with any other psychiatric disorder, workplace recognition is greatly enhanced by attention to shifts in an individual's personality, behavior, performance, and appearance. Workplaces that are alert to such changes are in a position to recognize the early warning signs of psychological distress, perhaps even before the distress progresses to the level of functional impairment. Work environments that incorporate periodic reviews as a matter of practice may be more likely to recognize psychological changes in an employee.

Affective disorders with psychotic features are characterized by hallucinations or delusions that accompany prominent depressive, manic, or mixed (irritable) mood symptoms. The symptoms of an affective disorder may be difficult to differentiate from psychotic symptoms (see Chapter Twenty-Two). For example, mania is often associated with grandiose ideas, which are on a continuum with grandiose delusions. The presence of psychotic features, such as hallucinations or delusions, may be mood congruent (for example, hearing voices saying "nobody likes you" as consistent with major depression) or mood incongruent (the grandiose delusions are inconsistent with major depression). Mood-incongruent symptoms are thought to be a poor prognostic indicator.

Effects of Symptoms in the Workplace

Individuals with an affective disorder may exert a stressor on the workplace environment. It can be a jarring experience for coworkers to experience the shift in mood and behavior that occurs as an individual develops symptoms of an affective disorder. It is unlikely that coworkers will become aware of psychotic features; often the individual will keep these experiences to himself or herself. A potential outcome is that coworkers may distance themselves from an individual who is experiencing a psychological disorder as they lose confidence in the individual's ability to complete tasks or because the individual has become difficult to relate to on an interpersonal level.

Psychiatric Management

Generally, there are three possible pharmacological treatment strategies for the treatment of affective disorders with psychotic features. Because antipsychotic medication may not be adequate to treat both the affective disorder and the psychotic features, an antipsychotic agent is often combined with an agent targeting the affective disorder—either an antidepressant or a mood stabilizer. Electroconvulsive treatment is also a highly effective treatment for major depression with psychotic features.

There have not been any attempts to evaluate specifically the effectiveness of psychotherapy in individuals diagnosed with affective disorders with psychotic features. The logical place to start, however, might be with adapting the treatments that have been found to be effective in the treatment of affective disorders without psychotic features to individuals diagnosed with affective disorders and psychotic features. Although more research has studied the benefits of psychosocial treatments in unipolar than bipolar depression, behavior therapy, CBT, and interpersonal therapy appear to be the most promising psychosocial treatments to date. Behavior therapy focuses on remediating maladaptive patterns of behavior, such as scheduling pleasant events and improving assertiveness skills. Specialized forms of behavior therapy include behavioral marital therapy or behavioral family therapy, which focus on building the skills of the whole family in an effort to improve problem-solving skills. CBT incorporates behavioral elements with the addition of focusing on building skills to identify and modify maladaptive patterns of thinking and psychoeducation about the illness and medication. Interpersonal therapy focuses on developing more effective ways of relating to other people. Some individuals and family members seem to benefit from involvement with self-help groups, such as the National Alliance for the Mentally Ill, although self-help has not been evaluated systematically in research studies.

Return to Work and ADA Reasonable Accommodation

Although the majority of individuals with affective disorders will be able to manage their illness with outpatient medication management and therapy, acute management may require hospitalization in some cases. Individuals with affective disorders are likely to have suicidal thoughts at some point in the history of their illness, and having psychotic symptoms may put someone at an even higher risk of suicidal thoughts or attempts. Although estimates of the percentage of individuals who successfully complete suicide are not available for individuals with psychotic features, individuals with major affective disorders have a 10 to 15 percent chance of committing suicide. Individuals with an affective disorder with psychotic features may require hospitalization at points in their illness due to medication nonadherence, increased stress resulting in symptom exacerbation, or biological changes that are associated with reduced effectiveness of medication or symptom resurgence. The majority of individuals respond well to treatment and can return to work once their symptoms stabilize.

SUBSTANCE-INDUCED PSYCHOTIC DISORDER

Other causes of psychotic symptoms include organic etiologies, as in psychotic disorder due to a general medical condition and substance-induced psychotic disorder. Several medical conditions can cause psychotic symptoms, including Huntington's disease, lupus erythematosus, epilepsy, thyroid disorders, and electrolyte imbalance. Psychotic symptoms may also be attributable to substance use or withdrawal, although the high rates of substance abuse and dependence in people diagnosed with schizophrenia or bipolar disorder suggest that careful assessment of symptoms is essential during periods free of substance use.

❖ Diagnostic Criteria for Substance-Induced Psychotic Disorder

A. Prominent hallucinations or delusions. *Note:* Do not include hallucinations if the person has insight that they are substance induced.

B. There is evidence from the history, physical examination, or laboratory findings of either (1) or (2):
   1. the symptoms in Criterion A developed during, or within a month of, Substance Intoxication or Withdrawal
   2. medication use is etiologically related to the disturbance

C. The disturbance is not better accounted for by a Psychotic Disorder that is not substance induced. Evidence that the symptoms are better accounted for by a Psychotic Disorder that is not substance induced might include the following: the symptoms precede the onset of the substance use (or medication use); the symptoms persist for a substantial period of time (e.g., about a month) after the cessation of acute withdrawal or severe intoxication, or are substantially in excess of what would be expected given the type or amount of the substance used or the duration of use; or there is other evidence that suggests the existence of an independent non-substance-induced Psychotic Disorder (e.g., a history of recurrent non-substance-related episodes).

D. The disturbance does not occur exclusively during the course of a delirium.

Reprinted with permission from the Diagnostic and Statistical Manual of Mental Disorders, Fourth Edition, Text Revision. *Copyright 2000 American Psychiatric Association.*

Case 3

John Trevor was a thirty-one-year-old single male who was laid off by the small computer company where he had worked as a software salesperson for three years. He was discouraged following the loss of his job and began drinking and gambling. John had been a heavy marijuana smoker in high school, but had not smoked since that time and had never used cocaine. Eventually, however, John did start using marijuana and cocaine. Once his unemployment benefits ran out, his friend helped him to obtain employment at his company. For the first few months of his employment, John abstained from using drugs and alcohol. He established good relationships with his customers, was enthusiastic about his work, and was seen as an asset to the company.

After a few months, however, John returned to a pattern of gambling and using alcohol and drugs and began procuring his own supply of marijuana and cocaine. He began having intermittent absences from work and appeared distant and jumpy when he was interacting with customers. Then one day, he confided in a coworker that he "would be keeping a low profile from now on" because there were people who "wanted to see him dead." Initially, his friend did not take this statement very seriously, although it occurred to him that John might have gotten in trouble with gambling debt. When John did not come to work the next day, he became concerned, and when he called John at home, John's phone had been disconnected. He went to John's residence and found John unshaven and the apartment in a shambles with the shades drawn and lines of cocaine on the coffee table. John told his friend that he needed to get out of town and indicated that he had been spending his days hidden in the event that the Drug Enforcement Agency (DEA) was keeping track of his movements. His friend convinced John to come for a ride with him in the car and took John to the local emergency room.

At the emergency room, John was treated with an antipsychotic and was referred to an inpatient psychiatric facility, where he was continued on the antipsychotic for one week. While in the hospital, he began attending Alcoholics Anonymous (AA) and Narcotics Anonymous (NA) meetings. After being in the hospital for one week, he was no longer fearful of the DEA. His antipsychotic medication was discontinued, and he remained in the hospital for another week without experiencing a resurgence of his paranoia. He was provisionally diagnosed with cocaine-induced psychotic disorder with delusions with onset during intoxication. He was referred for outpatient psychotherapy and continued his involvement with AA. John was unable to return to his previous place of employment because of his relatively short tenure there and its zero tolerance policy regarding illegal substance use.

Causes

Substance-induced psychosis is psychosis that is caused by the use of a substance of abuse. The drugs most commonly associated with psychosis are alcohol, stimulants (cocaine and amphetamines), ketamine and phencyclidine (angel dust), and hallucinogens (LSD and Ecstasy). Psychotic symptoms may become apparent on intoxication or withdrawal from a substance and symptoms typically remit with sustained abstinence from the substance of abuse.

Workplace Recognition and Referral

Workplace recognition of substance use may be facilitated by drug screening and drug-free policies. Often, however, attention to changes in the behavior and work performance of employees may be the best method for detecting substance abuse and concomitant psychological distress or psychosis.

Effects of Symptoms in the Workplace

Typically, an individual with a substance abuse problem devotes so much energy to acquiring and using substances that other responsibilities are not met. Furthermore, individuals may use substances in situations in which such use is dangerous (such as driving a car or operating other heavy machinery), potentially putting their safety and the safety of others at risk.

Psychiatric Management

Psychotic symptoms are typically treated with an antipsychotic medication. Because it is often difficult to determine whether the psychotic symptoms are the result of substance use or the start of a persistent psychotic disorder, it is important to observe the course of the psychotic symptoms once an individual has successfully abstained from substance use for a period of time.

Few medications have been shown to be effective in the treatment of substance abuse, and there are no medications currently available to treat certain types of substance abuse (cocaine is one of them). Behavioral and cognitive-behavioral therapy in combination with self-help groups like AA are the recommended mainstays of treatment for a substance use disorder. Individuals may also benefit from specific education about the association of psychotic symptoms and substance use in some people and the increased risk for a recurrence of psychotic symptoms with continued use.

Return to Work and ADA Reasonable Accommodation

Some workplaces may have policies that prohibit the use of substances of abuse, and in these cases it is likely that it will be difficult to have an individual with substance-induced psychosis return to the initial workplace. Workplaces that have more lenient policies can accommodate the needs of individuals with substance use disorders by permitting leave of absences for periods of inpatient detoxification.

SCHIZOPHRENIA SPECTRUM DISORDERS

Schizophrenia is one of several major psychiatric disorders characterized by psychotic symptoms. Positive symptoms (or psychotic symptoms) refer to hallucinations (false perceptions, such as hearing voices when no one is around), delusions (false beliefs, such as believing that the police intend to arrest you for having bad thoughts), and bizarre behavior (talking to oneself). Negative symptoms are characterized by deficits in emotional experience, expressiveness, and motivation. Common negative symptoms include anhedonia (diminished experience of pleasure), asociality (reduced social interest), anergia (decreased ability to initiate and follow through with plans), alogia (reduced speech production or reduced meaningful speech), and blunted affect (diminished emotional expressiveness). Cognitive impairments span the range of cognitive functions, including speed of information processing, attention and concentration, memory, abstract reasoning, and planning ability. Schizophrenia is a lifelong disorder that can have a major effect on the ability to work and to manage social relationships. Although there is a good deal of variability across individuals with schizophrenia in the severity and prominence of different symptoms, the disorder tends to be episodic, characterized by relapses that sometimes require inpatient treatment.

The diagnosis of schizophrenia is based largely on the presence of positive and negative symptoms, although there is growing appreciation for cognitive impairment as a critical feature of schizophrenia. The positive symptoms of schizophrenia are quite variable in their response to treatment; half of patients experience persistent symptoms despite being treated with medication. Negative symptoms, in contrast, tend to be much less responsive to medication, and few patients experience full remission of these symptoms between episodes of psychosis. The cognitive symptoms in schizophrenia tend to persist throughout the course of the illness, although their severity also increases during exacerbation of positive symptoms.

❧ Diagnostic Criteria for Schizophrenia

A. *Characteristic symptoms:* Two (or more) of the following, each present for a significant portion of time during a 1-month period (or less if successfully treated):
   1. delusions
   2. hallucinations
   3. disorganized speech (e.g., frequent derailment or incoherence)
   4. grossly disorganized or catatonic behavior
   5. negative symptoms, i.e., affective flattening, alogia, or avolition

Note: Only one Criterion A symptom is required if delusions are bizarre or hallucinations consist of a voice keeping up a running commentary on the person's behavior or thoughts, or two or more voices conversing with each other.

B. *Social/occupational dysfunction:* For a significant portion of the time since the onset of the disturbance, one or more major areas of functioning such as work, interpersonal relations, or self-care are markedly below the level achieved prior to the onset (or when the onset is in childhood or adolescence, failure to achieve expected level of interpersonal, academic, or occupational achievement).

C. *Duration:* Continuous signs of the disturbance persist for at least 6 months. This 6-month period must include at least 1 month of symptoms (or less if successfully treated) that meet Criterion A (i.e., active-phase symptoms) and may include periods of prodromal or residual symptoms. During these prodromal or residual periods, the signs of the disturbance may be manifested by only negative symptoms or two or more symptoms listed in Criterion A present in an attenuated form (e.g., odd beliefs, unusual perceptual experiences).

D. *Schizoaffective and Mood Disorder exclusion:* Schizoaffective Disorder and Mood Disorder With Psychotic Features have been ruled out because either (1) no

Major Depressive, Manic, or Mixed Episodes have occurred concurrently with the active-phase symptoms; or (2) if mood episodes have occurred during active-phase symptoms, their total duration has been brief relative to the duration of the active and residual periods.

E. *Substance/general medical condition exclusion:* The disturbance is not due to the direct physiological effects of a substance (e.g., a drug of abuse, a medication) or a general medical condition.

F. *Relationship to a Pervasive Developmental Disorder:* If there is a history of Autistic Disorder or another Pervasive Developmental Disorder, the additional diagnosis of Schizophrenia is made only if prominent delusions or hallucinations are also present for at least a month (or less if successfully treated).

Reprinted with permission from the Diagnostic and Statistical Manual of Mental Disorders, Fourth Edition, Text Revision. *Copyright 2000 American Psychiatric Association.*

In addition to the characteristic symptoms of schizophrenia, diagnostic criteria require impairment in functioning in major social roles (for example, worker, student, parent, spouse), impaired interpersonal relationships, a reduced ability to care for oneself, or minimal capacity to enjoy leisure activities. In addition to the characteristic symptoms and impairments, the diagnosis of schizophrenia requires a six-month period of impaired functioning. Therefore, at least some chronicity is incorporated into the definition of the disorder.

For many patients, problems in role functioning long predate the onset of the illness, which has its onset typically between the ages of sixteen and thirty years. Schizophrenia is closely related to three other disorders: schizoaffective disorder, schizophreniform disorder, and schizotypal personality disorder. Based on studies of mental illness in families and response to treatment, these disorders are grouped together as schizophrenia-spectrum disorders and are treated following the same guidelines. Individuals who meet the symptom and impaired functioning criteria for schizophrenia but whose impairment is less than six months duration (or who experience a full remission of symptoms with episodes lasting less than six months) meet diagnostic criteria for schizophreniform disorder. Individuals who meet criteria for schizophrenia during periods when their mood is normal but also have significant episodes of depression or mania meet diagnostic criteria for schizoaffective disorder. Schizotypal personality disorder resembles schizophrenia in many ways, although the severity of symptoms tends to be lower, and its course is less episodic and marked by less flagrant positive symptoms.

❖ Diagnostic Criteria for Schizoaffective Disorder

A. An uninterrupted period of illness during which, at some time, there is either a Major Depressive Episode, a Manic Episode, or a Mixed Episode concurrent with symptoms that meet Criterion A for Schizophrenia.

Note: The Major Depressive Episode must include Criterion A1: depressed mood.

B. During the same period of illness, there have been delusions or hallucinations for at least 2 weeks in the absence of prominent mood symptoms.

C. Symptoms that meet criteria for a mood episode are present for a substantial portion of the total duration of the active and residual periods of the illness.

D. The disturbance is not due to the direct physiological effects of a substance (e.g., a drug of abuse, a medication) or a general medical condition.

Specify type:

Bipolar Type: if the disturbance includes a Manic or a Mixed Episode (or a Manic or a Mixed Episode and Major Depressive Episodes)

Depressive Type: if the disturbance only includes Major Depressive Episodes

Reprinted with permission from the Diagnostic and Statistical Manual of Mental Disorders, Fourth Edition, Text Revision. *Copyright 2000 American Psychiatric Association.*

Case 4

Mary O'Neil was a twenty-seven-year-old single woman with a diagnosis of schizophrenia. She began hearing voices at age twenty, when she was in college and studying abroad, and noticed that she felt unreal and was having difficulty formulating her thoughts into words. Over a few months, she became increasingly anxious about being around other people, believing that they could read her thoughts and that she could read others' thoughts about her in public. She began hearing voices that she believed were the disparaging thoughts people around her were having about her, and she became socially withdrawn and stopped attending courses. When she stopped phoning her parents in the United States, they became concerned and alerted the director of the study-abroad program. She was sent home and hospitalized immediately.

Following her hospitalization, her symptoms stabilized with medication, and she began volunteering at a nonprofit corporation. She worked her way up to competitive employment as an administrative assistant in the agency, where she was known for reliable and competent work. After three years at the agency, she reluctantly accepted a promotion to become a billing clerk, and she experienced this change as stressful because she was not confident with computers.

Mary began coming into work early to spend more time on the computers, and her coworkers noticed that she was drinking a lot of coffee and was becoming more irritable. Although she was usually neatly dressed and groomed, she began looking more disheveled. Mary's supervisor attempted to speak to Mary regarding her concerns and found Mary to be very guarded. Mary had begun to believe that people were against her at work and that they wanted her to fail at her new job. Her thoughts became jumbled and confused, and she found it difficult to focus on what others were saying to her.

One day Mary was waiting in line at the cafeteria and was distressed by hearing voices instructing her to push her supervisor out of her way. Although Mary did not comply with this command hallucination, she decided that she could no longer handle work and without any explanation abruptly stopped coming to the office. When Mary attended her next scheduled appointment with her psychiatrist, her psychiatrist noticed the exacerbation in Mary's symptoms. He increased her medication and arranged for her social worker to refer her to an employment specialist for individuals with severe mental illness. The employment specialist helped Mary to regain her position at the nonprofit agency through coordination with the human resource department. Mary's supervisor and the employment specialist set up a line of communication with one another and created an action plan in the event that the supervisor noticed signs of an impending relapse. The supervisor would contact the employment specialist, who in turn would communicate with Mary's treatment team in the event that it appeared that she was experiencing an exacerbation of symptoms.

Causes

Schizophrenia is widely considered to be a biological disorder whose onset and outcome can be influenced by the environment, personal coping ability, medications, and commonly abused substances. The stress-vulnerability model is useful for conceptualizing the interactions of the biological factors, the environment, and the course of schizophrenia (Liberman et al., 1986; Zubin & Spring, 1977). According to this model, the course and severity of schizophrenia are determined by the interplay of biological vulnerability, environmental stress, and coping skills. Biological vulnerability is assumed to be determined early in life by a combination of genetic and perinatal factors. This vulnerability is critical to the development of schizophrenia; without it, the illness will not develop. When an individual has a biological vulnerability to schizophrenia, that vulnerability can be triggered by environmental stress, leading to the emergence of symptoms and characteristic impairments. Common examples of stress include major life events (moving away from home, starting a challenging job), tense and critical relationships with significant others, and lack of meaningful structure (jobless, out of school). After the onset of schizophrenia, exposure to stress can precipitate symptom exacerbations and further impair psychosocial functioning. The more effective coping skills the employee has, the less susceptible he or she will be to stress-induced relapses, because successful coping can eliminate the sources of stress or minimize its negative effects.

The stress-vulnerability model has several implications for understanding possible factors in the workplace that could contribute to symptom relapses and deterioration in functioning for persons with schizophrenia. Employees with schizophrenia who work at highly demanding jobs, with substantial expectations on productivity, time pressure, and rapid change to accommodate new opportunities, may find the pace and requirements of the job stressful, which could increase their risk of relapse. Jobs requiring changeable work hours, especially overtime work, extended hours, or work on little sleep, may similarly create stress. In addition, if the work environment is socially stressful, such as involving high levels of criticism from supervisors or tension among coworkers, employees may be at increased risk of relapse. The problem of social stress is of particular importance because employees with schizophrenia often have poor social perception skills (such as recognizing facial expressions, taking hints, interpreting others' motives), resulting in or exacerbating social problems. For example, they may mistakenly believe that their coworkers do not like them or value their work.

Although the stress-vulnerability model suggests stress in the workplace could contribute to symptom relapses in schizophrenia, it also indicates that the experience of working in a positive environment may confer protection against relapses as well. Research indicates that meaningful structure is associated with reduced levels of psychotic behavior (Rosen, Sussman, Mueser, Lyons, & Davis, 1981), and social support has been well established as a protective factor against relapses (Buchanan, 1995). Work that provides meaning and structure to employees may help to create a sense of purpose, thereby reducing stress. Positive and supportive social relationships at the workplace may result in similar benefits.

Workplace Recognition and Referral

Relapses in schizophrenia typically involve increases in psychotic symptoms, which are often accompanied by cognitive disorganization and mood instability. Severe relapses may prevent the patient from fulfilling job responsibilities altogether and possibly require hospitalization, but minor relapses can often be treated effectively, resulting in minimal disruption to work performance. The key to preventing major relapses, and thereby maintaining steady and good job performance, is good monitoring of the patient's psychiatric functioning and rapid action when changes are noted. This monitoring can be especially effective when it involves several people, including the case manager, supported employment specialist, the employer (when feasible), therapist, and family members.

Relapses tend to occur slowly over time, with small changes in mood, cognitive functioning, and behavior preceding the emergence or worsening of psychotic symptoms. These early warning signs of relapse are unique to each patient. Identifying these signs, monitoring them, and taking steps to address them when they emerge (for example, providing additional medication) can be effective in preventing full-blown episodes and maintaining functional capacity (Herz et al., 2000).

Effects of Symptoms in the Workplace

Schizophrenia can have a major impact on the ability of people to work, their performance at work, and their relationships with coworkers. Many employees with these symptoms and impairments are capable of excellent performance on the job, and work itself may have beneficial effects on reducing symptom severity (Bell, Lysaker, & Milstein, 1996). Thus, the presence of symptoms or associated problems should not be interpreted as suggesting problems in work are necessarily likely.

Individuals with apathy and anergia may seem as though they lack motivation and enthusiastic commitment to their work. It is important for supervisors and colleagues to recognize that these behaviors are part of the illness and should not be construed as reflecting that an individual is lazy or disinterested in staying employed. Although some people with schizophrenia work full time, part-time work may be more suitable for many employees because the overall effort required is less taxing. In addition, scheduled breaks may help employees maintain a steady level of energy throughout the workday.

Another negative symptom that can lead to misunderstandings at the workplace is blunted affect. People with schizophrenia often lack emotional expressiveness in their interactions with others and frequently have flattened facial expressions and minimal vocal inflection. These behaviors, which are common symptoms of schizophrenia, may give the false impression of not being interested, concerned, or responsive to others in what they have to say and can make interactions with such individuals less rewarding. Jobs that require strong customer service skills may not be a good match for individuals with blunted affect or impaired ability to read social cues.

Cognitive impairment in schizophrenia may have an impact on work performance in a variety of ways, depending on the tasks required and the specific nature of the deficits. A common problem is reduced speed of information processing and slower reaction time. This may be reflected in social interactions with the employee, in which the pace of conversation seems unnaturally slow. Jobs that require extensive interaction with others, including customers, or that require a rapid reaction time may not be a good match for employees with pronounced cognitive deficits. Other common cognitive problems include poor memory, difficulties in concept formation and abstract reasoning, and reduced planning ability.

There are several implications for these limitations at the workplace. Employees may require longer periods of time to learn how to perform a job, and the task may need to be broken down into small steps to simplify the learning process. Jobs that involve learning a large amount of information may require adaptation to overcome limits on memory. Work involving abstract concepts and rapid, creative decision making may be difficult or impossible for some employees to perform.

Positive symptoms, including delusions and hallucinations, are not frequent, but when they do occur, they can easily disrupt behavior at the workplace. With respect to delusions, employees may believe that others are talking about them or plotting against them, leading to suspicious behavior or avoidance. This pattern may disrupt relationships with coworkers and employers. Hallucinations can be problematic when employees respond to them publicly, such as talking back to voices or when the hallucinations distract the individual from focusing on work.

Impairments in social skills can have a significant effect on functioning in the workplace. Employees may be awkward when casually interacting with coworkers, responding to customers, seeking assistance in problematic situations, responding to criticism and negative feedback from supervisors, or speaking assertively with others. These problems can interfere with a good working atmosphere and, when the job involves direct customer interactions, job performance.

The common problem of substance abuse in schizophrenia can affect work functioning in a similar fashion as in the general population. Substance abuse can contribute to unexplained absences, reduced job performance due to the effects of substances or withdrawal, erratic behavior, and theft. Jobs in which alcohol consumption is considered part of normal socializing behavior among coworkers after work may be especially problematic for people with psychiatric disorders; evidence indicates that persons with schizophrenia are more sensitive to negative consequences from relatively moderate alcohol use (Mueser, Drake, & Wallach, 1998).

Psychiatric Management

Comprehensive treatment is needed for most employees with schizophrenia in order to attend to the wide range of their needs (American Psychiatric Association, 1997). The most common elements of treatment are case management, pharmacological treatment, and psychosocial rehabilitation.

Case Management. The role of case management is to identify patient needs, link patients to interventions, monitor outcomes, and advocate for patients, including obtaining entitlements (Mueser, Bond, Drake, & Resnick, 1998). The Assertive Community Treatment (ACT) model of more intensive case management is appropriate for patients with a recent history of multiple hospitalizations and poor psychosocial functioning (Allness & Knoedler, 1998; Stein & Santos, 1998). The ACT model is distinguished from standard case management by the lower clinician-to-patient ratio (one to ten in ACT versus one to thirty or more in standard case management) and shared caseloads across clinicians (rather than individual caseloads); in addition, most services are provided in the community rather than the clinic, there is twenty-four-hour coverage, and services are provided directly by the team rather than brokered to other providers. ACT has been found to reduce hospitalizations and symptom severity and to improve housing stability in multiple studies (Bond et al., 2001).

Pharmacological Treatment. Pharmacological treatment with antipsychotic medications, especially the newer atypical antipsychotics, is the mainstay of treatment for schizophrenia. Existing pharmacological treatments are more effective for the positive than for the negative symptoms of schizophrenia. In the past, antipsychotic medications were associated with a host of disruptive side effects. However, newer agents have improved side effect profiles, although substantial weight gain and sedation may occur in some individuals. Some patients also benefit from adjunctive medications, such as antidepressants or mood stabilizers (Rush et al., 1999). The vast majority of patients with schizophrenia experience considerable benefit from medication.

Psychosocial Treatment. Several interventions have been shown to improve outcomes in persons with schizophrenia:

• *Family psychoeducation* is appropriate for patients in regular contact with relatives and is aimed at developing a collaborative relationship between the treatment team and family, reducing stress, improving communication and problem solving, and helping members achieve personal and shared goals (Mueser & Glynn, 1999). Extensive research shows that family psychoeducation provided over an extended period of time (usually at least nine months) is effective at reducing relapses and rehospitalizations and improving the family environment (Pitschel-Walz, Leucht, Bäuml, Kissling, & Engel, 2001).

• *Social skills training* involves teaching new interpersonal skills, based on the principles of social learning theory, for improving social relationships and getting basic needs met (Bellack, Mueser, Gingerich, & Agresta, 1997). Multiple studies have shown that skills training is effective, especially when provided over more than six months. Skills training that targets specific work-related situations may be effective at improving interactions with coworkers, supervisors, and customers (Mueser, Foy, & Carter, 1986; Wallace, Tauber, & Wilde, 1999). In addition, interview skills training may be important for assisting individuals with schizophrenia to obtain employment, although extensive skills training prior to the initiation of the job search is not recommended.

• *Integrated treatment of dual disorders* (mental illness and substance use disorders) involves the use of outreach to engage patients in treatment, motivational strategies, nonconfrontational approaches, and group, individual, and family approaches to treat both disorders (Mueser, Drake, & Noordsy, 1998). Integrated treatment of both disorders is superior to separate treatment because it ensures that each disorder is addressed and minimizes possible inconsistencies between different groups of treatment providers. Research shows that integrated dual disorder treatment is effective at reducing substance abuse in patients with schizophrenia (Drake et al., 2001).

• *Cognitive-behavior therapy* for psychosis involves helping patients evaluate the evidence supporting delusional beliefs and developing more realistic and more adaptive ways of thinking. Other aspects of cognitive-behavior therapy include education about schizophrenia, coping skills training, and problem-solving skills training. Cognitive-behavior therapy is most appropriate for patients with persistent psychotic symptoms resulting in behavioral disruption or significant subjective distress. Research on cognitive therapy indicates that it reduces the severity of psychosis and in some studies lowers the risk of relapses and rehospitalizations (Gould, Mueser, Bolton, Mays, & Goff, 2001).

• *Training in illness management* provides patients with basic information about their psychiatric illness and principles of treatment, developing strategies for taking medication as prescribed, teaching relapse-prevention skills, and helping patients develop more effective ways of coping with persistent symptoms. Research on illness management training supports each of these core components of treatment (Mueser et al., in press).

• *Supported employment* is a vocational rehabilitation intervention used to assist people with schizophrenia and other psychiatric disorders in improving their work functioning (Becker & Drake, 1993; Bond, Drake, Mueser, & Latimer, 2001). Employment specialists work one-on-one with individuals who desire assistance in obtaining employment, or for those employed, in developing the skills and strategies for maintaining employment. Traditional vocational rehabilitation interventions emphasize prevocational assessment and training to prepare people with severe mental illness for employment. Supported employment, which helps people find employment directly, has shown higher rates of employment when compared to traditional vocational approaches such as prevocational work units and skills training, transitional employment, and sheltered work (Bond, Drake, Mueser, & Becker, 1997; Drake, Becker, Clark, & Mueser, 1999).

In supported employment, employment specialists assist people in identifying a good job match based on the person's preferences, skills, strengths, and unique challenges. The employment specialist may advocate directly with potential employers if the employee is willing to disclose her psychiatric status to employers. In some cases, when the employment specialist introduces himself, the name of his employer reveals that the employee has a disability. When contacting employers, the employment specialist is sometimes better able to advocate for a patient because of the social skills deficits inherent in schizophrenia. For example, the employment specialist can address with the employer an employee's apparent lack of enthusiasm in the job interview that is caused by flat affect from the illness. The supported employment specialist can also help the employee by acting as a liaison between the employer and employee once he or she is employed. Employment specialists work closely with other treatment providers to ensure that services are integrated at the level of patient delivery. The treatment providers form a team, meeting at least weekly, to share information, develop plans, and increase collaboration to support patients in different aspects of their lives, including employment. In this way, the employment specialist can be alerted if the employer begins to notice changes in the employee. In turn, the supported employment specialist can communicate with the treatment team.

The most common barrier to employment for people with schizophrenia is fear of losing governmental benefits such as Social Security Income, Social Security Disability Insurance, and Medicaid. The employment specialist helps the employee obtain accurate information about how his or her particular package of benefits will be affected by working. Many people work part time so that they do not lose their health insurance. The employee or employment specialist negotiates the desired number of hours with the employer.

The employee is provided individualized, time-unlimited support to maintain employment. The type of support varies according to the needs of the individual. Most support is provided away from the job site. People with schizophrenia sometimes feel stigmatized when the employment specialist is present at the job site. Furthermore, employees usually have little difficulty performing job duties if the job match is good. It is not surprising that taking an employee's preferences, interests, and strengths into account promotes job tenure. People with schizophrenia want to be treated like others without mental illness at the work site. In most cases, the employment specialist meets regularly with the employee away from the job site to review work progress. If the employee permits the employment specialist to speak with the employer, the employment specialist makes contact periodically to find out if the employee is performing satisfactorily at the job or to consult with the employer regarding any other job-related issues.

Overall, treatment for schizophrenia needs to be long term. The provision of supported employment services should also be long term, although the intensity of support may decrease as employees become better able to handle the demands of work on their own. Specific interventions can often be delivered on a time-limited basis. Family psychoeducational programs typically last between nine months and two years, although families (including employees) may also benefit from continued participation in support groups. Social skills training is usually provided in programs lasting between three or four months and over a year. Cognitive-behavioral treatment for psychotic symptoms and illness management programs generally lasts between six and twelve months, although some programs last even longer. Finally, integrated programs for comorbid substance abuse are usually relatively long term, lasting several years, with the duration of participation depending on when individual clients achieve stable remission of their substance use disorders.

Return to Work and ADA Reasonable Accommodation

The types of accommodations that people with schizophrenia request are typically low cost to the employer. An example is flexible work hours, such as adjusting the work schedule for appointments and medical leaves, providing more frequent breaks, and arranging time off without pay. Modification of the workspace and job tasks include minimizing distractions and noise, providing space to work alone, gradual introduction of tasks, and modification of job tasks. Crisis intervention includes procedures for emergency situations, telephone calls to employment specialists, and private space. The employment specialist, the employee, and the employer meet to create an individualized plan for the necessary workplace accommodations.

Psychotic disorders represent a diverse array of syndromes, each characterized by the presence of psychotic symptoms, such as hallucinations or delusions. Individuals may differ markedly in the range and severity of their symptoms and deficits. Effective pharmacological and psychosocial treatments exist for psychotic disorders that can minimize symptoms and impairments and facilitate the ability of individuals with these disorders to work. The majority of psychotic disorders respond to treatment, and many individuals with psychotic disorders can manage their illness successfully by participating in outpatient therapy and medication management.

Of particular relevance to successful vocational functioning for employees with schizophrenia is the availability of supported employment services. Supported employment involves assistance from an employment specialist in identifying and obtaining jobs in areas related to employees' interest, providing ongoing supports to manage job demands and the social environment of the workplace successfully, availability to employers to discuss job-related issues concerning the employee, and negotiating reasonable accommodations with employers. Supported employment services are most effective when they are integrated with other aspects of treatment and employment specialists function as members of clients' treatment teams. Although schizophrenia is a serious mental illness, comprehensive treatment, access to supported employment services, and a supportive work environment make many clients capable of being consistent and valued employees.

References and Additional Sources

Allness, D. J., & Knoedler, W. H. (1998). *The PACT Model of community-based treatment for persons with severe and persistent mental illness: A Manual for PACT Start-Up.* Arlington, VA: National Alliance for the Mentally Ill.

American Psychiatric Association. (1994). *Diagnostic and statistical manual of mental disorders* (4th ed. rev.). Washington, DC: Author.

American Psychiatric Association. (1997). American Psychiatric Association: Practice guideline for the treatment of patients with schizophrenia. *American Journal of Psychiatry, 154* (April suppl.).

Becker, D. R., & Drake, R. E. (1993). *A working life: The Individual Placement and Support (IPS) program.* Concord, NH: New Hampshire–Dartmouth Psychiatric Research Center.

Bell, M. D., Lysaker, P. H., & Milstein, R. M. (1996). Clinical benefits of paid work activity in schizophrenia. *Schizophrenia Bulletin, 22,* 51-67.

Bellack, A. S., Mueser, K. T., Gingerich, S., & Agresta, J. (1997). *Social skills training for schizophrenia: A step-by-step guide.* New York: Guilford Press.

Bond, G. R., Drake, R. E., Mueser, K. T., & Becker, D. R. (1997). An update on supported employment for people with severe mental illness. *Psychiatric Services, 48,* 335-346.

Bond, G. R., Drake, R. E., Mueser, K. T., & Latimer, E. (2001). Assertive community treatment for people with severe mental illness: Critical ingredients and impact on clients. *Disease Management and Health Outcomes, 9,* 141-159.

Buchanan, J. (1995). Social support and schizophrenia: A review of the literature. *Archives of Psychiatric Nursing, 9,* 68-76.

Drake, R. E., Becker, D. R., Clark, R. E., & Mueser, K. T. (1999). Research on the individual placement and support model of supported employment. *Psychiatric Quarterly, 70,* 627-633.

Drake, R. E., Essock, S. M., Shaner, A., Carey, K. B., Minkoff, K., Kola, L., Lynde, D., Osher, F. C., Clark, R. E., & Rickards, L. (2001). Implementing dual diagnosis services for clients with severe mental illness. *Psychiatric Services, 52,* 469-476.

Gould, R. A., Mueser, K. T., Bolton, E., Mays, V., & Goff, D. (2001). Cognitive therapy for psychosis in schizophrenia: A preliminary meta-analysis. *Schizophrenia Research, 48,* 335-342.

Heinssen, R. K., Liberman, R. P., & Kopelowicz, A. (2000). Psychosocial skills training for schizophrenia: Lessons from the laboratory. *Schizophrenia Bulletin, 26*(1), 21-46.

Herz, M. I., Lamberti, J. S., Mintz, J., Scott, R., O'Dell, S. P., McCartan, L., & Nix, G. (2000). A program for relapse prevention in schizophrenia: A controlled study. *Archives of General Psychiatry, 57,* 277-283.

Liberman, R. P., Mueser, K. T., Wallace, C. J., Jacobs, H. E., Eckman, T., & Massel, H. K. (1986). Training skills in the psychiatrically disabled: Learning coping and competence. *Schizophrenia Bulletin, 12,* 631-647.

Mueser, K. T., Bond, G. R., Drake, R. E., & Resnick, S. G. (1998). Models of community care for severe mental illness: A review of research on case management. *Schizophrenia Bulletin, 24,* 37-74.

Mueser, K. T., Corrigan, P. W., Hilton, D., Tanzman, B., Schaub, A., Gingerich, S., Copeland, M. E., Essock, S. M., Tarrier, N., Morey, B., Vogel-Scibilia, S., & Herz, M. I. (in press). Illness management and recovery for severe mental illness: A review of the research. *Psychiatric Services.*

Mueser, K. T., Drake, R. E., & Noordsy, D. L. (1998). Integrated mental health and substance abuse treatment for severe psychiatric disorders. *Practical Psychiatry and Behavioral Health, 4*(3), 129-139.

Mueser, K., Drake, R., & Wallach, M. (1998). Dual diagnosis: A review of etiological theories. *Addictive Behaviors, 23,* 717-734.

Mueser, K. T., Foy, D. W., & Carter, M. J. (1986). Social skills training for job maintenance in a psychiatric patient. *Journal of Counseling Psychology, 33,* 360–362.

Mueser, K. T., & Glynn, S. M. (1999). *Behavioral family therapy for psychiatric disorders* (2nd ed.). Oakland, CA: New Harbinger.

Pitschel-Walz, G., Leucht, S., Bäuml, J., Kissling, W., & Engel, R. R. (2001). The effect of family interventions on relapse and rehospitalization in schizophrenia—A meta-analysis. *Schizophrenia Bulletin, 27,* 73–92.

Psychosis, schizophrenia, schizoaffective disorder. Available on-line at: http://www.e-help.com/psychosis_and_schizophrenia.htm.

Rosen, A. J., Sussman, S., Mueser, K. T., Lyons, J. S., & Davis, J. M. (1981). Behavioral assessment of psychiatric inpatients and normal controls across different environmental contexts. *Journal of Behavioral Assessment, 3,* 25–36.

Rush, A. J., Rago, W. V., Crismon, M. L., Toprac, M. G., Shon, S. P., Suppes, T., Miller, A. L., Trivedi, M. H., Swann, A. C., Biggs, M. M., Shores-Wilson, K., Kashner, T. M., Pigott, T., Chiles, J. A., Gilbert, D. A., & Altshuler, K. Z. (1999). Medication treatment for the severely and persistently mentally ill: The Texas Medication Algorithm Project. *Journal of Clinical Psychiatry, 60,* 284–291.

Stein, L. I., & Santos, A. B. (1998). *Assertive community treatment of persons with severe mental illness.* New York: Norton.

Wallace, C. J., Tauber, R., & Wilde, J. (1999). Teaching fundamental workplace skills to persons with serious mental illness. *Psychiatric Services, 50,* 1147–1153.

Zubin, J., & Spring, B. (1977). Vulnerability: A new view of schizophrenia. *Journal of Abnormal Psychology, 86,* 103–126.

CHAPTER TWENTY-SEVEN

Emotion and Illness

The Psychosomatic Interface

Brian L. Grant

Only in recent years has a systematic approach started to unravel some of the age-old questions about the linkages between emotions and illness. Emotional distress causing physical symptoms (somatoform disorders), falsely represented symptoms (malingering), physical symptoms of other psychiatric disorders (panic disorder and others), controversial medical illness (multiple chemical sensitivity syndrome, fibromyalgia, and others), emotional causes of true physical disease (coronary artery disease and others), and toxic causes of behavioral symptoms are a fascinating but sometimes confusing group. Specific diagnosis and effective treatment depends on full awareness of the complex interaction among medical, psychiatric, psychodynamic, family, and cultural determinants. Workplace managers need to be sensitive to these issues in order to make appropriate decisions about employees with confusing physical symptoms. Even when the cause or severity of physical ailments is hotly disputed, the employee may still be suffering from a psychiatric disorder that requires professional attention.

Personality and physical factors have a reciprocal relationship with important workplace implications. Although modern medicine tends to distinguish and separate the mind from the body, this distinction is partial at best. In fact, true psychiatric and emotional conditions can be manifested through physical symptoms, and true physical disorders can be announced by emotional symptoms. This chapter examines these concepts.

SOMATOFORM DISORDERS: PHYSICAL SYMPTOMS OF EMOTIONAL ORIGIN

The somatoform disorders are a group of diagnoses where physical symptoms suggesting a medical condition are not explainable by a physical condition and are often present in general medical settings.

Pain Disorder

Case 1

John Hawkins, a fifty-three-year-old logger, experienced low back pain while moving a piece of machinery. When evaluated in an emergency room, he received a diagnosis of lumbosacral sprain. He left his job because of the pain and has not returned in the intervening seven years. John's pain complaints have progressed to his upper back, but multiple diagnostic evaluations have failed to produce conclusive evidence of physical pathology. John's complaints of pain were dramatic and presented in a pattern inconsistent with the anatomical distribution of back pain. He recoiled in apparent pain to a light touch on the skin and to direct downward pressure on the neck. He was enrolled in a multidisciplinary pain unit, which resulted in a brief but unsustained symptomatic improvement.

As a tenth-grade dropout, John had limited intellectual skills and equally limited work opportunities in sedentary occupations. His pain symptoms increased when he sat or stood for prolonged periods, prompting him to drop out of vocational retraining programs. John confined his activities to his home, light recreation, and visits with friends and family. His wife and children assumed the tasks of home maintenance. Workers' compensation benefits partially replaced his lost earnings. A multidisciplinary consultative examination concluded that John had a somatoform pain disorder.

Pain disorder may exist when a predominant complaint of pain is unsupported by any known cause. It may exist when an actual medical problem cannot account for the severity of the reported pain, resulting in social and occupational impairment. Some cases share the same psychodynamic and emotional underpinnings as conversion disorders (see page 551).

❖ Diagnostic Criteria for Pain Disorder

A. Pain in one or more anatomical sites is the predominant focus of the clinical presentation and is of sufficient severity to warrant clinical attention.

B. The pain causes clinically significant distress or impairment in social, occupational, or other important areas of functioning.

C. Psychological factors are judged to have an important role in the onset, severity, exacerbation, or maintenance of the pain.

D. The symptom or deficit is not intentionally produced or feigned (as in Factitious Disorder or Malingering).

E. The pain is not better accounted for by a Mood, Anxiety, or Psychotic Disorder and does not meet criteria for Dyspareunia.

Code as follows:

Pain Disorder Associated With Psychological Factors: psychological factors are judged to have the major role in the onset, severity, exacerbation, or maintenance of the pain. (If a general medical condition is present, it does not have a major role in the onset, severity, exacerbation, or maintenance of the pain.) This type of Pain Disorder is not diagnosed if criteria are also met for Somatization Disorder.

Specify if:

Acute: duration of less than 6 months
Chronic: duration of 6 months or longer
Pain Disorder Associated With Both Psychological Factors and a General Medical Condition: both psychological factors and a general medical condition are judged to have important roles in the onset, severity, exacerbation, or maintenance of the pain. The associated general medical condition or anatomical site of the pain . . . is coded on Axis III.

Specify if:

Acute: duration of less than 6 months
Chronic: duration of 6 months or longer

Reprinted with permission from the Diagnostic and Statistical Manual of Mental Disorders, Fourth Edition, Text Revision. *Copyright 2000 American Psychiatric Association.*

Somatization Disorder

Case 2

Sonia Thomas, a thirty-four-year-old woman, worked for one year as a bench mechanic for a large electronics company. In that year, she missed five weeks due to various illnesses. This was viewed as excessive absenteeism, so she was referred to the company physician for consultation. Among her many complaints were gastrointestinal complaints, chest pain, dizziness, frequent faintness, trouble walking at times, painful sexual intercourse, and extremely painful menstruation. She has been steadfastly ill since her early twenties, despite various diagnostic procedures and even exploratory surgery. She has vehemently resisted psychiatric referrals, citing the many physical problems that physicians had been unable to treat effectively. When she did finally consult with a psychiatrist, he diagnosed a somatization disorder. Realizing the importance of a good clinical relationship, he referred Sonia to a skilled and empathic family practitioner. In this way, unneeded and potentially dangerous medical interventions might be avoided.

A true somatization disorder (also referred to as Briquet's syndrome and hysteria) is rare and requires specific criteria. Physical complaints or the belief that one is sickly must be a well-established pattern before the age of thirty. There must be at least thirteen symptoms that have prompted medical evaluation or treatment, or alterations in lifestyle. There must be no organic disorder that can account for the symptoms or for their severity when actual pathology is observed. The symptoms may be centered in the gastrointestinal, cardiopulmonary, genitourinary, or female reproductive systems. They may take the form of conversion or fake neurological disorders.

❧ Diagnostic Criteria for Somatization Disorder

A. A history of many physical complaints beginning before age 30 years that occur over a period of several years and result in treatment being sought or significant impairment in social, occupational, or other important areas of functioning.

B. Each of the following criteria must have been met, with individual symptoms occurring at any time during the course of the disturbance:

1. *four pain symptoms:* a history of pain related to at least four different sites or functions (e.g., head, abdomen, back, joints, extremities, chest, rectum, during menstruation, during sexual intercourse, or during urination)

2. *two gastrointestinal symptoms:* a history of at least two gastrointestinal symptoms other than pain (e.g., nausea, bloating, vomiting other than during pregnancy, diarrhea, or intolerance of several different foods)

3. *one sexual symptom:* a history of at least one sexual or reproductive symptom other than pain (e.g., sexual indifference, erectile or ejaculatory dysfunction, irregular menses, excessive menstrual bleeding, vomiting throughout pregnancy)

4. *one pseudoneurological symptom:* a history of at least one symptom or deficit suggesting a neurological condition not limited to pain (conversion symptoms such as impaired coordination or balance, paralysis or localized weakness, difficulty swallowing or lump in throat, aphonia, urinary retention, hallucinations, loss of touch or pain sensation, double vision, blindness, deafness, seizures; dissociative symptoms such as amnesia; or loss of consciousness other than fainting)

C. Either (1) or (2):

1. after appropriate investigation, each of the symptoms in Criterion B cannot be fully explained by a known general medical condition or the direct effects of a substance (e.g., a drug of abuse, a medication)

2. when there is a related general medical condition, the physical complaints or resulting social or occupational impairment are in excess of what would be expected from the history, physical examination, or laboratory findings

D. The symptoms are not intentionally produced or feigned (as in Factitious Disorder or Malingering).

Reprinted with permission from the Diagnostic and Statistical Manual of Mental Disorders, Fourth Edition, Text Revision. *Copyright 2000 American Psychiatric Association.*

Epidemic Hysteria

Case 3

Over the course of several months, several dozen flight attendants for a major airline were partially overcome while flying in a particular type of jet on various routes. The first episode followed the leakage of a solvent and detectable fumes that entered an air intake. The odor did not disturb passengers or the flight crew, and only some of the attendants on that flight were affected. Although the condition was quickly corrected, the attendants continued to be overcome. Kindled by media attention, the problem reignited the animosity that remained several years after a long and bitter strike when management had obtained major labor concessions. Independent industrial hygienists, toxicologists, and physicians retained by the airline and government were unable to account for the symptoms on a physical basis, but felt that the incident was consistent with epidemic hysteria. Some of the flight attendants consulted with a self-described clinical ecologist, who felt that they were afflicted with multiple chemical sensitivity syndrome. This incident resulted in losses totaling many thousands of dollars in medical and legal fees and lost productivity.

This rare but fascinating syndrome of epidemic hysteria may occur when a group of people exposed to a common stimulus simultaneously present with common physical symptoms of psychological origin. Typically, those afflicted are highly suggestible and in a situation where they feel vulnerable or powerless. In a work setting, the stimulus may be a perceived toxic substance, noxious odors, an environmental stress such as extreme heat, or even an environment charged with prior emotional conflict.

Hypochondriasis and Body Dysmorphic Disorder

In addition to the three diagnoses illustrated in the cases, there are two additional diagnoses within the group of somatoform disorders in addition to an undifferentiated somatoform disorder. Hypochondriasis consists of a fear or preoccupation with having a serious disease, a misinterpretation of physical sensations or signs, and a lack of medical evidence to support the self-diagnosis. The so-called hypochondriac may seek multiple medical evaluations and investigations to validate these concerns. Body dysmorphic disorder concerns an imagined defect in appearance.

❖ Diagnostic Criteria for Hypochondriasis

A. Preoccupation with fears of having, or the idea that one has, a serious disease based on the person's misinterpretation of bodily symptoms.

B. The preoccupation persists despite appropriate medical evaluation and reassurance.

C. The belief in Criterion A is not of delusional intensity (as in Delusional Disorder, Somatic Type) and is not restricted to a circumscribed concern about appearance (as in Body Dysmorphic Disorder).

D. The preoccupation causes clinically significant distress or impairment in social, occupational, or other important areas of functioning.

E. The duration of the disturbance is at least 6 months.

F. The preoccupation is not better accounted for by Generalized Anxiety Disorder, Obsessive-Compulsive Disorder, Panic Disorder, a Major Depressive Episode, Separation Anxiety, or another Somatoform Disorder.

Specify if:

With Poor Insight: if, for most of the time during the current episode, the person does not recognize that the concern about having a serious illness is excessive or unreasonable

Reprinted with permission from the Diagnostic and Statistical Manual of Mental Disorders, Fourth Edition, Text Revision. *Copyright 2000 American Psychiatric Association.*

A Continuum of Disorders

As with many other psychiatric disorders, the somatoform disorders likely represent a continuum of underlying emotional conflict in complex individuals. The several diagnoses may overlap, lacking clear criteria in any particular patient. Common to all of these disorders is the use of physical symptoms as an expression of underlying emotional state and personality. The presence of a somatoform disorder does not rule out the coexistence of other medical and psychiatric problems. Despite their confusing or overlapping presentations, these are very real problems, and they often respond to appropriate treatment. The evaluating physician should take care not to reject or devalue the veiled emotional distress that these conditions often represent. Because somatization occurs without conscious intent, it is distinct from malingering, where conscious deception is the primary goal.

The incidence of somatoform disorders as a group is quite high. Although patients who meet the rigid formal criteria for somatization disorder may be rare, those who exhibit somatization traits or elements of somatization disorder are more common. Studies of family medical practices reveal a very high incidence of patients who express physical complaints when their primary problems are actually emotional in nature. In the workplace setting, the prevalence may be higher still.

FACTITIOUS DISORDERS AND MALINGERING: FALSELY REPORTED SYMPTOMS

The factitious disorders are characterized by the intentional feigning of physical or psychological symptoms in order to fulfill an inner emotional need to assume a sick role. This is done without external incentives such as greater economic status or improved well-being. These disorders thus differ from malingering, where symptoms are also falsely reported but in an effort to gain external rewards.

❖ Diagnostic Criteria for Factitious Disorder

A. Intentional production or feigning of physical or psychological signs or symptoms.
B. The motivation for the behavior is to assume the sick role.
C. External incentives for the behavior (such as economic gain, avoiding legal responsibility, or improving physical well-being, as in Malingering) are absent.

Code based on type:

With Predominantly Psychological Signs and Symptoms: if psychological signs and symptoms predominate in the clinical presentation
With Predominantly Physical Signs and Symptoms: if physical signs and symptoms predominate in the clinical presentation
With Combined Psychological and Physical Signs and Symptoms: if both psychological and physical signs and symptoms are present but neither predominates in the clinical presentation

Reprinted with permission from the Diagnostic and Statistical Manual of Mental Disorders, Fourth Edition, Text Revision. *Copyright 2000 American Psychiatric Association.*

True malingering is not an emotional disorder. It is the act of lying in a medical context. The primary criteria for malingering are the intentional production of grossly exaggerated physical and psychological symptoms and a desire for external gain, such as the avoidance of work or prosecution, access to medications, or monetary compensation. Malingering may be present when the physical findings are unsupported by objective measures, but such inconsistencies also may be found in the somatoform disorders. The somatoform disorders differ in that they assume a consistent presentation, even in unobserved private settings and are not conscious in nature. A malingerer feigns symptoms only as needed to attain certain conscious goals and might have normal functioning in unrelated settings.

❖ Diagnostic Criteria for Malingering

The essential feature of Malingering is the intentional production of false or grossly exaggerated physical or psychological symptoms, motivated by external incentives such as avoiding military duty, avoiding work, obtaining financial compensation, evading criminal prosecution, or obtaining drugs. Under some circumstances, Malingering may represent adaptive behavior—for example, feigning illness while a captive of the enemy during wartime.

Malingering should be strongly suspected if any combination of the following is noted:

1. Medicolegal context of presentation (e.g., the person is referred by an attorney to the clinician for examination)
2. Marked discrepancy between the person's claimed stress or disability and the objective findings

3. Lack of cooperation during the diagnostic evaluation and in complying with the prescribed treatment regimen
4. The presence of Antisocial Personality Disorder

Malingering differs from Factitious Disorder in that the motivation for the symptom production in Malingering is an external incentive, whereas in Factitious Disorder external incentives are absent. Evidence of an intrapsychic need to maintain the sick role suggests Factitious Disorder. Malingering is differentiated from Conversion Disorder and other Somatoform Disorders by the intentional production of symptoms and by the obvious, external incentives associated with it. In Malingering (in contrast to Conversion Disorder), symptom relief is not often obtained by suggestion or hypnosis.

Reprinted with permission from the Diagnostic and Statistical Manual of Mental Disorders, Fourth Edition, Text Revision. *Copyright 2000 American Psychiatric Association.*

Proving the existence of malingering is challenging and distasteful. Medical practitioners assume a spirit of mutual trust in the physician-patient relationship and often resist a search for dishonesty. Moreover, a resolution to the problem is more likely to lie in employer or legal action than in psychiatric treatment.

Case 4

George Casey, a thirty-eight-year-old steelworker, slipped on some grease, hit his head, and twisted his neck. Over the course of five months, he presented a left-sided partial paralysis requiring the aid of a cane and exhibited an inability to think or communicate clearly. His wife accompanied him to each examination, reporting that he had severely impaired memory and did little more than sit on the couch and watch television.

On examination, George appeared to be a very impaired man. He would respond in a nonsensical and childlike way to the examiner and would fall if not supported while walking. Some of those who examined him were perplexed by symptoms suggesting a serious head injury. The fall itself was not severe and was not accompanied by loss of consciousness or immediate symptoms. Physical examination did not reveal any evidence of stroke or tumor.

The employer chose to investigate the claim further. A private investigator set up video surveillance of George's activities. The investigator recorded George standing on and repairing a sloped roof and clearing land with a backhoe that he was observed to be operating, all requiring the use of four limbs and full neck motion. George was also observed engaging in animated conversations. The videotapes supported the conclusion by the attending and consulting physicians that George was malingering. The cost of George's claims to the employer and to the federal social security system exceeded $100,000 for medical benefits and time loss. George was successfully prosecuted for fraud.

Causes of Somatization

The somatoform disorders are outward manifestations of emotional distress, as determined by certain personality traits and cultural influences. Somatization is a psychological defense mechanism that provides some relief of emotional discomfort and simultaneously displays the discomfort outwardly through physical symptoms. Diseases of the body are regarded as fickle and uncontrollable things that happen to a person rather than as problems generated from within. Thus, physical symptoms permit a comforting perceived detachment from both underlying emotions and outward behavior.

Somatoform disorders are often associated with early or mid-childhood emotional trauma. The resulting intolerable feelings are suppressed from conscious thought to retain emotional equilibrium. When this suppression is incomplete, emotional conflicts and feelings may later emerge as physical complaints. The underlying trauma and resulting conflicts cannot be brought out and resolved without psychotherapy or a similar corrective experience. Somatization defenses and other maladaptive behaviors may become even more evident personality traits when a pattern of abuse reoccurs in later life.

Somatoform disorders also have cultural determinants. Every individual exists within the cultural framework of the greater society, a particular subculture, and a unique family. The family, that most compact and intimate cultural unit, defines the limits of interpersonal experience for the newborn and infant. The spoken and behavioral language of the family is the earliest form of communication for a child. The child learns to communicate by watching, listening, and imitating. Over time, this process widens to include playmates, classmates, friends, and even coworkers.

To understand the meaning of illness to the somatizing patient, it is important to learn about the illness behaviors of that person's family. Often there is a history of particular illnesses, pain disorders, and disability among family members. The expression of somatization may be a learned behavior, in addition to being a communication form determined by individual emotional defense structures. Verbal expression of emotional states and psychological discomfort is not well accepted in many families and cultures. In both the present and historical past, psychiatric disorders have often been attributed to other bodily organ systems. For instance, Western tradition has attributed depressed mood to "black bile," while some non-Western languages have limited psychological vocabularies, contributing to emotional distress being expressed in physical complaints and symptoms. Explanatory models of disease causation are developed in a manner consistent with the cultural or psychological experiences of the individual.

Workplace Relevance

The cultural and emotional determinants of somatization are important for understanding the workplace challenges of health, productivity, and disability. Since true somatoform disorders are not conscious, the primary gain for the individual is initially a reduction of emotional distress. Secondary gains may also accrue to the employee with symptoms, including reduced workplace demands, and otherwise unavailable emotional and financial supports. When there is a social or cultural resistance to the concept of psychological illness, the individual may be especially prone toward somatization.

Workplace problems and relationships offer a fertile field for the expression of emotional and interpersonal conflict through somatization. With little alteration, workers bring their unique personalities, experiences, and problems to work. A worker abused as a child might unwittingly experience even normal supervisory advice as a reminder of past abuse, which could lead to profound emotional distress around the supervisor and workplace. Somatic symptoms might then develop as a way of reducing emotional distress and finding an external explanation (the primary gain) for emotional discomfort. The symptoms can also be a way of countering supervisory pressure through the presentation of physical limitations, of eliciting coworker and family sympathy, as well as obtaining economic benefits (the secondary gain).

Workplace somatization takes on a new twist when it becomes entangled in formalized employee health and safety laws and established systems such as workers' compensation. A simple leg fracture due to a fall is a relatively unambiguous workplace injury. The bone is set, the fracture heals, and the worker returns to the job in due course. Complications can set in when a worker predisposed to unwitting somatization (or conscious malingering) sustains even such a straightforward injury. The worker may experience ongoing symptoms that do not follow the normal course of injury and attribute them to a particular injury or event that others perceive as inconsequential. Inexplicable and disabling physical complications may unexpectedly appear, often leading to a medical disability claim. Employers then find themselves with legal and economic responsibility for a confusing medical condition with ambiguous attribution. In addition to systemic benefits, the symptoms may have the effect of diverting the worker's attention from hidden emotional concerns, while attributing distress to externally caused physical symptoms.

Assessment

Diagnosis and treatment of somatoform disorders is challenging because of the inherent difficulties in identifying specific syndromal patterns from a confusing clinical picture. It is always essential to look carefully for other true medical and psychiatric diagnoses that may coexist with somatoform disorders. For instance, depression is a common concomitant of both incapacitating physical paralysis and the pseudoparalysis seen in conversion disorder. To ensure a cooperative effort at diagnosis and treatment, physicians must offer patients a mutually acceptable explanatory model of the disease. Most important, a patient's emotional need for a physical explanation requires special expertise in diagnostic interviewing. When there is persisting ambiguity, confusion, or overt conflict about the nature of the problem, effective treatment may be difficult or even impossible.

Consider the somatizing patient who experiences emotional problems as physical. This patient is engaged in a form of resistance that springs from a desire to avoid uncomfortable emotions, such as those associated with traumatic early experiences. The physician who deals only with the presented physical symptoms, discounting or ignoring any emotional basis for them, may not be very helpful in their resolution. Treatment that addresses the physical complaints and is inattentive to emotional factors may reinforce an incorrect focus of cause and fail as a result. Moreover, physically invasive treatments can leave their own residual scars, while paradoxically increasing distress by not addressing the root cause. And a correct but premature presentation of an emotional explanation may leave the patient feeling rejected or not understood by the physician and cause this person to seek care elsewhere.

The art of the effective physician involves an understanding of the factors that bring about a somatoform presentation. Diagnosis and treatment must be handled in a way that is both acceptable and helpful to the patient but without unwitting collusion or causing further harm. It is unrealistic for a physician to assume that a patient with a somatoform illness will readily acknowledge a psychological explanation for the problem. Because the patient's beliefs are often deeply held and not easily altered, the physician should consider working within the context of the patient's beliefs. For instance, recognizing the real, if partial, benefits of alternative or nonmainstream health care models and treatments may leave the patient feeling better understood and more comfortable with continuing medical care.

Psychiatric Management

Once the possibility of a somatoform diagnosis is raised, a psychiatric consultation can address the specific diagnostic possibilities. In addition to assessing comorbid psychiatric disorders, there are important differences among the various somatoform disorders. Effective treatment requires specific diagnosis, as well as a constant recognition of the patient's own explanatory model for their distress.

Treatments must be selected for specific diagnoses and individually for each patient. Treatment should simultaneously address the expressed physical symptoms as well as the emotional concerns that may be unstated. Pain and physical impairment can be treated with conservative physical therapy and behavioral pain therapies. Psychotherapy with the somatizing patient typically starts with a focus on the practical and emotional consequences of physical symptoms. The possibility of emotional causality is allowed to arise only much later when the patient starts to wonder about that possibility. Ultimately, psychotherapy seeks to uncover and thus relieve the hidden emotional fears that underlie the somatoform symptoms. As always, the psychotherapeutic process should be specific but gradual.

In conversion disorders, the specific symptom offers anxiety reduction through physical incapacity, as well as a symbolic representation of emotionally unacceptable hidden impulses. A classic example is of the angry worker (from an angry family) who has an impulse to punch his boss. Rather than hit the boss and suffer the retribution of getting fired, he unwittingly develops a paralysis of his arm. Unable to hit, he has less need to worry about punching or getting fired and may actually earn sympathy from the boss or others.

※ Diagnostic Criteria for Conversion Disorder

A. One or more symptoms or deficits affecting voluntary motor or sensory function that suggest a neurological or other general medical condition.

B. Psychological factors are judged to be associated with the symptom or deficit because the initiation or exacerbation of the symptom or deficit is preceded by conflicts or other stressors.

C. The symptom or deficit is not intentionally produced or feigned (as in Factitious Disorder or Malingering).

D. The symptom or deficit cannot, after appropriate investigation, be fully explained by a general medical condition, or by the direct effects of a substance, or as a culturally sanctioned behavior or experience.

E. The symptom or deficit causes clinically significant distress or impairment in social, occupational, or other important areas of functioning or warrants medical evaluation.

F. The symptom or deficit is not limited to pain or sexual dysfunction, does not occur exclusively during the course of Somatization Disorder, and is not better accounted for by another mental disorder.

Specify type of symptom or deficit:

With Motor Symptom or Deficit
With Sensory Symptom or Deficit
With Seizures or Convulsions
With Mixed Presentation

Reprinted with permission from the Diagnostic and Statistical Manual of Mental Disorders, Fourth Edition, Text Revision. *Copyright 2000 American Psychiatric Association.*

PSYCHIATRIC DISORDERS WITH FREQUENT PHYSICAL SYMPTOMS

Several distinct psychiatric disorders may present with somatic components. For instance, panic disorder may present with symptoms similar to those observed in coronary and respiratory diseases. A persistent misdiagnosis of a psychiatric disorder may lead to inappropriate and ineffective treatment for a real and treatable disorder, as well as a risk of harm from the wrong treatment. The psychiatric disorders examined here are discussed elsewhere in this book, but are briefly reviewed here to emphasize their importance when evaluating physical symptoms.

Panic Disorder

Panic disorder is a discrete form of anxiety whose features include attacks of great distress with at least four of the following physical symptoms: shortness of breath, dizziness, palpitation or fast heart rate, trembling or shaking, sweating, choking, nausea or abdominal distress, depersonalization or derealization, numbness or tingling sensations, hot flashes or chills, chest pain or discomfort, fear of dying, or fear of "going crazy" or doing something uncontrolled. If untreated, the disorder may progress to agoraphobia, the fear of going out in public. The physical presentation of the disorder, especially its unnerving cardiovascular symptoms, may prompt strenuous examinations for a cardiac problem. Panic disorder is readily treatable with certain medications and psychotherapy.

Schizophrenia

Schizophrenia is a thought disorder characterized by persistent psychotic delusions, hallucinations, loose communication, flat or blunted affect, and impaired social functioning. A wide variety of commonplace and bizarre physical symptoms can be reported. Patients with schizophrenia may sometimes harbor paranoid beliefs about family members, employers, or coworkers. It is nearly always unwise to dismiss such expressed concerns as delusional without an objective look at the facts. In particular, care should be taken not to discount legitimate concerns and job-related complaints because of known psychiatric illness. It is equally remiss to overlook the potential influence of psychological factors on the concerned employee.

Depression

Depressed patients commonly present for treatment of such physical complaints as weakness, anorexia, insomnia, or lightheadedness. This is especially prevalent in non-Western and lower socioeconomic groups. Chronic pain disorders such as headache, musculoskeletal dysfunction, and gastrointestinal distress also deserve special assessment for depression as a possible contributing factor. Chronic, vague, or nonspecific physical complaints should never be attributed to depression without appropriate medical examination. It is equally inappropriate to exclude depression from the diagnostic possibilities. When this diagnosis is overlooked, the continued distress can lead to needless suffering, unnecessary medical procedures, and even suicide.

CONTROVERSIAL MEDICAL ILLNESSES: FUNCTIONAL SOMATIC SYNDROMES

This is an emerging and often changing group of illnesses and syndromes that are controversial in terms of their existence and purported causes. They are characterized by conflict within the scientific and lay communities alike, especially when beliefs of proponents are challenged. They present with ill-defined features and frequently ascribe a cluster of subjective symptoms to some bodily organ or system. Members of this group include fibromyalgia, chronic fatigue syndrome, Gulf War syndrome, repetitive stress syndrome, multiple chemical sensitivity syndrome, chronic whiplash, breast implant response syndrome, and irritable bowel syndrome.

These functional somatic syndromes are promoted by four psychosocial factors: the belief that one has a serious disease; the expectation that one's condition is likely to worsen; the "sick role," including the impact of litigation and compensation; and the portrayal of the condition as catastrophic and disabling.

Several features make these syndromes controversial. First, there is disagreement about their existence as distinct entities, their prevalence, or their presence within a given patient. Second, there are healers and patients who think that the traditional medical establishment has ignorantly or intentionally disregarded patients who feel quite strongly about physical syndromes. Medical proponents of the syndromes may attract a great deal of attention. Afflicted patients often are elated that someone at last recognizes their physical, and therefore "real," problem. Ironically, these same practitioners are often criticized professionally for alleged bad science and patient exploitation. Since careful research cannot clearly verify either consistent physical findings or psychiatric syndromes, the controversy continues.

Even a modest selection of controversial medical illnesses will not meet with universal agreement or approval. The debate about the names, causation, and even the very existence of these diseases attracts strong advocates and detractors. Some take an organic approach, some psychological, and others a middle ground. There is the problem of hastily attributing a syndrome to an organic or external cause while ignoring or downplaying the cultural and psychological basis of causation, yet it would be dangerous to ascribe all symptoms to a psychological origin. This would foreclose exploration and discovery of true physical pathologies that might cause or complicate a patient's presentation. In the workplace, this could obscure the environmental factors that may cause or enhance symptoms of illness. Workplace factors can be both physical (physical conditions and substances) and social (corporate culture and employee relationships).

Multiple Chemical Sensitivity Syndrome

Case 5

Rebecca Greenson, a forty-three-year-old woman, worked as a laboratory technician at a college. When she developed a respiratory distress syndrome that she attributed to the formaldehyde preservative she used in the lab, she left her job and filed a workers' compensation claim. Supporting her claim was a physician who called himself a clinical ecologist. He diagnosed what he called multiple chemical sensitivity syndrome and attributed it to Rebecca's sensitivity to formaldehyde, as well as to most other synthetic chemicals found in urban and industrial settings. He prescribed treatment including vitamins, natural diet, and avoidance of synthetic fabrics and building materials. Rebecca left her urban home and settled in a cabin on the flanks of a mountainside. She became reclusive but made some friends in a support group of individuals with similar problems of hypersensitivity. When she made her rare trips to the city, usually for medical visits, she wore a carbon-filtered gas mask to trap airborne contaminants.

Multiple chemical sensitivity syndrome (MCSS) carries a primary complaint of inability to tolerate exposure to even small amounts of synthetic substances. Exposure may lead to a variety of severe, recurrent, and baffling toxicological reactions. The syndrome often follows an occupational or environmental exposure to chemicals, with substances such as formaldehyde frequently implicated. Consensus does not exist as to the definition of the syndrome, but certain diagnostic features have been observed. The onset of symptoms appears to be related to a documented environmental exposure, insult, or illness; symptoms involve more than one organ system; the symptoms recur and abate in response to predictable stimuli; symptoms are elicited by exposures to chemicals of diverse structural classes and toxic modes of action; symptoms are elicited by exposures that are demonstrable; noxious exposures are at very low levels (many standard deviations below average exposures known to cause adverse human responses); and symptoms cannot be explained by any widely available test of organ system function.

MCSS may be considered a subclass falling within the self-defined purview of clinical ecology. It describes itself as dedicated to the maintenance of health by recognition, management, and prevention of ecologic illness. "Ecologic illness is usually described as a polysymptomatic, multisystem chronic disorder manifested by adverse reactions to environmental excitants, as they are modified by individual susceptibility in terms of specific adaptation" (Occupational Safety and Health Administration, 2001).

Without judging causation, it is fair to say that some highly disabled people are among those who are thought to suffer from MCSS and other environmental illnesses. Many mainstream medical practitioners, lawyers, and administrators still harbor doubts as to the existence of the syndrome, much less its potential for causing disability. One must distinguish between the debatable syndromal label and the person involved. For whatever reason, many of those afflicted are extremely uncomfortable and severely limited in their ability to function.

It is likely that MCSS and environmental disease are in reality a subclass of a psychiatric disorder containing elements of somatization and anxiety disorders. In particular, panic disorder and associated phobias have been suggested by recent work. Patients with the syndromes are indeed ill, but not in a way that is acceptable to them. In fact, they would vehemently reject the possibility of any emotional component to their symptoms. Psychiatric illnesses are generally thought to originate within the individual, due to some combination of biological, genetic, developmental, situational, and personality factors. Although the symptoms and suffering are real, the explanatory model for MCSS deals with responses to environmental factors while failing to consider the psyche.

Chronic Fatigue Syndrome

Chronic fatigue syndrome (CFS) appears as a constellation of symptoms with a marked level of fatigue lasting longer than six months and frequent physical complaints including fever, sore throat, muscle aches, and impaired cognition. It is highly controversial and has enjoyed considerable attention in the lay media and scientific literature. The debate about CFS extends to the question of a still undiscovered physiological cause, whether it represents a form of conversion or somatization of emotional symptoms, and whether it is a variant of depression. Physical theories include infectious causes, notably the Epstein-Barr virus, and speculation about immunological responses caused by exposure to toxic agents. However, recent scientific studies that compared unaffected matched control groups to groups with CFS failed to demonstrate markedly different immunological or viral states. Despite subjective reports of cognitive loss and dysfunction, these have not been demonstrated by objective measurements. It is more interesting that depressive illness has been observed with a high frequency among those with the disease, although the question of depression as cause or effect of CFS remains unresolved.

It is possible that CFS is not a distinct entity but comprises several conditions with common symptoms. In some cases, an infectious condition might predominate, and in others, the cause may be primarily psychological. Clinical observation suggests that depression, especially chronic atypical depression, is a common contributor. Symptoms may respond to antidepressant medication and psychotherapy.

Fibromyalgia

Fibromyalgia may be an emotionally related subset of CFS. This disorder includes widespread musculoskeletal pain, sensitive areas on examination, and nonrestful sleep. Psychological causes may be at work when this disorder is the primary complaint and no other medical illness can be documented (forty-six medical conditions have been associated with fibromyalgia). In one British study, where twenty-one cases of primary fibromyalgia were followed for five years, all showed either a psychiatric disturbance or thyroid dysfunction. Women working in manual jobs were overrepresented, and none had been able to return to full-time work. Another study in the United States reported CFS subjects who were totally work disabled, but included subjects who retained a general ability to work in modified jobs.

The disability associated with this disorder seems to be affected, positively and negatively, by social and psychological factors. As CFS and its variations become more popularized, ill defined and controversial as they are, they are likely to become a more common source of disability claims and occupational dysfunction.

Assessment

In whole or in part, these disorders frequently represent a somatization of psychological symptoms, as shown in their physical manner of expression and concurrent denial of emotional issues. Those who diagnose controversial illnesses, as well as their patients, typically are quite resistant to a psychological explanation. Unfortunately, such resistance may be the strongest among mainstream physicians. Medical practitioners, due to their own biases or blind spots, may fail to recognize emotional factors in patients who present with vague or poorly defined physical complaints. They will scrupulously seek a physiological solution to the problem, while viewing an emotional line of inquiry as something approaching defeat.

The approach to such patients is made more difficult by their practiced resistance to emotional inquiry, much less psychiatric intervention. Psychiatric evaluation or consultation should be considered at the onset of such vague syndrome presentation. The treating physician or manager should present the idea of a referral in a way that neither minimizes nor challenges the patient's theory about the problem. It is best to suggest that psychiatric consultation can help the patient to better understand the meaning of the illness, while helping others to understand the problem in a way that would not be possible with a traditional medical approach. By taking an empathic approach to the patient, it may be possible to reach a shared alternate understanding of the cause of the problem and, as a result, achieve symptom reduction. Efforts to dissuade patients from their explanatory models are likely to fail in terms of reducing symptoms and maintaining a treatment relationship.

Psychiatric Management

Diagnosis and treatment rely on understanding the interactions of patient belief systems, nonmainstream therapies, medical illness, psychiatric disorders, and optimal interview technique. It is important to find common ground with a patient who espouses an alternative disease theory by listening to the patient, expressing an understanding of how the person feels, and agreeing that a significant problem exists. Culturally acceptable treatment alternatives will not usually impede effective treatment. Some conditions are self-limiting and responsive to suggestion. Suggestion can take the form of placebo medication or symbolic interventions.

It is always important to explore possible medical and psychiatric diagnoses fully. A long history of MCSS or CFS does not eliminate the possibility of a new or previously undiagnosed anemia, vitamin deficiency, hypothyroidism, anxiety disorder, or depression. Such disorders require specific and accurate diagnosis, but are readily responsive to treatment. At the same time, care must be taken to avoid prolonged or unnecessary medical diagnostic procedures. The psychiatrist's diagnostic interview and treatment selection keeps in mind the importance of the patient's beliefs and the realization that those beliefs will remain even after medication response. Common psychiatric disorders in these patients include major depression, atypical depression (dysthymia), and panic disorder (see Chapters Twenty-One and Twenty-Two).

At some point, it may become possible to pursue psychotherapeutic exploration of illness meaning and effects. Initial psychotherapy is dedicated to the reducing distortions and increasing self-knowledge and understanding. During a session, there may come a point where the focus can be shifted from disease and external factors to internal meanings and personal options. Ultimately, this may build self-esteem and reduce helpless feelings. Although patients will not soon change their firm beliefs about symptom causality, they will more quickly feel less distressed and in better control of their situation.

It is important to recognize when an illness belief is consciously or unwittingly used to avoid personal responsibility and accountability. In these cases, both the illness and the patient's complaints may be pernicious and persistent. For example, family members and others may have some interest in perpetuating the illness. When this happens, symptoms and disability become a patient's passport to external emotional, physical, or financial rewards.

Patients often seek primary health care from nonmainstream alternative health practitioners. Typically, these healers offer an explanatory model for disease along with a set of culturally acceptable treatments. With a different explanatory model for each patient or cultural group, the result can be a profusion of unconventional therapies. Scientific biomedicine does not enjoy a monopoly in the hearts and minds of all patients. Many regard biomedicine as impersonal and dangerous. Nonmainstream therapies that sometimes replace or supplement traditional medical care include naturopathy, chiropractic, acupuncture, curanderismo, shamanism, iridology, reflexology, faith healing, and Christian Science.

Exclusive reliance on these therapies can leave important illnesses undiagnosed and untreated and underlying emotional distress largely intact. But these therapies persist and are embraced by many because they do offer some helpful and socially acceptable benefits. Each approach is based on a theory of disease origins that may be venerated in one culture but abjectly dismissed in another that reveres science. However, many patients will concurrently accept and use multiple theories, for example, combining antibiotics with traditional herb medicines. Healing is an art and a science, and successful treatment may rely on the self-limiting nature of much disease and the patient's sense of psychological well-being that can be enhanced by a treatment consistent with their beliefs. Many nonmainstream therapies use therapeutic touch, which creates a human contact and bond between patient and therapist. This physical touch, whether applied as a laying on of hands or a spinal manipulation, may have effects that go beyond any physiological reaction. It can have a nonspecific but substantial positive psychological effect on the patient.

EMOTIONAL ASPECTS OF PHYSICAL DISEASE

Thus far, this chapter has focused on conditions that are primarily of psychiatric origin, most often known through physical symptoms or as syndromes of uncertain or multideterminant origin. It is also commonly accepted that emotions can bring on physical disease and, conversely, that physical disease can cause emotional disorders. Even the most mundane accident, cardiac failure, or tumor has direct psychological consequences and meaning to the patient. Often these disease processes gain momentum from lifestyle factors that are personality driven, and there can be causal emotional determinants. Among the specific diseases that have been widely studied for possible psychosomatic components are coronary artery disease, peptic ulcer, essential hypertension, asthma, thyroid disease, rheumatoid arthritis, irritable bowel syndrome, and ulcerative colitis. Knowledge of specific causal mechanisms remains limited. Much can be learned from illness in the workplace. This unique environment that is charged with experience and meaning provides an ideal backdrop for viewing the interactions of mind and body.

Coronary Artery Disease

Case 6
Samuel Bowden was an attorney who had founded and managed a small law firm. As a young man from a working-class family, he had driven himself very hard in school and work during the summers, on vacations, and during the school year. He graduated in the top quarter of his law school class, even while holding a full-time job. In time, he was offered a partnership in a large law firm but chose to go out

alone into practice. Considered an excellent business attorney, his clients were nearly as devoted to him as he was to them. Over the years, however, his pace and demanding personality burned out several attorneys and staff members. He had a low tolerance for the universal incompetence of those around him.

Samuel married in his early twenties, his wife assuming the traditional roles of supportive mother and homemaker. Their four children were born within a seven-year period but never spent much time with their father. Not content with the practice of law, Samuel invested in several working enterprises and maintained an active management role in each one. These included a small construction company and a cattle ranch with a second home. He typically spent more than eighty hours a week on his practice and businesses. At the age of forty-two, he had his first of several extramarital affairs. His wife saw them as typical behavior for a man of her husband's energy and drive. She tolerated these diversions as long as he did not let them interfere with their stable, though emotionally distant, home life.

Samuel avoided both long vacations and doctors, also tending to ignore occasional injuries, aches, and pains. He overlooked stabbing chest pains, which typically went away in a few seconds. One day, at age fifty-three, while dining with a client, the pain returned and persisted. The client insisted on bringing Samuel to an emergency room, where a heart attack was diagnosed. While in the coronary care unit, the hospital staff found him to be highly resistant to rehabilitative guidelines for moderation and lifestyle changes. He didn't think he had a serious illness.

When he was released from the hospital, Sam returned undeterred to his work, mistresses, and family distance. Six years later, he had a second heart attack. Suddenly conscious of his mortality, he became profoundly depressed. As he recovered, he religiously followed his cardiologist's advice, and joined a Type A behavior therapy group for heart attack survivors. Over many months, he gradually learned a more relaxed approach to work and attached a greater importance to his family life. He realized after a while that his fellow group members were really the closest buddies he had ever had.

Coronary artery disease (CAD) has received considerable attention as a model of the interaction of stress, environment, emotions, and disease processes. Many theories have linked the onset of CAD with certain character traits and the experience of external stress. In addition, loss of physical capacity and sick role demands of the cardiac patient can cause profound changes in activity, self-esteem, and economic status. Those changes can contribute to significant depression and anxiety.

One major theory of CAD describes a process that starts with repeated coronary arterial spasm and consequent damage and scarring of the arterial lining. Atherosclerotic plaques then obstruct blood flow. Eventually, the restricted blood flow provides inadequate oxygen, with resulting angina or heart attack. Risk factors for CAD include hypertension, increased serum cholesterol, smoking, age, family history, male gender, and Type A (coronary-prone) behavior.

Type A behavior traits include hostility, chronic impatience, overcompetitiveness, and excessive job involvement. These signs may be most evident when there are job-related time and responsibility pressures. Furthermore, Type A behavior is associated with denial of illnesses, avoidance of medical care, and premature return to work after heart attack. While many Type A behavior traits appear to serve the interests of an employee and employer, it is very important to distinguish the successful hard worker from the sometimes less successful hard-driving Type A.

Type A behavior is accompanied by increased physiological stress reactions. For instance, it may be associated with increased coronary arterial vasoconstriction in response to stress. It may also predispose to such other risk factors as smoking and serum cholesterol. Preventive measures commonly used to lower the risk of CAD are efforts to reduce or stop smoking, lower blood cholesterol levels, and relieve hypertension. Workplace-based efforts at risk factor reduction include programs for smoking, diet, hypertension, exercise, and cardiovascular risk assessment.

Low Back Pain Syndrome

The study of pain is a rich field that draws inspiration from the basic sciences of anatomy and physiology, as well as psychiatry and the social sciences. Researchers disagree about the relationship of psychiatric disorders and pain. Some studies suggest that pain causes psychiatric symptoms, and others that psychiatric symptoms cause pain. In reality, either approach may be valid to a greater or lesser degree, depending on the particular setting.

Pain is defined by the International Association for the Study of Pain as "an unpleasant sensory and emotional experience associated with actual or potential tissue damage, or described in terms of such damage" (Merskey & Bogduk, 1994, p. 209). Emotionally determined pain can sometimes exist without a specific physical focus. Whether it has a physiological cause or a purely emotional origin, pain is experienced subjectively in the mind. Pain cannot exist independent of the brain and cannot be measured except by indirect means, such as the skin, muscle, and neurological responses that occur with painful stimuli.

Many pain syndromes exist, but low back pain (LBP) is by far the most prevalent in the workplace. It may be called a crypto-illness, not because it is illusory, but because LBP is an inclusive term for an illness that defies categorization. Although LBP syndrome is not confined to the workplace, it is the most frequent cause of occupational losses, occurring in over 40 percent of the adult population each year, at an annual cost approaching $16 billion. In most cases, the LBP syndrome is self-limiting, with little or no social or occupational disruption. Most of the staggering losses can be attributed to a small percentage of the persons afflicted.

Like other pain syndromes, LBP presents a wealth of diagnostic possibilities, ranging from disorders with clear anatomic causes to complaints of pain that are unsupported by evidence of tissue pathology. When objective pathology is clearly present, LBP will frequently abate or improve with appropriate treatment and the passage of time. Treatment may include directed physical therapy, lifestyle modifications such as weight loss and exercise, postural and lifting training, and job modification. At times, specific medication or surgical intervention may be indicated, but bed rest is not considered a desirable treatment in most LBP cases. It may lead to deconditioning, prolong recovery, and contribute to a self-concept of disability. Pain medications can be useful and often essential, but their substantial potential for abuse makes it important to weigh risks and benefits carefully.

It is very important to consider comorbid and underlying psychiatric diagnoses. Depression and other psychiatric symptoms should be actively diagnosed and should never be written off as understandable consequences of physical pain. Major depression commonly presents with pain symptoms, and chronic physical pain can often lead to major depression, with further exacerbation of pain. Proper treatment of depression will greatly enhance pain response to other treatments. In fact, studies have shown that tricyclic antidepressants can be effective for subjective pain relief, even in the absence of diagnosed depression.

The LBP syndrome is the most frequent form of workplace somatization. It often serves to communicate other issues about the patient, especially when the complaints are chronic in nature. When an individual fails to recover or substantially improve after the initial stages of LBP, emotional factors should be considered. An episode of LBP syndrome could make it possible to avoid an unpleasant or intolerable workplace or supervisory situation. LBP symptoms might grant permission to avoid work or sanction an unconscious desire to perform in an unacceptable way. For example, a young mother who wants to care for her new baby may be burdened with expectations that she will hold a job. If she develops a persistent case of LBP, she might obtain implicit permission to stay home.

A further inducement for disability is the availability of wage-loss protection if LBP syndrome can be imputed to a work-related injury. In physically demanding trades, advancing age and the normal degenerative processes reduce the ability of older workers to tolerate everyday demands. An episode of LBP syndrome provides a way out. Another incentive for chronic LBP might be a declining labor market in a declining industry or depressed region. A poorly educated or illiterate worker may have few, if any, options for transfer or for retraining in a physically less demanding occupation. Even less strenuous jobs for poorly educated LBP sufferers tend to be in lower-paying service industries at little more than a minimum wage. Often the experienced manual tradesman has enjoyed wages that were two or three times greater. Large disparities in potential income can act as a further disincentive to LBP sufferers, who must recover in order to be reemployed. Malingering, when financial and other rewards are sought through conscious deception, can especially confuse clinical findings.

Irritable Bowel Syndrome

Irritable bowel syndrome is the most common gastrointestinal disorder encountered in the general patient population and in the workplace as well. Although the definitions and the symptoms vary, it is a continuous or recurring condition that involves abdominal pain. This distress is accompanied by defecation that varies in terms of appearance, frequency, composition, form, urgency, sensations, and other physical evidence of bowel disturbance. The validity of any diagnosis may be open to debate, since there may be an overlap with other medical or psychiatric illnesses.

Irritable bowel syndrome may reflect several forms of biological vulnerability to gastrointestinal distress, more likely to be active when there is a psychological predisposition. Patients thought to have irritable bowel syndrome often exhibit symptoms of autonomic arousal: weakness, dizziness, sleep disturbance, and other pain. While these symptoms have long been thought to suggest associations with anxiety and depression, research efforts have yielded inconsistent findings. More recently, though, there has been increasing clinical recognition of panic disorder in general and in irritable bowel patients. As a result, more recent studies have looked specifically for panic anxiety and have shown a high prevalence in irritable bowel syndrome. The gastrointestinal symptoms may represent specific physiological concomitants of panic anxiety, unlike the more emotionally complex symptoms of somatoform disorders and controversial medical illnesses. As a result, patients are often more accepting of psychiatric referral, medication, and psychotherapy.

ORGANIC BEHAVIORAL SYNDROMES

Many significant medical illnesses can often present with emotional or behavioral symptoms. Failure to diagnose the organic cause of such illnesses only sets the stage for a progression of the untreated problem. The workplace is a common site for initial appearance of the behavioral symptoms of medical illnesses. Underlying syndromes can be infectious, neoplastic (cancerous), metabolic, or toxic. Industrial chemicals can induce toxic syndromes, as can alcohol, illegal drugs, and prescription medications.

Chemical Toxicity

Undue exposure to common industrial and agricultural chemicals can induce behavioral change in the form of organic impairment. The effects of toxins on the central nervous system vary according to substance and dosage and may include dementia, delirium, psychosis, and depression. These toxins may enter the body by ingestion through the mouth, skin, and respiratory tract. Potentially harmful workplace substances include heavy metals such as lead, mercury, and arsenic. Of these, lead takes on the status of a general pollutant, found in many older homes and apartments and in certain water systems. The effects of lead on the central nervous system include headache, dizziness, sleep disturbance, impaired memory, and personality changes such as irritability. Mercury intoxication can produce irritability and tremors of varying intensity that can resemble symptoms of multiple sclerosis.

More complex poisons include the organic solvents, organophosphates, and certain gases. Thousands of organic compounds play a familiar role in everyday life and at times in contamination episodes. It is no small task to verify a toxic exposure and then to distinguish its purported effects from baseline personality and neurological functions. The difficulty is greater in cases involving only one person at low levels of exposure. A careful exposure history should accompany the toxicological screening whenever a previously healthy individual exhibits behavioral or neurological abnormalities. The likelihood of toxic exposure and appropriate treatment can be determined by correlating the findings with a sophisticated toxicological database.

Drug Toxicity

Alcohol, illegal drugs, and prescription medications can elicit a toxic response. Depending on the type of drug, common primary or side effects can include confusion, excessive stimulation, depression, anxiety, or psychosis. Drugs may have a synergistic effect if used in combination with other prescribed drugs or self-administered substances. For example, alcohol may potentiate the sedative effects of various antianxiety and antidepressant medications. Adverse drug responses may ensue not only from excessive dosages, but also at therapeutic and even subtherapeutic levels. Prescribed medications commonly known to affect the central nervous system should be used with extreme caution in settings where physical safety can be compromised, as in work involving heavy machinery or transportation. Potential drug toxicity must be considered by all who use or prescribe drugs, with potential benefits weighed against the risks to general health, safety, and performance in a particular job setting.

⁂ Diagnostic Criteria for Substance Intoxication Delirium

A. Disturbance of consciousness (i.e., reduced clarity of awareness of the environment) with reduced ability to focus, sustain, or shift attention.

B. A change in cognition (such as memory deficit, disorientation, language disturbance) or the development of a perceptual disturbance that is not better accounted for by a preexisting, established, or evolving dementia.

C. The disturbance develops over a short period of time (usually hours to days) and tends to fluctuate during the course of the day.

D. There is evidence from the history, physical examination, or laboratory findings of either (1) or (2):
   1. the symptoms in Criteria A and B developed during Substance Intoxication
   2. medication use is etiologically related to the disturbance

Reprinted with permission from the Diagnostic and Statistical Manual of Mental Disorders, Fourth Edition, Text Revision. *Copyright 2000 American Psychiatric Association.*

❧ Diagnostic Criteria for Substance Withdrawal Delirium

A. Disturbance of consciousness (i.e., reduced clarity of awareness of the environment) with reduced ability to focus, sustain, or shift attention.
B. A change in cognition (such as memory deficit, disorientation, language disturbance) or the development of a perceptual disturbance that is not better accounted for by a preexisting, established, or evolving dementia.
C. The disturbance develops over a short period of time (usually hours to days) and tends to fluctuate during the course of the day.
D. There is evidence from the history, physical examination, or laboratory findings that the symptoms in Criteria A and B developed during, or shortly after, a withdrawal syndrome.

Reprinted with permission from the Diagnostic and Statistical Manual of Mental Disorders, Fourth Edition, Text Revision. *Copyright 2000 American Psychiatric Association.*

❧ Diagnostic Criteria for Substance-Induced Persisting Dementia

A. The development of multiple cognitive deficits manifested by both
   1. memory impairment (impaired ability to learn new information or to recall previously learned information)
   2. one (or more) of the following cognitive disturbances:
      a. aphasia (language disturbance)
      b. apraxia (impaired ability to carry out motor activities despite intact motor function)
      c. agnosia (failure to recognize or identify objects despite intact sensory function)
      d. disturbance in executive functioning (i.e., planning, organizing, sequencing, abstracting)
B. The cognitive deficits in Criteria A1 and A2 each cause significant impairment in social or occupational functioning and represent a significant decline from a previous level of functioning.
C. The deficits do not occur exclusively during the course of a delirium and persist beyond the usual duration of Substance Intoxication or Withdrawal.
D. There is evidence from the history, physical examination, or laboratory findings that the deficits are etiologically related to the persisting effects of substance use (e.g., a drug of abuse, a medication).

Code [Specific Substance]-Induced Persisting Dementia:

(Alcohol; Inhalant; Sedative, Hypnotic, or Anxiolytic; Other [or Unknown] Substance)

Reprinted with permission from the Diagnostic and Statistical Manual of Mental Disorders, Fourth Edition, Text Revision. *Copyright 2000 American Psychiatric Association.*

Organically Induced Depression and Psychosis

Among the physical diseases that can produce depressive symptoms are thyroid disorders, several infectious and neurological diseases, malnutrition, and cardiovascular disease. In the elderly, depression may be among the presenting symptoms of dementia. Treatment is complicated by the fact that depressive symptoms are a side effect of many commonly used medications: central nervous system depressants such as barbiturates, drugs used in treatment of hypertension, such as the beta blockers (propranolol), and various sedatives, including alcohol. Undesirable side effects, such as depression and confusion, can result from combinations of therapeutic medications.

Psychosis can also appear as a component of several physical conditions, including lupus erythematosus, cerebral tumors, hyper- and hypothyroidism, and other endocrine abnormalities (see Chapter Twenty-Six). Attempts to treat organically induced depression or psychosis through psychotherapy or antidepressant medications alone will fail. Worse, they will delay appropriate treatment of an underlying disorder.

Organically Induced Dementia and Delirium

Slowed thinking, impaired decision making, reduced reaction times, confusional states, and memory lapses can have profound effects on performance and safety. Surprisingly, those symptoms can often progress gradually and quietly, until one day they have a dramatic effect. Too often, coworkers and employees notice early symptoms and assume a dementing process or some sort of understandable demoralization. Only the occurrence of an industrial accident, major judgment error, or clearly disturbed functioning will force action. While major depression is commonplace, primary dementia (Alzheimer's disease) is infrequently encountered in workers under age sixty-five. Drug abuse, including opiates and alcohol, is a far more common cause of cognitive symptoms. Confusion can also result from impaired cerebral blood flow brought on by arterial disease or stroke-inducing conditions. Toxic exposures, including those that occur in the workplace, may result in chronic and acute impairments of cognition and are a particular source of potential concern in some industries.

This chapter has examined a remarkable class of disorders: each involves the interaction of physical symptoms with emotional factors. To complicate the task of the physician or psychiatrist, these disorders often have complex cultural and familial origins. For effective diagnosis and treatment to take place, it is necessary to be aware of these factors and to use them in constructing an approach to underlying problems. Workplace managers need to be sensitive to these issues to make appropriate decisions regarding employees who present with psychosomatic disorders. Even when the cause or severity of physical ailments is hotly disputed, the employee may still be suffering from an emotional or psychiatric disorder that requires professional attention. Factitious disorders and malingering present the additional problem of willful falsification of symptoms. The psychosomatic disorders are real physical illnesses that may have emotional or behavioral determinants. It is vital to recognize that emotion and illness are linked: just as emotional states can evoke physical distress, a physical ailment can itself instigate psychiatric symptoms.

References and Additional Sources

Alemagno, S. A., Zynanski, S. J., Strange, K. C., Kercher, K., Medalie, J. H., & Kahana, E. (1991). Health and illness behavior of Type A persons. *Journal of Occupational Medicine, 33,* 891–895.

American Psychiatric Association. (1994). *Diagnostic and statistical manual of mental disorders* (4th ed.). Washington, DC: Author.

Barsky, A. J., & Borus, J. F. (1999). Functional somatic syndromes. *Annals of Internal Medicine, 130,* 910–921.

Blackburn, H., Watkins, L. O., Agras, W. S., Carleton, R. A., & Falkner, B. (1987). Task Force 5: Primary Prevention of Coronary Heart Disease. *Circulation, 76* (Suppl. 1), 1164–1167.

Cullen, M. R. (Ed.). (1987). *Occupational medicine: Workers with multiple chemical sensitivities.* Philadelphia: Hanley & Belfus.

Deyo, R. A. (Ed.). (1988). *Occupational medicine: Back pain in workers.* Philadelphia: Hanley & Belfus.

Glassman, A. H., & Shapiro, P. A. (1998). Depression and the course of coronary artery disease. *American Journal of Psychiatry, 155,* 4–11.

Kahn, J. P., Perumal, A. S., Gully, R. J., Smith, T. M., Cooper, T. B., & Klein, D. F. (1987). Correlation of Type A behaviour with adrenergic receptor density: Implications for coronary artery disease pathogenesis. *Lancet, 2,* 1937–1939.

Kleinman, A. (1988). *The illness narratives.* New York: Basic Books.

Merskey, H., & Bogduk, N. (Eds.). (1994). *Classification of chronic pain: IASP Task Force on Taxonomy.* Seattle: IASP Press.

Occupational Safety and Health Administration. (2001). *Multiple chemical sensitivities.* Available on-line at: http://www.osha-slc.gov/SLTC/multiplechemicalsensitivities/.

Rom, W. N. (Ed.). (1983). *Environmental and occupational medicine.* New York: Little, Brown.

Shepherd, J. T., Dembroski, T. M., Brody, M. J., Dimsdale, J. E., Eliot, R. S., Light, K. C., Miller, N. E., Myers, H. F., Obrist, P. A., & Schneiderman, N. (1987). Task Force 3: Biobehavioral Mechanisms in Coronary Artery Disease: Acute Stress. *Circulation, 76* (Suppl. 1.), 1150–1157.

Tollison, C. D. (Ed.). (1989). *Handbook of chronic pain management.* Baltimore: Williams & Wilkins.

Valciukas, J. A. (1991). *Foundations of environmental and occupational neurotoxicology.* New York: Van Nostrand Reinhold.

Walker, E. A., Roy-Byrne, P. P., & Katon, W. J. (1990). Irritable bowel syndrome and psychiatric illness. *American Journal of Psychiatry, 147,* 565–572.

Weiner, H. (1977). *Psychobiology and human disease.* New York: Elsevier.

Zenz, C. (Ed.). (1988). *Occupational medicine: Principles and practical applications* (2nd ed.). Chicago: Year Book Medical Publishers.

ABOUT THE EDITORS

Jeffrey P. Kahn, M.D., is president of WorkPsych Associates (www.WorkPsychCorp.com), an executive, corporate, and mental health consulting firm in New York City and Scarsdale, New York. His work encompasses executive assessment, development, coaching, and treatment and organizational, management, and benefits consultation for a wide range of corporations and individuals. He is clinical assistant professor of psychiatry at the Weill Medical College of Cornell University in Manhattan. He is past president of the Academy of Organizational and Occupational Psychiatry and one of its founders in 1990. He was a member of the American Psychiatric Association's Task Force on Business and continues on its successor Committee on APA/Business Relations. He is also an active member of the Society for Human Resource Management, the American College of Occupational and Environmental Medicine, and the New York Business Group on Health. He has written and spoken widely for business, mental health, lay audiences and the business press.

Alan M. Langlieb, M.D., M.P.H., M.B.A., is on the faculty of The Johns Hopkins University School of Medicine in Baltimore, Maryland, working in the areas of behavioral science, occupational health, and health service delivery. Previously, he had been a faculty member and completed a preventive medicine residency at The Bloomberg School of Public Health at Johns Hopkins.

After completing an American Psychiatric Assocation Bristol Meyers Squibb Fellowship in Public Psychiatry, he is now a member of the Committee on APA/ Business Relationships. He has lectured widely on the subject of preventive medicine and the use of strategic partnerships between business and academia to advance health promotion.

ABOUT THE CONTRIBUTORS

Howard E. Book, M.D., is a psychoanalytic organizational consultant and psychoanalytic psychiatrist who has lectured and offered workshops on emotional intelligence throughout Canada and the United States. He is a past board member of the International Society for the Psychoanalytic Study of Organizations and a founding member of Associates in Workplace Consultation, through which he offers consultation to medium- and large-sized organizations. He is the coauthor of *The EQ Edge: Emotional Intelligence and Your Success* (2000). He is an associate professor in the Department of Psychiatry and the Department of Health Policy, Management and Evaluation at the University of Toronto.

Corinne Cather, Ph.D., is a cognitive-behavioral therapist specializing in the treatment of residual symptoms in schizophrenia at the Schizophrenia Program of the Massachusetts General Hospital, Boston, and an instructor of psychiatry in the Department of Psychiatry at Massachusetts General Hospital and Harvard Medical School. She received her doctorate in clinical psychology from Rutgers University. Her other research interest is in the design and implementation of treatment approaches targeting weight gain and smoking cessation for individuals with schizophrenia.

David A. Deacon, M.B.A., worked for Morrison Associates, which examines personal, emotional, and business factors that interfere with or contribute to effective work, from 1989 to 1998. He spent fifteen years with a major money center bank in varied line and staff functions. then completed an M.B.A. at the University of Chicago and obtained a clinical psychology doctoral degree at the Illinois School of Professional Psychology.

Benjamin G. Druss, M.D., M.P.H., received medical postgraduate training in primary care medicine, psychiatry, and health services research and has been on the faculty of the Yale School of Medicine since 1996. His research has examined issues such as the work and general health costs of mental illness, quality of mental health care, and the quality and outcomes of general medical services for people with serious mental disorders. He has collaborated with, and consulted to, a number of public and private agencies including the National Center for Quality Assurance, the Robert Wood Johnson Foundation, and the American Psychiatric Association. He was the recipient of the 2000 American Psychiatric Association Early Career Health Services Research Award, the 2000 Association for Health Services Research Article-of-the-Year Award, and the 2001 Chairman's Award for Outstanding Performance from the Yale Department of Psychiatry.

Sara Eddy, Ed.D., J.D., is a member of the Law and Psychiatry Service at the Massachusetts General Hospital, Boston. Both an attorney and a psychologist, she acts as a consultant and mediator on issues arising in the workplace. She specializes in conducting sexual harassment investigations and frequently acts as a consultant in civil litigation matters. She received a law degree from Boston College and a doctoral degree from Boston University. She is on the staff of the Department of Psychiatry at the Massachusetts General Hospital and on the faculty of the Harvard Medical School.

Richard J. Frances, M.D., is medical director and chief executive officer of Silver Hill Hospital, New Canaan, Connecticut, and professor of clinical psychiatry at the New York University School of Medicine. He is the founding president of the American Academy of Addiction Psychiatry and coauthor of *Clinical Textbook of Addiction Psychiatry* (1998) and *Concise Guide to the Treatment of Alcoholism and Addictions* (2001).

Donald C. Goff, M.D., is the director of the Schizophrenia Program of the Massachusetts General Hospital, medical director of the Freedom Trail Outpatient Clinic of the Erich Lindemann Mental Health Center in Boston, and an associate professor of psychiatry at Harvard Medical School. He received his M.D. degree from UCLA Medical School and completed psychiatric residency training at the Massachusetts General Hospital. He oversees research projects in pharmacology, neuroimaging, cognitive-behavioral therapy, and genetics and pioneered the development of glutamatergic agents in the treatment of schizophrenia.

Robert P. Gordon, M.D., a psychoanalyst and organizational consultant, is on the faculties of the Chicago Institute for Psychoanalysis and the Department of Psychiatry of Northwestern University. He is a partner in Analytic Consultants, a consulting group that specializes in dealing with unconscious agendas that compromise organizational functioning. He is a board member and secretary of the Academy of Occupational and Organizational Psychiatry.

Brian L. Grant, M.D., is clinical associate professor in the University of Washington Department of Psychiatry and Behavioral Sciences. He completed his psychiatric residency training at the University of Washington and is in the private practice of Psychiatry in Seattle. In addition, he is the president and medical director of Medical Consultants Network, which provides multidisciplinary evaluations of injury and disability claims throughout the United States.

Barrie Sanford Greiff, M.D., is a consultant to the Harvard University Health Services and visiting professor of occupational psychiatry at the Institute of Living in Hartford, Connecticut. From 1968 to 1984, he was the psychiatrist to the Harvard Business School and in 1970 pioneered a unique course there, "The Executive Family." He has consulted and lectured to a wide range of organizations, chairs a committee of psychiatrists consulting to industry, and founded the Center for the Study of Work. He is a fellow of the American Psychiatric Association and a diplomate of the American Board of Psychiatry and Neurology.

Duane Q. Hagen, M.D., is chair of the Department of Psychiatry at St. John's Mercy Medical Center in St. Louis, Missouri. He has worked full time as a psychiatric consultant to various federal government agencies and has consulted to corporations. He has served as chair of the American Psychiatric Association Committee on Occupational Psychiatry and of the Group for the Advancement of Psychiatry Committee on Psychiatry in Industry.

Stephen H. Heidel, M.D., is the founder and chief executive officer of Integrated Insights, a behavioral health company providing employee assistance programs and occupational psychiatric services to organizations throughout the United States. He is a board-certified psychiatrist, certified by the American Society of Addiction Medicine, a fellow in the American Psychiatric Association, past president of the Academy of Organizational and Occupational Psychiatry, and associate clinical professor at the University of California San Diego Medical School.

Eric Hollander, M.D., completed a psychiatric residency at Mt. Sinai Medical School and a research fellowship at the New York State Psychiatric Institute and the Columbia-Presbyterian Medical Center. He is currently professor of psychiatry and director of the Siever Autism Center, Clinical Psychopharmacology, and the Compulsive and Impulsive Disorders Program at Mt. Sinai Medical School in New York City.

Nick Kates, M.B.B.S., is professor and vice chair of the Department of Psychiatry and Behavioural Sciences at McMaster University in Hamilton, Ontario, with a cross appointment in the Department of Family Medicine. He is director of the Hamilton regional psychiatry program and the Hamilton HSO Mental Health and Nutrition Program. He has consulted to many local organizations on work-related issues and is a consultant with a labor-sponsored plant closure adjustment program. He is a coauthor with Barrie Greiff and Duane Hagen of *The Psychosocial Impact of Job Loss.*

Gerald A. Kraines, M.D., is president and chief executive officer of the Levinson Institute, a Boston-based management consulting and leadership development firm. He is also on the faculty of Harvard Medical School and has written extensively on diverse subjects including brain chemistry, mental health administration, stress in the workplace, and the role of hierarchy in creating highly adaptive and accountable work systems. He is the author of *Accountability Leadership* (2001).

Robert C. Larsen, M.D., M.P.H., is a board-certified psychiatrist in San Francisco and the director of the Center for Occupational Psychiatry, an outpatient mental health group that provides services with a focus on career and job concerns. He frequently lectures on the topics of injury, disability, confidentiality, and fitness for duty related to emotional and behavioral presentations in the workforce. He is also an associate clinical professor in the Department of Psychiatry at University of California, San Francisco Medical Center, where he instructs residency and fellowship physician trainees in the field of forensic psychiatry.

Philip M. Liu, M.D., is a psychiatrist in private practice in Mountain View, California. He is the medical director of concern, an employee assistance program that has contracts with over 250 organizations in Silicon Valley. He graduated from the medical school of the University of Southern California and completed psychiatric residency training at the University of Colorado Medical Center. He is a member of the Academy of Occupational and Organizational Psychiatry. He has been an organizational consultant for numerous organizations throughout the United States.

Roy H. Lubit, M.D., Ph.D., is a psychiatrist, executive coach, and organizational consultant. He has been on the faculty of psychiatry departments and business schools, where he has taught managerial and leadership skills. He has written on narcissistic managers, scapegoating, difficult managerial behavior, knowledge management, organization design, stress management and coping with disasters. He has spoken at professional meetings in both psychiatry and business and appeared on TV and public radio. He is currently on the staff of the Department of Psychiatry at Saint Vincent's Hospital in Manhattan.

Avram H. Mack, M.D., is a postdoctoral fellow in psychiatry, College of Physicians and Surgeons of Columbia University, resident physician at New York–Presbyterian Hospital, and coauthor of *Concise Guide to the Treatment of Alcoholism and Addictions* (2001). He was twice the winner of the Harvard Longwood Academic Writing Award and is a trustee of the American Psychiatric Association.

Alan A. McLean, M.D. (deceased), was clinical associate professor of psychiatry at Weill Medical College of Cornell University, past president of the American College of Occupational Medicine, a member of the World Health Organization's Expert Advisory Panel on Occupational Health, and chair of the Committee on Occupational Psychiatry of the American Psychiatric Association. He was associated with IBM for most of his professional life in positions that included manager of medical programs, chief psychiatric consultant, and chair of its mental health advisory board. McLean was a founding member of the Academy of Organizational and Occupational Psychiatry and published nine books, including his classic volume, *Work Stress* (1979).

David E. Morrison, M.D., is a private consultant to major corporations and government groups. Morrison Associates, Ltd., in Palatine, Illinois, examines personal, emotional, and business factors that interfere with or contribute to effective work. It offers individual consultations for executives and middle managers, organizational consultations, seminars on a variety of topics, and speeches. He received his medical degree from the University of Southern California and completed psychiatric residency at the Menninger School of Psychiatry.

Kim T. Mueser, Ph.D., is a licensed clinical psychologist and a professor in the Departments of Psychiatry and Community and Family Medicine at the Dartmouth Medical School, Hanover, New Hampshire. He received his Ph.D. in clinical psychology from the University of Illinois at Chicago. He has given numerous lectures and workshops on psychiatric rehabilitation and is the coauthor of several books, including *Coping with Schizophrenia: A Guide for Families* (1994) and *Social Skills Training for Schizophrenia: A Step-by-Step Guide* (1997).

Steven E. Pflanz, M.D., received his medical degree from the University of Rochester School of Medicine. Since completing a psychiatric residency at Wilford

Hall USAF Medical Center in San Antonio, Texas, he has served as chief of mental health services at F. E. Warren Air Force Base in Cheyenne, Wyoming, where he is a major in the U.S. Air Force. He is board certified in psychiatry. He has published several papers on occupational psychiatry and presented numerous times on the topic of psychiatric illness in the workplace. His research protocols examine the relationship between work stress and mental health in the military.

David B. Robbins, M.D., M.P.H., is clinical associate professor of psychiatry at New York Medical College and former psychiatric consultant to the IBM Corporation. He completed Cornell University Medical College in 1960 and psychiatric residency at New York Hospital Cornell Medical Center. His publication subjects have included the assessment and management of psychiatric disability. He is a fellow of the American College of Occupational and Environmental Medicine, a former member of the Committee on Psychiatry in Industry of the Group for the Advancement of Psychiatry, and a member of the Academy of Organizational and Occupational Psychiatry.

Jeffrey S. Rosecan, M.D., is founder and director of the Cocaine Abuse and Chemical Dependency Treatment Program at Columbia University College of Physicians and Surgeons, where he is also assistant clinical professor of psychiatry. He is coauthor of the textbook *Cocaine Abuse: New Directions in Treatment and Research* (1987). He has been a drug abuse consultant to many corporations and organizations, including the National Football League, and has served as a professional in residence at the Betty Ford Center in Rancho Mirage, California.

Robert Rosenheck, M.D., is professor of psychiatry and public health at Yale Medical School, director of the Division of Mental Health Services Research in the Yale Department of Psychiatry, and director of the Veterans Administration's Northeast Program Evaluation Center. His interests are in the areas of cost-effectiveness analysis, dissemination of evidence-based practice in large health care systems, and systematic performance assessment. He has published widely and has won a number of national awards.

Ronald Schouten, M.D., J.D., is the director of the Law and Psychiatry Service of the Massachusetts General Hospital, Boston, and associate professor of psychiatry at Harvard Medical School. He has extensive experience as a teacher and consultant in the traditional areas of forensic psychiatry, as well as special expertise in the areas of sexual harassment, violence in the workplace, the Americans with Disabilities Act, domestic violence, and organizational consultation. He is a board-certified psychiatrist with added qualifications in forensic psychiatry and president of the Academy of Organizational and Occupational Psychiatry.

Carlotta Lief Schuster, M.D., is a member of the faculty of New York University, School of Medicine, and unit chief of the Recovery Clinic within the Division of Drug and Alcohol Abuse, Department of Psychiatry, at Bellevue Hospital in Manhattan. She is a graduate of the New York University School of Medicine. She has coauthored papers and book chapters on alcoholism and is the author of a monograph on alcohol and sexuality. Her clinical experience includes many years of working with corporations and employee assistant programs in the treatment of alcoholism.

Steven S. Sharfstein, M.D., M.P.A., is president and chief executive officer at the Sheppard Pratt Health System and clinical professor of psychiatry at the University of Maryland. A practicing clinician for over twenty years, he specializes in psychotherapy and psychopharmacology, especially for patients with long-term mental illness. He has written on a wide variety of clinical and economic topics.

Len Sperry, M.D., Ph.D., is clinical professor in the Department of Psychiatry and Behavioral Health and in the Department of Preventive and Occupational Medicine at the Medical College of Wisconsin. He is also professor of health services administration at Barry University. He is a member of the Committee on Psychiatry/Business Relations and is past chairman of the Committee on Psychiatry and the Workplace of the American Psychiatric Association. He is widely published and has received a number of awards, including the Harry Levinson Award from the American Psychological Association and the Alan McLean, M.D. Award from the Academy of Organizational and Occupational Psychiatry, both lifetime achievement awards for his contributions to leadership organizational consultation.

Dan J. Stein, M.D., Ph.D., received his undergraduate degree from the University of Cape Town and completed his psychiatry residency and research fellowship at the New York State Psychiatric Institute and the Columbia-Presbyterian Medical Center. He is director of the MRC Unit on Anxiety Disorders at the University of Stellenbosch, Cape Town, and research associate professor at the University of Gainesville, Florida.

Anne M. Stoline, M.D., is in private practice in Bel Air, Maryland. Her book *The New Medical Marketplace: A Physician's Guide to the Health Care Revolution* (1993) serves as an introduction to health care economics for medical professionals. She has also written on health policy issues. Her areas of interest are perinatal psychiatry, women's issues, and holistic psychiatric evaluation and treatment.

Mark P. Unterberg, M.D., is board certified in psychiatry and addiction psychiatry as well as a fellow of the American Psychiatric Association. He is executive medical director of Timberlawn Mental Health System, Dallas, where he also directs specialized inpatient treatment for professionals and executives. In addition, he is clinical associate professor of psychiatry at the University of Texas Southwestern Medical School and teaching instructor at the Dallas Psychoanalytic Institute. He is also team psychiatrist to the Dallas Cowboys and treating clinician of the National Football League's Program for Substance Abuse.

Thomas H. Valk, M.D., a board-certified psychiatrist, is chief executive officer and president of VEI, an occupational psychiatric consultation firm specializing in consultations to organizations assigning employees and families overseas. He has served as the assistant medical director for clinical psychiatry, overseeing the U.S. State Department's worldwide mental health system and performing occupational psychiatric duties, and in Cairo, Egypt, as regional psychiatrist for the Department of State. He is past president of the Academy of Organizational and Occupational Psychiatry and has written and lectured extensively on the subject of expatriate employees and families.

David A. Van Liew, M.D., is the president of Van Liew and Associates, a professional psychiatric service corporation in Seattle dedicated to maximizing personal and organizational development. His specialized practice emphasizes addressing conflicts of both individuals and companies from a practical, solution-oriented perspective. He is also the vice president of human resources for Applied Precision, a high-tech company, and an assistant clinical professor at the University of Washington, a former member of the Occupational Psychiatry Committee of the American Psychiatric Association, and a founding member of the Academy of Occupational and Organizational Psychiatry.

NAME INDEX

A

Adler, H., 74, 85
Agresta, J., 534, 538
Aiken, M., 138, 153
Alemagno, S. A., 566
Allen, H. M., 48–49, 58, 295
Allness, D. J., 533, 537
American Board of Examiners in Clinical
  Social Work, 35
American Management Association, 396
American Medical Association, 344, 349, 355,
  367
American Psychiatric Association (APA), 27,
  32, 210, 231, 336, 343, 357–358, 367, 384,
  409, 432, 435, 457, 479, 484, 503, 516, 533,
  537, 566
Amundsen, N., 137, 153
Anderson, V. V., 75, 85
Arterton, J., 384
Ash, P., 49, 57
Atay, J. E., 44, 46

B

Bachman, K., 258, 274
Badaracco, J., 394, 395, 403
Bailit, H. L., 49, 57
Balas, E. A., 51, 57
Balint, M., 219, 231

Ballenger, J. C., 432
Barber, M., 308, 312
Barling, J., 218, 231
Baron, R. A., 315, 327
Barsky, A. J., 57, 566
Bartlett, C., 172, 200
Bartolome, F., 259, 269, 274
Bäuml, J., 534, 539
Beck, A. T., 498
Becker, D. R., 535, 537, 538
Beer, M. D., 158, 169
Beiser, M., 312
Beitman, B. D., 27
Bell, M. D., 531, 538
Bellack, A. S., 534, 538
Bellak, L., 479
Bennis, W., 184, 200, 393, 403
Bentley, A., 290, 295
Benton, D., 101, 107
Berndt, E. R., 49, 57, 295
Bernstein, A. E., 27
Bhagat, R., 86
Bigos, S. J., 285, 294
Bion, W., 194, 200, 225, 231
Black, J. S., 258–259, 274
Blackburn, H., 566
Blazer, D. G., 55, 57, 279, 295
Bloomfield, H., 457

Bogduk, N., 560, 566
Bolles, R., 149, 153
Bolton, E., 535, 538
Bond, G. R., 533, 535, 538
Bonnie, R. J., 384
Book, H. E., 205, 208, 216, 218, 220, 224, 231, 232
Borgen, W., 137, 153
Bornstein, D., 83
Borus, J. F., 57, 566
Bostwick, J. M., 308, 313
Boyd, J. H., 159, 168
Boyle, P., 388, 403
Brakel, S. J., 343
Briggs, K. C., 172
Brill, P., 81
Brincat, C., 388, 403
Brittingham, A., 280, 295
Broadhead, W. E., 55, 57, 279, 295
Brody, M., 76, 85
Brooke-Gunn, J., 138, 153
Buchanan, J., 531, 538
Buckingham, M., 190, 200
Bunn, W., 165, 170
Burden, D. S., 258, 274
Bureau of Labor Statistics, 318–319, 328, 336
Burke, J., 392, 393, 394
Burke, R. J., 259, 274
Burling, T., 75–76, 85
Burlingame, C., 76, 80, 85
Burnam, M. A., 54, 59
Burns, D., 457
Burton, W. N., 56, 57, 279–280, 295
Bush, G. W., 223
Butler, T., 219, 232

C
Carbone, L. A., 57
Carter, L., 93, 107
Carter, M. J., 534, 539
Castillo, D. N., 344
Cather, C., 517
Centers for Disease Control, Office of Statistics and Programming, 319, 327
Chandra, P., 138, 154
Charan, R., 220, 231
Chawla, A. J., 24, 27, 56, 57
Chen, C. Y., 56, 57
Chowdhury, R., 280, 296
Chrisman, J. J., 218, 231
Chua, J. H., 218, 231
Clark, R. E., 535, 538
Claxton, A. J., 24, 27, 56, 57
Clemens, N., 83

Cloninger, C. R., 95, 107, 502, 516
Coffman, C., 190, 200
Colarusso, C. A., 479
Colledge, A. L., 331, 344
Collins, J., 172, 200, 218, 231
Collins, R., 77–78, 80, 85
Colvin, G., 220, 231
Committee on Medical Education, 69
Conti, D. J., 56, 57, 279–280, 295
Cook, R., 151, 153
Cooper, R. K., 216, 231
Cullen, M. R., 566
Culpin, M., 74, 85
Czander, W., 189, 200, 206, 231

D
Dalton, J., 86
Dauer, C., 279, 295
Davidson, J. A., 432
Davidson, L., 46
Davis, J. M., 531, 539
De Board, R., 225, 231
Deacon, D. A., 254
DePaulo, J. R., 48, 58, 457
Detsky, A. S., 51, 58
Deyo, R. A., 566
Dickerson, O., 85
Diorio, P. G., 367
Drake, R. E., 533, 534, 535, 537, 538
Drucker, P. F., 224, 231
Druss, B., 45, 46, 48–49, 54, 56, 58, 279, 280, 295
DuBose, E., 388, 403
Dunbar, E., 158, 169
DuPont, C. M., 432
DuPont, R. L., 157, 168, 432

E
Edington, D. W., 56, 57
Egdell, F. A., 367
Ellingson, S., 388, 403
Engel, R. R., 534, 539
Evans, P., 259, 269, 274
Everly, G., 301, 313

F
Faithorn, P., 479
Fallon, L. F., Jr., 367
Fein, R. A., 319, 327
Ferman, L., 138, 153
Fife, A., 57
Finkelstein, S. N., 49, 57, 295
Fishman, M., 512, 516
Folger, R., 315, 327

Fontaine, C. M., 158, 169
Fountain, D., 502, 516
Foy, D. W., 534, 539
Foyle, M. F., 158, 159, 169
Frances, R. J., 481, 498, 499
Frank, R., 44, 46, 52–53, 54, 55, 58
Franklin, G. M., 280, 296
Franklin, J. E., 499
Freud, S., 3–4, 84, 188, 194, 200, 411, 417, 479, 489, 498
Fricchione, G. L., 57
Friedman, H. S., 46
Frongillo, E., 138, 154
Frost, R., 194
Fullerton, C., 300, 313
Fulton-Kehoe, D., 280, 296

G
Gabbard, G. O., 479
Gastfriend, D. R., 512, 516
George, J., 216, 232
George, L. K., 55, 57, 279, 295
Gergen, K., 393, 403
Ghoshal, S., 172, 200
Giber, D., 93, 99, 100, 107
Giberson, L., 75, 85
Gilmore, T., 195, 201
Gingerich, S., 534, 538
Glassman, A. H., 566
Glynn, S. M., 534, 539
Goff, D. C., 517, 535, 538
Goffee, R., 209, 219, 220, 232
Gold, M. R., 58
Gold, S. R., 58
Goldberg, R., 145, 153
Golding, J. M., 54, 59
Goldman, H. H., 52–53, 54, 58
Goldman, W., 45, 46
Goldsmith, J., 200
Goldsmith, M., 93, 107
Goldstein, S. L., 49, 57
Goleman, D., 182, 200, 216, 232
Googins, B. K., 274, 275
Gordon, R., 83, 171
Gordus, J., 138, 151, 153
Gould, R. A., 535, 538
Grant, B. L., 347, 540
Greenberg, P. E., 24, 27, 279, 280–281, 295, 432
Greenfield, S. F., 503, 516
Greenwood, L., 74, 85
Greiff, B. S., 135, 153
Greist, J., 457
Griffith, E.E.H., 46

Griffith, J. H., 512, 516
Grinker, R., 76–77, 85
Guinn, D., 388, 403
Gullahorn, J. E., 157, 169
Gullahorn, J. T., 157, 169
Gyamfi, P., 138, 153

H
Haas, G., 308, 313
Hagen, D. Q., 135, 153
Haight, E., 107
Hall, R., 308, 313
Hall, R., 308, 313
Hammonds, K. H., 275
Hannigan, T. P., 165, 169
Harkavy-Friedman, J. M., 308, 313
Harlan, L. C., 367
Harlan, W. R., 367
Harrison, R., 137, 153
Harwood, H. J., 502, 516
Hay Group, 250
Hays, R., 296
Heidel, S. H., 82, 166, 170, 276, 297, 300, 301, 313
Hein, J., 86
Heinssen, R. K., 538
Heltberg, J., 157, 168
Henderson, M. J., 44, 46
Herman, R. C., 27
Herz, M. I., 531, 538
Herzog, A., 82
Hirshhorn, L., 195, 201
Hoffman, J. P., 280, 295
Hogan, J., 95, 107
Hogan, R., 95, 107
Hoge, M. A., 46
Holden, G. A., 319, 327
Hollander, E., 407, 432
Horrocks, F. A., 367
Horvitz, L. A., 48, 58, 457
House, J., 86
Howard, J., 318, 328, 344
Howland, M., 138, 153
Hurst, M. W., 282, 295
Huskamp, 44

I
Institute for Healthcare Improvement, 58
Integrated Benefits Institute, 368

J
Jackson, A., 138, 153
Jacobsen, D., 138, 153
Jacques, E., 195, 201

Jamison, K., 457
Jaques, E., 78, 86
Jarley, P., 138, 153
Jarrett, M., 74, 86
Jeffrey, M., 45, 46
Jenkins, C. D., 279, 282, 295
Jenkins, E. L., 344
Jenkins, R., 295
Johns, R. E., 331, 344
Jones, G., 209, 219, 220, 232
Jung, C., 172

K

Kahn, J. P., 3, 81, 83, 86, 91, 108, 113, 566
Kaminer, A. J., 290, 296
Kaminer, J., 85
Kanter, R. M., 209, 216, 218, 232
Kaplan, H. I., 479
Kasl, S., 86
Kates, N., 135, 153
Katon, W. J., 567
Kausch, O., 344
Kealey, D. J., 157, 165, 169
Keller, M. B., 49, 57
Kelloway, E. K., 218, 231
Kelly, R. F., 258, 275
Kennedy, S., 24, 27, 56, 57
Kernberg, O., 176, 187, 201, 225, 228, 230, 232, 479, 480
Kerr, C., 140, 153
Kessler, R., 52, 54, 55, 58, 278, 279, 295, 432
Kets de Vries, M.F.R., 134, 176, 177, 187, 201, 207, 209, 210, 232
Khantzian, E. J., 489, 499
Kieffer, C., 151, 154
Kirsh, S., 137, 153
Kissling, W., 534, 539
Kleinman, A., 566
Klerman, G. L., 27
Knoedler, W. H., 533, 537
Knotiss, L., 299
Kohut, H., 189
Kopelowicz, A., 538
Koran, L., 33, 46
Kotter, J., 209, 232
Kraines, G. A., 79, 233, 252
Kramer, P., 457
Krantz, J., 220, 232
Kraus, J. F., 318, 328, 344
Kraus, L., 83
Kretschmer, R.A.C., 57
Kruger, P., 220, 232

L

Langlieb, A. M., 28, 48
Larison, C., 280, 295
Larson, R. C., 60, 69, 329, 344
Lasswell, H., 171
Latimer, E., 535, 538
Lecrubier, Y., 432
Lee, K., 367
Lehmer, M., 290, 295
Leighton, A., 76, 86
Leighton, D., 76
Lentz, E., 76, 85
Leon, A., 308, 312
Leon, A. C., 54, 58
Leonard, S., 93, 94, 107
Leslie, D., 45, 46, 54, 58
Lesser, P., 78, 86
Lessler, D., 54–55, 59
Leucht, S., 534, 539
Levinson, D. J., 480
Levinson, H., 79, 236, 237, 245, 252, 253
Lewis, G., 142, 154
Liberman, R. P., 538
Liberty Mutual Insurance Research Center, 368
Liese, B. S., 498
Lilly, T. A., 275
Ling, T., 76, 86
Liu, P. M., 433
Livermore, G., 502, 516
Loewenthal, N. P., 158, 169
Lombardo, M., 99–100, 107
Longaker, W., 76, 85
Lopez, A. D., 51, 58, 434, 457
Lott, G., 76, 86
Lubit, R., 171, 178, 190, 201
Lyons, J. S., 531, 539
Lysaker, P. H., 531, 538
Lysgaard, S., 157, 169

M

Machiavelli, 389, 394–395
Mack, A., 481, 499
MacKinnon, R. A., 134
Mahoney, J. J., 280, 295
Malone, K., 308, 313
Manderscheid, R. W., 44, 46
Mann, J., 308, 313
Marzuk, P., 308, 312
Mays, V., 535, 538
McCall, M., 99–100, 107
McCulloch, J., 45, 46
McCurdy, D., 388, 403

McGuire, T. G., 44, 52–53, 58
McKenna, J. F., 258, 275
McLean, A. A., 1, 27, 71, 76, 78, 79, 80, 82, 86
McWilliams, P., 457
Mee-Lee, D., 512, 516
Mendenhal, M. D., 158, 169
Menninger, W., 274
Merrill, S., 140, 153
Merskey, H., 560, 566
Meyers, J. K., 159, 169
Michels, R., 134
Miller, D., 176, 187, 201
Miller, S., 498
Milstein, R. M., 531, 538
Minden, S. L., 57
Mindus, E., 78, 86
Mitchell, J., 301, 313
Monahan, J., 315, 320, 327, 384
Morris, B., 275
Morris, L. B., 210, 211, 232
Morrison, A., 99–100, 107
Morrison, D. E., 254, 259, 275, 344
Mossite, J., 344
Mueser, K. T., 517, 531, 533, 534, 535, 538, 539
Munoz, R., 82
Murray, C.J.L., 51, 58, 434, 457
Myers, I. B., 172

N

Nadler, M., 190, 201
Nash, L., 388, 391–392, 395, 396–403, 403
National Committee for Quality Assurance, 58
National Foreign Trade Council, 162, 169
National Institute for Mental Health (NIMH), 434
Nemeroff, C. B., 27
Nemiroff, R. A., 479
Newhouse, 44
Newman, C. F., 498
Nicholi, A. M., Jr., 480
Niemcryk, S. J., 282, 295
Noordsy, D. L., 534, 538
Normand, J., 280, 295
Normand, S. L., 52–53, 58
Norwood, A., 300, 313

O

Oberg, K., 156, 169
Oddoue, G. R., 158, 169
Offson, M., 434, 457
Oldham, J. M., 210, 211, 232
O'Neill, M., 101, 107

P

Palmer, R. H., 27
Pankratz, S., 308, 313
Pannzarella, J. P., 368
Parsons, P. E., 367
Pederson, P., 157, 169
Peek-Asa, C., 318, 328, 344
Pernice, R., 146, 154
Pflanz, S. E., 276
Phelan, G., 384
Pitschel-Walz, G., 534, 539
Pitt-Catsouphes, M., 274, 275
Platt, D., 308, 313
Pollack, E. S., 280, 296
Pomper, I. H., 290, 296
Porras, J., 172, 200
Portera, L., 54, 58, 308, 312
Postal, L. P., 344
Potter, J. M., 275
Potts, T., 100, 107
Potvin, J. H., 24–25, 27
Prosen, L., 390, 404
Prybeck, T., 95, 107

Q

Quick, J., 86
Quick, J., 86

R

Radomsky, E. E., 308, 310, 313
RAND Corporation, 433
Rappeport, J. R., 61, 69
Rath, F. H., Jr., 165, 169
Regier, D. A., 434, 457
Rennie, T., 76, 86
Resnick, P. J., 344
Resnick, S. G., 533, 538
Rice, D. P., 432
Richardson, W. S., 51, 58
Riley, J., 45, 46
Rischitelli, D. G., 344
Robbins, D. B., 290, 296, 347, 368
Rodgers, T. A., 163, 170
Rodriguez, E., 138, 154
Roethlisberger, F. J., 220, 232
Rogers, C. R., 220, 232
Rohrlich, J., 134
Rom, W. N., 566
Rose, R. M., 282, 295
Rosecan, J., 481, 499
Rosen, A., 321, 328
Rosen, A. J., 531, 539
Rosenheck, R. A., 45, 46, 48, 54, 58, 280, 295

Rothman, E. F., 314, 322, 328
Roy-Byrne, P. P., 49, 58, 567
Rush, A. J., 534, 539

S

Saarni, C., 216, 232
Sadock, B. J., 479
Salkever, D., 46
Salyards, S. D., 280, 295
Santos, A. B., 533, 539
Sawaf, A., 216, 231
Schatzberg, A. F., 27
Scheidemandel, P., 46
Schlesinger, M., 48–49, 58, 295
Schoenbaum, M., 52, 58
Schouten, R., 314, 322, 328
Schukit, M., 499
Schussler, T., 290, 296
Schuster, C. L., 502
Schwartz, H. S., 134, 191, 201
Searle, W., 165, 170
Shapiro, P. A., 566
Sharfstein, S. S., 28, 33, 46
Sharma, P., 218, 231
Shellenbarger, S., 299, 313
Shepherd, J. T., 566
Sheppard, H., 138, 153
Sherman, M., 74–75, 86
Shulman, G. R., 512, 516
Shultz, A. B., 56, 57
Simon, G. E., 52, 54, 59
Sisitsky, T., 432
Slater, F., 218, 231
Sledge, W. H., 45, 46, 54, 58, 280, 295
Slobodnik, A., 107
Slobodnik, D., 107
Smith, J. F., 331, 344
Smith, M., 74, 85
Snedden, N. L., 158, 169
Souetre, E., 24–25, 27
Southard, E., 1, 72, 74, 86
Speller, J. L., 134
Sperry, L. T., 27, 71, 81, 82, 83, 87, 91, 100, 102, 107, 186, 201, 210, 232, 387, 390, 403, 404
Spiegel, J., 76–77, 85
Spitz, H., 499
Spring, B., 539
SRI Selection Research International, 162, 169
Steadman, H. J., 315, 320, 327
Stein, D. J., 407, 432
Stein, L. I., 533, 539
Stein, S. J., 216, 220, 232
Stephens, K. G., 258–259, 274

Stephenson, P., 101, 107
Stewart, A., 296
Stiglin, L. E., 295
Stolar, M., 45, 46, 54, 58
Stoline, A. M., 28
Stone, A. A., 69
Stone, J., 151, 154
Stoner, J.A.F., 206, 210, 224, 232
Strock, M., 457
Sturm, R., 44, 45, 46, 47, 54, 55, 59
Substance Abuse and Mental Health Services Administration, 44
Sussman, S., 531, 539
Svrakic, D., 95, 107
Swackhamer, G., 76, 86
Sweeney, J. A., 308, 313
Swords, K., 384
Sykes, A., 100, 107

T

Tauber, R., 534, 539
Taylor, G., 76, 80, 86
Taylor, R., 140, 153
Thomander, L., 24–25, 27
Thomas, M. H., 331, 344
Tichy, N., 184, 201
Tollefson, G. D., 24–25, 27
Tollison, C. D., 567
Toscano, G., 336, 344
Triandis, H., 147, 154
Tsai, S. P., 279, 296
Tse, C. K., 55, 57, 279, 295
Tung, R. L., 162, 170
Tushman, M., 190, 201

U

U.S. Department of Health and Human Services (DHHS), 41–42, 47, 368
U.S. Department of Justice, 328
U.S. Department of Labor, 280, 296, 318–319, 328, 336
U.S. Occupational and Safety Administration, 348, 368, 554, 566
U.S. Public Health Service, 281, 296
U.S. Social Security Administration, 349, 368
U.S. Surgeon General, 48, 59, 434, 457
Unterberg, M. P., 113, 458
Ursano, R., 300, 313

V

Vaillant, G. E., 480, 489, 499
Valciukas, J. A., 567
Valk, T. H., 155, 157, 158–160, 164, 165, 166, 168, 170

Van Liew, D. A., 433
Vargas, L., 318, 328, 344
Verner, J. C., 49, 57
Vlahov, D., 494
Vossekuil, B., 319, 327
Voydanoff, P., 258, 275

W
Waldroop, J., 219, 232
Walker, E. A., 567
Walkup, J., 54, 58
Wallace, C. J., 534, 539
Wallach, M., 533, 538
Wankel, C., 206, 210, 224, 232
Warburton, J. W., 367
Ward, C., 170
Warner, G. M., 27
Warshaw, L. J., 344
Waternaux, C., 308, 313
Watson, J. P., 158, 169
Webb, G. R., 280, 296
Weber, W., 336, 344
Weiner, H., 567

Weinstein, M. C., 58
Weinstein, M. R., 368
Welch, S., 142, 154
Wells, K. B., 54, 55, 56, 57, 59, 281, 295
Werkman, S. L., 158, 170
Whyte, W. F., 76
Wickizer, T. M., 54–55, 59
Wike, V., 388, 403
Wilde, J., 534, 539
Wilson, R., 76, 85
Witherspoon, R., 103, 107
Witkin, M. J., 44, 46
Wolf, E., 189, 201
Woodward, L., 76, 86
Woodward, W., 77
Worthley, A., 387, 390, 404
Wright, F. D., 498

Z
Zaleznik, A., 187, 201
Zenz, C., 567
Zieman, G. L., 45, 47
Zubin, J., 539

SUBJECT INDEX

A

Absenteeism, 276; in Americans with Disabilities Act (ADA), 382; depression and, 48–49, 52, 55, 56, 279–280; from disability, 348; from family problems, 258; handling of, 293–294; from identified illness or injury, 277; as measure of productivity, 56; organizational acceptance of, 277; organizational culture and, 208; organizational effects of, 283–285; predictors of, 24–25, 48–49; psychosocial problems and, 281–282; substance abuse and, 280, 283, 505; types of, 277; from unclear reasons, 277. *See also* Workplace problems

Abstinence: for alcoholism, 511, 514; for drug addiction, 497–498

Academic research, history of occupational psychiatry and, 75–77, 79–80

Academy of Occupational and Organizational Psychiatry (AOOP), 32, 81, 82, 343, 346

Acamprosate, 498

Acceptance needs, 237

Access, to mental health care: enhancement of employee, 22, 292; state mandates for, 38–39

Access, to records, 68

Accidents, 276, 277; costs of, 284; family problems and, 262; medication and, 282; occupa-

tional psychiatry and, 74, 75; organizational culture and, 208; organizational effects of, 283–285; psychosocial problems and, 281–282; substance abuse and, 280, 283. *See also* Disability, psychiatric; Workers' compensation; Workplace problems

Accommodation, reasonable, 350; in Americans with Disabilities Act (ADA), 377–381, 405; for anxiety disorders, 413, 419, 423, 427, 431–432; for bipolar disorder, 456; for depressive disorders, 438, 447, 450, 456; interactive communication process of determining, 377–381; for psychotic disorders, 518, 520–521, 523, 526, 536–537; treatability and, 373–374. *See also* Americans with Disabilities Act (ADA)

Accountability: of managers, 240; organizational change and, 242, 252; organizational structures and, 224, 227–228

Achievement, compulsiveness and, 128–130

Action learning, 100

Action planning, in executive coaching, 102–103

Acute stress disorder, 299–300

Adaptation, 243–249; employees without capacity of, 249–250; human capabilities for, 243–244; personality traits and, 459–460. *See also* Flexibility

Adaptational problems: complexity of, 10–11; derailed employees and, 249–250

Adaptive readiness, 234, 243–249

Addiction: biopsychosocial approach to, 486–488; dependence and, 484–485; DSM-IV diagnostic criteria for dependence and, 484–485; models of, 485–488; psychiatric management of drug, 497–498; substance abuse emergencies and, 305–307. *See also* Alcohol abuse and dependence; Drug abuse; Substance abuse

Adjustment disorder with anxiety, 408–413; case example of, 408–109; causes of, 411–412; DSM-IV diagnosis of, 409–410; effects of, 412; psychiatric management of, 413; reasonable accommodation of, 413; return to work with, 413; workplace intervention in, 412–413; workplace recognition of, 412

Adjustment disorder with depressed mood, 433, 434, 435–438; bereavement *versus,* 435–436; burnout and, 434; case example of, 435; causes of, 436; diagnosis of, 435–436; effects of, 437; psychiatric management of, 438; reasonable accommodation of, 438; return to work with, 438; workplace intervention in, 437–438; workplace recognition of, 437. *See also* Burnout; Depression

Adjustment disorders: diagnosis of, 409–410; in expatriates, 157, 159; from traumatic disasters, 299–300

Administrative medical review, 362

Administrator-leaders, 186

Admiration, leaders with need of, 187, 189, 211–213

Adult Children of Alcoholics (ACOA), 513

Adverse drug responses, 563–564

Adverse selection, fee for service and, 38–39

Advice giving, insight-oriented psychotherapy and, 17

Affective disorders: alcohol abuse and, 509; in expatriates, 159. *See also* Anxiety; Anxiety disorders; Bipolar disorder; Depression

Affective disorders with psychotic features, 521–523; case example of, 521–522; causes of, 522; effects of, 522; psychiatric management of, 522–523; reasonable accommodation of, 523; return to work with, 523; workplace intervention in, 522; workplace recognition of, 522

Affiliative leadership style, 183, 184, 185

Afternoon, intoxication during, 508

Aggression: alcohol and, 305; antisocial personality disorder and, 466–469; assertiveness *versus,* 223; causes of, 179, 180–181; maladaptive, 336; in managers or leaders, 178–182, 187–188, 223; managing and working with, 180–182; narcissism and, 176, 179, 180; organizational effects of, 179–180; projection of, 194; styles of handling, 187–188; types of, 178; violence and, 314–327, 336–338. *See also* Violence

Aging: emotional intelligence and, 216; narcissism and, 176

Agoraphobia, 415–419. *See also* Panic disorder

Agricultural chemicals, 562–563

AIDS, 281

Al-Anon, 498, 507

Albert v. Runyon, 384

Alcohol abuse and dependence: addiction and, 488, 503; among expatriates, 160; anxiety and, 507–508, 509–510; case examples of, 503–504, 505–507, 512–514; causes of, 502–503, 507–508; with coexisting psychiatric disorders, 509–510, 515, 516; costs of, 502; depression and, 507–508, 509–510, 512–514; diagnosis of, 508–509; drug abuse combined with, 494, 509, 563; dual diagnosis, 509–510; effects of, 507–508; medical complications of, 511; prevalence of, 280, 481; psychiatric management of, 508–514; return to work with, 514–515; schizophrenia spectrum disorders and, 533; workplace environment and, 508, 514–515; workplace intervention in, 503–507; workplace problems caused by, 280, 503. *See also* Addiction; Substance abuse

Alcohol abuse treatment: detoxification and, 510; employee assistance programs for, 41, 506–507; hospitalization in, 497, 510, 511–514; inpatient *versus* outpatient, 511–514; medication for, 498, 510; workplace referral for, 503–507. *See also* Substance abuse treatment

Alcohol metabolism, 502–503, 510

Alcohol withdrawal, 305; detoxification and, 510; diagnosis of coexisting psychiatric problems and, 510; effects of, 507–508, 510, 564; treatment of, 510

Alcoholics Anonymous (AA), 488, 497–498, 526; in case studies, 504, 506, 507, 513–514; psychiatric treatment and, 514; return to work and, 514–515

Alliance, therapeutic, 17

Allies, 177

Allness, D. J., 537

Alprazolam, 418, 494, 495, 509

Alteer Chemical Company, 298–299

Alter ego, 189

Alternative health models, 557–558

Alzheimer's disease, 565

Ambition: family-driven, 267, 271–273; grandiosity and, 114–117, 475

Amego, EEOC v., 382, 384

American Academy of Occupational Medicine, 82

American Academy of Psychiatry and the Law, 343, 346

American College of Occupational and Environmental Medicine (ACOEM), 81, 82, 343; Code of Ethical Conduct, 61, 70; contact information for, 346

American Cyanamid, 77

American Journal of Psychiatry, 74–75, 76, 80, 84

American Psychiatric Association (APA), history of workplace psychiatry and, 77, 78, 79, 81–83, 84, 85, 86

American Psychiatric Association Biographical Directory, 32

American Psychological Association directory, 34

American Society of Addiction, patient placement criteria of, 512

AT&T, 258

AT&T, Gaul v., 377, 384

Americans with Disabilities Act (ADA), 106, 165, 325, 369–383; "absenteeism" in, 382; application of, 383; case law on, 371, 372, 373, 377–381; claims of, defenses against, 369–370; claims of, percentage of mental illness, 370; definitions in, 371–383; "direct threat" in, 382–383; "disability" in, 371–376; EEOC enforcement guidelines for, 370, 371–383; "essential functions" in, 376–377; fitness-for-duty examinations and, 331; historical evolution of, 370–371; impact of, 369; "impairment" in, 371–372; "major life activities" in, 374; "misconduct" in, 381–382; permissible termination under, 381–383; "poor performance" in, 382; purpose of, 369; "qualified individual" in, 376; "reasonable accommodation" in, 377–381, 405; "record of" in, 374; "regarded as" in, 375–376, 379–380; resources on, 386; substance abuse and, 497; "substantially limits" in, 372–373; "undue hardship" in, 382. See also Accommodation, reasonable

ADA Document Center, 386

ADA Technical Assistance, 386

Amphetamine abuse, 283, 482, 509, 525

Amygdala, 412

Anemia, 511

Anergia, 526, 532, 535

Angel dust, 525

Anger: aggressive behavior and, 179, 289, 317; conversion of, 551; family problems and, 263; job loss and, 146–147, 148; self-awareness of, 218–219

Anhedonia, 526

Anthrax scares, 299, 317

Antianxiety medication, 418–419; abuse of, 494–495, 509; expatriate use of, 159. See also Medication

Anticipatory anxiety, 415, 417, 418, 422

Anticipatory stage of job loss, 137–138, 150–152

Anticonvulsant medication, 455

Antidepressants, 18, 19; for affective disorders with psychotic features, 523; for anxiety disorders, 413, 418, 427; for bipolar disorder, 456; for compulsiveness, 129, 427; for dysthymia, 450; expatriate use of, 159; for major depressive disorder, 444–445; for pain relief, 561; for schizophrenia spectrum disorders, 534. See also Medication; Selective serotonin reuptake inhibitors

Antipsychotics: for affective disorders with psychotic features, 522–523; for delusional disorder, 520; expatriate use of, 159; for obsessive-compulsive disorder, 427; for schizophrenia spectrum disorders, 533–534; side effects of, 312, 533–534; for substance-induced psychotic disorder, 526

Antisocial personality disorder, 466–469; alcoholism and, 502; case examples of, 466–467; causes of, 468; diagnosis of, 467–468; DSM-IV diagnostic criteria for, 467–468; narcissism and, 468; psychiatric management of, 468–469; workplace intervention in, 468; workplace recognition of, 468

Antisocial traits, 466–469; aggressive behavior and, 179

Anxiety, 407–432; ability to tolerate, 219–220; alcohol abuse and, 507–508; anticipatory job loss and, 137–138; assessment of improvement of, 20; inadequate organizational structures and, 225, 227, 228, 229; irritable bowel syndrome and, 562; job loss and, 137–138, 142, 148; organizational change and, 246; paranoia and, 125–127; prevalence of, 279; recognition of, 11; somatoform disorders and, 551, 552; stress and, 9–10, 407–408; suppression of, 133; from trauma, 300

Anxiety disorders, 407–432; alcohol abuse and, 507–508, 509–510; causes of, 411–412, 417, 422, 426, 430; in expatriates, 159; functional somatic syndromes and, 555, 557; job loss and, 145; listed, 408; multiple chemical sensitivity syndrome and, 555; paranoid personality and, 127; prevalence of, 23; stress and, 408; treatment of, 13, 413, 418–419, 423, 427, 431; types of, 408–432; workplace problems caused by, 281. *See also* Adjustment disorder with anxiety; Generalized anxiety disorder; Obsessive-compulsive disorder; Panic disorder; Phobias; Posttraumatic stress disorder

Anxiety Disorders Association of America, 432

Apathy, in schizophrenia spectrum disorders, 532

Appetite suppressants, 489

Applied ethics, 388, 403. *See also* Ethics, organizational

Army Management Staff College, 93

Arterial disease, 558–560, 565

Assertive Community Treatment (ACT) model, 533

Assertiveness, 222–223

Assessment: executive, 92–97, 108–112; of functional somatic syndromes, 556; of job loss impact, 142–147, 150; methodologies of, 25; quality control and, 24–25; of somatoform disorders, 549–550; threat, 314–324; of traumatic stressors, 300; of treatment response, 19–22, 24–25; of workplace problems, 285–289. *See also* Diagnosis; Evaluation; Recognition; Screening

Attachments, change and, 245–247

Attitudes: toward authority, 188–189; toward work, job loss impact and, 146–147

Atypical depression. *See* Dysthymia

Authoritarian personalities and leaders, 183, 187, 223, 363

Authoritative leadership style, 183, 184, 185

Authority: attitudes toward, 188–189; in flat organizations, 195

Authorization for Release of Medical Information, 345

Autonomic arousal, 562

Avoidance: alcoholism and, 502; functional somatic syndromes and, 557; panic disorder and, 415, 418–419; resistance to change and, 132–134; social anxiety disorder and, 420, 422–423

Awareness programs, 12–13, 22

Axis I diagnoses, 93. *See also* Anxiety disorders; Depression

Axis II diagnoses, 93. *See also* Personality disorders and problems

B

Back pain, 285, 560–561

Backstabbing, 190

Balanced scorecard, 177

Bank robbery, 303, 304

Barriers, to treatment and referral, 7–8; in employee assistance programs, 42–43

Basic assumption group, dependency, 194–195, 225–227, 229

Behavior therapy, 13; for addiction, 497; for anxiety disorders, 418–419; in organizational consulting, 18; for psychotic disorders, 523, 526

Behavioral science, 72

Behavioral theories, of anxiety, 411–412, 417

Benefits, government, 536

Benefits, mental health care: human resource department and, 5; improving, proactive approaches to, 25–26; insurance arrangements and, 36–42; management and, 5; workers' compensation and, 364–367; for workplace problem prevention, 292. *See also* Funding sources; Insurance

Benign hierarchy, 92

Benzodiazepines, 159, 418, 419, 494, 497, 510

Bereavement, 435–436, 441

Beta blockers, 423

Binge drinkers, 510

Biological etiology. *See* Neurobiological etiology; Organic etiology

Biopsychosocial approach to addiction, 486–488

Bipolar disorder, 433–434, 450–456; case example of, 450–451; causes of, 453; depression and, 451, 454; diagnosis of, 451–453; as disability, 373; DSM-IV diagnostic criteria for, 451–453; effects of, 454; in expatriates, 165; psychiatric management of, 455–456; psychotic behavior in, 310–311, 338, 521–522; reasonable accommodation of, 456; return to work with, 456; workplace intervention in, 454–455; workplace recognition of, 453–454. *See also* Depression; Mania

Blaming: by CEOs, 212, 213, 219; culture of, 227–228

Blunted affect, 526, 532, 535

Body dysmorphic disorder, 544–545

Bomb threats, 317

Bombings, 298, 299, 325

Borderline personality disorder, 472–474; case example of, 472–473; causes of, 473; diagnosis of, 473; DSM-IV diagnostic criteria for, 473; psychiatric management of, 474; workplace intervention in, 473–474; workplace recognition of, 474

Boss. *See Executive headings;* Leaders; Managers; Superiors

Boston Psychopathic Hospital, 74

Bottom-line preoccupation, 396–397

Boundary issues, 194, 195

Brain chemistry. *See* Neurobiological etiology; Neurological problems

Brain drain, 235

Breast implant response syndrome, 553

Briquet's syndrome, 468, 542–543

Buffalo General Hospital, Glowacki v., 373, 384

Bultemeyer v. Fort Wayne Community Schools, 378, 384

Bunevitch v. CVS/Pharmacy, 372, 381–384, 384

Buprenorphine, 498

Buproprion, 129, 444

Burnout: depression and, 434; evaluation of mental illness and, 9–10; meaning of, 8, 9, 434. *See also* Adjustment disorder with depressed mood; Depression

Business ethics, 388. *See also* Ethics, organizational

Business meals, alcohol abuse and, 508

Business trips, alcohol abuse and, 508, 514–515

Business understanding, 100

Business unit performance, office politics and, 172

C

Cairo, U.S. Embassy at, 158–159, 163

California: confidentiality in, 61, 63; psychiatric disability in, 339; workplace violence in, 336

California Personality Inventory, 93

Canadian Business Review, 257

Canadian Roundtable on Mental Health and Economics, 82

Cancer, 281

Capitalism, covenantal ethics and, 395

Capitation: with health maintenance organizations, 39–41; with managed behavioral health care companies, 44–45

Career effects: confidentiality issues and, 61, 63–64; fear of negative, 7, 10, 283; of treatment for workplace problems, 290

Career enhancement programs, 17–18

Carnegie Fellowships in Industrial Psychiatry, 75–76

Carve-outs, 26, 44–45

Case management, 29; of schizophrenia spectrum disorders, 533

Causality determination, for psychiatric disability, 358–363

Causes, underlying: of affective disorders with psychotic features, 522; of aggressive behavior, 179, 180–181; of alcoholism, 502–503, 507–508; of antisocial personality disorder, 468; of anxiety disorders, 411–412, 417, 422, 426, 430; of avoidance, 133; of bipolar disorder, 453; of borderline personality disorder, 473; of competitiveness, 122, 124, 197–199; complexity of evaluation and, 10–11, 23; of compulsiveness, 129; defined treatment and, 11; of delusional disorder, 519; of depressive disorders, 360, 436, 441–442, 449, 453; displacement of emotions and, 131; of drug abuse, 482; of executive distress, 113–114; executive psychotherapy and, 105; family problems and, 257; of narcissistic dishonesty, 119–120; of narcissistic grandiosity, 115–117, 476; of obsessive-compulsive personality disorder, 462; of paranoid personality disorder, 127, 470–471; of psychosis, 311; of schizophrenia spectrum disorders, 530–531; of somatoform disorders, 547–548; of substance-induced psychotic disorder, 525; of workplace problems, 278–283. *See also* Family history; Neurobiological etiology; Organic etiology

Celebration, 245

Center for Occupational Mental Health, 79

Cerebellar atrophy, 511

Certification. *See* Credentialing and licensing

Challenger space shuttle tragedy, 398–399

Change: adapting to, 243–249; attachments and, 245–247; job loss and, 135–153; loss and, 245–247; phases of, 247–249; psychological resistance to, 132–134, 245–247

Change, organizational, 233–252; adaptive readiness for, 234, 243–249; alcohol abuse and, 507; casualties of, 249–250; depression and, 437; employee motivation and, 235–237; employees and, 233–252; factors in effective, 251; families and, 263; job loss and, 135–153; leadership of, 242–243, 250–251; leveraging employee potential during, 234, 235–236, 244, 245, 247–249; loss and, 245–247; managing, 240–243, 247–249; new demands and, 235, 245–247, 249–250;

Change, organizational, *continued*
organizational structures and, 224–225;
phases of, 247–249; psychological contract
and, 234, 236, 237–240, 245–247; resistance
to, 233–235, 245–247, 249–250; stress management and, 134; suicide risk in, 309; threat
and opportunity in, 244–245; trends in,
251–252. *See also* Culture, organizational;
Culture change

Change-in-scenario test, 397

Character: defined, 94, 393; executive, and
organizational ethics, 387, 393–395; leadership and, 184, 393–395; mature *versus*
immature, 95

Character assessment: executive, 93, 94–95,
97; interviews for, 97; inventories for, 95

Charismatic leaders, 187, 194; irrepressibly
self-confident CEOs and, 211–213; personal
conscience conflict and, 401

Chemical imbalance, 439, 442. *See also* Major
depressive disorder

Chemical plant fire, 301–302, 304

Chemical sensitivity, 553, 554–555

Chemical toxicity, 562–563, 565

Chief executive officer (CEO): emotional intelligence of, 216–224; employees' misperceptions of, due to inadequate organizational
structures, 225–229; hypervigilant, 214–216;
influence of, on organizational culture,
210–224, 230; interventions with, 224; irrepressibly self-confident, 211–213; overly conscientious, 213–214; personality types of,
210–216; role stresses of, 230

Child abuse, overseas, 163, 167

Child care issues, 258, 264–265

Childhood experience. *See* Family dynamics,
reenacted; Family history

Children: overseas, 160–161, 165; traumatic
disasters and, 300

Chlordiazepoxide, 510

Chronic fatigue syndrome (CFS), 281, 553,
555, 557

Chronic pain, 281. *See also* Low back pain
syndrome; Pain; Pain disorder

Chronic problems, 19–20

Church activities, 269

Cielo Bank, 303

Circuit Court of Cook County, Palmer v., 382,
385

Circuit-riding clinicians, overseas, 166, 167

City-funded hospital clinics, 29, 43

Civil commitment laws, overseas, 163–164

Client-therapist relationship, payment arrange-

ment and, 37. *See also* Physician-patient
relationship

Clinical psychologists. *See* Psychologists,
clinical

Clinics, public. *See* City-funded hospital clinics; Research clinics; State and local clinics

"Clockwork" model or organizations, 191

Clonazepam, 418

Coaching, executive, 17–18, 100–103; collaborative relationship in, 102, 103; executive
consultation *versus,* 100–101; models of, 101;
performance-based, 103; phases of, 102–103;
practice of, 101–103; psychotherapy *versus,*
100–101, 102, 105; skill-based, 103

Coaching leadership style, 184, 185

Cocaine abuse, 489–490; addiction and, 488;
alcohol abuse and, 509; case example of,
490–491; causes of, 482; cross addiction
with, 489, 509; effects of, 489–490; prevalence of, 481; psychotic symptoms with, 311,
524–525. *See also* Drug abuse

Cocaine Anonymous, 488, 491

Coercive leadership style, 182–183, 184, 185

Cognition, adaptation and, 243

Cognitive-behavioral therapy (CBT): for addiction, 497; for anxiety disorders, 413, 427,
431; for depression, 446; for psychotic disorders, 520, 523, 526, 534–535, 536

Cognitive impairment: organically induced,
565; in schizophrenia spectrum disorders,
526, 527, 532; in substance-induced persisting dementia, 564

Cognitive intelligence (IQ), 216, 217

Cognitive therapy, 14

Cole, Pettus v., 63, 69

Commitment: conditions for employee,
241–243; organizational change and,
235–236, 237, 239, 241–243; organizational
culture and, 208; schizophrenia spectrum
disorders and, 532

Committee on Occupational Psychiatry, American Psychiatric Association: history of workplace psychiatry and, 77, 81–82, 84, 85, 86.
See also Committee on Psychiatry in the
Workplace

Committee on Psychiatry/Business Relations,
American Psychiatric Association, 82–83, 84

Committee on Psychiatry in the Workplace,
American Psychiatric Association, 81–82, 83.
See also Committee on Occupational
Psychiatry

Communication: for fitness-for-duty examinations, 340–342

Communication, organizational: adaptation and, 243, 244; in anticipatory stage of job loss, 138, 151–152; dependency basic assumption and, 226–227; in expatriate communities, 162; fight-or-flight basic assumption and, 227–229; hidden agendas and, 192–193; during organizational change, 244, 247–249; subordinate-superior, 185–186

Communication skills, executive, 110, 184

Communities, expatriate, 161–162

Community mental health centers (CMHCs), 43

Community resources: for job loss, 136, 146, 149–150, 152; for suicidal behavior, 309; for traumatic events, 304

Company-employee relationship, psychological contract and, 234, 236, 237–240, 245–247

Compensation system. *See* Rewards system

Competition, excessive: anticipatory job loss and, 138; causes of, 122, 124, 197–199; intervention in, 122–123, 125; narcissism and, 176–177; Oedipal conflict and, 120–125; office politics and, 197–199; in organizational culture, 190; organizational effects of, 122, 125; prevention of, 122–123, 125; succession planning and, 123–125

Competitive advantage, adaptation as, 243

Complexity: impulse control and dealing with, 223–224; managing change and, 244

Compliance: antisocial personality disorder and, 468–469; coercive leadership and, 182–183; passive-aggressive personality disorder and, 477–478

Compromise formations, 459

Compulsions, 423–427, 485. *See also* Obsessive-compulsive disorder; Obsessive-compulsive personality disorder

Compulsive gamblers, 372

Compulsive personality style, 125, 128–130; causes of, 129; organizational effects of, 129–130; work functions and, 340. *See also* Obsessive-compulsive disorder; Obsessive-compulsive personality disorder

Conceptual thinking, 100

Conference Board of Canada, 258

Confidentiality issues, 1, 24, 26, 60–70; administrative influence and, 67–68; criminal conflict and, 67; of disability evaluation, 350–352, 380–381; of employee assistance programs (EAPs), 43, 482–483; of fitness-for-duty examinations, 330–332, 342–343, 380; legal revocation of confidentiality and, 350–351; medical ethics and, 61; organiza-

tional ethics and, 390; in organizational settings, 61–64; payment method and, 37; physician-patient relationship and, 61–64; professional ethics and, 61, 390; in referral situations, 65–68

Conflict, interpersonal, 276, 277–278, 282; evaluation of, 288, 289; organizational effects of, 283–285

Conflict, unconscious, 15, 16; therapist neutrality and, 17

Conflict avoidance, 186, 213–214

Conflict of interest: with employee assistance programs, 43; ethical perspectives, 391, 396–397; perceived, 66–67; in referral situations, 65–67

Conflict styles, 186, 213

Conscience, personal, 400–403

Consensus, leadership by, 92

Consent, informed, 61, 63, 64; lack of, 65; written, for fitness-for-duty examinations, 330–332, 341, 342, 345

Consultation, executive: coaching *versus*, 100–101; for excessive competition, 122–123

Conversion disorder, 549, 551; DSM-IV diagnostic criteria for, 551; treatment of, 551. *See also* Psychosomatic interface; Somatoform disorders

Coping skills, job loss and, 144, 147–148, 152

Cornell University: Medical College, 79, 81; School of Industrial and Labor Relations, 75–76

Coronary artery disease (CAD), 558–560

Corporate culture. *See* Culture, organizational

Cost-benefit analysis (CBA), 49–53; cost-effectiveness analysis *versus*, 50; value of, 49–50

Cost containment, 1; managed care and, 44–45, 54–55; quality of care issues and, 54–55; strategies of, 29

Cost crisis, factors in, 29

Cost-effectiveness, 1, 24; of depression treatment, 52–53; of mental health care, 56–57; quality of care and, 55

Cost-effectiveness analysis (CEA), 49–53; cost-benefit analysis *versus*, 50; measures in, 50–51; value of, 49–50, 52–53

Cost-effectiveness (C/E) ratio, 50, 51

Cost offsets, 53–54, 57; medical care, 25

Cost sharing, 29; health maintenance organizations and, 40

Costs: causal misattribution and, 361; of community mental health centers, 43; of depression in workplace, 48–49, 279–280, 281, 434;

Costs, *continued*
of disability, 347–348; in fee-for-service systems, 36–37, 38; of health maintenance organizations, 40–41; of mental illness, 282–283; of preferred provider organizations, 39; of psychosocial problems, 282–283; return on, 48–49; of substance abuse, 281, 496, 502; of workplace problems, 284–285

Counseling, supportive, 13, 14, 21, 23–24. *See also* Psychotherapy

Counselors: alcoholism, 36; historical overview of, 73–74; marriage and family, 36; mental health, 36; prevalence of, 74; selection of, 36

Counterphobia, 16

Countertransference, 15–16; as barrier to causal attribution, 360–361

Covenantal ethics, 389, 395

Covert aggression, 178

Coworkers: alcoholism and, 507, 508, 515; depression and, 443; effects of workplace problems on, 284; psychotic disorders and, 520, 522, 531; substance abusers and, 306; suicide and, 309. *See also* Organizational effects

Creativity: assessment of, 111; importance of, 120–121, 122; suppression of others', by executives, 120–125, 176–177, 213–214

Credentialing and licensing: counselor, 36; psychiatrist, 31; psychologist, 34; social worker, 35

Criado v. IBM, 373, 378, 384

Criminal conduct: confidentiality and, 67; narcissistic dishonesty and, 118, 120. *See also* Antisocial personality disorder

Crises, emotional. *See* Emotional crises

Crisis: Chinese word for, 244–245; organizational ethics and, 392

Crisis management plan, 325–326

Crisis management team, 326–327

Critical change, 244–249. *See also* Change; Change, organizational

Critical incident stress debriefing (CISD), 300–301, 303, 310

Cross-gender relationships, 196–197

Crypto-illness, 560

Cultural bridge, 162

Culture, national: competitiveness and, 198–199; delusional disorder and, 519; somatoform disorders and, 548

Culture, organizational, 205–231; of adaptive readiness, 234, 243–249; CEO's emotional intelligence and, 216–224; CEO's influence on, 210–224, 230; CEO's personality type

and, 210–216; competitiveness and, 198–199; compulsive personality and, 129; defined, 206–207; dependency basic assumption, 194–195, 225–227, 229; disability and, 363; espoused *versus* actual, 207; exclusive, 190; executive dishonesty and, 119–120; facilitative, 205, 208–210, 231; factors that shape, 190–191, 210–231; of fairness, 243; families and, 263; feeling states and, 206–207, 208; fight-or-flight, 194, 225, 227–229; fossilized, 213–214; functions and importance of, 189–190, 205; healthy, 189–190; hypervigilant CEOs and, 214–216; intolerant, 190; irrepressible, self-confident CEOs and, 211–213; narcissistic personality and, 177; noncooperative, 190; obstructive, 205, 207–208, 231; office politics and, 189–192; organizational resources and, 230; organizational structures and, 224–229; overly conscientious CEOs and, 213–214; persecuting/persecuted, 214–216; product and, 230; rigid, 190; slavish, 211–213; toxic, 190, 191–192. *See also* Organizational context; Workplace environment

Culture change, organizational, 18, 191, 263. *See also* Change, organizational

Culture shock syndrome, 155, 156–157, 166

CVS/Pharmacy, Bunevitch v., 372, 381–384, 384

Cynicism, 235, 242

D

Daddy track, 258

Dahill v. Police Department of Boston et al., 374, 384

Daley v. Koch, 372, 384

Death: bereavement and, 435–436; of well-liked executive, 302

Death, in family: organizational effects of, 263–264; workplace problems caused by, 283

Decade of the Brain, 434

Decision making improvement, as treatment response, 20–21

Defamatory statements, 315. *See also* Threats; Violence

Defense mechanisms, 16. *See also* Displacement; Projection; Somatoform disorders; Suppression

Defenses, psychological: in executives, 114; maladaptive personality traits and, 459

Delirium: organically induced, 565; substance intoxication, 563–564, 565; substance withdrawal, 510, 564

Delirium tremens, 510

Delivery systems, 1, 36–46; for expatriate populations, 166–167; overview of, 5–6; types of, 36–46. *See also* Mental health care; Treatment

Delusional disorder, 518–521; case example of, 519; causes of, 519; diagnosis of, 518–519; effects of, 520; persecutory-type, 520; prevalence of, 518; psychiatric management of, 520; reasonable accommodation of, 520–521; return to work with, 520–521; schizophrenia *versus*, 518; workplace intervention in, 520; workplace recognition of, 520

Delusions: in affective disorders with psychotic features, 522; in schizophrenia spectrum disorders, 526, 532, 534

Demands: excessive, workplace problems caused by, 282; family, 255, 264–270; organizational change and new, 235, 245–247, 249–250

Dementia: organically induced, 565; substance-induced persisting, 564

Demerol, 493–494

Democratic leadership style, 183, 184, 185

Denial, of addiction, 486

Depakote, 455

Dependence, substance, 484–485. *See also* Addiction; Alcohol abuse and dependence; Drug abuse; Substance abuse

Dependency basic assumption, 194–195, 225–227, 229

Dependency needs: CEO's, 230; dysfunctional leaders and, 187; group regression and, 194–195, 225–227, 229

Depressants, cocaine abuse and, 489

Depression, 433–456; absenteeism and, 48–49, 52, 55, 56, 279–280; alcohol abuse and, 507–508, 509–510, 512–514; burnout and, 10, 433–456; causes of, 360, 436, 441–442, 449, 453; compulsive personality and, 129; costs of, 48–49, 279–280, 281, 434; defined, 433; in expatriates, 159, 160; functional somatic syndromes and, 555, 557; irritable bowel syndrome and, 562; job loss and, 136–137, 142, 145; job performance problems and, 280–281, 283, 309; low back pain syndrome and, 561; narcissistic personality problems and, 114; organically induced, 565; paranoid personality and, 127; physical pain and, 561; prevalence of, 23, 434; productivity and, 48–49, 52–53, 54, 55, 56; psychotic behavior and, 312; recognition of, 8, 9, 10, 11, 309; somatic symptoms and, 442, 450, 549, 552; with substance abuse, 281, 442; suicide and,

309, 441; suppression and, 133; from trauma, 300; types of, 433–434; work function and, 339, 340. *See also* Adjustment disorder with depressed mood; Bipolar disorder; Dysthymia; Major depressive disorder

Depression era, 76

Depression treatment, 444–446, 450, 455–456; cost-effectiveness analysis of, 50, 51, 52–53; productivity and, 24–25, 50, 51, 52–53, 54, 56; response to, 20, 21, 434. *See also* Antidepressants; Psychotherapy

Deprivation, dealing with, after job loss, 147–148

Derailed employees, 249–250

Detachment, compulsive personality and, 129

Detail: attention to, 129–130; over-attention to, 213–214

Detoxification, 497, 510, 526

Devaluing of others: authoritarian leadership and, 187; narcissism and, 176

Developmental history review, in disability evaluation, 355

Diagnosis: of adjustment disorder with anxiety, 408–410; of adjustment disorder with depressed mood, 435–436; of alcoholism, 508–509; of antisocial personality disorder, 467–468; of bipolar disorder, 451–453; of borderline personality disorder, 473; of conversion disorder, 551; of delusional disorder, 518–519; DSM-IV system of, 11–12, 93, 210, 357–358, 405; of dysthymia, 447–449; of epidemic hysteria, 544; of factitious disorder, 546; of generalized anxiety disorder (GAD), 410–411; of histrionic personality disorder, 464–465; of hypochondriasis, 544–545; inaccurate, 21; of major depressive disorder, 439–441; of malingering, 546–547; of narcissistic personality disorder, 475–476; of obsessive-compulsive disorder, 424–426; of obsessive-compulsive personality disorder, 461–462; overview of, 10–11; of pain disorder, 541–542; of panic disorder, 414–417; of paranoid personality disorder, 470–471; of passive-aggressive personality disorder, 477–478; of phobias, 420–422; of post-traumatic stress disorder, 428–430; precise, 11, 23; from psychiatric disability evaluation, 357–358; of schizophrenia spectrum disorders, 527–529; of social anxiety disorder, 420–423; of somatization disorder, 542–543; of substance-induced psychotic disorder, 524; of substance intoxication delirium, 563–564. *See also* Assessment; Evaluation; Recognition; Screening

Diagnostic and Statistical Manual of Mental Disorders, Fourth Edition (DSM-IV), 12, 93, 210, 357–358, 405; adjustment disorders criteria of, 409–410; on alcoholism, 503, 508; Americans with Disabilities Act (ADA) definitions and, 372; antisocial personality disorder criteria of, 467–468; bipolar disorder criteria of, 451–453; borderline personality disorder criteria of, 473; conversion disorder criteria of, 551; delusional disorder criteria of, 518–519; dysthymic disorder criteria of, 448–449; factitious disorder criteria of, 546; generalized anxiety disorder (GAD) criteria of, 410–411; histrionic personality disorder criteria of, 464–465; hypochondriasis criteria of, 544–545; major depressive disorder criteria of, 439–441; malingering criteria of, 546–547; narcissistic personality disorder criteria of, 475–476; obsessive-compulsive disorder criteria of, 425–426; pain disorder criteria of, 541–542; panic disorders criteria of, 415–417; paranoid personality disorder criteria of, 470; passive-aggressive personality disorder criteria of, 478; phobias criteria of, 420–422; posttraumatic stress disorder criteria of, 336, 429–430; schizoaffective disorder criteria of, 528–529; schizophrenia criteria of, 527–528; somatization disorder criteria of, 528; substance-induced psychotic disorder criteria of, 524; substance intoxication delirium criteria of, 544–545; substance withdrawal criteria of, 545

Dialectical behavioral therapy, 497

Diet pills, 489

Directive command, 92

Directories: of psychiatrists, 32; of psychologists, 34; of social workers, 35. *See also* Referral resources

Disability, physical: Americans with Disabilities Act (ADA) and, 370, 371–376; emotional components of, 348; job loss and, 141–142, 145; somatoform disorders and, 549. *See also* Americans with Disabilities Act (ADA); Medical problems; Psychosomatic interface

Disability, psychiatric, 347–367; accommodation to, 350, 373–374, 377–381; adoption of role of, 362–363; Americans with Disabilities Act (ADA) and, 369–383; causality determination for, 358–363; costs of, 347–348; defined, in Americans with Disabilities Act (ADA), 371–376; defining, 349–350; employer perception of, 375–376, 379–380; evaluation for, 347, 350–363; external factors in, 363–364; impairment and, 349–350,

371–372; internal factors in, 364; legal issues of, 347, 349, 353, 358, 364–365, 371; legal meaning of, 349; mental illnesses associated with, 354–355; misattribution of, 359–363; prediction of, 366; prevalence of, 347–348; prevention of, 363–364; problems of, 347–348; progressive, 376, 381; qualification for, 376–377; state laws about, 371, 374; substance abuse and, 497; work environment and, 363–364; work function assessment and, 331, 339; workers' compensation and, 364–367. *See also* Accommodation, reasonable; Americans with Disabilities Act (ADA); Evaluation, psychiatric disability

Disability-adjusted life years (DALYs), 51

Disability Law Reporter, 386

Disability leaves, psychiatric: fitness-for-duty examinations for return to work after, 334–336; "reasonable accommodation" and, 377–381; second opinions related to, 334–335; treatability and, 373–374; treating physicians' role and, 351, 379. *See also* Accommodation, reasonable; Return to work

Disasters. *See* Traumatic disasters

Discounted FFS payment. *See* Preferred provider organizations (PPOs)

Dishonesty: intervention in, 120; in narcissistic executives, 118–120; organizational effects of, 120; prevention of, 120; underlying causes of, 119–120. *See also* Antisocial personality disorder

Disorganization phase of change, 247–248

Displacement, 105, 114; causes of, 131; in executives, 130–132; intervention in, 132; organizational effects of, 131–132; paranoia and, 127; prevention of, 132

Disruptive employees, fitness-for-duty examinations for, 333–334

Distance, employee-company, 238–239

Distorted perceptions, employees', of chief executive officer, 225–229

Divorce, organizational effects of, 261–262

Door County Summer Institute, 81

Dot-com fever, 235

Downsizing, 18

Dreams, 17

Drug abuse: addiction and, 484, 485–488; biopsychosocial approach to, 486–488; causes of workplace, 482; choice of drug and, 488–489; compulsion in, 485; continued use despite adverse consequences in, 485–486; definitions of, 484–488; denial of, 486; dependence and, 484–485; disability definitions and, 372, 497; DSM-IV diagnostic criteria for (dependency), 484–485; employee assistance programs for, 482–483, 500–501; individual drug-dependence syndromes and, 488–495; individual predisposition to, 487; legal issues of, 497; loss of control in, 486; overseas treatment of, 164, 165; polydrug, 485, 509, 563; prescription drugs and, 485, 493, 494, 563; prevalence of, 280, 481; psychiatric management of, 497–498; psychotherapies for, 497–498; treatment of, 497–498; workplace environment and, 488; workplace intervention in, 482–483; workplace problems caused by, 280, 283, 481–482. *See also* Addiction; Substance abuse

Drug and alcohol policy, 292

Drug testing, 280, 283, 292, 306, 495–496; pros and cons of mandatory, 496; sample policy for, 501; sample procedures for, 501

Drug toxicity, 563–564, 565

Du Pont, 74

Dual-career couples, overseas, 160

Dual diagnosis: of alcoholism with other drugs, 509; of alcoholism with psychiatric disorders, 509–510; integrated treatment of, 534, 536; of substance abuse with schizophrenia, 534

Dual roles, 401–402

Dysthymia, 18, 433–434, 447–450; case example of, 447; causes of, 449; diagnosis of, 447–449; DSM-IV diagnostic criteria for, 448–449; effects of, 449–450; functional somatic syndromes, 555, 557; psychiatric management of, 450; reasonable accommodation of, 450; return to work with, 450; workplace intervention in, 450; workplace recognition of, 449–450. *See also* Depression

E

Earthquake, 298

Easterson v. Long Island Jewish Medical Center, 344

Eastman Kodak Company, 77–78

Ecologic illness. *See* Multiple chemical sensitivity syndrome

Ecosystem distrust, 147

Ecstasy, 525

Educational programs, employee, 12–13, 22, 517–518

EEOC v. Amego, 382, 384

Efficiency, ethical dilemmas and, 397–399

Ego ideal. *See* Idealized self

Ego incentives, organizational ethics and, 399–400

Electroconvulsive treatment, 523

Electrocution, 301

Emotional climate, 206. *See also* Culture, organizational

Emotional crises, 297–312; discomfort with, 297–298; of psychotic behavior, 310–312; in substance abuse emergencies, 305–307; suicidal, 307–310; in traumatic disasters, 298–301; in traumatic work site events, 301–304; types of, 297

Emotional intelligence (EQ): CEO's, and culture shaping, 216–224; cognitive intelligence (IQ) *versus*, 216, 217; competencies of, for CEOs, 218–224; components of, listed, 217; defined, 216; for executive effectiveness, 92, 100, 218–224; importance of, 218

Emotional issues: causes of, 10–11; evaluation of, 9–12, 22–23; of expatriate employees and families, 156–162; functional somatic syndromes and, 553–558; of job loss, 135–153; of physical disease, 558–562; repression of, 114, 130–134; sensitivity to, 8–9; somatoform disorders and, 540–545, 547–548; in workplace *versus* home, 4, 10, 103–104, 256–257, 259. *See also* Mental illness

Emotionality, excessive, 463–466

Emotionally unstable personalities, 74

Emotions: displacement of, 105, 114, 130–132; rigid personalities and hidden, 125; self-awareness of, 218–219; suppression of, 114, 132–134

Empathic statements, 221–222

Empathy, 8–9; defined, 220; ego and, 399; as emotional intelligence competency, 220–222; as leadership requirement, 184, 220–222; narcissism and lack of, 175–176

Empire building, grandiosity and, 114–118

Employee assistance movement, 73–74

Employee assistance programs (EAPs), 41–43; for alcohol abuse, 41, 506–507; confidentiality issues of, 482–483; contracted-out, 42, 44; for drug abuse, 482–483, 500–501; goals of, 41–42; involvement of, in violence response team, 326; overview of, 5–6; pros and cons of, 42–43; for repatriation, 167; for return to work after psychiatric leave, 335–336; for suicide prevention, 309; for workplace problem prevention, 292

Employees: access of, to records, 68; derailed, 249–250; expatriate, 155–168; impact of layoffs on retained, 147; inadequate organizational structures and distorted perceptions of, 225–229; motivating, 209–210, 235–236; organizational change and, 233–252; valuing of, 208–210. *See also* Subordinates

Employer-funded services, 28. *See also* Benefits

Employment, supported, 535–536, 537

Employment specialists, 535–536, 537

Employment uncertainty, 135–153, 363. *See also* Job loss

Empowerment, employee, 18

Enforcement Guidance: Reasonable Accommodation and Undue Hardship Under the Americans with Disabilities Act (EEOC), 377–381

Enforcement Guidance on the Americans with Disabilities Act and Psychiatric Disabilities (EEOC), 370; on defining "disability," 371–376; on defining "reasonable accommodation," 371–376, 377–381; on threatening behavior, 371–376, 377–381, 382–383

England, history of workplace psychiatry in, 74, 78

Enron scandal, 119

Entitlement: aggressive behavior and, 179; antisocial personality disorder and, 467, 468; narcissistic, 118–120, 175–178

Entitlement, employee, 234, 240–241

Entrepreneurial leaders, 186

Environment: addiction and, 487, 488; schizophrenia spectrum disorders and, 530–531. *See also* Workplace environment

Environmental illnesses. *See* Chemical toxicity; Multiple chemical sensitivity syndrome

Epidemic hysteria, 543–544

Epstein-Barr virus, 555

Equal Employment Opportunity Commission, 106; Americans with Disabilities Act (ADA) and, 370–383; contact information for, 386

Equitable compensation, 242–243

Ethics: classification system of, 388–390; defined, 388

Ethics, executive: barriers to, 396–403; character and, 387, 393–395; narcissistic dishonesty and, 118–120; organizational ethics and, 387, 390–403; perspectives of, 390–391; suppressed fear and, 133

Ethics, organizational, 387–403; applied ethics and, 388, 403; bottom-line preoccupation and, 396–397; business ethics *versus*, 388; classification system for, 388–390; common issues of, in corporations, 391–392; conceptual framework for, 387–403; covenantal ethics and, 389, 395; dealing with conflicts in, 402–403; defined, 387, 388–390; ego incentives and, 399–400; examples of, 392; executive character and, 387, 393–395; executive ethics and, 387, 390–403; expediency pressures and, 397–399; field of, 387; general ethics *versus*, 388; organizational health and, 387; personal conscience—organizational policy conflicts and, 400–403; professional ethics *versus*, 389–390; systemic factors impacting, 396–403; *virtu* and, 389, 394–395; virtue ethics and, 389, 393–395

Ethics, professional, 1, 60–70; administrative influence and, 67–68; defined, 388–390; evaluation and, 94; medical, 61; moral conflict situations and, 65–68; organizational ethics *versus*, 389–391; physician-patient relationships and, 61–64. *See also* Confidentiality issues

Ethics codes: of American College of Occupational and Environmental Medicine, 61, 70; organizational, 390; professional, 61, 70, 390

Etiology. *See* Causes, underlying

Europe, history of workplace psychiatry in, 78–79

Evaluation: access and, 22; confidentiality in, 62–64; employee-initiated, confidentiality and, 69; of employees with workplace problems, 287–288; executive, 92–97; of organization and workplace environment, 72–73, 288, 291; overview of, 9–12; of workplace environment, 72–73, 288. *See also* Assessment; Diagnosis; Executive assessment; Fitness-for-duty examinations; Recognition; Screening

Evaluation, psychiatric disability, 347, 350–363; administrative medical review and, 362; Americans with Disabilities Act (ADA) and, 377–381; causality determination and, 358–363; conduct of, 353–358; confidentiality and, 350–352, 380–381; consultative examination for, 352–358; developmental history review in, 355; doctor-patient relationship and, 350–352, 353, 379, 380; employment history review in, 355–356; family history review in, 355; medical history review in, 356–357; mental status examination (MSE) in, 357; parties present at, 353–354; presenting problem identification in, 354; psychiatric history review in, 354–355; psychological testing in, 357; psychosocial history review in, 355–356; record and information review for, 354, 379–381; recording of, 354; social history review in, 355; summary, assessment, and recommendations of, 357–358; treating physician's role in, 350–352, 379; treatment and, 352–353. *See also* Americans with Disabilities Act (ADA); Disability, psychiatric

Evaluators, 23; for fitness-for-duty examinations, 340, 342–343, 346; for psychiatric disability evaluation, 352–353; psychiatrists as, 32–33; psychologists as, 33–34; social workers as, 35; types of providers and, 29–36, 73–74

Evans v. Federal Express Corp., 373, 384

Executive assessment, 92–97; for character, 93, 94–95; in coaching, 102; interviews for, 95–97; for personality, 93–94, 210; psychological testing in, 92–95, 112; reasons for, 92; sample report from, 108–112

Executive development, 17–18, 89, 91–112; assessment for, 92–97; coaching for, 100–103; expenditures on, 99; leadership development approaches to, 97–100; Oedipal conflict and, 120–125; on-the-job *versus* classroom, 99–100; personal treatment for, 103–106

Executive distress, 113–134; compulsive personality and, 128–130; dishonesty and, 118–120; displacement of emotions and, 130–132; grandiosity and, 114–118; narcissistic-level, 114–120, 175–178, 179; Oedipal conflict/competition and, 120–125; overview of, 113–114; paranoid personality and, 125–128; rigid personalities and, 125–130; suppression of emotions and, 132–134; typologies of dysfunctional leaders and, 187, 210–216; work function and, 340. *See also* Managers; Superiors

Executive effectiveness, 89; elements of, 91–92, 100, 106; family issues and, 103–104, 105, 130–132; productivity and, 106–107

Executive ethics. *See* Ethics, executive

Executive selection, 106; narcissistic grandiosity and, 117–118. *See also* Succession planning

Executives: aggression management by, 187–188; ethics and integrity in, 387, 390–395; psychological motivations of, 186–188; styles of, related to organizational growth stage, 186; styles of dysfunctional, 187. *See also* Chief executive officer; *Leader headings;* Managers; Superiors

Exhaustion: aggression and, 179, 180; family problems and, 254. *See also* Burnout; Fatigue

Expatriate Dual Career Survey Report, 160, 169

Expatriate employees and families, 155–168; costs of, 162; culture shock syndrome in, 155, 156–157, 166; dual-career, 160; early curtailment rates of, 162; expatriate community issues of, 161–162; family issues of, 155, 156, 160–161, 162, 164, 165, 258–259; mental health problems in, 158–160; mental

health problems of, 156–160; mental health service delivery to, 166–167; overseas mental health services and, 163–164; policies and procedures for, 164–168; predeparture training for, 166, 167; psychiatric evaluation of, 159–160; psychosocial issues of, 160–162; repatriation syndrome in, 155, 158, 166, 167–168; screening of, 164–165; spousal adjustment and, 160, 162, 165, 258–259

Expectations, treatment: low, 7, 8; unconscious, 15

Expediency, ethical dilemmas and, 397–399

Expertise building, 200

Exploitation, narcissism and, 175–176

Explosions, 301

Extroverts, 172, 173, 174

Exxon Valdez disaster, 392, 481

F

Facilitative cultures, 205, 208–210; CEO emotional intelligence competencies for, 216–224; feeling states in, 208; intrinsic motivation in, 209–210; signs of, 208–209, 231

Facilities, workplace, 209, 363–364. *See also* Workplace environment

Factitious disorders, 545–546

Fairness: compensation and, 242–243; culture of, 243; executive dishonesty and, 120; organizational change and, 242–243

Families: changing roles in, 256, 257, 258, 264–265, 268; impact of, on work, 254–274; impact of work on, 257; objective impacts of, 260; subjective impacts of, 260; as support for work, 256, 261–264; values conflict in, 268

Family and Medical Leave Act (FMLA), 335, 348, 369; application of, 383–384; medical certification for, 384; purposes of, 370, 383; requirements of, 383; substance abuse and, 497

Family business, 188

Family dynamics, reenacted, 114; Oedipal conflict and, 120–123; sibling rivalry and, 123–125, 188, 198

Family history: addiction and, 488; alcoholism and, 502; anxiety disorders and, 417; attitudes toward authority and, 188; of bipolar disorder, 453; childhood trauma in, 548, 549, 550; competitiveness and, 120–125, 197, 198; of depression, 442; fear of change and, 133; insight-oriented psychotherapy and, 15; narcissistic dishonesty and, 119–120; narcissistic grandiosity and, 116–117; obtaining,

Family history, *continued*
287; review of, in disability evaluation, 354–355; schizophrenia spectrum disorders and, 530; somatoform disorders and, 548

Family problems: categories of, 255; displacement of, 130–132; executive effectiveness and, 103–104, 105, 130–132; expatriate, 155, 160–161, 162, 164, 165, 166; of family-driven motivation to work, 255, 267, 271–273; of family needs interfering with work, 255, 264–270; interventions for, 273–274; job loss and, 141, 146; literature and research on, 256, 257–261; of loss of family support, 255, 261–264; organizational consequences of, 254–274; prevalence of, 23, 274; subtle consequences of, 257; symptoms of, expressed in workplace, 255, 273; treatment response and, 21–22; of workplace as substitute for unmet family needs, 255, 270–271; workplace distress and, 4, 10, 130–132; workplace influence on, 256

Family psychoeducation, 534, 536

Family systems approaches, 18; social workers and, 35

Family-work life relationship, 254–274; compensation in, 259, 269, 270–271; compulsiveness and, 130; conflict in, 259; critical factors in, 260; dimensions of, 259; independence in, 259; instrumentality in, 259; outcome measures of, 260; prevalence of difficulties in, 258; spillover in, 259

Fantasies, shared, 194, 195

Fathers, alcoholic, sons of, 502

Fatigue: chronic, 281, 553, 555; occupational psychiatry and, 74. *See also* Exhaustion

Fear: aggression and, 179, 180, 187; avoidance and, 132–134; of change, 132–134; organizational change and, 246; paranoia and, 125–127; threats of violence and, 316–317

Federal Express Corp., Evans v., 373, 384

Federal standards: for health maintenance organizations, 40; for parity, 45

Fee for service (FFS), 28, 37–39; costs under, 37–38; pros and cons of, 38–39

Feelers, 173, 174; affiliative leaders as, 183; superiors who are, 175

Feeling states, 206–207; in facilitative cultures, 208; in obstructive cultures, 208. *See also* Culture, organizational

Fibromyalgia, 281, 553, 555–556

Fight-or-flight basic assumption, 194, 225, 227–229

Fight-or-flight response to change, 247–248

Financial difficulties: of job loss, 138, 140–141, 144, 148; workers' compensation and, 367; workplace problems caused by, 281

Financial incentives: of health maintenance organizations, 40–41; working for family-driven need for, 272–273

Financial management, for coping with job loss, 148

Fires, workplace, 301–302, 304

First impressions, 199

First International Congress on Social Psychiatry, 79

Fit: fitness-for-duty examinations for testing, 329–330; leadership styles and, 184; testing for, 93, 329; understanding one's, 200

Fitness-for-duty examinations, 329–346; administrative minefields of, 342–343; appointment-making for, 341; for Family and Medical Leave Act (FMLA) requests, 384; guidelines for, 330–332; information exchange for, 340–342, 342; legal and confidentiality issues of, 330–332, 342–343, 380; for preemployment psychiatric screening, 333; after psychiatric leaves, 312, 334–336; "reasonable accommodation" and, 379, 380, 382–383; records release for, 341; selection of examiners for, 340, 342–343, 346, 380; situations appropriate for, 330, 332–338, 342; for threat assessment, 336–338, 382–383; work function assessment and, 338–340, 341

Flat organizations: boundary issues in, 195; competitiveness in, 198–199; organizational structures in, 227

FLEX exam, 31

Flexibility: in leadership styles, 92, 97, 110; in personality types, 210–211. *See also* Adaptation

Flexible schedules: for job search, 152; for schizophrenics, 532, 536

Flight attendants, epidemic hysteria in, 543–544

Floods, 298

Fluoxetine, 444

Fort Wayne Community Schools, Bultemeyer v., 378, 384

Fossilized cultures, 213–214

Fourteenth International Congress of Occupational Health, 78

Free association, 17

Freebase cocaine and crack, 488. *See also* Cocaine abuse

Frustration: ability to tolerate, 219–220; aggressive behavior and, 179, 180

Functional somatic syndromes, 553–558; assessment of, 556; psychiatric management of, 556–558; types of, 553–556. *See also* Chronic fatigue syndrome; Fibromyalgia; Irritable bowel syndrome; Multiple chemical sensitivity syndrome

Funding sources, 28–29; delivery systems and, 36–46. *See also* Benefits; Delivery systems

Future directions, for occupational psychiatry and associations, 82–83, 84–85

G

Garrity v. United Air Lines, 381, 384

Gatekeepers, 29–30; in employee assistance programs, 42–43; in health maintenance organizations, 40

Gaul v. AT&T, 377, 384

Gender differences, in alcoholism, 502–503

Gender identity disorders, 372

Gender roles: office politics and, 196–197; trends in families and, 257, 258, 264–265, 268

General Electric, 83

General ethics, 388

General Motors, 280

Generalized anxiety disorder (GAD), 408–413; alcohol abuse and, 509; case example of, 409; causes of, 411–412; DSM-IV diagnosis of, 410–411; effects of, 412; psychiatric management of, 413; reasonable accommodation of, 413; return to work with, 413; workplace intervention in, 412–413; workplace recognition of, 412

Glacier Metal Company studies, 78

Global economy, 89

Global Relocation Trends survey reports, 158, 160, 162, 166, 168, 169

Glowacki v. Buffalo General Hospital, 373, 384

Godfather, The, 240

Grandiosity, 114–118, 175–178; in affective disorders with psychotic features, 522; alcohol and, 311; in bipolar disorder, 310; intervention in, 117; narcissistic personality disorder and, 474–477; organizational effects of, 117, 175–177; prevention of, 117–118; spousal encouragement of, 269–270; underlying causes of, 115–117

Great Jackass Fallacy, The (Levinson), 236

Grief reaction, 299–300

Group for the Advancement of Psychiatry (GAP), 77, 81–82, 262, 275, 344, 499

Group process approaches, 18

Group psychology, 188–189, 194–195; bound-

aries and, 195; organizational structures and, 225–229; regression and, 194–195, 225–227

Groups, self-help, 13; for addiction, 488, 497–498, 514, 526; for psychotic disorders, 523, 526, 536; for unemployed workers, 150. *See also* Alcoholics Anonymous; Twelve-step groups

Groups, therapy, 62

Groupthink: in dependency basic assumption, 225–227, 229; in fight-or-flight basic assumption, 227–229

Guidance (EEOC). See Enforcement Guidance on the Americans with Disabilities Act and Psychiatric Disabilities

Guides to the Evaluation of Permanent Impairment (American Medical Association), 349, 355

Guilford of Maine, Inc., Soileau v., 373, 385

Gulf War syndrome, 553

H

Hallucinations: in alcoholic withdrawal, 510; in psychosis, 522, 526, 532

Hallucinogens, 525

Harassment, 317. *See also* Threats

Hardship, undue, 382

Harvard Business School, 79

Hawthorne effect, 257

Health maintenance organizations (HMOs), 28, 39–41; capitation and, 39–41; financial incentives and, 40–41; physician-patient relationship in, 62; pros and cons of, 40–41

Health Plan Employer Data and Information Set, 25

Heart disease, 281, 558–560, 565

Heavy metals, 563

Helplessness, job loss and, 148

Heroin, 482, 492–493, 509

Hidden agendas: competitiveness and, 198; hypervigilant CEOs and, 215; leader motivations and, 186–187; male-female relationships and, 197; Oedipal conflict and, 120; office politics and, 192–193

Hiring, for organizational culture, 191

History, of workplace psychiatry, 1, 3–4, 71–85; in 1920s, 74–75, 83; in 1930s and 1940s, 75–77; in 1950s and 1960s, 77–80, 83–84; in 1970s, 1980s, and 1990s, 80–82; in early 1900s, 74

Histrionic personality disorder, 340, 463–466; case example of, 463–464; diagnosis of, 464–465; DSM-IV diagnostic criteria for, 464–465; psychiatric management of,

Histrionic personality disorder, *continued* 465–466; workplace intervention in, 465; workplace recognition of, 465

Hoaxes, 317

Hogan Development Survey, 95

Hogan Personality Inventory, 95

Holihan v. Lucky Stores, 375, 384

Homicides, workplace, 318–319, 321, 336. *See also* Violence, workplace

Hospitalization: in alcoholism treatment, 510, 511–514; in drug addiction treatment, 497, 526; in psychosis, 520, 523, 526

Household Finance Corp., Weiler v., 372, 385

Human resource (HR) department: alcoholism treatment and, 505, 514, 515; role of, 5

Hurricane, 298

Hypervigilance: in chief executive officers, 214–216; paranoid personality disorder and, 471

Hypnotics, 494–495, 509

Hypochondriasis, 544–545

Hypomania, 165, 451, 452, 454. *See also* Bipolar disorder

Hysteria, 468, 542–543; epidemic, 543–544

I

IBM, 83

IBM, Criado v., 373, 378, 384

Idealized self, projection of, onto leader, 188–189, 194–195

Idealizing leaders, 187, 189

Identification: attachments and roots of, 245–246; with CEO personality type, 211. *See also* Projective identification

Illness, family: organizational effects of, 262; somatoform disorders and, 548. *See also* Medical problems

Illness, medical. *See* Disability, physical; Medical problems; Psychosomatic interface

Illness management training, 535

Image control, 199, 393

Immigrants, delusional disorder and, 519

Imminent-danger policies, overseas, 163–164, 167

Impairments: categories of psychiatric injuries and, 366; defined, 349; defining in Americans with Disabilities Act (ADA), 371–376; disability and, 349–350; guidelines for, 349; work-related, workers' compensation and, 364–367. *See also* Disability, physical; Disability, psychiatric

Impression management, 393

Improvement: assessment of, 19–22, 24–25; time frame for, 21, 24

Impulse control, 223–224

In-house programs, 5–6. *See also* Employee assistance programs

Inadequacy feelings, 246

Inadequate personalities, 74

Income jump, family-work relationship and, 266–267

Incomplete sentence forms, 93

Industrial chemicals, 562–563

Industrial Fatigue Research Board, 74

Industrial Medical Council for the State of California, 332, 344

Industrial psychiatry, history of, 74–85. *See also* Mental health care, workplace; Occupational psychiatry; Psychiatry

Industry Week, 258

Ineffective treatment experience, 7

Insight-oriented psychotherapy, 14–17; for anxiety disorders, 419, 427; for depression, 445–446; goals of, 15; names for, 14; for personality disorders, 463, 465–466, 468–469, 471–472, 474, 476–477, 478–479; session frequency of, 14–15; for somatoform disorders, 550–551; transference and countertransference in, 15–16, 17. *See also* Psychotherapy

Insights, 16

Insurance, health, 36–41; delivery systems and, 36–41; mental health care exclusions in, 36–37; parity in, 45. *See also* Benefits, mental health; Delivery systems; Funding sources

Integrity, executive: ethical perspectives and, 390–391; organizational ethics and, 387, 393–395. *See also* Character; Ethics, executive

Intelligence quotient (IQ), 216, 217, 357

International Association for the Study of Pain, 560

International Committee on Occupational Mental Health, 79

Interpersonal behavior: aggressive, 178–182, 223; assessment of improvement in, 20–21; displacement and, 130–132; oppositional, 250; suppression of fear and, 132–134, 179, 180. *See also* Conflict, interpersonal

Interpersonal deficits: job loss and, 142; in schizophrenia spectrum disorders, 528, 533

Interpersonal psychotherapy: for depression, 446; for psychotic disorders, 523

Interpretation, in insight-oriented psychotherapy, 16, 17

Intervention(s): for affective disorders with psychotic features, 522; for alcoholism, 503–507; for antisocial personality disorder, 468; for anxiety disorders, 412–413, 418, 423,

427, 431; for bipolar disorder, 454–455; for borderline personality disorder, 473–474; for CEO personality or emotional intelligence, 224; for depressive disorders, 437–438, 443, 450, 454–455; for drug abuse, 482–483; for executive competitiveness, 122–123, 125; for executive compulsiveness, 130; for executive displacement, 132; for executive emotional suppression, 134; for executive narcissistic grandiosity, 117; for executive or manager narcissism, 120, 177–178, 179; for executive paranoia, 127–128; for expatriate problems, 157; for family problems, 273–274; for histrionic personality disorder, 465; in job loss, 147–150; for narcissistic personality disorder or traits, 117, 120, 177–178, 179, 476; for obsessive-compulsive personality disorder, 462; for paranoid personality disorder, 127–128, 471; for passive-aggressive personality disorder, 478; for psychotic disorders, 520, 531; for psychotic emergencies, 311–312; in substance abuse emergencies, 306–307; for suicide, 309–310; for traumatic disasters, 300–301; for traumatic work site events, 304; for workplace problems, 289–291; for workplace violence and threats, 325–327. *See also* Treatment

Interview assessment: advantages of, 95–97; for executive assessment, 95–97; executive *versus* clinical, 97; psychological testing *versus*, 95, 97; sample report from, 108–111

Intoxication: diagnosis of substance intoxication delirium and, 563–564; onsite, 305–307, 507–508

Intrinsic motivation, 209–210, 235–237

Introverts, 172, 173, 174

Intuitives, 173, 174; authoritative leaders as, 183; superiors who are, 175

Invention, 244

Irrepressibly self-confident CEOs, 211–213

Irritable bowel syndrome, 553, 562

Isolation: CEO, 230; job loss and, 139; in obstructive culture, 208

J

Job Accommodation Network, 386

Job counseling, 152

Job description, written: for Americans with Disabilities Act (ADA) "essential functions" determination, 376–377; for work function assessment, 338, 341

Job dissatisfaction, 276, 278, 282; back pain and, 285; organizational effects of, 283–285. *See also* Workplace problems

Job loss, 89, 135–153; anticipatory stage of, 137–139, 150–152; assessment of impact of, 142–147, 153; community resources for, 136, 146, 149–150; coping with, 147–149; economic impact of, 138, 140–141, 144, 148; effects of, 135–142, 152–153; family issues and, 141, 146; identifying at-risk individuals in, 150; impact assessment of, 142–147, 153; impact of, 137–138; impact of, on retained employees, 147; integrated model of the impact of, 142, 143; intervention for, 147–150; losses in, 138–139, 147–148; meanings of, to individuals, 138–142; personal deficits and, 144–145; physical disability and, 141–142, 145; with preexisting emotional and psychiatric problems, 141–142, 144–145, 150; preventive interventions for, 150–152; probability of, 135; protective factors for, 142, 143; provoking factors for, 142, 143; psychological meaning of, 139; resources for, 149; role changes of, 139–140; routine and, 149; self-esteem and, 139, 140, 142, 148; social impact of, 138–139, 140, 141; social supports and, 146; strengths assessment in, 145–146, 148; stress of, 140–141, 142, 143, 144; systemic view of, 136; themes, 136; work attitudes and, 146–147; work skills and, 145; workplace problems caused by, 281–282. *See also* Termination, employee

Job performance problems, 276, 278; Americans with Disabilities Act (ADA) and, 382; depression and, 280–281, 283, 309; organizational effects of, 283–285; substance abuse and, 283. *See also* Workplace problems

Job search: job loss effects and, 137, 140; stress of, 140; support for, 149, 152

Johnson & Johnson: Credo, 395; Tylenol crisis, 392, 393, 403

Joint Commission on the Accreditation of Hospitals and Health Care Organizations (JCAHO), 390

Judgers, 173, 174; superiors who are, 175

K

Kleptomania, 372

Knoedler, W. H., 537

Koch, Daley v., 372, 384

L

L. L. Bean, 235

Laius, 121

Layoffs, 135, 138, 147, 150–152, 301. *See also* Job loss

LEAD model, 244, 251

Lead poisoning, 563

Leaders: influence of, on organizational culture, 210–224; managers *versus,* 187; psychological motivations of, 186–188; as transitional anchors, 246–247, 248; typologies of dysfunctional, 187, 210–216. *See also* Chief executive officer; *Executive headings;* Managers; Superiors

Leadership: adaptation and, 244; character and, 184, 393–395; of organizational change, 233–252; treatment response and improvement in, 20–21. *See also* Chief executive officer; *Executive headings;* Managers; Superiors

Leadership development, 97–100; best practices in, 100; combined with other executive development strategies, 98–99; on-the-job *versus* classroom, 99–100. *See also* Executive development

Leadership skills: assessment of, 96; development of, 100

Leadership styles, 182–185; assessment of, 97, 110; categories of, 182–185; flexibility in, 92, 97, 110; working with different, 184–185

Learning theory, 417, 534

Leaves of absence. *See* Disability leaves, psychiatric

Legal issues: of disability, 347, 349, 353, 358, 364–365, 366–367; of drug abuse, 497; of evaluation, 94; of fitness-for-duty examinations, 330–332, 342–343; of overseas mental health services, 163–164, 166, 167; of workers' compensation, 364–365, 366–367; of workplace violence, 337. *See also* Americans with Disabilities Act (ADA); Confidentiality issues

"Leisure nurse," 272–273

Lessons of Experience, The: How Successful Executives Develop on the Job (McCall et al.), 99–100

Leverage, during organizational change, 234, 235–236, 244, 245, 247–249

Levinson Institute, 79

Librium, 510

Licensing. *See* Credentialing and licensing

Life changes, major: adjustment disorder with depressed mood and, 436; trauma response and, 303; workplace problems caused by, 281

Listening, empathic, 220

Lithium, 159, 282, 445, 455–456

Liver function, 510, 511

Loneliness, grandiosity and, 115–116

Long Island Jewish Medical Center, Easterson v., 331, 344

Loss: bereavement and, 435–436; change and, 245–247; job, 135–153; organizational change and, 235, 245–247; psychological resistance to change and, 132–134

Low back pain (LBP) syndrome, 560–561

Lucky Stores, Holihan v., 375, 384

Lunches, alcohol abuse during, 508

M

MacArthur Study of Mental Illness and Violence, 320

Macy, R. H., department store, 75

Magellan Behavioral Health Services, 44

Major depressive disorder (MDD), 8, 11, 19, 433–434, 438–447; bereavement *versus,* 441; bipolar disorder and, 451; case example of, 438–439; causes of, 441–442; diagnosis of, 439–441; DSM-IV diagnostic criteria for, 439–441; effects of, 442–443; functional somatic syndromes and, 557; physical pain and, 561; psychiatric management of, 444–446; psychotic features with, 521; reasonable accommodation of, 447; return to work with, 447; subtypes of, 439; workplace intervention in, 443; workplace recognition of, 442–443. *See also* Depression

Male-female relationships, 196–197

Malingering, 359, 361–362, 546–547; case example of, 547; diagnosis of, 546–547; low back pain and, 561

Managed behavioral health care (MBHC) companies, 44–45

Managed care organizations (MCOs), 5, 44–45; assessment of, 26; physician-patient relationship in, 62; quality issues in, 24, 54–55; resource management methods of, 29–30

Management: mental health care, 8–9; role of organizational, 5

Managers: accountability of, 240; aggressive, 178–182; destructively narcissistic, 175–178, 179, 191; effects of workplace problems on, 284; leaders *versus,* 187; leadership styles of, 182–185; of organizational change, 240–243; psychological motivations of, 186–188; substance abuse and, 306. *See also Executive headings; Leader headings;* Superiors

Mania, 18, 451; in bipolar disorder, 451–456; in expatriates, 160, 165

Manic-depressive disorder. *See* Bipolar disorder

Manipulation: antisocial personality disorder and, 468; narcissism and, 175–178; threats used as, 317

Marijuana abuse, 491–492; case example of, 491–492; effects of, 492; prevalence of, 481, 491. *See also* Drug abuse

Market value, 30

Marriage and family counselors, 36

Massachusetts Commission Against Discrimination, 371, 374

Massachusetts Supreme Judicial Court, 374

Masters of the universe, 114–118

Mastery needs, 237

Meaning of work, enabling, 241–242

Media coverage, of workplace violence, 336

Medicaid, 536

Medical College of Wisconsin, 81

Medical departments, 6, 292

Medical history review, in disability evaluation, 356–357

Medical problems, 22; from alcoholism, 511; controversial, 553–558; emotional distress/mental illness with, 281, 357, 558–562; functional somatic syndromes and, 553–558; organic behavioral syndromes and, 562–565; prevalence of, as symptom trigger, 23; review of, in psychiatric disability evaluation, 356–357; somatoform disorders and, 540–545; workplace problems and, 281, 282. *See also* Disability, physical; Psychosomatic interface; Somatic symptoms

Medical review, administrative, 362

Medication: abuse of, 485, 493, 494; accidents caused by, 282; adherence to, 520–521, 523; for alcohol addiction, 498, 510; for anxiety, 413, 418–419, 423, 427, 494–495; attitudes toward, 19; for bipolar disorder, 455–456; combined with psychotherapy, 14, 18–19, 24, 51; conditions treatable with, 18–19; for drug addiction, 497, 498; expatriate use of, 159, 163, 167; for narcissistic grandiosity, 117; for pain, 561; psychiatrist evaluation for, 32–33; for psychotic disorders, 520–521, 522–523, 526, 533–534; side effects of, 312, 445, 456, 533–534; treatment response with, 21, 22. *See also* Antianxiety medication; Antidepressants; Antipsychotics

Memory loss, 511

Men: alcoholism in, 502; trends in family roles and, 257, 258, 264–265, 268

Menninger Foundation, 79

Mental health care, workplace: components of, 22–25; cost-effectiveness analysis of, 48–53; cost-effectiveness of, 56–57; for emotional crises, 297–312; for executives, 91–106; history of, 71–85; for job loss, 135–153; overseas, 155–168; overview of, 1, 3–27; program

of services for, 343; quality, 3–27; workplace violence and, 314–327. *See also* Delivery systems; Intervention; Occupational psychiatry

Mental health care exclusions, 36–37

Mental health care system, U.S., 28–29; delivery systems in, 36–46; providers in, 29–36

Mental Health in Industry, 80

Mental Health in the Workplace (Kahn), 81

Mental health professional roles, in threat assessment, 315–316. *See also* Counselors; Providers; Psychiatrists; Psychologists; Social workers

Mental health services, overseas, 163–164

Mental Hygiene, 74

Mental illness: associated with psychiatric disability, 354–355; attitudes toward, 3, 7–8; categories, in Americans with Disabilities Act (ADA), 372; common types of, among employees, 405–566; costs of, 282–283; defined, 11; evaluation of, 9–12, 23; of executives, 113–134; of expatriates, 156–162; impact of, on productivity, 48–49, 50; job loss and, 141–142, 145; medical illness with, 281, 357, 558–562; organizational change and, 250; physical symptoms of, 551–552; prevalence of, 274, 278–279; recognition of, 4–5; symptoms of, 279; from trauma, 300; in workplace, 4–5; workplace problems caused by, 276–294. *See also* Alcohol abuse and dependence; Anxiety disorders; Depression; Drug abuse; Emotional issues; Personality disorders; Psychosis; Psychosomatic interface; Substance abuse

Mental status examination (MSE), 357

Mentoring: executive, 100; expatriate, 168; office politics and, 199

Meperidine, 493–494

Mercury poisoning, 563

Mergers and acquisitions: in managed care sector, 44; organizational development and, 18

Methadone, 498

Methamphetamines, 283

Metropolitan Life Insurance Company, 75, 83

MHRI, Ward v., 382, 385

Michigan, worker compensation in, 78

Micromanagement, of overly conscientious CEOs, 213–214

Middle life, narcissism and, 176

Military, history of psychiatry in, 76–77

Millon Clinical Multiaxial Inventory, Version III (MCMI-III), 93

Mind-body connection. *See* Psychosomatic interface; Somatic symptoms; Somatoform disorders

Minnesota Multiphasic Personality Inventory-Revised (MMPI-2), 93
Mirroring, need for, 189
Misconduct, in Americans with Disabilities Act (ADA), 381–382
Mission, organizational, 238
Mob psychology, 188–189, 194–195
Mobil, 74
Mobilization, 244
Modeling, leader, 251
Monoamine oxidase inhibitors (MAOIs), 445
Mood changes: in expatriates, 157; in psychosis, 517
Mood disorders. *See* Anxiety disorders; Bipolar disorder; Depression
Mood stabilizers, 455–456, 523, 534
Moral conflict, mental health referral situations with, 65–68
Morale improvement, impact of families on, 257
Morale problems: CEO micromanagement and, 214; leader aggression and, 179–180, 223; managerial narcissism and, 176–177; organizational change and, 235; organizational structures and, 228
Morality, defined, 388. *See also Ethics headings*
Morton Thiokol, 398–399
Motivated bias, 172, 193
Motivation(s): bottom-line preoccupation and, 396–397; CEO, employees' distorted perceptions of, 225–229; employee, 209–210, 235–237; family-driven, 255, 267, 271–273; hidden agendas and, 192–193; human, 237; intrinsic, 209–210, 235–237; money as, 209–210; organizational ethics and, 396–397, 399–400; psychological, of leaders, 186–188; for threatening behavior, 316–317; unconscious, 186–188, 192–193
Mourning, 245; bereavement and, 435–436, 441
Multiple chemical sensitivity syndrome (MCSS), 553, 554–555, 557
Myers-Briggs Type Indicator (MBTI), 93, 112, 172–175, 210

N

Naltrexone, 498
Narcissism, healthy, 114–115, 175
Narcissistic leaders, 187
Narcissistic personality disorder, 114–120, 175–178, 474–477; aggressive behavior and, 176, 179, 180; case example of, 474–475; causes of, 115–117, 119–120, 476; coercive leadership style and, 183; diagnosis of, 475–476; dishonesty and, 118–120; DSM-IV

diagnostic criteria for, 475–476; in executives, 114–120, 187; grandiosity and, 114–118, 474–477; in managers, 175–178, 179; psychiatric management of, 476–477; strategies for working with, 177–178, 179; work function and, 340; workplace intervention in, 117, 120, 177–178, 179, 476; workplace recognition of, 476
Narcotics. *See* Opiate and opioid abuse
Narcotics Anonymous, 488, 494
National Aeronautics and Space Administration (NASA), 398–399
National Alliance for the Mentally Ill, 523
National Depression Screening Day, 434
National Institute for Mental Health (NIMH), 432, 443
National Register of Health Services Providers in Psychotherapy, 34
Needs, human, 237
NEO Personality Inventory (NEO-PI), 93, 94
Networks, office politics and, 199
Neurobiological etiology: of anxiety, 412, 417; of bipolar disorder, 453; of depression, 441–442, 449, 456; of obsessive-compulsive disorder, 426; of posttraumatic stress disorder, 430. *See also* Organic etiology
Neurological problems: of alcoholism, 511; chemical toxicity and, 562–563, 565; drug toxicity and, 563–564, 565
Neuropsychological testing, 357
Neurotransmitters: anxiety and, 412, 426; depression and, 441–442
Neutrality, therapist, in insight-oriented psychotherapy, 17
New York Occupational Medicine Association, 81
Newton, Urbaniak v., 331–332, 344
"No," leaders who can't say, 187
Nonmainstream alternative health, 557–558
Nonwork activities, 269
Not-invented-here syndrome, 190
Nuclear power plant disaster, 298

O

Oak Ridge, Tennessee, Industrial Community, 76
Observation, in interview assessment, 96–97
Obsessions, 424–427, 460–463
Obsessive-compulsive disorder (OCD), 18, 423–427; case example of, 423–424; causes of, 426; diagnosis of, 424–426; DSM-IV diagnostic criteria for, 425–426; effects of, 426–427; in expatriates, 159; prevalence of, 424; psychiatric management of, 427; rea-

sonable accommodation of, 427; return to work with, 427; workplace intervention in, 427; workplace recognition of, 426–427. *See also* Compulsive personality style; Obsessive-compulsive personality disorder; Rigid personalities

Obsessive-Compulsive Foundation, 432

Obsessive-compulsive personality disorder, 425, 460–463; case example of, 460–461; diagnosis of, 461–462; DSM-IV diagnostic criteria for, 461–462; etiology of, 462; psychiatric management of, 463; workplace intervention in, 462; workplace recognition of, 462. *See also* Compulsive personality style; Rigid personalities

Obstructionalism, workplace violence and, 314

Obstructive cultures, 205, 207–208; CEO personality types and, 210–216; inadequate organizational structures and, 224–229; signs of, 207–208, 231

Occupational Mental Health Notes, 79

Occupational psychiatry: confidentiality issues in, 62–64; history of, 71–85; trends in, 84–85. *See also* Mental health care, workplace; Psychiatry

Occupational Psychiatry Group (OPG), 79, 81

Oedipal conflict, 120–125

Oedipus, 121

Office of Vocational Rehabilitation, 77

Office politics, 11, 89, 97, 171–200; attitudes toward authority and, 188–189; boundary issues and, 194, 195; competition and, 197–199; concept of, 171–172; destructively narcissistic managers and, 175–178, 179, 191; in family businesses, 188; hidden agendas and, 192–193; impact of, 172, 199; leaders' unconscious motivations and, 186–188; leadership and, 187–188; leadership styles and, 182–185; male-female relationships and, 196–197; organizational culture and, 189–192; personal interests and, 171–172; personality problems and, 175–182; personality styles and, 172–185; regression and, 194–195; strategies for managing, 199–200; subordinate-superior relationship and, 185–186

Oklahoma City bombing, 299, 303

Open-ended questions, 96

Opiate and opioid abuse, 492–494; alcohol abuse and, 509; case example of, 493–494; causes of, 482; effects of, 492, 493; hospitalization for, 497; legal opiates and, 492, 493–494; treatment of, 497, 498; withdrawal from, 492–493

Opportunity, in change, 244–245

Oppositional behavior, 250. *See also* Aggression; Antisocial personality disorder

Organic behavioral syndromes, 562–565

Organic etiology: of behavioral syndromes, 562–565; of delirium, 565; of dementia, 565; of depression, 565; functional somatic syndromes and, 553–558; of psychotic disorders, 524, 530–531, 565. *See also* Neurobiological etiology

Organic impairment, testing for, 357

Organizational context: evaluation of, 11, 72–73, 288, 291; executive development and, 106; organizational consulting and, 18; risk factors for violence in, 323–324. *See also* Culture, organizational; Workplace environment

Organizational culture. *See* Culture, organizational

Organizational development, 18

Organizational dynamics, that impact organizational ethics, 396–403

Organizational effects: of aggressive behavior, 179–180, 223; of CEO emotional intelligence, 216–224; of CEO personality type, 210–216; of compulsive personality, 129–130; of displacement, 131–132; executive psychological problems and, 113–134; of family demands, 264–270; of family problems, 254–274; of inadequate organizational structures, 225–229; of loss of family support, 255, 261–264; of narcissism, destructive, 175–177, 191; of narcissistic dishonesty, 120; of narcissistic grandiosity, 117; of Oedipal conflict/competition, 122, 125; of paranoid personality, 127; of personality disorders, 458–460; of psychotic behavior, 311; of substance abuse emergencies, 306; of suicide, 309; of suppressed fear of change, 133; of traumatic workplace events, 304; of unmet family needs, 270–271; of workplace problems, 283–285. *See also* Absenteeism; Accidents; Conflict, interpersonal; Job dissatisfaction; Job performance problems; Productivity; Workplace problems

Organizational ethics. *See* Ethics, organizational

Organizational skill, for executive effectiveness, 92

Organizational structures. *See* Structures, organizational

Overinvolvement, 460–463. *See also* Obsessive-compulsive personality disorder

Overly conscientious CEOs, 213–214

Overseas employment, 89, 155–168. *See also* Expatriate employees

Oversuspicion. *See* Suspiciousness, over-
Overwhelm phase of change, 247
Oxazepam, 510

P
PA Preference Inventory, 210
Pacesetters, 184, 185
Pacific Rim, expatriates in, 258–259
Pain: abdominal, 562; defined, 560; depression
and, 561; emotionally determined, 560; low
back, 285, 560–561
Pain disorder, 541–542; case example of, 541;
diagnosis of, 541–542
Pairing, in groups, 194
Palmer v. Circuit Court of Cook County, 382,
385
Panic attack, 413–415, 417–419
Panic disorder, 11, 18, 413–419; alcohol abuse
and, 509; case example of, 413–414; causes
of, 417; diagnosis of, 414–417; effects of,
418; in expatriates, 159; functional somatic
syndromes and, 555, 557; impact of, on productivity, 49; job loss and, 145; multiple
chemical sensitivity syndrome and, 555;
prevalence of, 414; psychiatric management
of, 25, 418–419; reasonable accommodation
of, 419; return to work with, 419; somatic
symptoms of, 551, 552; workplace intervention in, 418; workplace recognition of,
418
Paranoid personality disorder and traits, 74,
125–128, 469–472; case example of, 469–
470; causes of, 127, 417, 470–471; diagnosis
of, 470–471; DSM-IV diagnostic criteria for,
470; intervention in, 127–128; narcissism
and, 176; organizational effects of, 127, 471;
paranoid psychosis *versus,* 127, 470; prevention of, 128; psychiatric management of,
471–472; work function and, 340; workplace
intervention in, 471; workplace recognition
of, 471
Paranoid psychosis, 310, 334; paranoid personality disorder *versus,* 127, 470
Parity, 45
Paroxetine, 104
Passive-aggressive personality disorder,
178–179, 477–479; case example of, 477;
diagnosis of, 477–478; DSM-IV diagnostic
criteria for, 478; psychiatric management of,
478–479; workplace intervention in, 478;
workplace recognition of, 478
Passive chief executive officers, 222–223
Pastoral counselors, 73
Patience, 200

Patient advocate, treating physician *versus,*
351, 379
Pay cuts, threatening behavior due to, 316, 317
Payment arrangements: client-therapist rela-
tionship and, 37; delivery systems and,
36–46. *See also* Funding sources; Insurance,
health
Peers, coping with narcissistic, 179
Pep pills, 489
Perceivers, 173, 174; superiors who are, 175
Perfectionism, 460–463
Performance-based coaching, 103. *See also*
Coaching, executive
Performance measurement, reward system
alignment with, 192
Performers, 186
Peripheral neuropathy, 511
Persecuting/persecuted cultures, 214–216
Persecutory leaders, 187
Personality, defined, 210
Personality change, as treatment response,
20–21
Personality disorders and problems, 93, 95,
458–479; aggressive behavior and, 180–181;
alcohol abuse and, 509; Americans with Disabilities Act (ADA) and, 372; development
of, 459–460; essential elements of, 479; in
executives, 114–130, 187; interpersonal functioning and, 339–340; job loss and, 145; in
managers, 175–182; organizational effects of,
458–460; personality types *versus,* 210–211;
violence and, 316. *See also* Aggression; Antisocial personality disorder; Borderline personality disorder; Compulsive personality
style; Histrionic personality disorder; Narcissistic personality disorder; Obsessive-
compulsive personality disorder; Paranoid
personality; Passive-aggressive personality;
Rigid personalities
Personality Research Form, 112
Personality Self-Portrait (Oldham & Morris),
210
Personality testing and inventories: Americans
with Disabilities Act (ADA) and, 376; for
executive character assessment, 95; for executive personality assessment, 93–94, 112,
210; for overseas assignments, 165–166; in
psychiatric disability evaluation, 357
Personality traits: adaptive, 459–460; addiction
and, 487; impact of, on career choice, 80;
maladaptive, 458–460; for overseas success,
165–166
Personality types: categorizations of, 172, 210;
of chief executive officers, 210–216; emo-

tional intelligence and, 216; Myers-Briggs categorization of, 172–175, 210; personality disorders *versus,* 210–211

Pettus v. Cole, 63, 69

Pharmacotherapy. *See* Medication

Phobias: causes of, 422; diagnosis of, 420–422; DSM-IV diagnostic criteria for specific, 421–422; effects of, 422–423; in expatriates, 159; prevalence of, 420; psychiatric management of, 423; reasonable accommodation of, 423; return to work with, 423; social anxiety disorder and, 419–423; workplace intervention in, 423; workplace recognition of, 422–423

Physical illness. *See* Disability, physical; Medical problems

Physician-patient relationship: disability evaluation and, 350–352, 353, 379, 380; ethics in, 61–64, 350–352, 390; in occupational psychiatry, 64; physician roles in, 61–64; traditional, 62. *See also* Psychiatrists

Physicians, psychiatric. *See* Psychiatrists

Planning skills, 111

Poisons, 562–563

Police Department of Boston et al., Dahill v., 374, 384

Policies and procedures: conflict between personal conscience and, 400–402; for emotional crises in the workplace, 298; for preventing workplace problems, 292; for substance abuse, 292, 306, 500–501, 505; for violence in workplace, 315, 325, 326–327

Politics, organizational, 11, 171–200; consulting psychiatrists and, 290–291; defined, 171. *See also* Office politics

Polydrug dependence, 485, 509, 563

Popularity, organizational change and, 234

Positive self-regard, 219–220

Postmodern identity, 393

Posttraumatic stress disorder (PTSD), 427–432; case example of, 427–428; causes of, 430; diagnosis of, 428–430; DSM-IV criteria for, 336, 429–430; effects of, 428–429, 430–431; psychiatric management of, 431; reasonable accommodation of, 431–432; return to work with, 431–432; stressors of, 428, 430; from traumatic disasters, 300; workplace intervention in, 431; workplace recognition of, 430–431

Power building, office politics and, 199–200

Power needs: aggressive behavior and, 180, 223; hidden agendas and, 192

Preexisting psychological problems: job loss and, 141–142, 144–145, 150; organizational change and, 250; traumatic workplace events and, 303

Preferred provider organizations (PPOs), 28, 39; physician-patient relationship in, 62; pros and cons of, 39

Presenteeism, 56

Prevention: of anxiety disorders, 412; of disability, 363–364; of executive competitiveness, 122–123, 125; of executive compulsiveness, 130; of executive displacement, 132; of executive emotional suppression, 134; of executive narcissistic dishonesty, 120; of executive narcissistic grandiosity, 117–118; of executive paranoia, 128; history of occupational psychiatry and, 75, 84; of job loss problems, 150–152; of psychotic behavior, 311–312; of substance abuse, 306, 307; of suicide, 309–310; of traumatic work site events, 304; of violence in workplace, 325–327, 337; of workplace problems, 291–294

Primary prevention, 84. *See also* Prevention

Privacy needs, 239

Privacy rights, drug testing and, 496. *See also* Confidentiality; Consent, informed

Private agencies, 29

Private-sector reimbursement mechanisms, 28, 37–43

Problem solving skills, 111

Procter & Gamble, 235

Productivity, 55–56; cultural factors in, 190; depression and, 48–49, 52–53, 54, 55, 56; disability and, 348; executive, 106–107; interpersonal conflict and, 278; measures of, 56; mental health and, 71–74, 85; mental illness and, 48–49, 50; obstructive culture and diminished, 207–208; office politics and, 172; substance abuse and, 55–56

Productivity improvement: with depression treatment, 24–25, 52–53, 54; as treatment outcome, 20–21, 24–25

Professional associations: for fitness-for-duty examiners, 343, 346; future directions for, 82–83; history of occupational psychiatry and, 77–78, 79, 81–82, 84

Profiles, for violence prediction, 321–322

Projection: authoritarian leadership and, 187; in groups, 194–195; narcissism and, 176; paranoia and, 125–128

Projective identification, 187, 188–189, 194. *See also* Identification

Promotion: narcissistic personalities and, 177; for organizational culture, 191. *See also* Succession planning

Providers: historical overview of workplace, 71–74; preferred, 39; in public sector, 43, 44; selection of delivery systems and, 36–37, 46; substitution of, 30; types of, 29–36. *See also* Counselors; Mental health professionals; Psychiatrists; Psychologists; Social workers

Prozac, 444

Psychiatric Consultation in the Workplace (Sperry), 81

Psychiatric disability. *See* Disability, psychiatric

Psychiatric fitness-for-duty examinations. *See* Fitness-for-duty examinations

Psychiatric nurse practitioners, 36

Psychiatric nurses, 36

Psychiatrists, 30–33; for assessing workplace problems, 285–289; confidentiality and, 62; consulting *versus* employee's personal, 285–286; credentialing and licensing of, 32; history of, in workplace, 74–85; prevalence of, 32, 84–85; referral sources for, 32; roles of, in workplace mental health, 71–74, 83–84; selection of, 32–33, 285–286; training of, 31–32. *See also* Physician-patient relationship

Psychiatry: beliefs about, 3, 7–8; history of workplace, 71–85; overview of, 3–4. *See also* Occupational psychiatry

Psychiatry in the World of Work (GAP committee), 82

Psychoanalysis, 31

Psychoanalytic/psychodynamic theory: on anxiety, 411–412; applied to groups, 194–195; applied to leadership, 188–189

Psychoanalytic psychotherapy. *See* Insight-oriented psychotherapy

Psychoanalytic training institutes, 29, 44

Psychobiological model, of phobias, 422

Psychodynamic psychotherapy. *See* Insight-oriented psychotherapy

Psychodynamics of Work and Organizations, The (Czander), 189

Psychoeducation, family, 534, 536

Psychological contract: changing, 234, 236, 237–240; dimensions of subordinate-superior relationship and, 237–239; marriage/family, 264–265, 266; organizational change and, 234, 236, 237–240, 245–247; relationships with, 240; violated, 239, 245–247

Psychological temperature, 206. *See also* Culture, organizational

Psychological testing: in executive assessment, 92–95, 112; interviews *versus,* 95, 97; in psychiatric disability evaluation, 357. *See also* Fitness-for-duty examinations

Psychologists, clinical, 33–34; credentialing and licensing of, 34; prevalence of, 34; referral sources for, 34; selection of, 34; training of, 33

Psychometric approaches: in executive assessment, 92–95; in organizational development, 18

Psychosis, 18, 517–537; affective disorders with, 521–523; causes of, 311, 519, 530–531; delusional disorder and, 518–521; in expatriates, 160, 165; organically induced, 565; prognosis of, 312; schizophrenia spectrum, 526–537; stress vulnerability model of, 519, 530–531; substance-induced, 524–526. *See also* Affective disorders with psychotic features; Delusional disorder; Paranoid psychosis; Psychotic behavior; Schizoaffective disorder; Schizophrenia; Schizophrenia spectrum disorders; Substance-induced psychotic disorder

Psychosis, Schizophrenia, Schizoaffective Disorder, 539

Psychosocial issues: adjustment disorder with depressed mood and, 435–436; bipolar disorder and, 453; costs of, 282–283; of expatriate populations, 160–162; in functional somatic syndromes, 553–558; major depression and, 442; review of, in disability evaluation, 355–356; workplace problems caused by, 281–282

Psychosocial treatment: for affective disorders with psychotic features, 523; for schizophrenia spectrum disorders, 534–536

Psychosomatic interface, 540–566; assessment of somatoform disorders and, 549–550; causes of somatization and, 547–548; in controversial medical illnesses, 553–558; depression and, 442, 450, 456, 549, 552; factitious disorders and, 545–546; in functional somatic syndromes, 553–558; malingering and, 546–547; organic behavioral syndromes and, 562–565; physical disorders with emotional aspects and, 558–562; psychiatric disorders with physical symptoms and, 551–552; somatoform disorders and, 540–545; treatment of somatoform disorders and, 550–551; workplace relevance of, 548–549, 561, 565–566. *See also* Disability, physical; Medical problems; Neurobiological etiology; Organic etiology; Somatic symptoms; Somatoform disorders

Psychotherapy, 12; for anxiety disorders, 413, 418–419, 423, 427, 431; for bipolar disorder,

455, 456; coaching *versus*, 100–101, 102, 105; cognitive, 14; combined with medication, 14, 18–19, 24, 51; for depressive disorders, 438, 445–446, 450, 455, 456; for drug addiction, 497–498; efficacy of, 24; for executives, 103–106; for functional somatic syndromes, 557; for personality disorders, 463, 465–466, 468–469, 471–472, 474, 476–477, 478–479; by psychiatrists, 32; for psychotic disorders, 520, 523, 526, 534–535; for somatoform disorders, 550–551; treatment response to, 21–22. *See also* Behavior therapy; Cognitive-behavioral therapy; Insight-oriented psychotherapy; Treatment

Psychotic behavior: affective disorders with, 521–523; in bipolar disorder, 310–311, 338, 521–522; causes of, 310, 311; effects of, on workplace, 311; examples of, 310; fitness-for-duty examinations for, 334; intervention in, 311–312; prevention of, 311–312; substance-induced, 524–526; workplace emergencies of, 297, 310–312. *See also* Psychosis

Public-sector mental health care, 29, 43–44

Publications, history of occupational psychiatry and, 80, 81, 84

Punishment, fear of, 7

Pyromania, 372

Q

"Qualified individual with a disability," 376–377

Quality, mental health care, 3–27; components of, 22–25; guidelines for, 22–26; improving, 25–26; recognizing, 25

Quality-adjusted years of life (QALYs), 50–51

Quality control, assessment and, 24–25

Quality of care: health maintenance organizations and, 40–41; in managed care, 45, 54–55

R

R. J. Reynolds Tobacco Company, 73

Ready, Fire, Aim: Avoiding Management by Impulse (Levinson), 245

Reasonable accommodation. *See* Accommodation, reasonable

Recalcitrants, 250

Recognition: of alcoholism, 503–507, 508–509; of anxiety disorders, 412, 418, 422–423, 426–427, 430–431; barriers to, 7–8; of bipolar disorder, 453–454; of depressive disorders, 437, 442–443, 449–450, 453–454; effective, 8–9; of family problems, 273;

issues of, 9–12; of mental health problems, 4–5; of personality disorders, 462, 465, 468, 471, 473–474, 476, 478; of psychotic disorders, 520, 522, 525, 531; of workplace problems, 291–292. *See also* Assessment; Diagnosis; Evaluation; Screening

Recognition, employee: grandiosity and, 115–116; organizational change and, 242–243; organizational culture and, 208, 209. *See also* Rewards system

Records, medical: employee access to, 68; release of, for fitness-for-duty examinations, 341; review of, for disability evaluation, 341, 379; separate storage of, 380–381

Recovery: alcoholism, 514–515; drug addiction, 497–498

Recovery phase of change, 248–249

Reduced-fee care, 29, 43–44

Reenactment. *See* Family dynamics, reenacted

Referral, for alcoholism treatment, 503–507; strategy for, 505–507; timing of, 504–505

Referral, outside, 6; barriers to, 7–8, 42–43; confidentiality and, 64, 65–68; effective, 8–9; employee assistance programs and, 42–43; for executive psychotherapy, 106; for workplace problems, 285–289

Referral, to employee assistance programs, 42–43, 380

Referral resources, 9; for executive psychotherapy, 106; for fitness-for-duty examiners, 343, 346; for psychiatrists, 32; for psychologists, 34; for social workers, 35

Regression, 194–195, 225–227

Reimbursement mechanisms. *See* Benefits; Funding sources; Insurance, health

Relationship problems, 281. *See also* Family problems; Interpersonal problems

Relationship skills: for executive effectiveness, 91–92, 106, 111; testing for, 93. *See also* Emotional intelligence

Relationships, loss of job and, 138–139, 141

Relaxation techniques, 413, 419

Release of information, 312

Relocation, family problems with, 265–266. *See also* Expatriate employees and families

Reorganization phase of change, 249

Repatriation syndrome, 155, 158, 166; dealing with, 167–168

Repetitive stress syndrome, 553

Repression, 16

Reputation, lingering, 21

Research clinics, 29, 44

Residency training, history of, 80–81

Resistance: in insight-oriented psychotherapy, 16; negative treatment response and, 21–22; to organizational change, 233–235, 245–247, 249–250; psychological, to change, 132–134, 245–247

Resources, organizational, impact of, on culture, 230

Retention, employee, office politics and, 172

Return to work, 405; with alcoholism, 514–515; with antisocial personality disorder, 468; with anxiety disorders, 413, 419, 423, 427, 431–432; with bipolar disorder, 456; with depressive disorders, 438, 447, 450, 456; employee assistance programs and, 335–336; fitness-for-duty examinations for, 334–336, 384; FMLA medical certification for, 385; with psychotic disorders, 312, 520–521, 523, 526, 536–537

Return-to-work agreement, after psychotic episode, 312

Revenge, 317

Rewards system: alignment of performance measurement with, 192; conditions of equitable, 242–243; ego incentives and, 399–400; intrinsic versus extrinsic motivation and, 209–210, 235–236; narcissistic personalities and, 177; organizational culture and, 191

Rigid personalities, 125–130; compulsive, 125, 128–130; paranoid, 125–128. See also Obsessive-compulsive disorder; Obsessive-compulsive personality disorder; Paranoid personality disorder

Robbery, 303, 304, 336

Robert Half International survey, 258

Role changes: due to job loss, 139–140, 141; in families, 257, 258, 264–265, 268

Role clarity, in organizational structure, 227–228

Rorschach test, 93

Rule breaking, executive dishonesty and, 118–120

Rumors: anticipatory job loss and, 138; in expatriate communities, 162

Runyon, Albert v., 384

S

Sabotage: aggressive CEOs and, 223; oppositional employees and, 250; passive-aggressiveness and, 178–179

San Francisco Examiner, 80

Scandinavia, history of workplace psychiatry in, 78

Scapegoating, 190

Schizoaffective disorder, 521; diagnosis of, 528–529; DSM-IV diagnostic criteria for, 528–529; schizophrenia versus, 527–528. See also Schizophrenia spectrum disorders

Schizoid personality, work function and, 340

Schizophrenia, 279, 311, 312, 526–537; case example of, 529–530; causes of, 530–531; delusional disorder versus, 518; diagnosis of, 527–528; DSM-IV diagnostic criteria for, 527–528; effects of, 531–533; negative symptoms of, 526, 527, 532; positive symptoms of, 526, 527, 532; somatic symptoms of, 552. See also Psychosis; Schizophrenia spectrum disorders

Schizophrenia spectrum disorders, 526–537; causes of, 530–531; diagnosis of, 527–529; effects of, on workplace, 531–533; listed, 528; medication for, 533–534; psychiatric management of, 533–536; psychosocial treatment of, 534–536; reasonable accommodation of, 536–537; relapse in, 531; return to work with, 536–537; substance abuse with, 533, 534; supported employment for, 535–536, 537; workplace intervention in, 531; workplace recognition of, 531

Schizophreniform disorder, 528

Schizotypal personality disorder, 528

Screening: of expatriate employees and families, 164–166; preemployment, Americans with Disabilities Act (ADA) and, 376; preemployment, fitness-for-duty examinations for, 333

Second opinions, related to psychiatric leaves, 334–335

Secondary prevention, 84. See also Prevention

Secrecy: in fight-or-flight basic assumption groups, 227–229; of hypervigilant CEOs, 215–216

Security, employee, 241

Sedatives, 494–495, 509

Selective serotonin reuptake inhibitors (SSRIs): for anxiety disorders, 413, 423, 427, 431; for depression, 444–445, 450. See also Antidepressants; Medication

Self-awareness, 218–219

Self-blaming, 213

Self-confidence: of charismatic CEOs, 211–213; executive work function and, 340; image of, 199; of managers versus leaders, 187; narcissism and, 175

Self-defeating behavior, 7–8, 20

Self-esteem: compulsive personality and, 129; in expatriates, 157; job loss and, 139, 140, 142, 148; in managers versus leaders, 187;

narcissism and, 175, 176; socioeconomic background and, 271; traumatic response and, 304

Self-help groups. *See* Groups, self-help

Self-insuring corporations: fee for service and, 36–39; workers' compensation and, 365

Self-medication: addiction and, 487, 489; of anxiety, 412

Self-protective behavior: executive, with subordinates, 123–125; in paranoid personality disorder, 471

Self-psychology, 189

Self-rating tools, 22

Self-reference, 125–128

Self-regard, positive, 219–220

Self-reliance, self-defeating, 7–8

Self-sabotage, unconscious, 268

Sensitivity, over-, 125–128, 176, 214–215

Sensors, 173, 174; superiors who are, 174–175

Separation issues, panic disorder and, 417

September 11, 2001, terrorist attacks, 223, 247, 298–299, 317

Serax, 510

Serotonin, 426

Session frequency, of insight-oriented psychotherapy, 14–15

Settings, organizational: delivery systems and, 36–46; with fee for service, 38; with health maintenance organizations, 39; physician roles and, 61–64; with preferred provider organizations, 39

Sexual behavior disorders, 372

Sexual harassment, 197, 508

Sexual intimacy, 270–271

Shame: in job loss, 140, 141, 147; narcissism and, 176

Shock, 247

Shootings, 298, 314, 365–366

Short-term thinking, 397–399

Shyness, 419–423. *See also* Social anxiety disorder

Sibling rivalry, 123–125, 188, 198

Sixteen PF Test (16-PF), 93, 94, 112, 210

Skill-based coaching, 103. *See also* Coaching

Skills training, for schizophrenia spectrum disorders, 534

Slavish organizations, 211–213

Sleep disturbance, 157, 440, 453

Smoking, 559, 560

"Snake pit" model of organizations, 191–192, 200

Social anxiety disorder, 419–423; case example of, 419; causes of, 422; diagnosis of, 420–423; DSM-IV diagnostic criteria for, 420–421; effects of, 422–423; prevalence of, 420; psychiatric management of, 423; reasonable accommodation of, 423; return to work with, 423; workplace intervention in, 423; workplace recognition of, 422–423

Social history: obtaining, 287; review of, in disability evaluation, 355

Social impairment, in schizophrenia spectrum disorders, 526, 528, 530–531, 533, 534, 536

Social learning theory, 534

Social phobia, 18, 104, 116, 419–423, 509. *See also* Social anxiety disorder

Social psychology, 72, 75–77

Social relationships, job loss and, 138–139, 140

Social Security Disability Insurance, 536

Social Security Income, 536

Social skills training, for schizophrenia spectrum disorders, 534, 536

Social support: job loss and, 146, 149; paranoid personality and, 127; schizophrenia spectrum disorders and, 531; trauma response and, 303

Social workers, 34–35; credentialing and licensing of, 35; referral sources for, 35; selection of, 35; training of, 34–35

Socialization, competitiveness and, 198. *See also* Culture, national

Sociopaths, 118, 120. *See also* Antisocial personality disorder

Soileau v. Guilford of Maine, Inc., 373, 385

Somatic symptoms: controversial medical illnesses and, 553–558; depression and, 442, 450, 549, 552; differential diagnosis of, 545; panic attack and, 415; in panic disorder, 551, 552; psychiatric disorders with, 551–552; as psychosocial defenses, 547–548; in schizophrenia, 552; social anxiety disorder and, 420; somatoform disorders and, 540–545. *See also* Psychosomatic interface

Somatic syndromes, functional, 553–558

Somatization disorder, 468, 542–543; case example of, 542; causes of, 547–548; diagnosis of, 542–543; disability issues and, 549; primary gains from, 548, 549; secondary gains from, 548, 549; treatment of, 551

Somatoform disorders, 540–545; assessment of, 549–550; causes of, 547–548; diagnosis of, 542–543, 549–550; psychiatric management of, 550–551; workplace relevance of, 548–549, 561

Southwest Airlines, 235

Spillover effect, of family satisfaction, 259

Splitting, 16, 194

Spousal adjustment, expatriate, 160, 162, 165, 258–259

Stage fright, 419–423. *See also* Social anxiety disorder

State and local clinics, 29, 43–44

State disability laws and enforcement, 371, 374

State hospital inpatient care, 29, 43

State-mandated coverage, 38–39; parity legislation and, 45

State psychological associations, 34

Status: ego incentives and, 399–400; job loss and, 138

Status quo, 122; acceptance of organizational change and, 239; resistance to organizational change and, 233–235

Stigma: depression and, 443; employee assistance programs and, 43; fears of, 7, 8, 10; treatment response and, 21; of unemployment, 141, 146

Stimulants, 489–491, 509, 525. *See also* Amphetamine abuse; Cocaine abuse

Strengths assessment, in job loss, 145–146, 148

Stress: aggression and, 179; Americans with Disabilities Act (ADA) and, 377; anxiety and, 9–10, 407–408; audit of workplace, 292–293; CEO, 230; executive, 89, 114, 125, 128, 132–134, 230; of expatriates, 156–157; family-work balance and, 258, 259; fear of change and, 132–134; of job loss, 135–153, 137–138; meaning of, 8, 9–10; narcissistic personalities and, 114; organizational change and, 246; rigid personalities and, 125, 128, 129; of single parents, 258; war, 75–77; work-related, workplace problems caused by, 282, 292–293; workplace environment and, 72–73, 78, 84, 292–293, 407, 530–531

Stress disorders: Americans with Disabilities Act (ADA) and, 372; from traumatic disasters, 299–300; from violence, 336. *See also* Anxiety disorders; Posttraumatic stress disorder

Stress management programs, 12–13; conditions appropriate for, 134; goal of, 407; for workplace problem prevention, 292–293

Stress vulnerability model: delusional disorder and, 519; schizophrenia spectrum disorders and, 530–531

Stroke, 281, 565

Structure, for schizophrenics, 530, 531

Structures, organizational: assessment of, 195; boundary issues and, 195; components of, 224; employees' distorted perceptions and, 225–229; functions and importance of, 224–225, 229; impact of, on organizational culture, 224–229; inadequate, consequences of, 225–229; misconceptions of, 224–225

Subordinate-superior relationship: attitudes toward authority and, 188–189; communication in, 185–186; organizational change and, 237–243; psychological contract and, 237–240

Subordinates: coping with narcissistic, 179; superiors' fear of, 123–125, 176–177, 211; tips for, on managing superiors, 185–186. *See also* Employees; Psychological contract

Substance abuse: absenteeism and, 280, 283; accidents and, 280, 283; addiction and, 484, 485–488; causes of, 305; costs of, 281, 496; with depression, 281, 442; effects of, in the workplace, 306; in expatriates, 159, 160, 164, 165; hiding of, 10; intervention in, 306–307; job loss and, 145; narcissistic personality problems and, 114; policies for, 292, 306, 500–501, 505; prevalence of, 23, 279, 280; prevention of, 306, 307; productivity and, 55–56; psychotic behavior from, 311, 524–526; with schizophrenia spectrum disorders, 533, 534; substance dependence and, 484–485; suppressed fear and, 132, 133; trauma-induced, 300; workplace emergencies due to, 297, 305–307. *See also* Addiction; Alcohol abuse and dependence; Drug abuse

Substance abuse treatment, 306–307; employee assistance programs for, 41–42; integrated dual disorder, 534, 536; mandated coverage of, 38

Substance-induced persisting dementia, 564

Substance-induced psychotic disorder, 524–526; case example of, 524–525; causes of, 525; diagnosis of, 524; effects of, 525–526; psychiatric management of, 526; reasonable accommodation of, 526; return to work with, 526; workplace intervention in, 525; workplace recognition of, 525

Substance intoxication delirium, 563–564, 565

Successful, need to be, 237, 242

Succession planning: fear of subordinates and, 123–125, 177; Oedipal conflict and, 120–125. *See also* Promotion

Suicide and suicidal behavior, 297, 307–310; in affective disorders with psychotic features, 523; alcohol abuse and, 508; depression and, 309, 441; effects of, on workplace, 309; examples of, 307–308; intervention in, 309–310; prevention of, 309–310; risk factors for, 308–309

Superiors: aggressive, 178–182; delusional disorder and, 520; destructively narcissistic, 175–178, 179, 191; leadership styles of, 182–185; managing one's, 185–186; personality styles of, 174–175; subordinate alcohol abuse and, 507; subordinate workplace problems and, 284, 285, 288. *See also* Chief executive officer; *Executive headings; Leader headings;* Managers; Subordinate-superior relationship

Supported employment, 535–536, 537

Supportive approaches, 13, 14, 21; efficacy of, 23–24

Suppression, emotional, 114; causes of, 133; of fear of change, 132–134; intervention in, 134; organizational effects of, 133; prevention of, 134

Survival scenarios, 398

Suspiciousness, over-: in executives, 125–128, 176; in fight-or-flight basic assumption groups, 227–229; in hypervigilant CEOs, 214–216; in subordinates, 189, 227–229

Sutton v. United Airlines, 374, 385

Symptomatic relief, 11

Symptoms: of alcoholism, 508–509; of anxiety disorders, 412, 418, 422–423, 426–427, 430–431; of bipolar disorder, 453–454; of depressive disorders, 437, 442–443, 449–450, 453–454; of family problems, 255, 273; of improvement, 20–21; of mental illness, 279, 283; of personality disorders, 462, 465, 468, 471, 473–474, 476, 478; psychiatric disability causal determination and, 359–360; of psychotic disorders, 520, 522, 525, 526, 531. *See also* Diagnosis; Somatic symptoms

Systems cost-effectiveness approach, 52–53

T

Task Force on Psychiatry and Business Relations, 82

Task Force on Psychiatry and Industry, 84

Tavistock Clinic, 78

Teaching clinics, 29, 44

Team building: narcissism and, 177; personality styles and, 174

Team-building skills, 100, 110–111

Teamwork: competitiveness and, 198–199; organizational culture for, 191. *See also* Group psychology

Telephone consultations, for expatriates, 166

Telepsychiatry, 166–167

Temperament and Character Inventory (TCI), 95

Termination, employee: Americans with Disabilities Act (ADA) and, 381–383; during organizational change, 249–250; for risk of violence, 320, 337. *See also* Job loss

Termination, psychotherapy, 15

Terrorism, 298–299; crisis management plan for, 325–326; substance abuse and, 481; threats of, 317

Tertiary prevention, 84. *See also* Prevention

THC, 491

Thematic Apperception Test (AT), 93, 94

Thiamine, 511

Thinkers, 173, 174; coercive leaders as, 183; pacesetters as, 184; superiors who are, 175

Threat, in change, 244–245

Threat assessment: Americans with Disabilities Act (ADA) and, 382–383; behavioral profiles for, 321–322; categorization system for, 318; definitions for, 314–315; fitness-for-duty examinations for, 336–338, 382–383; knowledge base for, 316–324; mental health professional roles in, 315–316; prevalence of workplace violence and, 318–319; variables for, 319–324. *See also* Violence, workplace

Threats, workplace, 314–327; Americans with Disabilities Act (ADA) and, 382–383; defined, 314–315; motivations for, 316–317; responding to, 325–327; types of, 316–317. *See also* Violence, workplace

360-degree assessment, 94, 100, 177

Thyroid disorders, 281

Time use, after job loss, 149

Timing, 8

Touch, therapeutic, 557, 558

Toxicity: chemical, 562–563, 565; drug, 563–564, 565

Toyota, 235

Toyota Motor Manufacturing v. Williams, 373, 385

Training: about drug abuse, 483; about psychiatric and workplace problems, 292; about psychosis, 517–518, 534; for expatriates, 166, 167–168; for schizophrenics, 534–536

Training, provider: in ethical conduct, 60; history of occupational psychiatry and, 75–76, 79, 80–81, 85; psychiatrists', 30–31; psychologists', 33; social workers', 34–35

Tranquilizers, 494–495; abuse of, 494–495; alcohol abuse and, 509; case example of addiction to, 495; effects of, 494–495; withdrawal from, 494

Transference, 15–16, 17

Transition skills, 111

Trauma, childhood, 548, 549, 550

Traumatic disasters: assessment of stressors in, 300; behavioral effects of, 299; cognitive effects of, 299; examples of, 298–299; intervention for, 300–301; physical effects of, 299; psychological effects of, 299; stressors of, 300. *See also* Posttraumatic stress disorder

Traumatic events, work site: disability causality and, 358, 365–366; effects of, on workplace, 304; examples of, 301–303; intervention for, 304; major life changes and, 303; mental illness from, 299–300; preexisting mental illness and, 303; prevention of, 304; previous, 303; response determinants for, 303–304; severity of, 303; social supports and, 303; violence and, 314–327, 336–337, 365–366; at work site, 301–304. *See also* Posttraumatic stress disorder; Violence

Treating the Self (Wolf), 189

Treatment: of anxiety disorders, 413, 418–419, 423, 427, 431; attitudes toward, 7–8, 19; barriers to, 7–8, 42–43; efficacy of, 23–24; of functional somatic syndromes, 556–558; nonspecific, 11; of personality disorders, 463, 465–466, 468–469, 471–472, 474, 476–477, 478–479; of psychotic disorders, 520, 522–523, 526, 527, 533–536; of somatoform disorders, 550–551; specific, 11, 23–24; techniques of, 12–19; for workplace problems, 290. *See also* Alcohol abuse treatment; Delivery systems; Depression treatment; Intervention; Medication; Mental health care; Psychotherapy

Treatment guidelines, 26

Treatment outcomes: assessment of, 19–22; barriers to positive, 21–22; negative, 21–22; positive, 20–21; for workplace problems, 290

Trust: hypervigilance and lack of, 215–216, 471; organizational change and, 248; personality and, 237; psychological contract and, 239

Turnover: job dissatisfaction and, 284–285; organizational culture and, 208

Twelve-step groups, 488, 497–498

2000 Diplomate Directory (American Board of Examiners), 35

Tylenol crisis, 392, 393, 403

Type A (coronary-prone) behavior, 559–560

U

U-curve hypothesis, 156–157

Uncertainty: anticipatory job loss and, 137–138; avoidance and, 132–134; employment, 135–153, 363; hidden agendas and,

193; inadequate organizational structures and, 225, 227, 228, 229; paranoia and, 125–126, 127

Unconscious conflict. *See* Conflict, unconscious

Unconscious motivations: competitiveness and, 198; hidden agendas and, 193; of leaders, 186–188

Uncovering psychotherapy. *See* Insight-oriented psychotherapy

Underachieving employees, 460–463, 477–478

Underlying causes. *See* Causes, underlying

Undue hardship, employer, 382. *See also* Accommodation, reasonable; Americans with Disabilities Act (ADA)

Unemployment. *See* Job loss

Unemployment benefits, 140

United Air Lines, Garrity v., 381, 384

United Airlines, Sutton v., 374, 385

U.S. Army, 72

U.S. Army Air Force, 76–77

U.S. Chamber of Commerce, 83

U.S. Congress, 317; Americans with Disabilities Act (ADA) and, 369, 370; Family and Medical Leave Act (FMLA) and, 383

U.S. Department of Labor, contact information, 386

U.S. Department of State, 158–160

U.S. Medical Licensing Exam, 31

U.S. Occupational and Safety Administration claim, 375

U.S. Postal Service, 280, 314

U.S. Senate, 398

U.S. Steel, 83

U.S. Supreme Court, 373, 374

University of Minnesota, Children, Youth and Family Consortium, 275

University of Santa Clara, 80

Unknown, fear of, 132–134

Urbaniak v. Newton, 331–332, 344

Urine screens: for alcohol abuse, 509; for drug abuse, 495–496, 501. *See also* Drug testing

Utah Power & Light, 280

Utilization management and review, 29; of preferred provider organizations, 39

V

Valproic acid, 455

Veterans, occupational psychiatry and, 77

Veterans Administration, 77

Violence, workplace, 314–327; Americans with Disabilities Act (ADA) and, 382–383; classification system for, 318; crisis management for, 325–326; defining, 314–315; fitness-for-duty examinations for assessing, 336–338, 382–383; follow-up to, 327; legal issues of, 337; organizational risk factors for, 323–324; policies and procedures for, 315, 325–327; prevalence of, 318–319; prevention of, 325–327, 337; profiles for predicting, 321–322; protective factors for, 324; psychotic behavior and, 311–312; responding to, 325–327; risk assessment for, 319–324, 336–338; risk factors for, 319–324, 337; scope of, 318–319; study limitations concerning, 321–324; threat assessment for, 314–324, 336–338; Type I, criminal intent, 318; Type II, customer/client-perpetrated, 318, 319; Type III, worker-on-worker, 318, 321, 322–323; Type IV, from personal relationships, 318, 319. *See also* Aggression; Threat assessment; Traumatic events

Virtu, 389, 394–395

Virtue ethics, 389, 393–395

Vocational rehabilitation, for schizophrenics, 535–536

Vocational Rehabilitation Act Amendments of 1943, 77

Voyeurs, 372

W

Wall Street Journal, 80, 250, 253

War stress, 75–77

Ward v. MHRI, 382, 385

Warnings, written, 505

Watson-Glaser Critical Thinking Appraisal, 112

Weiler v. Household Finance Corp., 372, 385

Weill Medical College, 81

What Color Is Your Parachute? (Bolles), 149

Whiplash, chronic, 553

Who's Who Directory of Medical Specialists, 32

Williams, Toyota Motor Manufacturing v., 373, 385

Withdrawal: alcoholic, 305; delirium with, 564; detoxification and, 497, 510; opiate, 492–493; tranquilizer, 494

Women in the workplace: alcoholism in, 502–503; office politics and, 196–197; single-parent, 258; stereotypes of, 196–197; trends in family roles and, 257, 258, 264–265, 268

Work ethic: families and, 256; job loss and, 139

Work-family life relationship. *See* Family-work life relationship

Work function assessment: fitness-for-duty examinations and, 338–340; information exchange for, 341; for psychiatric disability, 331, 339

Work history: obtaining, 287, 341; review of, in disability evaluation, 355–356

Work skills: job loss impact and, 145; repatriation and, 167–168; schizophrenics and, 534

Workers' compensation: benefits of, 365; disability and, 347–367; history of, 78; impairment and, 349; legal issues of, 364–365, 366–367; office politics and, 172; somatoform disorders and, 549; work-related impairments and, 364–367

Workplace: emotional crises in, 297–312; employee counseling in, 5–6; family problems and, 254–257; mental health issues in, 4–5; substance abuse emergencies at, 305–307; as substitute for unmet family needs, 255, 270–271; traumatic events at, 301–304, 336; trends in family roles and, 257, 258, 264–265, 268; violence in, 314–327, 336–338. *See also* Mental health care, workplace

Workplace environment: addiction and, 488; alcohol abuse and, 507, 508, 514–515; audit of stress in, 292–293; disability and, 363–364, 377; executive competition and, 122–123; executive compulsiveness and, 129; executive dishonesty and, 120; executive paranoia and, 127, 128; psychiatric evaluation and, 72–73, 288, 291; risk factors in, for violence, 323–324; schizophrenia spectrum disorders and, 530–531, 536–537; stress and, 72–73, 78, 84, 292–293, 377, 407–408, 530–531; traumatic response and, 304. *See also* Culture, organizational; Organizational context

Workplace problems: assessment of, 285–289; consulting on, 285–289, 290–291; delays in recognizing, 291–292; formulation of, 288–289; information gathering for, 286–287; interventions for, 289–291; mental illness and, 276–294; organizational effects of, 283–285; prevention of, 291–294; recognition of, 291–292; supervisor-employee agreements for handling, 289–290; types of, 276–278; underlying causes of, 278–283; work-caused, 281–282. *See also* Absenteeism; Accidents; Conflict, interpersonal; Job dissatisfaction; Job performance problems; Organizational effects

World Federation for Mental Health, 78–79

World Health Organization, 78

World War I, workplace psychiatry during, 72, 74
World War II, workplace psychiatry during, 75–77, 83
WorldCom scandal, 119

X
Xanax, 418, 494, 495, 509

Z
Zero tolerance, for violence, 325